CLASSROOM BEHAVIOR MANAGEMENT IN A DIVERSE SOCIETY

SECOND EDITION

HERBERT GROSSMAN

San Jose State University

MAYFIELD PUBLISHING COMPANY

Mountain View, California

London • Toronto

To Bill and Michele with love

Library of Congress Cataloging-in-Publication Data

Grossman, Herbert, Ph. D.
    Classroom behavior management in a diverse society / Herbert Grossman. —
2nd ed.
            p.   cm.
    Rev. ed. of: Trouble-free teaching. c1990.
    Includes bibliographical references.
    ISBN 1-55934-438-5
    1. Classroom management.   2. School discipline.   3. Problem children—
Education.   4. Behavior disorders in children.   I. Grossman, Herbert, Ph. D.
Trouble-free teaching.   II. Title.
LB3011.G76   1994
371.1'024—dc20   94-27460
                                                                    CIP

Manufactured in the United States of America

10   9   8   7   6   5   4   3   2   1

Mayfield Publishing Company
1280 Villa Street
Mountain View, California 94041

Sponsoring editor, Franklin C. Graham; production editor, Myrna Engler-Forkner; manuscript editor, Janet Greenblatt; text designer, Adriane Bosworth; cover designer, Gryphon Three; cover image, © David Young-Wolff/PhotoEdit; manufacturing manager, Aimee Rutter. The text was set in 10/12 Electra by Wilsted & Taylor and printed on 50# Ecolocote by Malloy Lithographing, Inc.

Text and photo credits appear on a continuation of the copyright page, p. 526.

♲   This book is printed on acid-free, recycled paper.

BRIEF
CONTENTS

DETAILED CONTENTS

CHAPTER 3   *Handling Potential Disruptions*   *74*

CHAPTER 4   *Contextually Appropriate Classroom Management*   *111*

CHAPTER 5   *Classroom Management for Students
from Diverse Ethnic and Socioeconomic
Backgrounds   141*

PART THREE   *Solutions to Individual Behavior Problems   377*

CHAPTER 11   *Conduct Problems   382*

PREFACE

This text is designed to provide preservice educators with the classroom management skills they will need to maintain environments that foster learning and enhance students' personal growth. The book suggests a three-stage approach to classroom management.

1. Because educators can avoid most behavior problems before they occur, the book begins by describing the management techniques that research indicates can help prevent problems.

2. Unfortunately, even the best management techniques do not completely avoid behavior problems. For this reason, the text also includes techniques that educators can use to solve behavior problems that occur even when they use good preventive management techniques.

3. Because no techniques work with all students, the book also introduces the skills teachers require to individualize their classroom management approaches.

Because the United States is such a diverse society, classroom management techniques that are effective with students from stable homes with two native-born, well-educated parents who understand the system and have the resources to help their children gain the maximum benefits from their school experiences will not work with all students. Many students do not grow up in these kinds of families or environments. Because the context of their lives is different, they do not adapt well to many classroom management approaches. Therefore, this text discusses how to adapt classroom management approaches to the contextual aspects of the lives of immigrant and refugee students, students who move from rural areas to urban areas, students from cultures that have a history of unequal cross-cultural relationships with European Americans, homeless and runaway students, abused and neglected students, and students whose parents are unable to provide them with adequate care.

Because our country is ethnically and socioeconomically diverse, students from different backgrounds come to school with diverse learning and behavior styles, values, interests, and goals. Most teachers and administrators are from European American middle-class backgrounds. Thus, many of the behavior styles that are acceptable to the students' families and communities are neither expected nor welcomed by teachers and other school officials. Also, classroom management techniques that are designed by European American middle-class teachers for European American middle-class students do not meet the needs of many non-middle-class non-European American students. This text helps preservice educators by providing insight into their preferred classroom management approaches and by helping them adapt their approaches to the needs of their ethnically and socioeconomically diverse students.

The text also deals extensively with the gender and sexual orientation issues that are involved in classroom management. Males and females behave differently both in and out of school, and teachers often use different classroom management techniques with males and females; they may prepare males and females for different roles. Some individuals believe that these behavioral differences are natural and desirable; others believe that they are the result of sexism. Some people believe that gender differences in classroom management are desirable because they reflect teachers' attempts to treat females and males according to their special needs; others believe that gender differences in classroom management are discriminatory and that they foster unacceptable gender stereotypical behavior and roles. This text confronts these issues head-on. It describes the ways in which males and females function differently in school, examines gender differences in teachers' classroom management techniques, helps preservice educators become more aware of their ideas about gender issues, and describes four alternative ways they can deal with gender differences when they manage their classrooms.

Although many students experience problems concerning sexual orientation, the topic is shunned by most teachers and administrators. This text discusses sexual orientation problems and how such problems can affect classroom management.

This book provides educators with both theoretical knowledge about the science of classroom management—the positions of well-known authors and the results of research investigations—and practical suggestions for implementing this knowledge in the classroom. However, the book does not leave readers with the impression that, having mastered its contents, they will be able to avoid or solve all classroom behavior problems. It acknowledges the limitations of the science of classroom management and discusses the factors beyond educators' control that affect their ability to solve the behavior problems that confront them. Research results that support suggestions in the text are listed in the reference section of each chapter rather than described in detail in the text.

The text includes a comprehensive view of classroom management that is wholistic and developmental. Instead of focusing on one age group, such as elementary or secondary school students, it is designed to provide readers with an understanding of students as complete human beings who are at a specific stage in the developmental process. By explaining why some techniques are more or less effective with students at particular levels of psychological, intellectual, and moral development, the text will help educators select techniques that are developmentally appropriate for their students. For example, readers will be better able to determine the extent to which their students are ready to participate in the establishment of classroom rules and objectives, to settle disputes among themselves without guidance and supervision, to use self-management techniques, to exercise self-control for intrinsic rather than extrinsic rewards, and to behave appropriately because that is the reasonable and ethical thing to do rather than to obtain a positive consequence or avoid a negative one.

This text is also comprehensive in terms of the broad range of classroom management techniques it offers. Instead of describing a limited number of techniques in great detail, the book includes the wide range of techniques that are available to deal with behavior problems. Teachers can select those that best suit their personalities, their philosophy of education, their values, the circumstances in which they work, and the developmental levels of their students.

The information in this book should empower educators to spend more time doing what they are supposed to do—teach, and their students should be able to spend more of their time doing what they are supposed to do—learn. The result should be measurable improvement in students' academic achievement and self-esteem.

The principles, concepts, strategies, and techniques included in the book come from my understanding of the writing and research of other professionals in the field, my training and experiences as a regular educator, special educator, clinical psychologist, and neuropsychologist, and my experience living and working with different ethnic and socioeconomic groups. They have proved effective with regular education students, mainstreamed students, and students in special education programs at both the primary and secondary levels. I sincerely hope they will be helpful to you.

Acknowledgments

I am grateful to the following reviewers of the text for their many excellent suggestions: Joann Adams, The Master's College; Karen D. Carpenter, Coastal Carolina University; Delores Gardner, Texas Women's University; and Frank Guldbrandsen, University of Minnesota, Duluth.

I am also grateful to my colleagues: to Nancy Cloud, Susan Pellegrini, and Jeri Traub for their constructive criticisms of earlier versions of the manuscript and to Henry Fishel, Harry Krohn, and George Singfield, who taught me so much when I was a classroom teacher. I also thank my sponsoring editor, Frank Graham, who helped me give my best to this text.

INTRODUCTION TO CLASSROOM MANAGEMENT

This introductory chapter begins by describing the components of an effective classroom management approach and the roles that educators assume to manage their classrooms well. Then it discusses the value and importance of basing classroom management techniques on behavior research.

Components of an Effective Approach

Because one picture is said to be worth a thousand words, let's begin by videotaping a typical day in the lives of certain teachers and their students to see if we can discover aspects essential to effective classroom management. We are in luck—the taping goes smoothly. Now it is time to review what we have recorded. Most teachers are doing an excellent job, but one seems less successful at maintaining order than her colleagues.

Avoiding Behavior Problems

Ms. Tucker is a good instructor with a flare for the dramatic. She chooses interesting material, and her students like her. Despite this, she lost her students' attention a number of times, and a few were even disruptive.

Let's study some specific incidents. Here is one: Seven or eight students are talking to each other; two are arguing over something. We rewind the tape to a few minutes earlier to see if we can discover why. Ms. Tucker is working with one student at her desk while the other students are working in their seats. Soon two students start talking, and then a few students near them look up to see what is going on. Ms. Tucker either does not hear them or chooses to ignore them. Pretty soon two more students start talking, then two more. By the time Ms. Tucker finally looks up, she has lost almost half the class. We can see from the tape that she should have intervened much earlier, before the talking had spread.

We review the tape again to find another incident. Here, Ms. Tucker is standing in the front of the room talking to one student while most of the others are either looking around or talking to one another. We rewind from here, and everything looks fine. Ms. Tucker is in front of the room talking, and everyone is paying attention. Oh, oh! Joe just passed a note to someone, and Ms. Tucker sees it. She interrupts her presentation and starts lecturing Joe about how many times she has told him not to do this. Joe defends himself, and she chastises him some more. Meanwhile, she is losing the students, at least those who are not interested in what she has to say about Joe, what Joe says back, or her response. Clearly, Ms. Tucker would have been better off if she had handled the situation without stopping the lesson. From this review of Ms. Tucker's class, we can conclude that *classroom management includes the use of good group management techniques that keep the group on task and functioning smoothly without too many interruptions or disruptions.*

Now let's study certain students to see what we can learn about classroom management from them. Most seem to be doing just what they are supposed to be doing. They work at their task and look about as content as most students are in school. But a few are obviously behavior problems. Right off, Teresa attracts our attention because her behavior from one class to another is so inconsistent. In three classes she did fine, but her behavior left much to be desired in Mr. Garcia's second-period social studies. Let's study her behavior in that class more closely.

Teresa is whispering to the person next to her. Now she is getting up to sharpen her pencil. There she is looking around the room and doodling in her notebook. Oops, she has taken out a comic book. Oh, oh! She is tapping the girl in front of her with a ruler, which starts another discussion. And so it goes.

Puzzled about why her behavior is so different in the social studies class, we study how each teacher works with her. This will help us figure out whether the way she behaves in social studies is related to the way Mr. Garcia deals with her or to other factors, such as the time of day or her level of interest in the subject.

After watching all four teachers, we discover that Mr. Garcia does not do some of the things that Teresa's other teachers do. Specifically, Teresa's other three teachers keep a watchful eye on her. One goes to Teresa's desk to see how her work is coming along. Another has Teresa working with a peer tutor. Aha! The third teacher gives Teresa seatwork that is different from what most of the other students are doing. Perhaps these teachers realize that Teresa will stray if she does not get more help than the other students. Although we cannot be sure from just viewing the video, it is beginning to look as if Mr. Garcia could have prevented Teresa's inattentive behavior by giving her the extra help she needed to stay on task. Studying the tape of Teresa has shown us that classroom management is more than just techniques for working with groups of students. *Classroom management includes using certain skills to keep individual students involved in productive work.*

Solving Behavior Problems

Now let's study another student, Hank, who is the most disruptive student on our tape. He calls out answers without being called on, grabs material from other students, pushes

Students who aren't engaged by the classroom instruction can become restless and bored and may end up misbehaving; however, involved, interested students seldom misbehave.

someone on a swing during recess who does not want to be pushed, and leaves his lunch bag and garbage on the cafeteria table, although the other students all clean up after themselves. In reviewing the tape to see if we can gain any insight into the problem, we can find nothing that any of his teachers did to provoke his disruptive behavior. We also cannot identify any early warning signs that his teachers might have used to intervene before he actually misbehaved. And finally, we see no inconsistencies in his behavior with different teachers in the classroom, during recess, or in the cafeteria. Hank is pretty much the same in all settings.

Although we cannot be 100% sure, it looks as if something about Hank himself would have to explain why he misbehaves consistently even though his teachers use the kinds of group and individual management techniques that prevent most behavior problems. These classroom management techniques, which work for most students, do not work for Hank. This leads us to realize that classroom management involves more than just avoiding problems. *Effective classroom management includes techniques for solving the behavior problems of students who don't respond to techniques that generally keep the group functioning smoothly and most students involved in productive work.*

Fostering Personal Growth

Finally, let's study one more teacher. Ms. Kelly has none of the problems we noticed in Ms. Tucker's tape. Her students almost always do what they are supposed to do without interruptions or disruptions. She clearly has much more control over students than Ms. Tucker, but it is obvious that her students are not happy. An example of their dissatisfaction is that while Ms. Kelly is talking, some students roll their eyes up, and others exchange knowing glances.

Let's rewind the tape to catch the beginning of this incident. Ms. Kelly is giving out homework. "I want all of you to put this assignment into your binders right now so no one loses it like the last one," she says in a clipped way. Some students begin to signal annoyance to each other. Three raise their hands, but Ms. Kelly continues without calling on them. "Do your own work. Follow the directions *exactly* as they are on the sheet, and remember what I said about no credit for assignments handed in late. No more excuses. You have two weeks to hand in your reports. That should be more than enough."

Now Ms. Kelly calls on one of the students, who asks, "Can we report on a book that isn't on the list if we . . . ?" "No!" Ms. Kelly interrupts gruffly, without giving the student a chance to finish. "You may only report on books from the list." Ms. Kelly's students grimace, while another student raises his hand. Ms. Kelly calls on him. "But you said we would have a month to do our book reports." "I know I did," Ms. Kelly responds. "However, I changed my mind because of the class play." At that, a sea of hands shoots up, and most of the students look annoyed. "There's no sense wasting valuable time discussing it," Ms. Kelly continues without slowing down, "that's the way it has to be." Some students express their disagreement by sighing and murmuring. Ms. Kelly ends the discussion by telling everyone to put their binders away and to take out their math books.

In contrast to Ms. Tucker, Ms. Kelly is certainly in control of her class and can keep her students on task. But there is clearly room for improvement in the way she is managing her class. Ms. Kelly helps us see that classroom management is more than classroom control and merely avoiding or solving behavior problems—though these are important and necessary goals. *Classroom management includes creating a positive classroom environment that enhances students' personal growth.*

The videotapes showed us that educators need to have at least three types of competencies to manage their classroom effectively: (1) the ability to avoid problems by having the group function smoothly without too many interruptions or disruptions and by keeping individual students involved in productive work; (2) the ability to solve the behavior problems of students who do not respond to the management techniques that avoid most behavior problems; and (3) the ability to create a classroom environment that enhances students' personal growth. The purpose of this book is to help educators acquire these abilities.

Three Aspects of the Educator's Role

In addition to the three competencies just described, Kounin (1) suggests that there are also three aspects of a teacher's roles vis-à-vis his or her students: an instructor, a manager, and a person. Applying Kounin's categories to the videotape, we can see that Mr. Garcia might have been able to avoid Teresa's behavior problems by using more appropriate instructional techniques. Ms. Tucker's students would probably have behaved better if she had used more effective group management techniques. And Ms. Kelly was too arbitrary and authoritarian in her personal relationships with her students.

In attending to all three aspects of the educator's role, this book describes instructional and managerial techniques that teachers can use to avoid as many behavior problems as possible, solve those that do occur, and enhance their students' personal growth. Specific discussions will provide you with tools to gain insight into your personality and the way it is likely to affect the way you perceive and react to your students' behavior. These discussions include suggestions on how you can use your personality to maximum advantage in the classroom.

Limitations to the Educator's Role

This book focuses on what you can do as an individual to solve your students' behavior problems. But the effects of your efforts will also be influenced—and possibly limited— by the total school context (ecology). For example, if the previous teachers of your second graders allowed students to approach the teacher's desk when they were confused or unsure about their seatwork and go to the bathroom whenever the bathroom pass was not being used, students will have an easier time adjusting if you set those same rules rather than if you require them to raise their hands and ask permission to do such things. Likewise, even if you feel comfortable with occasionally expressing your pride in your seventh-grade students or your concern about their feelings by some kind of physical contact, such as patting them on the back or placing an arm around their shoulders, you may hesitate to do this if your administrators frown on physical contact between teachers and students. Finally, even your best efforts to promote racial harmony among your students can fail if the rest of the faculty and school administration are not working toward the same goal.

You may find it necessary, on occasion, to explain to students why some of your methods differ from those of your colleagues. In general, paying attention to the total school environment will help you become a better classroom manager, and you will see how the school environment limits or fosters your role. Since the total school ecology often affects the results of your individual efforts, you may want to take an active role in helping develop schoolwide policies, attitudes, and approaches that support your efforts with your students.

The Value of a Research-Based Approach

Until fairly recently, classroom management was an art, not a science, and some teachers excelled at this art. Today, as a result of considerable research, we know enough about the science of behavior to put classroom management on a scientific basis (although, as any experienced teacher will tell you, classroom management remains partially an art).

Behavior research has revealed the weakness in some basic assumptions about classroom management. For example, until recently, many educators believed that students' behavior could be managed by rewarding desirable behavior and ignoring and/or punishing undesirable behavior. Recent research into the effects of reward and punishment on classroom behavior, however, shows that the relationship between rewards and punishment and their subsequent behavior is much more complex than had been supposed. Chapters 2 and 3 discuss the implications of these results in detail. I mention these findings here as an example of the role that theory and research play in improving classroom management approaches.

The following are some of the findings on using positive and negative consequences to manage students' behavior. Contrary to popular myth, extrinsic positive reinforcement (a reward that comes from outside the student) does not always increase desired behavior (2, 3). For example, praise from a teacher is likely to be ineffective if it is planned rather than spontaneous, if it is insincere, or if it is given effusively for trivial accomplishments. Under certain conditions, positive reinforcement can even have a detrimental effect on students' performance. In particular, students who are already motivated to learn and behave appropriately in the classroom may lose their intrinsic motivation to do so if they become too interested in earning extrinsic rewards (4–15). Positive reinforcement may increase students' learned helplessness and dependency if they come to rely excessively on their teachers' approval and opinions in place of their own motivation (16–18). And it can discourage creativity if students become more concerned about pleasing their teachers or conforming to their teachers' expectations than finding their own solutions to problems (19–22).

After reviewing the research on the effects of positive reinforcement, Deci concluded that

> extrinsic rewards whether money, praise, good player rewards, or gold stars—under varying circumstances—have deleterious effects on the intrinsic motivation and performance of the rewardee. . . . Many of the widespread practices and many of the widely espoused prescriptions for using extrinsic rewards to motivate people don't work the way practitioners and prescribers expect them to. (7, pp. 193–94)

The other tactic, negative consequences, may not reduce the incidence of undesirable behavior either (2), especially negative consequences that are harsh, excessive, or unfair. Even when negative consequences do reduce undesirable behavior, they can have unwanted side effects, causing students to lose interest in learning, become anxious, drop out of school, lose respect for their teachers, or try to turn other students against the teacher (23–27). And withdrawing attention or ignoring students when they misbehave is ineffective if their misbehavior is maintained by peer attention or other environmental reinforcements beyond the teacher's control (2, 3, 27).

The use of consequences to control students can insulate teachers from important feedback. For example, students might hide the fact that they are bored, frustrated, or angry because of the consequences they incur when they show their true reactions. As a result, educators might not realize that they need more emphasis on positive classroom management approaches, such as positive teacher-pupil relationships, effective instructional techniques, group management skills, and curriculum planning (28).

Students may also not experience consequences in the way their teachers intended.

For example, praising students in front of their peers may be counterproductive with some students. And suspending students who want to avoid school may encourage, not discourage, them to misbehave. As Brophy and Putnam explain in their discussions of reinforcements,

> Certain potential rewards, most notably teacher attention and praise and symbolic rewards, tend to be discussed as if they were universally rewarding. In fact, they are probably less rewarding than commonly believed. Many students find special attention or recognition from the teacher to be embarrassing or threatening rather than rewarding. (2, p. 53)

Findings show that the effectiveness of positive and negative consequences as a classroom management technique varies with student age, tending to be most effective with young children in kindergarten and first grade, somewhat less effective with older students, and least effective with secondary school students (2, 29, 30). The effectiveness of positive and negative consequences also depends, in part, on students' socioeconomic and ethnic backgrounds and their gender (see chapters 5 and 6). Finally, no one has shown that behavioral change brought about by positive and negative consequences in one situation generalizes to other situations (different classrooms, teachers, etc.) or is maintained when the extrinsic reinforcers are dropped (2, 31).

Despite research findings that question the widely held notion that positive and negative consequences are a fairly foolproof way of managing classrooms, the shelves of libraries and bookstores overflow with "how-to" books describing how to solve behavior problems using such techniques. Even when such suggestions are helpful, without scientific research it is difficult to determine under what conditions and with what types of students they are most likely and least likely to be effective. Research-based techniques are grounded in fact.

References

The following reference deals with three aspects of the educator's role.

1. Kounin, J. S. (1970). *Discipline and Group Management in Classrooms*. New York: Holt, Rinehart & Winston.

The following references discuss limited effectiveness of positive reinforcement.

2. Brophy, J. E., & Putnam, J. C. (1978). *Classroom Management in the Elementary Grades*. ERIC ED 167, 537.

3. Skiba, R. J. (1983). *Classroom Behavior Management: A Review of the Literature*. ERIC ED 236 839.

The following references deal with contradictory effects of positive reinforcement.

4. Condry, J., & Chambers, J. (1978). Intrinsic motivation and the process of learning. In M. R. Lepper & D. Greene (Eds.), *The Hidden Cost of Reward: New Perspectives on the Psychology of Human Motivation*. New York: Erlbaum.

5. De Charms, R. (1976). *Enhancing Motivation: Change in the Classroom*. New York: Irvington.

6. Deci, E. L. (1976). *Intrinsic Motivation*. New York: Plenum Press.

7. Deci, E. L. (1978). Applications of research on the effects of rewards. In M. R. Lepper & D. Greene (Eds.), *The Hidden Costs of Reward: New Perspectives on the Psychology of Human Motivation*. New York: Erlbaum.

8. Lepper, M. R., & Greene, D. (Eds.). (1978). *The Hidden Costs of Reward: New Perspectives on the Psychology of Human Motivation*. New York: Erlbaum.

9. Pittman, T., Boggiano, A., & Ruble, D. (1982). Intrinsic and extrinsic motivational orientations: Limiting conditions on the undermining and enhancing effects of reward on intrinsic motivation. In J. Levine & M. Wang (Eds.), *Teacher-Student Perceptions: Implications for Learning*. Morristown, NJ: Erlbaum.

10. Ross, M. (1976). The self-perception of intrinsic motivation. In J. H. Harvey, W. J. Ickes, & R. F. Kidd (Eds.), *New Directions in Attributional Research* (Vol. I). New York: Erlbaum.

Detrimental effects of praise on learning are considered in the following references.

11. Brophy, J. (1981). Teacher praise: A functional analysis. *Review of Educational Research, 51,* 5–32.

12. Condry, J. (1975). The role of initial interest and task performance on intrinsic motivation. In J. C. McCullers (Chair), *Hidden Costs of Reward*. A symposium presented at the American Psychological Association Convention, Chicago.

13. Good, T. L., & Grouws, D. A. (1977). Teaching effects: A process-product study in fourth-grade mathematics classes. *Journal of Teacher Education, 28,* 45–50.

14. McGraw, K. (1978). The detrimental effects of rewards on performance: A literature review and a prediction model. In M. Lepper & D. Greene (Eds.), *The Hidden Costs of Reward: New Perspectives on the Psychology of Human Motivation*. New York: Erlbaum.

15. Miller, L. B., & Estes, B. W. (1961). Monetary rewards and motivation in discrimination learning. *Journal of Experimental Psychology, 61,* 501–504.

Effects of praise on learned helplessness and dependency are discussed in the following references.

16. Ginott, H. G. (1972). *Teacher and Child*. New York: Avon.

17. Kruglanski, A. W. (1978). Endogenous attribution and extrinsic motivation. In

M. Lepper & D. Greene (Eds.), *The Hidden Costs of Reward: New Perspectives on the Psychology of Human Motivation*. New York: Erlbaum.

18. Weiner, B. (1979). A theory of motivation in some classroom experiences. *Journal of Educational Psychology, 71,* 3–25.

The following references discuss detrimental effects of praise on creativity.

19. Jenke, S., & Peck, D. (1976). Is immediate reinforcement appropriate? *Arithmetic Teacher, 23,* 32–33.

20. Johnson, D., & Johnson, R. (1975). *Learning Together and Alone: Cooperation, Competition, and Individualization*. Englewood Cliffs, NJ: Prentice-Hall.

21. Kruglanski, A. W., Friedman, I., & Zeevi, G. (1971). The effects of extrinsic incentive on some qualitative aspects of task performance. *Journal of Personality, 39,* 606–617.

22. Soar, R., & Soar, R. (1975). Classroom behavior, pupil characteristics, and pupil growth for the school year and summer. *JSAS Catalog of Selected Documents in Psychology, 5,* 873.

Negative consequences are discussed in the following references.

23. Fisher, C. W., Berliner, D. C., Filby, N. N., Marliave, R., Cohen, L. S., & Dishaw, M. M. (1980). Teaching behaviors, academic learning time, and student achievement: An overview. In C. Denham & A. Lieberman (Eds.), *Time to Learn*. Washington, DC: National Institute of Education.

24. Masden, C. H., Becker, W. C., Thomas, D. R., Koser, L., & Plager, E. (1968). An analysis of the reinforcing function of "sit down" commands. In R. K. Parker (Ed.), *Readings in Educational Psychology*. Boston: Allyn & Bacon.

25. Meacham, M. L., & Wiesen, A. E. (1969). *Changing Classroom Behavior: A Manual for Precision Teaching*. Scranton, PA: International Textbook Company.

26. Saunders, M. (1979). *Class Control and Behavior Problems*. Berkshire, England: McGraw-Hill.

Ignoring behavior is discussed in the following reference.

27. Jones, F. H., & Miller, W. H. (1974). The effective use of negative attention for reducing group disruption in special elementary school classrooms. *Psychological Record, 24,* 435–458.

The following reference deals with eliminating feedback.

28. Ryan, B. (1979). A case against behavior modification in the "ordinary classroom." *Journal of School Psychology, 17* (2), 131–136.

The following references discuss reinforcement and students' age.

29. Forness, S. R. (1973). The reinforcement hierarchy. *Psychology in the Schools, 10,* 168–177.

30. Stallings, J. (1975). Implementation and child effects of teaching practices in Follow Through classrooms. *Monographs of the Society for Research in Child Development, 40,* 7–8.

Generalization is considered in the following reference.

31. Emery, R., & Marholin, D. (1977). An applied behavior analysis of delinquency: The irrelevancy of relevant behavior. *American Psychologist, 32,* 860–873.

PART ONE

AVOIDING BEHAVIOR PROBLEMS

Introduction

As we noted in chapter 1, the first stage of an effective classroom management approach is to use techniques that avoid as many behavior problems as possible and to do this in ways that enhance students' personal growth. In many instances, the same techniques that educators use to prevent behavior problems also enhance their students' personal development; thus, these two goals are complementary. For example, helping students to be more responsible for their own behavior, more empathic about how their actions affect others, and more patient may also help them control their own behavior. But sometimes teachers use classroom management techniques that interfere with their students' personal growth. By using ridicule and sarcasm to control the students, for example, the teacher may lower their self-esteem. Or teachers may be so dominating and controlling that they stunt the development of their students' self-confidence, judgment, and initiative. Because certain techniques that help avoid behavior problems can also interfere with students' personal growth, it is important to be selective in the techniques you choose.

Enhancing students' personal growth can mean different things to different people. For purposes of this book, enhancing your students' personal growth will stand for fostering the development of the following 10 characteristics:

1. Self-esteem: self-acceptance, a healthy self-image, and a perception of self-worth that are reflected in personal, academic, and social behaviors
2. Self-confidence: confidence regarding personal and social skill development
3. Responsibility: reliability and investment of self in personal and social commitments
4. Initiative: the ability to undertake and sustain independent effort
5. Honesty/trust: the ability to express feelings honestly and openly to others
6. Empathy: the ability to respond to others with objectivity and understanding
7. Judgment: the ability to make appropriate decisions independently and to adapt behavior to the demands of a situation
8. Flexibility: the ability to adjust to change and to alter behavior constructively
9. Patience: the ability to accept differences during interaction with others; the ability to delay personal need gratification; the ability to handle frustration
10. Humor: the ability to employ humor appropriately, both in general and in situations involving conflict, to maintain perspective and release stress (1, p. 7)

This part introduces a four-step approach to avoid most behavior problems. You start by motivating students to want to behave appropriately because it's the right thing to do. Then you establish procedures for handling potentially disruptive situations. Next you establish rules that clarify how students are expected to behave. Finally, you convince students that it is necessary for them to comply with classroom rules and procedures.

Although all four steps contribute to avoiding behavior problems, motivating students to want to behave is the most important in a democratic society. Autocratic societies can rely on coercion and consequences to keep their citizens in line, but a democratic nation requires its citizens to voluntarily sacrifice their personal desires for the benefit of the group when necessary, accept the will of the majority, and respect the rights of others. This does not mean that enforcing the cost of misbehavior, the fourth step, is unnecessary—just that it should not be the most important or receive the most emphasis in a classroom management approach. To have classrooms approximate the real world and to prepare students for that world, educators should stress internal, not external, control and intrinsic, not extrinsic, motivation.

When students want to behave appropriately, they are more willing to exercise their self-control and improve their relationships with others. Educators can accomplish this by helping students to more willingly accept the rights of others, sacrifice their desires for others' benefits, and accept group goals. These motivational techniques also make students more able to assume responsibility for their own actions and accept the role their actions play in provoking responses from others.

With respect to their own goals, such techniques aid students in exercising more self-discipline and enable them to sacrifice a less important satisfaction of the moment to achieve a more important future satisfaction. They also prepare students to endure the difficult, frustrating, and distasteful but necessary aspects of life that we can't avoid if we want to accomplish worthwhile goals.

Students who have developed such self-control have many of the personal qualities needed to behave appropriately in school. Educators can use a number of techniques to foster this type of self-discipline in their students, including satisfying their students' basic needs, relating to their students in ways that enhance the development of their self-control, modeling appropriate behavior, promoting group cohesiveness, creating classroom environments that match students' needs, and increasing students' belief in the value of school. Chapter 2 describes techniques that educators can use to motivate their students to want to behave properly.

Chapter 3 explores techniques that manage such potentially disruptive situations as start-ups, transitions, obtaining permission, and distributing materials. The chapter describes how to lessen the likelihood that students will misbehave. Finally, for students still tempted to misbehave, they will be less likely to do so if the teacher enforces the cost of misbehaving. The chapter outlines techniques for convincing students that misbehaving would not be to their advantage, including making the rules explicit, making the rules acceptable to them, convincing students that they will be caught if they break the rules, and convincing students that, once caught, they will experience the consequences of their actions.

Chapters 4, 5, and 6 are extremely important in a diverse society such as ours. Chapter 4 describes how educators can avoid problems by adapting their classroom management approaches to the contextual aspects of their students' lives. Chapter 5 discusses how to accomplish this by taking into account the ethnic and socioeconomic diversity of the students. Chapter 6 examines the role of gender and sexual orientation in classroom management.

There is considerable controversy about whether school failure causes behavior problems or behavior problems cause school failure. The information in chapters 4, 5, and 6 shed light on this controversy. It is certainly true that students who experience less success in school, as measured by grades, achievement test scores, or the tracks they are assigned to, are more likely to misbehave in school; but there is considerable disagreement about whether there is a direct cause-and-effect relationship between the two factors. Many educators do not believe that schools cause students to fail or to misbehave. Some claim that a relationship exists between socioeconomic status and ethnic background on the one hand and both school success and misbehavior on the other. They believe that poor students and students from certain ethnic backgrounds, especially African Americans, Hispanic Americans, and Native Americans, do poorly in school and misbehave in school because of their backgrounds, not because of the schools they attend or the teachers that instruct them. Chapters 4 and 5 examine this point of view. Some educators who believe that misbehavior is a cause of school failure more often than the reverse deny that socioeconomic class and ethnic background are contributing factors. These educators see other causes of student misbehavior in school, and these causes are discussed in Part Three of this book.

The author believes that some behavior problems are caused by mismatches between what students need and what the schools offer them, whereas other students come to school predisposed to behave in ways that will interfere with their ability to succeed. This part describes techniques that educators can use to avoid behavior problems by helping all students to succeed, regardless of the context of their lives, their socioeconomic class and ethnic background, and their gender. Part Three explains how educators can help students who do not do well in school because of behavior problems that impede their learning.

MOTIVATING STUDENTS TO WANT TO BEHAVE APPROPRIATELY

You can avoid many behavior problems by motivating your students to want to behave appropriately. You can accomplish this by satisfying students' basic needs so they can attend to academic matters, maintaining positive student-teacher relationships, modeling the behavior that students should emulate, promoting group cohesiveness, creating a classroom environment that matches student needs, and enhancing students' belief in the value of school.

Satisfying Students' Basic Needs

All people have basic needs that they strive to fulfill, and students are more likely to behave appropriately when these needs are satisfied (2). This is because human needs are organized in a hierarchical way, so that people primarily concerned with meeting their basic needs are less likely to take care of higher level needs. Here is a hierarchically ordered list of human needs, starting with basic survival needs and working up from there:

1. Physiological satisfaction—taking care of hunger, thirst, rest

2. Safety—avoiding injury, physical attack, pain, extreme temperatures, disease, psychological abuse

3. Love and acceptance from others and a feeling of belonging to a group

4. Self-esteem, self-confidence, and a sense of purpose and empowerment

5. Self-actualization (3, 4)

15

When students are preoccupied with their physical well-being, safety, or pain, chances are they will be too concerned with these basic issues to care much about learning arithmetic skills or American history. In the classroom, they may act out their anger, resentment, and frustration at not having their basic needs fulfilled. And they may be jealous of their more fortunate peers and show this in a variety of ways.

Because, like all people, students have the right to have their basic needs satisfied and cannot be expected to function adequately in school if these needs are not satisfied, educators should place the highest priority on seeing that their students' basic needs are being met. Although educators do not have primary responsibility for ensuring that students' basic needs are satisfied, they do play an important role in this area of concern.

To play your part in seeing that your students' basic needs are met, be on the lookout for signs that your students are not being fed, clothed, or cared for adequately or that they are the victims of physical, sexual, or psychological abuse. You cannot solve these problems on your own, but you can—and are legally obligated to in most states—report your observations to those who can do something about the situation (see chapter 4).

On a personal level, you can provide students with some of the love, acceptance, and feeling of belonging we all require, and you can encourage other students to do the same. Enhance your students' sense of personal power by allowing them a role in the decision-making process in class. Improve their self-esteem and self-confidence by providing them with opportunities to solve their own problems, resolve their own conflicts with others, and experience success in activities they choose. Protect students who are ethnically, racially, religiously, economically, physically, or intellectually different from their peers from being laughed at, teased, or rejected (see chapters 4 and 5). And avoid using sarcasm, ridicule, and harmfully frank statements to control your students. Specific techniques for accomplishing the goals of meeting students' basic needs are described in subsequent chapters.

Positive Teacher-Student Relationships

The ways in which you choose to relate to your students in the three aspects of your role—as instructor, manager, and person—can increase your students' willingness to cooperate, learn, and behave appropriately and can motivate them to use you as a role model (5, 6). The following suggestions for establishing a positive teacher-student relationship are commonly found in the literature on classroom management. Research has not yet determined whether all of these suggestions always work, but experts have been virtually unanimous in recommending them.

Instructor

"A well-planned curriculum implemented by a well-prepared teacher who presents a study topic so that it holds the interest of the students has traditionally been considered a deterrent to disruptive behavior" (9, p. 21). This assertion in one form or another is shared by many writers on classroom management (10–16) and has been supported by research (7, 8). Although curriculum development and instructional techniques are not covered in a text on behavior problems, any discussion of how you can motivate students to want to behave has to involve the importance of your role as instructor—it is a key to unlocking your students' desire to behave.

Manager

Being in Charge   Teachers seen by their students as being in charge of their class have fewer behavior problems to contend with than those teachers seen as not being in charge. The critical distinction is that the teacher act as an authority and not as an authoritarian.

Educators seen as not in charge of their classrooms are described as noninterventionists (28) and even nonentities (29). They experience more behavior problems, possibly because their lack of classroom leadership tempts students to misbehave (18, 30, 38, 39).

In contrast, authoritative teachers maintain their authority and leadership, but they also provide students with a role in the decision-making process, seek consensus, and make sure that the students understand the rationale behind their decisions. Authoritarian teachers do just the opposite; they keep all the power to themselves and deny their students a role in the decision-making process. Goss and Ingersoll describe the difference between authoritarian and authoritative teachers in the following way:

> The authoritarian teacher exercises firm, rigid, autocratic control. The teacher dominates, but the domination is aloof and not directed at the positive personal growth of students. Students' self-esteem or self-concept is of little consequence. Because order and control are ends in and of themselves, control becomes repressive.

> The authoritative teacher also exercises firm control, but the control is paired with warmth and genuine concern for the well-being of the students. Order and control are seen as a means to an end. The teacher views classroom control as an element in providing an atmosphere in which students may experience positive personal growth.

> The authoritative teacher, as we define this person, establishes a degree of control and structure within the classroom that offers a sense of stability and security. Limits of acceptable behavior are clearly specified and the ramifications of violating limits are understood. The limits are not arbitrary and dogmatic; they are fair and reasonable. (32, p. 10)

Gnagey offers the following explanation for why some teachers are too authoritarian:

> Their primary concern is maintaining order. They tend to stereotype students in terms of their appearance, behavior, and parents' socioeconomic status. Despots perceive students as irresponsible, undisciplined people who must be controlled through punishment. These teachers view misbehavior in moralistic terms and take each violation as a personal affront. They maintain impersonal relationships with their students and expect them to accept the despot's decision without question. (29, p. 25)

If you have had experience managing groups of students, your answers to the self-quizzes that follow will help you determine whether you would be comfortable permitting your

*Self-Quiz: Students
and Decision Making*

Would you include your students in the following processes if they were sufficiently mature?

Establishing classroom rules

Determining the consequences of not following classroom rules

Setting up classroom routines

Deciding what should be included in the curriculum

Selecting teaching materials

Choosing class outings, trips, etc.

students to play a role in the decision-making process. If you find you would not, you might want to look into developing this capacity.

*Self-Quiz:
On Student Questions*

Would you encourage students to question you about these topics?

Is a rule necessary?

Is a punishment fair?

Is a homework assignment excessive?

Is seatwork just busy work?

Is some aspect of the curriculum irrelevant or boring?

Is a grade fair?

Is the amount of time allotted for certain assignments too short?

Should students who finish their work before the others be allowed to use their free time doing whatever they want?

Being Fair   Good managers are fair. They do not prejudge students based on ethnic, cultural, gender, socioeconomic, physical, or intellectual factors. They may consult their students' cumulative records or previous teachers about them, but they maintain an open mind and draw their own conclusions. (Chapter 5 discusses cultural differences in greater detail.)

Good managers also have realistic expectations for their students. They do not overestimate what outstanding students can accomplish or how well their model students can behave. They also avoid underestimating the potential achievements of students with learning problems.

Research indicates that educators tend to treat high achievers and low achievers differently. Specifically, teachers usually call on high achievers more often (19, 22, 31); give them more positive attention, feedback, praise, and approval (21, 23, 25, 33, 36); and both prompt them and wait longer for them to answer questions (35, 37). Educators also tend to seat high-achieving students closer to their desks (17, 24, 34), and research shows that students who sit closer to their teachers learn more (17, 24, 26, 40). To be a fair manager, try to avoid these tendencies, and treat all students equally.

Self-Quiz: On Fairness

Once you have had experience working with groups of students, your answers to the following questions will help you assess how free of bias your perceptions and expectations of your students are in the classroom.

- Are the behavior problems you identify always, or almost always, attributed to one group? Is it always boys who are most troublesome, Black children, girls, or Chicano children?
- Are your children divided in their seating, with the girls all on one side and the boys all on the other? Or the Black children all on one side and the white all on the other?
- Do you spend more time with one group than another? That is, do you stand and teach on the side of the room where one group sits? Do you direct your comments to and make pleasant eye contact with one group more than the other? Do you actually work more often with one group rather than the other?
- Have you indignantly dismissed, without serious consideration of the possibility that it may be true, an accusation by a child that you are prejudiced against a particular group?
- Do you teach literature to the children without including the work of minority writers?
- Do you teach history from the adopted textbook without making corrections and filling in omissions about minority groups?
- Do you use, without commenting about this to the children, reading books that do not include stories with minority-group characters? (27, pp. 91–92)

Self-Quiz: Working with Low Achievers

Your answers to the following questions about low achievers will help you evaluate how fair you are being in your work with them. Do you:

1. Call on low achievers less frequently to answer questions or demonstrate something?
2. Wait less time for them to answer?
3. Give them less encouragement or assistance after you have called on them?
4. Give them less praise when they answer correctly?
5. Praise them for answers that really aren't correct?
6. Criticize them more for incorrect answers?
7. Give them less feedback?
8. Interrupt them more often when they are reciting?
9. Maintain less eye contact with them when you lecture?
10. Allow them to do less work than others are expected to complete in order to receive credit?
11. Seat them far from you? (20, 22)

Person

Kounin (6) and other researchers (7) have demonstrated that students who like their teachers learn more and behave better than students who do not. While evidence does not support a particular list of personality traits that characterize popular and well-respected

Sometimes active listening may require you to encourage students to talk about things that you may not want to hear about or deal with.

teachers, researchers suggest that students are more likely to have positive feelings toward teachers who listen to them and encourage them to express themselves; are genuine, honest, and sincere; are friendly; communicate understanding, acceptance, and empathy; and maintain a sense of humor (29, 41–54).

Active Listening   Teachers who are good classroom managers know how to listen— and listen actively—to their students. Gordon defines active listening in the following way: "Active listening, as opposed to passive listening (silence), involves interaction with the student, and it also provides the student with proof (feedback) of the teacher's understanding" (45). According to Gordon, active listening involves (1) encouraging your students to communicate whatever is troubling them, (2) trying to discover the true meaning of what they have communicated if it is not clear, (3) checking with them to determine whether your understanding is correct, and (4) communicating your understanding to them. Gordon cites seven attitudes, or mental sets, that characterize an effective listener:

1. Have confidence in your students' abilities to solve their own problems.

2. Accept whatever feelings or ideas students express, regardless of whether you agree with them; otherwise students may be reluctant to express themselves.

3. Realize that these feelings are often transitory and that expression defuses them.

4. Try to help students, and provide time in your teaching schedule to do so.

THEORY FOCUS: GORDON ON TEACHER EFFECTIVENESS

Thomas Gordon's approach to classroom management is based on the assumption that students can, in most instances, solve their own behavior problems with guidance from their teachers. In his book *Teacher Effectiveness Training*, Gordon describes a nondirective approach. This strategy helps students to become aware of the inappropriateness of their behavior and its effects on others and to identify specific ways they can improve their behavior on their own.

Gordon advises educators to avoid power struggles with students. He believes that if a teacher wins, the result is that the students resent their teacher. But if educators give in to their students, this encourages more misbehavior. Instead of power struggles, he suggests that educators should aim for no-win exchanges in which they use active listening techniques to help students identify solutions to a problem that both teacher and student can agree on. Although Gordon is against the use of consequences to convince students to behave, he does feel that dangerous or disruptive situations call on educators to take a more directive role.

5. Empathize with your students' feelings without becoming too upset by them to be helpful.

6. Work toward becoming comfortable about hearing the real-life problems of your students.

7. Maintain the privacy and confidentiality of whatever your students reveal about themselves unless the law requires you to do otherwise, as in the case of suspected child abuse.

While it is usually a good idea to encourage students to talk about their thoughts, feelings, and problems, students from some ethnic backgrounds—for example, Asian Pacific Americans, Hispanic Americans, and Native Americans—may not be comfortable discussing such things with their teachers. In such cases it may be unwise to try too hard to encourage them to do so. (See the section on students' communication styles in chapter 5.)

Compare the following conversations between teachers and students. Can you see how the first teacher discouraged and the second teacher encouraged the student from sharing his thoughts and feelings?

STUDENT: I have a cousin staying over my house that's real weird.

TEACHER: He is?

STUDENT: Yeah! He does all kinds of drugs.

TEACHER: Like what?

STUDENT: Reefer and crack.

TEACHER: What do you think of him?

STUDENT: He's real chilly.

TEACHER: Really?

STUDENT: Sure.

TEACHER: You're kidding me, aren't you?

STUDENT: Yeah.

STUDENT: I have a cousin staying over my house that's real weird.

TEACHER: He is?

STUDENT: Yeah! He does all kinds of drugs.

TEACHER: Like what?

STUDENT: Reefer and crack.

TEACHER: What do you think of him?

STUDENT: He's real chilly.

TEACHER: You think he's chilly?

STUDENT: Yeah. Everyone likes him. He's a big shot.

TEACHER: Are you chilly too?

STUDENT: Yeah!

TEACHER: You mean you do drugs too?

STUDENT: What do you think, I'm crazy?

TEACHER: Do you think you're crazy?

STUDENT: Sometimes.

TEACHER: Why?

STUDENT: Because of what it says on TV about crack kills.

TEACHER: It sounds like you're worried about doing drugs.

STUDENT: Yeah.

Being Genuine   Almost everyone responds to a person who is genuine. Teachers are genuine when their words and actions express their true feelings and opinions. And when teachers are genuine, their students know they can trust what the teacher tells them.

Teachers have two basic reasons for not always being genuine. They may not be able to admit to themselves that they have certain feelings, or they may not be able to express their feelings to the students. Certain teachers may even hide their positive feelings from their students, but more often teachers are uncomfortable about expressing—or even feeling—their negative emotions.

If your answers to the following self-quiz suggest that you might have difficulty being genuine with your students, Chernow and Chernow (42) suggest that accepting the following three basic truths will help you be more honest with them:

Self-Quiz: Communication with Students

Do you think you would be able to communicate the following to your students in an appropriate way?

Disapproval of a student's behavior

Anger at the way the student relates to the opposite sex

Anger at the way the student treats other students

Anger at the way the student treats you

Disappointment that the student didn't keep a promise to you

Discouragement or frustration about your inability to motivate the student

Rage over your inability to control the student

Mistrust of the student's motives

Disbelief in what the student says

Which of the following do you think you would have trouble admitting even to yourself?

Dislike for a student as a person

Revulsion for a student's handicap

Preconceived notions about the student's honesty, motivation, potential, etc., based on the student's ethnic or socioeconomic background

Disappointment that the student doesn't appear to like you despite your efforts

1. In the natural course of events, students will sometimes make you uncomfortable, angry, and even furious.

2. You are entitled to have these feeling without also experiencing guilt or shame, because they are natural.

3. You are entitled to express your feelings as long as you do so in a way that doesn't harm your students.

To constantly "stuff your feelings"—that is, try to act as if nothing bothers you—can quickly lead to teacher burnout. The goal here is to express your real feelings in ways that help, not harm, your students. For example, suppose you are explaining to Tom why he shouldn't have picked on a younger student during recess. But instead of listening to you, Tom is looking around the yard and making it clear that he has no interest in what you're saying. You tell him that he is not listening, but he keeps looking around. You feel frustrated and more than a little upset. You tell yourself that he is just being defensive, that he is not purposely trying to get you angry. But that does not change your feelings, and a rage starts building inside of you. You recall that the last time you felt like this you walked away rather than express your feelings, but that only made you angrier because it seemed like that was what Tom wanted. Just remembering this makes you even angrier now. What should you do?

First, you need not feel guilty or think you are a poor teacher for being angry. Most people would get angry in that situation. Second, you should not try to mask your feelings behind a smile and walk away. Instead, tell Tom how you feel but in a way that does not attack him personally. You can do this by focusing on his behavior, not on him as a person.

"Tom, I'm getting angry. I feel you're not paying attention to what I'm saying, and that upsets me." This would be one acceptable way of expressing your feelings. Another good way would be to say, "Tom, when I see you looking everywhere but at me when I'm trying to tell you something important, it seems like you're not listening and don't care. That upsets me." Then a good follow-up, after expressing your feelings, is to set clear expectations for future behavior: "I'd like you to listen when I talk to you so we can get back to the business of you being a good student and me doing my job, too." Comments like "What's the matter with you, didn't anyone ever teach you to look at people when they talk to you?" and "Look at me when I'm talking to you" are two inappropriate ways of expressing yourself because they belittle him as a person.

By the way, failure to maintain eye contact is not always a sign of disrespect. As you will see in chapter 5, unlike European American children and youth who are taught to look at adults when they are being spoken to, African Americans and Hispanic Americans are brought up to look away when they are being reprimanded.

Being Friendly   Friendly teachers are effective managers. They are open, approachable, and available rather than closed, distant, and aloof. They are also interested in their students as people and are willing to listen to things that aren't directly related to their students' education. In turn, they reveal their interests and the kind of people they are by sharing their feelings, values, and opinions. This makes them "come alive" for their students. Although no teacher can actually be a friend of 30 students or six classes of 30 students, teachers can be friendly.

A word of caution is in order. Students are not all equally responsive to their teachers' friendly overtures. Some students, particularly from certain Asian Pacific American groups, are used to and prefer more formal relationships with their teachers. And some students with emotional problems are threatened by close relationships (see chapter 12). Therefore, if your attempts to be friendly with students are not accepted, it may be wiser to ask yourself why and back off, rather than redouble your efforts.

Shumsky (51) has identified two types of friendly teachers, one effective, the other ineffective. The first develop friendly relationships with students based on strength, respect, and trust while they maintain their role as the person in charge. The second type, motivated by a need to be accepted by students in order to build up their own self-esteem, reject taking charge and choose a weak role for themselves. The first type of friendly relationship with students is positive; the second is destructive, leaving the class lacking strong leadership.

Communicating Acceptance and Empathy   Accepting, empathic people feel good to be around. Teachers who are accepting treat all students with respect, regardless of the way the students behave or their achievement level. They accept their students, but not necessarily their students' behaviors. And when they disapprove of or reject certain behavior, they do not disapprove of or reject the students who acted inappropriately.

Notice the difference between the following statements. Those in the first column describe students' *behavior* in nonjudgmental ways. Those in the second column describe the *student* in judgmental terms. The first column rejects behavior. The second rejects the person.

You're interrupting.	You don't have any manners.
You're late again.	You're irresponsible.
You didn't hand in your work three times in the past two weeks.	You're lazy.
You are not contributing to your group by making suggestions.	You're selfish.
You're not paying attention to Latanya.	You're too self-centered.

Empathic educators try to understand their students from the students' point of view, and they often can appreciate the how and why of their students' thoughts and feelings. They understand that, given the circumstances and their students' developmental levels, their thoughts and feelings are both natural and normal. Empathic teachers can communicate their understanding of what their students are experiencing and their appreciation of why they feel and think as they do. But they don't always agree that their students should act on their thoughts and feelings. Here are some examples of empathic statements:

"I can appreciate how nervous you feel about performing the play in the auditorium today after forgetting your lines in practice yesterday. And I can understand that you don't want to participate. I remember how I felt when something like that happened to me. But I think you will do fine today, since you remembered all your lines this morning when Steve cued you."

"You look like you're ready to kill Harry for what he said about your mother. I don't blame you for being angry. But let's see if we can handle the situation in another way."

"I guess you feel pretty bad about breaking Aretha's project. Even though it really wasn't your fault, it still doesn't work anymore. But let's see what you can do to make it up to her. Okay?"

Modeling Desirable Behavior

The conventional view of teachers is that they stand in front of their students and teach them by telling them things. It may seem easier for teachers to tell students how to behave than to actually behave that way themselves, but students—especially younger ones—usually learn more from what their teachers do than from what they say (55–61). Here are alternative ways educators can handle problems in their classrooms. Which ones serve as more positive models for students?

- Harry starts a conversation while the teacher is explaining something to the class. The teacher:
  a. writes his name on the board, calling everyone's attention to his misbehavior.
  b. catches his eye and frowns slightly, conveying disapproval without calling attention to him.

- When the teacher calls on Cecilia, Cecilia says she can't answer because the teacher's directions weren't clear. The teacher:
  a. tells her to pay attention next time so she won't need to make excuses.
  b. asks her what part she didn't understand and goes over it again.

- Larry, the class clown, does something really funny. The teacher:
  a. laughs at his antics along with the other students in the class.
  b. ignores his behavior and suppresses a smile.

- Thomas, the class bully, pushes Jake. The teacher:
  a. steps in, separates them, and tells Thomas to stay in during recess so they can have a talk.
  b. yells at Thomas to stop, separates them, and scolds Thomas for his behavior.

- Rose has come to class without her homework for the third time in a week. When the teacher asks her to read the assignment, she says she left it at home. The teacher:
  a. says she doesn't believe her.
  b. says they will have to talk about the problem later in the morning.

- When the teacher tells Steve what his punishment will be for doing something wrong, Steve complains that the teacher isn't being fair. The teacher:
  a. stops the lesson for a while longer and asks Steve why he thinks he is being treated unfairly.
  b. tells Steve that the teacher, not he, is in charge, so there is no point in discussing it.

Promoting Group Cohesiveness

Research indicates that students will behave better if the class forms a cohesive group and adheres to positive group norms, such as not laughing when someone makes a mistake, not making fun of each other, and giving everyone—even poor players—a chance to play on a team during recess (62–64). Students form a cohesive group when they have a feeling of unity among them, when they think in terms of "we" as well as "I," when they experience a sense of oneness with the group, and when they are willing to accept some frustration, pain, and sacrifice of personal goals to help achieve group goals.

Group cohesiveness among students can reduce or eliminate many potential behavior problems that might otherwise arise if students feel less positive toward each other. Group cohesiveness decreases arguments between cliques; scapegoating of out-groups, minority students, and weaker students by in-groups, majority students, and dominant students; conflicts between males and females; disputes among students over minor issues; and tattling and name-calling (62). Group cohesiveness also makes students more willing to work cooperatively and put the group's goals ahead of personal goals. It increases students' willingness to conform to group norms and expectations. For all these reasons, a cohesive group that has accepted positive group norms exerts a strong influence on its members to behave appropriately out of loyalty and solidarity with the group. Thus, promoting group cohesiveness and the group's acceptance of positive norms will help you motivate your students to want to behave.

Working Together Cooperatively

The more students work together and communicate with each other in class, the more likely they are to form cohesive groups. So, even though competition is often the norm both inside and outside of school, include and stress cooperative learning experiences and group projects in your curriculum.

Although cooperative learning can enhance group cohesiveness if done properly, it can increase tension and hostility between males and females and between students from different ethnic backgrounds if done incorrectly. Female students are not always happy about cooperative learning, and there are many reasons for this. One reason is that in mixed-gender groups, females are less likely than males to participate in group discussions or assume leadership positions (69, 82–85). Another reason why females are often the losers in mixed-sex groups is that although they tend to be the providers of assistance, they are often rejected by males when they ask for assistance. In addition, in mixed-sex cooperative groups, females often revert to a pattern of not interacting with male students, allowing males to dominate them, and viewing themselves as less helpful, less important, and less visible (65, 67, 70–73, 75, 77). And there is some evidence that they may behave more competitively than they otherwise do (74). Males may actually learn more and perform better than females in cooperative mixed-sex groups because they often ignore females, contribute most of the ideas, do most of the talking, and typically function as the group leaders (66–68, 76). In mixed groups, girls tend to be equally responsive to requests from and reinforcement by either sex. However, boys are responsive primarily to other males (78–81).

These problems can be avoided. Females can benefit from mixed-gender cooperative groups when they have been given prior training on how to function as leaders of the group, when they have had prior experience with the group task, so that they are familiar with what is to be learned, and when educators have prepared students to function in a more egalitarian manner.

Cooperative learning experiences can definitely improve interethnic relationships (86,

87). Sometimes, however, the experiences of some African American and other non-European American students in mixed-ethnic cooperative groups can be similar to the negative experiences of many females (71, 88). Piel and Conwell claim:

> White children and black children may not be getting the same experience from a cooperative learning experience. . . . If white children assume leadership roles and black children assume more subservient roles then the purpose for cooperative groups seems to be somewhat diminished. (71, p. 14)

There is also evidence that some African American students are primed to cooperate with other African Americans and compete with European Americans (89). This can also defeat the purpose of cooperative learning.

To avoid these problems, teachers need to prepare their students to function in an egalitarian manner in their cooperative learning groups. Experts suggest the following guidelines to achieve a cooperative learning experience that will enhance and improve students' interpersonal relationships:

- Familiarize yourself with the variety of cooperative learning techniques available to teachers. The references at the end of this chapter are a good source of information.

- Inform students of the cooperative procedures they should follow, and teach them how to follow them.

- Prepare all students, especially those who are accustomed to accepting subservient positions, to assume the expert/leadership role.

- Sensitize students who are prone to use group situations to dominate others to the importance of allowing all students to take on all the roles available to group members.

- Monitor the groups closely to discourage the kinds of problems discussed earlier, and intervene as quickly as possible if problems arise.

You can involve students in the decision-making process to the degree that they are developmentally ready. This gives them opportunities to interact and work together as a group. If you work with younger students, instead of establishing classroom rules and selecting group activities by yourself, give your students the chance to work together by assigning them a role in the process. With older students, establish the general objective and let them figure out how to reach it under your supervision and guidance. For example, inform them that the class will take an outing or perform a play, but allow them to choose where to go or which play to perform from a list of alternatives you prepare in advance. Or advise them that they will be required to take a test on a particular topic within a specified period of time, but allow them to decide how much time they need to prepare for it. Finally, do not automatically intervene when students have disputes or differences of opinion if they are mature enough to settle their own disputes. Instead, encourage them to resolve the conflicts on their own with your assistance when it is possible for them to do so.

A creative teacher can devise many ways to involve students in cooperative activities.

When you allow a group of diverse students to resolve disputes in their own ways, do not be surprised if they do not agree on the best way to do so. As research presented in chapters 5 and 6 indicate, males and females and students from different ethnic backgrounds have somewhat different approaches to conflict resolution. Therefore, if you really want students to resolve their own conflicts, you may have to permit them to do so in ways that may not make you comfortable.

The importance of selecting developmentally appropriate classroom management techniques is stressed throughout this text. Unfortunately, many teachers do not pay close enough attention to their students' developmental level when they select classroom management and instructional techniques. For example, one study found that "only 20% of a randomly selected sample of public kindergarten classes met or exceeded a criterion of developmental appropriateness. Although another 20% of the classes were in close range to the criteria, the remaining 60% were below" (90, p. 798).

Minimizing Subgroup Formation

It is natural for some students to be attracted to one another and to want to work and play together, but make sure your students also work with students they may not select on their own. This helps them to perceive the larger "we" of the whole class as well as maintain loyalty to just their friends. Achieving this may mean playing an especially active role in getting younger boys and girls to work and play together, ensuring that the groups you assign students to are ethnically and socioeconomically heterogeneous and providing low-status students opportunities to work cooperatively with high-status students.

Another technique that helps minimize subgroups among your students is to de-emphasize ability grouping. Grouping by ability levels can be a divisive influence in the classroom. You can also make sure that all students participate in group activities so that you do not have participants and nonparticipants. For example, when selecting the list of plays for the class to choose from, make sure all the plays have a large number of parts and assign two or more students to share the main roles. And when students are playing during lunch or recess, encourage girls and boys to play group games such as kickball, punchball, jump rope, and other games together to discourage them from forming all-male or all-female groups (see chapter 6).

Create a climate of acceptance for individual differences in interests, abilities, opinions, cultural characteristics, and lifestyles in your classroom. Encourage your students to value diversity. Let them know that everyone can do something well, no one can do everything well, and by working together they can do great things. This will discourage the formation of subgroups based on differences. Teaching students to accept and value individual differences will prepare them to be better people and better citizens. It will also decrease the likelihood that individuals will be picked on or rejected because they are different.

Increasing the Value of the Group

Making the group more appealing and valuable in your students' eyes will increase cohesiveness. You can accomplish this by highlighting the positive aspects of the group. Tell them how much *they* have achieved, how well *they* are doing, and what *they* can achieve by *their* efforts. Plan appealing group activities, outings, challenges, and explorations. Assist the group to accomplish things that will be a credit to all its members, such as performing for other classes, raising money for good causes, developing a class project together, or creating a celebration for the entire class.

Maintaining Cohesiveness

Once achieved, you have to maintain group cohesiveness for it to continue. Conflicts among students are bound to occur, and so will group failures that make membership in the group less attractive. Fielding these challenges well maintains the group unity.

Settling Disputes   When conflicts develop, they should be resolved quickly with as much group participation as possible. Allow time in your schedule for students to solve the problems and conflicts that arise among them. Class time is not only for learning academic subjects; it is also for discovering how to resolve problems, which is a critical life-long skill.

Maintaining Faith in the Group   When your class fails to achieve its own or others' expectations, you can help your students put their lack of success in proper perspective. Instead of expressing disapproval, disappointment, or blame, ask students to investigate with you what the cause of the problem was. Did you or the group set expectations that were too high? Did you neglect to drill your students on the material they didn't do well on during the exam? Did your students allow themselves less time to complete a project or prepare for an exam than they actually needed? Did you wait too long before telling them to put the laboratory equipment away? Instead of lecturing the group about what they did wrong and urging or pressuring them to work harder or to be more cooperative, try to turn the problem into a learning experience. Help them to discover what their mistakes were, to learn that mistakes are a natural part of the learning process, and to decide what they can do to succeed next time.

Improving Interethnic Group Relations

Interethnic group conflict in the school reduces group cohesiveness and interferes with student functioning. In some ways, relationships between students from different ethnic backgrounds are no better and perhaps worse than before schools were integrated. While school classrooms are integrated, informal voluntary segregation is commonplace in the school yard, cafeteria, in other nonacademic areas, and during many school activities. Gang fights and other forms of even more serious violence between youths of different ethnic backgrounds have increased. These animosities and rivalries between students spill over into the classroom, reducing group cohesiveness and affecting the students' motivation to behave appropriately, their ability to attend to their studies, and their respect for educators.

There are many useful approaches to improving interethnic group relations. These approaches include discussing the similarities and differences among different ethnic groups, including aspects of students' cultures in the curriculum, taking proactive steps to counter and correct bias and prejudice, and preparing students to emancipate themselves and transform society.

Discussing Differences and Similarities   Teaching students that all people have similar needs, desires, and problems but have different ways of satisfying and solving them can increase respect for diversity and reduce prejudice among students (91–93). According to Glimp and Hicks,

> Children must be provided the concepts and experiences which are necessary to assist them in realizing the extent of the similarities, and the nature of the differences in their various human associations. In this manner, children are encouraged to develop an understanding and appreciation of human diversity. (91, p. 4)

Younger students can study how all people need to eat but may eat different foods and prepare them differently; how all humans need to keep warm and protect themselves against the elements but use many different and equally effective ways of accomplishing these goals. They can tell each other what they like to do to have a good time, what their favorite foods are, and the like. Older students can study the different ways people organize themselves into groups, handle interpersonal conflicts, schedule activities, and so on. They can describe how things are done at home: how respect is shown in their families, what is embarrassing and distasteful, how late is late, and what happens when children do not do what they are supposed to do (how parents discipline children). They can learn how different students like to have things done at school—whether they prefer a lot of teacher supervision and feedback or very little, lectures or discussions, individual or group work, and so on.

Some educators are not comfortable with this approach, believing that it is better to focus on the similarities among people. They want educators to avoid discussing differences among people because they are concerned about the divisive effect it can have on relationships between different groups. The available evidence indicates that discussing similarities and differences increases appreciation and respect for diversity. There is no evidence that it causes the kinds of problems that concern its critics.

Including Students' Cultures in the Classroom   Many educators believe that American schools contribute to ethnic strife by failing to include non-European American cultures in the curriculum and have made a variety of suggestions for how teachers can include students' cultures in the classroom (94–101).

Educators who include aspects of their students' cultures in the curriculum teach units on the foods, clothing, stories, legends, dances, and arts of the major American ethnic groups. They select textbooks and other educational materials that include pictures of and stories about different ethnic groups. Students listen to the music of different ethnic groups, discuss and celebrate their holidays, note their historical and current contributions, and bring to class such things as pictures, foods, games, photos, jewelry, pets, money, and musical instruments from home.

These activities should not be included in special units or only on special occasions, but as part of the ongoing, daily curriculum. According to Banks,

> When educators add ethnic heroes and fragmented ethnic content to the curriculum, ethnic heroes and content are assumed to be nonintegral parts of the mainstream U.S. experience. Consequently, it is assumed sufficient to add special units and festivals to teach about ethnic groups and their cultures. Particularly in elementary social studies, ethnic content is taught primarily with special lessons and pageants on holidays and birthdays. Blacks usually dominate lessons during Black History Week or on Martin Luther King's birthday, but they are largely invisible in the curriculum during the rest of the year. (94, p. 533)

When including information about diverse cultures, educators should avoid teaching students superficial or inaccurate stereotypes. Thus, Pepper advises:

> Bias about Indians is often the result of inaccurate information. The realities of American Indian and Alaskan Native life are often oversimplified and distorted. Stylized accounts of Indian life reinforce the "buckskin and feather" and the "Eskimo and igloo" stereotypes. With such instruction, students are certain to develop misguided impressions of Indians. (98, p. 1)

Merely celebrating special days, learning about selected heroes, eating ethnic foods, and building tepees and igloos does not help students understand the experiences, attitudes, problems, lifestyles, and so on, of different groups. Therefore, especially in middle school and high school, teachers should focus more on these real-life current problems. As Mendenhall puts it,

> Focusing on the strange and exotic traits and characteristics of ethnic groups is likely to reinforce stereotypes and misconceptions. The making of tepees does not reveal anything significant about contemporary American Indian values, cultures, or experiences. It merely adds to the classical Indian stereotype, which is so pervasive on television and in the wider society. (97, p. 86)

And here is what Banks has to say on the subject:

> The infusion of fragmented ethnic content into the curriculum . . . results in the trivialization of ethnic cultures. The study of Mexican-American food or of native American tepees will not help students develop a sophisticated understanding of Mexican-American culture and of the tremendous cultural diversity among native Americans. (94, p. 533)

Taking Proactive Steps for an Antibias Curriculum   Acknowledging a variety of cultures in the classroom and discussing why various ethnic and socioeconomic characteristics are equally acceptable help reduce prejudice, discrimination, and intergroup hostility in the classroom. However, to really accomplish these goals, teachers must take positive steps specifically designed to help resolve hostility, animosity, and suspicion between students from different cultural backgrounds (102–108). Research indicates that taking specific steps to improve students' relationships and perceptions of each other is more effective than merely talking at students or teaching them a unit about prejudice. More is accomplished by teaching students about the realities of prejudice in the United States than by simply including students' cultures in the curriculum. And a schoolwide approach that is designed to influence all students and to change the climate of the school is better than an approach that only involves a single class or group of students.

Eliminating the bias found in the materials you use in class and in the content of the courses you teach can help prevent student bias. There are many published guidelines you can refer to for assistance (109–115). The following sources of bias are a good place to begin:

- Representing certain groups in an unflattering or demeaning manner (Jews are money-mad and stingy, Mexican Americans are lazy, African Americans are on welfare, gang members are only African Americans or Hispanic Americans)

- Overgeneralizing (African American families are always headed by females; Hispanic Americans always have many children)

- Omitting non-Europeans altogether or underrepresenting them

- Revising the illustrations in a book to include significant numbers of non-European Americans without otherwise changing the book's content

- Darkening illustrations of people with obvious European facial features to make them appear ambiguous

- Stereotyping in instructional material (presenting non-Europeans in stereotypical roles at work and play; attributing stereotypical personality traits, such as studious Asian Americans or athletic African Americans)

- Assigning certain ethnic groups roles that imply that they have limited abilities and potential or are less valuable to society (European Americans perform leadership roles, take the initiative, play the key roles in solving problems, give aid and assistance; non-European Americans are their helpers and the recipients of their assistance)

- Omitting the roles of non-Europeans in history, their contributions to science, and so on

- Describing all cultural heritage from a European American point of view (presenting only a European American perspective on wars and other conflicts between groups, calling Native American victories massacres and their defeats battles)

- Presenting problems such as drug abuse, poverty, homelessness, and crime as if they were restricted to non-European communities

- Including only a few non-European works in basal readers, literary anthologies, and language arts kits

- Glossing over or ignoring such controversial or troublesome issues as slavery, oppression, poverty, prejudice, and injustice

- Setting information about non-European Americans off in boxes, away from the main body of the text, which remains biased and one-sided

- Describing families as two-parent families that live in suburban, middle-class neighborhoods and in which the father goes to work in a suit and the mother stays home

- Employing only middle-class standards of success, such as a college degree and working as a professional, executive, or entrepreneur

Informing students about racism in the United States can make them less biased. Nieto suggests:

> Although the beautiful and heroic aspects of our history should be taught, so must the ugly and exclusionary. Rather than viewing the world through rose-colored glasses, anti-racist multicultural education forces both teachers and students to take a long, hard look at everything as it was and is. (107, pp. 208–209)

A great deal has been written about how to teach students about prejudice in general. Proponents of antibias curricular approaches have offered teachers the following suggestions (105, 107, 116, 117):

- Make discussions of racism and discrimination an explicit aspect of the curriculum. Do not allow the truth about these problems to be swept under the carpet as something too ugly or un-American for discussion.

- Introduce pertinent incidents of prejudice and discrimination in the news or your particular field of study into the curriculum on a regular and timely basis.

- Have students examine TV programs, movies, magazine articles, and their textbooks for prejudice, bias, and stereotyping.

- Invite guest speakers who perform roles that counteract stereotypes. Talks by African American and Hispanic American lawyers and physicians can reduce students' stereotypes of such groups.

- Eliminate stereotypes by informing students about people who do not fit the stereotypical view of the groups to which they belong.

- Organize discussions in which students describe the prejudice that they have suffered.

- Use role-playing activities to help students experience rejection and prejudice.

- Have students divide into groups on the basis of some arbitrary characteristic, such as hair color, height, or alphabetical order, and assign superior and subordinate roles to each group.

Many published materials have proved effective (118–128). Exposing students to the life experiences of the refugee and immigrant students whom they often ridicule and reject helps the class to understand these students and reduces prejudice against them. Themes such as Coming to America, Forced Out, Homeland Histories, and Our Lives have been used to encourage immigrant and refugee students to describe their experiences through art projects, murals, plays, and oral reports. Published materials specifically designed to teach students about the immigrant and refugee experience are also available (122). It is also possible to request guest speakers from such groups as Children of War.

The guest speakers provided by Children of War are children who have been victims of war themselves. They participate in workshops throughout the United States designed to help other students understand the experiences of refugee children and their problems. Many cities have local chapters that can provide this service to the local schools (124). Of course, teachers can do the same thing by having refugee students in the school describe their experiences in class or as part of an assembly program.

Another helpful approach is to encourage interethnic group interaction. Forming interethnic groups in class and at recess and pairing students in English as a second language or bilingual classes with students in regular classes on a weekly or monthly basis to discuss life experiences or engage in multicultural activities have all been used successfully.

Many teachers prefer to avoid dealing with discriminatory incidents or intergroup friction in the form of fights, name-calling, and threats. However, many experts suggest that teachers handle these problems head-on. They advise teachers not to merely tell students, "We don't call others names in this room" or something to that effect. Rather, teachers should discuss such incidents not as isolated incidents, but as a reflection of the society in which students are growing up. According to Suzuki,

> Teachers generally avoid discussing such issues as racial name-calling, or peer relationships and how they develop among students. Yet, such issues are often the more potent aspects of the immediate social reality of students and can be used by teachers to give

students a deeper, more personal understanding of broader social issues. By personaliz-
ing learning in this way, I believe that students will gain not only cognitive knowledge,
but equally important, they will also develop greater empathy and sensitivity. (93,
p. 313)

Interethnic group conflicts can be handled within the classroom or by means of various schoolwide entities. Student mediation panels, composed of student volunteers who
have been trained to mediate intercultural problems between students, have proved successful. Interethnic advisory boards and forums made up of students, parents, staff, and
community members are another effective way to respond to conflicts (124).

It is also possible to use a case study method to examine how prejudice, discrimination, and ethnic conflict occur and to discover how they can be avoided and resolved.
Educators can prepare cases on their own or choose from those that are available in the
literature (129). To develop a case study for use in your classroom, include the following
questions for your students to consider:

How does the situation look from the points of view of the students involved?

What went wrong?

What could have been done to avoid the problem?

What should be done now?

Research indicates that the goal of improving interethnic group relations and resolving
intergroup conflicts cannot be fully achieved in a one-time or one-classroom approach (99,
107, 130). Nieto suggests:

The entire "culture" of the school must be changed if the impact of multicultural education is to be felt, including curriculum and materials, institutional norms, attitudes
and behaviors of teachers and other staff, counseling services, the extent to which parents are welcome in the school (107, p. 253)

There are a number of schoolwide programs designed to reduce prejudice and discrimination and improve intergroup relations (124). Project REACH is a year-long, four-
phase program that has been used successfully with middle school students (124). In the
human relationship skills phase, students complete activities designed to enhance their
self-esteem, self-awareness, interpersonal communication skills, and understanding of
group dynamics. This is followed by the cultural self-awareness phase, in which students
examine their own culture, ethnicity, family history, or community. The third phase—
multicultural awareness—is based on a set of booklets, the *Ethnic Perspectives* series, designed to present American history from diverse ethnic points of view. In the final phase,
cross-cultural experience, students engage in dialogue and exchange with students and
adults from different ethnic backgrounds. Students who have completed the program have
a greater sense of pride and know more about other cultures than do students who have
not taken the program. They are more accepting of ethnic differences and more interested
in learning about students from other backgrounds. And they engage in fewer incidents of
putting down other students, name-calling, and ethnic slurs (121, 123).

A World of Difference provides a number of services, including community action and school-based programs, one of which is a 40-lesson program for secondary-level students on American beliefs and values; prejudice, stereotyping, and discrimination; and scapegoating and racism (124). The Green Circle Program provides schools with workshops run by trained facilitators that guide students through understanding how they can include rather than exclude certain groups of individuals who appear to be different because of their religion, ethnic background, or disability (124).

Taking an Emancipatory and Transformational Approach   Some educators believe that students, especially those who are the victims of prejudice, should be taught how to resist and combat it. This approach has been called emancipatory education and education for empowerment (93, 95, 131–134). According to Sleeter,

> Education for empowerment demands taking seriously the strengths, experiences, strategies, and goals members of oppressed groups have. It also demands helping them to analyze and understand the social structure that oppresses them and to act in ways that will enable them to reach their own goals successfully. . . . Education for empowerment also means teaching students how to advocate effectively for themselves as individuals as well as collectively. (133, p. 6)

Some educators suggest that resistance is insufficient. They favor an approach called transformational education and social reconstructionist education (95, 131–134). To their way of thinking, teachers should prepare students to change the biased discriminatory aspects of society:

> A transformative curriculum cannot be constructed merely by adding content about ethnic groups and women to the existing Eurocentric curriculum or by integrating or infusing ethnic content or content about women into the mainstream curriculum. When the curriculum is revised using either an additive or an infusion approach, the basic assumptions, perspectives, paradigms, and values of the dominant curriculum remain unchallenged and substantially unchanged, despite the addition of ethnic content or content about women. . . . A curriculum designed to empower students must be transformative in nature and help students to develop the knowledge, skills, and values needed to become social critics who can make reflective decisions and implement their decisions in effective personal, social, political, and economic action. (95, pp. 130–131)

Classroom Environments That Motivate Students

Students learn more and behave better in schools that provide for their educational needs. Providing an educational program that suits the individual needs of thousands of diverse students in the same building is a challenging task. Providing a classroom atmosphere, instructional strategies, curriculum, and classroom management techniques that work for a class of diverse students is almost as difficult and very time-consuming. However, successful teachers who achieve this goal avoid many potential behavior problems.

Some aspects of the school environment that can cause students to be uncomfortable in school and dampen their motivation to behave appropriately are inherent to the nature of schools in our society; others can be avoided.

Inherent Difficulties

The demands placed on youngsters in school are different from those placed on them in the "real world" (135). These school-related demands can cause youngsters who are fine elsewhere to have problems even in the best-run schools and classrooms.

Interpersonal Relationships   At home, most youngsters have to learn to live with only a few people—their parents and siblings. These relationships are usually stable and develop over a long period of time. In school, though, students have to contend with new teachers each year, as well as those teachers' own ways of managing and relating to students. At home, children are gradually prepared by their parents to fulfill the roles their parents assign them. In school, new teachers expect students to adjust quickly to their ways even if these conflict with what the students are used to at home. Youngsters are also very special to their parents at home. In school, they are one of many students. Whereas at home youngsters receive personal attention and usually a lot of it, at school they receive much less, and what they do get tends to be much more impersonal. If, like many children, they are used to receiving their parents' praise and encouragement for almost everything they do at home, they may react poorly to their teachers' more realistic appraisals of their accomplishments and to the inevitable comparisons children make between themselves and their peers.

Structure   The structure in and out of school is also very different. Although definite limits exist at home, children and teenagers have more opportunity to choose what to do, how to do it, when to do it, and when to stop doing it there. Even when it comes to such things as cleaning up their rooms or doing chores, youngsters have some say about when they will do them and how fast they will work, even though their parents may not like it. In school, the same youngsters have precious little choice. Their teachers decide what they will do, how they will do it, when they will do it, and how long they will spend doing it. Instead of being able to pace themselves, students are usually obliged to keep up with the group—to start when the group starts, whether they are ready or not, and to stop when the group stops, whether they have finished or not.

In the world outside of school, children and teenagers can gradually choose to engage in activities they like and do well in and avoid those that are hard for them. In school, students must participate in all classroom activities and study all subjects, whether they like them and do well in them or not. Outside school walls, they are generally allowed to question the authority of their parents, scout leaders, camp counselors, and so on, to some extent. In school, questioning teachers' authority is often taboo. At home, when they are doing their homework, students can move around as they wish, take breaks, and listen to music or talk and laugh. In school, they probably are not given such freedom. The structure of school may often be necessary, but it is certainly unnatural and extremely constricted and restrictive.

Tasks   The tasks required of youngsters in school are also very different from what they are asked to do at home. While they certainly learn a great deal from their play, for example, playing outside of school and learning in school are quite different. At school, learning is likely to involve learning by listening or by reading. In addition, the tasks youngsters confront in school are both more complex and more abstract. It's much easier for most children to learn how to make their bed, fold their clothes, take care of their younger brothers and sisters, figure out the rules of their new board games, and hit and catch a baseball than it is to learn to spell, print or write, speak and read a foreign language, or solve algebra problems. To do a good job of learning in school, youngsters need even more chances to set their own paces and more individualized help than they need outside of school. Unfortunately, they rarely receive this extra amount of choice and help.

Private Versus Public Time   Outside of school, children and teenagers can have private time. By closing a door, they can shut out others if they want to be alone when they are upset, need time to themselves, or want to do or try things they aren't ready for other people to witness. In school, everything students do is scrutinized by their teachers and peers. Even when they have private thoughts, they may be disciplined for being off-task.

Atypical Students   Most students gradually adjust to the special demands school makes on them within a reasonable period of time. Others continue to have difficulty adjusting to school long after their peers have made the adjustment and have accepted schooling on its own terms. It is these students, who have problems for a variety of reasons discussed in this and the following chapters, that will require some kind of individualized response from you.

Avoidable Difficulties

Unfortunately, in the imperfect world we live in, few schools or school systems are run as well as they could be. Many suffer from one or more of the following failings, which naturally impact on students (136–143).

Underfinancing, Overcrowding, and Undertraining   As a result of substantially reduced financial support to education, too many school systems are unable to provide the educational services students require. Lower school budgets have also led to overcrowded classrooms and inadequate teacher salaries. These factors, in turn, have made it difficult for school systems to attract and retain high-caliber educators and to provide the in-service training teachers need to improve their skills.

Schools that serve poor students are particularly likely to be underfinanced and overcrowded. Local and state governments spend less money on educating poor and non-European American students and provide them with less adequate instructional materials and equipment, especially in the areas of computer technology and science (144–156). Per-pupil expenditures for schools serving students in poor and non-European communities are considerably below those for European American middle-class students. In Kentucky, for example, the per-pupil cost ranged from a low of $1,800 to a high of $4,200. In Texas, the per capita expenditure on education in the 100 poorest school districts was less than $3,000 compared to the more than $7,000 spent on pupils attending the 100 richest school districts. In New Jersey, the gap between the amount of money spent per pupil by the richest and poorest districts was over $10,000 (151). The per-pupil expenditure for students in New York City, with a predominantly non-European American, poor student population, was $4,351 compared to $6,605, $6,539, and $5,852 in the three surrounding suburban counties (154). The results of these disparities are reflected in the availability of equipment and materials for academic courses, especially computers and science laboratory equipment, the availability of nonacademic course offerings, the quality of the educational staff, and so on. Karp describes the effects of these disparities in spending for education:

> These numbers translate into daily injustices for school kids. Princeton's high school science students study in seven modern, well-equipped labs and student athletes can play golf, field hockey and lacrosse in addition to baseball, basketball and football. In Jersey City, middle-school science students have no labs at all while in East Orange, NJ, the track team practices in a second floor corridor. In rural Kentucky, elementary schools have done without music and art teachers. In one poor Texas district students study computer science by pretending to type on an artificial paper replica of a computer keyboard. (157, pp. 1, 14)

While many students excel in school despite the effects of these problems, others fall victim to them.

Inadequate Physical Environments   As Gordon states,

> Most classrooms unfortunately are designed, constructed, and furnished in ways that make it difficult for students to stay motivated and involved in the learning process; and when students are distracted and bothered by the classroom environment, many of their coping mechanisms turn into behavior unacceptable to teachers and interfere with efforts to teach. (138, p. 156)

Poor Instruction and Management Techniques   Students' behavior is influenced by how well their teachers instruct them, how interesting and relevant the courses are, how effectively teachers manage their classrooms, how often teachers resort to punishment, how available and approachable teachers are, how well teachers match the difficulty level of individual students' work to their level of functioning, and how fair teachers are. Research clearly demonstrates that "better" teachers have fewer discipline problems than "poorer" teachers (139, 140, 142).

In reviewing the instructional errors teachers make, Jones suggests that one mistake is especially damaging:

> Almost all the chronic motivation problems and overt helplessness in any classroom are a by-product of one simple thing—the way a teacher helps a student who is stuck. . . .

It is universally assumed that when students are stuck, you explain to them what they do not understand and then help them to do it right. Unfortunately, this unexamined and ordinary piece of teacher behavior is an unmitigated educational disaster. (139, p. 23)

Jones explains that rushing in to help students reinforces their helplessness by giving them teacher time and attention; it keeps them from learning how to solve problems for themselves and uses time that should be spent on group instruction and supervision.

Unnecessary Anxiety and Stress   Anxiety and stress can cause students to misbehave (137, 141, 143). Although we probably can't make schools totally stress free, many students are subjected to unnecessary levels of anxiety and stress. Phillips (143) has identified a number of stress-causing situations in school. Among them are the students' inability to understand and learn what they are taught when teachers proceed too rapidly, academic competition between students, not fulfilling teachers' academic expectations, being laughed at for giving the wrong answer, taking tests, and having teachers report to parents.

Students Lacking Readiness Skills   Some children enter school without the social and academic skills their teachers and the school system expect them to have. Certain preschoolers and kindergartners may not, for example, have experienced and accepted many of the rules and routines (such as waiting in line or taking turns) that educators rely on to manage large groups of students. Others may not be used to the pace at which the group functions. Some young students may find it hard to adjust to teachers who treat them differently from the way their parents do. Often this happens when teachers don't give a child as much individual attention, assistance, praise, or freedom as the child is used to. In other cases, the teacher may not hold the same opinion as a student's parents do about the relative value of cooperation versus competition, the rights of the individual versus the rights of the group, or the best methods to manage a group or to discipline youngsters.

Some preschoolers and kindergartners, especially from poor and non-European American families, may not have the academic skills necessary to succeed in school at the same level as their peers. Unless educators are willing and able to individualize their social and academic expectations for students and work with each one at their entering level, many students will not have the skills they need to succeed. This, in turn, may cause them to become tense, anxious, angry, rebellious, or withdrawn (173).

Teachers in the upper grades face similar problems with students who function below grade level. Secondary school teachers often have to deal with the problems that result when students are allowed to enroll in their courses without the necessary prerequisites. Accommodating one's teaching techniques and instructional materials to different levels of functioning can solve many behavior problems; however, this is often difficult to accomplish, especially at the secondary level, without the cooperation of one's colleagues and administrators.

If a kindergartner or first grader is having difficulty learning, seems anxious and tense, and daydreams or talks instead of staying on-task, this student may not be able to function at the level of the other students in the class. To determine whether you are giving a student work that he or she isn't ready for, you can do an informal assessment of what the student

THEORY FOCUS: JONES ON POSITIVE CLASSROOM DISCIPLINE

Fredric Jones derived many of his ideas about classroom management from working as a clinical psychologist with youngsters who had emotional problems, but his two volumes entitled *Positive Classroom Discipline* and *Positive Classroom Instruction* were written specifically for educators. Jones's main emphasis is on managing group behavior to reduce disruptions and increase cooperative behavior. The four major elements in his approach are classroom structure, limit setting, responsibility training, and backup systems.

According to Jones, educators can avoid many behavior problems by establishing good classroom structure. This includes not only rules, routines, and standards of appropriate behavior but also good teacher-student relations that are positive, gentle, and cooperative. When students misbehave despite good classroom structure, Jones advises setting limits, expecting and teaching students to assume responsibility for their behavior, and finally using backup systems (positive consequences) to motivate them. Because Jones believes that educators can motivate students enough by providing them with the opportunity to gain or lose positive consequences, he feels it's unnecessary to punish them.

Jones describes the four major aspects of his approach to classroom discipline as follows:

1. *Preliminary structure:* "Natural" teachers make "proactive" into an art form. They know exactly what they want done, and they have routines for getting things done that are simple and effective. Preliminary structure includes such things as specific choreography to the first hour, day, and week of the school year, room arrangement, the organization of chores, the clarification of rules and values, and the communication of those rules and values to parents. Common to all, however, is an investment in getting to know the students and an ongoing effort to make the learning environment personal, safe, and comfortable.

2. *Limit-setting:* Limit-setting or "meaning business" is the teacher's physical demeanor that communicates to the students at all times that the teacher is "in charge." Limit-setting . . . is body language—the sum total of the teacher's body language that is visible at all times and can be read like a book by any two-year-old.

   Body language is the language of emotions and intentions both conscious and unconscious. It is part of our biological equipment—neither invented nor changeable. We either understand it and use it to our advantage or experience exhaustion and exasperation as "creative" students use it to their advantage.

   There are two keys to understanding limit-setting:
   a. Effective discipline management begins at the *emotional* level.
   b. *Calm is strength whereas upset is weak-*

knows and doesn't know and can and can't do. Then compare the results with the skills needed to succeed at the level of your expectations. Or you could use one of the many formal assessment procedures that appear valid for evaluating students' readiness skills (174–177, 180, 181).

If your assessment of the student indicates that the student lacks certain readiness skills, accommodate your expectations, materials, and teaching techniques to the student's actual level of functioning. Research indicates that accomodating to students' readiness

THEORY FOCUS: JONES ON POSITIVE CLASSROOM DISCIPLINE *(continued)*

ness. When you consider that your body is designed to get upset when provoked (a "fight-flight" reflex that becomes nagging and threatening as soon as we add dialogue), it is clear that our "natural equipment" is a considerable liability when social power rather than physical power is the issue.

3. *Building patterns of cooperation:* To be positive, discipline management must ultimately be voluntary on the part of students. We ask for cooperation thousands of times a day as we ask the entire class to be at the right place at the right time with the right materials doing the right thing. If we want all of this cooperation, we must answer one eternal question over and over again . . . "Why should I?" We will need very good answers to reach all the students in the class.

   Those answers are called incentives. Yet incentives as they typically exist in classrooms are inadequate. They expect the students to behave appropriately in order to get some type of reinforcer. Any kid who will "prime the pump" by giving cooperation before they get anything doesn't need much management to start with. How do you get noncooperative students to repeatedly do what you want them to do the first time you ask by using learning as the reinforcer? This will require the more sophisticated incentives we refer to as Responsibility Training.

4. *Back-up systems:* What do you do when

push comes to shove in discipline management . . . ? The answer to this question is the stuff of which school discipline codes are made. Warnings, detentions, trips to the office, suspensions—it hasn't changed in 75 years, and 5 percent of the student body still produce 90 percent of office referrals. So what's new?

It would be new if our within-classroom back-up system prevented the need for continual reliance upon the school site back-up system. It would be new if teachers had a specific and effective plan for responding to common provocations so that they got smaller rather than larger.

But first think of limit-setting and remember that at its foundation discipline management is emotional, and calm is strength. If you "lose it" and demean the student in front of their peers due to your "upset," you will pay and pay fast. There is no such thing as win/lose in discipline. Either you and the students win together, or the students will guarantee that you pay more dearly than they do.

But exactly how do you respond in the heat of the moment to diffuse a rough situation—to protect the student in order to protect yourself? Don't expect your "biological equipment" to be of any help. It will take a lot of training and practice to overcome the fight/flight reflex. (F. Jones, personal communication)

levels can help avoid the kinds of educational difficulties that often cause young students to misbehave (172, 178, 179).

Mismatched Learning and Teaching   Research has clearly demonstrated that students learn more efficiently when they are taught in ways that conform to their learning styles—conditions in which they learn most efficiently (182, 184, 187, 191, 194, 195, 198, 201, 202, 204–206). Many differences among students' learning styles have been substan-

Self-Quiz: On Personal Characteristics

Kauffman, Pullen, and Akers identify eight teacher characteristics that contribute to student misbehavior:

a. Inconsistency in management techniques
b. Reinforcement of the wrong behavior
c. Formation of inappropriate expectations for children
d. Nonfunctional or irrelevant instruction
e. Insensitivity to children's legitimate individuality
f. Demonstration or encouragement of undesirable models
g. Irritability and overreliance on punishment
h. Unwillingness to try new strategies or to seek suggestions from other professionals (208, p. 2)

If you have had teaching experience, answer the following eight questions about yourself. Your answers may give you insight into the way you function in class.

1. Am I consistent in responding to children's behavior?
2. Am I rewarding the right behavior?
3. Are my expectations and demands appropriate for children's abilities?
4. Am I providing instruction that is useful to children?
5. Am I tolerant enough of children's individuality?
6. Are children seeking desirable models?
7. Am I generally irritable and overreliant on punishment as a control technique?
8. Am I willing to try a different tack on the problem or to seek the help of colleagues or consultants?

tiated by research, including the finding that some students prefer to work independently, whereas others want more feedback and supervision from their teachers (200) (see chapters 5 and 6). Also, although many students seem to respond well to competition, many others function better in cooperative situations, especially if they come from a culture that encourages cooperation (200). Research has shown that not all students are motivated by the same types of rewards. Material rewards such as candy, toys, and trips are effective with some students, but others are more responsive to interpersonal rewards, such as praise and teacher attention (200). In terms of learning modality, although kindergarten students are kinesthetic learners and learn best by doing, touching, feeling, and manipulating (182), by the time they reach the upper elementary grades, some students learn better when material is presented to them orally. Others, however, learn more when material is presented visually (193, 199, 206). Another area in which students differ is whether they require silence or sound to do their best work. Some are distracted by the sounds around them; others concentrate best when the radio, tape deck, or television is on (198).

Other findings show that some students concentrate best in bright light, whereas others do better when the light is dim (194). Like adults, students tend to be day or night people. Night owls do better late in the day, and early birds function best in the morning (183, 199). Students who prefer a formal atmosphere like to work at their desks or at a table in the library, but students who enjoy informality do better lying or sitting on the floor, lounging in a chair, or reading in bed (199, 202).

In addition, students work at different paces. Some are comfortable working fast; others learn more when they are allowed to proceed at a slower pace than most students (203).

Kindergartners tend to be kinesthetic learners, but older students have a variety of learning styles.

A related characteristic is that while some students can sit still for long periods of time, others function better when they can move about fairly often (188). In general, students become less impulsive and more reflective as they mature, but students tend to be either reflective or impulsive throughout their educational careers (207). Students who are reflective need to think for a while before answering questions and beginning activities, whereas impulsive students "get off the mark" almost immediately (192, 196). Certain students can concentrate for long periods of time on one activity, whereas others require periodic breaks to maintain their concentration (188). Analytical students use a step-by-step approach to solve problems and understand things. In contrast, global students need to see the big picture before they can deal with the details (187, 189, 205).

Because students learn more effectively when the teaching style matches their learning style, some behavior problems occur when students have to consistently function in ways that hinder rather than enhance their learning. In such cases, teachers can improve their students' behavior by individualizing their teaching styles as much as possible. When you feel that your students may be misbehaving because your teaching style doesn't match their learning styles, you can assess them informally or use published instruments. The Learning Style Inventory—regular and primary versions—is one example of instruments designed to assess students' learning styles (190, 197, 201). The Learning Style Inventory involves students in the assessment process by having them state whether or not various statements apply to them. Here are sample items from the instrument:

I remember things best when I study them early in the morning.

Noise usually keeps me from concentrating.

The things I remember best are the things I hear.

I like to be given choices of how I can do things.

I like to be told exactly what to do.

Once you have identified your students' learning styles and compared them with your usual teaching style, you can accommodate your teaching techniques to your students' needs as much as possible so that they can learn more effectively (182, 185, 186, 190, 194, 198, 200, 202, 204, 205). For example, if you frequently use competition and material rewards, you can make an effort to include more cooperative learning and interpersonal rewards in your classroom activities. If you basically lecture students as your primary instructional strategy, you can supplement your usual presentation with visual materials—pictures, films, reading materials—for the visual learners among your students. Such changes should lead to improvements in their behavior.

Behavior Problems   Numerous authors have provided anecdotal descriptions of the ways in which such things as underfinancing, overcrowding, inadequate physical environments, and poor instruction and classroom management techniques cause students to misbehave (157–162). Research has confirmed many of these anecdotal descriptions. For example, as students progress through the grades, they often perceive themselves as doing schoolwork because they are required to do so to receive good grades, not because they are interested in the material (157). They also become less proud of their work, less likely to believe they are doing as well as they should, less likely to say they are trying their best, less likely to feel positive about school, and more likely to say they are discouraged about their school careers (163, 164, 170, 171). Naturally, students who feel and think these ways about themselves are unlikely to give their all in school. African American, Hispanic American, Native American, and poor students are particularly likely to be disillusioned about school (209–213).

Failing students have an especially difficult time in school. Lack of success or outright failure is an experience that all students react to poorly. Although most youngsters can handle an occasional setback, constant repetitive failure, even if it occurs only in one area or subject, is something few children or adolescents can easily cope with. The experience of failure can be even more devastating when teachers show preference for students who do well.

Sometimes students react to failure by doubling their efforts to succeed. All too often, they become anxious and insecure. They may, if possible, avoid challenging situations. Or they may blame themselves for their failure and feel guilty or depressed. They may also defend themselves against such feelings by blaming the situation, their teachers, or their peers for the difficulty they experience and then feel angry and resentful (136, 137).

By the time they are teenagers, some students are so far behind they see little, if any, point to school. Some are willing to put the time in until they can drop out legally. But many others are unwilling to continue to play the part of the well-motivated, well-behaved student.

No wonder students who score high on tests and who get high grades behave better than those who do poorly (136, 137, 140). Research indicates that students' misbehavior both in school (166, 167, 169) and out (165, 168) is related to their school experiences to a considerable degree. For example, Rutter et al. (169) found that students who were well matched with each other when they entered school differed dramatically in terms of both the frequency and seriousness of their misbehavior after a few years, depending on the school they attended and their experiences in school.

Suggestions for improving your classroom management techniques and decreasing student anxiety and stress are included throughout this book. These suggestions should help you to avoid many behavior problems.

Case Studies

The following case studies illustrate how students' behavior problems that are caused by educational difficulties can be avoided.

Carlos   Carlos, a third-grade student, immigrated to the United States from El Salvador when he was 3. He was transferred from a bilingual class to a regular class after second grade because he passed an English proficiency test. But his third-grade teacher, Ms. Allen, described Carlos as "requiring excessive teacher direction, feedback, and praise" to complete learning tasks. Typically, he raised his hand or went up to the teacher's desk three or four times during a 30-minute period to ask if he was doing his assignment correctly. If he wasn't able to get such feedback, he stopped what he was doing and waited. His teacher felt he was overly dependent on her and couldn't work independently enough to succeed in a class of 33 students.

Initially, Ms. Allen attributed Carlos's dependency to "insecurity and anxiety caused by a low self-concept." But after having Carlos in class for 2 months, she realized that Carlos had much more self-confidence than she had given him credit for: He made friends easily, volunteered for a part in the class play, was always eager to read books that were difficult for him because of his earlier lack of English proficiency, and seemed to expect that she would tell him he was on the right track whenever he asked her for feedback about how he was doing.

Carlos's former bilingual education teacher agreed that he had a good self-concept and thought that he probably wasn't unusually anxious about being in an all-English class. Rather, she assumed that Carlos's behavior was a reflection of his field-sensitive learning style, a characteristic of many Hispanic American students, and suggested that Ms. Allen compare his learning style with her teaching style. When she did, Ms. Allen concluded that she was not encouraging cooperative learning enough or expressing enough physical and verbal approval for many of the students in her class. So she decided to change her approach with both the entire class and Carlos. First, she stopped her unnecessary attempts to build up Carlos's self-confidence, and she accommodated to his requests for her feedback. At the same time, she also told him that in the United States, students are expected to work more on their own, which would prepare him for success in other classrooms. And she made a point of praising him whenever he completed assignments without asking her opinion. By the end of the school year, Carlos was working much more independently, although he continued to show her his finished work more often than most other students.

Jo Ann   Jo Ann was doing worse in the sixth grade than she had done before in school. Instead of getting mostly B's with an occasional A or C, she was earning all C's except for D's in math and science. Mr. Davidson, a second-year teacher, noticed that she rushed through her assignments, made many careless errors, almost never volunteered answers, daydreamed a lot, and seemed extremely anxious during tests.

Thinking that she might have been experiencing problems outside of school that were affecting her functioning in class, he contacted her parents. They said that as far as they knew, Jo Ann had no serious problems, but they also reported that she had been complaining about school for the first time since third grade. When pressed by Mr. Davidson, they said that Jo Ann felt that her teacher was going too fast, gave students tests before they were ready, and didn't like them to ask questions about things they didn't understand.

After thinking about what he had heard, Mr. Davidson decided to slow down the pace. He told the class he wanted them to ask questions if they didn't understand something and made a point of commenting, "That's a good question" or "I guess I didn't explain that too well" when they did. He also conducted a review before each test. Although he never spoke individually to Jo Ann about the problem, he noticed a dramatic improvement in her behavior and test scores within just a few weeks.

Frank   Ms. Russo, Frank's 11th-grade social studies teacher, found him to be a "fresh," "impudent," "rebellious" student. Yet when she spoke to his other teachers, none reported any problems with him. Concerned about whether it was the subject matter, the time of day, or just the chemistry between them, Ms. Russo did some self-evaluation. This led her to admit that she was intensely uncomfortable with the way Frank related to the girls in the class. She especially disliked the way he strutted in as if he were "God's gift to women," smiling at each pretty girl as he passed. She was also revolted by bits and pieces of conversation she overheard between Frank and some of the girls.

In giving this more thought, Ms. Russo decided she didn't have the right to allow her feelings about Frank's relationships with the girls to affect the way she dealt with him, especially since he was earning an A in her course. She met with him after class, expressed her opinion about his behavior, and stated that she was wrong to have let it influence the way she dealt with him. Then she suggested that they start all over. Although her opinion of him remained the same, their relationship improved somewhat so that it was at least bearable. At times, though, Ms. Russo had the feeling that Frank purposely did things to annoy her.

Enhancing Students' Belief in the Value of School

Many educators believe that a significant portion of the disruptive behavior, inadequate motivation, lack of participation, and high dropout rates that many poor, African

American, Hispanic American, and Native American middle school and high school students demonstrate are caused in part by their loss of faith in the school system. These educators claim that the more time these students spend in school, the more they suffer biased and sexist treatment by their teachers and the clearer it becomes to them that the school system is structured in ways that make it difficult for them to succeed, regardless of how hard they try. These educators maintain that these groups of students will continue to function in these problematic ways until educators treat them as fairly as they treat other students and schools are reorganized to serve their interests as much as those of the European American middle class.

This section describes various reasons why many students devalue school. Chapters 4 through 6 describe what teachers can do to avoid these problems.

Prejudice and Discrimination

As the research indicates, prejudice and discrimination against non-European American and poor students are still rampant. The discrimination that these students experience in school is summarized here and dealt with at greater length in chapters 4 through 6.

Educators tend to believe that middle-class students are more intelligent than poor students and expect them to do better in school. They attribute more learning potential to European American and Asian Pacific American students than to African American or Hispanic American students. And they expect that non-European American students, especially African Americans, will be more disruptive and deviant than European Americans. Teachers tend to evaluate the academic performance of African American, Hispanic American, and poor students in a biased manner and assign them to low-ability groups. Teachers also judge the exact same transgressions as more severe or deviant when they are committed by African American males than when they are committed by other students.

No one knows the exact degree to which behavior problems in school are caused by prejudice. However, when the evidence is considered as a whole, it is inconceivable that the discriminatory manner in which many students are treated by their teachers does not affect their attitudes and behavior. Therefore, elimination of teacher prejudice is one of the most important steps educators can take to eliminate disciplinary problems.

Ineffective Educational Approaches

Some school systems contribute to behavior problems in other ways. Because schools tend to be geared to the needs of mainstream students, they often provide other students with educational services that do not match the context of their lives. Thus, they fail to offer the education needed by poor students, students from broken homes, students who have been neglected or abused, homeless students, and immigrant, refugee, migrant, rural, and urban students. (See chapter 4 for suggestions on how to deal with these problems.) Because schools tend to be designed with European American middle-class students in mind, the educational approaches employed by many teachers often do not match the learning, behavioral, and communication styles of students from other ethnic or socioeconomic backgrounds. (See chapter 5 for suggestions on how to deal with these problems.)

And reflecting the sexism that still pervades the greater society, schools tend to utilize sexist educational techniques. (See chapter 6 for suggestions on how to deal with these problems.)

In many schools, students with limited English proficiency are placed in the regular education program, where they are taught in English without regard to their linguistic needs instead of being placed in an English as a second language (ESL) program or a sheltered English program. Submerged in English without the skills necessary to profit from the instruction they receive, these students are at risk for joining the ranks of students who tune out their teachers, misbehave, cut classes, and drop out of education before graduating from high school.

A student in such an English submergence program reported:

> I just sat in my classes and didn't understand anything. Sometimes I would try to look like I knew what was going on, sometimes I would just try to think about a happy time when I didn't feel stupid. My teachers never called on me or talked to me. I think either they forgot I was there or else wished I wasn't. I waited and I waited, thinking someday I will know English. (214, p. 62)

Two other students made the following comparison between their experiences in an ESL program and a regular class taught in English:

> My ESL teacher helped me a lot in my first year here. I could relax there. I wasn't afraid. . . . In my other classes I was always confused and lost and I didn't want to ask anything because of my bad English. (214, p. 62)

> My first school I didn't want to go, just to stay home. When I went I just sat there and didn't understand anything. . . . No one talked to me and I couldn't say anything. I didn't know what was going on. My second school had an ESL teacher who taught me from the ABCs and helped me learn many more things. (214, p. 62)

Structured Reproduction

Many educators believe that schools unwittingly reproduce the inequalities found in society at large by perpetuating the prevailing biased societal views and values about ethnicity, socioeconomic class, and gender. Some educators believe that this is done purposefully, not unwittingly. They believe that it is only one of many discriminatory structures that the European American middle and upper class (especially males) have set up throughout society to maintain their economic and social power and position. That is, they believe that those who exercise control and power in our society—middle- and upper-class European American males—structure its institutions, including schools, to maintain their special positions by reproducing the inequality that serves their interests (215–225).

Some of these reproduction theorists suggest that society and schools are not equally biased against all non-European students. They believe that the European American dominant class differentiates between voluntary immigrants and involuntary, subordinated castelike groups such as African Americans, Native Americans, Puerto Rican Americans, and Mexican Americans. Voluntary immigrants, according to these theorists, are those who chose to come to the United States. Involuntary immigrants are those who were brought here as slaves (e.g., African Americans) or who were incorporated into the United States against their will by conquest (e.g., Native Americans and Mexican Americans). Voluntary immigrants are likely to be accepted into society as equals once they have assimilated. And they tend to be the preferred non-European Americans because they most resemble the original northern European American settlers of the continent. Involuntary groups, however, are unlikely to be accepted as equals for three reasons: the history of their relationship with the dominant European Americans; the myths that European Americans have created about their innate inferiority to justify the conquest of their land, the eradication of their culture, and the enslavement of their ancestors; and the fact that they do not resemble European Americans in either looks or behavior.

European Americans are willing to accept voluntary immigrants into their country clubs and into some high-status positions. And school personnel are willing to tolerate their cultural differences at least to some degree. Involuntary castelike groups are not treated as well socially or vocationally. And in school, their cultural differences are devalued, disliked, and squashed because these groups have been deemed inferior for hundreds of years.

Thus, these theorists believe that the people in power use schools to maintain an ethnic, class, and gender division of labor that works against involuntary immigrants, poor students, and females. According to them, schools provide these students with the kinds of educational experiences that maintain them as a source of cheap, though well-prepared, labor for their enterprises, while the more affluent European American males are trained to be the leaders of society. And at the same time, schools teach poor, involuntary immigrant, and female students to accept the status quo—their economic and social inferiority. Grant and Sleeter claim:

> School plays a major role in the culture students develop. Like the family and neighborhood, school affects how students understand and pursue their life chances. It provides an institutional ideology, socializing agents, and an experiential context within which students define and shape the way they think about their personal dreams. The school context, containing social relations defined by race, social class, and gender, can produce a student culture in which young people accept and live out their parents' place in a stratified society, in spite of the school's espoused mission as equalizer and escalator to a better life. (220, p. 19)

Reproduction theorists believe that two of the most effective techniques that those in power use to accomplish their ends, in addition to the discriminatory and inappropriate education provided to certain groups of students, are the lower level of funding provided schools that serve students from poor and non-European American neighborhoods and the use of tracking and ability grouping to separate European American middle-class students from other students. They also claim that females, especially those who are poor or who belong to involuntary immigrant groups, are exposed to two separate but related forces in the schools: those designed to maintain middle- and upper-class hegemony over the poor and those designed to maintain male hegemony over females.

These theorists also suggest that while students are being exposed to ethnic, socioeconomic, and gender biases in school and society at large, egalitarian ideas are available in the media, in the materials students read in school, and in the ideas presented to them by teachers who do not believe in the current socioeconomic, ethnic, and gender biases. Because of these additional messages, students do not passively accept the biases presented to them. Instead, they are constantly involved in a process of accommodating to some messages and resisting others (226–243).

According to reproduction theorists, many students who are alienated, distrustful, angry, and disillusioned about school also know that even if they do well in school, a society stratified along ethnic, socioeconomic, and gender lines will not afford them the same benefits that European American upper-class males receive from succeeding in school. Therefore, instead of acquiescing to the educational system for payoffs they do not believe will be forthcoming, they battle against the system to maintain their own sense of identity.

Thus, while some students accept their assigned place and role, others actively resist the biased education they receive and the inferior position it threatens to place them in. Some students resist schools in nonconstructive ways. They purposefully misbehave in aggressive or sexual ways, tune out their teachers, refuse to do their homework, come late to school, drop out before graduating, decide not to participate in higher education, and so on (107, 227, 238, 239, 241).

Other students battle the same forces in constructive ways. They reject the biased ideas they are exposed to. They assert their own experiences, heighten their own sense of self-worth, and leave school with a new understanding of their ethnic, gender, and socioeconomic identity and with the knowledge, skills, value, and self-awareness they require to contribute to transforming society (223, 233, 235).

According to the theory, students from the subordinated involuntary immigrant groups are less willing to play the educational game according to the rules established by their oppressors. They are most likely to reject and resist school because of the prejudicial treatment they receive regardless of how much they accomplish academically.

There is a great deal of evidence that the structure of American schools does indeed contribute to the reproduction of ethnic and socioeconomic inequality. As already noted, schools provide many students with inappropriate and discriminatory educational services. Local and state governments spend less money on educating poor and non-European American students and provide them with less adequate instructional materials and equipment (244–253). Per-pupil expenditures for schools serving students in poor and non-European communities are considerably below those for European American middle-class students. The results of these disparities are reflected in the availability of equipment and materials for academic courses, the availability of nonacademic course offerings, the quality of the educational staff, and so on. Even programs specifically designed to serve poor students are underfinanced. At the height of their financial support, compensatory educational programs served only 57% of the 9 million eligible students. Head Start only reaches 18% of eligible students (245).

Poor and non-European American students are much more likely to be placed in slow-track and low-ability groups than are European American middle-class students. Research on these approaches indicates that they typically do more harm than good (252, 254–261). Students placed in low-ability groups do not learn better. They experience a loss of self-esteem and a worsening of their attitude toward school. They do not receive the instructional approaches and attention they require. In fact, research clearly demonstrates the opposite. Schools spend less money on students in low-ability groups. These students are counseled less often and are exposed to a watered-down curriculum. Moreover, they are treated poorly by their teachers, who call on them less often, criticize them more often, praise them less frequently, give them less help and feedback, and expect less from them.

Self-Quiz: Critical Incidents

It is not always easy to apply one's ideals or principles to a real-life situation. Describe how you think you would handle each of the following critical incidents, and explain why you would handle it that way:

1. An African American 10-grade male in a predominantly poor neighborhood school tells you in no uncertain terms to get off his case and stop telling him about the value of graduating high school. He insists that a high school diploma does not help African Americans. The next day the student brings in an article that confirms that African American males who graduate high school do not earn significantly more than those who do not.

2. You overhear two seniors say that they plan to protest the prejudice they experienced in school by wearing some outlandish clothes to the graduation ceremony rather than the conservative clothes and cap and gown prescribed by the school administration.

Management problems are typically increased rather than diminished by grouping students into low-ability groups and tracks because students tend to be more disruptive and teachers tend to interrupt the academic work more often to deal with discipline problems.

Finally, students are not placed in ability groups in an accurate and fair manner. On the contrary, as already noted, non-European American and poor students are often assigned to low-ability groups in a biased manner. And in some cases, ability grouping is used to resegregate students in desegregated schools, not to enhance their learning.

The claim that many non-European and poor students are alienated, distrustful, angry, and disillusioned about the schools they attend, believing that even if they do well in school, they will not obtain the same benefits that European American upper-class males receive, appears to be true (262–266). African American middle school and high school students feel alienated and distrustful about their teachers, the schools they attend, and the American political system (264). Research also suggests that while African American students think that getting a good education is important, many of them do not believe that education necessarily leads to a good job (262, 263). In one study, over 50% of the 10- to 15-year-old African American students surveyed did not believe that a high school diploma led to a good job (262). And the authors of another study observed that many African American high school males had similar doubts, speculating that "if African American male youth feel that racism hampers the 'cashing in of their educational check,' it is probably valid to assume that they will not take full advantage of the educational opportunities that their schools have to offer" (263, p. 12).

There is also evidence that Native American and African American high school graduates do not reap the benefits a high school diploma affords European American students. For example, a recent study indicated that, with rare exceptions, Native American students who graduated from high school obtained the same "menial or service-industry positions" as dropouts (266).

One may believe that schools *simply reflect* the biases that permeate society. Or one may agree that European American middle- and upper-class males *purposely* structure schools in ways that reproduce their power in society. Whether the current situation is purposeful or not, it is clear that despite the progress that has occurred in providing equal educational opportunities to all students, the educational system perpetuates inequality in school and in the larger society and causes many students to misbehave, tune out, and drop out.

Therefore, eliminating discriminatory and inappropriate educational practices and removing the structures in the greater society that reproduce inequality will help convince students of the value of an education, motivate them, and avoid many behavior problems. Individual teachers cannot change society. But they control their own classes and can contribute to the improvement of the educational practices in the schools and systems in which they work. Thus, teachers can employ the techniques provided in chapters 4 through 6 for eliminating discriminatory and inappropriate educational practices. They can speak out against ability grouping and tracking in the schools. And they can use emancipatory and social reconstructionist education to help empower students and prepare them to become agents of change in school and in the greater society.

Summary

Students' desire to behave appropriately can be improved by satisfying their basic needs, maintaining positive relationships with them, and modeling the behavior expected from them. Increasing the value of the group by maintaining group cohesiveness, minimizing subgroup formation, and improving interethnic group relations is also helpful. Creating classroom environments that match students' needs and enhancing students' belief in the value of school can be powerful motivating techniques.

Activities

I. Interview several teachers or students in your class about their preferences for cooperative, competitive, and individualistic learning. Investigate whether they are aware of the gender and ethnic disparities that can result during unstructured cooperative learning activities.

II. Ask some of your classmates who attended elementary, middle, or high schools with diverse student populations whether their schools offered programs to improve interethnic group relations. Ask them which, if any, of the programs described in this chapter they would like to see employed in schools.

III. Find out if your local schools offer bilingual, ESL, and sheltered English programs or if they submerge students with limited English proficiency in regular classes taught in English.

IV. Poll your classmates regarding their opinions about tracking and ability grouping. If you interview an ethnically diverse group of students, determine whether their ethnic backgrounds influence their opinions.

V. Think of an empathic response to each of the following situations.

1. A second-grader refuses to sit at a table with three classmates of the opposite sex.

2. A student becomes frustrated during seatwork, crumples her paper noisily, and throws it on the floor, attracting everyone's attention.

3. A student storms out of the room, slamming the door behind him, after some classmates laugh at the mistakes he makes during oral reading.

4. A student throws his snack at another student who teased him about the "exotic" food he brought from home.

5. A student sulks because she wasn't called on in class during sharing time, and she had something special to tell her classmates.

References

The following reference discusses personal growth.

1. Ontario Department of Education. (1986). *Behavior: Resource Guide*. ERIC ED 284 386.

The following references discuss satisfying basic needs.

2. Braun, C. (1976). Teacher expectations: Socio-psychological dynamics. *Review of Educational Research*, 46 (2), 185–213.

3. Maslow, A. H. (1960). Some basic propositions of a growth and self-actualization psychology. *Association of Supervision and Curriculum Development Yearbook*. Alexandria, VA: Association of Supervision and Curriculum Development.

4. Maslow, A. H. (1970). *Motivation and Personality* (2nd ed.). New York: Harper & Row.

References that discuss teacher-student relationships follow.

5. Brophy, J. E., & Putnam, J. G. (1978). *Classroom Management in the Elementary Grades*. ERIC ED 167 537.

6. Kounin, J. S. (1970). *Discipline and Group Management in Classrooms*. New York: Holt, Rinehart & Winston.

The following references deal with the educator as instructor.

7. Anderson, L. M., Evertson, C. M., & Emmer, E. T. (1979). *Dimensions in Classroom Management Derived from Recent Research.* ERIC ED 175 860.

8. Coker, H., Medley, D. M., & Soar, R. S. (1980). How valid are expert opinions about effective teaching? *Phi Delta Kappan, 62* (2), 131–134.

9. Davis, J. E. (1974). *Coping with Disruptive Behavior.* Washington, DC: National Education Association.

10. Jones, F. (1987). *Positive Classroom Discipline.* New York: McGraw-Hill.

11. Jones, V. F., & Jones, L. S. (1986). *Comprehensive Classroom Management: Creating Positive Learning Environments* (2nd ed.). Boston: Allyn & Bacon.

12. Mauer, R. F. (1985). *Elementary Discipline Handbook: Solutions for the K–8 Teacher.* West Nyack, NY: Center for Applied Research in Education.

13. Sabatino, D. A., Sabatino, A. C., & Mann, L. (1983). *Discipline and Behavior Management: A Handbook of Tactics, Strategies, and Programs.* Rockville, MD: Aspen.

14. Tanner, L. N. (1978). *Classroom Discipline for Effective Teaching and Learning.* New York: Holt, Rinehart & Winston.

15. Tobin, K. G., & Capie, W. (1980). *Student Engagement in Middle School Science Classrooms.* ERIC ED 194 522.

16. Unruh, A. (1977). Teachers and classroom discipline. *NASSP Bulletin, 61* (406), 84–87.

These references discuss the educator as manager.

17. Adams, R., & Biddle, B. (1970). *Realities of Teaching: Explorations with Video Tape.* New York: Holt, Rinehart & Winston.

18. Anderson, L. H., Evertson, C. M., & Emmer, E. T. (1979). *Dimensions in Classroom Management Derived from Recent Research.* ERIC ED 175 860.

19. Brophy, J. E., & Good, T. L. (1970). Teachers' communication of differential expectations for children's classroom performance: Some behavioral data. *Journal of Education Psychology, 61,* 365–374.

20. Brophy, J. E., & Good, T. L. (1974). *Teacher-Student Relationships: Causes and Consequences.* New York: Holt, Rinehart & Winston.

21. Chaikin, A., Sigler, E., & Derlega, V. (1974). Nonverbal mediators of teacher expectancy effects. *Journal of Personality and Social Psychology, 30,* 144–149.

22. Cooper, H., & Good, T. L. (1983). *Pygmalion Grows Up.* White Plains, NY: Longman.

23. Cornbleth, C., David, O. L., Jr., & Button, C. (1974). Expectations for pupil achievement and teacher-pupil interaction. *Social Education, 38,* 54–58.

24. Daum, J. (1972). *Proxemics in the Classroom: Speaker-Subject Distance and Educational Performance.* Paper presented at the annual meeting of the Southeastern Psychological Association.

25. de Groat, A., & Thompson, G. A. (1949). A study of the distribution of teacher approval and disapproval among sixth-grade pupils. *Journal of Experimental Education, 18,* 57–75.

26. Delefes, P., & Jackson, B. (1972). Teacher-pupil interaction as a function of location in the classroom. *Psychology in the Schools, 9,* 119–123.

27. Epstein, C. (1979). *Classroom Management and Teaching: Persistent Problems and Rational Solutions.* Reston, VA: Reston Publishing.

28. Glickman, C. D., & Wolfgang, C. H. (1979). Dealing with student misbehavior: An eclectic review. *Journal of Teacher Education, 30* (3), 7–13.

29. Gnagey, W. J. (1981). *Motivating Classroom Discipline.* New York: Macmillan.

30. Goldstein, J. M., & Weber, W. A. (1979). *Managerial Behaviors of Elementary School Teachers and Student On-Task Behavior.* Paper presented at the American Education Research Association, San Francisco.

31. Good, T. L. (1970). Which pupils do teachers call on? *Elementary School Journal, 70,* 190–198.

32. Goss, S. S., & Ingersoll, G. M. (1981, February). *Management of Disruptive and Off-Task Behaviors: Selected Resources.* Washington, DC: ERIC Clearinghouse on Teacher Education, Sp. 017 373.

33. Hoen, A. (1954). A study of social class differentiation in the classroom behavior of nineteen third grade teachers. *Journal of Social Psychology, 39,* 269–292.

34. Rist, R. (1970). Student social class and teacher expectations: The self-fulfilling prophecy in ghetto education. *Howard Educational Review, 40,* 411–451.

35. Rosenthal, R. (1973). The Pygmalion effect lives. *Psychology Today, 7,* 56–63.

36. Rothbart, M., Dalfren, S., & Barrett, R. (1971). Effects of teachers' expectancy on student-teacher interaction. *Journal of Educational Psychology, 62,* 49–54.

37. Rowe, M. (1974). Wait-time and rewards as instructional variables, their influence on language, logic and fate control: Part one, wait-time. *Journal of Research in Science Teaching, 11,* 81–94.

38. Ryans, D. G. (1952). A study of criterion data. *Educational and Psychological Measurements, 12,* 333–344.

39. Thompson, G. G. (1944). The social and emotional development of preschool children under two types of educational programs. *Psychological Monograph, 56* (5), Whole No. 258, 1–29.

40. Schwebel, A., & Cherlin, D. (1972). Physical and social distancing in teacher-pupil relationships. *Journal of Educational Psychology, 63,* 543–550.

The following references discuss the educator as a person.

41. Aspy, D. N., & Roebuck, F. N. (1977). *Kids Don't Learn from People They Don't Like*. Amherst, MA: Human Resource Development Press.

42. Chernow, F. B., & Chernow, C. (1981). *Classroom Discipline and Control: 101 Practical Techniques*. West Nyack, NY: Parker.

43. Ginott, H. G. (1972). *Teacher and Child: A Book for Parents and Teachers*. New York: Macmillan.

44. Glasser, W. (1969). *Schools Without Failure*. New York: Harper & Row.

45. Gordon, T. (1974). *Teacher Effectiveness Training*. New York: Wyden.

46. Kleinfeld, J. (1972). *Instructional Style and the Intellectual Performance of Indian and Eskimo Students*. Final Report, Project No. 1-J-027. Office of Education, U.S. Department of Health, Education, and Welfare.

47. Kohut, S., Jr., & Range, D. G. (1979). *Classroom Discipline: Case Studies and Viewpoints*. Washington, DC: National Education Association.

48. Norman, J., & Harris, H. (1981). *The Private Life of the American Teenager*. New York: Rawson, Wade.

49. Rogers, C. R. (1969). *Freedom to Learn*. Columbus, OH: Merrill.

50. Schmuck, R., & Schmuck, P. A. (1979). *Group Processes in the Classroom*. Dubuque, IA: Brown.

51. Shumsky, A. (1968). *In Search of Teaching Style*. New York: Appleton Century Croft.

52. Weber, W. A. (1982). *The Classroom Management Project: A Technical Report*. Princeton: Educational Testing Services.

53. Weber, W. A., Roff, L. A., Crawford, J., & Robinson, C. (1983). *Classroom Management: Reviews of the Teacher Education and Research Literature*. Princeton: Education Testing Services.

54. Wolfgang, C. H., & Glickman, C. D. (1986). *Solving Discipline Problems: Strategies for Classroom Teachers* (2nd ed.). Boston: Allyn & Bacon.

The following references discuss modeling appropriate behavior.

55. Bryan, J., & Walbek, N. (1970). Preaching and practicing generosity: Children's actions and reactions. *Child Development, 41*, 329–353.

56. Charles, C. M. (1981). *Building Classroom Discipline*. White Plains, NY: Longman.

57. Clarizio, H. F., & Yelon, L. S. L. (1976). Learning theory approaches to classroom management: Rational and intervention techniques. *Journal of Special Education, 1*, 267–274.

58. Cullinan, D. A., Kauffman, J. M., & La Fleur, N. K. (1975). Modeling: Research with implications for special education. *Journal of Special Education, 9,* 209–221.

59. Good, T., & Brophy, J. (1984). *Looking in Classrooms* (3rd ed.). New York: Harper & Row.

60. Prentice, N. M. (1972). The influence of live and symbolic modeling on prompting moral judgment of adolescent delinquents. *Journal of Abnormal Psychology, 80,* 157–161.

61. Scheiderer, E. G., & O'Connor, R. D. (1973). Effects of modeling and expectancy of reward on cheating behavior. *Journal of Abnormal Child Psychology, 1,* 257–266.

Group cohesiveness is discussed in the following references.

62. Johnson, L. V., & Bany, M. A. (1970). *Classroom Management: Theory and Skill Training.* New York: Macmillan.

63. Schmuck, R. A., & Schmuck, P. A. (1975). *Group Processes in the Classroom.* Dubuque, IA: Brown.

64. Stanford, G. (1980). *Developing Effective Classroom Groups.* New York: A & W Visual Library.

These references discuss gender relationships in mixed gender groups.

65. Charlesworth, W. R., & LaFrenier, P. (1983). Dominance, friendship utilization and resource utilization in preschool children's groups. *Ethology and Sociobiology, 4,* 175–186.

66. DeVries, D. K., & Edwards, K. J. (1974). Student teams and learning games: Their effects on cross-race and cross-sex interaction. *Journal of Educational Psychology, 66* (5), 741–749.

67. Lockheed, M. E., & Harris, A. M. (1984). Cross-sex collaborative learning in elementary classrooms. *American Educational Research Journal, 21* (2), 275–294.

68. Lockheed, M. E., Harris, A. M., & Nemceff, W. P. (1983). Sex and social influence: Does sex function as a status characteristic in mixed-sex groups of children? *Journal of Educational Psychology, 75,* 877–888.

69. Moody, J. D., & Gifford, V. D. (1990). *The Effect of Grouping by Formal Reasoning Ability, Formal Reasoning Ability Levels, Group Size, and Gender on Achievement in Laboratory Chemistry.* ERIC ED 326 443.

70. Peterson, P., & Fennema, E. (1985). Effective teaching, student engagement in classroom activities, and sex-related differences in learning mathematics. *American Educational Research Journal, 22* (3), 309–334.

71. Piel, J. A., & Conwell, C. R. (1989). *Differences in Perceptions Between Afro-American and Anglo-American Males and Females in Cooperative Learning Groups.* ERIC ED 307 348.

72. Powlishta, K. (1987). *The Social Context of Cross-Sex Interactions*. Paper presented at the biennial meetings of the Society for Research in Child Development, Baltimore.

73. Siann, G., & Macleod, H. (1986). Computers and children of primary school age: Issues and questions. *British Journal of Educational Technology, 17,* 133–144.

74. Skarin, K., & Moely, B. E. (1974). *Sex Differences in Competition-Cooperation Behavior of Eight-Year-Old Children.* ERIC ED 096 015.

75. Underwood, G., McCaffrey, M., & Underwood, J. (1990). Gender differences in a cooperative computer-based language task. *Educational Research, 32* (1), 44–49.

76. Webb, N. (1984). Microcomputer learning in small groups: Cognitive requirements and group processes. *Journal of Educational Psychology, 76* (6), 1076–1088.

77. Wilkinson, L. C., Lindow, J., & Chiang, C. P. (1985). Sex differences and sex segregation in students' small-group communication. In L. C. Wilkinson & C. B. Marrett (Eds.), *Gender Influences in Classroom Interaction.* New York: Academic Press.

Gender differences in responsiveness to peers' requests and reinforcement are discussed in the following references.

78. Fagot, B. I. (1985). Beyond the reinforcement principle: Another step toward understanding sex roles. *Developmental Psychology, 21,* 1097–1104.

79. Lamb, M. E., Easterbrook, A. M., & Holden, G. W. (1980). Reinforcement and punishment among preschoolers: Characteristics, effects, and correlates. *Child Development, 51,* 1230–1236.

80. Serbin, L. A., Sprafkin, C., Elman, M., & Doyle, A. B. (1984). The early development of sex differentiated patterns of social influence. *Canadian Journal of Social Science, 14* (4), 350–363.

81. Wilkinson, L. C., & Marrett, C. B. (Eds.), (1985). *Gender Influence in Classroom Interaction.* New York: Academic Press.

Gender differences in leadership assumption and participation in mixed-sex groups are treated in the following references.

82. Lockheed, M. E. (1977). Cognitive style effects on sex status in student work groups. *Journal of Educational Psychology, 69,* 158–165.

83. Lockheed, M. E. (1985). Sex and social influence: A meta-analysis guided by theory. In J. Berger & M. Zeldich (Eds.), *Status, Attributions, and Rewards.* San Francisco: Jossey-Bass.

84. Lockheed, M. E., & Hall, K. P. (1976). Conceptualizing sex as a status characteristic: Application to leadership training strategies. *Journal of Social Issues, 32* (3), 111–124.

85. Webb, N. M., & Kinderski, C. M. (1985). Gender differences in small group interaction and achievement in high- and low-achieving classes. In C. Wilkinson & C. B. Marrett (Eds.), *Gender Influence in Classroom Interaction*. New York: Academic Press.

The positive effects of cooperative learning on interethnic group relationships are reported in these references.

86. Johnson, D. W., & Johnson, R. T. (1985). The internal dynamics of cooperative learning groups. In R. Slavin, S. Sharan, S. Kagan, R. H. Lazarowitz, C. Webb, & R. Schmuck (Eds.), *Learning to Cooperate, Cooperating to Learn*. New York: Plenum.

87. Slavin, R. E. (1985). An introduction to cooperative learning research. In R. Slavin, S. Sharan, S. Kagan, R. H. Lazarowitz, C. Webb, & R. Schmuck (Eds.), *Learning to Cooperate, Cooperating to Learn*. New York: Plenum.

The experiences of different ethnic groups in cooperative learning groups are discussed in these references.

88. Conwell, C. R., Piel, J. A., & Cobb, K. B. (1988). *Students' Perceptions When Working in Cooperative Problem Solving Groups*. ERIC ED 313 455.

89. Fry, P. S., & Coe, K. J. (1980). Achievement performance of internally and externally oriented black and white high school students under conditions of competition and cooperation expectancies. *British Journal of Educational Psychology, 50*, 162–167.

The following reference documents the developmentally inappropriateness of many teachers' classroom management techniques.

90. Bryant, D. M., Clifford, R. M., & Peisner, E. S. (1991). Best practices for beginners: Developmental appropriateness in kindergarten. *American Educational Research Journal, 28* (4), 783–803.

These references are concerned with discussions about differences and similarities among people.

91. Glimps, B., & Hicks, J. (1983). *Planning for a Culturally Sensitive Program in the Preschool Setting*. ERIC ED 230 009.

92. Grossman, H. (1984). *Educating Hispanic Students: Cultural Implications for Instruction, Classroom Management, Counseling, and Assessment*. Springfield, IL: Thomas.

93. Suzuki, B. H. (1984). Curriculum transformation for multicultural education. *Education and Urban Society, 16*, 294–322.

These references discuss including students' cultures in the classroom.

94. Banks, J. A. (1987). Social studies, ethnic diversity, and social change. *Elementary School Journal, 87* (5), 531–543.

95. Banks, J. A. (1991). A curriculum for empowerment, action, and change. In C. Sleeter (Ed.), *Empowerment Through Multicultural Education*. Albany, NY: State University of New York Press.

96. Loridas, L. (1988). *Culture in the Classroom: A Cultural Enlightenment Manual for Educators*. ERIC ED 303 941.

97. Mendenhall, P. T. (1982). Bicultural school organization and curriculum. In R. Barnhardt (Ed.), *Cross-Cultural Issues in Alaskan Education Vol. II*. Fairbanks: University of Alaska, Center for Cross-Cultural Studies.

98. Pepper, F. C. (1990). *Unbiased Teaching About American Indians and Alaska Natives in Elementary Schools*. Charleston, WV: ERIC/CRESS.

99. Pine, G. J., & Hilliard, A. G., III. (1990). Rx for racism: Imperatives for America's schools. *Phi Delta Kappan*, 71 (8), 593–600.

100. Sleeter, C. E., & Grant, C. A. (1988). *Making Choices for Multicultural Education*. Columbus, OH: Merrill.

101. Thomas, M. D. (1981). *Pluralism Gone Mad*. Bloomington, IN: Phi Delta Kappa Educational Foundation.

The following references stress the importance of proactive antibias and antiracism approaches.

102. Banks, J. A. (1988). *Multiethnic Education: Theory and Practice* (2nd ed.). Boston: Allyn & Bacon.

103. Brandt, G. L. (1986). *The Realization of Anti-Racist Teaching*. London: Falmer Press.

104. Cohen, O. P., Fischgrund, J. E., & Redding, M. A. (1990). Deaf children form ethnic, linguistic and racial minority backgrounds: An overview. *American Annals of the Deaf*, 135 (2), 67–73.

105. Mitchell, V. (1990). *Curriculum and Instruction to Reduce Racial Conflict*. New York: Teachers College, Columbia University, ERIC Clearinghouse on Urban Education.

106. Moultry, M. (1988). *Multicultural Education Among Seniors in the College of Education at Ohio State University*. ERIC ED 296 634.

107. Nieto, S. (1992). *Affirming Diversity: The Sociopolitical Context of Multicultural Education*. New York: Longman.

108. Olneck, M. R. (1990). The recurring dream: Symbolism and ideology in intercultural and multicultural education. *American Journal of Education*, 98 (2), 147–174.

The following references offer guidelines, checklists, and suggestions for detecting prejudice and bias in curricular materials and instructional techniques.

109. Banks, J. A. (1984). *Teaching Strategies for Ethnic Studies*. Boston: Allyn & Bacon.

110. California State Department of Education. (1988). *Ten Quick Ways to Analyze Children's Books for Racism and Sexism.* Sacramento, CA: Author.

111. California State Department of Education. (n.d.). *Standards for Evaluation of Instructional Materials with Respect to Social Content.* Sacramento, CA: Author.

112. Cotera, M. P. (1982). *Checklists for Counteracting Race and Sex Bias in Educational Materials.* ERIC ED 221 612.

113. Ferguson, H. (1987). *Manual for Multicultural Education.* Yarmouth, ME: Intercultural Press.

114. National Education Association. (n.d.). *How Fair Are Your Children's Books?* Washington, DC: Author.

115. Office of Intergroup Relations. (1977). *Guide for Multicultural Education: Content and Context.* Sacramento, CA: California State Department of Education.

The following describe techniques for increasing respect for diversity and reducing prejudice, animosity, and alienation and their effectiveness.

116. Cummins, J. (1988). From multicultural to anti-racist education: An analysis of programmes and policies in Ontario. In T. Skutnabb-Kangas & J. Cummins (Eds.), *Minority Education: From Shame to Struggle.* Philadelphia: Multilingual Matters.

117. Kanpol, B. (1992). The politics of similarity within difference: A pedagogy for the other. *Urban Review, 24* (2), 105–131.

Programs and approaches to reduce prejudice and improved interethnic and intercultural relationships are described in the following references.

118. Anti-Defamation League of B'nai B'rith. (1986). *The Wonderful World of Difference: A Human Relations Program for Grades K–8.* New York: Author.

119. Byrnes, D. A., & Kiger, G. (Eds.). (1992). *Common Bonds: Anti-Bias Teaching in a Diverse Society.* Wheaton, MD: Association for Childhood Education International Publications.

120. Cole, J. (1990). *Filtering People: Understanding and Confronting Our Prejudices.* Philadelphia: New Society Publishers.

121. Howard, G. (1989). Positive multicultural outcomes: A practitioner's report. *Multicultural Leader, 2* (1), 12–16.

122. Jorgensen-Esmaili, K. (1988). *New Faces of Liberty: A Curriculum for Teaching about Today's Refugees and Immigrants.* Berkeley, CA: Graduate School of Education, University of California, Berkeley.

123. Lynch, J. (1987). *Prejudice Reduction and the Schools.* New York: Nichols.

124. Olsen, L., & Dowell, C. (1989). *Bridges: Promising Programs for the Education of Immigrant Children.* San Francisco: California Tomorrow.

125. Panel of Americans. (1991). *No Dissin' Allowed.* New York: Author.

126. San Francisco Study Center. (n.d.). *Voices of Liberty*. San Francisco: Author.

127. Southern Poverty Law Center. (1991). *Teaching Tolerance*. Montgomery, AL: Author.

128. Teidt, I., & Teidt, P. (1986). *Multicultural Teaching: A Handbook of Activities, Information, and Resources*. Needham, MA: Allyn & Bacon.

Descriptions of materials that can be employed in a case study approach for dealing with ethnic conflict are included in the following reference.

129. Kleinfeld, J. (1990). *The Case Method in Teacher Education: Alaska Models*. Charleston, WV: ERIC/CRESS.

The following reference includes evidence that schoolwide approaches reduce prejudice and improve interethnic group relations in school.

130. Pate, G. S. (1989). Reducing prejudice in the schools, *Multicultural Leader, 2* (20), 1–3.

The works of authors who favor a transformational education or social reconstructionist education multicultural approach are listed below.

131. Mullard, C. (1985). Racism in society and school: History, policy, and practice. In F. Rizvi (Ed.), *Multiculturalism as an Educational Policy*. Victoria, Australia: Deakin University Press.

132. Quality Education for Minorities Project. (1990). *Education That Works: An Action Plan for the Education of Minorities*. Cambridge, MA: MIT Press.

133. Sleeter, C. (Ed.). (1991). *Empowerment Through Multicultural Education*. Albany, NY: State University of New York Press.

134. Wood, G. H. (1984). Schooling in a democracy: Transformation or reproduction: *Educational Theory, 34* (3), 219–239.

Inherent difficulties are discussed in the following reference.

135. Brophy, J. E., & Putnam, J. G. (1978). *Classroom Management in the Elementary Grades*. ERIC ED 167 537.

Avoidable difficulties are discussed in these references.

136. Duke, D. I. (1976). Who misbehaves? A high school studies its discipline problems. *Educational Administration Quarterly, 12*, 65–85.

137. Gnagey, W. J. (1978). *Attitudes, Motives, and Values of Facilitators and Inhibitors*. Paper presented at the annual conference of the American Educational Research Association, Toronto, Canada.

138. Gordon, T. (1974). *Teacher Effectiveness Training*. New York: Wyden.

139. Jones, F. H. (1987). *Positive Classroom Instruction*. New York: McGraw-Hill.

140. Jorgenson, G. W. (1977). Relationship of classroom behavior to the accurate match between material difficulty and student ability. *Journal of Educational Psychology, 69* (1), 24–32.

141. Leffingwell, R. J. (1977). Misbehavior in the classroom: Anxiety a possible cause. *Education, 97* (4), 360–363.

142. Moore, T. (1966). Difficulties of the ordinary child in adjusting to primary school. *Journal of Child Psychology and Psychiatry, 7,* 17–38.

143. Phillips, B. (1978). *School Stress and Anxiety: Theory, Research and Intervention.* New York: Human Science Press.

The following references deal with the inadequate educational services provided to non-European middle-class students.

144. Ascher, C. (1989). *Urban School Finance: The Quest for Equal Educational Opportunity.* New York: ERIC Clearinghouse on Urban Education.

145. Bastian, A., Fruchter, N., Gittell, M., Greer, C., & Haskins, K. (1986). *Choosing Equality.* Philadelphia: Temple University Press.

146. Becker, H. J. (1986). *Computer Survey Newsletter.* Baltimore, MD: Johns Hopkins University, Center for the Social Organization of Schools.

147. Center for the Social Organization of Schools. (1983). *School Uses of Microcomputers: Reports from a National Survey, No. 3.*

148. Darling-Hammond, L. (1985). *Equality and Excellence: The Status of Black American Education.* New York: College Entrance Examination Board.

149. Furr, J. D., & Davis, T. M. (1984). Equity issues and microcomputers: Are educators meeting the challenges? *Journal of Educational Equity and Leadership, 4,* 93–97.

150. Hood, J. F. (1984). *Update on the School Market for Microcomputers.* Westport, CT: Market Data Retrieval.

151. Karp, S. (1991). Rich schools, poor schools & the courts. *Rethinking Schools, 5* (2), 1–15.

152. Mickelson, R. A. (1980). Social stratification processes in secondary schools: A comparison of Beverly Hills High School and Morningside High School. *Journal of Education, 162* (4), 83–112.

153. National Assessment of Education Progress. (1988). *Computer Competence: The First National Assessment.* Princeton, NJ: Educational Testing Service.

154. New York City Board of Education (1989). *A New Direction: 1989–1990 Budget Request.* New York.

155. Oakes, J. (1983). Limiting Opportunity: Student race and curricular differences in secondary vocational education. *American Journal of Education,* May, 328–355.

156. O'Brien, E. M. (1989). Texas legislators impatient to solve unfairness of school financing system. *Black Issues in Higher Education, 6* (16), 23.

The citations below deal with the subject of the negative effects of poor schooling based on anecdotal descriptions.

157. Cormany, R. (1975). *Guidance and Counseling in Pennsylvania: Status and Needs*. Lemoyne, PA: ESEA Title III Project, West Shore School District.

158. Hargreaves, D. H., Hester, S. K., & Mellor, F. J. (1975). *Deviance in Classrooms*. Boston: Kegan & Paul.

159. Holt, J. (1979). *The Underachieving School*. New York: Pitman.

160. Laurence, J., Steed, D., & Young, P. (1984). *Disruptive Children, Disruptive Schools*. New York: Nichols.

161. Melton, D. (1975). *Burn the Schools—Save the Children*. New York: Thomas Crowell.

162. Purkey, W., & Novak, J. (1984). *Inviting School Success: A Self-Concept Approach to Teaching and Learning* (2nd ed.). Belmont, CA: Wadsworth.

The following references are research studies that document the negative impact that poor schooling can have.

163. Blumenfeld, P., Pintrich, P., Meece, J., & Wessels, K. (1982). The formation and role of self-perceptions of ability in elementary classrooms. *Elementary School Journal*, 82, 400–420.

164. Currence, C. (1984). School performance tops list of adolescent worries. *Education Week*, 3, 8.

165. Heal, J. (1978). Misbehavior among school children: The role of the school in strategies for prevention. *Policy and Politics*, 6, 321–332.

166. Johnson, K. D., & Krovetz, M. L. (1976). Levels of aggression in a traditional and a pluralistic school. *Educational Research*, 18 (2), 146–151.

167. Laurence, J., Steed, D., & Young, P. (1977). *Disruptive Behavior in a Secondary School*. London: University of London Goldsmiths College.

168. Reynolds, D. (1976). The delinquent school. In M. Hammersley & P. Woods (Eds.), *The Process of Schooling: A Sociological Reader*. London: Routledge & Kegan Paul.

169. Rutter, M., Maughan, B., Montimore, P., Ouston, J., & Smith, A. (1979). *Fifteen Thousand Hours: Secondary Schools and Their Effects on Children*. Cambridge, MA: Harvard University Press.

170. Stake, R., & Easley, J. (1978). *Case Studies in Science Education* (Vols. 1 & 2). Urbana, IL: Center for Instructional Research and Curriculum Evaluation.

171. Stanwyck, D., & Felker, D. (1974). *Self-Concept and Anxiety in Middle Elementary School Children: A Developmental Survey*. Paper presented at the Annual American Education Research Association Convention, Chicago.

The references cited below deal with the readiness skills of high-risk students.

172. Au, K. H. (1974). *A Preliminary Report on Teaching Academics Readiness*. ERIC ED 158 852.

173. Caspari, I. (1976). *Troublesome Children in Class*. London: Routledge & Kegan Paul.

174. Colligan, R. C. (1976). Prediction of kindergarten reading success from preschool reports of parents. *Psychology in the Schools, 13* (3), 304–308.

175. Hayes, M., Mason, E., & Covert, R. (1975). Validity and reliability of a simple device for readiness screening. *Educational and Psychological Measurement, 35,* 495–498.

176. Ireton, H., Kampen, M., & Shing-Lun, K. (1981). Minnesota Preschool Inventory: Identification of children at risk for kindergarten failure. *Psychology in the Schools, 18* (4), 394–401.

177. Nagle, R. J. (1979). The predictive validity of the Metropolitan Readiness Tests, 1976 Edition. *Educational and Psychological Measurements, 39* (4), 1043–1045.

178. Pheasant, M. (1985). *Aumsville School District's Readiness Program: Helping First Graders Succeed*. ERIC ED 252 967.

179. Terens, S. (1984). *Second Year Full Day Kindergarten Program Evaluation, Laurence Public Schools, Number Four School*. ERIC ED 251 177.

180. University City School District, Missouri. (1970). *Primary Mental Abilities and Metropolitan Readiness Tests as Predictors of Achievement in the First Primary Grade*. ERIC ED 043 683.

181. Wood, C. M. (1979). *Cognitive Style, School Readiness and Behavior as Predictors of First Grade Achievement*. ERIC ED 182 014.

The citations that follow discuss the learning styles of high-risk students.

182. Carbo, M. (1980). *An Analysis of the Relationship Between the Modality Preferences of Kindergarteners and Selected Reading Treatments as They Affect the Learning of a Basic Sight-Word Vocabulary*. Unpublished doctoral dissertation, St. John's University, Jamaica, NY.

183. Carruthers, S., & Young, A. (1980). Preference of condition concerning time in learning environments of rural versus city eighth-grade students. *Learning Styles Network Newsletter, 1* (2), 1.

184. Cofferty, E. (1980). *An Analysis of Student Performance Based on the Degree of Match Between the Educational Cognitive Style of the Students*. Unpublished doctoral dissertation, University of Nebraska, Lincoln, NE.

185. Dixon, C. N. (1977). *Matching Reading Instruction to Cognitive Style for Mexican-American Children*. ERIC ED 158 269.

186. Domino, G. (1970). Interactive effects of achievement orientation and teaching styles on academic achievement. *ACT Research Report, 39,* 1–9.

187. Douglass, C. B. (1979). Making biology easier to understand. *The American Biology Teacher, 41* (5), 277–299.

188. Dunn, R. (1983). Learning style and its relation to exceptionality at both ends of the spectrum. *Exceptional Children, 49*, 496–506.

189. Dunn, R., Cavanough, D., Eberle, B., & Zenhausern, R. (1982). Hemispheric preference: The newest element of learning style. *American Biology Teacher, 44* (5), 291–294.

190. Dunn, R., & Dunn, K. (1978). *Teaching Students Through Their Individual Learning Styles: A Practical Approach.* Reston, VA: Reston Publishing Company.

191. Gregorc, A. (1982). *An Adult's Guide to Style.* Maynard, MA: Gabriel Systems.

192. Kagan, J. (1966). Reflection-impulsivity. *Journal of Abnormal Psychology, 71*, 17–24.

193. Keefe, J. W. (1979). Learning style: An overview. In *Student Learning Styles: Diagnosing and Prescribing Programs.* Reston, VA: National Association of Secondary School Principals.

194. Krimsky, J. S. (1982). A *Comparative Analysis of the Effects of Matching and Mismatching Fourth Grade Students with Their Learning Styles Preferences for the Environmental Element of Light and Their Subsequent Reading Speech and Accuracy Scores.* Unpublished doctoral dissertation, St. John's University, Jamaica, NY.

195. McCarthy, B. (1980). *The 4Mat System: Teaching to Learning Styles with Right/Left Mode Techniques.* Oak Brook, IL: Excel.

196. Messick, S. (1970). The criterion problem in the evaluation of instruction. In M. C. Wittrock & D. E. Wiley (Eds.), *The Evaluation of Instruction: Issues and Problems.* New York: Holt, Rinehart & Winston.

197. Perrin, J. (1982). *Learning Style Inventory: Primary Version.* Jamaica, NY: St. John's University.

198. Pizzo, J. (1981). *An Investigation of the Relationships Between Selected Acoustic Environments and Sound, an Element of Learning Style, as They Affect Sixth Grade Students' Reading Achievement and Attitudes.* Unpublished doctoral dissertation, St. John's University, Jamaica, NY.

199. Price, G. (1980). Which learning style elements are stable and which tend to change? *Learning Styles Network Newsletter, 1* (3), 1.

200. Ramirez, M., & Castañeda, A. (1974). *Cultural Democracy, Bicognitive Development and Education.* New York: Academic Press.

201. Renzulli, J., & Smith, L. (1978). *The Learning Style Inventory: A Measure of Student Preference for Instructional Techniques.* Mansfield Center, CT: Creative Learning Press.

202. Shea, T. C. (1983). *An Investigation of the Relationship Among Preferences for the Learning Style Element of Design, Selected Instructional Environments, and Reading Achievement of Ninth Grade Students to Improve Administrative Deter-*

minations Concerning Effective Educational Facilities. Unpublished doctoral dissertation, St. John's University, Jamaica, NY.

203. Shumsky, A. (1968). *In Search of Teaching Style.* New York: Appleton-Century-Crofts.

204. Tannenbaum, R. (1982). *An Investigation of the Relationships Between Selected Instructional Techniques and Identified Field Dependent and Field Independent Cognitive Styles as Evidenced Among High School Students Enrolled in Studies of Nutrition.* Unpublished doctoral dissertation, St. John's University, Jamaica, NY.

205. Trautman, P. (1979). *An Investigation of the Relationship Between Selected Instructional Techniques and Identified Cognitive Style.* Unpublished doctoral dissertation, St. John's University, Jamaica, NY.

206. Urbschat, K. S. (1977). *A Study of Preferred Learning Models and Their Relationship to the Amount of Recall of CVC Trigrams.* Unpublished doctoral dissertation, Wayne State University, Yellow Springs, OH.

207. Witkins, H. A., Goodenough, D. R., & Kays, S. A. (1967). Stability of cognitive style from childhood to young adulthood. *Journal of Personality and Social Psychology, 1,* 291–300.

This reference relates to the self-quiz on personal characteristics.

208. Kauffman, J. M., Pullen, P. L., & Akers, E. (1986). Classroom management: Teacher-child-peer relationships. *Focus on Exceptional Children, 19* (1), 1–10.

Alienation among African American, Native American, and poor students is the focus of the following references.

209. Ginsberg, E., Berliner, H. S., & Ostrow, O. (1988). *Young People at Risk: Is Prevention Possible?* Boulder, CO: Westview Press.

210. Harris, W. G., & Blanchard, R. (1990). *A Select Group of African American Males' Perceptions of Barriers to Successfully Achieving the Typical Male Familial Role—Implications for Educators.* Paper presented at the annual meeting of the National Association for Multicultural Education, New Orleans.

211. Hirsch, B. J., & Rapkin, B. D. (1987). The transition to junior high school: A longitudinal study of self-esteem, psychological symptomatology, school life, and social support. *Child Development, 58,* 1235–1243.

212. Segrave, J. O., & Hastad, D. N. (1983). Evaluating structural and control models of delinquency causation. *Youth & Society, 14* (4), 437–456.

213. Utah researcher blames discrimination for Native American high school dropout rate. (1992). *Black Issues in Higher Education, 9* (9), 3.

This reference discusses the problems of limited-English-proficient students who are submerged in classes taught in English.

214. Olsen, L. (1988). *Crossing the Schoolhouse Border: Immigrant Students and the California Public Schools.* San Francisco: California Tomorrow.

References that discuss the role of schools in the reproduction of inequities in society are listed below.

215. Apple, M., & Weis, L. (Eds.). (1983). *Ideology and Practice in Schools.* Philadelphia: Temple University Press.

216. Connell, R. W. (1989). Curriculum politics, hegemony, and strategies of social change. In H. A. Giroux & R. I. Simon (Eds.), *Popular Culture, Schooling and Everyday Life.* Granby, MA: Bergin & Garvey.

217. Deem, R. (1978). *Women and Schooling.* Boston: Routledge Kegan Paul.

218. Giroux, H. A. (1981). Hegemony, resistance, and the paradox of educational reform. In H. A. Giroux, A. N. Penna, & W. F. Pinar, *Curriculum & Instruction: Alternatives in Education.* Berkeley, CA: McCutchan.

219. Giroux, H. A., &: Penna, A. N. (1988). Social education in the classroom: The dynamics of the hidden curriculum. In H. A. Giroux (Ed.), *Teachers as Intellectuals: Toward a Critical Pedagogy of Learning.* Granby, MA: Bergin & Garvey.

220. Grant, C. A., & Sleeter, C. E. (1988). Race, class, and gender and abandoned dreams. *Teachers College Record, 90* (1), 19–40.

221. Irvine, J. J. (1989). *Black Students and School Achievement: A Process Model of Relationships Among Significant Variables.* ERIC ED 310 220.

222. Valli, L. (1986). *Becoming Clerical Workers.* Boston: Routledge & Kegan Paul.

223. Weiler, K. (1988). *Women Teaching for Change: Gender, Class & Power.* Granby, MA: Bergin & Garvey.

224. Witt, S. H. (1979). Native women in the world of work. In T. Constantino (Ed.), *Women of Color Forum: A Collection of Readings.* ERIC ED 191 975.

225. Wolpe, A. (1981). The official ideology of education for girls. In M. McDonald, R. Dale, G. Esland, & R. Fergusson (Eds.), *Politics, Patriarchy and Practice.* New York: Falmer Press.

The following references deal with student resistance to school.

226. Anyon, J. (1984). Intersections of gender and class: Accommodation and resistance by working class and affluent females to contradictory sex-role ideologies. *Journal of Education, 166* (1), 25–48.

227. Arnot, M. (1982). Male hegemony, social class and women's education. *Journal of Education, 164* (1), 64–89.

228. Comer, J. P. (1990, October). What makes the new generation tick? *Ebony, 45,* 34–38.

229. Ford, D. Y. (1991). *Self-perceptions of Social, Psychological, and Cultural Determinants of Achievement Among Gifted Black Students: A Paradox of Underachievement.* Unpublished doctoral dissertation, Cleveland State University, Cleveland.

230. Ford, D. Y. (1992). The American achievement ideology and achievement differentials among preadolescent gifted and nongifted African American males and females. *Journal of Negro Education, 61* (1), 45–64.

231. Fordham, S. (1988). Racelessness as a strategy in Black students' school success: Coping with the burden of "acting White." *Urban Review, 18,* 176–207.

232. Fordham, S., & Ogbu, J. U. (1986). Black students' school success: Coping with the "burden of acting white." *Urban Review, 18* (3), 176–203.

233. Gaskell, J. (1985). Course enrollment in high school: The perspective of working class females. *Sociology of Education, 58* (1), 48–59.

234. Gibson, M. A. (1987). The school performance of immigrant minorities: A comparative view. *Anthropology and Education Quarterly, 18* (4), 262–275.

235. Kessler, S., Ashenden, R., Connell, R., & Dowsett, G. (1985). Gender relations in secondary schooling. *Sociology of Education, 58* (1), 34–48.

236. MacLeod, J. (1987). *Ain't No Makin' It: Leveled Aspirations in a Low-Income Neighborhood.* Boulder, CO: Westview Press.

237. Matute-Bianchi, M. E. (1986). Ethnic identities and patterns of school success and failure among Mexican-descent and Japanese-American students in a California high school: An ethnographic analysis. *American Journal of Education, 95* (1), 233–255.

238. Ogbu, J. U. (1986). The consequences of the American caste system. In U. Meisser (Ed.), *The School Achievement of Minority Children: New Perspectives.* Hillsdale, NJ: Erlbaum.

239. Ogbu, J. U. (1987). Variability in minority school performance: A problem in search of an explanation. *Anthropology & Education Quarterly, 18* (4), 312–334.

240. Ogbu, J. U. (1990). Minority education in comparative perspective. *Journal of Negro Education, 59,* 45–57.

241. Simon, R. (1983). But who will let you do it? Counter-hegemonic possibilities for work education. *Journal of Education, 165* (3), 235–256.

242. Suarez-Orozco, M. M. (1987). Becoming somebody: Central American immigrants in the United States. *Anthropology and Education Quarterly, 18* (4), 287–299.

243. Weis, L. (1985). Excellence and student class, race and gender cultures. In P. Altbach, G. Kelly, & L. Weis (Eds.), *Excellence in Education: Perspective on Policy and Practice.* Buffalo: Prometheus Press.

The following references deal with the inadequate educational services provided to non-European middle-class students.

244. Ascher, C. (1989). *Urban School Finance: The Quest for Equal Educational Opportunity.* New York: ERIC Clearinghouse on Urban Education.

245. Bastian, A., Fruchter, N., Gittell, M., Greer, C., & Haskins, K. (1986). *Choosing Equality*. Philadelphia: Temple University Press.

246. Becker, H. J. (1986). *Computer Survey Newsletter*. Baltimore, MD: Johns Hopkins University, Center for the Social Organization of Schools.

247. Darling-Hammond, L. (1985). *Equality and Excellence: The Status of Black American Education*. New York: College Entrance Examination Board.

248. Furr. J. D., & Davis, T. M. (1984). Equity issues and microcomputers: Are educators meeting the challenges? *Journal of Educational Equity and Leadership, 4*, 93–97.

249. Karp, S. (1991). Rich schools, poor schools & the courts. *Rethinking Schools, 5* (2), 1–15.

250. National Assessment of Educational Progress. (1988). *Computer Competence: The First National Assessment*. Princeton, NJ: Educational Testing Service.

251. New York City Board of Education (1989). A *New Direction: 1989–1990 Budget Request*. New York.

252. Oakes, J. (1983, May). Limiting opportunity: Student race and curricular differences in secondary vocational education. *American Journal of Education*, 328–355.

253. O'Brien, E. M. (1989). Texas legislators impatient to solve unfairness of school financing system. *Black Issues in Higher Education, 6* (16), 23.

These references are concerned with the effects of tracking and ability grouping.

254. Chun, E. W. (1988). Sorting black students for success and failure: The inequity of ability grouping and tracking. *Urban League Review, 11* (1–2), 93–106.

255. Gamoran, A. (1986). *The Stratification of High School Learning Opportunities*. Paper presented at the annual meeting of the American Educational Research Association, San Francisco.

256. Lake, S. (1985). *Update on Tracking and Ability Grouping*. ERIC ED 274 708.

257. Lee, V. (1986). *The Effect of Tracking on the Social Distribution of Achievement in Catholic and Public Secondary Schools*. Paper presented at the annual meeting of the American Educational Research Association, San Francisco.

258. Oakes, J. (1985). *Keeping Track: How Schools Structure Inequality*. New Haven: Yale University Press.

259. Oakes, J. (1988). Tracking in mathematics and science education: A structural contribution to unequal schooling. In L. Weis, *Class, Race, and Gender in American Education*. Albany, New York: State University of New York Press.

260. Simpson, W. (1990). *Black Male Achievement: Strategies for Ensuring Success in School*. Paper presented at the annual meeting of the National Black Child Development Institute, Washington, DC.

261. Slavin, R. (1986). *Ability Grouping in Elementary Schools: A Best Evidence Synthesis*. Baltimore: Johns Hopkins University Press.

Alienation among African American, Native American, and poor students is the focus of the following references.

262. Ginsberg, E., Berliner, H. S., & Ostrow, O. (1988). *Young People at Risk: Is Prevention Possible?* Boulder, CO: Westview Press.

263. Harris, W. G., & Blanchard, R. (1990). *A Select Group of African American Males' Perceptions of Barriers to Successfully Achieving the Typical Male Familial Role—Implications for Educators*. Paper presented at the annual meeting of the National Association for Multicultural Education, New Orleans.

264. Hirsch, B. J., & Rapkin, B. D. (1987). The transition to junior high school: A longitudinal study of self-esteem, psychological symptomatology, school life, and social support. *Child Development, 58,* 1235–1243.

265. Segrave, J. O., & Hastad, D. N. (1983). Evaluating structural and control models of delinquency causation. *Youth & Society, 14* (4), 437–456.

266. Utah researcher blames discrimination for Native American high school dropout rate. (1992). *Black Issues in Higher Education, 9* (9), 3.

HANDLING POTENTIAL DISRUPTIONS

This chapter describes techniques to handle potentially disruptive situations—such as start-ups, transitions, and obtaining permission—in ways that avoid behavior problems. It also suggests techniques you can use to reduce the potential for disruption inherent in certain instructional methods. The chapter offers effective procedures for establishing rules and helping students comply with them. It also includes exercises to help you gain insight into how your personality will influence the way you try to manage potentially disruptive situations.

If not handled well, some situations could tempt generally well-behaved students to misbehave. Here are some examples of potentially disruptive situations:

Beginning class at the start of the day or period, after recess, or after lunch

Transition times between activities

When students are waiting to request permission for certain activities

Times when students are called from class by the office or leave early for medical appointments

Late arrivals

Fire drills

Handing in late assignments

Informing students about what was covered and the homework they missed during an absence

Unanticipated schedule changes due to bad weather, audiovisual equipment break-down, teacher work days, standardized testing, and so on

The discussion begins by focusing on three typical potentially disruptive situations: starting up the class, transitions between activities, and obtaining permission. These three situations show how valuable it is to establish procedures before disruptions occur.

Start-Ups

The first few minutes of class as the day begins, right after recess, or following lunch at the elementary or intermediate level can be a waiting time for students who arrive early or settle down quickly. Having optional work on the board for them to do can keep them busy until everyone is ready. Options include new vocabulary words, map research for social studies, an interesting puzzle, or a special "stumper problem." You can also let students work on their journals, get a head start in silent reading, or select a learning center to work at for the first few minutes.

Transitions

Transitions—the times when students are finishing one activity and preparing for and actually starting the next activity—often find students not actively engaged in productive work. When transitions are not smooth—when students are waiting to be told what to do, are confused about what to do next, or do not have enough time to end one activity and prepare for the next or when teachers are attending to distributing or putting away things rather than attending to the students in the class—disruptive behavior problems are more likely to occur (1–4). Transitions can be especially disruptive if they occur without any warning or when the bell for recess, lunch, or dismissal sounds while students are still working. At such times, students are ready and eager to leave and reluctant to delay their departure to put things away, to hear what the homework assignment is, and so on.

When transitions are smooth, however, students switch from one activity to another quickly and without disruptions. They will also have more time for learning. Paying attention to transitions is classroom management time well spent.

Four Common Mistakes

Kounin (3) identifies four common mistakes teachers make during transitions. He names these *thrusts*, *dangles*, *flip-flops*, and *fragmentations*.

Thrusts These occur when the teacher suddenly interrupts an activity with no warning: "Time's up," "Everyone stop working," "Close your books," "It's recess time." When teachers end activities without warning, students in the middle of their work may interfere with the transition by expressing their reluctance to end what they were busy doing. In some instances, they may continue working on the earlier activity and not hear the directions that they will need to do the next activity well.

You can avoid such situations by giving your students advanced notice that an activity will end soon. Telling your students they will have to stop in 5 minutes or advising them

Students often welcome the opportunity to help out during transitions.

not to start another problem if they won't be able to finish it in the next 2 minutes are simple ways of avoiding thrusts.

Dangles   Educators leave students "dangling" when they get too involved in setting up materials, reviewing lesson plans, conversing with a student who needs extra attention, or making students wait too long for the next activity. The students are ready, but they have nothing to do except wait patiently or "get into trouble."

Sidestep having students dangle during transitions by having the materials you will need to use or distribute handy so you will not have to look for them. Use transparencies and an overhead projector instead of having students wait while you write things on the board. Establish automatic routines with your students for putting things away, collecting and distributing materials, and other classroom activities to reduce students' waiting time during transitions.

Another option instead of giving out all of the laboratory equipment, athletic equipment, or art supplies yourself is to assign two or three monitors to help if your students are old enough to assume that kind of responsibility. Establishing automatic routines using

THEORY FOCUS: KOUNIN ON CLASSROOM MANAGEMENT

Jacob Kounin investigated how teachers' behavior affects the ways their students behave. He introduced the practice of videotaping classrooms to study how students react to different types of classroom management techniques. He discovered that effective classroom management was characterized by four factors he labeled "with-it-ness," overlapping, smoothness, and momentum. These increase students' on-task behavior. In contrast, classroom management characterized by dangles, flip-flops, bottlenecks, fragmentations, and desist orders that are rough, unclear, and untimely lead to off-task and disruptive behavior. Kounin's book *Discipline and Group Management in Classrooms* is considered by many to have initiated the scientific study of classroom management.

students' assistance will reduce waiting time and free you to attend to the students rather than to housekeeping chores.

Another strategy is to avoid bottlenecks during transitions by putting materials in an easy-to-reach spot and by having more than one distribution point where students can pick up or check out what they need. Also arrange the furniture and equipment in the classroom so that it does not block traffic when students have to move from one place to another.

Stainback, Stainback, and Froyen suggest testing out the traffic pattern:

> Teachers can identify major traffic routes by "walking through" the activities that are likely to occur during the course of a school day. They may find that furniture and equipment placed in close proximity to storage areas, the cloakroom, or the classroom door must be relocated to allow for smooth, unobstructed travel. Likewise, traffic pattern testing may suggest a classroom plan or rule that can eliminate some congestion or disruption, for example, "No more than three students are allowed in the cloakroom at one time," "Enter the cloakroom from the left and exit from the right." (4, p. 13)

If you are working with younger students, arrange their cubbies, coat hangers, lockers, and other access areas so that groups of them can get to these areas at the same time without having to wait too long for turns. You can help kindergartners and students in early elementary grades by identifying storage locations with color codes or pictures.

Flip-Flops These occur when educators direct their students' attention back to a previous activity after they have started a new one. Examples of flip-flops include stopping a lecture about Native Americans to give the math homework after math has ended or interrupting a lesson to answer questions from students who do not know what they should be doing because they were not paying attention while the class was being prepared for the activities. Such flip-flops readily interfere with the momentum of the lesson and can make it difficult to get the class back on track.

To avoid flip-flops, make sure you complete all aspects of one activity before moving to the next one. Check that all students are paying attention while you are preparing them for the next activity, and double-check that all of them know what they are supposed to

TRANSITIONS	
Effective Management Techniques	*Ineffective Management Techniques*
Warning students that an activity will end shortly—5-minute warning	Ending an activity abruptly without warning
Shortening transition time by having materials ready in advance, using transparencies, etc.	Poor housekeeping procedures or stopping to write things on the board
Using several distributors and distribution points	Bottlenecks caused by students waiting to receive materials
Arranging the room to facilitate student movement, providing easy access to cubicles or lockers, color coding storage areas	Traffic jams
Completing all aspects of an activity before beginning a new one; making sure everyone is attending before giving directions or initiating an activity	Interrupting one activity to return to an earlier one
Preparing all students for an activity simultaneously; assigning self-directed activities if students have to wait	Moving the group along piecemeal
Monitoring students' attention span	Requiring students to continue an activity they can't concentrate on
Providing self-directed activities for students who finish early	Requiring faster students to wait idly
Providing slow workers other chances to complete their work	Penalizing slow workers for incomplete assignments

do. Whenever you discover that you have omitted something after you have changed activities, ask yourself if you really need to deal with it at the moment or if you can wait for a less disruptive time.

Fragmentations   Fragmentation refers to moving the group along piecemeal instead of together. Educators can fragment the group by having the class start a new activity one row at a time or by preparing the Robins for their reading assignment while having the Blue Jays wait their turn to be told what to do. Again, when students are waiting with nothing to do, they may be tempted to pass the time doing things that they wouldn't ordinarily do if they were actively engaged in learning activities.

You can avoid fragmentations by preparing your whole class simultaneously for a new activity. If you have to work with different groups separately before they can start, have the Blue Jays engage in a self-directed activity while you are giving the Robins their instructions and/or materials.

Timing

Determining when to end an activity and begin another one is just as important as determining how to make the transition between two activities. Because attention spans differ, students are not all capable of working efficiently and cooperatively for the same amount of time. Thus, whether students are working individually at their seats or in small or large groups, it is important to end the activity before they are no longer able to cooperate and start misbehaving.

One way to determine when students "have had it" with an activity is to identify a "steering criterion group" (5–7)—that is, a few students who represent those with the shortest attention span—and monitor them. Another way is to monitor the group as a whole for signs that some of them are fading. Signs that would indicate this include fidgeting, looking around, combing hair, talking to others, and writing or exchanging notes.

It is just as important to give your fast-working students self-directed activities to engage in while they wait for their less speedy peers to complete seat assignments. Slow workers, who are unable to complete seatwork in the allotted time, may be more willing to proceed to the next activity without resisting if you give them an opportunity to complete their assignments at a later, more convenient time (see chapter 13).

When the whole group requires more time to work at an activity than they are able to devote to it without becoming restless, you might try boosting their interest. Helpful comments include: "I know you guys must be almost pooped, but we can finish this in a few more minutes" or "We're almost done—let's try to finish up before we quit." If this doesn't help, you can give the group a short break and then return to the activity if your schedule permits.

Obtaining Permission

When teachers are busily involved with helping a student, working with a group of students, or doing work at their desks, they may not notice that a student is waiting to ask permission to sharpen a pencil, get a drink, go to the bathroom, and the like. Young students with low frustration tolerances or strong needs (to use the bathroom) may not be able to wait very long before interrupting their teachers or expressing their frustration in disruptive ways.

One way you can handle such situations is to allow students to attend to certain needs without obtaining your permission. This will cut down on your students' waiting time and the potential for associated disruptions. But because some students may abuse the freedom to move around the room without consulting you, you may prefer to have students obtain your permission in these situations. In that case, establish routines that enable students to gain your attention as quickly and unobtrusively as possible. This will cut down on their waiting time and maintain your control over their movements. You can also establish routines that minimize the need for students to leave their seats by handing out sharpened pencils at the beginning of the class and meeting other anticipated needs before they arise.

Which of these three approaches will work best for you depends in part on your personal style. Whichever you emphasize, though, the following suggestions should help:

1. Make a conscious choice—ahead of time—about how you wish to handle each of the situations just described. You may decide to allow students to get up without permission to do certain things in the room but not others or allow students to move around the room freely but not leave the room without permission.

2. Whatever choice you make, organize the classroom environment to minimize disruptions. For example, select pencil sharpeners that do not make a lot of noise and locate several so that students can reach them easily. Follow the same principle with movable storage cabinets, wastepaper baskets, and so on.

3. Maximize activities in which students can be self-directed. Minimize those for which students must obtain permission. This gives you more time for important things and also fosters your students' personal growth.

4. If you want to allow students to do some things without asking permission, make sure they are mature enough to handle this privilege. Younger children may be able to use the pencil sharpener without any problem, but allowing them to get materials from storage cabinets could cause difficulties. Monitor students closely, especially at the beginning of the school year, to make sure they can handle the privilege and don't abuse it.

In general, students should not be permitted to pester others while moving around, nor should they be allowed to absent themselves from the classroom by repeated trips or long visits to the water fountain or bathroom. One way of supervising when, how often, and how long students leave the room is to locate one or two larger passes for the drinking fountain and the bathroom in a place you can monitor. If students do not abide by the rules you have set up, employ the techniques in Part Two that you think will solve the problem.

Teaching Students Procedures

As noted in the previous sections, you can avoid many potentially disruptive problems by establishing procedures for doing such things as starting activities, distributing materials, moving from place to place, and obtaining permission. However, just telling students about certain procedures is not enough. The younger your students are, the more you need to teach them how to follow procedures and give them opportunities to practice. Typical procedures include where students line up for a fire drill, how materials are distributed, and what students do when they come late. The best time to teach such procedures is during the first few days of the school year. It may seem that having students practice the procedures you want them to follow uses up time at the beginning of the year and is less interesting and more tedious than other activities, but doing this will make your class more trouble free for the rest of the year.

Young children are not the only students who may have to be taught procedures. Any students who are not familiar with school routines may need to learn them. As will be seen in chapters 4 and 5, this may apply to immigrant and refugee students, especially those who have never attended school. Native Americans who transfer or graduate from schools that serve and are staffed by Native Americans to schools that serve and are staffed primarily by European Americans, as well as students who move from rural to urban areas and any other students who are not used to the procedures in their new schools, may also have to learn them.

Techniques for assisting students to follow procedures and rules are discussed in more detail a little later in this chapter, in the section "Establishing Rules."

Three Instructional Approaches

Each of the methods teachers use for instruction has certain inherent characteristics that may stimulate behavior problems if not handled properly. Three of the most common approaches educators use to instruct students are assigning students seatwork to be done individually; lecturing students interspersed with question-and-answer periods (direct instruction); and stimulating student interaction through group discussions, debates, group projects, cooperative learning, and the like. (This latter is high student involvement instruction.)

The following discussion is designed to help you use these instructional strategies in ways that maximize their effectiveness while minimizing their potential for disruptiveness.

Seatwork

Students who cannot continue working on their own because they need help with a particularly difficult problem or a step in a process or need to have their work checked before going on to another activity may not always wait patiently for their teacher to notice and attend to them. The following suggestions can help you avoid any problems that this might create (8–11):

1. Establish routines that enable students to gain your attention as quickly as possible.

2. Instead of requiring students to keep their hands raised while waiting for you to notice, establish an alternative signal, for example, a small cardboard stand they

can place on their desks. If you know that a number of students will require your assistance with a particular project or assignment, use a take-a-number system or have them add their names to a list in a prominent place so you can attend to them in order.

3. Give students feedback about their work efficiently. Checking students' work before permitting them to go on may be educationally sound, as you can determine if they have mastered a particular skill and can move ahead. But this approach uses up a lot of class time that you could spend teaching, and it means that students have to wait for you if you can't respond to them immediately. As an alternative, allow them to place completed work that does not require your immediate feedback in a to-be-checked folder for you to review at a more convenient time.

To handle fast-working students who may get into trouble if they have nothing to do but wait, you can instruct students to proceed to the next group of problems or questions when they finish if the assignment allows for this. If that is not feasible, you can permit them to select an acceptable activity at their desks or at a learning center of their choice. The latter can create more problems than it solves if it motivates students to be more interested in finishing fast to gain free time than in doing their work well. To avoid this possibility, you will have to monitor the quality of your fast-working students' work.

Sometimes you can give students who work a little slower than their peers a little extra time to finish. Or you might allow these students to complete some of their work at home or excuse them from having to complete every single problem in an assignment. In particular, slow readers may require a head start if they are going to finish something that the whole group will be discussing. (See chapter 13 for additional suggestions on managing fast- and slow-working students.)

Direct Instruction

Most behavior problems occur when the teacher is lecturing or other students are reciting, and students' thoughts drift. Instead of listening to what is being said, students can become management problems by daydreaming, scribbling, engaging in side conversations, writing, passing notes, and so forth (12–14).

The following techniques will help you maintain your students' attention when you lecture:

- Select topics and materials that are interesting and relevant to your students.

- Adjust your method of presentation to your students' developmental levels.

- Use proper pacing and timing.

- Actively involve your students in the learning process by encouraging them to react to your presentation, directing them to query you when they are confused or in doubt, and asking questions periodically to evaluate the effectiveness of your presentation.

Why are the students whispering? Is the lecture boring? Do they already know the work? Does one of them have some news that can't wait?

The following techniques will enable you to maintain the group's attention during question-and-answer periods, but they should be used only with students for whom they are appropriate:

- Vary the procedure you follow to select students to call on: Ask for volunteers at times, call on students randomly at other times, or call them in order. Calling students randomly maintains their attention, since they will not know if they will be asked to recite. This also keeps them actively thinking because they cannot just sit back and passively wait to hear what the volunteers have to say.

  This technique is not appropriate for all students. As discussed in chapter 5, some Asian Pacific American and Native American students may be extremely uncomfortable about reciting in class if they have not volunteered. And students with emotional problems may be threatened by having to answer questions when they are not ready to do so.

- Ask the question first, give students a few moments to think about it, and then call on someone. This will maintain your students' attention better than calling on someone and then asking the question, because the students won't know whether they will be the one you call on.

- Call on students in order only when a question has many possible answers, as in naming the 50 states, the 13 colonies, the 10 reasons why, and so on. Then ask your students not to repeat any of the states, colonies, or reasons given by other students.

- Intersperse group recitation with individual recitations. Have everyone in class express his or her opinions or vote on a decision by a show of hands.

    This technique is also culturally inappropriate for some students. Hispanic American and Native American students, for example, tend to be reluctant to express their opinions if they differ from those expressed by their peers. They may also resist voting on decisions if they are accustomed to arriving at group decisions through consensus building. (See chapter 5.)

Group Discussion

Probably the most challenging instructional strategies for classroom management are those that have students working together, but these are also highly engaging for the students. This group of techniques will assist you in maintaining the group's attention when students are interacting with each other:

- Teach students to talk to the rest of the class, not only to you, when they recite.

- Have them face the other students, not you.

- Make sure they wait until everyone is paying attention before beginning.

- Check to see whether everyone can hear and whether they understand what their peers have said. Students have no reason to pay attention when their peers recite if they can't hear or understand them.

- Have students comment about what the other students have said. This technique should be used on a voluntary basis, because many students are uncomfortable commenting about their peers' contributions, especially if their comments may seem critical.

Establishing Rules

Like procedures, rules are expectations for how students should behave. But procedures describe routines that students should follow in carrying out certain tasks that are basically functional and that may vary considerably from school to school and teacher to teacher. Rules, on the other hand, describe appropriate behavior. For example, students should wait their turn, work independently during tests, and respect the property of others. Rules typically describe how students should relate to each other and to their teachers or how they should behave in certain situations. Cangelosi (22) suggests that rules serve four purposes: to maximize on-task behavior and minimize off-task behavior; to provide students

THEORY FOCUS: THE CANTERS ON ASSERTIVE DISCIPLINE

In their book *Assertive Discipline*, Lee and Marlene Canter propose an approach to classroom management that includes the following principles:

- Teachers have the right to determine the environment, structure, routines, and rules that will facilitate learning in their classrooms.
- Teachers have a right to expect and insist that students will conform to their standards.
- Teachers should prepare a discipline plan in advance that includes explicit statements of their expectations, routines, and rules and the intervention approach to be used if and when students misbehave.
- Students don't have the right to interfere with the rights of others or to impede their learning.
- When students don't conform to teachers' expectations, teachers can respond in several ways: They can react nonassertively—passively surrendering to their students; hostilely—responding angrily and vindictively; or assertively—calmly insisting and assuming that students will fulfill their expectations.
- Since students who misbehave know the rules and so choose to behave inappropriately, with very few exceptions teachers should not accept the excuses students offer for their misbehavior. To do so only encourages students to misbehave more.

- Teachers should use consequences—positive if possible, negative if necessary—to convince students that it is to their benefit to behave appropriately.
- Teachers shouldn't feel guilty about asserting their rights and using harsh negative consequences when necessary. They should keep in mind that students want their teachers to help them control themselves.
- When necessary, teachers also have the right to ask for and receive help from parents and school administrators in order to handle students' behavior problems.

The Canters describe their work in the following way:

> We developed Assertive Discipline to give classroom teachers a systematic plan for dealing with student misbehavior. When a plan is in place, students know exactly what behaviors are expected in the classroom, and they can make a choice: to behave and enjoy the rewards or to misbehave and pay the consequences. . . . As teachers become more skilled at managing their classrooms, they can then provide better instruction and hone in on the individual needs of their students. (Lee and Marlene Canter, personal communication)

with a safe and comfortable learning environment; to prevent students from disturbing other students in the school; and to maintain acceptable standards of decorum.

Necessary Rules

Experts in the field agree that rules are necessary (15–20). Without rules, students would not know how to behave appropriately because expectations of acceptable behavior in and outside of school can differ (17). For example, outside of school it may be totally appropriate for students to move around and take breaks whenever they want to while doing their homework, for more than one person to speak at a time, or for students to express themselves in four-letter words. But in school, these behaviors are likely to be unacceptable.

While rules are necessary, some are more necessary than others. Sometimes teachers establish rules that reflect their particular preferences and desires rather than what is necessary for classrooms and groups to function effectively. These kinds of rules may seem arbitrary and unnecessary to students and cause them to feel resentful, particularly at the high school level. Therefore, if you decide to establish a rule that is somewhat unique to your class, it would be helpful, if not imperative, to explain your reasons to your students and to encourage them to discuss their thoughts and feelings about it.

Effective Rules

Most experts agree that to be effective, rules should be reasonable, observable, positive, and few in number (21–26).

Reasonable Rules   Rules are reasonable if they are necessary and not arbitrary. For example, it is necessary for students to be silent during fire drills, to keep their hands off other students during class, and to respect the property of others. But is it reasonable to prohibit students from chewing gum, from wearing clothes in class that may make teachers uncomfortable, or from swearing? Educators disagree about the reasonableness of such prohibitions. See chapter 9 for a more detailed discussion of how and why educators disagree about whether certain behaviors should or should not be permitted in school.

Observable Rules   Some authors (23, 24, 26) suggest that certain rules—for example, that students should be polite, respectful, responsible, and the like—are difficult for students to conform to because ideas about what polite, respectful, and responsible mean vary widely. For example, people disagree about whether one must always say please and thank you to be polite or always hand in homework on time to be responsible. The authors cited believe that because students may be confused about exactly what to do and not to do when they are told to be polite, responsible, and so on, rules should be observable. Examples of observable rules are "Walk, don't run, in the hallways" and "Do your own work on tests." Brophy and Putnam (21) and others, however, suggest that more general rules applicable to many situations, such as "Keep the classroom neat," and "Treat others with courtesy and respect," are preferable because they avoid a long and unnecessary list of specific things to do and not to do.

Positive Rules   To the extent possible, rules should state what students are to do rather than what they should not do. The value of this approach is that it will provide students with guidelines on how to behave correctly. For example, "Raise your hand and wait to be called on" is preferable to "Don't call out" because it teaches a procedure. In certain cases, though, negative statements are necessary: for example, "Don't spit" versus "Keep your saliva in your mouth."

Few Rules Most experts suggest that a few good rules are better than many detailed rules. First, students may experience a long list of rules as oppressive. Also, they may not be able to remember and follow them, especially in the primary grades.

Ethnically, Contextually, and Gender-Appropriate Rules

Students come to school with their own particular learning, behavioral, and motivational styles, which are influenced by their ethnic background, the contextual factors in their lives, their gender, and so on. By the time they begin school, they have also become accustomed to the management and disciplinary styles used by the adults who have been responsible for caring for them. (See chapters 4, 5, and 6.) As a result, some of the rules and expectations that seem necessary, appropriate, and acceptable to teachers and most students may be unfamiliar and appear unnecessary and arbitrary to some students who do not share their teachers' background and experiences. With such students, you may want to consider whether some of your rules are unnecessary or whether they should apply equally to all students (see chapters 4, 5, and 6). It will certainly be beneficial to explain to these students why rules that are unfamiliar to them are necessary and to help them learn how to follow such rules (see chapter 9).

Who Should Establish Rules?

Many educational theorists suggest that students should participate in developing classroom rules (27–31). To support their approach, these authors typically cite one or more of the following reasons. First, participating in the development of rules teaches students how to function in a democratic society. Such participation also helps students understand why specific rules are necessary, which in turn makes them more willing to abide by them. And students, like all people, are more willing to accept rules they help formulate. In fact, teacher-formulated rules can engender hostility and rebellion in some students who have difficulty obeying authority.

Other authors believe that educators should formulate rules on their own and explain them to their students (32–37). The reasons these authors give to support their position include the idea that educators cannot achieve their educational goals unless they possess the power to maintain classroom environments that suit them as individuals. Thus, educators have the right to establish the conditions necessary for them to succeed. In addition, these authors believe that teachers, not students, know what behaviors and standards have to be enforced so that students can learn. They also suggest that teachers, not students, are responsible for the classroom. Thus, allowing students to help set standards of behavior abrogates the teacher's responsibility.

These theorists also point out that by the time students have been attending school for a while, they realize that a schoolwide set of norms exists for almost all aspects of their behavior. To pretend that they are actually helping formulate such classroom rules is hypocritical, and students readily perceive that they are merely being manipulated and subtly

---

THEORY FOCUS: BROPHY RESEARCHES PRACTICE

Jere Brophy has authored or coauthored a dozen books about classroom management and instruction, including *Looking into Classrooms, Student Characteristics and Teaching, Teacher Behavior and Its Effects, Teachers Make a Difference, Teachers' General Strategies for Dealing with Problem Students, Recent Research on Teaching,* and *Learning from Teaching: A Developmental Prospective.* He and his coauthors have probably conducted, reported on, and evaluated more research on classroom management than any other group of individuals in the field.

Brophy's books are designed to enable teachers to base their decisions about classroom management strategies and techniques on scientific knowledge. Following the path cut out by Jacob Kounin, Brophy and his coauthors have contributed much toward our present understanding of effective classroom management and have helped bridge the gap between what theorists claim are good management techniques and what research indicates actually works in practice. For example, Brophy has led the way in establishing developmentally appropriate expectations and classroom management techniques for students at different grade levels, and he has also helped to establish the limitations of such techniques as using consequences and ignoring students to modify students' behavior.

---

coerced into agreeing with already-established rules. Students go along with the pretense of agreeing to the rules, but their acquiescence to the process doesn't necessarily affect their behavior.

Another point is that while it may be feasible to involve students in developing rules in elementary school, secondary school teachers cannot function adequately with a different set of rules each period of the day. And finally, students in a democratic society have to learn to abide by rules that are formulated by others.

Unfortunately, very little research exists regarding these conflicting opinions. The research that has been done indicates that classroom rules help students behave appropriately regardless of how they are formulated (30–40). Some research indicates that, at least in the lower grades, student participation in developing classroom rules increases the likelihood that the students will abide by them (33, 35, 36). But no evidence shows that teacher-formulated rules do not work, too.

When to Establish Rules

Most theorists suggest that classroom rules should be established and taught as early as possible in the school year (41). For example, Brophy and Putnam state:

Rules need to be stressed on the first day of school and again periodically during the new few weeks, as necessary, until they are working satisfactorily. There is no need for a teacher to be artificially strict or threatening (there is no support for the "don't smile until Christmas" notion), but students should be clear about what the rules are and should receive assistance in remembering and following them, if necessary. Especially in the early grades, getting the year off to a good start may require the teacher to show students what to do and give them practice in doing it rather than just telling them. (46, p. 37)

Four reasons are typically cited for establishing classroom rules early. The first is that establishing rules early could avoid some misbehavior that occurs simply because students don't know what is expected of them. Second, the sooner students know the rules, the sooner they will start following them. Third, students are more receptive to learning rules at the beginning of the year. And finally, criticizing students' behavior before they have been told what is expected of them is unfair.

In contrast to this approach, a few authors suggest that the teacher should establish rules during the year as the occasion arises because students are more likely to see and understand the reason for a rule that is set up in response to a real, current problem. A second reason for this policy is that students may feel oppressed by being given a long list of rules at the beginning of the school year. The limited research evidence regarding these two positions favors establishing rules at the outset rather than intermittently as the occasion arises.

Teaching Rules

Experts in the education field agree that students in the primary grades need to be taught how to abide by class rules (42, 43). Merely telling them the rules is insufficient. Here are some suggestions for teaching rules to students in the lower grades:

- Describe and demonstrate the desired behavior. Do not tell students to "be good" or to "behave themselves." Describe specifically what they should do to behave themselves and demonstrate and model the behavior you desire.

- Provide students with opportunities to practice the desired behaviors. Have them go through activities in which the rules come into play or role-play interpersonal situations in which they apply. This will help them learn how to behave appropriately and enable you to determine when they have learned to do so.

- Give students feedback about how they are doing and correct their mistakes.

- Wait until students know your rules and can comply with them before you begin to enforce them by means of consequences.

- Post the rules if students are young enough to need a reminder. Provide students with their own copy of the rules if you think it would be helpful.

Such procedures are usually unnecessary with older students, who have been exposed to a wide variety of school rules for many years. If you employ these procedures with high school students, they may perceive you, with some justification, as talking down to them. This does not mean that you should not inform them of your expectations. They need to

THEORY FOCUS: GLASSER'S REALITY THERAPY

William Glasser believes that students are in control of their own behavior and choose whether to behave appropriately or not. Because students misbehave when they make poor choices, Glasser's approach, as described in his book *Reality Therapy*, is designed to help students make better choices. Like the Canters, he advises educators not to accept students' excuses for their behavior. Instead, he provides educators with a 10-step process for helping students focus on the results, not the causes, of their actions. This process may or may not involve consequences. For example, students who are unaware of how their behavior affects others may agree to change their behavior once they know the results of their actions. Students who already know that their behavior is unacceptable and are unwilling to modify it may require increasingly severe consequences to motivate them toward change.

One of the many techniques Glasser suggests for giving students insight into their behavior and applying pressure to change is the class meeting. Glasser feels that a regular class meeting, conducted weekly or even more often, can provide students with feedback about how their behavior affects others, a variety of ideas and plans to select from for improving their behavior, and the peer support and pressure that could help them make significant changes. Whichever technique the teacher uses, the key to successful behavioral change, as Glasser sees it, is for students to accept responsibility for their behavior and to develop a written plan that indicates the behavior to be modified and the consequences that will result from following or not following the agreed-upon plan.

know which of the many rules that they have learned during their school careers they will be expected to follow in your class. However, unless you institute a new and somewhat unique rule, older students will not need to learn how to follow it.

Schoolwide Rules

Schoolwide rules that are consistently enforced by all faculty and staff are more likely to be accepted and followed by students. Rules that are not schoolwide can seem arbitrary to students, and teachers who establish and enforce them may seem strict and unfair. On the other hand, teachers who ignore schoolwide rules may be surprised that their students perceive them as weak and overly lenient, not as a "good guy." This may be true even if the rules make students unhappy, as long as students believe that the rules are necessary and fair.

Therefore, all things being equal, your rules will be more effective if they conform to those established and enforced by your colleagues. And you will appear to be doing the job you are supposed to do if you enforce schoolwide rules to the same extent as your colleagues.

You may not always agree with all the schoolwide rules you are expected to enforce. For example, you may feel that the rules concerning the way males and females can relate to each other during recess are either too permissive or too restrictive. You have a number of options when you do not agree with a particular schoolwide rule. You might decide to enforce it. You can attempt to avoid situations in which it is likely to apply. And you can attempt to get the rule changed. Whatever option you select, your choice should be based on thoughtful consideration of the alternatives.

Achieving Compliance

For rules to be effective, teachers have to enforce them. As Carson and Carson have said,

> Even if rules are short, positively stated, conspicuously posted, and are reasonable expectations of behavior, rules are ineffective if they cannot be enforced with appropriate consequences. Effective teachers therefore have rules that specify both behavior and the consequences for compliance with or violation of rules. (23, p. 135)

Not all students, though, will require the same amount of enforcement to get them to comply with rules. For certain students to follow the rules, they have to expect that they will be caught if they break the rules and will also have to pay consequences for their transgressions. But many other students will obey school rules without close supervision simply because they are motivated to do so—unless there are extenuating circumstances. Teachers who believe that most students can be encouraged to want to behave appropriately emphasize techniques that motivate students toward appropriate behavior and deemphasize enforcement. Teachers who perceive students as less than willing to abide by the school rules stress the expectation that the rules will be enforced. The point of view espoused in this book is that enforcement (extrinsic motivation) plays an essential role in classroom management, but increasing students' motivation to want to behave (intrinsic motivation) should take precedence as essential preparation for life in a democratic society.

Rule enforcement involves two steps: monitoring students' behavior and intervening when they misbehave. The sections that follow discuss these two key aspects of rule enforcement.

Monitoring Behavior

Kounin (3) and others (44–49) have demonstrated that students are more likely to abide by classroom rules if they believe that their teachers will notice when they misbehave. Kounin describes teachers as "with it" when their students believe that the teacher knows what is going on in the class. Teachers who have "with-it-ness" seem to have eyes in the back of their heads. They can attend to more than one thing at a time. And even while working with one student or a small group, they notice what other students are doing. When something starts to go wrong, they intervene right away before things get out of hand and the problem spreads. If more than one student is involved, the teacher focuses on the

The closer students are to the teacher, the easier it is to monitor their behavior and intervene in a timely fashion when they misbehave.

instigator or initiator, not the followers. In all these ways, with-it teachers convince their students that it is pointless to try to get away with things.

The following suggestions are aimed at helping you convince students of two important points: You will catch them if they misbehave, and you will intervene quickly and effectively:

1. Arrange the classroom furniture and your desk so you can see and hear what is going on.

2. Maintain eye contact with your students and move around the room to use your physical presence as a way of discouraging misbehavior.

3. Keep your eyes and ears open and periodically scan the class while you are working with individuals or small groups.

4. Be on the lookout for signs of impending trouble, such as scowls and frowns, students looking around the room, or a small flurry of energy, and intervene *before* anything actually happens.

5. As soon as a disruptive incident occurs, intervene before it becomes serious or spreads to other students.

6. When you intervene, focus your attention on the instigator of the problem, not an innocent victim if there is one. Specifically, intervene with the student who actually passed a note, asked to see someone's answers during an exam, or made a remark about a student's mother—not with the unwitting recipient, the student who says, "Do your own work," or the one who says, "Don't say anything about my mother or else."

7. When two disruptive events occur simultaneously—a student reading a comic in one part of the room and two students teasing a third elsewhere—attend to the more serious misbehavior first.

Intervening with Consequences

Although research shows that students are less likely to behave inappropriately when their teachers observe them and intervene appropriately, educators differ on what form such interventions should take. Many authors take the position that the cause of the infraction is irrelevant (50–54). They maintain that regardless of the cause, teachers should handle misbehavior by immediate, automatic, and consistent consequences. Here are some representative examples of this point of view:

> There must be consistent *consequences* for rule fulfillment or infraction. . . . Bending the rules for specific pupils or situations should be avoided unless this has been planned with students in advance. (53, p. 92)

> Peer pressure, inadequate parenting, learning disabilities, personal stress, and poor health are just some of the factors that make it more difficult for some students to be on-task than it is for other students. However, it is a fallacy that the presence of such factors excuses students from being responsible for their own behavior. (50, p. 31)

> There is no excuse for bad behavior. All students, except for some with known brain dysfunction, can behave acceptably. Behavior is a matter of choice. Students choose to behave the way they do. Consequences are not arbitrary punishment. They are results that students choose just as they choose their behavior. (52, pp. 211, 213)

Other authors disagree; they argue that teachers should match their intervention techniques to the causes of their students' misbehavior (55–57). Goss and Ingersoll state:

> The teacher must be aware of the underlying causes of behavior. For example, aggression that results from trouble at home should be treated differently from aggression resulting from boredom. Teacher control and interventions are alerted in relation to the interpretation of the reasons for a behavior. Intervention is neither arbitrary nor capricious. (55, p. 11)

At present, no research evidence indicates which of these two approaches is the more effective. Thus, the choice of whether you use consequences routinely or match intervention techniques to the causes of your students' misbehavior will probably depend on your personality and your perception of how best to manage students' disruptive behavior.

The point of view of this book is that educators should select intervention techniques that are appropriate for the causes of their students' problems (see Part Three). It is true that the application of immediate, routine, and consistent consequences is a useful and necessary technique for students who need to be discouraged from misbehaving because they have not yet acquired the intrinsic motivation necessary to abide by rules. But it is equally, if not more, important to motivate these students to want to behave even in the absence of consequences. (How to do this is the subject of chapter 11.) This idea is well expressed in the following statement by Jones and Jones:

> Behavior that violates accepted rules should be dealt with by discussing the matter with the child. This does not mean that reasonable punishments should not be employed, but when dealing with unproductive behavior we must help children examine both their motivations and the consequences of their actions. . . . In a very real sense, a punishment orientation reinforces a low level of moral development and does not help children develop a higher, more socially valuable level of morality. (26, pp. 195–196)

Moral Development

The importance of adapting your techniques to your students' motivational development levels was discussed in the previous chapter. This section covers how you can adapt your classroom management techniques to the moral development of students. (See chapter 11 for additional information.)

Three Stages

Many factors affect the pace and final form of an individual's moral development. Two of them, ethnic background and gender, are discussed shortly. Despite these individual and group differences, however, it is possible to identify various stages that typify the moral development of most people.

Piaget (67), Kohlberg (66), and others (58–73) have researched and described the stages children go through in relation to the reasons for conforming to societal expectations. Although these authors disagree on certain points, in general their work indicates that children's moral development includes at least three stages. (Keep in mind, though, that just as children learn to walk and talk at somewhat different ages, the ages at which they pass through these stages also vary with each individual.)

THEORY FOCUS: KOHLBERG ON MORAL DEVELOPMENT

Lawrence Kohlberg is one of the world's foremost researchers on moral development throughout the life span. In such books as *The Psychology of Moral Development, The Stages of Ethical Development: From Childhood through Old Age, The Measurement of Moral Judgment,* and *Moral Education, Justice and Community: A Study of Three Democratic Schools,* he has contributed much to our understanding of the different types of moral thinking that individuals are capable of at various stages of their development. He has also studied the evaluation of moral development and how to foster moral growth. Although the process of moral development now appears to be more influenced by cultural factors and is less universal than Kohlberg had originally thought, his work has contributed a great deal to our understanding of how to improve youngsters' moral functioning.

First Stage: Extrinsic Consequences   Children are in the first stage of moral development until the age of 7 or 8. Able to see the world from their own perspective only, they cannot control their behavior by empathizing with others (putting themselves in the other person's shoes) or by accepting the idea that others also have rights. Their level of morality, called moral realism, is based on the question, What will adults do to me if I do such and such? In this stage, children do what is expected of them because adults have authority over them, and positive consequences follow "good" behavior and negative consequences follow "bad" behavior.

Toddlers: Even this preliminary kind of morality takes years to develop in children. Infants do whatever they want, but by the toddler age, youngsters have to submit to authority. Toddlers control themselves for three basic reasons. First and perhaps foremost, adults force their will on them. By taking things out of their hands, putting things beyond their reach, dressing them in certain clothing, holding onto them firmly in public buildings, and so on, adults teach toddlers that they can both keep them from doing things and force them to do things. When children realize this, they are less likely to engage in power struggles that they know they cannot win. Second, adults teach toddlers that when they do what they are told, they get such positive reinforcements as smiles, hugs, praise, sweets, and the like. But when they do not do as they told, they are scolded, smacked on the hand, deprived of their toys, or given "time out" away from the others. Finally, adults model the way they want toddlers to behave and give them enough attention, nurturance, and love to motivate them to want to copy adults.

Preschool students: Educators use the same three techniques with preschoolers. They teach children to submit to authority by means of positive and negative consequences; they model the behavior they want the students to copy and motivate them to want to copy it. Though preschoolers have a greater capacity to control themselves, the type of self-control they are capable of is still very much like the self-control of toddlers. That is, when they are told not to do something—especially if they are told repeatedly—they generally respond appropriately. But they still cannot be relied on to exercise self-control without others there to tell them what to do and what not to do.

The words that adults use with toddlers are almost invariably a command like "Don't," "Stop," or "No." Preschoolers are ready for more advanced types of commands, such as "Wait," "Just a minute," "Later," and "Do it," "Pick it up," "You do it." Thus, toddlers can begin to learn that they cannot do everything they want, but preschoolers can also learn to wait and to do things for themselves or to at least help out a little.

Primary-grade children: When students are in kindergarten and first grade, typical self-control issues they struggle with include waiting to be called on, taking turns, not interrupting others, listening when other students are reciting, and sharing materials. Fortunately, by this time they can remember the consequences of their previous behavior. As a result, teachers have a fourth method they can use to teach these students to behave appropriately: They can remind them what happened the last time they did the wrong thing or did not wait.

Primary-grade students can also understand, although at a basic level, the ideas that people cannot all fit through one door at the same time and no one can be heard if everyone talks at once. This gives educators a fifth technique: They can explain the reasons why certain rules and procedures are necessary. Lacking experience and maturity, these youngsters have only a limited capacity to understand and recall the reasons their teachers give them for certain behaviors. But explaining the whys and wherefores to them in a way they can understand may still be helpful. Such explanations can help them progress to the next stage, since submitting to authority is only a basic beginning in a democratic society that calls for citizens with a higher level of moral development.

Second Stage: Natural Consequences   Students who are between 7 and 11 are usually in the second stage of moral development, sometimes referred to as the cooperative, reciprocal, or constructive stage. In this stage, students are much more able to understand why rules are necessary. They can readily see that they have to be quiet so their classmates can hear the speaker or that they must put things back where they belong so they can find them the next time they need them. But once students can appreciate why some rules are necessary, they may question the necessity for other rules that seem arbitrary to them. For example, they may want to know why they cannot chew gum in class or dress the way they want to if it does not hurt or interfere with anyone else. During this stage, they want to be told why they should or should not do certain things, and they are less willing to do things just because their teachers say so. Educators who rely too often on power to control students who have progressed beyond moral realism may find that their techniques spark dissatisfaction or outright rebellion in students who want to be treated more maturely.

Because students at this stage can appreciate why rules are necessary, they are able to distinguish between necessary and arbitrary rules and can see other people's points of view and empathize with their feelings. They can also understand concepts of justice, fair play, and so on, and so are able to participate in making classroom rules and determining the consequences when students do not abide by them. As we will see in chapter 7, this kind of experience can help prepare students to function fully in a democratic society.

Third Stage: Intrinsic Consequences   When students enter the final stage of moral development (usually when they enter junior high school), they begin to behave appropriately because it's the "right" or "good" thing to do. Instead of conforming just because of what teachers will do to them and what other students will think about them, they begin to exercise self-control and behave appropriately even if no one will know what they do or no one rewards or punishes them. As a result, at this stage educators can place greater emphasis on rational discussion and appeals to social responsibility instead of positive and negative consequences when attempting to motivate their students. They can now encourage their students to behave appropriately for the good of the class or because it's the "right" way to behave.

A democratic society cannot function properly unless its citizens have reached this stage of development, and so one goal of education should be to help students attain this level of morality. Overreliance on extrinsic consequences and failure to provide students with the opportunity to exercise the third stage of moral self-control may stunt their development. Class discussions about moral issues and taking part in projects that right injustices and reduce inequality, such as feeding the poor and confronting prejudice, can foster students' moral development (see chapter 11).

Ethnic and Gender Differences

While it is true that students tend to progress through the three moral stages we have just described, there are significant ethnic and gender differences in their moral development and approaches. Cross-cultural research has revealed significant differences in the pace at which children and youth pass through these stages in different parts of the world. (See chapter 5 for additional discussion of other ethnic differences.) And although the research about gender differences in moral development and behavior is inconclusive, it appears that girls tend to develop more rapidly than boys. They score higher than boys on tests of moral judgment, and many people believe that they behave somewhat differently (74–90). Adults describe girls as telling the truth more consistently, following through on what they say they are going to do more often, and empathizing more with others. Adults see boys as more prone to maintain a double standard (demanding that others behave more morally than they do), less self-critical of their behavior, and more likely to cheat.

There is some evidence that these "observed" differences between the genders may be more apparent than real—the product of observer bias and unfounded preconceptions. For example, research shows that teenage girls do commit less overt aggression than boys, but they engage in more covert aggression. Research also suggests that girls may not cheat less than boys when they think they can get away with it.

Although females score higher than males on tests of moral reasoning, the fact that they can reason morally is no guarantee that they will behave morally (see chapter 11). So far, the research evidence about this issue is inconclusive and offers little guidance to educators.

Some individuals have suggested that males and females use somewhat different moral approaches. Thus, Gilligan believes that male morality is based on abstract, impersonal, inflexible principles, whereas female morality is organized around notions of sensitivity to the feelings and needs of others, a sense of responsibility for others, and a desire and willingness to care for others (80, 81). This supposed difference between male and female morality has been described in the following way:

> Men evoke the metaphor of "blind justice" and rely on abstract laws and universal principles to adjudicate disputes and conflicts between conflicting claims impersonally,

impartially, and fairly. Women reject the strategy of blindness and impartiality. Instead, they argue for an understanding of the . . . needs of individuals . . . and the particular experiences each participant brings to the situation. (80, p. 8)

Lyons believes that in male morality, "issues, especially decisions of conflicting claims between self and others (including society), are resolved by invoking rules, principles, or standards." Men's moral decisions and actions are evaluated by considering "whether values, principles or standards are (were) maintained, especially fairness." In female morality, "problems are generally construed as issues of relationships or of response, that is, how to respond to others in their particular terms. They are resolved through the activity of care." And women evaluate their actions in terms of "maintaining connections of interdependent individuals to one another or promoting the welfare of others or preventing their harm; or relieving the burdens, hurt, or suffering (physical or psychological) of others" (86, p. 136).

Lyons illustrates the difference between male and female morality by the responses she received to the question, "What does morality mean to you?" A male responded, "Morality is basically having a reason for or a way of knowing what's right, what one ought to do and when you are put into a situation where you have to choose from among alternatives . . . having a reason for choosing among alternatives." A female responded, "Morality is a type of consciousness, I guess, a sensitivity to humanity, that you can affect someone else's life . . . and you have a responsibility not to endanger other people's lives or hurt other people" (86, p. 125).

Adapting to Students' Moral Development

Very little research has studied the effects of adapting management techniques to students' stages of moral development. Yet so many authors have suggested these adaptations and so many teachers have reported that they seem to work that using them until research either supports or refutes them seems reasonable. This section discusses using and adapting management techniques that correspond to the three stages of moral development.

Students in the first stage of moral development—preschool and primary-grade students—respond to consequences. Rewarding them for behaving appropriately and applying negative consequences when they misbehave help teach them about the real world. Thus, although consequences should not be the teacher's main approach to classroom management, they do play an important role with young students.

Older students who have not been exposed to life's lessons at home or elsewhere and come to school believing they can "get away with" doing whatever they please also need to learn that, at least in school, they have to abide by rules. But such students are only a small fraction of the school population. These students also need to develop intrinsic motivation so they will not want to get away with things. Knowing that there will be consequences if one misbehaves is also needed to keep many well-behaved students on track, just as knowing that the IRS may audit one's taxes or the parking meter attendant may ticket one's car helps citizens abide by the laws. In general, however, negative consequences should play an extremely minor, insignificant, and primarily deterrent role with upper elementary and secondary school students. Educators who punish older students excessively or who rely heavily on the threat of punishment for control risk making students resentful and rebellious about being treated like "babies" or "criminals." Such educators also neglect their responsibility to help students develop the intrinsic motivation needed to function as true citizens in a democratic society.

Because upper elementary and secondary students can understand why it is necessary to behave appropriately, follow rules, and be good group members, they should be approached—at least in part—as rational people capable of managing their own behavior once they know how they should behave and why it is necessary for them to behave that way. Secondary school teachers in particular should foster their students' intrinsic motivation. This is not meant to imply that secondary school teachers and administrators can dispense with consequences. Consequences are a fact of life. What it means, once again, is that after the primary grades, consequences should play a minor, deterrent role.

The Educator's Personality and Background

Research indicates that educators' personalities, values, beliefs, and so on, help determine the ways they manage their classrooms (91–93). Specifically, educators differ in terms of how much movement and talking they allow in their classes, the kinds of activities students can engage in without obtaining their permission, the types of instructional approaches they use, how much they emphasize acquiring basic skills and knowledge or improving interpersonal skills, whether they use authoritative or authoritarian classroom management techniques, the relative emphasis they place on fostering students' intrinsic motivation to behave appropriately as opposed to using extrinsic consequences, the roles they assign students in developing classroom rules, and whether they emphasize cooperation or competition to motivate their students.

There is evidence that educators' gender influences their instructional and classroom management styles in many ways (94–109). Male teachers are generally more direct with their students and more subject centered; female teachers are more indirect and more student centered. Males lecture more; females ask more questions and involve themselves more often in classroom discussions. Females use cooperative learning more than males, who are more likely to employ competitive learning. Females are more likely to praise students for answering correctly but less likely to give students feedback when their answers are wrong. Males are more likely to criticize wrong answers, offer explanations designed to help students correct their responses, and give students another chance to respond correctly.

Female teachers are more available to students during class time; they make more eye contact and maintain less distance from their students. They are more sensitive to students' needs and feelings, more accepting, and less critical and harsh. When organizing students into groups, female teachers are more likely than males to assign students to specific groups, while males are more likely to allow students to form their own groups.

Female teachers are less comfortable than males with assertive and active behavior. When dealing with disruptive behavior, females are more likely to provide students with

Self-Quiz: Student Feedback

Here are some sample statements you can use to find out how your students perceive you when you are student teaching or have your own class. The actual statements that you use would depend on what you are interested in learning from your students as well as on their developmental level. You might ask older students to rate you on a scale of 1 to 10, 1 to 5, or as excellent, good, fair, poor, or very poor. But younger students might relate better to single, double, triple, home run or always, usually, sometimes, never.

I am friendly.

I am polite and respectful.

I don't lose my temper.

I am fair.

I make you feel good about yourself.

I am not sarcastic.

I don't embarrass you in front of your classmates.

I listen to your complaints, discuss them, and tell you whether I agree with you or not and why.

I call on you as often as I call on other students.

I listen to your answers and comments and give you my honest reactions to them.

I give you permission to do the things you want to do when you want to do them.

I allow you to participate in making decisions that affect you, such as when tests will be given and where we will go on class trips.

I encourage you to talk to me about whatever is on your mind, even if it isn't related to school.

I do my best to make time before, during, or after class for you to discuss whatever you want with me.

I give you my honest opinions when we discuss things.

I understand how you feel about things.

I act the way I expect you to act.

I encourage everyone in class to get along and to cooperate with each other.

I encourage students to solve the conflicts between them on their own.

I praise and criticize you only when you deserve it.

I make sure the class knows what to do when they come in at the start of the day, at the beginning of the period, after lunch, and after recess.

I give you enough time to complete your work.

I don't require you to ask for permission to do certain things you can do on your own.

I don't make you wait too long when you need help with difficult work or want permission to do something.

I allow you to help decide the class rules and the consequences for breaking them.

Classroom rules are clear.

Classroom rules are fair.

I am in charge of the class.

I know who is doing what in class.

I don't expect too little or too much from you.

I expect you to act your age, not younger or older.

I treat you like someone your age should be treated.

information about the effects of their behavior on others. They also tend to prefer techniques that provide students with external control. Males teachers tend to reinforce young boys for stereotypical male behaviors more than females do. They are more tolerant of males' aggressive and disruptive behavior and less likely to send aggressive or disruptive boys to the office or to refer them to special education. But they reprimand students more than females and do so more publicly.

Ethnicity also influences educators' instructional and classroom management styles. For example, Hispanic Americans function differently than European Americans in a number of ways (99, 110–114). Hispanic Americans are more cooperative and more sensitive to the feelings and opinions of others than are European Americans. They are more likely to believe that behavior is controlled on a conscious level. And believing that behavior is subject to conscious control, they are more likely to utilize behavior modification techniques to control children's behavior rather than techniques designed to change children's dynamics or resolve their underlying problems. Hispanic Americans are also more likely to give children and teenagers feedback about their behavior in private rather than in public because a public negative message is an affront to Hispanic Americans' self-respect and an attack on their family pride. Hispanic American parents tend to speak more politely and indirectly when they criticize or discipline their children.

When dealing with behavior problems, Hispanic Americans prefer to provide flexibility, accommodate to individual differences, and provide students with alternatives. As already noted, they are more likely to use consequences to convince students to modify their behavior. They are also more concerned about preventing future problems from occurring.

Research indicates that African Americans also have preferred ways of functioning (112–123). Compared to European Americans, African Americans use more authoritarian disciplinary techniques with children and are more sensitive to and concerned about the feelings of others. When dealing with classroom management problems, African Americans favor explaining the reasons why students should or should not behave in a particular way and helping students understand the effects of their behavior on others.

There is also evidence that instructors' gender and ethnic background influence what they teach teachers-in-training about the most effective ways to manage their classroom (124).

Summary

By handling potentially disruptive situations, such as start-ups, transitions, and obtaining permission properly, it's possible to sidestep many potential classroom behavior problems. Establishing procedures and rules can also help you eliminate problems. To ensure that students will comply with established procedures and rules, it's necessary to monitor the students' behavior and intervene when they misbehave. Such intervention techniques should be suited to your students' level of moral development and their ethnic and gender background. It is also helpful to be aware of and modify, if necessary, your personal preferences regarding classroom management techniques.

Activities

I. List some activities you could assign students at the beginning of the school day, after recess, or after lunch that would help avoid potential problems during start-ups. Use the class or program you plan to work in to establish the students' ages.

II. Review the arguments for and against each of the following controversial practices. Formulate your opinion, and state the reasons for your decision.

- Including versus not including students in developing classroom rules

- Establishing rules at the beginning of the school year versus later in the term

- Intervening immediately, automatically, and consistently when students misbehave versus taking the causes of students' misbehavior into consideration

III. List the management techniques that you can use to help students behave appropriately at each of the following levels of moral development: stage 1, extrinsic consequences; stage 2, natural consequences; stage 3, intrinsic consequences.

References

These references deal with effective transitions.

1. Anderson, L. M., Evertson, C. M., & Brophy, J. E. (1979). An experimental study of effective teaching in first grade reading groups. *Elementary School Journal*, 79 (4), 1, 193–223.

2. Arlin, M. (1979). Teacher transitions can disrupt time flow in classrooms. *American Educational Research Journal*, 16 (1), 42–56.

3. Kounin, J. (1970). *Discipline and Group Management in Classrooms*. New York: Holt, Rinehart & Winston.

4. Stainback, W., Stainback, S., & Froyen, L. (1987). Structuring class to prevent disruptive behaviors. *Teaching Exceptional Children*, 19 (4), 12–16.

The references below deal with steering criterion groups.

5. Arlin, M., & Westbury, I. (1976). The leveling effect of teacher pacing on science content mastery. *Journal of Research in Science Teaching*, 13, 213–219.

6. Dahloff, U. (1971). *Ability Grouping, Content Validity and Curriculum Planning Analysis*. New York: Teachers College Press.

7. Lundgren, U. P. (1977). *Model Analysis of Pedagogical Process*. Stockholm: CWK Gleerup.

These articles discuss managing waiting time.

8. Berliner, D. (1978). *Changing Academic Learning Time: Clinical Intervention in Four Classrooms*. Paper presented at the annual meeting of the American Educational Research Association, Toronto, Canada.

9. Brophy, J. E., & Evertson, C. M. (1976). *Learning from Teaching: A Developmental Perspective*. Boston: Allyn & Bacon.

10. Brophy, J. E., & Putnam, J. G. (1978). *Classroom Management in the Elementary Grades*. ERIC ED 167 537.

11. Yinger, R. (1979). Routines in teacher planning. *Theory into Practice, 18*, 163–169.

The following sources cover maintaining group focus.

12. Good, T. (1978). *The Missouri Mathematics Effectiveness Project: A Program of Naturalistic and Experimental Research*. Paper presented at the annual meeting of the American Educational Research Association, Toronto, Canada.

13. Kounin, J. S. (1970). *Discipline and Group Management in Classrooms*. New York: Holt, Rinehart & Winston.

14. Kounin, J. S., & Doyle, P. H. (1975). Degrees of continuity of a lesson's signal system and the task involvement of children. *Journal of Educational Psychology, 67*, 159–164.

Necessary rules are discussed in these references.

15. Canter, L., & Canter, M. (1976). *Assertive Discipline*. Seal Beach, CA: Canter & Associates.

16. Dreikurs, R., & Grey, L. (1968). *A New Approach to Discipline: Logical Consequences*. New York: Hawthorne Books.

17. Gnagey, W. J. (1981). *Motivating Classroom Discipline*. New York: Macmillan.

18. Masden, C., & Masden, C. (1970). *Teaching/Discipline*. Boston: Allyn & Bacon.

19. Morgan, D. P., & Jenson, W. R. (1988). *Teaching Behaviorally Disordered Students: Preferred Practices*. Columbus, OH: Merrill.

20. Tikunoff, W. J., Word, B., & Dasho, S. (1978). *Three Case Studies*. (Report A78-7). San Francisco: Far West Laboratory for Educational Research and Development.

The references below discuss effective rules.

21. Brophy, J. E., & Putnam, J. G. (1978). *Classroom Management in the Elementary Grades*. ERIC ED 167 537.

22. Cangelosi, J. S. (1986). *Cooperation in the Classroom: Students and Teachers Together*. Washington, DC: National Education Association.

23. Carson, J. C., & Carson, P. (1984). *Any Teacher Can: Practical Strategies for Effective Classroom Management.* Springfield, IL: Thomas.

24. Charles, G. M. (1981). *Building Classroom Discipline: From Models to Practice.* White Plains, NY: Longman.

25. Gnagey, W. J. (1981). *Motivating Classroom Discipline.* New York: Macmillan.

26. Jones, V. F., & Jones, L. S. (1986). *Comprehensive Classroom Management: Creating Positive Learning Environments.* Boston: Allyn & Bacon.

Procedures for establishing rules with students are included in the following references.

27. Glasser, W. (1969). *Schools Without Failure.* New York: Harper & Row.

28. Guarnaccia, V. J. (1972). The effectiveness of school rule codes in reducing misbehavior in elementary school classes. *Dissertation Abstracts International 33* (6–B) 2810 (Order No. 72–31–955).

29. Jensen, R. E. (1975). Cooperative relations between secondary teachers and students: Some behavioral strategies. *Adolescence, 10,* 469–482.

30. Schmuck, R., & Schmuck, P. A. (1979). *Group Processes in the Classroom.* Dubuque, IA: Brown.

31. Tjosvold, D. (1980). Control, conflict, and collaboration in the classroom. *Education Digest, 45* (8), 17–20.

The articles that follow describe establishing rules without student participation.

32. Bloom, R. B. (1980). Teachers and students in conflict. The CREED Approach. *Phi Delta Kappan, 61,* 624–626.

33. Canter, L., & Canter, M. (1976). *Assertive Discipline.* Seal Beach, CA: Canter & Associates.

34. Dobson, J. (1970). *Dare to Discipline.* Wheaton, IL: Tyndale House.

35. Englander, M. E. (1986). *Strategies for Classroom Discipline.* New York: Praeger.

36. Johnson, L. V., & Bany, M. A. (1970). *Classroom Management Theory and Skill Training.* New York: Macmillan.

37. McDaniel, T. R. (1982). How to be an effective authoritarian: A back to basics approach to classroom discipline. *Clearing House, 55,* 245–247.

These references discuss the efficacy of rules.

38. Masden, C. H., Jr., Becker, W. C., & Thomas, D. R. (1986). Rules, praise and ignoring: Elements of elementary classroom control. *Journal of Applied Behavior Analyses, 1,* 139–150.

39. O'Leary, K. D., Becker, W. C., Evans, M. B., & Sudargas, R. A. (1969). A token reinforcement program in a public school: A replication and systems analysis. *Journal of Applied Behavior Analyses, 2,* 3–13.

40. Walker, H. M. (1979). *The Acting-Out Child: Coping with Classroom Disruption*. Boston: Allyn & Bacon.

The citation below focuses on establishing rules early.

41. Emmer, E., Evertson, C., & Anderson, L. (1980). Effective management at the beginning of the school year. *Elementary School Journal, 80*, 219–231.

These references discuss how to teach students rules.

42. Emmer, E. T., Evertson, C. M., Sanford, J. P., Clements, B. S., & Worsham, M. E. (1989). *Classroom Management for Elementary Teachers*. Englewood Cliffs, NJ: Prentice-Hall.

43. Emmer, E. T., Evertson, C. M., Sanford, J. P., Clements, B. S., & Worsham, M. E. (1989). *Classroom Management for Secondary Teachers*. Englewood Cliffs, NJ: Prentice-Hall.

These references discuss monitoring students' behavior.

44. Borg, W. R., & Ascione, F. R. (1982). Classroom management in elementary mainstreaming classrooms. *Journal of Educational Psychology, 74*, 85–95.

45. Brophy, J. E., & Evertson, C. M. (1976). *Learning from Teaching: A Developmental Perspective*. Boston: Allyn & Bacon.

46. Brophy, J., & Putnam, J. (1978). *Classroom Management in the Elementary Grades*. Research Series Number 32. East Lansing, MI: Institute for Research on Teaching, Michigan State University.

47. Crawford, J., Gage, N., Corno, L., Stayrook, N., & Mitman, A. (1978). *An Experiment on Teacher Effectiveness and Parent-Assisted Instruction in Third Grade* (preliminary draft). Stanford, CA: Center for Research at Stanford, Stanford University.

48. Emmer, E., & Evertson, C. (1981). Synthesis of research on classroom leadership. *Educational Leadership, 38*, 342–347.

49. Evertson, C. M., & Emmer, E. T. (1982). Effective management at the beginning of the school year in junior high classes. *Journal of Educational Psychology, 74* (4), 485–498.

The references below include information about intervening with consequences.

50. Cangelosi, J. S. (1988). *Classroom Management Strategies: Gaining and Maintaining Students' Cooperation*. New York: Longman.

51. Carson, J. C., & Carson, P. (1984). *Any Teacher Can: Practical Strategies for Effective Classroom Management*. Springfield, IL: Thomas.

52. Charles, C. M. (1981). *Building Classroom Discipline: From Models to Practice*. White Plains, NY: Longman.

53. Kerr, M. M., & Nelson, C. M. (1983). *Strategies for Managing Behavior Problems in the Classroom*. Columbus, OH: Merrill.

54. Masden, C. H., Jr., & Masden, C. K. (1970). *Teaching/Discipline*. Boston: Allyn & Bacon.

These references deal with matching causes and interventions.

55. Goss, S. S., & Ingersoll, G. M. (1981). *Management of Disruptive and Off-Task Behaviors: Selected Resources*. Washington, DC: ERIC Clearinghouse on Teacher Education.

56. Johnson, L. V., & Bany, M. A. (1970). *Classroom Management: Theory and Skill Training*. New York: Macmillan.

57. Redl, F. (1975). Disruptive behavior in the classroom. *School Review, 83* (4), 569–594.

The typical stages of moral development are described in these references.

58. Aronfreed, J. M. (1968). *Conduct and Conscience: The Socialization of Internalized Control over Behavior*. New York: Academic Press.

59. Bear, G. B., & Richards, H. C. (1981). Moral reasoning and conduct problems in the classroom. *Journal of Educational Psychology, 73,* 664–670.

60. Brockman, J., et al. (1978). *The Developmental Relationship Among Moral Judgment, Moral Conduct, and a Rationale for Appropriate Behavior*. ERIC ED 165 051.

61. DePalma, D. J., & Foley, J. M. (Eds.). (1975). *Moral Development: Current Theory and Research*. New York: Erlbaum.

62. Edelman, E. M., & Goldstein, A. P. (1981). Moral education. In A. P. Goldstein, E. G. Carr, W. S. Davidson, & P. Wehr (Eds.), *In Response to Aggression*. New York: Pergamon.

63. Freeman, S. J. M., & Biebink, J. W. (1979). Moral judgment as a function of age, sex and stimulus. *Journal of Psychology, 102,* 43–47.

64. Gibbs, J. C., Arnold, K. D., Ahlborn, H. H., & Cheesman, F. L. (1984). Facilitation of sociomoral reasoning in delinquents. *Journal of Consulting and Clinical Psychology, 52,* 37–45.

65. Hoffman, M. L. (1970). Moral development. In P. H. Mussen (Ed.), *Manual of Child Psychology, Vol. 2* (3rd ed.). New York: Wiley.

66. Kohlberg, L. (1984). *The Psychology of Moral Development*. San Francisco: Harper & Row.

67. Piaget, J. (1965). *The Moral Judgment of the Child*. New York: Free Press.

68. Rest, J. R. (1983). *Morality*. In P. H. Mussen (Ed.), *Handbook of Child Psychology* (4th ed.). New York: Wiley.

69. Rothman, G. (1972). The influence of moral reasoning on behavioral choice. *Child Development, 43,* 397–406.

70. Staub, E. (1979). *Positive Social Behavior and Morality*. New York: Academic Press.

71. Tanner, L. N. (1978). *Classroom Discipline for Effective Teaching and Learning*. New York: Holt, Rinehart & Winston.

72. Turiel, E. (1974). Conflict and transition in adolescent moral development. *Child Development, 45*, 14–29.

73. Zimmerman, D. (1983). Moral education. In A. P. Goldstein (Ed.), *Prevention and Control of Aggression*. New York: Pergamon.

The following references deal with gender differences in moral attitudes, judgments, and behavior.

74. Belenky, M. F., Clinchy, B. M., Goldberger, N. R., & Tarule, J. M. (1986). *Women's Ways of Knowing: The Development of Self, Voice, and Mind*. New York: Basic Books.

75. Brabeck, M. (1983). Moral judgement: Theory and research on differences between males and females. *Developmental Review 3*, 274–91.

76. Brandes, B. (1986). *Academic Honesty: A Special Study of California Students*. ERIC ED 272 533.

77. Brockman, J., Anderson, T., & Armstrong, S. 1978. *The Developmental Relationship Among Moral Judgement, Moral Conduct and a Rationale for Appropriate Behavior*. ERIC ED 165 051.

78. Feshbach, N. D., & Feshbach, S. (1987). Affective processes and academic achievement. *Child Development, 58*, 1335–1347.

79. Gibbs, J., Arnold, K. D., & Burkhart, J. E. (1984). Sex differences in the expression of moral judgement. *Child Development 55* (3), 1040–1043.

80. Gilligan, C. (1982). *In a Different Voice. Psychological Theory and Women's Development*. Cambridge, MA: Harvard University Press.

81. Gilligan, C. (1982). New maps of development: New visions of maturity. *American Journal of Orthopsychiatry, 52* (2), 199–212.

82. Gilligan, C., Langdale, S., & Lyons, N. (1982). *The Contribution of Women's Thought to Developmental Theory: The Elimination of Sex-Bias in Moral Developmental Theory and Research*. Final report to the National Institute of Education, Washington, DC. ERIC ED 226 301.

83. Kitchener, K. S., King, P. M., Davison, M. L., Parker, C. A., & Wood, P. K. (1984). A longitudinal study of moral and ego development in young adults. *Journal of Youth and Adolescence, 13* (3), 197–211.

84. Kohlberg, L. (1981). *The Philosophy of Moral Development: Moral Stages and the Idea of Justice*. San Francisco: Harper & Row.

85. Krebs, R. L. (1977). Girls—more moral than boys or just sneakier? In J. Pottker & A. Fishel (Eds.), *Sex Bias in the Schools: The Research Evidence*. Cranbury, NJ: Associated University Presses.

86. Lyons, N. P. (1983). Two perspectives: On self, relationships, and morality. *Harvard Educational Review, 53* (2), 125–145.

87. Rest, J. R. (1983). Morality. In J. Flavell & E. Markham (Eds.), *Manual of Child Psychology* (vol. 4). New York: Wiley.

88. Smye, D. M., & Wine, J. D. (1980). A comparison of female and male adolescents' social behaviors and cognitions: A challenge to the assertiveness literature. *Sex Roles, 6* (2), 213–230.

89. Socoski, P. M. (1984). *Responses to Sex-Bias Criticism in Cognitive Moral Theory*. ERIC ED 278 881.

90. Tavris, C., & Wade, C. (1984). *The Longest War: Sex Differences in Perspective* (2nd ed.). New York: Harcourt Brace Jovanovich.

The references below document the relationship between teachers' personalities and their classroom management styles.

91. Dobson, J. E., & Campbell, N. J. (1979). The relationships of teachers' philosophy of human nature and perception and treatment of behavioral problems. *Humanist Educator, 18* (1), 23–31.

92. Jury, L. E., Willower, D. J., & Delacy, W. J. (1975). Teacher self-actualization and pupil control ideology. *Alberta Journal of Educational Research, 21* (4), 295–301.

93. Rohrkemper, M. M., & Brophy, J. E. (1979). *Classroom Strategy Study: Investigating Teacher Strategies with Problem Students*. ERIC ED 175 857.

Gender differences in instructional and classroom management styles are described in these references.

94. Allen, J. L., O'Mara, J., & Long, K. M. (1987). *The Effects of Communication Avoidance, Learning Styles and Gender upon Classroom Achievement*. ERIC ED 291 111.

95. Brophy, J. (1985). Interaction of male and female students with male and female teachers. In L. C. Wilkinson & C. B. Marrett (Eds.), *Gender Influences in Classroom Interaction*. New York: Academic Press.

96. Engstrom, G. A. (1981). *An Examination of the Viability of Class Climate as a Useful Construct in Secondary Schools. A Study of Schooling in the United States*. Technical Report Series No. 23. ERIC ED 214 891.

97. Etaugh, C., Collins, G., & Gerson, A. (1975). Reinforcement of sex-typed behaviors of two-year-old children in a nursery school setting. *Developmental Psychology, 11*, 255.

98. Grossman, H. (1994). *Gender Issues in Education*. Needham, MA: Allyn & Bacon.

99. Grossman, H. (1994). *Professors' Preferences for Classroom/Behavior Management Techniques: Consensus and Ethnic, Gender, Socioeconomic Class and Field of Instruction Differences*. Final Report. San Jose, CA: San Jose State University.

100. Kajander, C. (1976). The effects of instructor and student sex on verbal behavior in college classrooms. *Dissertation Abstracts International*, 37 (5-A): 2743–2744.

101. Karp, D., & Yoels, W. (1976). The college classroom: Some observations on the meanings of student participation. *Sociology and Social Research*, 60, 421–439.

102. McIntyre, L. L. (1988). Teacher gender: A predictor of special education referral? *Journal of Learning Disabilities*, 21 (6), 382–383.

103. Meece, J. L. (1987). The influence of school experiences on the development of gender schemata. *New Directions for Child Development*, 38, 57–73.

104. Moos, R. H. (1979). *Evaluating Educational Environments*. San Francisco: Jossey-Bass.

105. Pratt, D. L. (1985). Responsibility for student success/failure and observed verbal behavior among secondary science and mathematics teachers. *Journal of Research in Science Teaching*, 22 (9), 807–816.

106. Richardson, L., Cook, J., & Macke, A. (1981). Classroom management strategies of male and female university professors. In L. Richardson & V. Taylor (Eds.), *Issues in Sex, Gender, and Society*. Lexington, MA: Heath.

107. Stake, J., & Katz, J. (1982). Teacher-pupil relationships in the elementary school classroom: Teacher-gender and pupil-gender differences. *American Educational Research Journal*, 19, 465–471.

108. Sternglanz, S., & Lyberger-Ficek, S. (1977). Sex differences in student teacher interactions in the college classroom. *Sex Roles*, 3, 345–352.

109. Wardle, F. (1991). Are we shortchanging boys? *Child Care Information Exchange*, 7 (79), 48–51.

These references deal with Hispanic American instructional and classroom management styles.

110. Condon, E. C., Peters, J. Y., & Sueiro-Ross, C. (1979). *Special Education and the Hispanic Child: Cultural Perspectives*. Philadelphia: Temple University, Teacher Corps Mid-Atlantic Network.

111. Grossman, H. (1986). *Educating Hispanic Students: Cultural Implications for Instruction, Classroom Management, Counseling, and Assessment*. Springfield, IL: Thomas.

112. Grossman, H. (1990). *Trouble Free Teaching: Solutions to Behavior Problems in the Classroom*. Needham, MA: Allyn & Bacon.

113. Grossman, H. 1995. *Special Education in a Diverse Society.* Needham, MA: Allyn & Bacon.

114. Ramirez, M., & Price-Williams, D. (1974). Cognitive styles of children of three ethnic groups in the United States. *Journal of Cross-Cultural Psychology, 5,* 212–219.

Differences between the instructional and classroom management styles of African Americans and European Americans are the focus of the following references.

115. Bacon, M. M. (n.d.). *Coping Creatively with Adolescence: Culturally Relevant Behavior Management Strategies for the Twenty-First Century.* Unpublished manuscript. Palo Alto, CA: Palo Alto Unified School District.

116. Gitter, A. G., Black, H., & Mostofsky, D. (1972). Race and sex in the perception of emotion. *Journal of Social Issues, 28,* 63–78.

117. Hale-Benson, J. E. (1986). *Black Children: Their Roots, Culture, and Learning Styles* (rev. ed.). Baltimore: Johns Hopkins University Press.

118. Hilliard, A. (1976). *Alternatives to I.Q. Testing: An Approach to the Identification of Gifted Minority Children.* Sacramento, CA: California State Department of Education.

119. Lubeck, S. (1988). Nested contexts. In L. Weis (Ed.), *Class, Race, and Gender in American Education.* Albany, NY: State University of New York Press.

120. Robbins, H. A. (1976). *A Comparison Study of Cognitive Styles Across Educational Levels, Race and Sex.* Unpublished doctoral dissertation, East Texas State University.

121. Shade, B. J. (1979). *Racial Preferences in Psychological Differentiation: An Alternative Explanation to Group Differences.* ERIC ED 179 672.

122. Simpson, A., & Erickson, M. (1983). Teachers' verbal and nonverbal communication patterns as a function of teacher race, student gender, and student race. *American Educational Research Journal, 20,* 183–198.

123. Triandis, H. C. (Ed.) (1976). *Variations in Black and White Perceptions of Social Environment.* Urbana, IL: University of Illinois Press.

The relationship between professors' ethnic background and gender and their preferences for behavior management techniques is discussed in the reference below.

124. Grossman, H. (1994). *Professors' Preferences for Classroom/Behavior Management Techniques: Consensus and Ethnic, Gender, Socioeconomic Class and Field of Instruction Differences.* ERIC ED 364 537.

CONTEXTUALLY APPROPRIATE CLASSROOM MANAGEMENT

The classroom management techniques that most educators use are typically designed for middle-class students from stable homes with two native-born, well-educated parents who understand the way schools work and have the time and resources to help their children gain the most that they can from their school experiences. However, many students do not grow up in this kind of family or environment. Because the context of their lives is different, they do not adapt well to many classroom management approaches.

This chapter discusses the effects of various contextual factors on students' school experiences and the problems that many students face because of the context of their lives. It also suggests specific ways in which educators can adapt their classroom management approaches to the contextual aspects of their students' lives.

Immigrant, Immigrant-Like, and Refugee Students

The immigrant and refugee population in the United States has been increasing dramatically (see chapter 5). Immigrant and refugee students experience many contextual problems in American schools that affect their learning and behavior. Teachers should be sensitive to these potential contextual problems.

Culture Shock

When people have to adjust to a culture that is significantly different from their own, they often become confused, anxious, and frustrated because they don't know what is expected of them in different situations. They often cannot solve interpersonal problems and

111

In some states, non-European American students are the majority.

do not know what is and is not acceptable behavior in the new culture. They may become angry at people whose behavior they can't understand. They can also feel anxious and fearful about not being able to function adequately in the new culture or sad and depressed over the loss of their familiar way of life. This disorientation and confusion is called culture shock (1, 3, 4).

Students who immigrate to the United States from other countries can suffer culture shock in school. They may become angry, anxious, sad, or depressed. Some students may withdraw from their teachers and the other students or act aggressively toward them. The difficulties of the Hispanic American student who suffers culture shock are evident from the following description:

> The very first day in the first grade the Mexican American child starts with a handicap no humane society should place on the shoulders of a mere child. English is the language of the classroom. He speaks no English or he speaks inadequate English. The whole program is designed to make him an Anglo. . . . He doesn't want to become an Anglo or he doesn't know how. . . . The Anglo concepts and values that prevail are unintelligible to him. . . . There is nothing in the atmosphere from which he can draw any comfort. Nothing he can relate to. . . . He is one scared kid. (10, p. 3)

Imposing the school's culture on students without regard to the culture they bring with them can cause them to experience even greater degrees of culture shock than they already do. But building bridges between their home culture and the culture of the classroom can help manage the severity of the culture shock they will have to suffer.

One way to bridge the gap is to pair students with culture brokers—bicultural individuals, usually other students, assistant teachers, or parent volunteers who are equally knowledgeable about and comfortable in both the non-European American students' culture and the culture of the school. Culture brokers can tell students how to behave in problematic situations. They can explain why some of the ways the students are accustomed to behaving are unacceptable in American schools and help them understand the rationale behind American rules and norms of behavior. Recent immigrants, second-generation Americans, Native Americans, and others who are not knowledgeable about the ways of European American schools have been helped to adjust to unfamiliar school environments in this way (15, 16, 19).

The following statement by a Hispanic American student with a mixed African American, European American, and Native American background illustrates the usefulness of a culture broker:

> My first day in school I didn't understand anything at all. I didn't speak English, I didn't understand the black students. I didn't understand the white students and there were hardly any Latinos. I was real scared. Then they assigned me a buddy. She was black and Latino like me and she was in the eighth grade too. I went to all of her classes with her and never went anywhere during recess, lunch, or any time without her.
>
> She told me that the other students were trying to figure out what I was, black, Latino or what. I looked like I could be black but didn't speak or act black. She helped me understand things. She taught me what to do when people started up with me. She taught me how to do things right in school. And she explained why the black kids acted that way.
>
> Little by little I learned how to act in school. I even learned how to be black. Now I can act Latino, black or white. (12)

Cultural assimilators have also helped students who are unfamiliar with American school practices to understand and adjust to them. Cultural assimilators typically consist of a series of problematic situations with a number of alternative ways of behaving in the situation or perceiving the situation. Students decide which alternative they would choose. Then they discuss each alternative's advantages and disadvantages, appropriateness or inappropriateness, and accuracy or inaccuracy in America (13, 14, 17, 18).

It is also helpful to include aspects of students' home culture in the classroom. By putting up pictures of their native country and arranging for classroom demonstrations of the cooking, music, or dancing of your students' place of birth, you can make the classroom environment a little less strange and help smooth your students' transition. Accept behavior caused by culture shock, so long as it isn't too disruptive, to avoid putting extra pressure on students to adjust faster than they are able. Provide alternatives when the activity of the moment is not appropriate for or acceptable to students. Some students may not be ready for coed recreational activities, competitive games, or showering nude in front of others. Provide alternative foods and snacks for students whose religion prohibits them from eating certain foods or who are simply unaccustomed to eating certain foods. This

Cultural Assimilators

The following scenarios are typical of those found in cultural assimilators.

What should you do?

- You are sitting in the classroom talking with classmates when your teacher enters the room.
- Your teacher gives out papers to the class and you don't get one.
- Your teacher is talking to the class, and you don't understand part of his lecture.

- Your teacher gives you a homework assignment that you aren't able to do. It's due the next day.

How should you feel?

- You see an American classmate walking toward you. You stop and say hello. Your classmate smiles, says "Hello, how are you," and continues walking.

Why do people behave that way?

- One of your female teachers sometimes sits on her desk when teaching, wears slacks to class, and often talks with students informally after class.

(14)

will demonstrate your concern and respect for students and their customs and avoid placing them in a conflict situation. Suggestions for helping immigrant and refugee students adjust to and succeed in school can be found in the resource material listed in the reference section (20–24).

Identity Conflicts

Many immigrant students may experience identity conflicts during the acculturation process if they are pressured at home and in their community to maintain the traditional values of their culture while at the same time being pressured at school to accept new cultural values (25–27). Although some immigrant and second-generation students are brought up by parents who want them to assimilate totally to the culture of the school, many others are torn between conflicting messages and pressures regarding the right and wrong ways to live their lives. Some students adopt the culture of the school and try to abandon the traditions of their families. If they do this, they may be punished by their parents and suffer from feelings of guilt and shame. Other students may reject the pressures of school and satisfy their parents. But by so doing, they risk getting into trouble with their teachers and school administrators (27) and being ostracized by classmates.

A Chinese American high school student who immigrated to the United States when she was 10 years old expressed her identity conflict this way:

I don't know who I am. Am I the good Chinese daughter? Am I an American teenager? I always feel I am letting my parents down when I am with my friends because I act so

Teaching others about their cultures can increase students' pride in themselves.

American, but I also feel that I will never really be an American. I never feel really comfortable with myself anymore. (26, p. 30)

The school's role in exacerbating immigrant students' identity conflicts can be described this way:

Cultural conflicts between home and school cause youth to either choose one or the other. This causes conflicts in personality, adjustment, etc. He needs to act one way at school and when he gets home, uses a different language and a different set of cultural values. If the school allowed him to be himself, he wouldn't have the problem. (25, p. 122)

You can reduce the severity of your students' identity conflicts by not placing them in situations that create identity conflicts. Do not pressure them to do things the way you are used to having them done or use management techniques that are new and unacceptable to them when their culturally influenced ways are just as effective. Examples of inappropriate techniques may include calling on students who do not volunteer or feel comfortable speaking up in class, criticizing their answers or behavior in front of others, or requiring students to admit their mistakes and apologize for them verbally. Using techniques for reducing culture shock and using teaching and classroom management styles that are familiar to students reduce pressure on students to either assimilate completely at the expense of their original cultures or reject the school's culture to maintain their own.

Language and Teaching Style Differences

Having to adjust to a new language and a strange teaching style can be traumatic for some students. This is especially true of immigrant students who have never attended school because they come from rural areas or internment camps and/or grew up in cultures that have no written language. If these students feel anxious, angry, resentful, or ashamed of their difficulties and act out their emotions, they may become behavior problems in school. Consider the emotional toll paid by a Chinese American immigrant student: "I started to hate myself when I failed to answer the teacher's questions . . . because I couldn't express my answers in English. Then I began to hate everything in the world, including my parents because they took me to this country" (5, p. 25).

Wei describes some of the difficulties Vietnamese American students often experience in American schools:

> The American teachers' friendliness and informality are shocking to the Vietnamese students and hard for them to accept. The absence of honorific terms in the English language compounds the problem and makes the Vietnamese students feel uneasy and uncomfortable when talking with their teachers. They are reluctant to ask questions in class because such behavior seems aggressive and disrespectful to them. Their confusion is increased when, to their surprise, their teachers reward such behavior in class.
>
> Since they are not accustomed to talking in front of the class, they are shy and uncomfortable when asked to do so in the American classroom. They do not volunteer answers because they have been taught to be modest. If they need help, they probably will not ask for it.
>
> The language problem can be very acute when there is only one or very few Vietnamese students in the school. The lack of communication or understanding between the child and the school authority can cause a small misunderstanding to grow into a large emotional or discipline problem. . . . The language barrier also limits the child's social contacts with American peers. (11, pp. 13–14)

Research indicates that instructing students for part of the day in their native language while they are learning English as a second language helps them adjust better than if they attend schools where almost every transaction is in English (8). The Bilingual Education Act of 1988 provides that limited-English-proficient students may be instructed bilingually for 3 years and up to 5 years, if needed, to bridge the transition from their native language to English. When bilingual education is not a viable option, students can be placed in programs that combine sheltered English instruction, in which basic English is used to teach students their academic subjects, with English as a second language instruction to improve their advanced English skills. While not as desirable as bilingual education, these programs are preferable to merely submerging non-English-proficient students in regular classes taught in English, where they either swim or sink.

Adapting your instructional and classroom management techniques to the learning styles of these students while they acquire the skills necessary to learn in American classrooms can enhance their learning. It may also reduce the likelihood that students will be frustrated, angry, anxious, or resentful in class.

Previous Educational Experiences

There are vast differences between the educational experiences of immigrant students. Some have attended school before they arrive in the United States. Many others are too young to have participated in the educational programs of their countries of origin. Immigrant students from industrialized countries such as Taiwan and Korea, typically have very different school experiences than those who come from Haiti, El Salvador, Laos, and Cambodia. A nonindustrialized environment may not provide students with the knowledge they require here.

The different school experiences of immigrant children are described in the following quotation:

> Some have been exposed to one hour a day of political indoctrination as their sole education, while others have put in eight-hour school days, six days a week, covering all major academic areas. . . . There are dramatic contrasts between rural and urban education. For example, in Mexico . . . 75% of those in urban areas finish the 6th grade, compared to only 15% of those in rural areas. In El Salvador most rural area schools don't go beyond second grade and operate with few materials or trained teachers. . . .
>
> Most students from Southeast Asia in the past decade have had disrupted school histories because of war, and have lived for a period in refugee camps. Depending on the camp's location and who ran it, a student may have had a few hours a day or less of instruction. Most camps had minimal if any books or instructional materials and few educated teachers. (26, p. 21)

Immigrant students who are accustomed to philosophies of life and education far different from those that prevail in the United States may have adjustment problems in school. This may be especially true of students from communist or former communist countries, such as Cuba and Russia, where students have been taught such very different ideas about economics, history, international relations, interpersonal relationships, and so on (7, 8):

> Three important objectives of present Cuban education are to determine the types of crimes that "American imperialism" has committed in different parts of the world, to explore the many advantages of socialism over capitalism and to recognize other people's struggles against imperialism around the world. (8, p. 37)

As already noted, immigrant students' academic readiness skills and knowledge will be different from those of most students in their classes. If they have not attended school prior to coming to the United States, they will lack a great deal of knowledge and skill that children acquire in school. If they attended school irregularly, there will be huge gaps in what they know and can do. And even if they attended regularly, they will not have learned many of the things that are included in the curriculum of the typical American school.

Therefore, it is essential to provide these students with a curriculum that is as individualized to their needs as possible. This can be done by starting at the student's current level of functioning, including the concepts and skills the student has acquired, being on the lookout for and filling in gaps, and using teaching techniques that complement the student's learning styles.

Conflicting Demands

Immigrant students often are faced with demands that conflict with those of the schools they attend. If they are the only person in the family who can speak some English, they may have to interpret for their parents during school hours at meetings with community agencies. If they are the oldest child, they may have to care for their siblings instead of attending school. And if they came to the United States on their own as unaccompanied minors, they may have family back home who are dependent on them. According to the National Coalition of Advocates for Students,

> At quite an early age . . . children serve as interpreters for their parents and help their families confront many adult tasks. For example, if their tenement has no heat in the winter, the school child who knows English might be the one to place a telephone call . . . these immigrant children face much more responsibility and pressure than the average American school child. (5, p.21)

It is important to take these conflicting demands into consideration when working with immigrant students. As much as possible, teachers should try to relieve students of as many of their outside burdens as possible. Teachers can assist families to obtain interpreters and child-care services so that their students may be free to attend class. They can help parents understand that in the United States, it will be difficult for their children to succeed in school unless they attend regularly.

When despite their teachers' best efforts, students are caught between conflicting demands, teachers can also adjust their expectations and demands to their students' realities. Adapting schedules, deadlines, and workloads to students' outside schedules can be especially helpful.

Encouraging or pressuring students to avoid and resist outside demands on their time, however, can be counterproductive. In many cases, such pressure exacerbates the conflict in their lives without providing them with ways of solving their dilemmas.

Impoverished Living Conditions

The living conditions of many immigrant and most refugee students are not conducive to success in school. Many of their parents arrive in the United States with few economic resources to support them. Too often, they do not find employment. Those that do are likely to earn very low wages. As a result, many children grow up in relatively impoverished environments that can seriously impede their ability to succeed in school. Too often, parents do not have the financial resources to provide children with an adequate diet, health care, decent sleeping arrangements, materials necessary to progress in school, and so on. The home environment is often too crowded and noisy for students to prepare their lessons. As To explains,

> Immigrants tend to settle in relatively deteriorating areas of inner cities where educational facilities are already poor and heavily used. In the absence of sufficient additional assistance, the influx of immigration adds an almost unbearable burden on the resources of the school. The home living condition of immigrant children is equally a serious drawback in terms of learning environment. Many of these immigrants live in crowded houses and apartments occupied by more than one family. The children may have no quiet place at home to do their homework or to study. (9, p. 7)

To succeed with students who are living in impoverished conditions, it is important for teachers to adapt their methods and expectations to these students' realities. The following section on homeless students includes many suggestions for accomplishing this.

Illegal/Undocumented Immigrants

The children of illegal immigrants are particularly prone to problems in school. Their parents are especially likely to work as migrant laborers or in jobs that pay low wages. Although these children are entitled to a free education, they are not always afforded their rights (5, 36–39). As an attorney who advocates for children reports, "One way or another, vigilante principals and people who are misinformed are asking kids for their papers and denying them access to schooling on the basis that they do not have them, or refuse to produce them" (5, p. 41).

Enforcement of immigration laws can also interfere with students' education. A child advocate reports:

> There appears to be a pattern developing with INS [Immigration and Naturalization Service] focusing their attention around school sites. Last spring . . . the school was a site for an immigration raid. Approximately 10 parents were arrested . . . they were taking their children there . . . of course, after that . . . many went down and pulled their children out of school for several weeks. (5, p. 64)

Because many undocumented immigrants live in fear of being discovered and deported, educators should avoid requesting information about students' immigration status or documents related to immigration questions. And they should assure students and their families that their immigration status is confidential.

Immigrant-Like Students

Native American students who grow up on reservations and attend schools run by and designed for European American students are in a position that is somewhat analogous to that of immigrant students (28–30). Like foreign-born students, they, too, live in a region separate from mainstream America, where they speak a language other than English. And they, too, are ill prepared to adjust to and profit from the education typically offered in mainstream schools. This is especially true if the curriculum is culturally irrelevant, encourages beliefs and values that conflict with those of their communities, and is taught by teachers who are unfamiliar with their culture and unable to speak their native languages.

Rural children who move to urban areas often have similar experiences (31–35). For example, the following problems have tended to characterize many Appalachian students and their families who have moved to urban northern cities:

> Appalachian youth are less likely to seek, or readily accept, school personnel support such as sponsorship or encouragement by a particular teacher or counselor. . . . They are less likely to participate in school activities.
>
> Youth do not identify with their schools especially in junior and senior high school, since most youth are placed in an unfamiliar neighborhood. . . . Familism requires that family situations take priority over education. . . . High absenteeism is at least in part a result of youth being needed at home to help care for siblings and household matters. The traditional migration process, in the three to five years after initial settlement in urban areas . . . can mean moving several times to find satisfactory neighborhoods, jobs, schools, doctors, and shopping areas. Class differences cause Appalachian youth to feel "looked down on" and the lack of attention given to Appalachian culture only adds to a defeated self-image. Differences in language, dress, and values are seen by other classes as deficiencies or inferiority. (33, pp. 99–101)

Students who are bused from one ethnic or socioeconomic neighborhood to another and students who move from middle America to the coasts or from the South to the North (and vice versa) can suffer similar problems, albeit to a lesser degree.

Refugees

Refugee students who have experienced war, famine, persecution, and other forms of suffering in their native lands or internment camps prior to coming to the United States bring to school additional problems that can interfere with their functioning and cause them to present serious behavior problems in school (5, 6, 40, 41). Nguyen explains some of the problems that refugee students experience:

> Vietnamese students came to the United States not only as immigrants to this new land, but also as refugees. Immigrants leave their homeland on their own volition, with many possibilities of motivation for the move, whereas refugees have "no choice but to leave or to suffer." Refugees are in fact "driven away from their homeland"—they are "pushed out."
>
> Studies have shown that this type of forced migration and the experience of being uprooted involuntarily causes more psychological problems to refugees than to immigrants. With this in mind, an educator must be concerned about the mental well-being of students who have lived in conditions of violence and sociopolitical turmoil before coming to this country. Such students have been exposed to loss, extended violence, prolonged threat, and terrorization. They may have witnessed violence inflicted on members of their family or to close friends. Their exodus to this country has been paved

with dangers and life threatening situations such as poverty, starvation, drowning at sea, rape, murder, piracy, life in a refugee camp, and the possibility of the separation of the family. (6, p. 1)

Describing school life in Central America, a Salvadorian has stated:

There are countless situations where children . . . were in the classroom where their teachers . . . were killed by armed people in different countries in Central America. And that is something that definitely affects a kid's performance and the overall ability for them to adapt into the school system. (5, p. 22)

Life in Cambodia for school children has been described this way: "Many teachers were executed . . . schools were destroyed and children sent to live on 'work farms' often separated from their families . . . almost half the population died, either by starvation, disease, execution, or the war" (5, p. 22).

Educators can make the class a safe haven for students who have suffered the traumatic experiences that cause families to leave their homelands precipitously. Students who do not yet feel secure in their new surroundings and who are frightened by physical aggression or threats of aggression or even verbal conflicts among students may need to feel that their teachers will protect them from the possibility that they will be caught up in these events. If they are unable to handle discussions on themes such as war, starvation, and crime, they may need to be allowed to engage in another activity or leave the class until the discussion has terminated.

Students who have survived the ordeals or refugee camps by becoming hard and tough and engaging in activities that in this country would be considered delinquent require understanding when they continue to behave in these ways in school. Although educators should not accept the behavioral patterns that refugee students acquired to survive terrible situations, they should not view the students as bad or punish them. A more appropriate and fairer approach would be to explain that although their behavior may have been necessary while they were refugees, their situation in the United States is different and they no longer need to behave that way.

Prejudice

Many immigrant students experience ethnic prejudice in American schools. Native American students who leave their reservations to attend schools run by and attended by European Americans, and rural students who migrate to urban areas, often have similar experiences. Students may react in many different ways to the prejudicial treatment they receive from other students. They may withdraw from contact with their peers, become sullen and depressed, or form self-protective gangs. If they also receive prejudicial treatment from teachers and/or other school personnel, they may react in the ways described in chapter 12.

Consider the experiences reported by a Chinese American limited-English-proficient student (13, p. 34):

American students always picked on us, frightened us, made fun of us and laughed at our English. They broke our lockers, threw food on us in cafeteria, said dirty words to us, pushed us on the campus. Many times they shouted at me, "Get out of here, you Chink, go back to your country." Many times they pushed me and yell on me. I've been pushed, I had gum thrown on my hair. I've been hit by stones, I've been shot by air gun. I've been insulted by all the dirty words in English. All this really made me frustrated and sad.

And a Cambodian American student has reported:

The Americans tell us to go back to our own country. I say we don't have a country to go back to. I wish I was born here and nobody would fight me and beat me up. They don't understand. I want to tell them if they had tried to cross the river and were afraid of being caught and killed and lost their sisters, they might feel like me. (13, pp. 34–35)

According to Gibson,

In school, Punjabi teenagers are told they stink, directly by white students and indirectly by their teachers. They are told to go back to India. They are accused of being illegals. They are physically abused by the majority students, who spit at them, refuse to sit by them in class or on buses, crowd in front of them in line, stick them with pins, throw food at them and worse. They are labelled troublemakers if they defend themselves. . . . They are criticized for their hairstyle, their diet, and their dress. They are faulted because they place family ahead of individual interests, defer to the authority of elders, accept arranged marriages, and believe in group decision making. (2, p. 268)

Immigrant and immigrant-like students should not have to suffer experiences like those just described. Chapter 3 provided many suggestions for eliminating prejudice in the schools.

Strengths

While it is true that immigrant and refugee students experience many contextual problems that can interfere with their functioning in school, they also have unique strengths (2, 42). Those that leave their native lands to immigrate to the United States tend to be the active strivers and survivors—those who are best prepared to make sacrifices for their family's future. Compared to many native-born Americans, immigrant students and their parents are more likely to view education as the major and often only way for them to improve their vocational and economic status. Immigrant students see education as a way to repay their parents for the sacrifices they made to bring them to this country and to help those family members left behind. And they appreciate the opportunity that was often denied their parents in their native countries to obtain an education (2, 42).

Identifying Immigrant, Immigrant-Like, and Refugee Students

While almost all of the students discussed in this section experience at least some of the problems described above when they first begin school, none of them experience all of these problems. And some students who have had time to adjust to the American school system may no longer experience these problems. Therefore, it is important to understand the particular circumstances and contextual problems of each of your students and to treat them as individuals.

Immigrant students who have spent the first years of their lives somewhere else require a number of years to adapt to the way things are done in the United States, even if they and their parents want to learn the new ways as quickly as possible. Thus, you can assume that their classroom functioning will be affected by at least some of the problems described previously. You can also expect that students who have recently arrived and are just beginning to attend school will experience some degree of culture shock. The same would apply to many other students who have to adjust to unfamiliar school environments, including Native American students, rural students, and students who attend schools that serve children and youth from a different socioeconomic class.

Students' cumulative folders may contain information about whether they attended school prior to coming here and, if so, the kind of school experiences they had. This is extremely important for refugee students who may have spent 2, 3, 4, or more years in refugee camps where there were no schools and for students from rural areas in developing countries, where schooling may not have been compulsory or even available. If students' cumulative folders do not contain this information, you should be able to obtain it from the students themselves, if they are old enough, or from their parents or guardians.

You can obtain some information about your Native American or rural students from their cumulative folder. However, you may have to rely on the students themselves, their parents, and sometimes agencies that are working with the students for most of the information you need.

Educators who work with refugee and immigrant students, Native American students who have grown up on reservations, and rural students in urban areas should adapt their instructional and classroom management approaches to the context of their students' lives. They also need to accept a certain amount of problematic behavior, which students cannot control while they are adjusting to their new educational environment.

Unequal Cross-Cultural Relationships

The history of the relationship between a student's group and the group the teacher represents, usually the dominant culture, can affect a student's classroom behavior and success in school. Students who have personally experienced prejudice, oppression, rejection, or abuse by European Americans or who have been brought up to anticipate and be wary of such treatment may be suspicious of the teacher's motives. They may reject the teacher's friendship, act provocatively and disrespectfully, or rebel against the teacher's authority. This certainly could apply to African American, Hispanic American, and Native American students, who have experienced first- or secondhand the discriminatory treatment described in chapter 2: "Growing up Indian in white America entails learning legends about historical atrocities committed by whites against Indians as well as personally experiencing white prejudice and discrimination in daily encounters" (30, p. 18).

Some Vietnamese American students have been told by their parents to be wary of Americans, who betrayed them by withdrawing from the war and leaving behind many

Vietnamese people who fought alongside them and supported them. And as a result of the damage that Korean American businesses suffered in Los Angeles in 1992, some Korean American students may harbor resentments against African American teachers.

Speaking of the attitude of some Hispanic American students toward their teachers, a Hispanic American educator states:

> Chicanos are intolerant of, and hostile toward, whites who approach them with the usual racist stance in terms of language, attitudes, and behavior. Because of their new self-perception, they are apt to cause whites, particularly those who harbor residuals of racism, a great deal of anxiety. Therefore, the educator who is unable or unwilling to acknowledge the new concept of this group is apt to be ineffectual in relating to them. (25, p. 121)

Another Hispanic American educator states:

> The Anglo image of Latin Americans is very similar to that of Chicanos. Both are seen as foreign and inferior. When our children start school, they are made to feel inferior merely because they are different from the Anglos. (25, p. 151)

Writing about the attitudes of Hispanic American immigrant parents toward school, a third Hispanic American educator writes:

> I have found that many Mexican immigrants who do not have legal documentation to be in this country often are unwilling to question any educational practice, are afraid and/or unable to come to school . . . are reluctant to answer questions about their family or give any information they think could lead to deportation. (25, p. 152)

An individual teacher may not merit such feelings on the part of his or her students, but their existence in the students' attitudes can adversely affect how they function in class and in school. Students who are alienated, hostile, and suspicious of another group, such as the dominant society and its institutions and organizations, can bring this hostility to school. They may disbelieve and reject out of hand much of what they are taught in class. For example, even at a young age, they may already disbelieve the concept "your friend, the police officer." As they progress through the grades, they may reject both their teachers' and the textbooks' interpretations of American and world history (e.g., the role of Christopher Columbus, the causes of the Civil War, desirability of American intervention in Central America, labeling the events in Los Angeles a riot rather than a rebellion) as well as the standard explanations of how the American economic and political systems function. Their opinions about the best way to solve the current issues facing America and the world may be at odds with those of their teachers. They may believe, sometimes with justification, that their teachers are insensitive to their cultural needs and indifferent—or even prejudiced—toward them. As a result, they may be suspicious of their teachers' motives.

Although some students keep their feelings to themselves in class, many others—especially the older ones—act them out. They may repeatedly challenge their teachers' statements and demonstrate a lack of respect and disregard for their teachers' authority by not following rules, acting bored, making sarcastic and provocative comments, and purposely disrupting the class. Some students may withdraw from what they consider to be an irrelevant and prejudicial education by tuning their teachers out, arriving late, and cutting class. These students may behave this way in your class regardless of whether you merit their reactions because of what you represent to them—at least until they get to know and trust you.

If some of your students are alienated or if you are the recipient of their anger, resentment, and distrust of the system, tell them that you understand how they feel and why they might feel that way, but explain how things are different in your classroom. If students act out their anger or resentment in class, tolerate behavior problems that do not seriously disrupt the class. But make it clear that although you understand how they feel, they will not be allowed to interfere with other students' right to learn. When students withdraw from classroom participation, tune you out, come late, cut classes, and so on, explain that there are better ways of expressing their feelings and solving the problem than denying themselves an education.

Earn your students' trust and confidence by utilizing a multicultural approach when you manage their behavior. And advocate for their rights when they are mistreated or victimized by prejudice. It is also important to correct any misperceptions students' families may have about you and develop positive relationships with them before it becomes necessary to solve problems and resolve issues. Communicating the positive accomplishments of their children, inviting them to visit the class and to participate in class events, and seeking their input and feedback about your class can help establish a relationship of mutual respect and confidence.

Migrant Students

Migrant students' dropout rate, which has been estimated at between 45% and 57%, is the highest rate of any group in the United States (46, 48). Even while they are attending school, they often fail to actualize their potential for learning because of both the contextual aspects of their lives and the school system's inability or unwillingess to provide them with a contextually appropriate education (43–56). Dyson has described some of the unique contextual problems that migrant students must deal with:

> Imagine the problems a migrant child must face as he shifts from one school to another—perhaps as many as three times a year. Very often the migrant child does not use English as the primary language; he is not accepted readily by his classmates because he is "different"; educational approaches and textbooks tend to vary from school to school; and many times instructors are not willing to bother with a student who will be in the classroom only a few weeks. (45, p. 1)

The negative results of these problems are all too prevalent:

> Inevitably this constant interruption of learning, lack of continuity, absence from school during travel time, and often blatant discrimination by local communities and school personnel all contribute to migrant students falling behind . . . and getting disinterested

Self-Quiz: Contextual Problems of Immigrant, Immigrant-Like, and Refugee Students

List and compare the possible contextual problems that each of the following students may be experiencing. Although there is insufficient information to really understand these students, it is possible to be sensitive to the potential problems that they may be facing because of the context of their lives.

- Martín, a 5-year-old Hispanic American student in a bilingual kindergarten program, was born in a rural town in Mexico and came to the United States with his parents when he was 3. Very little is known about Martín's parents because they resist providing information to school authorities. However, it is known that both parents speak only Spanish.

- Jewel is a 5-year-old African American student. She lives in a predominantly poor African American neighborhood. Both parents dropped out of high school when they were 16 and 17.
- Rashid is a 9-year-old African American student who lives in a predominantly middle-class African American neighborhood. His parents are both college graduates.
- Hoa is a 6-year-old Vietnamese American student who came to this country when she was 4 years old. She comes from a rural area. After escaping from Vietnam by boat, she was kept in a camp for refugees for 17 months before coming to the United States.
- Mai is an English-proficient 9-year-old Vietnamese American student. She was born in the United States. Both of her parents were born in Vietnam and came here when the U.S. forces left Vietnam in the 1970s.
- Thomas is a 14-year-old who recently moved from a rural area to a large city when his father lost his job in a coal mine.

in an educational system which cannot provide the needed continuous education. (52, p. 4)

It is a mistake to generalize about all migrant students. They are not equally susceptible to these problems. Students who live in rural areas, whose families are the poorest, and whose parents are born in Mexico are much more likely to have difficulty in school than those who live in urban areas and have parents who are born in the United States (51).

These problems can be ameliorated to a considerable degree by educational programs geared to the needs of migrant students. Unfortunately, schools often add to students' problems rather than contribute to solving them. As Dyson puts it, "It is an unfortunate but undeniable reality that our educational system has been developed for, and geared toward, the permanent community resident" (45, p. 1).

Many of the techniques for helping immigrant students are also appropriate for migrant students. The following additional suggestions for adapting educational approaches to the context of migrant students' lives appear repeatedly in the literature (43–49, 54–56):

- Utilize a multicultural approach to make the classroom more relevant to students and to help students bridge the gap between their experiences and the culture of the school (see chapter 2).

- Because migrant students tend to be characterized by inconsistent enrollment and attendance in a number of different schools, do not assume that students are accustomed to, understand, or are able to conform to the procedures that you or your school employ.

- Provide students with successful role models by inviting individuals who have escaped the vicious cycle that many migrant families are caught in to be guest speakers, tutors, and so on.

- Help students become acquainted with the community, the services that the community offers, and how their life can be improved by making use of those services. Field trips can be especially useful.

- Help students understand that it is possible for them to aspire to other careers besides farmwork.

Middle-Class, Affluent, Suburban Students

Many educators tend to overlook the contextual problems facing students who grow up in middle-class, affluent suburbs. Contrary to the view presented in many basal readers, television programs, magazine articles, and education textbooks, children and youth who live in middle-class, affluent suburbs often lead lives that are far from idyllic. In some cases, their parents are too involved in their own careers to provide them with the supervision, support, attention, and affection they need. Parents who are concerned that if their children do not get into the right preschool they will not be in the track leading to the right college and the right career may have great difficulty accepting their children's disabilities. They may pressure these children when they are older to study more than they can, learn faster than they are able, and earn higher grades than they are capable of obtaining.

Students who live in four-parent families with shared custody over them may find themselves living disjointed, unstable lives. Unless they have duplicates of all the educational support materials they require at both of their homes, whether or not they can complete a particular assignment may depend in part on which home they are living in during a particular week. If they spend some nights of the week in one home and the remainder in another, they may forget to bring all of their school materials and books with them when they go from one to the other.

Growing up in more affluent circumstances, they may have more money at their disposal to abuse drugs, alcohol, cars, and so on. They may have the wherewithal to spend their time in amusement arcades instead of attending school, and they may have more expensive electronic games at home to tempt them away from their schoolwork.

For these and other reasons, you should be as concerned about your more affluent students as you are about any other groups of students. When you understand the contextual reasons why some students behave as they do, you may find that the management techniques described in chapters 9 and 13 are particularly appropriate.

Inadequate, Neglectful, and Abusive Child Care

The number of abused and neglected children and youth has risen precipitously in recent years. Although about 2 million cases of child abuse and neglect are officially reported annually, conservative estimates suggest that the number of children and adolescents who actually suffer abuse and neglect is two to three times that number. Thus, between 10% and 15% of American children and adolescents suffer from maltreatment (58). Whether this reflects a real increase in the prevalence of these problems or merely a greater willingness to report them is somewhat unclear. However, it is clear that far too many students suffer the effects of neglect and psychological, physical, and sexual abuse.

There are many reasons why students do not receive adequate child care. Through no fault of their own, very poor families are often unable to provide their children with the same nutrition and medical care that more advantaged children receive. And many parents cannot give their children the financial support they need to succeed in school.

Students do not have to be poor to suffer inadequate child care. Many middle-class and upper-class parents do not adequately care for their children. Divorced parents may use their children as pawns in their battles with each other. Parents who abuse drugs and alcohol are often unable to care for their children while they are under the influence of these substances. And they may be unable to care for their children financially and psychologically even when they aren't under the influence if their lives are consumed by drug problems. In some cases, the inadequate care that students receive amounts to neglect or abuse.

While neglected children have many problems, those who suffer actual abuse are much worse off. Fink and Janssen describe the effects of abuse on adolescents:

> Systematic abuse causes significant dysfunction in intellectual, emotional, developmental, and motoric ability. Systematic abuse creates substantial "at risk" conditions among adolescents for psychological, interpersonal, academic, medical, and legal problems. Self-image, motivation, personal satisfaction, and success in the workplace are negatively impacted. Systematic maltreatment is an experience that dominates and delimits personal competence and effectiveness. (59, p. 32)

Abused students tend to demonstrate serious behavior problems in school. However, the form their behavior problems take depends on how they react to the abuse. Those who act out against others tend to be aggressive and abusive toward others; if they have been sexually abused, they may abuse others sexually or at least act out sexually. Those who turn away from others are likely to reject friendly overtures from others and withdraw from interpersonal relationships.

Whatever the outward manifestations of their problems, abused students tend to mistrust others, especially adults. They have low self-esteem and poor self-concepts, and compared to nonabused students, they are more likely to develop conduct and emotional problems (see chapters 11 and 12), to abuse drugs and alcohol, to lack the motivation and energy necessary to succeed in school, and to misunderstand and be suspicious of the behavior and intentions of others.

Their tendency to misperceive others makes it especially necessary for teachers to be careful when selecting classroom management techniques for them. Because these students have been maltreated in the past, they are less able to tolerate any kind of negative consequences, even mild ones. Students who have been locked up alone may have extreme difficulty coping with time-out in an isolated area. Corporal punishment can have disastrous repercussions, especially with students who have been physically abused.

Abused students may experience authoritative teachers who take charge of their classrooms as abusive. And they may even experience praise as manipulative attempts to control them.

Students who have been sexually abused may be threatened by friendly and warm teachers. They may recoil from any form of physical contact, no matter how innocent. Some of them may imagine that their teachers are on the verge of abusing them.

To avoid these potential problems and to help students overcome them, educators need to know which, if any, of their students have been victims of abuse or neglect. Although others may be the source of such information, educators are often the first persons to suspect and report possible cases of child abuse and neglect to the appropriate authorities. Every state has passed laws that require educators to report observations that lead them to suspect the possibility of child abuse. Because most teachers need additional training to be able to identify the signs of possible child abuse (62), it is important that they seek such training from their school districts or teacher preparation programs. Educators can also take advantage of some of the material currently available to improve their level of competency (57, 64, 65, 66).

There are a number of ways you can help students who are known to have been abused (60, 61, 63, 67–69). Begin by maintaining a classroom climate that makes abused students feel comfortable and secure. Avoid using classroom management techniques that can have unexpected negative effects. Determine whether students have actually suffered any of the potential negative results of child abuse that can interfere with their cognitive functioning, powers of attention and concentration, ability to relate positively to others, and so on, and deal with their negative results. As Wolverton states,

> As a teacher you are entrusted with a real treasure—a child's spirit. It can grow and flourish or it can be crushed. For the abused child, the school may be the only avenue of escape, a place where s/he can feel safe. Your classroom can support the child's needs if you:
> Promote an accepting environment in your classroom.
> Be warm and loving.
> Create an individualized program for the maltreated child.
> Give the maltreated child additional attention wherever possible. (69, p. 3)

Identifying Neglected and Abused Students

The following physical and behavioral symptoms should alert educators to the possibility of child abuse and the need for additional investigation. However, they may also be caused by other problems.

Signs of Physical Abuse

Unexplained cuts, bruises, burns, fractures, and welts

Wary of adult contact

Apprehensive when other students cry

Aggressiveness or withdrawal

Resists going home

Fear of parents

Reports of abuse by parents

Signs of Physical Neglect

Consistent hunger

Poor hygiene

Inappropriate dress

Consistent lack of supervision

Unattended physical or medical problems

Abandonment

Begging or stealing food

Early arrival and late departure from school

Constant fatigue, listlessness, or falling asleep in class

Alcohol or drug abuse

Delinquency

Reports of parental neglect

Signs of Sexual Abuse

Difficulty in walking or sitting

Torn or stained clothing

Pain or itching in genital area

Venereal disease

Pregnancy

Unwilling to change for gym

Withdrawal, fantasy, or infantile behavior

Bizarre, sophisticated, or unusual sexual behavior, preoccupations, or knowledge

Poor peer relationships

Running away

Reported sexual abuse

Signs of Emotional Maltreatment

Speech disorders

Lag in physical development

Failure to thrive

Sucking, biting, rocking

Antisocial, destructive behavior

Sleep disorders

Compulsions, phobias, obsessions

Behavior extremes—compliant, passive, demanding, aggressive

Mental or emotional developmental lag

Attempted suicide

(Adapted from 68)

When it is desirable or necessary to discuss students' abusive experiences with them, reassure these students that it is not their fault and they are not in trouble, have done nothing wrong, and are not bad persons because of the actions of others. Avoid asking prying questions and making judgmental statements about the adults who abused them. If students describe their abusive experiences, do not appear shocked, surprised, or horrified.

Report your discussion in a timely manner to the person who has been legally designated by the school administration.

Runaway and Homeless Children and Youth

Between 1 million and 1.5 million children and youth run away from home each year (94). These children and youth suffer a great many problems (81, 94, 103, 105). Prior to running away, they may have suffered severe maltreatment, including physical and sexual abuse. Compared to children and youth who live at home, they are more likely to engage in self-destructive behavior, to abuse drugs and alcohol, to have medical and psychological problems, to attempt suicide, to be involved in illegal activities to obtain money, and to have serious school problems. Because they attend school erratically, move from place to place, do not have the documents required by schools, and lack parents or guardians to speak and sign for them, they are also much less likely to receive the education services that they require.

Estimates of the number of homeless children range from 272,773 to 1.6 million (76, 77). The plight of homeless children and youth is especially horrendous (70–80, 82–106). Compared to students who live in homes, homeless students are more likely to be aggressive and noncompliant, shy and withdrawn, anxious, tired, and restless. They have greater difficulty forming relationships with others. They are also more likely to exhibit symptoms associated with stress and low self-esteem. Studies indicate that approximately 50% of them are clinically depressed, over 50% have contemplated suicide, and between 31% and 50% of them need psychiatric evaluation. Although they have four times as many health problems and twice as many chronic diseases, they have less access to medical care and are less able to follow the health regimes prescribed by physicians.

The contextual problems that confront homeless children interfere with their schooling to the point that anywhere from 28% to 43% do not even attend school. According to Heflin & Rudy,

> The combination of physical, psychological, intellectual, and behavioral outcomes of homelessness for children and youth may make it difficult for them to achieve in school. Homelessness has been described as a "breeding ground" for disabling conditions. . . . Although they are clearly at risk for academic failure, the transient nature of most homeless students makes the time-consuming task of assessment and referral for special services almost impossible. . . . A variety of legal, financial, bureaucratic, social, and familial barriers serve to effectively exclude homeless children and youth from accessing educational opportunities. (85, pp. 15–17)

Therefore, to be effective, educators have to adapt their classroom management approaches to the contextual realities of these students' lives. The following suggestions have been offered by experts in the field:

- *Make sure students' basic needs are met.* Students who are struggling with problems around transportation to school, food, clothing, sleep, and school supplies are unable to give their all to their studies. Assist students and their families to obtain the social, medical, financial, and other support services they require. Be discreet to avoid embarrassing them. And use techniques that empower parents to deal with social agencies in order to strengthen their child-care role and foster more positive parent-child relationships. However, if necessary, advocate for families who meet with resistance from service agencies.

- *Provide students a safe environment in which they can feel secure, relax their guard, act their age, and be themselves.* Runaway and homeless students often have learned to distrust adults who may have been unable or unwilling to care for them. They may be on their guard against anticipated disappointments, rejections, and abuse. And they may have had to assume adultlike responsibilities before they were ready to do so.

- *Assign students personal space.* Since homeless and runaway students are unlikely to have space of their own—their own room, closet, bed, place at a dinner table, and so on—providing them with a space in their classroom that they can call their own and mark with symbols of their identity can improve their sense of self-worth and stability.

- *Assess students' skills, knowledge, abilities, and strengths and weaknesses in great detail.* While this is desirable for all students, it is especially important for students who attend school irregularly, enroll in many different schools, and often do not complete assignments when they do attend.

- *Encourage students to become autonomous and independent so that they come to believe that they can be in control of their own lives.* Runaway and homeless students' living conditions tend to lead them to develop an external locus of control.

- *Maintain the kinds of flexibility necessary to incorporate students into your program for whatever amount of time they are able to attend.* Allowing students to progress at their own pace, individualizing their assignments, and using modules and computerized instruction are tools that can provide needed flexibility.

- *Encourage and assist students to attend your program even when it becomes difficult for them to do so.* However, do not penalize students who are unable to attend, complete assignments, and so on, because of contextual problems.

- *Work closely with other agencies that are assisting your students and their families.* Collaborative efforts are more effective than individualistic, uncoordinated approaches.

Summary

Many students are faced with contextual problems that can seriously impede their ability to succeed in school. Immigrant and refugee students, students who move from rural areas to urban areas or who have lived on reservations but must attend European American schools, students from cultures that have a history of unequal cross-cultural relationships with European Americans, homeless and runaway students, abused and neglected students, and students whose parents are unable to provide them with adequate care all need contextually appropriate classroom management.

Activities

I. Interview some local school district officials to find out about the procedures and policies they follow to identify and report cases of suspected child abuse.

II. Enhance your understanding and appreciation of homeless and runaway students by visiting a local shelter for homeless families or runaway youth.

References

The following references describe the problems of immigrant/refugee students and their families.

1. Adler, P. S. (1975). The transitional experience: An alternative view of culture shock. *Journal of Humanistic Psychology, 15*, 13–23.

2. Gibson, M. A. (1987). The school performance of immigrant minorities: A comparative view. *Anthropology and Education Quarterly, 18* (4), 262–275.

3. Juffer, K. A. (1983). Culture shock: A theoretical framework for understanding adaptation. In J. Bransford (Ed.), *Monograph Series: BUENO Center for Multicultural Education, 4*, 136–149.

4. Mostek, K. (1985). *Exploring the Definition of Culture Shock and Second Language Learning in Elementary School—Grades 4–8.* ERIC ED 270 975.

5. National Coalition of Advocates for Students. (1988). *New Voices: Immigrant Students in U. S. Public Schools.* Boston, MA: Author.

6. Nguyen, T. P. (1987). Positive self-concept in the Vietnamese bilingual child. In M. Dao (Ed.), *From Vietnamese to Vietnamese American: Selected Articles.* San Jose, CA: Division of Special Education and Rehabilitative Services, San Jose State University.

7. North Carolina Department of Public Instruction. (1983). *Here They Are . . . What Do We Do?* Raleigh, NC: Author.

8. Silva, H. (1985). *The Children of Mariel from Shock to Integration: Cuban Refugee Children in South Florida Schools*. ERIC ED 261 136.

9. To, C. (1979). *The Educational and Psychological Adjustment Problems of Asian Immigrant Youth and How Bilingual-Bicultural Education Can Help*. Paper presented at the annual conference of the National Association of Asian American and Pacific Island Education, San Francisco.

10. Ulibari, S. (1970). *Stereotypes and Caricatures*. Paper presented at the National Education Task Force de La Raza Staff Training Institute. Albuquerque, New Mexico.

11. Wei, T. T. D. (1980). *Vietnamese Refugee Students: A Handbook for School Personnel* (2nd ed.). ERIC ED 208 109.

Techniques and materials for reducing culture shock are included in the following references.

12. Aranguri-Oshiro, R. (1987). Personal communication.

13. Fiedler, F., Mitchell, T., & Triandis, H. C. (1971). The culture assimilator: An approach to cross-cultural training. *Journal of Applied Psychology, 55*, 95–102.

14. Ford, C. K., & Silverman, A. M. (1981). *American Cultural Encounters*. San Francisco: Alemany Press.

15. Gentemann, K. M., & Whitehead, T. L. (1983). The culture broker concept in bicultural education. *Journal of Negro Education, 52* (2), 118–129.

16. Herzog, J. D. (1972). The anthropologist as broker in community education: A case study and some general propositions. *Council on Anthropology and Education Newsletter, 3*, 9–14.

17. Rosita, A., & Adamopoulos, J. (1976). An attributional approach to culture learning: The culture assimilator. *Topics in Cultural Learning IV*. Honolulu: East West Culture Learning Institute.

18. Triandis, H. C. (1975). Culture training, cognitive complexity and interpersonal attitudes. In R. W. Brislin, S. Bochner, & W. J. Lonner (Eds.), *Cross-Cultural Perspectives on Learning*. Beverly Hills, CA: Sage.

19. Wyatt, J. D. (1978–1979). Native involvement in curriculum development: The Native teacher as cultural broker. *Interchange: A Journal of Educational Studies, 9*, 17–28.

Suggestions for helping immigrant and refugee students adjust to and succeed in school and lists of books, materials, films, and so on, that are concerned with immigrants and refugees are listed below.

20. California Tomorrow. (1989). *Bridges: Promising Programs for the Education of Immigrant Children*. San Francisco, CA.

21. Chang, H. N. (1990). *Newcomer Programs: Innovative Efforts to Meet the Educational Challenges of Immigrant Students*. San Francisco, CA: California Tomorrow.

22. Friedlander, M. (1991). *The Newcomer Program: Helping Immigrant Students Succeed in School*. Washington, DC: National Clearinghouse for Bilingual Education.

23. Jorgensen-Esmaili, K. (1988). *New Faces of Liberty: A Curriculum for Teaching About Today's Refugees and Immigrants*. Berkeley, CA: Graduate School of Education, University of California, Berkeley.

24. National Council of La Raza. (1986). *Beyond Ellis Island: Hispanics—Immigrants and Americans*. Washington, DC.: Author.

Identity conflicts of immigrant students are discussed in the following references.

25. Grossman, H. (1984). *Educating Hispanic Students: Cultural Implications for Instruction, Classroom Management, Counseling, and Assessment*. Springfield, IL: Thomas.

26. Olsen, L. (1988). *Crossing the Schoolhouse Border: Immigrant Students and the California Public Schools*. San Francisco, CA: California Tomorrow.

27. Ramirez, M., & Castañeda, A. (1974). *Cultural Democracy, Bicognitive Development and Education*. New York: Academic Press.

These references describe the experiences of Native American students in non-Native American settings.

28. Bureau of Indian Affairs. (1988, March). *Report on B. I. A. Education: Final Review Draft*. Washington, DC: Department of the Interior.

29. Chavez, R. C., Belkin, L. D., Hornback, J. G., & Adams, K. (1991). Dropping out of school: Issues affecting culturally, ethnically, and linguistically distinct student groups. *Journal of Educational Issues of Language Minority Students, 8*, 1–21.

30. Lin, R. (1987). A profile of reservation high school girls. *Journal of American Indian Education, 26* (2), 18–28.

The adjustment problems of rural students in urban settings are the focus of the following references.

31. Obermiller, P. J., Borman, K. M., & Kroger, J. A. (1988). The lower price community school: Strategies for social change from an Appalachian street academy. *Urban Education, 23* (2), 123–132.

32. Maloney, M. E., & Borman, K. M. (1987). Effects of schools & schooling upon Appalachian children in Cincinnati. In P. J. Obermiller & W. W. Philliber (Eds.), *Too Few Tomorrows: Urban Appalachians in the 1980's*. Boone, NC: Appalachian Consortium Press.

33. McCoy, C. B., & McCoy, H. V. (1987). Appalachian youth in cultural transition. In P. J. Obermiller & W. W. Philliber (Eds.), *Too Few Tomorrows: Urban Appalachians in the 1980's.* Boone, NC: Appalachian Consortium Press.

34. Swift, D. (1988). *Preparing Rural Students for an Urban Environment.* Las Cruces, NM: New Mexico State University, ERIC CRESS.

35. Vaughn, D., & Vaughn, P. R. (1986). *Preparing Rural Students for an Urban Work Environment.* ERIC ED 270 243.

The special difficulties facing illegal immigrants and refugees are documented and discussed in the references below.

36. Carrera, J. W. (1989). *Education of Undocumented Children: A Review of Practices and Policies.* Las Cruces, NM: ERIC CRESS, University of New Mexico.

37. Gardner, C., & Quezada-Aragon, M. (1984). *Undocumented Children: An Ongoing Issue for the Public Education System.* Las Cruces, NM: New Mexico State University, ERIC CRESS.

38. Padilla, A. (1987, spring). Human rights in the human service of Central Americans. *Spanish Speaking Mental Health Research Center,* 1–4.

39. Stepick, A., & Portes, A. (1986). Flight into despair: A profile of recent Haitian refugees in South Florida. *International Migration Review, 20* (2), 329–350.

The stress experienced by refugees from countries engaged in civil wars is the focus of the following references.

40. Cervantes, R. C., Salgado de Snyder, V. N., & Padilla, A. M. (1988). *Post-Traumatic Stress Disorder Among Immigrants from Central America and Mexico.* Spanish Speaking Mental Health Research Center. Occasional Paper No. 24. Los Angeles, CA: Spanish Speaking Mental Health Research Center, University of California, Los Angeles.

41. Padilla, A. M. (1987, spring). Post traumatic and psychosocial stress: The Central American experience. *Spanish Speaking Mental Health Research Center,* 5–6.

The strengths of immigrant and refugee students are described in the following reference.

42. Suarez-Orozco, M. M. (1987). Becoming somebody: Central American immigrants in the United States. *Anthropology and Education Quarterly, 18* (4), 287–299.

Migrant students and their families are discussed in the following references.

43. Center for Educational Planning. (1989). *Migrant Education Dropout Prevention Project Final Report.* ERIC ED 321 951.

44. Chavkin, N. F. (1991). *Family Lives and Parental Involvement in Migrant Students' Education.* Las Cruces, NM: New Mexico State University, ERIC CRESS.

45. Dyson, D. D. (1983). *Migrant Education: Utilizing Available Resources at the Local Level*. Las Cruces, NM: ERIC CRESS.

46. Henderson, A. (1987). *The Evidence Continues to Grow: Parent Involvement Improves Student Achievement*. ERIC ED 315 199.

47. Herrington, S. (1987). How educators can help children of the road. *Instructor*, 97, 36–39.

48. Interstate Migrant Education Council. (1987). *Migrant Education: A Consolidated View*. ERIC ED 285 701.

49. Interstate Migrant Secondary Services Program. (1985). *Survey Analysis: Responses of 1070 Students in High School Equivalency Programs, 1984–1985*. ERIC ED 264 070.

50. Johnson, F., Levy, R., Morales, J., Morse, S., & Prokop, M. (1986). *Migrant Students at the Secondary Level: Issues and Opportunities for Change*. ERIC ED 270 242.

51. Manaster, G. J., Chan, J. C., & Safady, R. (1992). Mexican-American migrant students' academic success: Sociological and psychological acculturation. *Adolescence*, 27 (105), 123–136.

52. Mattera, G. (1987). *Models of Effective Migrant Education Programs*. Las Cruces, NM: New Mexico State University, ERIC CRESS.

53. Migrant Attrition Project. (1987). *Migrant Attrition Project: Abstract of Findings*. Oneonta, NY: State University of New York at Oneonta.

54. Rasmussen, L. (1988). *Migrant Students at the Secondary Level: Issues and Opportunities for Change*. Las Cruces, NM: New Mexico State University, ERIC CRESS.

55. Salerno, A. (1991). *Migrant Students Who Leave School Early: Strategies for Retrieval*. Las Cruces, NM: New Mexico State University, ERIC CRESS.

56. Simich-Dudgeon, C. (1986). *Parent Involvement and the Education of Limited-English-Proficient Students*. ERIC ED 279 205.

The following references discuss the educator's role in identifying and helping students who have been abused.

57. Caplan, P., Watters, J., White, G., Parry, R., & Bates, R. (1984). Toronto multi-agency child abuse research project: The abused and the abuser. *Child Abuse and Neglect: The International Journal*, 8, 343–351.

58. Fink, A. H., & Janssen, K. N. (1990). *Abused/Neglected Adolescents: Programming for Their Educational Needs*. Paper presented at the National Conference on Adolescents with Behavior Disorders, Miami.

59. Fink, A. H., & Janssen, K. N. (1992). The management of maltreated adolescents in school settings. *Preventing School Failure*, 36 (3), 32–36.

60. Garabino, J., & Authier, K. J. (1987). The role of educators. In J. Garabino, P. E. Brookhouser, & K. J. Authier (Eds.), *Special Children Special Risks: The Maltreatment of Children with Disabilities*. Hawthorne, NY: Aldinede Gruyter.

61. Hurwitz, B. D. (1985). Suspicion: Child abuse. *Instructor, 94* (4), 76–78, 81, 125.

62. McIntyre, T. (1990). The teacher's role in cases of suspected child abuse. *Education and Urban Society. 22* (3), 300–306.

63. National Center on Child Abuse and Neglect. (1984). *The Educator's Role in the Prevention and Treatment of Child Abuse and Neglect*. Washington, DC: U.S. Department of Health and Human Services, Administration for Children, Youth, and Families, Children's Bureau.

64. National Clearinghouse on Child Abuse and Neglect. (1991). *Curricula*. Washington, DC: Author.

65. National Clearinghouse on Child Abuse and Neglect. (1991). *Prevention Programs: Training Materials*. Washington, DC: Author.

66. Ohman, L. (1988). The NEA: Professional organization and advocate for teachers. In A. Maney & S. Wells (Eds.), *Professional Responsibilities in Protecting Children: A Public Health Approach to Child Sexual Abuse*. New York: Praeger.

67. Shaman, E. J. (1986). Prevention programs for children with disabilities. In M. Nelson & K. Clark (Eds.), *The Educator's Guide to Preventing Child Sexual Abuse*. Santa Cruz, CA: Network Publications.

68. Warger, C. L., Tewey, S., & Megivern, M. (1991). *Abuse and Neglect of Exceptional Children*. Reston, VA: Council for Exceptional Children.

69. Wolverton, L. (1988). *Teaching the Abused Migrant Child: What's a Teacher to Do?* Las Cruces, NM: New Mexico State University, ERIC CRESS.

These references concern the educational problems of homeless and runaway children and adolescents.

70. Bass, J. L., Brennan, P., Mehta, K. A., & Kodzis, S. (1990). Pediatric problems in a suburban shelter for homeless families. *Pediatrics, 85* (1), 33–38.

71. Bassuk, E. L., & Gallagher, E. M. (1990). The impact of homelessness on children. In N. A. Boxill (Ed.), *Homeless Children: The Watchers and the Waiters*. Binghamton, NY: Haworth.

72. Bassuk, F., & Rosenberg, L. (1988). Why does family homelessness occur? *American Journal of Public Health, 78*, 783–788.

73. Bassuk, F., & Rosenberg, L. (1990). Psychosocial characteristics of homeless children and children with homes. *Pediatrics, 85*, 257–261.

74. Bassuk, F., & Rubin, L. (1987). Homeless children: A neglected population. *American Journal of Orthopsychiatry, 57* (2), 279–286.

75. Bowen, J. M., Purrington, G. S., Layton, D. H., & O'Brien, K. (1989). *Educating Homeless Children and Youth: A Policy Analysis*. Paper presented at the annual conference of the American Educational Research Association, San Francisco.

76. Burns, S. (Ed.). (1991). Homelessness demographics, causes and trends. *Homewords, 3* (4), 1–3.

77. Cavazos, L. F. (1990). *U.S. Department of Education Report to Congress on the Education for Homeless Children and Youth Program for the Period October 1, 1988 through September 30, 1989*. Washington, DC: U. S. Department of Education.

78. Children's Defense Fund. (1988). *What Every American Should Be Asking Political Leaders in 1988: About Children and the Future, About Leadership and Vision, About National Values and Priorities*. Washington, DC: Author.

79. Eddowes, A., & Hranitz, J. R. (1989). Educating children of the homeless. *Childhood Education: Infancy through Early Adolescence, 65* (4), 197–200.

80. Ely, L. (1987). *Broken Lives: Denial of Education to Homeless Children*. Washington, DC: National Coalition for the Homeless.

81. Faber, E., McCoard, D., Kinast, C., & Baum-Falkner, D. (1984). Violence in families of adolescent runaways. *Child Abuse and Neglect, 2* (3), 173–192.

82. Friedman, L., & Christiansen, G. (1990). *Shut Out: Denial of Education to Homeless Children*. ERIC ED 320 987.

83. Gewirtzman, R., & Fodor, I. (1987). The homeless child at school: From welfare hotel to classroom. *Child Welfare, 66* (3), 237–245.

84. Hall, J. A., & Maza, P. L. (1990). No fixed address: The effects of homelessness on families and children. In N. A. Boxill (Ed.), *Homeless Children: The Watchers and the Waiters*. Binghamton, NY: Haworth.

85. Heflin, L. J., & Rudy, K. (1991). *Homeless and in Need of Special Education*. Reston, VA: Council for Exceptional Children.

86. Jackson, S. (1989). *The Education Rights of Homeless Children*. Cambridge, MA: Center for Law and Education.

87. Kayne, A. (1989). *Annotated Bibliography of Social Science Literature Concerning the Education of Homeless Children*. Cambridge, MA: Center for Law and Education.

88. Layzer, J. I., Goodson, B. D., & deLange, C. (1986). Children in shelters. *Children Today, 15*, 6–11.

89. Linehan, M. F. (1989). Homeless children: Educational strategies for school personnel. *PRISE Reporter, 21* (2), 1–2.

90. Mihaly, L. K. (1991). *Homeless Families: Failed Policies and Young Victims*. Washington, DC: Children's Defense Fund.

91. Miller, D. S., & Linn, E. H. B. (1988). Children in sheltered homeless families: Reported health status and use of health services. *Pediatrics, 81,* 668–673.

92. Neiman, L. (1988). A critical review of resiliency literature and its relevance to homeless children. *Children's Environments Quarterly, 5* (19), 17–25.

93. Palenski, J. E., & Launer, H. M. (1987). The "process" of running away: A redefinition. *Adolescence, 22* (86), 347–362.

94. Powers, J. L., Eckenrode, J., & Jaklitsch, G. (1988). *Running Away from Home: A Response to Adolescent Maltreatment.* ERIC ED 296 228.

95. Rafferty, Y., & Rollins, N. (1989). *Learning in Limbo: The Educational Deprivation of Homeless Children.* Long Island City, NY: Advocates for Children of New York.

96. Rafferty, Y., & Rollins, N. (1990). *Homeless Children: Educational Challenges for the 1990's.* ERIC ED 325 589.

97. Rescoria, L., Parker, R., & Stolley, P. (1991). Ability, achievement and adjustment in homeless children. *American Journal of Orthopsychiatry, 61* (2), 210–220.

98. Rivlin, L. G. (1990). Home and homelessness in the lives of children. In N. A. Boxill (Ed.), *Homeless Children: The Watchers and the Waiters.* Binghamton, NY: Haworth.

99. Rosenman, M., & Stein, M. L. (1990). Homeless children: A new vulnerability. In N. A. Boxill (Ed.), *Homeless Children: The Watchers and the Waiters.* Binghamton, NY: Haworth.

100. Russell, S. C., & Williams, E. U. (1988). Homeless handicapped children: A special education perspective. *Children's Environments Quarterly, 5* (1), 3–7.

101. Schumack, S. (Ed.). (1987). *The Educational Rights of Homeless Children.* ERIC ED 288 915.

102. Stronge, J. H., & Helm, V. M. (1990). *Residency and Guardianship Requirements as Barriers to the Education of Homeless Children and Youth.* ERIC ED 319 845.

103. Stronge, J. H., & Tenhouse, C. (1990). *Educating Homeless Children: Issues and Answers.* Bloomington, IN: Phi Delta Kappa Educational Foundation.

104. Waxman, L. D., & Reyes, L. M. (1987). *A Status Report on Homeless Families in America's Cities: A 29-City Survey.* ERIC ED 296 018.

105. Witt, V. (Ed.). (1988). *Children's Defense Budget: FY 1989. An Analysis of Our Nation's Investment in Children.* Washington, DC: Children's Defense Fund.

106. Wright, J. D. (1990). Homelessness is not healthy for children and other living things. In N. A. Boxill (Ed.), *Homeless Children: The Watchers and the Waiters.* Binghamton, NY: Haworth.

CHAPTER 5

CLASSROOM MANAGEMENT FOR STUDENTS FROM DIVERSE ETHNIC AND SOCIOECONOMIC BACKGROUNDS

The population of the United States is rapidly becoming less European American (1–5). By the year 2000, non-European Americans are expected to account for one third of the U.S. population. The three fastest growing groups are Hispanic Americans, African Americans, and Southeast Asian Americans. The two largest non-European American groups, 30 million African Americans and 20 million Hispanic Americans, will make up almost a third of the total school enrollment. Currently, non-European American students are the majority in the 25 largest school districts in the country.

The number of children and youth living in poverty is also continuing to rise. Between 1979 and 1989, the numbers of Hispanic American, European American, and African American children living in poverty increased by 29%, 25%, and 6%, respectively, leading to an overall increase of 19%.

Classroom management approaches that are designed with European American middle-class students in mind are unlikely to serve the needs of the ever-increasing numbers of students from non-European and/or low-income backgrounds. This chapter is designed to help educators take their students' ethnic and socioeconomic backgrounds into consideration when they select classroom management techniques. It begins by noting that many educators relate to students from non-European or low-income backgrounds in a discriminatory manner. Then it describes how educators can misperceive and misunderstand students' behaviors and use inappropriate responses to deal with those behaviors when they interpret their students' behavior from their own ethnic or socioeconomic perspective. The next section describes some of the ethnically and socioeconomically influenced student characteristics that educators should be aware of to understand why students are behaving in a particular way and what techniques might help them to behave differently. This is followed by discussions of field-sensitive and field-independent learning and teaching styles and techniques for identifying ethnically diverse students. The next section discusses four different strategies that educators can use to resolve differences between the ethnically and socioeconomically influenced ways students function and their expectations for and beliefs about how students should function. The final section uses Hispanic American students as an example of how the concepts and principles discussed in the chapter can be applied to different ethnic groups.

Prejudice and Discrimination in the Educational System

Most, but not all, studies indicate that many teachers treat non-European American and poor students unfairly. The following are some of the ways many educators discriminate against African American, Native American, and Hispanic American students (7–10, 12–16, 18–27).

Teachers praise African American students less and criticize them more than European American students. The praise they give them is more likely to be routine, rather than feedback for a particular achievement or behavior. And when teachers praise them for a specific behavior, it is more likely to be qualified ("Your work is almost good enough to be put on the board") or, in the case of females, more likely to be for good behavior than for academic work.

Educators are less likely to respond to African American male students' questions than to the questions of European American students, and they are also less likely to direct questions to them. Unlike the preferential treatment many teachers give their brightest European American students, they give bright African American students, especially females, the least attention and criticize them the most. While European American teachers typically demonstrate considerable interest in European American females' academic work, they pay less attention to African American females' academic work than to their social behavior. Teachers encourage European American female students in intellectual and academic areas, while they encourage and praise African American females in areas involving social skills. In addition, European American females are more likely to receive trusted lieutenant duties and special high-prestige assignments; African American female students' duties typically involve social responsibilities.

Educators tend to use different classroom management techniques with African American and European American students. In general, teachers of classes with high percentages of African American students are more likely to be authoritarian and less likely to use an open classroom approach. Teachers spend more time on the lookout for possible misbehavior by African American students, especially males. When male students misbehave, educators are especially prone to criticize the behavior of African American males and to use more severe punishments, including corporal punishment and suspension. And when females misbehave, teachers treat African Americans more harshly than European Americans.

Teachers relate to Hispanic American students in a biased manner. Although Hispanic American students tend to prefer more positive reinforcement and feedback from their teachers than most European American students, teachers praise them less often and give them less positive feedback when they answer correctly or perform well. Teachers are also less likely to encourage them when they need encouragement, to accept their ideas, and to direct questions to them.

Research about the ways in which teachers treat Native Americans is sparse. There is some evidence that teachers and their aides tend to speak to and attend to them less than to European American students (16). However, this may be partly the result of teachers' failure to recognize the nonverbal ways that Native American students ask for help and attention.

Poor students also receive unfair treatment in school (6, 11, 17, 20). Teachers give them fewer rewards. They provide poor students, especially males, fewer social and instructional contacts, but more disciplinary and control contacts. And teachers in schools that serve predominantly poor students are more likely to recommend or use corporal punishments, verbal punishments, or suspension than teachers in middle-class schools.

Avoiding Culturally Inappropriate Educational Approaches

Educators do not have to be prejudiced to use biased classroom management techniques with students. Well-meaning teachers who are not aware of the different behavioral, disciplinary, and communication styles of the various ethnic and socioeconomic groups in their classrooms can misperceive and misunderstand students' behaviors when they interpret them from their own perspective. They can perceive behavior problems that do not exist, not notice problems that do exist, misunderstand the causes of students' behaviors, and use inappropriate techniques to deal with students' behavior problems.

Misperceptions

Nonexistent Problems   Students who come from different ethnic or socioeconomic backgrounds than their teachers and school administrators may have values, goals, and interests that are acceptable to their families and communities but not to the school system. As a result, educators may not be able to accept behavior that the students and their parents find completely appropriate. For example, teachers may incorrectly think that students brought up not to be assertive or to volunteer their opinions unless encouraged by adults are shy or insecure. And they may believe that students who are encouraged at home to work independently rather than with others and to judge their accomplishments for themselves rather than rely on the opinions of others do not care about others. Let us consider some specific examples of how educators may perceive nonexistent problems in the case of African American, Hispanic American, and Asian Pacific American students.

African American students are especially prone to have difficulty in school because of incompatibilities between the way many of them are encouraged to behave in their communities and the expectations of their teachers (28, 30, 31, 33, 35, 38). Many African American males, and females as well, express their emotions much more intensely than most European Americans. When European American teachers observe African American males behaving aggressively and assertively, too many of them assume that the students are much angrier or upset than they actually are. Attributing a level of anger to African American students that would be correct for European American students who behaved in a similar way, the teachers can become uncomfortable, even anxious, and concerned about what they incorrectly anticipate will happen next. As a result, they intervene when no intervention is necessary. If teachers appreciated the cultural context of African American males' seemingly aggressive behavior toward others and understood that African American students displaying such behavior are unlikely to come to blows, they would be less likely to feel the need to intervene. This would lessen the likelihood that African American males would get into trouble needlessly. Here is how two African American professionals see it:

> Urban schooling patterns, for the most part, promote quietness and docility. Such classrooms are therefore designed to suit the learning norms of children from white families and opposed to the characteristics of Black children, making it difficult for them to comply with the demands made upon them by that system. . . . A troubled teacher-pupil relationship is the outcome. The resentful teacher and the balking student's interactions erode with daily incidents. School policy leads to a compilation of a dossier on these students so as to build up a string of minor offenses, which, when presented all at once, appear to be a massive campaign of misdeeds. (38, pp. 51–52)

> Most teachers are unprepared to accept the active, aggressive behavior of Black boys. The aggressive behavior of a Black child is immediately interpreted as hostile. The teacher's expectation is that the student should be compliant, docile, and responsive to authority. The student is expected to conform to a standard of behavior that the teacher is familiar with, the compliant child standard that was indicative of the teacher's upbringing. It is as though the teacher makes an unwritten contract with the student, "If you don't behave, I won't (or can't) teach you."
>   The next step in the process is that the teacher will make futile attempts to control the aggressive, active behavior, but abandon those efforts very quickly and conclude that the child is unmanageable. The child resists the teacher's efforts to control the behavior. More often than not, the behavior becomes more unmanageable. As the disruptive behavior increases, the amount of time and effort available to devote to attending to the instructions and acquiring academic skills decreases. In all likelihood the student prefers to avoid the academic work. Within a short period of time it becomes apparent that this unmanageable student is not functioning at grade level. This then can be interpreted, depending on the tolerance level of the teachers, as a learning problem and a justification for referral for special placement. The longer the time span involved, the greater the learning problem. (28, pp. 78–79)

An African American educator describes how other behavior patterns that are acceptable in the African American community can cause problems for students in school:

> Blacks are accustomed to integrating mental, emotional, and physical activities. Schools tend to encourage compartmentalizing these areas. The Black child's involvement in cognitive classroom activities is likely to be signaled by vocal responses, exuberance, and physical movement. Teachers consider this behavior disruptive because they expect that one can be highly stimulated to intellectual activities without involving affective or psychomotor dimensions.
>   What teachers view as total chaos and noise may be structured activity to Blacks. What teachers consider planned activities may be perceived by Black students as prohibiting constraints. The problem of perception stems from different sets of expectations and cultural sensibilities. (30, pp. 32–33)

Elaborating on the way that blacks respond to others when they are reciting, performing, and so on, Gay and Abrahams state:

There is more total interaction involved; all those in the social environment must play some active response role if it is only through such responses as "right on brother." . . .

The Black child in performing looks for verbal and kinesthetic support from his peers. The teacher hears noise and is threatened. The child's success is measured by his peers by the extent to which he stimulates the others to provide responses. When this behavior is manifested, teachers see an undisciplined and discourteous group of Blacks.

This situation arises because contrarily in white, middle-class culture the relationship between a performer and his audience demands a show of passivity on the part of the latter. . . . When Black children's classroom behavior is assessed using this frame of reference, the conclusions are foreordained. The culturally determined Black ways of demonstrating interest and involvement are interpreted as restlessness, inattentiveness, and sometimes hostility. (31, p. 338)

A final example of the many incompatibilities between acceptable African American behavior at home and the expectations of the schools is the verbal dueling games such as "playing the dozens," "ribbin' and jivin'," and so on, that African American students play. Although they know that these are merely competitive games, European American and other non-African American teachers often perceive them as a prelude to a fight (35).

Commenting on the way European American teachers may misperceive the origin and meaning of the field-sensitive/dependent relationship style of Hispanic American students, Jaramillo states:

An Anglo teacher is likely to consider many of the Spanish speaking children in his class dependent in a negative sense, or perhaps he will say they are immature, or that they are retarded in their social development. In reality, these differences are purely cultural, and viewed from another perspective, these children are perfectly normal and mature for their age. (34, p. 13)

Wong provides insight into the kinds of cultural misperceptions that educators can make about Chinese American students:

The child does not volunteer to answer. He just sits and waits for his teacher to call upon him. So in the eyes of the American teacher, Asian children, as compared to the American students, are dull, passive, unresponsive, and lack initiative. Most of the time, Chinese (Asian) students are ignored because of their absolute silence in class. (41, p. 11)

The kinds of cultural misperceptions that educators can make about Southeast Asian American students are illustrated by Nguyen:

The Vietnamese literal equivalent of the English word "Yes" is "Da" (pronounced "Ya" in the Southern Vietnamese dialect). However, whereas the English "Yes" means unequivocally "Yes," the Vietnamese "Da" means a variety of things. In the final analysis, it can mean "Yes," but in general usage it merely means "I am politely listening to you," and it does not at all mean that "I agree with you." The listener may disagree with what he hears, but due to his politeness, cannot say no. His English "Yes" for him conveys the polite and noncommittal Vietnamese "Da," but to the American it can carry only its English meaning. Thus, the Vietnamese may appear insincere, or even stupid, to the American. (39, pp. 6, 7, 19)

It is easy to understand how educators who do not know these facts could misinterpret their students' responses. For example, they may think that their students have just agreed to do what they have been asked to do and so become angry and frustrated when the students don't follow through after saying "yes."

Unnoticed Problems   Educators who are not tuned in to the ways students from other cultures communicate can miss a request for help or assistance. They may not even realize that their students have problems. As noted previously, Hispanic American and Asian Pacific American students are usually brought up not to ask teachers for help: Hispanic Americans are expected to be sensitive to the needs, feelings, and desires of others, making it unnecessary for others to be embarrassed by asking for help; and Asian Pacific American students believe that to ask for help would insult their teachers.

Incorrect Causes

Educators may mistakenly attribute behavior problems that are culturally determined to other causes. For example, educators who are unaware of their students' identity conflicts may attribute their behavior to lack of interest and motivation to succeed in school, lack of respect for teachers, poor parenting, and other causes. Then, instead of responding with understanding to their students' identity conflicts or helping them resolve these conflicts, they are likely to use inappropriate techniques to squash the objectionable behavior. Some of the ways that non-African American teachers can misunderstand the causes of African American students' behavior are revealed in the reactions of the faculty of a desegregated school:

> The Black children displayed unfamiliar behavior that teachers found difficult to adjust to and cope with. At one time or another teachers commented:
> "There's so much pent-up anger in them."
> "They talk so loud."
> "When he came here he was totally nonverbal."
> "Did you ever see such antsyness?"
> Teachers called attention to kids who used "foul" language ("I'll never get used to that"), to children who spoke out in class, to antisocial behavior (fighting, spitting at other children, stealing), to short attention spans, to immaturity (e.g., thumb sucking). Each of these behaviors made the job of teaching much more difficult than it had been prior to desegregation. . . . The first and most basic teacher response to the number of problems presented by the Black children was to devise some personal explanation for the unfamiliar behavior. While these explanations varied somewhat from teacher to teacher, a common theme emerged. On several occasions unfamiliar and disturbing behavior (whether antisocial actions or difficulty mastering classroom work) was attributed to problems in a child's environment. Comments such as "I think Ben is brutalized at home" were offered as explanations for children's actions or attitudes. To a lesser extent I heard references made to children's previous schools not having demanded enough of them. Whether these explanations accurately represented fact or not, they made the problems understandable and to some extent served to legitimate the approach taken by the teachers to ameliorate the problems. (37, p. 21)

Now consider some possible causes of behavior problems that teachers should bear in mind when they interpret the behavior of Asian Pacific American students:

When a Southeast Asian student misbehaves this misbehavior may be the result of one or more of the following sources of tension: frustration due to language problems and misunderstanding, imitation out of a desire for rapid adaptation, behavior learned in refugee camps where survival was paramount and included stealing and violent self-defense, intragroup historical animosity among various Southeast Asian groups, adjustment difficulties because school rules here are less strict and well-defined, culture-gap in the family resulting from different rates of assimilation. (29, p. 58)

One teacher was puzzled by an Asian child, because he responded with a smile when scolded. Asian children tend to "camouflage" their embarrassment by smiling. (36, p. 1)

Finally, Ortiz and Yates remind educators not to overlook the possibility that some of the behavior problems of limited-English-proficient students can be caused by their language difficulty: "Problem behaviors such as difficulty following directions, poor eye contact, inattention, and daydreaming could be associated with a handicapping condition, but they could also reflect a lack of English proficiency" (40, p. 52).

Incompatible Techniques

Even when educators recognize when students' behavior problems are culturally determined, they may still respond with techniques that are incompatible with the way students are accustomed to being treated. For example, many European Americans and Hispanic Americans speak differently to children and teenagers:

Hispanic parents tend to speak more politely and indirectly when they criticize or discipline their children. In the United States educators are much more gruff and direct with students. . . . Some Hispanic students, especially males, may interpret the gruff or more direct manner of Anglos as an indication that educators do not consider them worthy or deserving of a proper relationship. When educators speak to them in a matter-of-fact or authoritarian manner, they may feel insulted, angry, or resentful and lose respect for these educators and the desire to cooperate or conform. (32, p. 102)

At times, the very techniques that teachers choose to motivate individual students backfire because of different cultural values. For example, rewarding Hawaiian American students for appropriate behavior can cause them to behave in less desirable ways to avoid being singled out for praise and recognition. On the other hand, rewarding the whole group for the improvement of one or more members of the group can cause those individuals who are not behaving appropriately to behave in a more desirable manner.

Diverse Student Characteristics

The following are some of the ways in which students' characteristics differ. Knowledge of how ethnic and socioeconomic factors influence these characteristics may help you understand how students actually behave, why they behave as they do, and which management techniques might be most effective with them.

Disciplinary Style

Students from different ethnic backgrounds come to school with very dissimilar expectations about and preferences for disciplinary styles because people from different cultures have their own standards of acceptable and unacceptable behavior, attribute behavior problems to different causes, and use different techniques to motivate children and youth to behave in acceptable ways. Some ethnic groups believe that children and adolescents consciously and willfully choose to misbehave. Others admit the possibility that students can be physiologically disposed to behave in undesirable ways or are driven to behave inappropriately because of emotional and psychological problems. Some groups rely heavily on the use of consequences to modify children's behavior; others do not. Some are quick to resort to punishments; others emphasize rewards. Some stress materialistic rewards; others train children and youth to respond to more personal ones. Therefore, it is helpful to know the kinds of disciplinary techniques that students are accustomed to in their homes and communities. Many authors have discussed how this principle applies to African American students (46, 50, 53):

> Many districts offer a single program for improving the behavior of all students based on the assumption that the student population is homogeneous. But . . . it is likely that those activities necessary to improve the behavior of African-American students will involve efforts that address those behavioral differences. Identifying alternative disciplinary actions is perhaps the most difficult of the tasks included in this approach because it involves trying to determine what actions may be more effective.

> The difficulty of the task partially reflects the reluctance of schools to develop and use strategies that specifically address the needs and problems of African-American students because they fear that they will be charged with having dual standards of discipline. (53, p. 34)

> In many instances white teachers are unable to discipline Black children because they do not "connect" culturally; the teachers do not behave as Black children expect authority figures to behave. . . . It seems that when white teachers practice the disciplinary techniques they are taught in college, Black children "run over them." (46, p. 172)

A number of disciplinary style differences have been observed in diverse groups of students.

Permissive Versus Strict Management   Although educators are being advised to be more accepting and understanding of their students' behavior problems, some educators believe that a lenient, permissive approach to classroom management can backfire with students who are used to a more authoritarian approach (29, 46, 52). For example, speaking of African American students, Bacon advises that "those who are accustomed to a more authoritarian approach to behavior management are particularly difficult to control in an atmosphere of permissiveness, of being given freedom to choose prematurely and without training" (42, p. 7).

In a somewhat similar vein, Tharp advises that teachers of Hawaiian Americans need to be tough:

> To be tough, the teachers must be firm, clear, and consistent in insisting that the children comply with their directions and requests. They must dispense contingently the resources they control, such as recess, access to peers, and praise. (52, p. 354)

However, Tharp reports that the opposite is true for Navajo students:

> For Navajos, neither extreme of "tough" or "nice" is appropriate, and the reinforcing and punishing value of identical teacher behaviors is often reversed. Navajo adults are more reserved in their affectionate displays but are highly respectful of children's individuality and of children's sovereignty over their own persons. Punishment, contingent reward, or any openly manipulative effort to control the behavior of others—including children—is a violation of cultural values. (52, p. 354)

Positive Consequences   How much praise and reward do students receive from adults? Will students expect to be rewarded and praised more often, less often, or about as often as teachers habitually praise and reward them? Providing students with less than their customary amount of praise and rewards may cause them to think that their teachers do not value them or their work. On the other hand, rewarding and praising students excessively can cause learned helplessness. Educators understand the importance of using praise to motivate students. Their problem lies in the fact that what is an unnecessary or excessive amount of praise for some students may be just the amount or less than what others are accustomed to receiving. For example, Southeast Asian American children usually are not rewarded and praised as often as children from many other cultures:

> The child should not receive rewards for the behaviors he is expected to demonstrate. Accomplishments are usually acknowledged in the form of parent encouragement to do even better and strive for higher levels of achievement. This attitude is also reflected in the family discouragement of praising oneself or family members in the presence of non-family members. When a child (or adult) is given a compliment, it is often dismissed or negated by immediate discussion of one's faults through self-deprecating remarks. (49, p. 4)

Students' ethnic backgrounds also affect which consequences they do and do not experience as rewarding or punishing: "'Time-out' from the social interaction of recess or in-class activities is a sharp punishment for Hawaiian children. In Navajo classrooms, children are quite content to be alone" (52, pp. 354–355).

There are many other questions that educators should consider when they make decisions about whether and how to reward students. Are students brought up to strive for individual recognition, or is anonymity stressed? Will students respond better when the individual is rewarded or when the group is praised and rewarded? Should teachers recognize students' accomplishments or those of the group as a whole? When recognizing students' accomplishments, should teachers do so publicly, by placing their work on the walls, referring to their achievement, and using them as peer models, or privately? Many non-European students—especially Asian Pacific Americans, Hawaiian Americans, Hispanic Americans, and Native Americans—and European American females have such difficulty in classrooms that stress individual goals and individual recognition that it is often better to recognize their achievement in a less public manner (32, 51).

Are students accustomed to receiving personal or impersonal rewards at home? Will they respond better to personal, positive reinforcements, such as statements of approval, smiles, and pats on the back, or impersonal ones, such as treats, toys, gold stars, and sweets? Is it possible that students aren't changing their behavior because they are relatively indifferent to praise and criticism from others?

Negative Consequences   Educators should also be aware of their students' characteristics when they decide to use negative consequences. There are a number of important issues to consider. What kinds of negative consequences do adults use to discipline youngsters: physical punishments (spanking and slapping); loss of affection, attention, or the possibility of social interaction (statements of disappointment and anger, removal from the presence of others); loss of privileges (being grounded, loss of TV); or loss of material things (desserts, allowances)? What kinds of negative consequences will work best with the students? Which ones will be unacceptable to them or their parents? Here are a few examples of cultural differences among Hispanic Americans, Native Americans, and Southeast Asian Americans:

> Hispanics tend to use corporal punishment more and deprivation of love and affection less when disciplining their children. (32, p. 161)

> Native American children are seldom if ever, struck by an adult: no parents, uncles, aunts, no adults. (43, p. 45)

> Such forms of punishment as locking the child outside the house, isolating the child from the family social life, shaming the child, scolding or guilt induction that results in a "loss of face" are commonplace in Southeast Asia. (48, p. 145)

What are the acceptable and unacceptable ways of criticizing or punishing children and teenagers? Can students accept direct criticism or only indirect and subtle feedback? Can they tolerate being criticized in public or will they only respond positively to private criticism? Should educators write students' names on the blackboard when they misbehave and comment about their inappropriate behavior in front of others, or should they only correct students in private to make sure they do not "lose face"?

Many non-European American students may react quite negatively to public criticism. Consider the likely response of Filipino American students to criticism:

> Correction of students' mistakes must be done tactfully. Pilipino students often have difficulty detaching themselves from their work and may view adverse comments as direct criticisms of themselves. . . . Pilipino children are particularly sensitive to criticism. When embarrassed the child may withdraw and become uncooperative. The teacher may be frustrated in all attempts to discover what is wrong. (47, p. 19)

What tone of voice do adults use when they discipline and criticize children and teenagers? Are they gruff, emotional, and direct? Or are they gentle and indirect? European Americans tend to be more emotional and direct than many other groups. For example, among Native Americans, "Talking loud, especially while correcting children, is highly disapproved" (43, p. 45).

Group Consequences   To what extent are students motivated by the attitude of their peer group? Can teachers motivate students to change their behavior by showing its effect on the peer group? As already noted, many non-European Americans are more sensitive than European Americans to the effects of their behavior on their peers:

> What motivates Hispanics to be punctual are not impersonal reasons such as it's efficient for everyone to arrive at the same time and begin at the same time. Hispanics may feel that the meeting or work could have started without them if necessary. . . . On the other hand, personal relationships do concern them. For example they may be very concerned that their lack of punctuality not be interpreted as a sign of disrespect or a lack of courtesy toward others and arrive on time to make sure they do not seem disrespectful. . . . Statements such as "if you respect your classmates you will get here when we need you" may have more effect than statements such as "we could not finish on time" or "we wasted fifteen minutes because we had to wait for you." (37, p. 95)

Shame and Guilt   Do parents emphasize guilt—feeling bad about oneself for misbehaving—or shame—feeling bad because others know one has misbehaved—or neither when they discipline children? When motivating students to behave well, should educators focus on what the students themselves should think about their behavior (guilt), how others will think of them (shame), or neither? Educators are typically advised not to make students feel guilty or to shame them even in private. In fact, many readers may feel that this discussion of possibly using guilt or shame to motivate students is inappropriate. However, shame and its avoidance can be a very effective and acceptable motivator with some Hispanic American, Native American, and Southeast Asian American students (34, 43, 44, 48, 49):

> For Native Americans, warnings about the consequences of bad behavior are couched in community terms like, "What will people say—they will laugh at you." . . . Shame, otherwise known as embarrassment, is a common disciplinary tool with Native Americans. (43, p. 48)

> Shame is, indeed, a powerful instrument for discipline in Hispanic culture . . . where the threat of a failing grade or detention may not succeed in producing the desired change of behavior with the student, a private and strong reminder of his family obligations may do wonders. (44, pp. 72–73)

Perception of Authority Figures   Are students expected not to speak unless spoken to, not to ask questions, and to obey their elders just because they are the authorities? Or can they disagree with adults and ask their elders to justify why they are requiring them to do certain things or punishing them? Can teachers expect students to accept their opinions, rules, and consequences simply because they are in charge, or are they expected to justify themselves to their students?

Although many experts advise teachers to be authoritative rather than authoritarian, students from other cultures may require help in adjusting to an adult who is authoritative and not authoritarian. These students may also have difficulty participating in democratic classrooms, in which the students are actively involved in establishing rules, procedures, and consequences. For example, a Filipino American teacher states:

Especially to a small child from grade one to grade six, the democratic atmosphere that is being provided here is an entirely new aspect. Perhaps, during the first months the Filipino student is somewhat lost. He doesn't know what to do. The Filipino child may feel insecure. In the Philippines, the teacher usually says, "do this, make this." (45, p. 21)

Is the relationship between adolescents and adult authority figures more like that between children and adults or between adult and adult? What special rights and privileges do adolescents enjoy that are denied to children? What special instructional and classroom management techniques should teachers use with adolescents? Which techniques that are appropriate with younger students are inappropriate with adolescents?

Are the authority roles of male and female adults the same? Is one gender the authority figure and the other the nurturer? Does each gender express and enforce its authority in the same way or in different ways? Are students ready to accept teachers of either gender as authority figures? Are students prepared to accept the same disciplinary techniques from teachers, regardless of their teachers' gender? A Hispanic American educator offers the following comment about Hispanic American males' perceptions of their female teachers: "One should be conscious of a male Chicano's lack of understanding in trying to take orders from a female teacher. He will really look up to or listen with better interest if an adult male is talking to him" (32, p. 104).

Because some Hispanic American males may have difficulty accepting the authority of female teachers, some educators suggest that females use nonauthoritarian methods, such as requesting rather than ordering, and perhaps request that a male administrator intervene if it becomes necessary to deal in a stern way with male students (32).

How do students express their respect for authority? In some cultures, looking an adult in the eye is a sign of respect and submission. In other cultures, avoiding eye contact communicates the same message. As a result, teachers may misinterpret the nonverbal messages communicated by students from other cultural backgrounds. The way that African American, Asian Pacific American, Hispanic American, and other non-European American students are taught to show respect is typically different from the way European American students are expected to behave.

Relationship Style

While human nature governs how we relate to each other, its rules are flexible. An appreciation of the different relationship styles that can exist among different ethnic and socioeconomic groups can enhance teachers' classroom management efforts.

Individual Versus Group Rights   Are the rights of individuals or the obligations of individuals to the group stressed? Are youngsters encouraged to establish their own goals and strive for individual excellence, or are they expected to be sensitive and responsive to the needs and desires of the group? Are students likely to sacrifice their desires for the benefit of their classmates?

Which group rights are respected? Some cultures expect individuals to consider the effect of their actions on other people's sensibilities. Cultures that stress people's individuality—their right to determine for themselves the way to satisfy their desires—require their members to learn to tolerate the inconvenience that the rights of others may create for them. Thus, some children are taught to be considerate of others by keeping the volume on the TV or stereo low so as to avoid disturbing others. And other children are taught to be considerate of others by learning how to do what they have to do even when the volume is high. Teachers who are unaware of this difference may mistakenly believe that some students are inconsiderate and self-centered rather than merely behaving in a culturally approved manner. The following description shows the different approaches of many African Americans and European Americans in this respect:

> Whites have been taught that to act on behalf of their own feelings is unjustified if someone else's sensibilities might become offended as a result. So strongly ingrained is this rule that it has the force of a moral injunction. Rather than violate it and feel guilty . . . whites will hold back what they truly feel even if this will result in an injustice to their feelings or create for themselves an unwanted social situation.
>
> From a black standpoint, individuals asserting themselves in accordance with their feelings are seen not as violating the sacred rights of others but, rather, as preserving the sacred rights of self. (55, pp. 121, 123)

How should educators deal with this issue? Should they teach students to be tolerant of each other's styles or to be sensitive to the needs and sensibilities of others? Some students have great difficulty coping when others express strong feelings. Other students may have strong needs to express themselves. How should educators reconcile the conflicting needs of students in such situations?

Giving and Sharing   Some cultures bring up children to be better sharers than others. Some cultures train children to be generous with their possessions because it is better to give than to receive. Other cultures stress private ownership and property rights. Some students have more practice in sharing because their cultures do not provide many experiences in private ownership and personal space. Instead of having their own room, area, chair, and so on, they have to share space, belongings, and the like. Their different experiences at home can affect how they prefer to function in school.

To what extent are children and youth expected to share their things with others? How prepared are students to share their belongings with others? Will they also expect their peers to reciprocate? How will students react if their peers do not share their things with them?

> Humanism in Hispanic children is . . . expressed in their unusual generosity with toys and other personal belongings, an openness of attitude which they frequently discover is not reciprocated by their Anglo-Saxon peers. (44, p. 75)

> When educators attempt to resolve sharing difficulties among students by explaining the rights of owners—emphasizing private property or what's mine is mine and what's yours is yours, Hispanic students may feel bewildered, confused or even rejected and insulted. (32, p. 89)

Do students think that helping a friend during a test is bad, cheating, and dishonest or a way of demonstrating their helpfulness, friendliness, and brotherhood? Some Hawaiian American and Hispanic American students may feel that helping friends during a test or when they are called on to recite is necessary despite their teachers' view that it is cheating (32, 54).

How should educators react to students whose ethnic backgrounds lead them to have different attitudes about sharing their belongings and helping their peers when they are called on to recite or are taking a test? Should teachers treat all students the same, regardless of the students' beliefs, or take their beliefs into consideration when they establish rules, procedures, and expectations?

Relationships with the Opposite Sex   How do children and youth relate to the opposite sex at different ages? The brother-sister and male-female relationships in the Hispanic American community have been described as follows:

> Older boys for instance, tend to assume a protective and responsible attitude toward their sisters—escorting them to and from school, dispensing lunch money to them, and defending them against intruders; as a result of their protective upbringing, girls tend to be shy and submissive toward their brothers and other boys. Neither of these typical male and female Hispanic behaviors meets the wholehearted approval of the egalitarian Anglo-American educator who tends to translate them as overaggressiveness on the one hand, and excessive dependence on the other. (44, p. 61)

At what age are students comfortable relating to peers of the opposite sex? Should they be allowed to choose to work in same-sex groups or required to participate in groups with the opposite sex? Does the students' age or the nature of the activity play a role in their ability to participate comfortably in mixed-gender groups?

In recent years, an increased emphasis on nonsexist coeducational activities in the schools has been required by Title IX of the Education Amendments Act and supported by the courts (see chapter 6). Yet, students from some cultural backgrounds may resist being required to engage in activities that are reserved for the opposite sex in their cultures. They may also balk at being made to engage in coed activities that are usually carried out in sexually segregated groups in their home culture. Consider the problems that many Native American and East Indian American students experience in mixed-gender groups:

> At a school dance in which Anglo teachers were instructing Navajo students in the expected social behavior of adolescents in the dominant society, these harbingers of "culture" randomly selected young males and females and forced them to dance together. As some of these students were from the same clan, this physical contact was akin to a sexual encounter. In their minds, incestuous relations were forced upon these students. (57, p. 23)

> East Indian American students expressed great discomfort about working with someone of the opposite sex on a class assignment about how to run a household as a married couple. The Indian culture segregates males and females in all environments especially until they are married. Thus coming from a culture that believes it would be wrong to work in close contact with each other it is uncomfortable for most students to do so. All of the European American students felt totally comfortable with the project and stated that it would be a great learning experience. (58, p. 3)

How should educators deal with the requirements of Title IX? Should they respect students' ethnic preferences, encourage students to comply with Title IX, or require them to do so?

How do males and females express interest in one another? What one group may consider an insulting form of attention or show of interest, other groups may deem acceptable. This is especially true of African Americans and Hispanic Americans. Thus, *piropos*, compliments said to females who one does not know, about how great they look or how sexy they are, are acceptable in many Hispanic American and African American communities, but insulting to many European Americans (55, 56). How should educators deal with the problems that occur when males relate to females from different ethnic backgrounds in ways that the males think are acceptable but which make the females feel insulted or harassed?

Social Space   People from different backgrounds prefer different amounts of personal space between them and the individuals with whom they are interacting. Thus, European American educators may find that some Hispanic American students make them uncomfortable by standing too close to them, while the students feel rejected every time a teacher backs away to feel more comfortable. These same teachers may have the exact opposite experience with some Asian Pacific American students, who require even more personal space than they do:

> The concept of social space is interpreted in widely different manners in Hispanic and American societies, with the former opting generally for a narrower interaction distance than that preferred by the latter. . . . Many an Anglo American has reacted negatively without realizing it to the "crowding" behavior of Latino children, and his instinctive withdrawal has been interpreted by them as a sign of exclusion from the inner circle of favorite students. (44, p. 65)

> In the classroom situation, Oriental American students, particularly those newly arrived, have often demonstrated uneasiness when teachers sit too close to them. This is because they are not used to proximity between an adult and a youngster. In Asia, teachers are respected by both students and their parents, and the size of the spatial bubble is rather extensive. Oriental teachers seldom mingle with students to help them with schoolwork. (59, pp. 68–69)

Communication Style

Mismatches between communication styles can make it difficult for educators to understand what their students are telling them about how they feel or think. And sometimes these mismatches lead to misunderstandings. Students who are unfamiliar with their teachers' communication styles may not be able to distinguish when their teachers are serious and when they are joking. Therefore, educators should be aware of the differences in communication style between them and their students. The following are some communication style differences that educators should keep in mind when they manage their classrooms (60–70).

Formal Versus Informal Communication   While all cultures have rules that people are expected to follow when they communicate with each other, some cultures are much more flexible than others. Some groups expect strict adherence to communication conventions in certain situations, such as when children are addressing parents and other adults or when subordinates are communicating with those who have more status and/or power than they have. Other cultures are much more relaxed and informal about communication codes. Strict codes of communication may be designed to show respect for others, to avoid open demonstrations of conflict and disagreement, or to avoid causing individuals to "lose face."

The communication styles of Hispanic Americans and some Asian Pacific American groups tend to be much more formal than either the African American or European American communication styles:

> Because one of the ways in which Hispanics demonstrate their respect for each other is through the maintenance of certain formal conventions like the use of the formal *usted* rather than the informal *tu* in conversation, Hispanics may mistake an Anglo's less formal approach to interpersonal relationships as a sign of disrespect. (32, p. 130)

> In Asian cultures the communication interaction is very structured and predictable. . . . The individual's status in the situation will define the role that he or she is expected to play in communication. These roles are usually defined by tradition and are often highly formalized. For communication to proceed smoothly, each participant must behave in the expected manner by using verbal and nonverbal behaviors appropriate to one's role. (67, p. 46)

Emotional Versus Subdued Communication   When people communicate, are they expected to be considerate of other people's sensibilities—their reactions to what is being communicated and how it is being communicated? Or are the right of individuals to express their feelings, regardless of how it might affect others, considered more important? Some cultures protect individuals' rights to express their feelings and require their members to learn to tolerate, accept, and deal with the expression of intense feelings. Cultures that are more concerned with protecting people's sensibilities expect feelings to be communicated in a subdued way. African Americans and European Americans tend to be very different in this regard:

> Whites want social interaction to operate at an emotionally subdued level. To realize this goal they first establish the rule that expressive behavior shall be subdued, which develops sensibilities capable of tolerating only relatively subdued outputs. . . . Black cultural norms desire levels of public interaction that are more emotionally intense. Consequently they allow individuals to express themselves at the level at which feelings are felt. (55, p. 117)

Although students are allowed to protest the decisions of their teachers, they are expected to do so in an acceptable manner. When African American students express their positions passionately, European American teachers, who tend to value coolheaded reasoning, may perceive these expressions as being beyond the bounds of acceptability (55).

Direct Versus Indirect Communication   Do people express themselves directly, openly, and frankly, or do they speak indirectly and politely in order to maintain smooth interpersonal relationships? Should teachers be indirect or frank when they have to criticize students' work or behavior?

As the following remarks indicate, many Asian Pacific American groups shun European American frankness:

American straightforwardness is considered at best impolite if not brutal. In Indochina, one does not come directly to the point. To do so is, for an American, a mark of honesty and forthrightness while a person from Indochina sees it as a lack of intelligence or courtesy. (39, p. 6)

The [Filipino] student will sometimes employ a mediator in communicating with the teacher. While this procedure may appear strange to the Anglo teacher, the child may have had numerous experiences at home with difficult-to-approach adults which have required the services of a mediator. This may be especially true if the teacher is held in high esteem. (65, p. 19)

If educators use an indirect approach to tell students when they want them to do something, will the students who are accustomed to a more direct approach understand that they are actually expected to comply? For example, African American students and students from poor backgrounds, who are accustomed to being told directly what they should and should not do, may not understand just how serious their teachers are when they are spoken to in an indirect manner (70).

Honesty Cultures have very different ideas about exactly what is honest communication and even whether honest communication is desirable. No culture expects people to be completely honest. Other issues besides honesty, such as the relative importance placed by the culture on maintaining one's honor or one's face, avoiding disagreement and conflict, or avoiding personal responsibility, influence a group's opinion about how honest communication should be. In fact, in some cultures, when people communicate it is more important to maintain smooth interpersonal relationships than to tell the truth:

Falsehood carries no moral structure for a Cambodian, Laotian, or Vietnamese. The essential question is not whether a statement is true or false, but what the intention of the statement is. Does it facilitate interpersonal harmony? Does it indicate a wish to change the subject? Hence, one must learn the "heart" of the speaker through his/her words. (39, pp. 6, 7)

Even within cultures, subgroups have different attitudes about honest communication. In the European American culture, some individuals feel that people should take responsibility for, pay the price for, and stand up for one's actions, whereas many politicians believe that it is appropriate to use such techniques as damage control, spin control, and plausible deniability to color the truth and even hide it from the voters.

In some cultures, a promise to do something or to comply with an expectation may not be meant literally. If a refusal would lead to an uncomfortable interpersonal moment or even insult someone, especially someone in a position of authority, a promise may be little more than a way of maintaining smooth interpersonal relationships. Thus, some students do not have the slightest intention of complying with a behavioral plan that they have agreed to or a contract that they have signed.

Response to Guilt and Accusations When individuals are accused of doing the wrong thing, how do they express guilt and remorse or proclaim their innocence? European American students tend to express guilt by lowering their eyes and avoiding eye contact. When they are falsely accused, they may issue strong denials. Kochman describes the

European American reaction in the following way: "If they are innocent, they issue a vigorous and defensive denial—especially if the charge is serious. If they are guilty and are not trying to pretend otherwise, their response is subdued and embarrassed" (55, p. 93).

As previously noted, African American students lower their eyes as a sign of respect, not as an admission of guilt. And they do not experience the same need to proclaim their innocence by emotional statements when they are not guilty. Because European Americans and African Americans respond differently when they admit or deny guilt, they can each assume that the other has communicated their guilt when they have not.

Educators who do not know that African American students tend to avoid direct eye contact with authority figures or elders as a sign of respect and submission may judge their students' behavior by their own standards, exemplified by the expression "Look me in the eye and tell me the truth." When African American students avert their eyes while being confronted about their behavior, teachers may misinterpret their lack of eye contact as indicating insincerity and guilt. African Americans may also misinterpret their European American students' communication styles, as the following quote illustrates:

> When whites . . . issue a vigorous and defensive denial—the kind that whites often use when they feel *falsely* accused—blacks consider this a confirmation of guilt since they believe only the truth would have been able to produce a protest of such intensity. (55, p. 92)

Topics for Discussion

All cultures have unwritten rules about what should or should not be talked about and with whom. Because teachers and students may have culturally determined different expectations about what students should be willing to discuss with their teachers or their peers, it is important to know what students are and are not comfortable discussing. The following are examples of themes that some students may be reluctant to discuss with teachers.

Ability to Express Needs   In some cultures, people are so sensitive to others' needs that it is unnecessary for individuals to be open and direct about their needs. Thus, it is important for teachers to know whether their students are accustomed to expressing their needs openly or if they expect others to be sensitive to their feelings and problems. This is especially true for Hispanic Americans:

> Mexican American children seldom ask for help. Their socialization has accustomed them to the expectation that their needs will be noticed and help provided without its having to be asked for. This type of socialization results in children learning to be sensitive to the needs and feelings of others. (69, p. 15)

> Educators should be tuned into these subtle expressions of need. They should not assume that because Hispanic students have not expressed a need for help or understanding in a direct and forthright manner, they do not need special attention or consideration. (32, p. 96)

Admission of Errors and Mistakes   Do people admit when they are wrong or have made a mistake? Although students may have difficulty accepting responsibility for their errors and mistakes or apologizing to others for cultural reasons, they may be misperceived as defiant or stubborn.

In Spanish-speaking countries, language forms make it easy for people to avoid accepting responsibility for their mistakes. A Hispanic American educator explains it this way:

> Let's pretend I missed the plane which brought me to this conference. Maybe it was my fault, and maybe not. Perhaps my husband turned off the alarm. Or perhaps my car would not start. But whatever rationalization I use, if I express myself in English it is my fault. The only way I can express what happened in English is to say "I missed the plane." So I think it would be better to express myself in Spanish. That way I don't have to feel guilty about what happened. I simply say, "El avion me dejó." That means the plane left me. . . . If I were to drop this glass, some of you would say to yourselves, "she dropped the glass," implying that I'm clumsy. Others of you would say, "*se cayó el vaso.*" Somehow the glass managed to slide out of my hand and break itself. (34, pp. 6–7)

Should students be required to admit that they made a mistake or to apologize for something they did? Would that make students lose face? Perhaps students should learn to verbally accept responsibility for their behavior as well as accept the consequences of their behavior. But some students may be willing to accept the consequences of their behavior while resisting admitting their responsibility to others. In such cases, it may be more effective to permit them to avoid having to admit their errors and mistakes.

Disagreement, Unwillingness, and Inability   Are people expected to say when they are unwilling or unable to do something? Are they likely to express disagreement? When people say that they, too, feel or believe as others do or that they will do something, do they mean it? Or is this just their way of avoiding an unpleasant moment?

> In the midst of a great cultural emphasis on harmony and respect in Japan one speaker will rarely directly contradict another or even answer a question with a direct "no." Even in situations in which Americans can perceive "nothing personal" to be conveyed by a "no" answer, the Japanese will usually find one of at least 16 different ways of saying "no" without using the literal equivalent. (63, p. 47)

> Hispanics often find themselves in difficulty if they disagree with an Anglo's point of view. To them, direct argument or contradiction appears rude and disrespectful. On the surface they seem agreeable, manners dictating that they do not reveal their genuine opinion openly unless they can take time to tactfully differ. (32, p. 131)

Can teachers count on students to do the things they commit themselves to do? Some students are brought up to believe that not following through on promises and saying something that is not so are acceptable behaviors when they contribute to interpersonal harmony or help someone save face. When students do not fulfill a contract, do they think of it as lying or irresponsible behavior? Or do they believe that their behavior is appropriate?

> An American who is not familiar with the Filipino culture might become annoyed when a Pilipino speaker says he or she will "try to come" and does not appear for the appointment. . . . The American probably does not know that when the Pilipino

speaker says "I'll try" he or she usually means one of the following: 1. "I cannot do it, but I do not want to hurt your feelings by saying no." 2. "I would like to, but I am not sure you really want me to come. Please insist that I do." 3. "I will probably come, but I will not say yes because something may prevent me from coming. I have no control over what may happen." (62, pp. 32–33)

Will students be able to ask questions or request help when they do not understand something? "A Japanese youth . . . will not insult the teacher's efforts by saying, 'I don't understand.' Will nod politely even while not understanding and attribute the difficulty to his or her own lack of diligence" (70, p. 19).

Facts Versus Feelings   Many cultural groups frown on displays and discussions of feelings, expecting their members to discuss matters of fact:

> In the USA as well as in northern European cultures and many oriental groups, the expression of emotion is limited. Southern European cultures and some Latin American groups seem to permit the incredible in this matter of expressing emotions. (56, p. 4)

When students have problems, it is important to know if they are as comfortable discussing their feelings (such as resentment, anger, shame, or guilt) as discussing the facts.

Sensitive and Controversial Topics   How well do individuals have to know each other and what kind of relationship do they have to have to be able to discuss sensitive or intimate topics? Under what circumstances will students be willing to discuss sensitive topics with their teachers? In some cultures, people will discuss sensitive issues only with family members and extremely close friends.

Group Processes

There are no hard and fast rules about group processes that apply to all ethnic groups. Ethnic groups can function very differently.

Making Decisions   How do groups arrive at decisions? Do groups have leaders? Do leaders make decisions or lead the group to arrive at their own decisions? Are differences of opinion discussed openly, or are they sidestepped? Would students be comfortable participating in the decision-making process, or would they prefer to have decisions made by their teachers? Would they feel comfortable expressing opinions and feelings that differ from others in the group? Would they be able to participate in discussions of controversial issues or feel comfortable about deciding group issues by a public vote? Students who have been trained to avoid public conflicts and disagreements may be unable to participate in discussions of controversial issues, express opinions that are different from a previous speaker, or even vote on what the group should or should not do.

Group process as practiced in Asian Pacific American and Hispanic American groups can often differ from the typical European American approach:

Because being a member of a group is so important, the ability to work harmoniously with a group is highly valued. . . . The goal of group problem solving is to reach consensus, not to compete for acceptance and approval of one's idea or position at the expense of others in the group. Directness and forthrightness are not valued, and people who display these traits are considered to be rude and impolite. (56, p. 47)

When a group of Hispanics disagree they may resolve the issue by continuing to discuss it until it becomes apparent that a consensus has been reached without polling the group or calling for a vote. . . .

This is much better than bringing out the differences of opinion among people by requiring them to take a stand—stand up and be counted, show which side you're on, etc. This can increase conflict and often does. (32, pp. 100–101)

How many people speak at a time? European Americans expect that even in group situations, only one person will speak and the others will wait their turn and listen. This is not true of all cultures:

In Arab countries and in many Latin American ones, conversations are invitations for everybody to join. (56, p. 4)

In a heated discussion, blacks frequently make their points whenever they can enter the discussion. Deference is given to the person who considers his or her point most urgent. Turn-taking is the style of whites, who usually raise their hands to be recognized. Teachers find black students impolite, aggressive, and boisterous when they cut off another student or fail to restrain themselves so that every student can have a turn to talk. (33, p. 29)

Many European Americans expect groups to function quietly. However, African Americans, Mediterranean Americans, and Hispanic Americans are comfortable with much higher levels of what may seem like noise to European Americans.

Resolving Conflicts   Are conflicts faced and dealt with in a straightforward manner, or swept under the table? Should teachers bring conflicts between students into the open to resolve them? At home, are youngsters who disagree allowed or encouraged to argue or fight it out, or are they required to settle their differences peacefully and shake hands and make up? Is it better to intervene when students have conflicts or permit them to settle their conflicts themselves? Should students be required to shake hands and "make friends"? African American students are brought up to settle their conflicts in a much more open manner than many European American middle-class students and teachers. Teachers' intolerance of their behavior contributes to their being mislabeled behavior disordered.

Taking Turns   The time a person must wait to begin to respond or to introduce a new topic after another person has completed a statement varies with different cultures. Students from cultures that require longer pauses may feel left out or blocked out of classroom discussions because others who are used to shorter pauses take the floor before they do (70).

Nonverbal Communication

Educators are often unaware of the cultural differences in students' nonverbal communication styles. This is unfortunate because people's nonverbal communication can be an even more important clue to their thoughts, feelings, and attitudes than their actual words.

Expressing Emotion   Cultures differ in the way people are expected to express their emotions. In some Asian Pacific cultures, students laugh or giggle when they are embarrassed. Some cultures bring up males and females to express their feelings differently. For example, in some groups only males can express anger; females never talk sharply or snap at others. When they are angry, they smile and their voices become softer.

Because cultures differ in how people express emotions and feelings, educators cannot always judge how students are feeling based on how they themselves behave when they are upset, embarrassed, angry, and so on. To understand their students' feelings, they need to be sensitive to the subtle and often not so subtle clues that are obvious to those who are able to recognize them.

Expressing Affection   Do people demonstrate affection easily? Do they do so verbally or physically? Would students welcome or reject their teachers' display of affection? What are the acceptable ways teachers can express their affection for students? Is a pat on the back, an arm on the shoulder, and so on, acceptable, or are displays of affection limited to verbal statements? Although many students welcome physical touching, it is "taboo" behavior in some cultures. For example, the Hispanic American culture encourages more physical displays of affection than the European American culture:

> Hispanics tend to show affection and acceptance through touching. Friends are likely to kiss when they meet. Males are likely to hug each other or pat each other on the back as well as shake hands. And it is not unusual for people to hold others by the arm or place their hands on their shoulders when conversing. Therefore, educators should utilize physical contact when expressing approval and acceptance of their Hispanic student, especially the young ones. (32, p. 97)

Expressing Defiance   European Americans typically express anger and defiance by silent stares. African Americans roll their eyes, and many Asian Pacific Americans force a smile when they are angry. As Johnson explains, among African Americans, especially females,

> Rolling the eyes is a non-verbal way of expressing impudence and disapproval of the person who is in the authority role and of communicating every negative label that can be applied to the dominant person. . . . Often white teachers (who are in an authority role and who have contact with Black children) will miss the message communicated by Black children when they roll their eyes. (66, pp. 18, 57)

African American (and Hispanic American) females will also stand with their hands on their hips when they are angry or defiant. Johnson advises, "Most Black people know to 'cool it' when Black women take this stance. The non-verbal message communicated when a Black female takes this stance is: 'I'm really mad, now. You better quit messing with me'" (66, p. 57).

Expressing Submissiveness   How do students express their respect for authority? In some cultures, looking an adult in the eye is a sign of respect and submission. In other cultures, avoiding eye contact communicates the same message. As a result, teachers may misinterpret the nonverbal messages communicated by students from other cultural backgrounds. The way that African American, Asian Pacific American, Hispanic American, and other non-European American students are taught to show respect and submission is typically different from the way European American students are expected to behave. For example:

> Asians generally tend to use repeated head nodding, avoidance of direct eye contact, and minimal spontaneous verbalization, and to refrain from making critical comments, as a way of showing deference toward an authority figure. (67, p. 49)

> Occasional avoidance of eye contact by Oriental children may be classified as submissive behavior . . . such avoidance of eye contact provides others with a distorted image of an Oriental child—as being timid, shy, insecure, suspicious, undependable, and lacking self confidence. (59, p. 69)

> Avoidance of eye contact by a Black person communicates "I am in a subordinate role and I respect your authority over me," while the dominant culture member may interpret avoidance of eye contact as "Here is a shifty, unreliable person I'm dealing with." (66, p. 18)

The way some African American males walk away from a reprimand can also reveal whether or not they have accepted it:

> If the young Black male walks away in a natural manner then the reprimand was received positively; if he walks away with a "pimp strut" it means that the young Black male has rejected the reprimand and in fact is non-verbally telling the authority person to "go to hell." (66, p. 19)

In some cultures, youngsters may behave submissively while grumbling about the fact that they have to comply; in other cultures, grumbling would be a sign of severe disrespect (64).

Expressing Agreement and Disagreement   How do people communicate yes and no, agreement and disagreement, willingness and unwillingness, and so on?

> There is a marked tendency on the part of Westerners to feel that the meaning of head-nods are universal, up-and-down to mean "yes" and side-to-side to mean "no." . . . Hawaiians raise their eyebrows to say "yes," sometimes simultaneously jerking the head back slightly and lowering the corners of the mouth. (60, p. 4)

Physical Contact   Compared to European Americans, non-European Americans are more likely to touch each other in many different situations. Differences in this regard between European Americans and Haitian and Hawaiian Americans are evident:

Haitian children are very physical . . . we use our hands. . . . If a child wants to speak, instead of saying: "Hi, Johnny," he will touch the other child automatically. (68, p. 62)

Children will often simply lay a friendly hand on an adult they are trying to reach, rather than make a verbal approach. For Western teachers such touching on the part of Hawaiian youngsters can cause discomfort and is often not understood, leaving the teacher with a vague sensation of being pawed at or hung on, and the child with a feeling of having been ignored.

One part of the body not commonly touched by Hawaiians is the head, which is considered tabu throughout Polynesia. . . . By contrast, one of the few touching gestures which is natural and comfortable for Westerners is a friendly pat on the head or tousling a youngster's hair. . . . Although not on a conscious level Hawaiians react quite negatively to such behavior, with emotions ranging from a vague feeling of discomfort to resentment and anger and a feeling of physical violation. (60, p. 2)

Field-Sensitive and Field-Independent Students

Researchers often identify the characteristics we have described as either field sensitive (field dependent) or field independent. Here are some of the ways in which field-sensitive and field-independent students display different behavioral, relationship, communication, and learning styles:

Whether students rely more on internal clues—their own feelings, ideas, values, and the like—to understand the world around them (field independent) or on information from their surroundings (field dependent/sensitive)

Whether they prefer solitary activities, personal time, and more distant, aloof relationships (field independent) or are sociable, gregarious, and interested in helping people (field dependent/sensitive)

Whether they work better individually (field independent) or in groups (field dependent/sensitive)

Whether they are relatively indifferent to the feelings, ideas, opinions, attitudes, and so on, of others when they decide what to do or how to do it (field independent) or are sensitive to and responsive to what others feel and think and how their actions might affect others (field dependent/sensitive)

Whether they prefer to maintain considerable physical distance when they talk with others (field independent) or to be in close proximity to them (field dependent/sensitive)

Whether they are indifferent to praise and criticism from others (field independent) or react intensely to being praised and criticized (field dependent/sensitive)

FIELD INDEPENDENT	FIELD DEPENDENT
Internal cues	External cues
Solitary activities	Group activities
Indifferent to others' feelings and opinions	Sensitive to others' feelings and opinions
Considerable physical distance	Close proximity
Indifferent to praise and criticism	Responsive to praise and criticism
Competitive	Cooperative
Self-motivated	Seek feedback and guidance
Abstract, theoretical tasks	Humanized problems
Impersonal rewards	Personalized rewards

Whether they function better in competitive situations (field independent) or under cooperative conditions (field dependent/sensitive)

Whether they prefer to work independently (field independent) or seek feedback, guidance, and approval from others (field dependent/sensitive)

Whether they prefer abstract, theoretical tasks, such as math computational problems (field independent), or tasks that involve human issues and concerns, such as math word problems (field dependent/sensitive)

Whether they respond better to impersonal rewards like money, toys, candy, time off, and so on (field independent) or personal rewards such as praise, smiles, pats on the back, and the like (field dependent/sensitive) (73, 77–79, 85–90, 92, 93, 98, 99)

Although research indicates that these field-sensitive and field-independent learning and behavioral style differences exist among people, it's clear that no individual is completely field independent or field sensitive. People—and even an entire culture—may function in a predominantly field-sensitive or field-independent way, but still incorporate aspects of the opposite learning and behavioral styles.

Depending on the learning or behavioral style that predominates in their culture, some students may have learning styles that clash with their teachers' teaching styles. For example, research indicates that African American students tend to be field-dependent/sensitive learners. Some researchers (93, 97, 98) attribute this to their African roots. African Americans tend to rely on external cues and information when forming judgments, opinions, and so forth (81, 91, 94, 95). They also tend to be more people oriented, sensitive to others' feelings, gregarious, sociable, and interested in helping others (82, 84, 96). As an expression of this, they maintain less physical distance between themselves and others (71, 72). In addition, they are more sensitive to both praise and criticism than field-independent people (74, 80).

Although some individuals are put off by assertions that different ethnic groups have their own behavioral and learning styles, others are not. The following quotes typify this second position, beginning with a list of field-sensitive traits that Hale views as typical of African American students:

Is highly affective

Uses language requiring a wide use of many coined interjections (sometimes profanity)

Expresses herself or himself through considerable body language

Relies on words that depend upon context for meaning and that have little meaning in themselves

Prefers using expressions that have several connotations

Adopts a systematic use of nuances of intonation and body language such as eye movement and positioning

Prefers oral-aural modalities for learning communication

Is highly sensitive to others' nonverbal cues

Seeks to be people oriented

Is sociocentric

Uses internal cues for problem solving

Feels highly empathetic

Likes spontaneity

Adapts rapidly to novel stimuli (83, p. 38)

Is there a black learning style, a learning style especially suited to innercity students? I believe there is. Use of such a style does not mean lowering standards or expectations, however. It does mean recognizing the students' strengths and utilizing them. (75, p. 755)

Afro-Americans apparently attend to different facial cues, different emotional overtones, and receive different sets of information from people or words. This apparent greater people sensitivity suggests that field-dependency is the cognitive style orientation most often in use. (96, pp. 10–11)

Because many—if not most—teachers employ a field-independent teaching style and use primarily visual materials to teach, they unknowingly condemn many of their African American students to have learning and behavioral problems in school. (As we will see later in this chapter, the same applies to large numbers of Hispanic American students.) When students with one learning or behavioral style are taught by teachers who use a different teaching style, the students often have difficulty learning the material in the way it's presented and in conforming to their teachers' behavioral expectations. Like many students who aren't succeeding in school, they may feel stupid and lose their motivation to succeed in school and to conform to the classroom rules and regulations. This may help explain why teachers like and relate better to students whose learning styles match their teaching styles (76). Since the predominant teaching style in American schools is field independent,

African American, Hispanic American, and other field-dependent/sensitive students are the ones most at risk for problems resulting from a mismatch.

Ramirez and Castañeda have developed a behavior rating scale that is designed to evaluate whether students are field sensitive or field independent (92). Although the instrument was designed for use with Hispanic American students, it can be used to evaluate students from other ethnic groups. It is also a useful tool to examine gender stereotypes, since many, though not all, females prefer a field-sensitive learning style, whereas males tend to be more field independent (see chapter 6).

The scale also has items to evaluate whether teachers employ field-sensitive or field-independent teaching styles. By using both the teacher and student sections of this instrument, teachers can determine whether their style matches a particular student's characteristics. Here are some sample items from the Ramirez and Castañeda Behavior Rating Scale:

FIELD SENSITIVE	FIELD INDEPENDENT
	STUDENT
Likes to work with others to achieve a common goal	Prefers to work independently
Seeks guidance and demonstration from teacher	Likes to try new tasks without teacher's help
Is sensitive to feelings and opinions of others	Is task oriented; is inattentive to social environment when working
	TEACHER
Encourages cooperation and development of group feeling; encourages class to think and work as a unit	Encourages competition between individual students
Humanizes curriculum; attributes human characteristics to concepts and principles	Relies on graphs, charts, and formulas
Is sensitive to children who are having difficulty and need help	Encourages independent student achievement; emphasizes individual effort

Identifying Ethnically Diverse Students

Ramirez and Castañeda (92) have pointed out that diverse students have three options for resolving their cultural identity conflicts. They can maintain the values, beliefs, and practices of the home and reject the mainstream culture (traditional); they can reject the culture of the homeland and adopt the mainstream culture (assimilated); or they can identify with and accept both cultural systems and use each in appropriate situations (bicultural). Each choice has implications for classroom behavior and teaching.

Students who are assimilated or bicultural are still non-European Americans, but their learning and behavioral styles may parallel majority students. Thus, merely knowing a student's surname, ethnic background, skin color, and so on, isn't enough to determine whether she or he should be considered culturally different. The following process can help you determine whether cultural differences may be contributing to students' behavior problems.

Informal Assessment

Observe the students' behavior. Comparing your problem students' behavior to the typical ways nonassimilated youngsters of their cultures behave can help you pinpoint whether their problems are characteristic of students with their cultural backgrounds or are likely to be caused by other factors. If you aren't sure, answer the following questions about their behavior:

1. Do students socialize only with students from their same ethnic or social backgrounds, only with students from the mainstream culture, or with all types of students?

2. What language do bilingual students prefer to use when they aren't in class (at lunch, recess, after school): English only, another language, or a mixture of both?

3. Do students dress like mainstream students or in ways that identify them as members of a different group?

4. What do the statements students make about the mainstream culture and the culture of their homes reflect about their cultural identity? Do they express pride in their ethnic or racial background or reject it? Do they comment positively or negatively about the mainstream culture?

5. Do students' reactions to national and ethnic holidays indicate a bicultural identity or a preference for one type of holiday over the other?

6. Are the students' behavior problems typical of students with their cultural background?

Interview the Student   Ask students if any of the classroom procedures, routines, rules, or social patterns conflict with how they are used to doing things at home or in school. You can also ask students if they ever feel pressured in school to behave in ways that make them uncomfortable because they behave differently at home or in their neighborhoods.

Consult with Colleagues   If you aren't knowledgeable about your students' cultures, ask colleagues (other teachers, paraprofessionals, etc.) who are to observe the students and tell you whether they think cultural differences could be contributing to their behavior problems.

Formal Assessment

There are numerous formal assessment instruments for evaluating students' acculturation (100, 102, 103, 105–109, 111, 112). These instruments study the extent to which students are involved in their original culture and the European American culture by requiring them to respond to a series of questions about their friendships both in and out of school, the activities they engage in, their recreational habits, the language or languages they speak, their attitudes and values, the way they identify themselves, and so on. Typical items include:

- "What is the ethnic origin of your friends?" (Exclusively Hispanic, Vietnamese, or Chinese Americans; mostly Hispanic, Vietnamese, or Chinese Americans; both Hispanic, Vietnamese, or Chinese Americans and European Americans; mostly European Americans; exclusively European Americans)

- "How do you call yourself?" (Hispanic, Vietnamese, or Chinese; Hispanic, Vietnamese, or Chinese American; American)

- "What kind of music do you prefer to listen to?" (Hispanic, Vietnamese, or Chinese, or European American)

Some instruments also include questions about students' parents, such as their citizenship, the languages they speak, the kind of jobs they work at, the amount of education they have completed, and the number of children they have, because assimilated and non-assimilated families tend to differ along these lines. One instrument is based on a series of questions designed to determine whether the persons being assessed consider themselves to be "insiders" or "outsiders" in relation to the dominant culture (105).

The students' answers are then compared with those of a sample group of students from similar backgrounds, enabling educators to determine the extent to which students have remained traditional, become assimilated, or become bicultural and whether they are growing up in a home that is atraditional (assimilated), traditional, or bicultural.

Until recently, most experts viewed acculturation as a process of change along a continuum from unassimilated to highly assimilated (101–104, 106, 108, 110–112). Therefore, most instruments indicate students' acculturation along this continuum—the extent to which they are traditional, assimilated, or bicultural. Because these instruments yield a score that indicates students' general level of acculturation, they can easily be misinterpreted. We now realize that students and others do not assimilate at the same pace in all areas of their lives. Thus, an overall score can underestimate the extent of their assimilation in one area and overestimate their adaptation in another. As Mendoza and Martinez state,

> Some cultural traits tend to be assimilated more rapidly than others. Language usage, dress customs, and technological necessities, for instance, are generally incorporated much faster than abstract or less tangible qualities that involve values, sentiments, esthetic preferences, or attitudes on various socialization practices. (107, p. 73)

Despite the limitation of the instruments currently available, the information they provide can serve as a starting point for continued examination of the ways in which students deal with cultural incompatibilities. Most of the instruments currently available assess Hispanic Americans. However, they can be adapted, and translated if necessary, for use with other ethnic and language groups.

These formal and informal procedures will provide you with a place to begin. They will give you a general understanding of the degree to which students are assimilated. And they will help alert you to possible cultural differences. However, they cannot tell you if your students are characterized by a particular cultural trait—information that would help you choose the most effective educational approaches to use with them. This kind of detailed information comes from the way the individual students function in school.

Strategies for Dealing with Ethnic and Socioeconomic Differences

Most educators would probably agree that teachers should not treat students in a discriminatory manner. Most educators would likely agree that teachers should avoid perceiving behavior problems that do not exist, not noticing problems that do exist, misunderstanding the causes of students' behaviors, and using ineffective techniques to deal with behavior problems. However, there is considerable disagreement among educators about how teachers should handle the incompatibilities between students' culturally influenced disciplinary, relationship, and communication styles and those that prevail in most classrooms.

There are at least four different ways in which educators can resolve these incompatibilities. They can *accommodate* their methods to students' characteristics, help students to adjust to the approaches that are typically found in American schools (*assimilation*), assist students to become *bicultural*, or *empower* them to resolve the incompatibilities in their own ways. The section examines the arguments for and against each of these approaches.

Accommodation

Many educators believe that teachers must understand and treat their students as individuals in order to be successful classroom managers. Teachers need to know how students' religious beliefs, values, and customs, as well as their discipline, communication, and learning styles, affect their learning and behavior; how the trauma that many refugee students have experienced prior to arriving in the United States affects their behavior in school; how the problems that migrant students face (moving with their parents from job to job) affect their ability to succeed in school; how the economic problems of students living in poverty affect their learning and behavior; and so on.

They advise educators to adapt their management techniques to students' ethnic, socioeconomic, contextual, gender, and other individual characteristics to help them learn more efficiently, behave appropriately, and feel better about themselves. They believe that when there are mismatches between teachers' classroom management styles and their students' behavioral and disciplinary styles, teachers should adapt, or accommodate, their educational approaches to their students. They feel that students will be more accepting of their teachers' management approaches when they are managed in ways that are familiar to them. They caution that when students are exposed to unfamiliar and inappropriate classroom management techniques, they are more likely to reject their teachers' management approaches and less likely to change their behavior.

The arguments in favor of accommodation and the research that supports it appear throughout the text. For example, chapter 4 discusses how educators can accommodate their classroom management approaches to the contextual aspects of students' lives and the reasons why they should do this. The present chapter describes how educators can adapt their management techniques to the disciplinary, relationship, and communication styles of different ethnic and socioeconomic groups and the benefits that result. And chapter 6 presents the arguments for accommodating management approaches to gender differences.

Criticisms   Other educators have reservations about accommodating to ethnic and socioeconomic differences. Some of them believe that it is impractical. Others believe that even if accommodation were feasible, it is undesirable. Their reasons are discussed below.

There are no monolithic cultures in the United States.

Some individuals argue that even within such groups as Asian Pacific Americans, Hispanic Americans, and African Americans, people are so different that it is not possible to accommodate educational techniques to the cultural needs of any ethnic group. This point of view is presented in the following statement about Hispanic Americans, but it applies to other ethnic groups as well:

> Latin America is composed of developed industrialized countries such as Argentina and Chile and basically under-developed countries such as Bolivia, Honduras, Belize and Panama. Some countries have a strong European cosmopolitan influence, others have an American influence and others are still predominantly Indian. Some have high rates of illiteracy while others have well-developed educational systems which are as fine or better than those found in some states in the U.S. How then can we talk about a Hispanic culture in the U.S. when Hispanics come here from such diverse countries? (32, pp. 9–10)

Other educators grant that there is great variability among members of a particular ethnic group. But they claim that as important as these differences are, there are also many important similarities among the members. As a Hispanic American educator put it, "When I am with a group of fellow Latinos I'm conscious of our differences. Cubanos, Mexicanos, Puerto Riqueños, Colombianos, we are all different. Yet when I find myself among non-Latinos I realize how much alike we Latinos are" (32, p. 10).

As you will see throughout this text, research studies consistently reveal educationally relevant differences between different ethnic, socioeconomic, and regional groups. While these characteristics may not apply to all individuals in a particular group, they are common enough so that educators should be alert to the *possibility* that they may be applicable to an individual student or parent.

> *It is impossible to accommodate educational approaches to the needs of the many ethnic groups found in any particular school system or often within a particular classroom.*

Many people do not believe that educators can accommodate their methods and techniques to the different ethnic groups with whom they work. Some of their reasons are found in the following remarks by a teacher:

> My school district, the Los Angeles County School District, has over one hundred different language/culture groups. How can anyone be expected to know about all these different cultures, and how can anyone be expected to apply what they do know? . . . How can I teach my Anglo students one way, my Latino students a second way, my Vietnamese students a third, my Korean students a fourth way, my Hmong, my Portuguese, etc., at the same time? Impossible! (32, pp. 15–16)

Other educators believe that it is possible. They do not agree that each culture requires a unique educational approach. They point out that alternative methods of instructing students, organizing classrooms, and counseling parents are limited. For example, educators can encourage or require their students to work individually or in groups; they can motivate them through the use of competitive games or cooperative settings; they can allow them to work at their own pace or encourage them to work as quickly as possible; they can attempt to develop close personal relationships with them or maintain a "professional distance"; they can correct and criticize them in front of their peers or privately; they can encourage them to discuss controversial issues and express differences of opinion or emphasize similarities of experience and opinion; and they can teach abstract concepts or utilize methods that stress the concrete and learning by doing. Believing that educators are always choosing between alternatives as limited as these, proponents of accommodation contend that educators can easily adapt their methodology to the cultural needs of their students.

There is little research to support either position. We do not know how effective educators can be when they must accommodate their techniques simultaneously to many different groups in the same classroom (140).

> *It would not be a good idea for professionals involved in educating non-European American students to use misleading and even prejudicial descriptions of their cultures.*

Some people are concerned that when educators attempt to be culturally relevant, they often believe misleading and outdated stereotypes about their students' cultures and adapt their educational practices to these incorrect beliefs. Some teachers do accept outdated or fictionalized versions of their students' cultures and focus on the quaint or unusual aspects of their lifestyles. For example, some teachers may believe that their Native American students have lifestyles like those depicted in Hollywood westerns (124). However, this merely suggests that educators should take care to avoid such problems. It does not mean that they should not attempt to learn as much as they can about their students' cultural background.

Many educators are also concerned that educators will fall victim to prejudicial stereotypes of non-European American students. The following statement reflects their view: "I believe enough good research has been done to dismiss bigoted stereotypes. . . . I, personally, get very tired of having to defend my culture against the mythical themes of the 'hot blooded, lazy, Latin'" (32, p. 11).

As the following statements indicate, many other educators maintain that one of the most effective ways of combating such prejudice is to provide educators with accurate descriptions of the cultural characteristics of ethnic groups:

> Regardless of the benefits that may accrue from public institutions refusing to acknowledge, *in public*, general descriptions of ethnic traits, it is my conviction that this very refusal has fostered the continued use of incorrect and often unjust stereotypes about ethnic groups. (126, p. 10)

> To identify differences related to Afro-Americans is, of course, a controversial issue; regardless of the disclaimers, values of good or bad, inferior or superior, are so ingrained in our society that the issue will still lead to reinforcement of stereotypes. . . . However, if we are to engage in an educational revolution aimed at promoting the success of a larger percentage of the Afro-American population, it is an area that must be explored. (135, p. 238)

Cultural descriptions can lead to misleading overgeneralizations.

Some educators are concerned that teachers may think that their knowledge of the cultural characteristics of different ethnic groups and socioeconomic classes is sufficient for them to understand an individual student or parent. This concern is expressed in the following statement:

> There are many common stereotypes of the Hispanic person such as never being on time, being deeply religious, etc. Those who work with Hispanics should be aware of this and guard against a generalized, stereotyped view of those they work with. This is not to say that a specific stereotype (like being deeply religious) may not apply to an individual. Rather, the individual should always be dealt with as a unique human being who may or may not exhibit certain attitudes, habits, and beliefs.
>
> A list of over-general attributes which describe certain socioeconomic sub-groups of Hispanics such as the poor who may be more apt to have certain problems in school or the Indian who may be more apt to believe in La Llorona will not make educators more sensitive. Educators must recognize that children come to us from an infinitely varied array of backgrounds and not assume that all Hispanic students come from poor or Indian backgrounds. (32, p. 12)

The possibility of overgeneralization is an ever present danger. However, as the following statement indicates, many people nevertheless believe that educators should be aware of the cultural traits that may characterize their students:

> It is important for educators to be aware of our culture just so long as they refrain from thinking that we are all exactly alike. Just as knowing one Anglo would not enable a Hispanic to know all Anglos, so too knowing a few Hispanic students does not enable an

Accommodation: An Example of a Culturally Compatible Educational Approach

Hawaiian American students are often perceived as lazy and uninvolved by teachers who are unaware of the cultural incompatibilities that they experience in schools. In school, teachers constantly supervise students, set rules, make assignments, and regulate the classroom's resources. But at home, when a Hawaiian American parent wants something done, he or she tells the children to do it and lets them organize themselves and take care of it. When teachers act more like Hawaiian American parents by withdrawing their supervision and assuming that the students will act responsibly,

Hawaiian American students involve themselves in the classroom activities. The following approach has been used successfully to make the classroom routines more culturally compatible and involve Hawaiian American students in classroom activities:

- The teacher models a routine or task and explains the procedure.
- The teacher instructs the students to perform the desired task, then withdraws as quickly as possible from supervising the group.
- The teacher lets the group determine how the task will be done, who the leader will be, who will perform which aspects of the task, and so on.
- The teacher does not interfere to impose his or her own cultural values about such things as fair play, sharing the workload equally, and so on. (123)

Anglo educator to "know" all Hispanic students either as a group or individually. (32, p. 13)

To treat some students differently than others is discriminatory.

Some critics of accommodation argue that since all people are basically the same, they should be treated the same. Not to do so, in their opinion, is unfair and discriminatory.

Proponents of accommodation disagree. They acknowledge that human beings are basically the same; they prefer success to failure, praise and recognition to criticism or condemnation, and acceptance and attention to rejection and inattention. However, those who believe in accommodation maintain that people's behavior in these situations is influenced by different cultural veneers. They have different criteria for success. They find different forms of praise and recognition rewarding. They differ in terms of when, where, why, and how they are willing to accept criticism or condemnation. And they express acceptance and rejection in their own culturally influenced ways. Therefore, if teachers expect all individuals to behave the same way or are unaware that they are interpreting everyone's behavior from their culturally influenced point of view, they may fail to respond to the unique needs of many of their ethnic minority students.

In addition, the result of treating all students the same may be that those who do not fit the model used by their teachers are treated in a discriminatory manner: "When teachers ignore students' race and claim that they treat all children the same, they usually mean that their model of the ideal student is white and middle-class" (38, p. 54).

For example, Hilliard (121) suggests that educators who provide students the same instructional techniques, classroom management approaches, and so on, have the mistaken notion that they are treating their students equally and being fair to them. However,

Self-Quiz: Management Techniques and Student Characteristics

With which of the following ways of accommodating management techniques to students' behavioral characteristics would you feel comfortable?

- Being authoritarian with some students and authoritative with others
- Being tough with some students and lenient with others

- Using time-out as a negative consequence with some students, but not with others
- Recognizing some students' achievements, progress, and improvements publicly and those of others privately
- Using shame, guilt, corporal punishment, scolding, or peer pressure with students who are accustomed to such forms of discipline at home and in their communities

Do you agree that female educators should use less direct management techniques with those Hispanic males who are not accustomed to direct disciplinary approaches from females?

they are not treating all students the same, but are dealing with some students in a culturally appropriate manner and others in a biased manner. Hilliard suggests that there is a more valid way of treating students the same, which is to provide all students with culturally appropriate educational approaches. According to him, while this may make it appear that students are being treated differently, they are actually being treated the same and in a nondiscriminatory manner.

Treating groups of students differently can result in lower expectations and standards for some non-European American groups.

Anecdotal evidence that needs updating suggests that these are valid concerns (82, 99). In an attempt to be culturally relevant, some well-meaning educators do lower their standards for students. However, these teachers are not following the advice of educators who caution them to maintain realistic standards for non-European American students and not expect them to behave in an antisocial manner or to achieve less than others while they educate them in a culturally appropriate manner (126).

Assimilation

A great many educators believe that the best way to deal with cultural incompatibilities in students' learning styles, behavioral styles, and communication styles is for students to adopt the school's European American culture. Here are the reasons they typically cite for believing that assimilation should be the ultimate goal.

Students will learn more effectively if they adapt to the learning and behavioral styles that prevail in schools.

Many educators believe that for non-European students to actualize their potential in school, "they must aspire to enter the middle class, adopt the middle-class lifestyle, and use the middle-class value standard as a reference to judge their own behavior" (139, p. 20). There is little evidence to support this hypothesis. In fact, there is evidence that among some non-European groups, those who are most likely to be well adjusted and to succeed in school are not those who reject their ethnic identity, but those who identify with their own ethnic group (115–117, 123, 125, 128, 129, 133, 137, 139, 142, 143, 145). The reasons for this have not been well studied, but here are some possible explanations:

- Students who have not assimilated bring the positive aspects of their cultures to the educational situation.

- Students who assimilate may substitute the poor attitudes toward school that characterize many European American students for the positive attitudes that prevail in their original culture.

- Students who maintain their cultural identity have more self-esteem and self-confidence than those who reject their cultural background.

- Compared to monocultural students, bicultural students have a larger repertoire of learning strategies and coping techniques to apply to the tasks and challenges of school.

- Assimilated students may experience conflicts with their parents as well as identity conflicts, resentment, anger, and rebelliousness, all of which can interfere with students' learning.

Schools should not accommodate their expectations and approaches to those of disadvantaged or inferior non-European American cultures.

Some educators believe that schools should not accommodate to the cultural needs of non-European American students because the European American culture is superior to other cultures. Instead they should encourage non-European American students and their parents to give up those cultural characteristics that have held back the progress of their native countries or ethnic groups.

The idea that some cultures, especially the African American, Hispanic American, and Native American cultures, are inferior, deprived, or disadvantaged has almost no support in the research literature (146–166). Students from so-called disadvantaged cultures have different, not inferior, language skills and experiences. They do not have poor self-concepts or low aspirations when they begin school. Research indicates that poverty, prejudice, culturally inappropriate educational approaches, and lack of financial support to schools that serve so-called disadvantaged students account for most of the differences in school outcomes among different ethnic groups.

Non-European American students and their families should adapt to the mainstream culture in the schools because people living in the same country should all speak the same language, follow the same laws, and share the same morality.

This idea is embodied in the following statements:

We cannot survive as a culture with different laws for different people. Everyone must pay taxes, serve in the army, respect private property and the rights of others regardless of where they were born or what religion they profess. (32, p. 13)

Pluralism in our society has produced a moral climate that tells everyone to establish a sense of what is right and wrong *for you*. This trend has a way of blurring the limits of a moral code. In the educational arena this trend has produced a no-fault morality and relativistic values. . . . Schools, if they are to survive, must protect and articulate moral standards, ethical behavior, and historical principles of social cohesion. It is their function to teach the common beliefs that unite us as a free nation. (141, pp. 15–16)

These concerns are based on the incorrect assumption that persons who favor pluralistic approaches believe in complete cultural relativism. Pluralists typically recommend that diversity should be balanced against higher and universal values (120, 131, 132, 138). Two examples of this position follow:

Because each cultural group proceeds from a different context, we can never reach total agreement on the "best" or most appropriate ways in which to lead our lives. . . .

Nevertheless, it should also be stressed that above and beyond all cultures there are human and civil rights that need to be valued and maintained by all people. These rights guarantee that all human beings are treated with dignity, respect, and equality. Sometimes the values and behaviors of a group so seriously challenge these values that we are faced with a dilemma to reject it or to affirm the diversity it represents. If the values we as human beings hold most dear are ultimately based on extending rights rather than negating them, we must decide on the side of those more universal values. (131, pp. 278–279)

I believe in a form of cultural pluralism in which universal and particularistic values would be dialectically balanced against each other. In particular, I believe that the universal values of equality, freedom, and democracy, which are among the most important values that have been promulgated under the concept of common school, should be balanced against the particularistic values associated with the maintenance of cultural diversity. But the freedom of an individual must be restrained to the extent that it imposes detrimentally on the freedom of others. Unfortunately, this two-sided nature of cultural pluralism is rarely underlined and, as a consequence, it is sometimes misunderstood as licence for runaway ethnicity, rather than as a way of avoiding such ethnocentric behavior. (138, pp. 300–301)

The contention that accommodating to cultural differences in the classroom necessarily leads to two or more national languages and different laws for different cultural groups is also incorrect. Instructing students in their native languages while they learn English, permitting them to work at their own pace, developing the kinds of interpersonal relationships with them that make them feel comfortable, allowing them to choose whether to behave competitively or cooperatively, and so on, does not necessarily lead to adopting two or more national languages, moral codes, or sets of laws.

Adapting educational approaches to students' cultural characteristics does not prepare them to function effectively in the mainstream European American–dominated society.

Educators who support this position argue that the real world is not nearly as tolerant or as flexible as some educators would like it to be. They maintain that because employers and others require individuals to conform to mainstream expectations and norms, accommodating to students' culturally influenced behavior patterns, learning styles, communication styles, concepts of punctuality, and so on, dooms them to be uncompetitive and disadvantaged in the real world.

There is some truth to this concern. Americans do live in an imperfect society. Despite federal and state laws against discrimination, too many people with supervisory and administrative power continue to expect and insist that those over whom they have influence conform to their culturally determined standards. However, does that mean that educators should prepare their students to acquiesce to the prejudicial attitudes of these individuals? Who has the right to decide whether students should be encouraged and helped to submit to such abuse or to fight it: the teachers or the students themselves? (See the section on empowerment.)

Criticisms   Critics of the assimilation position offer the following reasons for preferring alternative solutions to cultural incompatibilities (113, 114, 118, 119, 127, 130, 144):

- Many students do not want to replace their values, attitudes, learning and behavioral styles, and so on, with those of the European American middle class. Requiring them to do so can cause them to become angry, resentful, suspicious, and rebellious and to tune out their teachers or drop out of school.

- If students believe that their culture is inferior and that they should change their culturally determined ways of functioning, they may suffer a loss of self-esteem and self-confidence.

- Even if students want to change, it is no easy task to change one's lifestyle and values. Thus, Longstreet maintains,

   There is a limited capability within each of us to modify the ethnic traits we absorb as children. We may change our accent or the way we smile but we cannot, intellectually or emotionally, change the multitude of traits that would have to be altered to change our basic ethnicity. (126, p. 20)

- Even if students succeed in changing, their efforts can create serious problems and unwanted side effects. When non-European American students act in ways that are less natural to them than to European American middle-class students, who were brought up from their earliest years to behave in these ways, they can become tense and nervous. And they may experience the guilt, shame, and anxiety that often results from rejecting one's culture.

- Students may experience identity conflicts if they are exposed to conflicting pressure from home and community and the schools.

- Students who assimilate may suffer the loss of friendship and outright hostility from peers who accuse them of trying to be "coconuts, oreos, or bananas" (brown, black, or yellow on the outside and white on the inside). This is especially likely to happen if there is movement within the students' culture toward increasing the group's cultural pride or if there is a history of conflict and oppression between the students' ethnic group and the European American power structure.

   An African American high school student who lived in a poor neighborhood and attended a predominantly white middle-class preparatory school described the experience this way:

   When trying to live in two different worlds, one is in peril of not belonging to either of them. . . . Being put in a position of changing one's character every morning and afternoon to adapt to two different worlds endangers one's identity. (130, p. 337)

Assimilation: An Example of a Less Stressful Approach to Changing Students

Papago parents teach their children through nonverbal means, such as modeling and gesturing and economical speech. In school, children are expected to be verbal. At home and in their community, Papago children enjoy considerable autonomy. They are not rebuked by adults for interfering with their work or conversations, nor are they forced to bow to the wishes of their elders. Because children are raised with few limitations on their freedom, they are not accustomed to being controlled, reprimanded, or punished by adults. In school, Papago children are expected to conform to many rules and procedures, and they are exposed to punitive consequences if they do not.

Papago preschool teachers whose goal was to prepare Native American students to transit to European American schools did so without creating undue stress for them. For example, the teachers respected and accepted the students' desire not to participate and recite in class. They allowed children to learn by doing and by observing how their teachers did things. However, they also explained how things should be done. They combined phys-ical activities with verbal activities, such as dancing and singing simultaneously. And they exposed them to the behavior that would eventually be required of them by presenting them with activities designed to entice them into improving their verbal skills and self-assertive classroom participatory behavior.

Teachers taught students to conform to school rules and procedures. But because students were unaccustomed to so many limitations on their freedom, teachers did not use consequences to enforce rules. Instead, they repeatedly reminded students what was expected of them and patiently waited for them to conform. In these ways, teachers helped students to gradually adjust to the school's culture without unduly confronting the culturally determined learning and behavioral styles that these students brought with them to school. Here is how Macias describes the teachers' approach:

> Teachers continuously present their students with experiences which are typical of mainstream education and which necessitate the child's adjustment to culturally different ways of behaving and learning. Yet, of most importance, these same teachers act to mitigate the discontinuity of the necessary preschool experiences and ensure that the child's appreciation of his own culture is not eroded. (127, p. 378)

- There is little reason to assume that assimilation can work. It has been tried for years with very little success. This concern was expressed quite some time ago by one of the pioneers in the field of multicultural education:

> Schools' past efforts to acculturate culturally different children have failed miserably. These children as a whole are still not being educated, and the school system cannot continue to ignore its ethical, legal, moral, and professional responsibilities to accommodate children as they are. It is highly presumptuous for any school system to assume the responsibilities of acculturating children when the potential emotional consequences of forced acculturation are so pernicious. If most educators realized the way in which they risk the mental health of culturally different children by insisting on acculturating them, they would look more favorably on their potential role in developing a culturally pluralistic society. (114, p. 555)

Biculturalism

Since the 1970s, some educators have been rejecting both accommodation and assimilation (92, 134). They disagree that the school's way is best. They do not think that schools can accommodate to an unlimited number of cultural differences. And they do not believe that non-European American students should be required to choose between the ways of their family and the way school officials expect them to function. They propose a third alternative—biculturalism. Instead of having to choose between maintaining the values, beliefs, and practices of the home while rejecting the mainstream culture of the schools or rejecting the culture of their home while adopting the school culture, students can identify with and accept both cultural systems and use each in appropriate situations.

There are two different bicultural approaches. Some educators who favor biculturalism believe that while neither the school's culture nor the students' culture is superior, the school's culture is more appropriate in school and the students' culture is more appropriate at home and in their neighborhoods. Thus, they recommend that teachers prepare students to function one way at home and another way at school. Other educators view biculturalism as a process of mutual accommodation. They maintain that teachers should expect students to adjust to only some of their procedures while they also accommodate to some aspects of their students' culture. Proponents of this form of biculturalism do not believe that students must leave all of their cultural characteristics at the school door—only those that conflict with the effective operation of the educational process (131, 134).

Nieto's conception of biculturalism is an example of this second approach:

> Mutual accommodation means accepting and building on students' language and culture as legitimate expressions of intelligence and as the basis for their academic success. On the part of students and families, it means accepting the culture of the school in such areas as expectations about attendance and homework and learning the necessary skills for work in school. (131, p. 259)

Proponents of mutual accommodation believe that both school and students are enriched by it. Teachers expand their repertoires of instruction and classroom management techniques. And bicultural students acquire a second way to react to challenges and tasks. Thus, they are able to adapt their approaches to the requirements of the situation (e.g., being cooperative or competitive, assertive or nonassertive, as needed).

In actual practice, this second approach to biculturalism is different from the first only in the degree to which teachers accommodate to students' cultural characteristics or require students to adjust to the school's culture. It does allow for some accommodation on the part of the school. However, it still requires students and their parents to acknowledge that the school's way is necessary if not superior in some areas.

Criticisms   Some educators see problems associated with both of these bicultural approaches. They do not believe that either one is as fair as it appears at first glance. They ask why only one cultural perspective has to predominate at all in schools that serve a pluralistic society and why the European American way should be the accepted way in school. They assert that although teachers may think that they are communicating to students that neither the school's way nor their home's way is more desirable, by stating that the European American way is best for even some school situations, they are communicating that it is generally the better way. Critics also maintain that both bicultural approaches can place students in conflict situations if students' parents and friends do not believe that there should be only one cultural perspective in school or that the European American way is the best approach in any areas of the educational setting.

Empowerment

Some educators believe that the accommodation, assimilation, and bicultural models create problems for students because they are too teacher directed. They prefer to empower students to choose how to resolve their cultural conflicts (136). This approach involves exposing students to the fact that there are various ways they may function, educating them about the possible advantages and disadvantages of each way, and helping them to select the solution that they themselves favor.

Criticisms   Many educators who appreciate the good intentions of those who wish to empower students to make important decisions for themselves question whether the approach can work. They doubt that teachers can be neutral and impartial regarding students' choices, especially when the values involved are important to them. They wonder whether teachers can avoid communicating their preferences to students. And they ask if teachers can accept students' choices that interfere with the smooth progress of their class or the rights of others.

Critics of the empowerment approach are also skeptical about students' abilities to make reasonable choices. They point out that until students reach adolescence, they are not mature enough to evaluate the alternatives from which they must choose. Critics also worry about the results of allowing even the best prepared students to choose for themselves. They find it difficult to believe that students who are relative strangers to the United States can appreciate the ramifications of different alternatives. They ask whether adolescents can project themselves into the future and imagine how employers might react if, as a result of choosing to remain true to their cultural backgrounds, they were unable or unwilling to engage in competitive behavior, to work at the same pace as others, to acknowledge their mistakes and errors, to discuss difficult interpersonal issues without a mediator, to accept public criticism, and so on.

Critics also point out that the empowerment approach may have only a limited positive effect on students' identity problems. It may assist teachers to avoid placing students in conflict situations by not pressuring them to choose one culture over another. However, it will not help students avoid identity conflicts if the choices they make conflict with those that their parents or peers prefer.

Individual Differences Among Educators

In actual practice, educators do not use the same approach with each and every case of cultural incompatibility that occurs in their classes. Their response to each situation depends on such factors as the importance they place on the particular cultural incompatibility or issue involved, the effect that their students' behavior has on the classroom environment, and the attitude of the students or their parents toward the particular cultural trait. For example, most educators would probably be willing to accommodate their approaches to students who feel uncomfortable in competitive situations or who prefer to work independently rather than in groups. These culturally influenced styles do not seriously impede the progress of the group as a whole.

Educators may be a little less likely to accommodate students who work at a slow pace, request a great deal of feedback and direction, express their needs only in extremely subtle, indirect ways, or resist admitting that they don't know or understand something. These culturally influenced styles do not impede the progress of the group, but they do require extra work and sensitivity on the teacher's part. Educators are probably least likely to accommodate to students who prefer to settle their differences by fighting or who think it is better to be assertive and aggressive than compliant and conforming. These behaviors seriously interfere with the rights of others and tend to impede teachers' ability to manage the class.

Some educators may be less willing to accommodate cultural differences that go against their deeply held beliefs. Educators who prefer students to function in androgynous rather than gender-stereotypical ways may be reluctant to empower students to choose their own solutions to cultural conflicts when the students' culture encourages males to act like men and females to be ladies.

Educators may refrain from encouraging the children of Hispanic migrant workers to function biculturally if they and their parents do not plan to stay in the United States. They may also avoid attempting the assimilation and bicultural approaches with African American and Native American students who do not believe that European American values and lifestyles are desirable:

> Historically, American Indians have resisted acculturation and assimilation more than any other ethnic group. What this means is that by retaining traditional values and beliefs that are important to them, a natural conflict is set up in the classroom that must be handled by children of a very sensitive age. (122, pp. 45–46)

Hispanic American Students: An Example

Space does not permit us to discuss all the various ethnic groups represented in American schools today. The discussion that follows of the Hispanic American culture is offered as an example of how information about students' ethnic and contextual characteristics can help educators do a better job of adapting techniques to their students' cultural characteristics. Although not all Hispanic American students are alike, and what is true for some Hispanic American students isn't true of all Hispanic American students, this section offers suggestions for helping Hispanic American students whose behavior problems are caused by culture shock, the frustration of being taught in a foreign language or in an

Self-Quiz: Critical Incidents

This self-quiz is designed to provide you with some insight into the approaches you might use to resolve acculturation issues. First describe how you think the teacher involved should handle each of the following critical incidents. Then disregard the teacher's point of view. Instead, put yourself in the teacher's place; imagine what your own viewpoint would be; and state how you would deal with the problem. Then decide which of the following alternatives best describes each of your solutions: assimilation, accommodation, biculturalism, or empowerment. If you prefer a number of different approaches to the incidents, try to determine the factors that led you to select the particular approaches you would use in each critical incident.

1. A second-grade Filipino American student who has been brought up to respect and depend on adult authority figures appears to be unable or unwilling to make choices such as selecting a book to bring home from the school library, choosing a partner, and selecting which learning center to work at during free time without her teacher's guidance. The teacher feels that one of the educator's roles is to help young children learn to function more independently.
2. A parent who is representing the parents of all four of the Chinese American students in a third-grade class asks the teacher not to require their children to express their opinions in class because they are in school to learn what the teacher knows. He tells the teacher that Chinese Americans believe that children should be taught to respect the knowledge and opinions of adults. And, he adds, it is not a good idea for children to discuss their personal views of things about which they have little knowledge. The teacher believes that students should be participants in the learning process, not merely banks into which teachers deposit information. The teacher also thinks that presenting problems and having students share their opinions about them is an effective technique for developing students' critical thinking skills.
3. After hearing a seventh-grade student tell his classmate that he would "get him" after school for what he said about his mother, the teacher tells the two students that they should settle their arguments without fighting. The teacher reminds them that fighting is against the rules and warns them that if they fight after school, they will get into trouble. The student who did the threatening answers that his parents expect him to stand up for himself, especially when someone says something derogatory about his family.
4. An eighth-grade student in a predominantly poor neighborhood complains that her teacher is too tough on her. She accuses the teacher of being insensitive to the students in the class because the teacher gives them too much homework. And she insists that as long as she does okay on tests, she should not be marked down every time she does not complete an assignment, because she has to work after school to earn money for the family. Although the teacher realizes that the student is telling the truth, the teacher also feels that teachers in urban schools should expect as much from their students as teachers in more affluent suburban schools. In the teacher's opinion, to expect less of students is to condemn them to life as second-class citizens.
5. An African American 10th-grade male in a predominantly poor neighborhood tells his teacher in no uncertain terms to get off his case and stop telling him about the value of a high school diploma. He insists that a high school diploma does not help African Americans. The teacher tells the student that he is wrong. The next day the student brings in some articles that confirm that African American males who graduate high school do not earn significantly more than those who do not graduate.

unfamiliar teaching style, culturally influenced differences in readiness skills, identity conflicts, and a history of unequal cross-cultural relationships. The section lists cultural traits that research indicates are more likely to characterize Hispanic American students than non-Hispanic American students and makes suggestions for when and how to adapt classroom management techniques to these cultural differences. It also describes some typical ways that educators misperceive the behavior of their Hispanic American students.

The material included in this section is based on a variety of published sources (5, 32, 34, 44, 69, 71, 73, 77, 85, 88, 90, 92, 93, 167–193). The quoted excerpts are edited statements from the literature about the education of Hispanic American students. In a national survey, approximately 400 Hispanic American educators, counselors, and psychologists as well as non-Hispanic American professionals with considerable experience working with Hispanic American students agreed with both the quotations about Hispanic American cultural characteristics and the quotations that followed them on how to help Hispanic American students cope with the acculturation process in school (32).

Culture Shock

Since Hispanic students are used to foods, music, holidays, language, and customs which are very different from what Anglos are accustomed to, Hispanic students may have difficulty relating to the Anglo-oriented classroom. . . . Students from families with low incomes may suffer cultural shock in school because of the differences between what is available to them at home, where they may have to wear out, make do, or do without, and what is provided by the school system. These differences may do harm to these students' self-concepts and make it difficult for these students to adjust to school. (32, pp. 69, 70, 74)

Educators should take pains to reduce or eliminate those aspects of their classroom environment, teaching materials, and teaching techniques which might cause cultural shock. They should make the classroom culturally relevant to these students so as to ease their entrance into the world of school. (32, p. 70)

Language and Teaching Style

The two excerpts that follow relate to language—how Hispanic American students relate to their native language and what they need to do well in schools:

Many Hispanic parents have considerable pride in being both Latin and belonging to "La Raza." This pride is often expressed in attempts to maintain the use of the Spanish language at home and in the community even after many years of residence in the United States. Some Hispanic parents may have not acquired enough English to speak to their children in English because of not having lived in the United States for enough time or because of having lived in a neighborhood-barrio where English fluency was unnecessary. As a result, some Hispanic students are not fluent enough in English when they start school to profit from instruction in arithmetic, science, social studies, etc., when the language of instruction is English. Immersing them in a completely English program may cause them to fall behind their English-speaking peers in these subject areas and make it difficult for them to adjust to school. (32, pp. 59–60)

Research indicates that bilingual education helps students learn a second language more efficiently.

Therefore, such limited English proficient students should receive a bilingual education. They should be taught such subjects as math, science, etc. in Spanish while they are being helped to become proficient enough in English to profit from English language instruction in these subject areas. (32, p. 61)

Cultures, through their members, have characteristic ways of passing on information and skill. Educators who know about and use a teaching style that "speaks to" how their diverse students usually learn in their home culture are likely to be successful with these students:

The Hispanic culture emphasizes learning by doing. As a result, some Hispanic students learn more by touching, seeing, manipulating, and experiencing concrete objects than by discussing or reading about ideas. Therefore, educators should deemphasize the lecture approach and emphasize direct experiences with these Hispanic students. (32, p. 57)

Readiness Skills

Prior to their entrance into school, Hispanic students may be exposed to the richness of the Hispanic culture at home rather than to the many cultural concepts that are expected and valued by the Anglo school system. Therefore, educators should adapt their curriculum and instruction techniques to the knowledge and experiences Hispanic students bring to school. This will prevent them from being educationally behind as soon as they enter the school system. (32, p. 67)

Unequal Cross-Cultural Relationships

History, geography, social roles, etc. are often studied exclusively in terms of the Anglo point of view. Too often, students are taught that Columbus rather than the Native Americans discovered America, that Ponce de Leon was a fool who was looking for a fountain of youth, and that Latin Americans are lazy procrastinators who live in small underdeveloped pueblos. . . . When their foods are not mentioned during discussions of what are good foods to eat in order to have a balanced diet, their music is not played during assemblies and music appreciation classes, etc., Hispanic students may feel that they and their culture are inferior in the eyes of their teachers. (32, pp. 73–74)

Therefore, educators should include the Hispanic contribution in the curriculum, correct inaccurate and prejudicial stereotypes of Hispanics, and include as much of the Hispanic foods, music, language, values, etc. as possible in the daily curriculum. And they should act as advocates for Hispanic students when they are confronted by discrimination. (32, p. 75)

Interpersonal Relationships

Each culture has characteristic patterns for all relationships that set the tone and possibly content. Information about these patterns will help you realize "where your students are coming from." The following excerpts describe children's usual relationship with adults in Hispanic American cultures:

Hispanic children tend to have formal respectful relationships with adults. As a result, they may be uncomfortable with the less formal relationships usually observed between Anglo teachers and Anglo students. Therefore, educators should not attempt to develop informal relationships with their Hispanic students who are not comfortable with such relationships. However, they should also explain to them that although formal relationships may be appropriate at home, a less formal relationship is more typical of the classroom. (32, pp. 98–100)

Hispanic children are brought up to look up to their elders, especially their parents, and respect their wishes, opinions, attitudes, and advice and to model themselves after adults whom they like. As a result, they may function better when adults are involved and supportive and provide encouragement and feedback about how they are doing. Hispanic parents tend to discourage their children from showing too much initiative or independence or expressing their own ideas and opinions without consulting their elders first. They are much more likely than Anglo children to ask their parents and other adults for their advice and suggestions when they have to make important decisions. As a result some Hispanic students may have difficulty when educators want them to form their own opinions and make their own decisions independently of their teachers. Therefore, educators should try to encourage these students to be less dependent on the opinions and approval of adults so that they can begin to learn to function more independently. However, until they are able to do so, educators should provide these students with the guidance and approval they need in order to make decisions in the classroom and the encouragement and feedback about how they are doing they require in order to work effectively. (32, pp. 45–48)

Because the Hispanic culture tends to be patriarchal, some Hispanic male students, especially adolescents, may have difficulty complying with female authority figures. Therefore, female educators should stress nonauthoritarian methods such as requesting rather than ordering for managing the classroom behavior of these Hispanic male students. (32, pp. 104–105)

How does the individual relate to a group? This is a key question because the answer will explain and even help predict students' classroom behavior:

Hispanic children are brought up to believe in the importance of the extended family; to sacrifice their own desires for the good of the family; and to expect that the family will support and aid them when they are in need. This upbringing tends to make Hispanic students more cooperative and group oriented than other students. As a result, Hispanic students may allow other students to copy their homework or their answers on examinations in order to show their helpfulness, brotherhood, and generosity. They may not consider this to be bad behavior. (32, pp. 80–81)

Educators should explain that while working on homework assignments together and helping each other when they are being evaluated may be acceptable in some cultures, it is not acceptable in the school system they are attending. (32, p. 83)

Hispanics tend to believe that it is bad manners to try to excel over others in the group or to attempt to be recognized for their individual achievement. As a result, many Hispanic students will avoid competing with their peers for fear of being criticized or rejected by them. . . . Because of their belief that it is bad manners to try to excel over others, some Hispanic students may not volunteer answers or they may even pretend not to know the correct answer when called upon. (32, pp. 84–86)

Educators should deemphasize competition and stress cooperation when attempting to motivate some Hispanic students. They should praise and reward students for cooperative behavior as much as for individual achievement. They should also be sensitive to the needs of those Hispanic students who prefer not to be singled out in front of the group and recognize their achievements in a less public manner. One way of doing this would be to communicate their praise to their students' families. (32, pp. 85–86)

Hispanic boys are taught to be protective of their sisters and other girls, escorting them to and from school, protecting them from other boys, handling their money, etc.; Hispanic girls are encouraged to assume a submissive role toward brothers and other boys. As a result, both sexes may feel uncomfortable when they are required to work and play together as equals. They may prefer to work in school in groups of their own sex and feel uncomfortable when well-meaning egalitarian nonsexist Anglo educators require that the sexes work or engage in athletic activities together. However, despite their discomfort, educators should require that the sexes work and play together in class. (32, pp. 111–112)

Communication Style

Our usual way of communicating seems so natural that it's hard to realize that, in fact, it has particular rules and values that are not shared by all cultures. European Americans tend to be direct and straightforward and to value this approach. Other cultures favor indirectness:

Anglos are taught to value openness, frankness, and directness. They are much more likely to express themselves simply, briefly, and frequently bluntly. The traditional Hispanic approach requires the use of much diplomacy and tactfulness when communicating with another individual. . . . Hispanics often find themselves in difficulty if they disagree with an Anglo's point of view. To them, direct argument or contradiction appears rude and disrespectful. On the surface they may seem agreeable, manners dictating that they do not reveal their genuine opinion openly unless they can take time to tactfully differ. . . . Hispanics are less likely to state their unwillingness to do what others ask or expect from them. This is especially true of children and adolescents who are taught to respect their elders. Therefore, educators should not assume that because Hispanic students have verbally acquiesced to their expectations or demands, they either agree with them or plan to carry them out. Instead, educators should take into consideration the vast array of nonverbal communications that some Hispanic students use to express their disinclination or disagreement. (32, pp. 91, 93, 131)

What does one express, and what does one keep to oneself? The answer very much depends on where one is born and grows up:

Hispanics are less likely to verbally acknowledge responsibility for mistakes and errors or to apologize when they have wronged someone. Instead of blaming themselves for errors, they frequently attribute it to adverse circumstances. . . . Educators should not assume that Hispanic students who do not "own up" to their errors, mistakes, and wrongdoings are either unaware of them or too rebellious and recalcitrant to admit them and apologize for them. They should not shame Hispanic students by requiring them to make verbal acknowledgements of their mistakes and wrongdoings in ways which are culturally unacceptable to them. (32, pp. 114–116)

Hispanics, especially males, also tend not to admit to not knowing something or being unable to do something. Therefore, educators should not assume that Hispanic students who have not said that they do not understand something or cannot do something or have not asked for help actually understand their lessons and can do their assignments without help. Rather, educators should be sensitive to the subtle clues which indicate that they are in need. (32, pp. 115–116)

Warmth, affection, and touching are more acceptable in some cultures than others:

Hispanics tend to show affection and acceptance through touching. Friends are likely to kiss when they meet. Males are likely to hug each other or pat each other on the back as well as shake hands. And it is not unusual for people to hold others by the arm or place their hands on their shoulders when conversing. Therefore, educators should utilize physical contact when expressing approval and acceptance of their Hispanic students, especially the young ones. (32, p. 97)

How do people usually act in groups? What are the ways in which groups function? The answers to these questions will help you understand why your students behave as they do:

In the Hispanic culture it is not impolite for more than one person to speak at a time during group discussions. Multiple conversations may be carried out simultaneously without anyone being considered rude or discourteous. However, despite this, educators should explain to Hispanic speakers that while it may be all right for more than one person to speak at a time at home, in school students are expected to wait their turn before speaking. (32, p. 100)

When a group of Hispanics disagree, they may resolve the issue by continuing to discuss it until it becomes apparent that a consensus has been reached without polling the group or calling for a vote. Therefore, when working with groups of Hispanic students, educators should allow them to arrive at a consensus in whatever manner is most comfortable for them. Educators should not insist that decisions be made by voting. (32, pp. 100–101)

Time

Does the student's home culture stress the present or the future? Emphasis on either has an effect on school, which tends to be future oriented:

Hispanics tend to be more present time oriented. Finishing a conversation now may be more important than keeping an appointment later. Living to the fullest now and enjoying what the present has to offer may be more important than saving, planning, and striving for future satisfactions and security. The anticipation of a large reward or satisfaction in the future may be much less motivating than a smaller satisfaction in the here and now. Therefore, educators should provide immediate feedback, approval, recognition, and reward to Hispanic students. (32, pp. 50–52)

The pace at which people work is also influenced by culture and even by location:

Hispanics tend to be more concerned with doing a job well, regardless of the amount of time required, than they are in finishing rapidly so they will have more time for the next task. They tend to prefer to work at a relaxed pace even if it means taking longer to finish something. At home, Hispanic children are permitted to do things at their own pace without adhering to strict time schedules. As a result, Hispanic students may not complete classroom work as fast as their Anglo peers. When required to rush or stop working before they have finished in order to begin the next task with their peers, they may become anxious, nervous, rebellious, etc. . . . Therefore, educators should not rush Hispanic students when they are called on to answer questions in class. However, they should not allow Hispanic students to spend as much time as necessary to complete class assignments. Instead they should help such students adjust to the time orientation which they encounter in school and which will govern their lives in the dominant culture. This should include helping them to adjust to the pressures of time limits. (32, pp. 52–54)

Ideas about time include what being "on time" means. This simple-sounding concept can have quite different meanings:

The Hispanic concept of punctuality is different than the Anglo concept. If a meeting is called for two o'clock, people are expected to arrive sometime after that. If a party or dance is set for nine o'clock, people may be expected to arrive at eleven or even later.

An agreement to repair a TV for Wednesday means that it will probably be ready sometime after Wednesday. Because of this, educators should inform Hispanic students that although the Hispanic concept of punctuality is fine for their homes and community, in school and other similar situations it would be best if they adapted to the dominant culture's expectations of punctuality. (32, pp. 54–55)

Discipline

Children are taught and disciplined according to patterns in their culture. An effective form of discipline for some youngsters, therefore, may backfire with students from another culture:

Some Hispanic parents tend to use physical punishment rather than deprivation of love and affection when disciplining their children. Moreover, once they have punished their children, they tend to forgive them rather than to remain angry, resentful, or to hold a grudge. . . . Therefore, educators should not use deprivation of affection to manage Hispanic students. (32, pp. 101–102)

Hispanics tend to be more interested in and dependent on the approval of others than Anglos who are more likely to be receptive to more impersonal and materialistic forms of recognition. . . . Therefore, educators should stress the fact that Hispanic students' families will be proud of them and share the honor of their accomplishments. And they should use praise, hugs, pats on the back, and other personal rewards with Hispanic students more than checks, gold stars, and materialistic forms of reinforcement such as sweets and toys. (32, pp. 37, 40)

Hispanic students may be much more willing and able to accept criticism, direction, and discipline from educators with whom they have a close personal relationship. Therefore, educators should not maintain an impersonal, objective, aloof, or distant relationship with Hispanic students. (32, p. 94)

Role of Education

Hispanics place a high value on education. However, Hispanic children also have a very active role to play in the family. They may be responsible for helping to take care of the younger children and may have many chores to do. When their parents do not speak English, they may be required to serve as translators when the adults have to meet with doctors, agencies, businessmen, etc. When these responsibilities interfere with the students' attendance at school or homework and study time, Hispanics tend to view the students' responsibilities to the family as more important than their responsibility to the school. . . . Therefore, when Hispanic students miss school or come unprepared, educators should determine when conflicting family responsibilities are the cause and accommodate their expectations and teaching methods to the students' and parents' realities. They should not lower course grades or punish Hispanic students in other ways when family responsibilities prevent them from completing assignments, arriving on time, or attending class. Nor should they pressure students to choose between their responsibilities to their families and the school by insisting that they attend school and complete assignments even when family responsibilities interfere. However, they should talk with the Hispanic parents and try to help them to shift their priorities somewhat so that the students' responsibilities at home do not interfere with their success in school. (32, pp. 105–107)

Cultural Misperceptions

Because of the cultural differences between the Hispanic American and European American cultures, educators who teach Hispanic American students but know little or nothing about the Hispanic American culture may have some misperceptions. For example, the Hispanic American culture requires good students to be passive learners—to sit quietly at their desks, pay attention, learn what they are taught, and speak only when called on. In contrast, European American educational methods often call on students to be active learners—to show initiative and leadership, to volunteer questions and answers, and to question the opinions of others. As a result, teachers may incorrectly perceive Hispanic American students who can't assume this more active role as insecure, shy, or excessively passive.

In another example, Hispanic American students who are trained to be dependent on the opinions, values, and decisions of adults may seem to be overly dependent, immature, or even slow. Or Hispanic American students who are brought up to be cooperative rather than competitive in their relationships with their peers may be seen as too passive and nonassertive in school activities. In addition, Hispanic Americans who are not necessarily expected to admit responsibility or apologize when they have made a mistake or wronged another person may resist doing so, especially in front of their peers. Educators can misperceive this unwillingness as recalcitrance, stubbornness, or defiant behavior. Another potential area for mistaken perception is in doing schoolwork. Hispanic American students who help each other when they are called on, during examinations, or with their homework may seem to be cheating rather than cooperating to a teacher unfamiliar with the Hispanic American culture.

Cultural conflicts between Hispanic American and European American expectations for children and adolescents may cause identity problems for Hispanic American youth. Some resolve these identity crises by adopting rebellious, exaggerated behavior patterns designed to express their individuality. When students demonstrate these behaviors in school, they may threaten educators, who may think that these Hispanic American youth have emotional or behavioral problems.

When Hispanic American students are made to compete against their will, are criticized in front of their peers, are denied the dependent relationship they are accustomed to having with adults, and are coerced into other behaviors that are culturally at odds with theirs, they may feel rejected, abused, or picked on by their teachers. They may become insecure and anxious, they may rebel against such treatment, or they may withdraw from further attempts to succeed in school or relate to their teachers. Educators can misperceive such situational, emotional, and behavioral problems as personality problems. Teachers can believe that students who do not complete assignments or attend school when family responsibilities prevent them from doing so are unmotivated or irresponsible. They can also see students who work at the slower, more relaxed Hispanic American pace as lazy or slow, instead of as working in what to these students is "the right way."

Self-Quiz: Hispanic American Students

This exercise is designed to help you apply the information about Hispanic American characteristics to actual students. For each of the three students described, state which of the nine problems in the list could be caused by contextual or cultural factors.

Martín is a 6 1/2-year-old student whose parents immigrated to the United States from a rural area in Mexico when he was 4 years old. His parents, neither of whom graduated high school, speak only Spanish at home. They live in a Hispanic barrio. Martín was enrolled in a bilingual education program for kindergarten. At the time that his teacher described him as having problems, he was about to complete a bilingual first-grade class.

José is a 6 1/2-year-old student who was born in the United States. José's mother and father immigrated to the United States when they were 7 and 9. His mother dropped out of school when she was 16, but his father graduated high school. At home the family usually speaks English; however, they also speak Spanish because José's parents want him to be bilingual. José is completely proficient in English and has been attending classes taught in English since kindergarten. Almost all of his friends are Hispanic Americans.

Michael is a 6 1/2-year-old student who was born in the United States. His ancestors were living in Texas when Mexico ceded it to the United States. Both of his parents are teachers. At home the family speaks English. Michael's parents are proud of their Hispanic American heritage. However, they choose to live in an upper middle-class, primarily European American nieghborhood. Michael is completely proficient in English and has been attending classes taught in English since kindergarten. While many of his friends are Hispanic Americans, he does not choose his friends on the basis of their ethnic background.

1. He works so fast when writing letters and numerals that his work is almost illegible.
2. He often miscounts when he uses his fingers to do simple addition and subtraction.
3. He constantly asks the teacher to check over his work to see if he is doing it correctly, even though he is almost always on track.
4. He almost never volunteers questions, answers, or comments in class. But when the teacher calls on Juan or Carlos, his two best friends, he will whisper the correct answers to them.
5. He often enters the room noisily and roughhouses with his friends before taking his seat.
6. He will not check out books from the school library unless the teacher encourages him and helps him select the books.
7. He sometimes takes things from his peers' cubbies.
8. He has difficulty sharing toys and materials with other students and resists relinquishing materials when it is another student's turn to use them.
9. He hits his peers when he is angry and teases the weaker children in the class.

Summary

There are many ways that educators can improve their classroom management approaches with students from diverse ethnic and socioeconomic backgrounds. Since many educators contribute to students' behavior problems by relating to them in a discriminatory manner, they can correct their ethnic and socioeconomic biases. Rather than interpreting students' behavior from their own perspective, educators can avoid misperceiving and misunderstanding students' behaviors by taking students' behavioral styles into consideration. They can select culturally appropriate classroom management techniques to solve the problems that confront them. And they can make conscious, rational decisions about whether assimilation, accommodation, biculturalism, or empowerment is the most appropriate strategy with a particular student in a given situation.

Activities

I. Ask some of your classmates or friends from different backgrounds to describe their disciplinary, relationship, and communication style preferences. Do you notice any of the characteristics reported in this chapter?

II. Using the characteristics included in "Hispanic American Students: An Example" as a guide, prepare descriptions of the traits that you believe are characteristic of an ethnic group. Then ask a few of your colleagues, peers, or students to review your list and tell you which traits they do and do not accept as being characteristic of their group.

III. Interview individuals from an ethnic group that interests you, and prepare a description of the characteristics that these individuals think educators should consider when they select management techniques.

IV. Ask your fellow students to answer the self-quiz on accommodating management techniques to student characteristics. Do you observe any differences between persons of different ethnic backgrounds? How do your answers compare to theirs?

V. List the various classroom/behavior management techniques that your instructors tend to use with students. Compare the techniques they use with the needs and preferences of their students.

References

These references discuss population trends.

1. Bureau of the Census. (1988). *The Black Population in the United States. Current Population Reports, Series P-20, No. 442.* U.S. Department of Commerce, Washington, DC: U.S. Government Printing Office.

2. Bureau of the Census. (1988). *Hispanic Population in the United States: Current Population Reports, Series P-20, No. 438.* U.S. Department of Commerce, Washington, DC: U.S. Government Printing Office.

3. Bureau of the Census. (1988). *Money, Income and Poverty Status in the United States: (Advance Data from the March 1989 Current Population Survey). Current Population Reports, Series P-60, No. 166.* U.S. Department of Commerce, Washington, DC: U.S. Government Printing Office.

4. National Information Center for Children and Youth with Handicaps. (1988). *Minority Issues in Special Education: A Portrait of the Future.* Washington, DC: Author.

5. Puente, T. (1991). Latino child poverty ranks swell. *Hispanic Link Weekly Report,* 9 (35), 1, 2, 8.

Discussions about prejudice in schools are found in the following references.

6. Appleford, B., Fralick, P., & Ryan, T. J. (1976). *Teacher-Child Interactions as Related to Sex, Socio-Economic Status and Physical Attractiveness.* ERIC ED 138 869.

7. Barba, L. (1979). A *Survey of the Literature on the Attitudes Toward the Administration of Corporal Punishment in Schools.* ERIC ED 186 538.

8. Bennett, C., & Harris, J. J. (1982). Suspension and expulsion of male and black students: A case study of the causes of disproportionality. *Urban Education, 16* (4), 399–423.

9. Bickel, F., & Qualls, R. (1981). *The Impact of School Climate on Suspension Rates in the Jefferson County Public Schools.* Paper presented at the annual meeting of the American Educational Research Association, Boston.

10. Buriel, R. (1983). Teacher-student interactions and their relationship to student achievement: A comparison of Mexican-American children. *Journal of Educational Psychology, 75,* 60, 889–897.

11. Friedman, P. (1976). Comparison of teacher reinforcement schedules for students with different social class backgrounds. *Journal of Educational Psychology, 68,* 286–293.

12. Glackman, T., Martin, R., Hyman, I., McDowell, E., Berv, V., & Spino, P. (1980). *Corporal Punishment in the Schools As It Relates to Race, Sex, Grade Level and Suspensions.* Philadelphia: Temple University, National Center for the Study of Corporal Punishment in the Schools.

13. Grant, L. (1984). Black females' "place" in desegregated classrooms. *Sociology of Education, 57,* 98–110.

14. Grant, L. (1985). Race-gender status, classroom interaction, and children's socialization in elementary school. In L. C. Wilkinson & C. B. Marrett (Eds.), *Gender Influences in Classroom Interaction.* New York: Academic Press.

15. Grossman, H., & Grossman, S. (1994). *Gender Issues in Education.* Needham, MA: Allyn & Bacon.

16. Guilmet, G. M. (1979). Instructor reaction to verbal and nonverbal styles: An example of Navajo and Caucasian children. *Anthropology and Education Quarterly, 10,* 254–266.

17. Hamilton, S. (1983). The social side of schooling. *Elementary School Journal, 83,* 313–334.

18. McGhan, B. R. (1978). *Teachers' Use of Authority and Its Relationship to Socioeconomic Status, Race, Teacher Characteristics, and Educational Outcomes.* ERIC ED 151 329.

19. Moody, C. D., Williams, J., & Vergon, C. B. (1978). *Student Rights and Discipline: Policies, Programs and Procedures.* ERIC ED 160 926.

20. Moore, W. L., & Cooper, H. (1984). Correlations between teacher and student background and teacher perception of discipline problems and disciplinary techniques. *Psychology in the Schools, 21,* 386–392.

21. National Black Child Development Institute. (1990). *The Status of African American Children: Twentieth Anniversary Report.* Washington, DC.: Author.

22. Richardson, R. C., & Evans, E. T. (1991). *Empowering Teachers to Eliminate Corporal Punishment in the Schools.* Paper presented at the annual conference of the National Black Child Development Institute, Washington, DC.

23. Simpson, A. W., & Erickson, M. T. (1983). Teachers' verbal and nonverbal communication patterns as a function of teacher race, student gender and student race. *American Educational Research Journal, 20* (2), 183–198.

24. Stevens, L. B. (1983). *Suspension and Corporal Punishment of Students in the Cleveland Public Schools, 1981–1982.* Cleveland, OH: Office of School Monitoring and Community Relations.

25. Taylor, M. (1979). Race, sex and the expression of self-fulfilling prophecies in a laboratory teaching situation. *Journal of Personality and Social Psychology, 37* (6), 897–912.

26. Washington, V. (1982). Racial differences in teacher perception of first and fourth grade pupils on selected characteristics. *Journal of Negro Education, 51,* 60–72.

27. Woolridge, P., & Richman, C. (1985). Teachers' choice of punishment as a function of a student's gender, age, race and I. Q. level. *Journal of School Psychology, 23,* 19–29.

Misperceptions and misunderstandings that can affect teachers' choices of management approaches are discussed in the following references.

28. Dent, J. L. (1976). Assessing black children for mainstream placement. In R. L. Jones (Ed.), *Mainstreaming and the Minority Child.* Reston, VA: Council for Exceptional Children.

29. ERIC Clearinghouse on Urban Education. (1985). The social and psychological adjustment of Southeast Asian refugees. *Equity and Choice, 1* (3), 55–59.

30. Gay, G. (1975, October). Cultural differences important in the education of Black children. *Momentum*, 30–33.

31. Gay, G., & Abrahams, R. D. (1973). Does the pot melt, boil, or brew? Black children and white assessment procedures. *Journal of School Psychology, 11* (4), 330–340.

32. Grossman, H. (1984). *Educating Hispanic Students: Cultural Implications for Instruction, Classroom Management, Counseling, and Assessment.* Springfield, IL: Thomas.

33. Irvine, J. J. (1991). *Black Students and School Failure: Policies, Practices, and Prescriptions.* New York: Praeger.

34. Jaramillo, J. L. (1973). *Cautions When Working with the Culturally Different Child.* ERIC ED 115 622.

35. Johnson, S. O. (1980). Minorities and discipline games. *High School Journal, 63* (5), 207–208.

36. Koh, T., & Koh, S. D. (1982). A note on the psychological evaluation of Korean school children. *P/AAMHRC Research Review, 1* (3), 1–2.

37. Kritek, W. J. (1979). Teachers' concerns in a desegregated school in Milwaukee. *Integrated Education, 17,* 19–24.

38. Morgan, H. (1980). How schools fail black children. *Social Policy, 10* (4), 49–54.

39. Nguyen, L. D. (1986). Indochinese cross-cultural adjustment and communication. In M. Dao & H. Grossman (Eds.), *Identifying, Instructing and Rehabilitating Southeast Asian Students with Special Needs and Counseling Their Parents.* ERIC ED 273 068.

40. Ortiz, A. A., & Yates, J. R. (1988). *Characteristics of Learning Disabled, Mentally Retarded, and Speech-Language Handicapped Hispanic Students at Initial Evaluation and Reevaluation.* ERIC ED 298 705.

41. Wong, M. K. (1978). Traditional Chinese culture and the behavior patterns of Chinese students in American classrooms. In *Second Annual Forum on Transcultural Adaptation (Proceedings): Asian Students in American Classrooms.* Chicago: Illinois Office of Education.

The following references discuss disciplinary styles that educators should consider when selecting classroom/behavior management approaches.

42. Bacon, M. M. (n.d.). *Coping Creatively with Adolescence: Culturally Relevant Behavior Management Strategies for the Twenty-First Century.* Unpublished manuscript. Palo Alto, CA: Palo Alto Unified School District.

43. Burgess, B. J. (1978). Native American learning styles. In L. Morris, G. Sather & S. Scull (Eds.), *Extracting Learning Styles from Social/Cultural Diversity: A Study of Five American Minorities.* Norman, OK: Southwest Teacher Corps Network.

44. Condon, E. C., Peters, J. Y., & Sueiro-Ross, C. (1979). *Special Education and the Hispanic Child: Cultural Perspectives.* Philadelphia: Temple University, Teacher Corps Mid-Atlantic Network.

45. Geschwind, N. (1974). *Cross-Cultural Contrastive Analysis: An Exploratory Study.* Unpublished master's thesis, University of Hawaii, Honolulu.

46. Hale-Benson, J. E. (1986). *Black Children: Their Roots, Culture, and Learning Styles* (rev. ed.). Baltimore: Johns Hopkins University Press.

47. Howells, G. N., & Sarabia, I. B. (1978). Education and the Pilipino child. *Integrated Education, 16* (2), 17–20.

48. Morrow, R. D. (1987). Cultural differences—Be aware. *Academic Therapy, 23* (2), 143–149.

49. Morrow, R. D., & McBride, H. J. (1988). *Considerations for Educators in Working with Southeast Asian Children and Their Families.* ERIC ED 299 730.

50. Robinson, S. (1989). Quoted in E. Wiley III. Educators call for fairer, more effective means of discipline in schools: Black males most likely to be punished. *Black Issues in Higher Education, 5* (21), 3, 16.

51. Swisher, K. (1990). Cooperative learning and the education of American Indian/ Alaskan Native students: A review of the literature and suggestions for implementation. *Journal of American Indian Education, 29* (2), 36–43.

52. Tharp, G. (1989). Psychocultural variables and constants: Effects on teaching and learning in schools. *American Psychologist, 44* (2), 349–359.

53. Williams, J. (1989). Reducing the disproportionately high frequency of disciplinary actions against minority students: An assessment-based policy approach. *Equity and Excellence, 24* (2), 31–37.

These references discuss relationship styles that educators should consider when selecting classroom/behavior management approaches.

54. Chan, K., & Rueda, R. (1979). Poverty and culture in education: Separate but equal. *Exceptional Children, 45,* 422–427.

55. Kochman, T. (1981). *Black and White Styles in Conflict.* Chicago: University of Chicago Press.

56. Leggio, P. (n.d.). *Contrastive Patterns in Nonverbal Communication Among Different Cultures.* Trenton, NJ: Office of Equal Opportunity, New Jersey State Department of Education.

57. Medicine, B. (1985). Child socialization among Native Americans: The Lakota (Sioux) in cultural context. In *Indian Studies.* Cheney, WA: Eastern Washington University.

58. Sra, D. (1992). *A Comparison of East Indian American and European American Students.* San Jose, CA: Unpublished manuscript, San Jose State University, Division of Special Education.

59. Yao, E. L. (1979). Implications of biculturalism for the learning process of middle-class Asian children in the United States. *Journal of Education, 16* (4), 61–72.

These references describe differences in verbal and nonverbal communication styles.

60. Anthony, A. P. (n.d.). *Hawaiian Nonverbal Communication: Two Classroom Applications*. Honolulu, HI: University of Hawaii at Manoa, Department of Indo-Pacific Languages.

61. Boseker, B. J., & Gordon, S. L. (1983). What Native Americans have taught us as teacher educators. *Journal of American Indian Studies, 22* (3), 20–24.

62. California State Department of Education. (1986). *Handbook for Teaching Pilipino-Speaking Students*. Sacramento, CA: Author.

63. California State Department of Education. (1987). *Handbook for Teaching Japanese-Speaking Students*. Sacramento, CA: Author.

64. Goodwin, M. H. (1990). *He-Said-She-Said: Talk as Social Organization Among Black Children*. Bloomington, IN: Indiana University Press.

65. Howells, G. N., & Sarabia, I. B. (1978). Education and the Pilipino Child. *Integrated Education, 16* (2), 17–20.

66. Johnson, K. R. (1971, spring/fall). Black kinetics: Some nonverbal communication patterns in the Black culture. *Florida Reporter,* 17–20, 57.

67. Matsuda, M. (1989). Working with Asian parents: Some communication strategies. *Topics in Language Disorders, 9* (3), 45–53.

68. National Coalition of Advocates for Students. (1988). *New Voices: Immigrant Students in U.S. Public Schools*. Boston, MA: Author.

69. Rodriguez, J. (n.d.). *An In-Service Rationale for Educators Working with Mexican American Students*. Stanford, CA: Chicano Fellow, Stanford University.

70. Wolfram, W., & Adger, C. T. (1993). *Language Differences Across Dialects*. Baltimore City Public Schools.

These references deal with field-sensitive and field-independent students.

71. Aiello, J. R., & Jones, S. E. (1971). Field study of the proxemic behavior of young school children in three subcultural groups. *Journal of Personality and Social Psychology, 19,* 351–356.

72. Bauer, E. (1973). Personal space: A study of blacks and whites. *Sociometry, 36,* 402–408.

73. Buriel, R. (1975). Cognitive styles among three generations of Mexican-American children. *Journal of Cross-Cultural Psychology, 6* (4), 417–429.

74. Cooperman, M. L. (1975). Field-dependence and children's problem-solving under varying contingencies of predetermined feedback. *Dissertation Abstracts International, 35,* 2040–2041.

75. Cureton, G. O. (1978). Using a Black learning style. *The Reading Teacher, 31* (7), 751–756.

76. DiStefano, J. J. (1970). Interpersonal perceptions of field-independent and field-dependent teachers and students. *Dissertation Abstracts International, 31*, 463A–464A.

77. Dixon, C. N. (1977). *Matching Reading Instruction to Cognitive Style for Mexican-American Children.* ERIC ED 158 269.

78. Dunn, R. V., & Dunn, K. (1978). *Teaching Students Through Their Individual Learning Styles: A Practical Approach.* Reston, VA: Reston Publishing.

79. Dunn, R. V., & Dunn, K. (1979). Learning styles/teaching styles: Should they?—can they?—be matched? *Educational Leadership, 36*, 238–244.

80. Ferrell, J. G. (1971). The differential performance of lower class, preschool, Negro children as a function of sex of E, sex of S, reinforcement condition, and the level of field dependency. *Dissertation Abstracts International, 32*, 3028B–3029B.

81. Gill, N. T., Hertner, T., & Lough, L. (1968). Perceptual and socioeconomic variables, instruction in body part orientation and predicted academic success in young children. *Perceptual Motor Skills, 26*, 1175–1184.

82. Gitter, A. G., Black, H., & Mostofsky, D. (1972). Race and sex in the perception of emotion. *Journal of Social Issues, 28*, 63–78.

83. Hale, J. E. (1981). Black children: Their roots, culture, and learning styles. *Young Children, 36* (2), 37–50.

84. Hilliard, A. (1976). *Alternatives to I.Q. Testing: An Approach to the Identification of Gifted Minority Children.* Sacramento, CA: Final report to the California State Department of Education.

85. Holtzman, E. H., Goldsmith, R. P., & Barrera, C. (1979). *Field-Dependence/Field-Independence: Educational Implications for Bilingual Educators.* Austin, TX: Dissemination and Assessment Center for Bilingual Education.

86. Hsi, V., & Lim, V. (1977). A *Summary of Selected Research on Cognitive and Perceptual Variables.* ERIC ED 145 003.

87. Hwang, B. (1978). Examplars of instructional units for cultural diversity. In L. Morris, G. Sather, & S. Scull (Eds.), *Extracting Learning Styles from Social/Cultural Diversity.* Southwest Teach Corps Network.

88. Kagan, S. (1974). Field dependence and conformity of rural Mexican and Anglo American children. *Child Development, 45*, 765–771.

89. Kagan, S., & Zahn, L. C. (1975). Field dependence and the school achievement gap between Anglo-American and Mexican-American children. *Journal of Educational Psychology, 67* (5).

90. Knight, G. P., Kagan, S., Nelson, W., & Gumbiner, J. (1978). Acculturation of second- and third-generation Mexican-American children: Field independence,

locus of control, self-esteem and school achievement. *Journal of Cross-Cultural Psychology, 9* (1), 87–97.

91. Perney, V. (1976). Effects of race and sex on field dependence-independence in children. *Perceptual and Motor Skills, 42,* 975–980.

92. Ramirez, M., & Castañeda, A. (1974). *Cultural Democracy, Bicognitive Development and Education.* New York: Academic Press.

93. Ramirez, M., & Price-Williams, D. (1974). Cognitive styles of children of three ethnic groups in the United States. *Journal of Cross-Cultural Psychology, 5,* 212–219.

94. Ritzinger, C. F. (1971). *Psychological and Physiological Differentiation in Children Six to Eleven Years of Age.* Unpublished doctoral dissertation, East Texas State University, Commerce, TX.

95. Schratz, M. (1976). *A Developmental Investigation of Sex Differences in Perceptual Differentiation and Mathematic Reasoning in Two Ethnic Groups.* Unpublished doctoral dissertation, Fordham University, New York, NY.

96. Shade, B. J. (1979). *Racial Preferences in Psychological Differentiation: An Alternative Explanation to Group Differences.* ERIC ED 179 672.

97. Triandis, H. C. (Ed.). (1976). *Variations in Black and White Perceptions of the Social Environment.* Urbana, IL: University of Illinois Press.

98. Valentine, C. (1971). Deficit difference and bicultural model of Afro-American behavior. *Harvard Educational Review, 41,* 137–157.

99. Witkins, H., Moore, C. A., Goodenough, D. R., & Cox, P. W. (1978). Field-dependent and field-independent cognitive styles and their educational implications. *Review of Educational Research, 47* (1), 1–64.

These references discuss various ways of evaluating students' acculturation.

100. Cloud, N. (1990). *Measuring Level of Acculturation in Bilingual, Bicultural Children.* Paper presented at the annual meeting of the American Educational Research Association, Boston.

101. Cloud, N. (1991). Acculturation of ethnic minorities. In A. M. Ambert (Ed.), *Bilingual Education and English as a Second Language: A Research Handbook 1988–1990.* New York: Garland.

102. Cuellar, I., Harris, L. C., & Jasso, R. (1980). An acculturation scale for Mexican American normal and clinical populations. *Hispanic Journal of Behavioral Sciences, 2* (3), 199–217.

103. Franco, J. N. (1983). An acculturation scale for Mexican-American children. *Journal of General Psychology, 108,* 175–181.

104. Lin, K., & Masuda, M. (1983). Impact of refugee experience: Mental health issues of Southeast Asian refugees. In R. F. Morales (Ed.), *Bridging Cultures.* Los Angeles: Asian American Health Center.

105. Mainous, A. G., III. (1989). Self concept as an indicator of acculturation in Mexican Americans. *Hispanic Journal of Behavioral Sciences, 11* (2), 178–189.

106. Martinez, R., Norman, R. D., & Delaney, H. D. (1984). A children's Hispanic background scale. *Hispanic Journal of Behavioral Sciences, 6* (2), 103–112.

107. Mendoza, R. H., & Martinez, J. L. (1981). The measurement of acculturation. In A. Baron, Jr. (Ed.), *Explorations in Chicano Psychology.* New York: Holt.

108. Olmedo, E. L. (1980). Quantitative models of acculturation: An overview. In A. M. Padilla (Ed.), *Acculturation: Theory, Models, and Some New Findings.* Boulder, CO: Westview Press.

109. Olmedo, E. L., & Padilla, A. M. (1978). Empirical and construct validity of a measure of acculturation for Mexican Americans. *Journal of Social Psychology, 105,* 179–187.

110. Padilla, A. M. (1980). The role of cultural awareness and ethnic loyalty in acculturation. In A. M. Padilla (Ed.), *Acculturation: Theory, Models, and Some New Findings.* Boulder, CO: Westview Press.

111. Suinn, R. M., Rickard-Figueroa, K., Lew, S., & Vigil, P. (1987). Asian Self-Identity Acculturation Scale: An initial report. *Educational and Psychological Measurement, 47,* 401–407.

112. Szapocznik, J., Kurtines, W. M., & Fernandez, T. (1979). *Bicultural Involvement and Adjustment in Hispanic American Youth.* ERIC ED 193 374.

The following references discuss the different ways students and educators can respond to cultural incompatibilities in school and examine their advantages and disadvantages.

113. Alley, J. (1980). Better understanding of the Indochinese students. *Education, 101,* 111–114.

114. Bernal, E. (1974). In A dialogue on cultural implications for learning. *Exceptional Children, 40,* 552–563.

115. Buriel, R. (1984). Integration with traditional Mexican-American culture and sociocultural adjustment. In J. L. Martinez, Jr. & R. H. Mendoza, *Chicano Psychology* (2nd ed.). Orlando, FL: Academic Press.

116. Buriel, R., & Saenz, E. (1980). Psychocultural characteristics of college bound and non-college bound Chicanos. *Journal of Social Psychology, 110,* 245–251.

117. Cloud, N. (1991). Acculturation of ethnic minorities. In A. M. Ambert (Ed.), *Bilingual Education and English as a Second Language: A Research Handbook 1988–1990.* New York: Garland.

118. Ellis, A. A. (1980). *The Assimilation and Acculturation of Indochinese Children into American Culture.* ERIC ED 213 484.

119. ERIC/CUE. (1985). The social and psychological adjustment of Southeast Asian Refugees. *Urban Review, 17* (2), 147–152.

120. Higham, J. (1984). *Send These to Me: Immigrants in Urban America.* Baltimore, MD: Johns Hopkins University Press.

121. Hilliard, A. G., III. (1992). *Language, Culture, and Valid Teaching.* Paper presented at the Topical Conference on Culturally and Linguistically Diverse Exceptional Children, Minneapolis.

122. Hornett, D. M. (1990). Elementary-age tasks, cultural identity, and the academic performance of young American Indian children. *Action in Teacher Education, 12* (3), 43–49.

123. Jordan, K., Tharp, R. G., & Baird-Vogt, L. (1991). Cross-culturally compatible schooling. In M. Saravia-Shore & S. F. Arvizu (Eds.), *Cross-Cultural Literacy: Ethnographies of Communication in Multiethnic Classrooms.* New York: Garland.

124. Kleinfeld, J. (1975). Positive stereotyping: The cultural relativist in the classroom. *Human Organization, 34* (3), 269–274.

125. Landsman, M., Padilla, A., Clark, C., Liederman, H., Ritter, P., & Dornbusch, S. (1990). *Biculturality and Academic Achievement Among Asian and Hispanic Adolescents.* Paper presented at the annual meeting of the National Association for Bilingual Education, Tucson.

126. Longstreet, W. S. (1978). *Aspects of Ethnicity.* New York: Teachers College Press.

127. Macias, J. (1987). The hidden curriculum of Papago teachers: American Indian strategies for mitigating cultural discontinuity in early schooling. In G. Spindler & L. Spindler (Eds.), *Interpretive Ethnography of Education: At Home and Abroad.* Hillsdale, NJ: Erlbaum.

128. Melville, M. B. (1980). Selective acculturation of female Mexican migrants. In M. B. Melville (Ed.), *Twice a Minority: Mexican American Women.* St. Louis: Mosby.

129. Morales, R. F. (Ed.). (1983). *Bridging Cultures.* Los Angeles: Asian American Health Training Center.

130. Niera, C. (1988). Building 860. *Harvard Educational Review, 58* (2), 337–342.

131. Nieto, S. (1992). *Affirming Diversity: The Sociopolitical Context of Multicultural Education.* New York: Longman.

132. Patrick, J. L. (1986). Immigration in the curriculum. *Social Education, 50* (3), 172–176.

133. Santiseban, D., & Szapocznik, J. (1982). Substance abuse disorders among Hispanics: A focus on prevention. In R. M. Becerra, M. Karno, & J. I. Escobar (Eds.), *Mental Health and Hispanic Americans: Clinical Perspectives.* New York: Grune & Stratton.

134. Saville-Troike, M. (1978). *A Guide to Culture in the Classroom.* Rosslyn, VA: National Clearinghouse for Bilingual Education.

135. Shade, B. J. (1982). Afro-American cognitive style: A variable in school success. *Review of Educational Research, 52,* 219–244.

136. Sleeter, C. (Ed.) (1991). *Empowerment Through Multicultural Education.* Albany, NY: State University of New York Press.

137. So, A. Y. (1987). High-achieving disadvantaged students: A study of low SES Hispanic language minority students. *Urban Education, 22* (1), 19–35.

138. Suzuki, B. H. (1984). Curriculum transformation for multicultural education. *Education and Urban Society, 16,* 294–322.

139. Szapocznik, J., Kurtines, W. M., & Fernandez, T. (1979). *Bicultural Involvement and Adjustment in Hispanic American Youths.* ERIC ED 193 374.

140. Thomas, E. W. (1978). English as a second language—for whom? *The Crisis, 85* (9), 318–320.

141. Thomas, M. D. (1981). *Pluralism Gone Mad.* Bloomington, IN: Phi Delta Kappa Educational Foundation.

142. Torres-Matrullo, C. M. (1980). Acculturation, sex-role values and mental health among mainland Puerto Ricans. In A. M. Padilla (Ed.), *Acculturation: Theory, Models, and Some New Findings.* Boulder, CO: Westview Press.

143. Vigil, J. D. (1982). Chicano high schoolers: Educational performance and acculturation. *Educational Forum, 47* (1), 58–73.

144. Wei, T. T. D. (1980). *Vietnamese Refugee Students: A Handbook for School Personnel.* ERIC ED 208 109.

145. Wong-Rieger, D., & Quintana, D. (1987). Comparative acculturation of Southeast Asian and Hispanic immigrants and sojourners. *Journal of Cross-cultural Psychology, 18* (3), 345–362.

Criticism of the concept that some cultures are deprived, culturally disadvantaged, or educationally disadvantaged is contained in the following references.

146. Adams, M. J. (1986). Teaching thinking to Chapter 1 students. In B. I. Williams, P. A. Richmond, & B. J. Mason (Eds.), *Designs for Compensatory Education: Conference Proceedings and Papers.* ERIC ED 293 913.

147. Bowles, S., & Gintis, H. (1976). *Schooling in Capitalist America: Educational Reform and the Contradictions of Economic Life.* New York: Basic Books.

148. Braroe, N. W. (1975). *Indian and White: Self-Image and Interaction in a Canadian Plains Community.* Stanford, CA: Stanford University Press.

149. Calfee, R. (1986). Curriculum and instruction: Reading. In B. I. Williams, P. A. Richmond, & B. J. Mason (Eds.), *Designs for Compensatory Education: Conference Proceedings and Papers.* ERIC ED 293 912.

150. Cummings, S. (1977). Explaining poor academic performance among black children. *Educational Forum, 41* (3), 335–346.

151. Datcher-Loury, L. (1989). Family background and school achievement among low income blacks. *Journal of Human Resources, 24* (3), 528–544.

152. Doyle, W. (1986). Vision and reality: A reaction to issues in curriculum and instruction for compensatory education. In B. I. Williams, P. A. Richmond, & B. J. Mason (Eds.), *Designs for Compensatory Education: Conference Proceedings and Papers.* ERIC ED 293 918.

153. Evans, F. B., & Anderson, J. G. (1973). The psychocultural origins of achievement and achievement motivation: The Mexican-American family. *Sociology of Education, 46,* 396–416.

154. Goodwin, L. (1976). A critical comment on success-value research. *American Journal of Sociology, 81,* 1151–1155.

155. Grossman, H. (1994). *Special Education in a Diverse Society.* Needham, MA: Allyn & Bacon.

156. Healy, G. W., & DeBlassie, R. R. (1974). A comparison of Negro, Anglo, and Spanish American adolescents' self-concepts. *Adolescence, 33,* 15–24.

157. Heaps, R. A., & Morrill, S. G. (1979). Comparing the self-concepts of Navajo and white high school students. *Journal of American Indian Education, 18* (3), 12–14.

158. Kandel, D. B. (1971). Race, maternal authority, and adolescent aspiration. *American Journal of Sociology, 76* (6), 999–1020.

159. Larned, D. T., & Muller, D. (1979). Development of self-concept in Mexican American and Anglo students. *Hispanic Journal of Behavioral Sciences. 1* (2), 179–185.

160. Luftig, R. L. (1982). *The Effects of Schooling on the Self-Concept of Native American Students.* ERIC ED 220 227.

161. Parry, R. (1982). Poor self-concept and differential academic achievement: An inadequate explanation of school performance of black and Native American children. *Canadian Journal of Native Education, 10* (1), 11–24.

162. Passow, A. H. (1990). *Enriching Compensatory Education Curriculum for Disadvantaged Students.* New York: ERIC Clearinghouse on Urban Education, Teachers College, Columbia University.

163. Patton, S. M., Walberg, H. J., & Yeh, E. G. (1973). Ethnicity, environmental control, and academic self-concept in Chicago. *American Educational Research Journal, 10,* 85–91.

164. Poussaint, A. R. (1974, August). Building a strong self-image in the black child. *Ebony,* 136–143.

165. Rodman, H., & Voydanoff, P. (1978). Social class and parents' range of aspirations for their children. *Social Problems, 25,* 333–344.

166. Wells, E. E. (1978). *The Mythical Negative Black Self-Concept.* San Francisco: R & E Research Associates.

The following references apply specifically to Hispanic students.

167. Aragon, J., & Marquez, L. (1973). *Spanish American: Language and Culture.* Reston, VA: Council for Exceptional Children.

168. Aramoni, A. (1972, January). Machismo. *Psychology Today,* 69–72.

169. Baca, L., & Lane, K. (1974). A dialogue on cultural implications for learning. *Exceptional Children, 40* (8), 552–563.

170. Bryant, B., & Meadow, A. (1979). School-related problems of Mexican-American adolescents. *Journal of School Psychology, 14* (2), 139–150.

171. Cross, W. C., & Maldanado, B. (1971). The counselor, the Mexican-American and the stereotype. *Elementary School Guidance and Counseling, 6* (1), 27–31.

172. De Blaisse, R. R. (1976). *Counseling with Mexican-American Youth.* Austin, TX: Learning Concepts.

173. Felder, D. (1970). The education of Mexican-Americans: Fallacies of the mono-cultural approach. *Social Education, 34* (6), 639–647.

174. Flores, J. M. (1980). *Chicano Education: Clearer Objectives and Better Results.* ERIC ED 198 968.

175. Henkin, C. S., & Henkin, A. B. (1977). Culture, poverty and educational problems of Mexican-Americans. *Clearing House, 50,* 316–319.

176. Hepner, E. M. (1970). *Self-Concepts, Values and Needs of Mexican-American Underachievers or Must the Mexican-American Child Adopt a Self-Concept That Fits the American Schools?* ERIC ED 048 954.

177. Hosford, R. E., & Bowles, S. A. (1974). Determining culturally appropriate reinforcers for Anglo and Chicano students. *Elementary School Guidance and Counseling, 8* (4), 240–300.

178. Kagan, S., & Madsen, M. C. (1971). Cooperation and competition of Mexican, Mexican-American and Anglo-American children at two ages under four instructional sets. *Developmental Psychology, 5* (1), 32–39.

179. Keller, G. D. (1974). *The Systematic Exclusion of the Language and Culture of Boricuas, Chicanos and Other U.S. Hispanos in Elementary Spanish Grammar Textbooks Published in the United States.* Ypsilante, MI: Bilingual Press. Editorial Bilingue, Department of Foreign Languages and Bilingual Studies, Eastern Michigan University.

180. LeVine, E. S., & Bartz, K. W. (1979). Comparative child rearing attitudes among Chicano, Anglo and Black parents. *Hispanic Journal of Behavioral Sciences, 1* (2), 165–178.

181. Maes, W. R., & Rinaldi, J. R. (1979). Counseling the Chicano child. *Elementary School Guidance and Counseling*, 8 (4), 279–284.

182. Martinez, J. L. (Ed.). (1977). *Chicano Psychology*. New York: Academic Press.

183. Martinez, J. L., & Mendoza, R. H. (Eds.). (1984). *Chicano Psychology* (2nd ed.). New York: Academic Press.

184. Masden, M. C. (1971). Developmental and cross-cultural differences in the cooperative and competitive behavior of young children. *Journal of Cross-Cultural Psychology*, 2 (4), 365–371.

185. Mendiville, M. (1979, February). A Hispanic perspective on curriculum reform and design. *Social Education*, 108–110.

186. Ortiz, F. I., & Morelan, S. J. (1974). *The Effects of Personal and Impersonal Rewards on the Learning Performance of Field Independent-dependent Mexican-American Children*. Paper presented at the annual meeting of the American Educational Research Association, Chicago.

187. Padilla, A. M., et al. (1985). *Acculturative Stress in Immigrant Students: Three Papers*. Los Angeles: Spanish Speaking Mental Health Research Center.

188. Prago, A. (1973). *Strangers in Their Own Land: A History of Mexican-Americans*. New York: Four Winds.

189. Roberts, A. H., & Greene, J. E. (1971). Cross-cultural study of relationships among four dimensions of time perspective. *Perceptual and Motor Skills*, 33, 163–173.

190. Smith, G. W., & Caskey, O. L. (Eds.). (1972). *Promising School Practices for Mexican-Americans*. ERIC ED 064 003.

191. Stewart, I. S. (1976). Cultural differences between Anglos and Chicanos. *Education Digest*, 41, 29–31.

192. Wagner, H. A. (1977). A comparison of selected differences in adolescence in Mexico and the United States. *Adolescence*, 12 (47), 381–384.

193. Vigil, D. (1979). Adaptation strategies and cultural lifestyles of Mexican-American adolescents. *Hispanic Journal of Sciences*, 1 (41), 375–392.

GENDER-APPROPRIATE CLASSROOM MANAGEMENT

Males and females behave differently both in and out of school. Some individuals believe that these behavioral differences are natural and desirable; others believe that they are the result of sexism.

Teachers use different classroom management techniques with males and females. People also disagree about whether or not gender differences in classroom management are desirable. Some individuals believe that they foster unacceptable gender-stereotypical behavior. Others believe that they reflect teachers' attempts to treat each gender according to its special needs. Therefore, any discussion of gender-appropriate classroom management procedures needs to examine gender differences in both the way students behave and the way teachers manage their behavior, including the full range of opinion about these differences.

This chapter describes the ways in which males and females function differently in school. Then it explores the desirability of these differences. An examination of gender differences in classroom management techniques comes next, followed by alternative ways that teachers can deal with gender differences in their classrooms. The chapter also includes a discussion about sexual orientation.

Avoiding Misleading Stereotypes

Although the focus of this chapter is on the ways in which males and females behave differently and fulfill different gender-specific roles both in school and in the larger society, it is important to avoid speaking about and acting on misleading gender stereotypes. No gender difference applies to all females and all males.

Different ethnic groups expect different gender-specific behavior from their members.

For example, European American students are more likely to be exposed to nontraditional role models (models that do not conform to those that were common 20 or more years ago) than their Hispanic American and Asian American peers, who are often brought up in families and communities that have more traditional values, beliefs, and expectations about gender roles. Thus, students brought up by parents who were born in other countries or by parents who belong to ethnic groups that do not share the values and expectations of European American middle-class parents may learn to behave in the gender-specific ways of their own ethnic group rather than in the ways typical of the European American majority.

Subgroups within larger ethnic groups also differ. Although not all students fit the following generalization, Mexican American students tend to be exposed to much more traditional role models than the Nicaraguan American students, who were brought up in the atmosphere of relative equality between the genders that was encouraged by the Sandinistas after they assumed power.

There is diversity among students brought up in families with similar ethnic backgrounds. Parents who want their children to maintain their own ethnic identities may encourage and even pressure them to maintain traditional values, attitudes, and behavior patterns to a much greater degree than parents who want their children to assimilate into the American mainstream. For example, Mexican migrant workers and their children who plan to return to Mexico may be less motivated to adopt European American values and behavior patterns than those who hope to remain in the United States.

Students from different socioeconomic backgrounds are also influenced by dissimilar cultural experiences. In addition, the change in attitude toward gender-specific roles that has occurred in the United States during the past 20 or 30 years has been primarily a middle-class phenomenon. As a result, students from working-class backgrounds are more likely to be brought up to fulfill traditional roles than are middle-class students.

Students from the same socioeconomic class may not be equally motivated to maintain their cultural heritage. Students in upwardly mobile, low-income families and those who want to join the middle class may be less likely to aspire to traditional gender roles than students who are content with their economic situation.

Regional differences create diversity within ethnic and socioeconomic groups. Mexican American students who live in "border towns" in Texas, New Mexico, and Arizona are much more likely to be exposed to the traditional Latino cultural lifestyles and attitudes than students who live in other parts of the country. As a result, they may have more traditional points of view about gender roles. Likewise, because students from low-income families growing up in Appalachia have less exposure to middle-class values and behavior patterns than do students who live in large cities such as Chicago, Detroit, or Atlanta, their attitudes, values, and behavior may be somewhat different from their city peers.

Prejudice can discourage students from aspiring to certain gender-stereotypical roles or prevent students from fulfilling the roles to which they do aspire. For example, racism in employment discourages many working-class African American male students from hoping to fulfill traditional male roles because they know that they are less likely than European Americans to have the opportunity to be the "breadwinner" of the family and to enjoy the status associated with being the primary source of financial support. And poor parents who can barely afford to have one child attend college may persuade their daughters to sacrifice their desire for higher education and the roles open to them as a result so that their brothers can obtain a college or university degree.

While it is true that generalizations about gender differences can be misleading, some gender differences cut across class, ethnic, and geographical boundaries and tend to apply to the majority of most groups' members. These generalizations can sensitize educators to the possibility that their students may behave in certain gender-specific ways. As long as educators do not assume that all of their students will conform to a particular stereotype, generalizations about gender differences can be useful. However, it is as important to avoid relating to students on the basis of incorrect gender stereotypes as it is to avoid being insensitive to the influence that gender may have on students' lives.

Gender Differences

In most respects, male and female students behave similarly. However, some of the differences in the way they behave and the roles they fulfill have important implications for classroom management.

Gender differences do not appear all at once. They develop gradually, each stage influencing the next, to help produce the gender differences we see among adults.

By the time boys and girls begin school, many striking differences exist between the sexes. During preschool, kindergarten, and early elementary school years, boys and girls engage in different play activities (1–12). Boys prefer to play with airplanes, blocks, water and sand, and trucks and cars. Girls prefer dolls, beads, makeup, cradles, and kitchen toys. During their free time, boys engage in more physical rough-and-tumble play. They also tend to select self-initiated, loosely structured activities with few externally imposed rules or guidelines, such as running in a pack to put out a fire. Girls organize more structured activities, such as playing Little Mermaid, in which they assign each other roles and follow a story. Boys tend to engage in more exploratory behavior. They like digging in a sandbox and taking toys apart. While playing or engaged in other activities, boys are also more physically active (13–15).

Male and female preschoolers relate to others in different ways (16–28). Girls tend to be more polite and helpful and less aggressive and assertive than boys. Boys get their way with others by physical means—pushing, posturing, and demanding; girls are more likely to use verbal manipulation ("You can't be my friend. I'm not going to invite you to my party"), verbal persuasion, and polite suggestions. Boys tend to demand and order others ("Do that," "This is for the shot [injection] I'm gonna give you"); girls are more indirect ("Could you do that?", "This is for the shot I'm gonna give you, okay?").

Girls are likely to let the group select activities; boys tend to make more independent choices. While girls are responsive to feedback from teachers and peers of either sex, boys are much less interested in and responsive to their teachers and appear to lack interest in and ignore feedback from girls. In mixed-gender groups, girls became more passive than they usually are and acquiesce to the boys. In general, girls are more responsive to the desires of boys than boys are to the desires of girls.

As children mature, many of the gender differences observed in preschools become more pronounced, and additional differences appear. As a result, the behavior of male and female students becomes increasingly different during their school years.

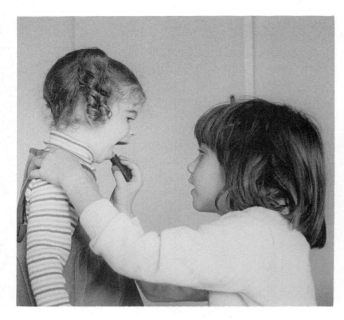 

The play of many young children fulfills current sex role stereotypes.

Emotional Style

Elementary and secondary school girls and boys have somewhat different emotional styles (29–41). With many exceptions, school-age girls are more fearful and anxious than boys. In school, this difference is especially noticeable when students take tests. Female students are more willing to express their fears and anxieties. But when boys express emotions, they do so more intensely. Girls also tend to experience themselves as sad or depressed more than boys, who are angry more often than girls.

Relationship Style

The gender differences observed among preschoolers in how they relate to others continue throughout students' school careers. Boys are more assertive, aggressive, and concerned about dominance (22, 39, 42–51). Girls tend to be more altruistic and helpful, especially when strength is not involved and the help required is not seen as being in the male domain (e.g., science and mathematics homework). Girls are more likely to share things such as school supplies with others and to be supportive when their classmates are confronted with problems, disappointments, and so on (52–61). With many exceptions, girls are also less competitive than boys (62–66). Girls generally tend to avoid conflicts with others rather than deal with them openly (67).

Girls appear to be more interested than boys in obtaining the approval of others (68–72). Some evidence that needs updating suggests that in comparison to elementary school boys, they tend to be more willing to conform to obtain their teachers' approval (71). They tend to actively seek the assistance and approval of adults, including their teachers, more than boys do (68–70, 72). And they demonstrate higher levels of achievement when adults are present than when they are absent (68). As adults, females are more likely to use learned helplessness as a way of influencing others, especially males, and gaining their assistance (73, 74).

In mixed groups, girls tend to be equally responsive to requests from and reinforcement by either sex. However, boys are responsive primarily to other males (5, 23, 28, 75, 76). Males continue to exercise a dominant role in mixed-sex groups throughout their educational careers (77–79). Boys initiate and receive more of the interaction, do more of the talking, are more influential in the decision-making process than girls, especially girls who are generally acquiescent to others, and are more likely to assume leadership positions. While girls tend to be equally responsive to the requests of either sex, boys continue to be responsive primarily to other males.

Some evidence, mostly anecdotal, suggests that many of these differences apply to a greater degree to Hispanic American and Asian American females, many of whom are brought up in families that adhere to traditional ideas about gender roles, than to European American middle-class females. But these differences appear less often or not at all in other ethnic groups that do not bring up their children to fulfill these gender-specific roles (80–86). For example, African American females do not relate to others in these gender-specific ways (84–85). Many African American females do not act passively, allow males to dominate mixed groups, or use learned helplessness as a way of obtaining their aims.

Moral Style

As noted in chapter 3, it appears that girls' moral development tends to proceed more rapidly than that of boys. Girls score higher than boys on tests of moral judgment. Adults believe that they behave somewhat differently. And some individuals have suggested that males and females use somewhat different moral approaches.

Communication Style

European American males and females employ somewhat different communication styles that tend to mirror the different ways they relate to others (9, 27, 87–97). Most girls' language is more polite, with fewer four-letter and forceful words. Research that should be updated indicates that compared to boys, girls tend to suggest and hint rather than command, expressing themselves less directly. When they enter into ongoing conversations, they do so in a more polite, less intrusive manner. According to Maccoby,

> Boys in all-boy groups, compared with girls in all-girl groups, more often interrupt one another, more often use commands, threats, and boasts of authority, more often refuse to comply with another child's demand, more often give information, heckle a speaker, tell jokes or suspenseful stories, "top" someone else's story, or call another child names. Girls in all-girls groups, on the other hand, more often express agreement with what another speaker has just said, pause to give another girl a chance to speak, and acknowledge what another speaker has said when starting a speaking turn. It is clear that speech

serves more egoistic functions among boys and more socially binding functions among girls. (9, p. 758)

As in the case of gender differences in relationship styles, gender differences in communication styles are most likely to apply to Hispanic American and Asian Pacific American females who are brought up in families that believe in traditional values. Females from these ethnic groups who are brought up in less traditional families and females from certain other ethnic backgrounds do not behave in these gender-stereotypical ways. African American females, for example, do not behave passively or allow males to dominate mixed-gender groups.

Both culture and racism help to explain the difference. Culturally, African Americans do not expect the genders to behave differently in these ways, nor do parents model these differences to the extent that European Americans do (82, 83). Lewis explains:

> The Black child, to be sure, distinguishes between males and females, but unlike the white child he is not inculcated with standards which polarize behavioral expectations according to sex. . . . Many of the behaviors which whites see as appropriate to one sex or the other, blacks view as equally appropriate to both sexes or equally inappropriate to both sexes; and the sex differences that do exist are more in the nature of contrasts than of mutually exclusive traits. (83, p. 228)

Racism also plays a part. Many people believe that African American females tend to be brought up to be independent, aggressive, and assertive because racism has so disabled African American males economically that females cannot rely on males to the extent and in the ways that European American females can (85, 86). According to Simpson,

> The American caste system has historically enforced the underemployment of Black males. Cognizant of this fact, these Black women were taught that they must be economically independent, regardless of their marital status.
>
> White oppression of Black people has created a situation in which, compared to Whites, the underemployment and lower income of Black males and the higher incidence of marital disruption makes it difficult for Black women to anticipate an economically dependent full-time homemaking role with equanimity. (85, pp. 126–127)

Learning Style

Girls react less positively than boys to difficult and challenging situations and are less likely to take risks (98–101). They are less persistent and perform less adequately than boys following failure or the threat of failure (102–105). They also tend to be less self-confident than males. (See following section on self-concept and self-esteem.)

Compared to males, females, especially those from working-class backgrounds, are more cooperative and may learn better in cooperative situations. In group settings they are more oriented toward group rather than individualistic goals. Boys respond better to competitive situations (106–118).

On balance, girls are more likely than boys to modify their opinions and attitudes to conform to others (119–123) and to copy what others model, though some research indicates the contrary (123). Boys tend to maintain their ideas and opinions despite what others may think or feel.

Self-Concept and Self-Esteem

Gender differences in self-concept and self-esteem have been the focus of a great deal of research (124–145). Although it is not true of African Americans, in most ethnic groups females tend to be less self-confident than males in many school situations. These include competitive situations and courses that are thought to be in the male domain, especially when they lack objective information about how well they have done or can do (38, 128, 130, 132, 134, 136, 139, 142, 145). Females are not less self-confident than males in courses such as *reading*, which are not perceived to be in the male domain, and in situations that involve their perceived ability to develop friendly relationships with others, to be popular, to resolve conflicts with others, to break bad habits, to gain insight, and so on.

It is unclear whether there are also gender differences in students' overall self-concepts and self-esteem. Some studies have found that males have higher self-concepts and self-esteem (125, 135, 139, 140). Some studies have found no differences between the self-concepts and self-esteem of African American, European American, and Native American males and females (131, 137, 138, 143). One study found that females, especially African Americans, have more positive self-concepts and higher self-esteem than males (144).

Students differ in terms of the extent to which they believe they are in control of, and responsible for, what happens to them in their lives. Some studies have found that females are more likely than males to believe that they are in control of their lives (138, 151). Some studies have found the opposite (144, 150, 155). And some researchers have found no gender differences for either African American or European American students (162, 166). Thus, there is no reason to believe that males and females differ in this respect.

Studies that have examined how students explain their school-related experiences (rather than events in their personal lives) paint a different picture. While a few researchers have found no gender differences (148, 153, 165), most studies indicate that males and females attribute their academic successes and failures to different factors. Researchers who have compared males' and females' beliefs about whether they or external factors have greater influence over their general school performance have found that in comparison to males, females, especially those from a working-class background, are more likely to attribute their general academic performance to internal factors (147, 154, 164). However, in courses such as math and science, which are thought to be in the male domain, females tend to attribute their poor performance to internal factors, such as lack of ability, and their success to external factors, such as luck, rather than effort or ability (100,146, 149, 152, 156, 158, 160, 161, 167). Males' attributions are different. They are more likely to attribute their failures to external factors and their success to internal factors across courses and subjects (157, 159–161, 163).

Motivation to Avoid Success

Although the evidence is somewhat inconsistent, it appears that males and females have different reactions to success in school (170–172, 174). Many European American

THEORY FOCUS: GILLIGAN ON WOMEN'S PSYCHOLOGY

Carol Gilligan is the founder of the Harvard Project on Women's Psychology and Girls' Development. Her pioneering book *In a Different Voice: Psychological Theory and Women's Development* helped bring women's voices into psychological theory and women's lives into research on human development. Through studies such as "Understanding Adolescents: A Study of Urban Teens Considered to Be at Risk" and "Women and Girls: A Project to Strengthen Connections Between Teenage Girls and Adult Women," she and her colleagues at the Harvard Project have added to our knowledge of the relationship between gender and ethnic and socioeconomic factors and methods for assisting females to overcome the problems they face in a prejudiced society.

females, especially those from less affluent and working-class backgrounds, have mixed feelings about, and are uncomfortable with, success in courses or occupations traditionally thought of as being in the male domain. This applies to a lesser degree to African American females.

Research indicates that there are at least two reasons for this (51, 168–170, 173, 174). One is that some females are concerned that they may seem less feminine and be less popular with males if they outperform them in these areas. An example of this is a study that found that African American females' stories about a successful African American heroine included concerns that she

> must not only contend with boyfriends who become upset and feel inferior, but also with other males in her class who feel they should not have to compete with a woman. Success also leads to a questioning of feminine identity in that the heroine fears being seen as a freak . . . this successful girl is seen either as an obnoxious misfit who had nothing better to do or as one whose greatest dilemma is now finding a man who is her equal. (170, p. 708)

A second reason why some females are uncomfortable with success is that success provokes a conflict between their desires to achieve and their more traditional perception of the ideal female as less oriented to achievement and individualism than to collaboration and egalitarianism. In this vein, Tannen explains:

> Appearing better than others is a violation of the girls' egalitarian ethic: People are supposed to stress their connection and similarity. . . . It is no wonder that girls fear rejection by their peers if they appear too successful and boys don't. Boys from the earliest age, learn that they can get what they want—higher status—by displaying superiority. Girls learn that displaying superiority will not get them what they want—affiliation with their peers. For this they have to appear the same as, not better than, their friends. (51, pp. 217–218)

Males may also be uncomfortable with success in certain situations. There is some evidence that males may avoid success if their peer group devalues school success or if they perceive success in school as a feminine characteristic (175).

Desirability of Gender Differences

Educators disagree about the desirability of many of the gender differences described in the previous section. For example, some individuals feel that males should be less assertive, aggressive, and competitive and behave more cooperatively; others believe that females should become more assertive and competitive; and still others find the differences between the genders natural, understandable, and totally acceptable. Although individuals may think that some differences are desirable and others unacceptable, their attitudes about gender differences tend to be consistent.

Pro

Certain commentators assert that women and men are most happy and fulfilled when acting out different roles. Woodward claims:

> Mothers who don't want to be mothers and "liberated" women who feel their daughters ought not to learn feminine ways . . . are robbing their daughters of their sexual identities. . . . The forces arrayed against sexual roles in general seem formidable: the more militant women's liberationists for whom mothering is a form of indentured servitude; overachieving fathers for whom inflation is a goad to still longer hours at work; and an increasingly androgynous youth culture that seeks psychological security by deliberately blurring sexual distinctions.(179, p. 28)

Schlafly believes:

> The overriding psychological need of a woman is to love something alive. A baby fulfills this need in the lives of most women. If a baby is not available to fill that need, women search for a baby-substitute. This is the reason why women have traditionally gone into teaching and nursing careers. They are doing what comes naturally to the female psyche. The schoolchild or the patient of any age provides an outlet for a woman to express her natural maternal need. (178, pp. 50–51)

Con

Bem takes a different view:

> In American society, men are supposed to be masculine, women are supposed to be feminine, and neither sex is supposed to be much like the other. If men are independent, tough, and assertive, women should be dependent, sweet, and retiring. A womanly woman may be tender and nurturant, but no manly man may be so. . . .
>
> I have come to believe that we need a new standard of psychological health for the sexes, one that removes the burden of stereotype and allows people to feel free to express

THEORY FOCUS: SCHLAFLY ON BOYS' EDUCATION

No stranger to controversy, Phyllis Schlafly has spoken and written on a wide variety of issues facing women, including sex role differences, women's liberation, and abortion. Many of her 12 books express her views on these subjects. Her impact on women's issues has also resulted from her membership and service on such committees and organizations as Stop ERA, Illinois Commission on the Status of Women, and former president Reagan's Defense Policy Advisory Group.

Though most authors have written about the effects of sex roles on female students, Schlafly is equally concerned that males should receive an appropriate education. According to her,

at the age that formal schooling begins for most Americans, little boys lag at least a year behind little girls in maturity. Yet no provision is made for this gender difference either in our compulsory school attendance laws or in the curriculum of kindergarten and first and second grades. It is unnatural for little boys of that age to be expected to sit quietly at a desk and do neat pencil-and-paper work as little girls can so easily do.

This equality of treatment is grievously unfair to the boys, and often causes a deep sense of failure and frustration. When boys cannot compete successfully with

girls at their assigned tasks, they seek other (perhaps antisocial) ways of using their excess energies. The result is that boys outnumber girls 13 to 1 in learning failure classes and 8 to 1 among the emotionally disturbed.

Early school entry is harmful to both boys and girls because it makes them peer dependent, but it is twice as harmful to boys. This is only the beginning of the regulations, curricula, and customs of public schools which try to teach a gender neutrality that is contrary to human experience. Coed sports and coed sex classes that pretend a gender neutrality are harmful both physically and psychologically. School materials that induce role reversals, such as showing men as househusbands and women as construction workers, teach false notions far from reality.

Teachers used to believe they were doing a good thing by trying to make left-handed children right-handed. We now know that is unwise. Likewise, it is unwise to ignore gender identity and try to teach gender neutrality. Gender differences cannot be eradicated, and mixed-up children are the results of those who try.

(Phyllis Schlafly, personal communication)

the best traits of men and women. . . . In fact, there is already considerable evidence that traditional sex typing is unhealthy. For example, high femininity in females consistently correlates with high anxiety, low self-esteem, and low self-acceptance. And although high masculinity in males has been related to better psychological adjustment during adolescence, it is often accompanied during adulthood by high anxiety, high neuroticism, and low self-acceptance.

Traditional sex typing necessarily restricts behavior. Because people learn, during their formative years, to suppress any behavior that might be considered undesirable or inappropriate for their sex, men are afraid to do "women's work," and women are afraid to enter a "man's world." Men are reluctant to be gentle, and women to be assertive. In contrast, androgynous people are not limited by labels. They are able to do whatever they want, both in their behavior and their feelings. (176, p. 32)

And consider the following remarks:

> The masculine imperative, the pressure and compulsion to perform, to prove himself, to dominate, to live up to the "masculine ideal"—in short, to "be a man"—supersedes the instinct to survive. . . .
>
> A man's psychological energy is used to defend *against*, rather than to express, what he really is. His efforts are directed at proving to himself and others what *he is not*: feminine, dependent, emotional, passive, afraid, helpless, a loser, a failure, impotent and so on. . . . The repression of emotion, the denial and suppression of vulnerability, the compulsive competitiveness, the fear of losing, the anxiety over touching or any other form of sensual display, the controlled intellectualizing, and the general lack of spontaneity and unself-conscious playfulness serve to make the companionship of most men unsatisfying and highly limited. Men are at their best when a task has to be completed, a problem solved, or an enemy battled. (177, pp. 91, 93)

Gender-Biased Classroom Management Approaches

Research clearly and conclusively indicates that teachers foster many of the gender differences described by treating male and female students differently.

Teacher Attention and Feedback

Beginning in preschool, boys receive more attention from their teachers (180–204). One reason boys receive more attention is that teachers spend more time disciplining them for misbehavior (192, 204, 206). Much of the difference, however, is due to the positive attention that teachers provide males. Teachers are more likely to call on males when they volunteer to recite and even when they do not volunteer. When students recite, teachers are also more likely to listen to and respond to the males more. Teachers also use more of the males' ideas in classroom discussions and respond to them in more helpful ways (196).

Beginning in preschool, teachers ask males more questions and give them more individual instruction, acknowledgment, praise, encouragement, corrective feedback, opportunities to answer questions correctly, and social interaction (180, 187, 189, 191, 201). The pattern of giving more attention to males is especially prevalent in science and mathematics classes. In mathematics classes, teachers wait longer for males to answer questions before calling on someone else. They reward females for performing computational skills and males for higher level cognitive skills, demonstrate more concern about giving males remedial help, and expect males to be more interested in math and better at solving math problems.

Gender differences in teacher attention and feedback do not favor males in all subjects.

Self-Quiz: Gender Differences

What is your opinion about the observed differences in the gender roles of students? For each of the following differences, state whether you think it is innate or learned, desirable or undesirable. Indicate whether you believe it should be encouraged, accepted, or discouraged.

Play Style

Females engage more often in play activities that involve dolls, beads, makeup, cradles, and kitchen toys and less often in activities that involve airplanes, trucks, cars, blocks, water, and sand.

Interpersonal Relationships

Males are more competitive and less cooperative.

Males share less.

Males express less support for their classmates.

Females are less likely to deal openly with conflicts.

Females are less assertive.

Females are less physically aggressive.

In their relationships with males, females are less competitive, more submissive, and allow them to dominate the conversation.

Males are less compliant toward adults.

Females are more likely to seek the attention and assistance of adults.

Males are less motivated to behave appropriately to obtain approval.

Females use learned helplessness to influence others more often.

Emotional Style

Females are more fearful and anxious.

Females are more willing to express their fears and anxieties.

Females are more likely to experience themselves as sad or depressed.

Males are angry more often.

(continued)

In reading, a course traditionally seen as being in the female domain, teachers tend to spend more time attending to females (191, 199).

How do females interpret their teachers' apparent disinterest in them? Boudreau's conclusion about the message girls receive may be correct: "The idea conveyed to girls is, although subtle, quite clear. What boys do matters more to teachers than what girls do" (182, p. 68).

Teachers also provide males and females different kinds of attention. Again, the difference favors males. Teachers give boys more praise and attention for high levels of achievement and correct responses (183–185, 186, 188). In fact, teachers give high-achieving girls the least amount of attention, praise, and supportive feedback and the largest number of disparaging statements compared to low-achieving girls and all boys (188, 200). They praise girls more for neatness, following instructions exactly, and raising their hands. Even when they give the wrong answer, girls are often praised for raising their hands and volunteering (198). Many teachers avoid criticizing girls' responses, even when they

Moral Style

Females' moral development tends to proceed more rapidly.

Females tell the truth more consistently, following through on what they say they are going to do more often.

Males maintain a double standard (demanding that others behave more morally than they do).

Males are less self-critical of their behavior and more likely to cheat.

Male morality is based on abstract, impersonal, inflexible principles, while female morality is organized around notions of sensitivity to the feelings and needs of others, a sense of responsibility for others, and a desire and willingness to care for others.

Communication Style

Girls' language is more polite.

Girls tend to suggest rather than command.

Girls express themselves less directly.

Boys interrupt one another more often.

Females allow males to dominate the conversation.

Learning Style

Females react less positively to difficult and challenging situations and are less likely to take risks.

Females perform less adequately than boys following failure or the threat of failure.

Females are less self-confident than males, especially in situations that are in the "male domain."

Females are more likely to attribute their poor performance to lack of ability rather than lack of effort or motivation.

Females are more cooperative and may learn better in some cooperative situations.

Females are more oriented toward group rather than individualistic goals.

Males respond better to competitive situations.

Females are more likely to modify their opinions and attitudes to conform to others and to copy what others model.

are wrong (198). This is unfortunate because girls learn better when they receive corrective feedback (190).

There is some evidence that these gender biases in teacher attention are more characteristic of European American teachers than of African Americans (220). This may be one more example of the fact that "Blacks are less gender-typed and more egalitarian than whites" (194, p. 61).

What do teachers communicate to female students when they relate to them in these ways? Are they telling them that they do not expect them to be able to perform well in academic areas? Are they implying that they do not believe that females can respond correctly? Are they saying that females are too fragile to be criticized? Any and all of these explanations are possible in the absence of research data.

How do female students interpret their teachers' bias? With the exception of courses in the "female domain," female students are still getting the message that teachers do not expect them to do as well as boys.

The message that African American females receive is even more destructive

(205–208). Teachers, especially European American teachers, perceive and treat African American females in an even more biased manner than they do European American females (205, 207, 208). These teachers seem to be telling African American females that all they are good for are the stereotypical roles that European Americans have historically assigned to them, such as that of housekeeper, maid, and child-care provider.

Gender and ethnic differences in teacher attention, feedback, expectations, and evaluations can have other negative effects on students (127, 129, 209, 210). They may help explain why girls are more likely than boys to react poorly to failure or the threat of failure and to attribute their poor performance to lack of ability rather than lack of effort. They may also contribute to females' high anxiety during testing situations. And they may be one reason why European American females enroll in fewer math and science courses.

Encouragement of Behavioral Differences

Although all teachers want their students to be well behaved, research conducted from the 1970s to the mid-1980s indicates that teachers have different standards for males and females. Beginning in preschool, teachers tend to encourage gender-stereotypical behavior (75, 182, 211–214). Teachers praise boys more than girls for creative behavior and girls more than boys for conforming behavior. Boys are rewarded for functioning independently, while girls are rewarded for being obedient and compliant. Boudreau believes that this form of discrimination harms females: "The pattern of reinforcement that young girls receive may lead them to stake their sense of self-worth more on conforming than personal competency" (182, p. 73). To the extent that these research findings still prevail, teachers who encourage these gender differences can certainly cause problems for girls in situations that require creativity, assertiveness, or independence.

Teachers accept different kinds of inappropriate behavior from males and females. Huffine, Silvern, and Brooks found that kindergarten teachers discipline males and females for different kinds of misbehavior:

> Aggression in boys is acceptable while in girls it is not. The reverse seems to be true of disruptive talking. Teachers expect and/or accept talking from girls, at least much more so than from boys. Thus, the stereotypical behaviors, aggressiveness and loquacity, may be acquired and/or maintained by the differential teacher responses to these behaviors. (213, p. 34)

Intolerance of Male Behavior Patterns

Boys get into trouble with their teachers more frequently than girls. There are two reasons for this: Boys are less prepared to behave in the ways their teachers desire, and teachers react more often to the misbehavior of males than of females (182, 215–217, 222–225).

Boudreau (182) points out that girls and boys come to school with different behavior styles, and this is likely to cause them to have different kinds of problems:

Girls, on the average, enter school better equipped to play the student role than boys. The nonassertive, nonaggressive behavior that is part of girls' socialization fits right in with the structured routine of the classroom. The competitive, self-assertive behavior for which boys have been rewarded outside the classroom creates greater adjustment problems for them. Boys are more likely to "get into trouble" than girls. Paradoxically, the very behavior that allows girls to fit into school more easily also functions to make them less visible, inhibits their learning process, and leads to differences in self-expectancies for success. (182, p. 98)

Educators, especially female educators, tend to be less tolerant of "male-typical" behaviors (226, 227). African American males are especially likely to suffer the consequences of teachers' intolerance. Many African American males, and females as well, express their emotions much more intensely than most European Americans. As noted in the previous chapter, when European American teachers observe African American males behaving aggressively and assertively, they tend to assume that the students are much angrier or upset than they actually are. When teachers interpret such situations from their own perspective, they intervene when no intervention is necessary. If teachers appreciated the cultural context of African American males' seemingly aggressive behavior toward others and understood that such behavior is unlikely to cause the fight (or whatever else they expect to occur) between African American students, they would not feel so compelled to intervene. This, in turn, would lessen the likelihood that African American males would get into trouble needlessly.

Biased Disciplinary Techniques

Teachers tend to reprimand males more often than females, and differently as well (20, 182, 185, 213, 217). They tend to speak softly and privately to girls but harshly and publicly to boys. With younger children, they tend to use physical methods like poking, slapping, grabbing, pushing, and squeezing with boys and negative comments, disapproving gestures, and other forms of nonverbal communication with girls (213). Teachers are more likely to use even harsher disciplinary techniques, such as corporal punishment and suspension, with poor, African American, and Hispanic American males than with middle-class European American males (213, 217, 218–221). This is unfortunate because public and harsh reprimands, physical forms of discipline, and severe punishments can cause students to react rebelliously to punishments that they feel are too harsh for their "crimes." This may help explain why males get into trouble in school and are referred to special education programs for students with behavior and emotional problems much more often than females. It may also help explain why males from poor backgrounds and some non-European American backgrounds tend to get into even more trouble than European American middle-class males (222–225).

Gender Segregation/Separation

Studies done in the late 1970s and mid-1980s revealed that some teachers discouraged male-female interaction. Instead of encouraging mixed-gender groups, some teachers assigned certain chores to boys and other chores to girls. For example, girls put things in order while boys moved furniture. Some teachers separated boys and girls when assigning seats or areas to hang up clothes and when forming study and work groups and committees (202, 228, 231). Lockheed and Harris reported a particularly sexist management approach: "In classrooms, assignment to mixed-sex seating adjacencies or groups often is used as a punishment designed to reduce student interaction instead of as a learning technique designed to foster cooperative interaction" (229, p. 276).

Roberts explains why some educators follow such practices:

> The physical separation of boys and girls can be interpreted in a variety of ways. At one level, teachers continue this practice because of their belief that a certain degree of mischief and teasing will be avoided. Also, some teachers feel that girls need this kind of protection and insulation from supposedly aggressive boys who might take advantage of and dominate the girls. Another explanation of teacher and school policy that separates the sexes is the fear that boys and girls will become involved in sexual games together. For many teachers this very terrifying possibility is avoided by turning girls and boys into "natural" rivals, and by accentuating stereotypical behavior differences. This process helps to prevent girls and boys from developing open, healthy friendships with one another. (202, pp. 156–157)

It is unclear how many teachers engaged in these practices in the past and whether teachers continue to do so now. Research is needed to determine if these practices continue and if they are widespread.

Conclusions

The data clearly indicate that many teachers use different classroom management approaches for males and females. These differences can cause problems for both groups and foster stereotypical gender roles. As Meece puts it:

> Schools have been slow in adapting to recent changes in the social roles of men and women. As a result, schools may be exposing children to masculine and feminine images that are even more rigid and more polarized than those currently held in the wider society. Furthermore, the school setting does not seem to provide children with many opportunities to perform behaviors not associated with their gender. Therefore, schools seem to play an important role in reinforcing rigid gender distinctions. (194, p. 67)

Positions on Gender Differences

While no evidence as yet directly supports the following suppositions, it seems probable that few educators would disagree that teachers should:

Self-Quiz: Gender-Appropriate Classroom Management

What is your opinion about the gender issues discussed in this chapter? Your answers to the following questions should provide you with some of the insight you need to avoid using gender-biased classroom management approaches.

Should males and females be separated for some activities?
Are some topics better dealt with in single-gender groups?

Should students be allowed to sit, play, or work in same-gender groups if they appear to prefer them?

Should teachers ask males to do the physical work, such as moving furniture, and females to decorate the room, organize the bulletin board, clean up, or do other traditional female chores?

Should females act like ladies and males like gentlemen?

When males are dominating the group by monopolizing the conversation and making most of the suggestions and decisions, should teachers intervene on the females' behalf and encourage them to take a more active role in the group?

Should teachers discourage males from dominating females?

Should teachers encourage female students who are passive or docile to be more assertive and competitive and to take more risks?

Should teachers encourage boys to be less competitive and assertive and more cooperative?

Should teachers encourage all students to behave in a conforming, quiet manner?

Should educators be as concerned about the female-typical behavior of passive, inhibited, quiet, withdrawn, timid, or overdependent students as they are about the male-typical behavior of overactive, overly assertive, or overly aggressive students?

Should teachers be equally accepting of students who are assertive and students who are passive, of students who are competitive and those who are cooperative, and of students who prefer to work alone and those who like to work in groups?

When there is a conflict between students, should they face it head-on or "sweep it under the carpet"?

Should students try to find a compromise solution to disagreements or stand up for their rights as they see them?

Should teachers use the same or different disciplinary approaches with males and females?

Are the more severe forms of punishment more appropriate for males than for females?

Do you think that educators should use the same rewards for male and female students, or do you believe that some rewards are more appropriate for one gender than for the other?

- Pay equal attention to boys and girls who volunteer answers or ask questions.
- Provide the same amount and kind of help to students, regardless of their gender.
- Praise male and female students equally for high achievement and creativity.
- Attribute the cause of students' poor performance accurately.

- Be equally attentive to the misbehavior of boys and girls.

- Avoid using public and harsh reprimands with all students.

- Discourage dependent, helpless, and overconforming behavior in all students.

Less agreement exists among educators about whether they should:

- Separate boys and girls during certain activities.

- Permit males and females to choose to work and play in homogeneous groups.

- Encourage, permit, or discourage boys and girls from engaging in activities that reflect societal gender stereotypes.

- Encourage, permit, or discourage gender differences in cooperative versus competitive behavior, assertive versus passive behavior, risk-taking, politeness, emotional expressiveness, conformity, and docility.

- Encourage students to conform to the same standards of behavior, regardless of their gender.

- Use the same disciplinary classroom management procedures with males and females.

The controversy about gender differences in society at large is reflected in people's attitudes regarding what, if anything, educators should do about gender differences in the schools despite Title IX, which requires the elimination of differential treatment in schools based on gender (230). Individuals who feel that the gender differences discussed earlier in this chapter are natural basically favor leaving things as they were 20, 30, or 40 years ago. Individuals who don't approve of gender differences, at least to the extent that they currently exist in our society, criticize educators who they believe help maintain a sexist society.

Excluding the practices that most educators would probably agree are unfair, here are the four most common positions that have appeared in the literature about whether teachers should treat females and males the same:

1. *Educators should not treat males and females the same* (238–240). Educators should prepare the genders to fulfill different societal roles because there are natural, physiological differences between the sexes. And educators should accommodate their methods to these existing gender differences. The author of the following quotation argues that males are being feminized because schools treat both genders the same:

> Boys who rise to the top in school often resemble girls in many important ways. . . .
> Scholastic honor and masculinity, in other words, too often seem incompatible. . . .
> The feminized school simply bores many boys: but it pulls some in one of two opposite directions. If the boy absorbs school values, he may become feminized himself. If he resists, he is pushed toward school failure and rebellion. (239, pp. 13, 33)

Do you agree that being a "real boy" is incompatible with being a good student? Do you agree that being a "real boy" in the sense that the term is usually used is a desirable personality characteristic? What is your opinion about the author's concern that schools feminize males?

Educators who believe that boys should be allowed to be boys and girls allowed to be girls may avoid some disagreements and conflicts with their students by not trying to change their behavior. For example, educators who permit boys to behave less politely, less compliantly, and more aggressively than girls don't need to scold and discipline them as much as educators who require the same compliant, nonassertive behavior from both genders. Educators who permit girls to feign helplessness and act dependently may avoid the battles of wills that could result from attempts to get them to change their behavior. And educators who allow girls and boys to maintain the kinds of relationships with each other that they have outside of school, even though it means looking the other way when girls submit to male domination, may avoid the hassles that could come with trying to change their relationships. But going along with the prevailing gender stereotypes can also be detrimental to students if it results in allowing and encouraging females to submit to male domination or if it confirms female students' beliefs that it is appropriate for them to be dependent and helpless.

2. *Educators should cease fostering gender differences that are unnatural, outdated, and harmful* (119, 231, 232, 235, 237). Educators should prepare students for the androgynous roles that are increasingly available to them in society and perhaps even encourage and prepare students to do what is necessary to transform our sexist society into a less sexist one. Bem's viewpoint is repeated here:

> In American society, men are supposed to be masculine, women are supposed to be feminine, and neither sex is supposed to be much like the other. If men are independent, tough, and assertive, women should be dependent, sweet, and retiring. A womanly woman may be tender and nurturant, but no manly man may be so. . . . I have come to believe that we need a new standard of psychological health for the sexes, one that removes the burden of stereotype and allows people to feel free to express the best traits of men and women. . . .
>
> Traditional sex typing necessarily restricts behavior. Because people learn, during their formative years, to suppress any behavior that might be considered undesirable or inappropriate for their sex, men are afraid to do "women's work" and women are afraid to enter a "man's world." Men are reluctant to be gentle, and women to be assertive. In contrast, androgynous people are not limited by labels. They are able to do whatever they want, both in their behavior and their feelings. (231, p. 32)

Brooks-Gunn and Matthews argue that "if docility, obedience, and conformity are undesirable traits for boys, surely they are undesirable for girls as well." (233, p. 188) Carson and Carson further suggest:

> It is senseless to expect boys to misbehave simply because they are boys or to expect girls to behave simply because they are girls. . . . Such sexual stereotyped thinking often causes problems for everyone. . . . Viewing a child's behavior on the basis of his or her sex is unfair to the uniqueness of the child. Furthermore, labeling the child as "sweet, good, little girl" or "all boy" rather than describing the specific behavior is a judgment that serves no important purpose other than establishing sexist and confining behavioral expectations. (234, p. 125)

Schools can discourage gender differences.

Do you agree that students should be encouraged to become androgynous? If you do, you probably favor discouraging students from accepting and acting out any gender-stereotypical roles, whatever they may be.

Eliminating gender stereotypes can help students. For example, convincing girls that they can do well in math, science, and computer courses or convincing boys that it's okay for them to express their anxieties and fears can be beneficial. But pressuring girls to take courses that they feel they can't do well in or to engage in rough sports that they think are unfeminine or pressuring boys to take home economics or to expose their feelings to others when they feel they shouldn't, can create, not solve, problems.

3. *Educators should decide for themselves whether they want to prepare students to fulfill different gender roles or encourage students to fulfill similar roles* (236). The desirability or lack of desirability of gender roles is something for the individual professional or the group to decide:

> If we value the higher levels of aggressiveness in males, then schools should encourage aggression, competition, and assertion more in females. This might mean more emphasis on competitive athletics for girls, perhaps beginning in early elementary school, or perhaps even in the preschool years. In the academic classroom, it might mean encouraging reticent girls to speak up more forcefully in debates or to become more competitive about their success in mathematics courses. If, on the other hand, we value the low level of aggressiveness of females, we might seek to reduce the level of aggressiveness in boys, while simultaneously encouraging peaceful cooperation for them. . . .

We might want to de-emphasize competitive sports in favor of cooperative sports or noncompetitive ones such as jogging. In the classroom, we would avoid competitively structured learning and work toward cooperatively structured learning. . . . Which of these alternatives is chosen, of course, is a matter of values. (236, pp. 64–65)

Do you agree that gender roles are inherently neither desirable nor undesirable, but depend on the values of different individuals and societies? If so, does that mean that societies have the right to establish different expectations for their male and female members? Does it also follow that different ethnic and socioeconomic groups have the right to expect the schools to respect their freedom to bring up their children to fulfill the gender roles they believe most appropriate? Or should the greater society determine the gender roles for all the subgroups living within its boundaries?

4. *Educators should empower students to decide for themselves whether to conform to any particular gender role or to be androgynous.* Educators who favor this position believe that only the students themselves have the right and the self-knowledge to make decisions about their gender roles:

> To force everyone into the new mold may violate the individual as much as to force them into the older stereotypes. . . . Freedom to choose according to individual need would seem to be the preferred way of dealing with the complex problem of man/woman roles. (239, p. 202)

Should teachers encourage and enable their students to make their own decisions, or should teachers involve themselves in shaping their students' attitudes about gender roles? Do students, especially younger ones, have the necessary experience and maturity to make thoughtful decisions in this area?

Cautions When Dealing with Gender Differences

When dealing with gender differences in school, it's worth keeping the following things in mind. First, only a fine line separates *encouraging* students to change and *pressuring* them to do so. What an educator thinks is encouragement, students can experience as pressure. Second, by encouraging students to behave in ways that their families and friends think is totally inappropriate, well-meaning educators may place students in conflict situations between the school on one side and the home and community on the other. This can cause students to experience the same kinds of identity conflicts as culturally different students. Third, while it is clear that some of the observed differences in behavior between female and male students are learned, unnecessary, and harmful, considerable controversy still exists over the origin of other differences. For example, after reviewing the available research, Maccoby and Jacklin (193) suggest that the observed differences between males and females in aggressiveness may be biologically determined; many other authors, however, reject this possibility. Basically, we do not at present know for sure which, if any, gender differences are biologically based and which are socially learned.

THEORY FOCUS: MACCOBY STUDIES GENDER ROLES

In addition to serving as the codirector of the Maccoby-Jacklin longitudinal study of behavioral differences among males and females, Eleanor Maccoby has brought together the research in the area of sex or gender role differences in her pioneering works *The Development of Sex Differences* and *The*

Psychology of Sex Differences. Through these and other publications, she has contributed significantly to our objective knowledge about what sex role differences actually exist and to our ability to begin to apportion the origins of these differences between genetic and environmental causes.

Even if some of the observed differences do have a biological basis, it's still unclear whether these biological factors *require* people to behave in certain ways or merely incline people to behave in these ways unless they are taught to behave differently. Until we know more about which gender differences are biologically based and which are learned and the extent to which even biologically based behavior patterns are modifiable, educators' decisions to accommodate to or change gender differences in behavior will continue to be based on their preferences, values, and biases rather than on a body of proved scientific fact.

Finally, virtually no research has been done to determine the most effective techniques to help students change behavior that fits a particular gender stereotype, to deal with identity conflicts, or to prepare students' classmates, friends, and families to accept and welcome their new behavior. Until we have more reliable information, a cautious, sensitive approach seems the wisest course.

Legal Requirements

Title IX of the Education Amendments Act was designed to correct the biased treatment that males and females receive in school. Some of the provisions of Title IX that protect students from gender bias also restrict the rights of educators to decide for themselves about how to respond to certain gender issues (230).

Title IX requires schools to provide equal educational opportunities to all students, regardless of gender. As it did in the 1970s and 1980s, Title IX serves as the main legal basis for efforts to eliminate gender-discriminatory educational practices. Its requirements include the following:

- Students may not be denied admission to schools or subjected to discriminatory admissions practices on the basis of their gender.

- Once admitted, students may not be excluded from participation in, be denied the benefits of, or be subjected to discrimination while participating in, any academic,

---

Self-Quiz: Modeling

Since research indicates that students' behavior is sometimes influenced more by what teachers do than by what they say, you may want to learn about the kind of model you present to your students. When you have your own class, ask a colleague to observe and rate you in terms of the behavioral differences typically observed among males and females.

---

extracurricular, research, occupational training, or other educational program or activity.

- All courses and activities, except human sexuality courses, must be open to all students, regardless of their gender. If offered, human sexuality courses must be available to all students, but they can be taught separately to males and females.

- Standards for student participation in physical education activities and ability groupings within these activities must be objective and applied equally to all students, regardless of gender. Separate athletic teams may be provided for males and females for contact sports or for other sports when the separation is justified by differences in skills. However, if a school has a contact sport for males only, a noncontact alternative team sport for females must be provided.

- Dress codes must be applied equally to males and females.

- Graduation requirements must be the same for both genders.

- Textbooks and other instructional materials are exempted from Title IX regulations owing to potential conflicts with freedom of speech rights guaranteed by the First Amendment and other legislation.

Sexual Orientation

In addition to gender issues, many teachers, especially those who teach in secondary schools, are also confronted with issues around adolescents' emerging sexual drives and sexual orientation. Educators disagree about how these problems should be managed. They even disagree about whether these topics are fit for discussion in school. Sexuality, and especially sexual orientation, is a forbidden subject in many schools, and many individuals and community groups demand that it remain so. For example, only 1 out of 28 local school district boards in the New York City public school system voted to include in their schools the central board of education approved elementary school curriculum that deals with homosexual orientation (242).

Self-Quiz: Critical Incidents

This self-quiz is designed to provide you with some insight into the approaches you might use to resolve gender issues. First describe how you think the teacher involved should handle each of the following critical incidents. Then put yourself in the teacher's place, disregarding the original teacher's point of view. Instead, imagine what your viewpoint would be and how you would deal with the problem. If you prefer a number of different approaches to the incidents, try to determine the factors that led you to select the particular approaches you would use in each critical incident.

1. The father of an Asian American preschool student is angry because his son told him that his teacher encouraged him to play in the housekeeping/dollhouse area. He tells the teacher that he does not want his son to play "girls' games" or with "girl things." The teacher believes that doll and housekeeping play are important for all children because they foster caring and nurturing qualities in children and androgynous gender roles.
2. A group of second-grade girls does not want any boys to join in their game in the school yard because the boys play too rough. The teacher wants to encourage boys and girls to play together.
3. A fourth-grade student suggests that the class should have a spelling bee with the boys against the girls, like some other classes do. The teacher feels that the students are already too competitive and wants them to learn to be more cooperative. In addition, the teacher believes in bringing the genders together rather than identifying them as competing groups.
4. A fifth-grade Hispanic American girl says that she does not want to participate in physical education classes because she feels that girls should not participate in sports or physical fitness exercises. The teacher believes that physical activities and sports are appropriate for both sexes.
5. After raising her hand repeatedly to volunteer answers to her teacher's questions without being called on, a sixth-grade student complains that her teacher is unfair because the teacher always calls on the boys to answer the difficult questions. The teacher does not believe that the student is correct.
6. One of a teacher's best students, a ninth-grade Hispanic American female in a program for gifted and talented youth, informs the teacher that she is not going to continue in the program in high school because she is not planning to go to college. When the teacher asks why, the student replies that in her family and culture, college is for boys. She says that her plans are to finish high school, find a job for a while, get married, have four or five children, and stay home. The teacher believes that females should be encouraged to go on to college so that they can have the career and other opportunities that a college degree provides.
7. The immigrant mother of a 15-year-old female refuses to give her daughter permission to attend school dances or go on coeducational school outings because she believes that her daughter is too young to understand and deal with the physical desires of male teenagers. She explains that in her country, girls are expected to avoid such situations until they are much older.

Problems

Although research indicates that there are no innate reasons why lesbian, gay, and bisexual students should have more problems than other students, society's homophobic attitudes condemn many of them to a very difficult adolescence (243–246, 249–251, 256, 257, 260–262, 264). They experience a great deal of discrimination and prejudice both

Self-Quiz: An Incident on the Playground

The following incident was reported by a school principal:

> Allen attended a parochial school where the playgrounds were segregated by gender. In one playground the girls skipped and jumped rope; in the other, the boys played football. Allen often stood on the sidelines and chatted with several other non-athletic boys. Allen's teacher was concerned and arranged privately with several of the male athletes to include Allen and his friends in the daily football game. The teacher warned that if they failed to do so, all of the boys in the class would be punished. (241, p. 208)

How do you feel about the gender separation that existed on the playgrounds? What is your opinion about the way the teacher responded to Allen and his friends' behavior? What might have been the teacher's reason for responding in that manner? How would you have responded?

in and out of school, and they also have a great deal of difficulty adjusting to their sexual orientation.

Because gay and lesbian students are brought up in a homophobic society and have little access to information that portrays lesbians and gays in a positive way, many of them suffer from homophobia and believe that they are sick, evil, inferior, and disgusting. These ideas can lead to emotional problems such as depression, shame, guilt, low self-esteem, self-hatred, or at least ambivalence toward their sexual orientation. In turn, their emotional problems can cause them to drop out of school, abuse substances, and even commit suicide. Some homosexual students attempt, usually unsuccessfully, to change their sexual orientation. Most students hide their homosexuality, thereby living in fear that they will be discovered. Kissen describes their plight:

> If, like most gay adolescents, they try to hide their identity, they live in constant fear that someone will discover they are gay. Even if they are successful at concealment, they must live every day as a lie, pretending to be someone they are not, and surrounded by homophobic jokes. . . . Anyone who spends time in a high school is surely aware that homophobia—fear and hatred of gay people—is the last "acceptable" form of bigotry among adolescents. Young people who would not dream of uttering (or would not dare to utter) a racial or religious epithet still unthinkingly toss around "queer" and "faggot," probably the most often heard insults in any high school. (253, p. 2)

Sometimes, gay, lesbian, and bisexual students declare their sexual orientation to others (come out). This can make them feel that they have been true to themselves and enable them to have relationships with others based on honesty and trust. However, coming out can cause family conflicts and parental rejection, and many of these students run away from home. Loss of the friendship of (and indeed abuse by) their heterosexual peers often follows. Ross-Reynolds offers this description of the problems faced by a gay and a lesbian student:

> Andy is a middle-class, White sixteen-year-old who ran away from his family home in Oregon after suffering years of abuse from his father after the man read his son's love letters from another boy. . . . Andy worked in a fast food restaurant in the evenings and

attended high school during the day, resolving to complete high school and get his diploma, despite the obstacles caused by the relocation. Instead of a supportive environment at his new school, Andy found his peers hostile and harassing. Openly gay to his classmates and teachers, Andy was mocked during class time by other students, and received no support from teachers. After he was physically assaulted at the bus stop after school Andy felt pushed to the point of either quitting school or demanding action.

Nina is a Black fifteen-year-old from Harlem. She had difficulty coping with the rejection she faced in her inner-city high school because she was up front about being a lesbian. . . . Name-calling, harassing notes, and verbal threats of violence, including rape, began to turn an upbeat, cheerful girl into a jumble of dysfunction and misery. As Nina faced the unpleasant task of steeling herself for two more years of such assaults, she found herself moving toward leaving school. (262, pp. 444–445)

Gay, bisexual, and lesbian students, as well as those students who are worried about their sexual orientation, need as much help and understanding as any other student with serious problems. However, many educators believe that school is not the place to deal with differences in sexual orientation. That may be why sexual orientation problems and the presence of lesbian, bisexual, and gay students are denied or unnoticed at best. Dunham describes the situation in the schools as follows:

While mental health professionals have worked to create positive and meaningful programs for the gay and lesbian population, educational systems have been considerably less eager to recognize and respond to the needs of this minority group. Public schools have continued to treat homosexuality as a forbidden subject. (247, p. 3)

Solutions

What, if anything, should teachers do about these issues in their classrooms? Educators have offered the following suggestions for helping students who are concerned about their sexual orientation (245, 246, 248, 254, 259, 262):

- Resist community pressure to avoid relating to the needs of students who are concerned about their sexual orientation.

- Protect students from harassment, criticize such incidents when they occur, and express disapproval of jokes about gays.

- Modify homophobic attitudes. Since values are caught, not taught, teach students to accept each other regardless of sexual orientation by modeling acceptance.

- Include issues and topics that affect gay and lesbian students in the curriculum (e.g., gay rights and contributions in social studies classes, gay lifestyles in health and psychology courses, and gay and lesbian authors in English courses).

- Oppose censorship of texts and library materials that demonstrate respect for lesbian and gay rights and lifestyles.

- Dispel myths about people with nonheterosexual orientations.

- Have students experience the effects of discrimination and homophobic attitudes on students by role playing.

Myths About Gay and Lesbian Students

Effeminate boys and masculine females and those who like to cross-dress or play with toys that are thought of as in the domain of the opposite gender grow up to become gay and lesbian. Research indicates that although some gay and lesbian students are more likely to exhibit cross-gender behaviors when they are children and adolescents, many do not, and many children who exhibit these behaviors do not grow up to be gay or lesbian.

One homosexual experience means that a person is and will be homosexual. In reality, neither homosexual nor heterosexual experimentation is unusual. Human sexuality exists along a continuum from completely heterosexual to completely homosexual, with many people somewhere between the extremes but close to the heterosexual end.

Discussing gay and lesbian issues encourages students to become homosexuals. There is no evidence to support this notion.

Lesbian and gay teachers provide role models that encourage students to become lesbians and gays. Homosexuality is not caught by observing lesbian and gay models.

Gay and lesbian adults sexually abuse children and recruit them to their lifestyles. Children and adolescents are much more likely to be abused by heterosexual adults.

Homosexuality is a sickness or a disorder. The American Psychological Association and the American Psychiatric Association both state that homosexuality is not a disorder.

Homosexual behavior is rare in most animal species. Research indicates that the opposite is true.

Because gays are incapable of establishing long-term relationships, they lead lonely, isolated lives. Many gay and lesbian couples enjoy long-term relationships.

Homosexuality is a choice that one makes. Research indicates that in our society, most homosexuals at first reject their homosexuality and resist thinking of themselves as homosexuals (252, 258, 263).

- Advocate for students' rights.
- Include homosexual role models:

    A healthy socialization process involves positive role models. Ideally, the socialization experiences for gay and lesbian adolescents will include learning from competent gay and lesbian adults. Observing how successful adults develop productive and ethical lifestyles, resolve problems of identity disclosure, obtain support, manage a career, and build relationships can be extremely valuable for teenagers. (249, p. 121)

- Refer students to community agencies and resources where they can obtain assistance.

It is not easy for educators to carry out these suggestions, as Rofes points out:

Because many educators believe that homosexuality is sick, sinful, or criminal, it is tremendously difficult for them to truly adopt an "objective" stance when addressing gay

---

Self-Quiz:
Gay and Lesbian
Sexual Orientations

1. What is your opinion about the following statement?

   In a democratic country no citizen should be forced to live under the fear

of homophobia. Fear is unhealthy for the individual and our democracy. . . . We need not endorse particular private sexual acts to protect the civil rights of all citizens. (255, p. 285)

2. Should sexual orientation issues be included in the curriculum? Should educators discuss their students' sexual orientation problems with them?

---

and lesbian issues in the classroom. . . . By allowing positive treatment of homosexuality in the classroom, teachers are vulnerable to witch-hunts by parents and school committees attempting to root out homosexual teachers. In certain parts of the nation, laws have been proposed and successfully passed that forbid positive discussion of homosexuality in public school classrooms. (263, p. 451)

In addition, since "Gay and lesbian adolescents continue to be socialized to conceal their identities—educated to be invisible within the school community and the community at large" (247, p. 5), they are often reluctant to come out—to disclose their sexual orientation to others.

If you teach in a secondary school, sexual orientation issues will probably arise in your classes at various times during your teaching career. How will you handle them? You may decide to avoid them. Or you may tackle them head-on, perhaps following many of the suggestions listed here. The final self-quiz in this chapter is designed to help you resolve this important issue.

Summary

Significant differences show up in the ways boys and girls behave in school. Many, but not all, people believe that this is a reflection of gender stereotypes that exist in society at large. These individuals claim that educators either knowingly or unknowingly contribute to maintaining such stereotypes, and they offer specific suggestions for overcoming and eliminating them in school. Accepting and accommodating to gender differences can help educators avoid some behavior problems, but it can also cause other problems. But then, attempting to eliminate gender differences can help students and yet can cause problems for them as well.

It seems reasonable to assume that the more educators are aware of the relationship between gender stereotypes and behavior problems, the more they can help their students. Yet, to date, little scientific knowledge shows which gender differences are natural and which are learned, when and how to accommodate to necessary differences, and when and how to eliminate unnecessary ones. Much of what goes on in classrooms behind closed doors regarding the encouragement and discouragement of gender differences is based on the preferences and values of individual educators. Therefore, it is imperative that educators become aware of their preferences and values regarding gender differences and do what is best for their students, not what makes them personally most comfortable.

Although adolescents have many problems concerning their sexual orientation, sexual orientation is a forbidden subject in many schools. Some educators believe that this is as it should be. Many others fault the schools for failing to help students with their problems. They suggest that educators should modify their own homophobic attitudes and those of their students, protect students from harassment, advocate for homosexual students' rights, include homosexual role models and topics that affect gay and lesbian students in the curriculum, oppose censorship of texts and library materials that demonstrate respect for lesbian and gay rights and lifestyles, and dispel myths about people with non-heterosexual orientations. In today's environment, this will not be an easy thing for educators to accomplish.

Activities

I. Ask some of your classmates in this class or other courses you may be taking to respond to the critical incidents in the self-quiz. Do you notice any gender or ethnic differences in their responses?

II. How knowledgeable are your classmates about Title IX? Make up a short quiz on the subject and administer it to them. Do you notice any gender differences in the extent of their knowledge?

III. Ask some gay or lesbian students or friends whether they have experienced any of the problems described in this chapter. Ask them if any of their teachers knew about their sexual orientation, how those teachers reacted to the information, and how they would have preferred their teachers to have reacted.

IV. Compose a questionnaire based on the myths about homosexuality, and administer it to some of your friends or other students. Do they believe the prevalent myths, or do they know the facts? Do you notice any gender differences in their beliefs?

References

Gender differences in play preferences are discussed in the following references.

1. Cameron, E., Eisenberg, N., & Kelly, T. (1985). The relations between sex-type play and preschoolers' social behavior. *Sex Roles, 12* (5), 601–615.

2. Carpenter, C. J. (1979). *Relation of Children's Sex-Typed Behavior to Classroom and Activity Structure.* ERIC ED 178 173.

3. Charlesworth, W. R., & Dzur, C. 1987. Gender comparisons of preschoolers' behavior and resource utilization in group problem-solving. *Child Development, 58*, 191–200.

4. DiPietro, J. A. (1981). Rough and tumble play: A function of gender. *Developmental Psychology, 17* (1), 50–58.

5. Fagot, B. I. 1985. Beyond the reinforcement principle: Another step toward understanding sex roles. *Developmental Psychology, 21*, 1097–1104.

6. Giddings, M., & Halverson, C. F. (1981). Young children's use of toys in home environments. *Family Relations, 30*, 69–74.

7. Harper, L. W., & Sanders, K. M. (1975). Preschool children's use of space: Sex differences in outdoor play. *Developmental Psychology, 11* (1), 119.

8. Johnson, J. E., & Ershler, J. (1981). Developmental trends in preschool play as a function of classroom program and child gender. *Child Development, 52* (3), 995–1004.

9. Maccoby, E. E. (1988). Gender as a social category. *Developmental Psychology, 24* (6), 755–765.

10. O'Brien, M., & Huston, A. C. (1985). Development of sex-typed play behavior in toddlers. *Developmental Psychology, 21* (5), 866–871.

11. Pellegrini, A. D. (1983). *Children's Social Cognitive Play Behavior: The Effects of Age, Gender, and Activity Centers.* ERIC ED 245 814.

12. Varma, M. (1980, July). Sex-stereotyping in block play of preschool children. *Indiana Educational Review*, 32–37.

These references indicate that males are the more active sex.

13. Maccoby, E. E., & Feldman, S. S. (1972). Mother-attachment and stranger-reactions in the third year of life. *Monographs of the Society for Research in Child Development, 37*.

14. Pedersen, F. A., & Bell, R. Q. (1970). Sex differences in preschool children without histories of complications of pregnancy and delivery. *Developmental Psychology, 3*, 10–15.

15. Smith, P. K., & Connolly, K. (1972). Patterns of play and social interactions in preschool children. In N. Blurton-Jones (Ed.), *Ethological Studies of Child Behavior.* Cambridge, England: Cambridge University Press.

Differences in the way the sexes relate to others are the focus of the following references.

16. Becker, J. A., & Smenner, P. C. (1986). The spontaneous use of "thank you" by preschoolers as a function of sex, socioeconomic status, and listener status. *Language in Society, 15* (4), 37–45.

17. Charlesworth, W. R., & La Frenier, P. (1983). Dominance, friendship utilization and resource utilization in preschool children's groups. *Ethology and Sociobiology, 4*, 175–186.

18. Cook, S. A., Fritz, J. J., MacCormack, B. L., & Visperas, C. (1985). Early gender differences in the functional use of language. *Sex Roles, 12* (9), 909–915.

19. Esposito, A. (1979). Sex differences in children's conversation. *Language and Speech, 22* (3), 213–220.

20. Fagot, B. L., & Hagan, R. (1985). Aggression in toddlers: Responses to the assertive acts of boys and girls. *Sex Roles, 12* (3), 341–351.

21. Feldbaum, C. L., Christenson, T. E., & O'Neal, E. D. (1980). An observational study of the assimilation of the newcomer to the preschool. *Child Development, 51*, 497–507.

22. Hyde, J. S. (1984). How large are gender differences in aggression? A developmental meta-analysis. *Developmental Psychology, 20*, 722–736.

23. Jacklin, C. N., & Maccoby, E. E. (1978). Social behavior at 33 months in same-sex and mixed-sex dyads. *Child Development, 49*, 557–569.

24. Jennings, K. D., & Suwalsky, J. T. (1982). Reciprocity in the dyadic play of three-year-olds. In J. W. Lay (Ed.), *The Paradox of Play*. West Point, NY: Leisure Press.

25. King, L. A., & Barnett, M. A. (1980). *The Effects of Age and Sex on Preschoolers' Helpfulness*. ERIC ED 188 779.

26. Maccoby, E. E., & Jacklin, C. (1980). Sex differences in aggression: A rejoiner and reprise. *Child Development, 51*, 964–980.

27. Sachs, J. (1987). Preschool boys' and girls' language use in pretend play. In S. U. Philips, S. Steele, & C. Tanz (Eds.), *Language, Gender, and Sex in Comparative Perspective*. Cambridge, England: Cambridge University Press.

28. Serbin, L. A., Sprafkin, C., Elman, M., & Doyle, A. B. (1984). The early development of sex differentiated patterns of social influence. *Canadian Journal of Social Science, 14* (4), 350–363.

The following references describe gender differences in emotional reactions.

29. Baron, P., & Perron, L. M. (1986). Sex differences in the Beck Depression Inventory scores of adolescents. *Journal of Youth and Adolescents, 15* (2), 165–171.

30. Brody, L. R. (1984). Sex and age variation in the quality and intensity of children's emotional attributions to hypothetical situations. *Sex Roles, 11* (1), 51–59.

31. Choquet, M., & Menke, H. (1987). Development of self-perceived risk behavior and psychosomatic symptoms in adolescents: A longitudinal approach. *Journal of Adolescence, 10*, 291–308.

32. Czerniak, C., & Chiarelotti, L. (1984). *Science Anxiety: An Investigation of Science Achievement, Sex and Grade Level Factors*. ERIC ED 243 672.

33. Hadfield, O. D., & Maddux, C. D. (1988). Cognitive style and mathematics anxiety among high school students. *Psychology in the Schools, 25*, 75–83.

34. Harlow, L. L., Newcomb, M. D., & Bentler, P. M. (1986). Depression, self-derogation, substance use and suicide ideation: Lack of purpose in life as mediational factor. *Journal of Clinical Psychology, 42*, 353–358.

35. Haynes, N. M., Comer, J. P., & Hamilton-Lee, M. (1988). Gender and achievement status differences on learning factors among Black high school students. *Journal of Educational Research, 81* (4), 233–237.

36. Holden, C. (1987). Female math anxiety on the wane. *Science, 236* (4802), 660–661.

37. Marsh, H. W. (1987). *The Content Specificity of Math and English Anxieties: The High School and Beyond Study.* ERIC ED 300 402.

38. Matyas, M. L. (1984). *Science Career Interests, Attitudes, Abilities, and Anxiety Among Secondary School Students: The Effects of Gender, Race/Ethnicity, and School Type/Location.* ERIC ED 251 309.

39. Reynolds, W. (1984). Depression in children and adolescents. *School Psychology Review, 13*, 171–182.

40. Worchel, F., Nolan, B., & Wilson, V. (1987). New perspectives on child and adolescent depression. *Journal of School Psychology, 25* (4), 411–414.

41. Wynstra, S., & Cummings, C. (1990). *Science Anxiety: Relation with Gender, Year in Chemistry Class, Achievement, and Test Anxiety.* ERIC ED 331 837.

Gender differences in aggressiveness, assertiveness, and dominance are discussed in the following references.

42. Barrett, D. E. (1979). A naturalistic study of sex differences in children's aggression. *Merrill Palmer Quarterly, 25* (3), 193–204.

43. Burdett, K., & Jensen, L. C. (1983). The self-concept and aggressive behavior among elementary school children from two socioeconomic areas and two grade levels. *Psychology in the Schools, 20* (3), 370–375.

44. Eagly, A. H. (1987). *Sex Differences in Social Behavior: A Social Role Interpretation.* Hillsdale, NJ: Erlbaum.

45. Hyde, J. S., & Linn, M. C. (1986). *The Psychology of Gender: Advances through Meta-Analysis.* Baltimore: Johns Hopkins University Press.

46. Olson, S. L. (1984). The effects of sex-role taking on children's responses to aggressive conflict situations. *Sex Roles, 10* (9), 817–823.

47. Parke, R. D., & Slaby, R. G. (1983). The development of aggression. In P. H. Mussen & E. M. Hetherington (Eds.), *Handbook of Child Psychology: Socialization, Personality and Social Development* (4th ed.). New York: Wiley.

48. Sheldon, A. (1990). Pickle fights: Gendered talk in preschool disputes. *Discourse Processes, 13*, 5–31.

49. Smye, D. M., & Wine, J. D. (1980). A comparison of female and male adolescents' social behaviors and cognitions: A challenge to the assertiveness literature. *Sex Roles, 6* (2), 213–230.

50. Sprafkin, J., & Gadow, K. (1987). An observational study of emotionally disturbed and learning-disabled children in school settings. *Journal of Abnormal Child Psychology, 15* (3), 393–408.

51. Tannen, D. (1990). *You Just Don't Understand.* New York: Morrow.

References that deal with gender differences in sharing, helpfulness, and other forms of altruistic behavior follow.

52. Barnett, M. A. (1978). *Situational Influences and Sex Differences in Children's Reward Allocation Behavior.* ERIC ED 172 081.

53. Dederick, W. E., Dederick, J. G., & Zalk, S. R. (1977). *Interpersonal Values of Intellectually Gifted Adolescent Females: Single-Sex Co-Education.* ERIC ED 140 523.

54. Harris, M. B., & Siebel, C. E. (1975). Affect, aggression, and altruism. *Developmental Psychology, 11,* 623–627.

55. O'Bryant, S. L., & Brophy, J. E. (1976). Sex differences in altruistic behavior. *Developmental Psychology, 12,* 554.

56. Radke-Yarrow, M., Zahn-Waxler, C., & Chapman, M. (1983). Children's prosocial dispositions and behavior. In E. M. Hetherington (Ed.), *Handbook of Child Psychology* (4th ed.) (Vol. 4). New York: Wiley.

57. Shegetomi, C. (1982). Children's Altruism. Doctoral dissertation, University of Utah.

58. Shegetomi, C., Haitmann, D. P., & Gelfand, D. M. (1981). Sex differences in children's reputation for helpfulness. *Developmental Psychology, 17,* 434–437.

59. Skarin, K., & Moely, B. E. (1976). Altruistic behavior: An analysis of age and sex differences. *Child Development, 47* (4), 1159–1165.

60. Weissbrod, C. S. (1980). The impact of warmth and instructions on donation. *Child Development, 51,* 279–281.

61. Zarbatany, L., Hartmann, D. P., Gelfand, D. M., & Vinciguerra, P. (1985). Gender differences in altruistic reputations: Are they artifactual? *Developmental Psychology, 21* (1), 97–101.

The references that follow focus on gender differences in competitive and cooperative behavior.

62. DeVoe, M. W. (1977). Cooperation as a function of self-concept, sex and race. *Educational Research Quarterly, 2* (2): 3–8.

63. Kagan, S., & Madsen, M. C. (1972). Rivalry in Anglo-American and Mexican children of two ages. *Journal of Personality and Social Psychology, 24,* 214–220.

64. Moely, B. E., Skarin, K., & Weil, S. (1979). Sex differences in competition-cooperation behavior of children at two age levels. *Sex Roles, 5* (31), 329–342.

65. Pepitone, E. A. (1973). *Patterns of Interdependence in Cooperative Work of Elementary School Children.* ERIC ED 091 047.

66. Skarin, K., & Moely, B. E. (1974). *Sex Differences in Competition-Cooperation Behavior of Eight-Year-Old Children.* ERIC ED 096 015.

Gender differences in reactions to conflict are the topic of the following article.

67. Miller, P. M., Danaher, D. L., & Forbes, D. (1986). Sex-related strategies for coping with interpersonal conflict in children aged five and seven. *Developmental Psychology, 22* (4), 543–548.

Gender differences in seeking teacher and adult feedback and approval are the focus of the following references.

68. Caplan, P. (1979.) Beyond the box score: A boundary condition for sex differences in aggression and achievement striving. In B. Maher (Ed.), *Progress in Experimental Personality Research* (Vol. 9). New York: Academic Press.

69. Carpenter, C. J., & Huston-Stein, A. (1980). Activity structure and sex-typed behavior in preschool children. *Child Development, 51,* 862–872.

70. Eiszler, C. F. (1982). *Perceptual Preference as an Aspect of Adolescent Learning Styles.* ERIC ED 224 769.

71. Harter, S. (1974). Effectance motivation reconsidered: Toward a developmental model. *Human Development, 21,* 34–64.

72. Huston, A. C., Carpenter, C. J., Atwater, J. B., & Johnson, L. M. (1986). Gender, adult structuring of activities, and social behavior in middle childhood. *Child Development, 57,* 1200–1209.

Females' use of helplessness to influence others is the subject of the following references.

73. Johnson, P. (1976). Women and power: Toward a theory of effectiveness. *Journal of Social Issues, 32* (3), 99–110.

74. Parsons, J. E. (1982). Sex differences in attributions and learned helplessness. *Sex Roles, 8* (4), 421–432.

Gender differences in responsiveness to peers' requests and reinforcement are discussed in the following references.

75. Lamb, M. E., Easterbrook, A. M., & Holden, G. W. (1980). Reinforcement and punishment among preschoolers: Characteristics, effects, and correlates. *Child Development, 51,* 1230–1236.

76. Wilkinson, L. C., & Marrett, C. B. (Eds.). (1985). *Gender Influence in Classroom Interaction.* New York: Academic Press.

Gender differences in behavior in mixed-sex groups are treated in the following references.

77. Lockheed, M. E. (1977). Cognitive style effects on sex status in student work groups. *Journal of Educational Psychology, 69,* 158–165.

78. Lockheed, M. E. (1985). Sex and social influence: A meta-analysis guided by theory. In J. Berger & M. Zeldich (Eds.), *Status, Attributions, and Rewards.* San Francisco: Jossey-Bass.

79. Webb, N. M., & Kinderski, C. M. (1985). Gender differences in small group interaction and achievement in high- and low-achieving classes. In L. C. Wilkinson & C. B. Marrett (Eds.), *Gender Influence in Classroom Interaction.* New York: Academic Press.

The following references deal with ethnic differences in female roles.

80. Dao, M. (1987). From Vietnamese to Vietnamese American. Unpublished manuscript, San Jose, CA: San Jose State University.

81. Grossman, H. (1984). *Educating Hispanic Students: Cultural Implications for Instruction, Classroom Management, Counseling and Assessment.* Springfield, IL: Thomas.

82. Kunkel, P., & Kennard, S. S. (1971). *Sprout Spring: A Black Community.* New York: Holt, Rinehart & Winston.

83. Lewis, D. (1975). The black family: Socialization and sex roles. *Phylon, 36* (3), 221–237.

84. Scanzoni, J. H. (1971). *The Black Family in Modern Society.* Boston: Allyn & Bacon.

85. Simpson, G. (1984). The daughters of Charlotte Ray: The career development process during the exploratory and establishment stages of Black women attorneys. *Sex Roles, 11* (1/2), 113–139.

86. Staples, R. (1971). The myth of the impotent Black male. *The Black Scholar, 2* (10), 2–9.

References concerning gender differences in communication styles follow.

87. Andersen, E. S. (1978). Learning to Speak with Style: A Study of the Socio-Linguistic Skills of Children. Doctoral dissertation, Stanford University.

88. Eakins, B., & Eakins, R. G. (1978). *Sex Differences in Human Communication.* Boston: Houghton Mifflin.

89. Fishman, P. M. (1978). Interaction: The work women do. *Social Problems, 25* (4), 397–406.

90. Goodwin, M. H. (1980). Directive-response sequences in girls' and boys' task activities. In S. McConnell-Ginet, R. Borker, & M. Furman (Eds.), *Women and Language in Literature and Society.* New York: Praeger.

91. Goodwin, M. H., & Goodwin, C. (1987). Children's arguing. In S. U. Philips, S. Steele, & C. Tanz (Eds.), *Language, Gender, and Sex in Comparative Perspective*. Cambridge, England: Cambridge University Press.

92. Hall, J. C. (1978). Gender effects in decoding nonverbal cues. *Psychological Bulletin, 85*, 845–857.

93. Leet-Pelligrini, H. M. (1980). Conversational dominance as a function of gender and expertise. In H. Giles, W. P. Robinson, & P. M. Smith (Eds.), *Language: Social Psychological Perspectives*. Oxford, England: Pergamon.

94. Rosenthal, R., Hall, J. A., Di Matteo, M. R., Rogers, P. L., & Archer, D. C. (1979). *Sensitivity to Non-Verbal Communication*. Baltimore: Johns Hopkins University Press.

95. Sachs, J. (1982). 'Don't interrupt': Preschoolers' entry into ongoing conversations. In C. E. Johnson & C. L. Thew (Eds.), *Proceedings of the Second International Congress for the Study of Child Language*. Lanham, MD: University Press of America.

96. Thorne, B., & Henley, N. (1975). *Language and Sex: Differences and Dominance*. Rowley, MA: Newbury House.

97. Zimmerman, D. H., & West, C. (1975). Sex roles, interruptions and silences in conversation. In B. Thorne & N. Henley (Eds.), *Language and Sex: Differences and Dominance*. Rowley, MA: Newbury House.

The focus of the following references is on gender differences in reaction to challenges and risk taking.

98. Ginsburg, H. J., & Miller, S. M. (1982). Sex differences in children's risk-taking behavior. *Child Development, 53* (2), 426–428.

99. Harter, S. (1975). Mastery motivation and need for approval in older children and their relationship to social desirability responses tendencies. *Developmental Psychology, 11*, 186–196.

100. Licht, B. G., Kistner, J. A., Ozkaragoz, T., Shapiro, S., & Clausen, L. (1985). Causal attributions of learning disabled children: Individual differences and their implications for persistence. *Journal of Educational Psychology, 77* (2), 208–216.

101. Licht, B. G., Linden, T. A., Brown, D. A., & Sexton, M. (1984). *Sex Differences in Achievement Orientation: An "A" Student Phenomenon*. ERIC ED 252 783.

Gender differences in reactions to failure are discussed in the following references.

102. Dweck, C. S., & Goetz, T. E. (1978). Attributions and helplessness. In J. H. Harvey, W. Ickes, & R. F. Kidd (Eds.), *New Directions in Attribution Research*. Hillsdale, NJ: Erlbaum.

103. Miller, A. (1986). Performance impairment after failure: Mechanisms and sex differences. *Journal of Educational Psychology, 78* (6), 486–491.

104. Nicholls, J. G. (1975). Causal attributions and other achievement-related cognitions: Effects of task outcome, attainment value, and sex. *Journal of Personality and Social Psychology, 31,* 379–389.

105. Reyes, L. H. (1984). Affective variables and mathematics education. *Elementary School Journal, 84* (5), 558–581.

Gender differences in reactions to competition and cooperation are discussed in the following references.

106. Allen, J. L., O'Mara, J., & Long, K. M. (1987). *The Effects of Communication Avoidance, Learning Styles and Gender upon Classroom Achievement.* ERIC ED 291 111.

107. Alvino, J. (1991). An investigation into the needs of gifted boys. *Roeper Review, 13* (4), 174–180.

108. Dalton, D. W., Hannafin, M. J., & Hooper, S. (1989). Effects of individual and cooperative computer assisted instruction on student performance and attitudes. *Educational Technology Research and Development, 37* (2), 15–34.

109. Englehard, G., Jr., & Monsas, J. A. (1989). Performance, gender and the cooperative attitudes of third, fifth, and seventh graders. *Journal of Research and Development in Education, 22* (2), 13–17.

110. Fennema, E. H., & Peterson, P. L. (1985). Autonomous learning behavior: A possible explanation of gender-related differences in mathematics. In L. C. Wilkinson & C. B. Marrett (Eds.), *Gender Influences in Classroom Interaction.* New York: Academic Press.

111. Harpole, S. H. (1987). *The Relationship of Gender and Learning Styles to Achievement and Laboratory Skills in Secondary School Chemistry Students.* ERIC ED 288 728.

112. Johnson, D. W., & Johnson, R. T. (1987). *Learning Together and Alone: Cooperation, Competition and Individualization* (2nd ed.). Englewood Cliffs, NJ: Prentice-Hall.

113. Kagan, S., Zahn, G. L., & Gealy, J. (1977). Competition and school achievement among Anglo-American and Mexican-American children. *Journal of Educational Psychology, 69* (4), 432–441.

114. Lockheed, M. E., Harris, A. M., & Nemceff, W. P. (1983). Sex and social influence: Does sex function as a status characteristic in mixed-sex groups of children? *Journal of Educational Psychology, 75,* 877–888.

115. Peterson, P., & Fennema, E. (1985). Effective teaching, student engagement in classroom activities, and sex-related differences in learning mathematics. *American Educational Research Journal, 22* (3), 309–334.

116. Strube, M. J. (1981). Meta-analysis and cross-cultural comparison: Sex differences in child competitiveness. *Journal of Cross-Cultural Psychology, 12* (1), 3–20.

117. Webb, N. M., & Kenderski, C. M. (1985). Gender differences in small-group interaction and achievement in high- and low-achieving classes. In L. C. Wilkinson & C. B. Marrett (Eds.), *Gender Influences in Classroom Interaction*. New York: Academic Press.

118. Wilkinson, L. C., Lindow, J., & Chiang, C. P. (1985). Sex differences and sex segregation in students' small-group communication. In L. C. Wilkinson & C. B. Marrett (Eds.), *Gender Influences in Classroom Interaction*. New York: Academic Press.

Sex differences in conformity are the focus of the following articles.

119. Becker, B. J. (1986). Influence again: An examination of reviews and studies of gender differences in social influence. In J. S. Hyde & M. C. Linn (Eds.), *The Psychology of Gender*. Baltimore: Johns Hopkins University Press.

120. Cooper, H. M. (1979). Statistically combining independent studies: A meta-analysis of sex differences in conformity research. *Journal of Personality and Social Psychology, 37,* 131–146.

121. Eagly, A. H. (1978). Sex differences in influenceability. *Psychological Bulletin, 85,* 85–116.

122. Eagly, A. H., & Carli, L. L. (1981). Sex of researchers and sex-typed communications as determinants of sex differences in influenceability: A meta-analysis of social influence studies. *Psychological Bulletin, 90,* 1–20.

123. Van Hecke, M., Tracy, R. J., Cotter, S., & Ribordy, S. C. (1984). Approval versus achievement motives in seventh-grade girls. *Sex Roles, 11* (1), 33–41.

Gender differences in students' self-concepts and self-esteem are discussed in the following references.

124. Armstrong, J. M., & Kahl, S. (1980). *A National Assessment of Performance and Participation of Women in Mathematics*. Washington, DC: National Institute of Education.

125. Berryman, C., Larkins, A. G., & McKinney, C. W. (1983). *Self Concept and Sex of Rural Children*. ERIC ED 231 585.

126. Brush, L. (1980). *Encouraging Girls in Mathematics: The Problem and the Solution*. Boston: Abt.

127. Eccles (Parsons), J., Adler, T. F., Futterman, R., Goff, S. B., Kaczala, C. M., Meece, J., and Midgley, C. (1983). Expectations, values, and academic behaviors. In J. T. Spence (Ed.), *Perspective on Achievement and Achievement Motivation*. San Francisco: Freeman.

128. Eccles, J., Adler, T. F., & Meece, J. L. (1984). Sex differences in achievement: A test of alternate theories. *Journal of Personality and Social Psychology, 68,* 119–128.

129. Fox, L. H., Brody, L., & Tobin, D. (Eds.). (1980). *Women and the Mathematical Mystique.* Baltimore: Johns Hopkins University Press.

130. Hare, B. R. (1979). *Black Girls: A Comparative Analysis of Self-Perception and Achievement by Race, Sex and Socioeconomic Background.* Report No. 271. ERIC ED 173 503.

131. Harter, S. (1982). The Perceived Competence Scale for Children. *Child Development, 53,* 87–97.

132. Hyde, J., & Fennema, E. (1990). *Gender Differences in Mathematics Performance and Affect: Results of Two Meta-Analyses.* Paper presented at the annual meeting of the American Educational Research Association, Boston.

133. Lenney, E. (1977). Women's self-confidence in achievement settings. *Psychological Bulletin, 84,* 1–13.

134. Levine, G. (1990). *Arithmetic Development: Where Are the Gender Differences?* Paper presented at the annual meeting of the American Educational Research Association, Boston.

135. Loeb, R. C., & Horst, L. (1978). Sex differences in self- and teachers' reports of self-esteem in preadolescents. *Sex Roles, 4* (5), 779–788.

136. Meece, J. L., Parsons, J. E., Kaczala, C. M., Goff, B., & Futterman, R. (1982). Sex differences in math achievement: Toward a model of academic choice. *Psychological Bulletin, 91,* 324–348.

137. Olszewski, P., Kulieke, M. J., & Willis, G. B. (1987). Changes in the self-perceptions of gifted students who participate in rigorous academic programs. *Journal for the Education of the Gifted, 10* (4), 287–303.

138. Prawat, R. S., Grissom, S., & Parish, T. (1979). Affective development in children, grades 3 through 12. *Journal of Genetic Psychology, 135,* 37–49.

139. Richman, C. L., Clark, M. L., & Brown, K. P. (1984). General and specific self-esteem in late adolescent students: Race × gender × SES effects. *Adolescence, 20* (79), 555–566.

140. Robison-Awana, P., Kehle, T. J., & Jenson, W. R. (1986). But what about smart girls? Adolescent self-esteem and sex role perceptions as a function of academic achievement. *Journal of Educational Psychology, 78* (3), 179–183.

141. Sherman, J. (1980). Mathematics, spatial visualization, and related factors: Changes in girls and boys, grades 8–11. *Journal of Educational Psychology, 72,* 476–482.

142. Stevenson, H. W., & Newman, R. S. (1986). Long-term prediction of achievement and attitudes in mathematics and reading. *Child Development, 57,* 646–659.

143. Sullivan, J. L. (1979). *Perceptions of Students' Self and Ideal Self by Teachers and Students at the Red Lake Indian Reservation.* ERIC ED 244 759.

144. Tashakkori, A., & Thompson, V. D. (1990). *Race Differences in Self-Perception and Locus of Control During Adolescence and Early Adulthood*. ERIC ED 327 806.

145. Travis, C. B., McKenzie, B. J., & Wiley, D. L. (1984). *Sex and Achievement Domain: Cognitive Patterns of Success and Failure*. ERIC ED 250 601.

The following references deal with students' perceptions of their ability to exert control over their lives and their attribution of the cause of their successes and failures in school.

146. Dweck, C. S., & Reppucci, N. D. (1973). Learned helplessness and reinforcement responsibility in children. *Journal of Personality and Social Psychology, 25,* 109–116.

147. Dyal, J. A. (1984). Cross-cultural research with the locus of control construct. In H. M. Lefcourt (Ed.), *Research with the Locus of Control Construct, vol. 3: Extensions and Limitations.* New York: Academic Press.

148. Evans, E. D., & Engleberg, R. A. (1988). *Journal of Research and Development in Education, 21* (2), 45–54.

149. Frey, K. S., & Ruble, D. N. (1987). What children say about classroom performance: Sex and grade differences in perceived competence. *Child Development, 58,* 1066–1078.

150. Gordon, D. A., Jones, R. H., & Short, N. L. (1977). Task persistence and locus of control in elementary school children. *Child Development, 48,* 1716–1719.

151. Lao, R. C. (1980). Differential factors affecting male and female academic performance in high school. *Journal of Psychology, 104,* 119–127.

152. Lewis, M. A. (1989). *Consistency of Children's Causal Attributions across Content Domains.* ERIC ED 306 488.

153. Lewis, M. A., & Cooney, J. B. (1986). *Attributional and Performance Effects of Competitive and Individualistic Feedback in Computer Assisted Mathematics Instruction.* ERIC ED 271 287.

154. Lopez, C. L., & Harper, M. (1989). The relationship between learner control of CAI and locus of control among Hispanic students. *Educational Technology Research and Development, 37* (4), 19–28.

155. Lykes, M. B., Stewart, A. J., & LaFrance, M. (1981). *Control and Aspirations in Adolescents: A Comparison by Race, Sex and Social Class.* ERIC ED 212 948.

156. McMahan, I. D. (1982). Expectancy of success on sex-linked tasks. *Sex Roles, 8,* 949–958.

157. Powers, S., & Wagner, M. J. (1983). *Achievement Locus of Control of Hispanic and Anglo High School Students.* ERIC ED 230 355.

158. Reyes, L. H., & Padilla, M. J. (1985). Science math and gender. *Science Teacher, 52* (6), 46–48.

159. Ryckman, D. B., & Peckman, P. D. (1986). Gender differences in attribution patterns in academic areas for learning disabled students. *Learning Disabilities Research, 1* (2), 83–89.

160. Ryckman, D. B., & Peckman, P. D. (1987). Gender differences in attribution for success and failure. *Journal of Early Adolescence, 7,* 47–63.

161. Ryckman, D. B., & Peckman, P. D. (1987). Gender differences in attribution for success and failure across subject areas. *Journal of Educational Research, 81,* 120–125.

162. Sewell, T., Farley, F. H., Manni, J., & Hunt, P. (1982). Motivation, social reinforcement, and intelligence as predictors of academic achievement in Black adolescents. *Adolescence, 17* (67), 647–656.

163. Stipek, D. J. (1984). Sex differences in children's attributions for success and failure on math and spelling tasks. *Sex Roles, 11* (11–12), 969–981.

164. Turner, R. R. (1978). Locus of control, academic achievement, and follow through in Appalachia. *Contemporary Educational Psychology, 3,* 367–375.

165. Wahl, M., & Besag, F. (1986). *Gender, Attributions and Math Performance.* ERIC ED 276 620.

166. Wildstein, A. B., Thompson, D. N., & Holzman, T. G. (1982). *Locus of Control and Expectation Set on Two Aptitude Measures.* ERIC ED 277 739.

167. Willig, A. C., Harnisch, D. L., Hill, K. T., & Maehr, M. L. (1983). Sociocultural and educational correlates of success-failure attributions and evaluation anxiety in the school setting for Black, Hispanic and Anglo children. *American Educational Research Journal, 20* (3), 385–410.

References that deal with gender differences in motivation to avoid success are listed next.

168. Burlew, K. A. (1977). Career educational choices of Black females. *Journal of Black Psychology, 3,* 89–106.

169. Crovitz, E. (1980). A decade later: Black-white attitudes toward women's familial roles. *Psychology of Women Quarterly, 5* (2), 170–176.

170. Fleming, J. (1978). Fear of success, achievement related motives and behavior in Black college women. *Journal of Personality, 46,* 694–716.

171. George, V. D. (1981). *Occupational Aspirations of Talented Black Adolescent Females.* ERIC ED 206 976.

172. George, V. D. (1986). Talented adolescent women and the motivation to avoid success. *Journal of Multicultural Counseling and Development, 14* (3), 132–139.

173. Horner, M. S. (1972). Toward an understanding of achievement-related conflicts in women. *Journal of Social Issues, 28* (2), 157–175.

174. Roberts, L. R. (1986). *Gender Differences in Patterns of Achievement and Adjustment During Early Adolescence.* ERIC ED 288 134.

175. Stockard, J., Schmuck, P. A., Kemper, K., Williams, P., Edson, S. K., & Smith, M. A. (1980). *Sex Equity in Education*. New York: Academic Press.

The desirability of gender role differences is discussed in the references below.

176. Bem, S. L. (1983). Traditional sex roles are too restrictive. In B. Leone & M. T. O'Neill (Eds.), *Male-Female Roles: Opposing Viewpoints*. St. Paul, MN: Greenhaven Press.

177. Goldberg, H. (1979). *The New Male: From Self-Destruction to Self-Care*. New York: Morrow.

178. Schlafly, P. (1977). *The Power of the Positive Woman*. New York: Arlington House.

179. Woodward, K. L. (1983). Children need to learn traditional sex roles. In B. Leone & M. T. O'Neill (Eds.), *Male-Female Roles: Opposing Viewpoints*. St. Paul, MN: Greenhaven Press.

The references below deal with gender differences in teacher attention and feedback.

180. Becker, J. (1981). Differential treatment of males and females in mathematics classes. *Journal of Research in Mathematics Education, 12*, 40–53.

181. Benz, C. R., Pfeiffer, I., & Newman, I. (1981). Sex role expectations of classroom teacher, grades 1–12. *American Educational Research Journal, 18* (3), 289–302.

182. Boudreau, F. A. (1986). Education. In F. A. Boudreau, R. S. Sennott, & M. Wilson (Eds.), *Sex Roles and Social Patterns*. New York: Praeger.

183. Brophy, J. E. (1985). Interaction of male and female students with male and female teachers. In L. C. Wilkinson & C. B. Marrett (Eds.), *Gender Influences in Classroom Interaction*. New York: Academic Press.

184. Brophy, J. (1986). Teaching and learning mathematics: Where research should be going. *Journal for Research in Mathematics, 17*, 323–346.

185. Eccles, J. S., & Blumenfeld, P. (1985). Classroom experiences and student gender: Are there differences and do they matter? In L. C. Wilkinson & C. B. Marrett (Eds.), *Gender Influences in Classroom Interaction*. New York: Academic Press.

186. Fennema, E., & Peterson, P. L. (1986). Teacher student interactions and sex-related differences in learning mathematics. *Teaching and Teacher Education, 2* (1), 19–42.

187. Fennema, E., Reyes, L., Perl, T., Konsin, M., & Drakenberg, M. (1980). *Cognitive and Affective Influences on the Development of Sex-Related Difference in Mathematics*. Symposium presented at the annual meeting of the American Educational Research Association, Boston.

188. Frey, K. S. (1979). *Differential Teaching Methods Used with Girls and Boys of Moderate and High Achievement Levels*. Paper presented at the annual meeting of the American Educational Research Association, Minneapolis.

189. Gore, D. A., & Roumagoux, D. V. (1983). Wait-time as a variable in sex-related differences during fourth-grade mathematics instruction. *Journal of Educational Research, 76* (5), 273–275.

190. Hodes, C. L. (1985). Relative effectiveness of corrective and noncorrective feedback in computer assisted instruction on learning and achievement. *Journal of Educational Technology Systems, 13* (4), 249–254.

191. Leinhardt, G., Seewald, A. L., & Engel, M. (1979). Learning what's taught: Sex differences in instruction. *Journal of Educational Psychology, 71* (3), 432–439.

192. Lockheed, M. (1982). *Sex Equity in Classroom Interaction Research: An Analysis of Behavior Chains.* Paper presented at the annual meeting of the American Educational Research Association, New York City.

193. Maccoby, E. E., & Jacklin, C. N. (1974). *The Psychology of Sex Differences.* Stanford, CA: Stanford University Press.

194. Meece, J. L. (1987). The influence of school experiences on the development of gender schemata. *New Directions for Child Development, 38*, 57–73.

195. Minuchin, P. P., & Shapiro, E. K. (1983). The school as a context for social development. In P. Mussen, & E. M. Hetherington (Eds.), *Handbook of Child Psychology* (Vol. 4, 4th ed.). New York: Wiley.

196. Morrison, T. L. (1979). Classroom structure, work involvement and social climate in elementary school classrooms. *Journal of Educational Psychology, 71*, 471–477.

197. Morse, L. W., & Handley, H. M. (1985). Listening to adolescents: Gender differences in science classroom interaction. In L. C. Wilkinson & C. B. Marrett (Eds.), *Gender Influences in Classroom Interaction.* New York: Academic Press.

198. Parsons, J. E., Kaczala, C. M., & Meece, J. L. (1982). Socialization of achievement attitudes and beliefs: Classroom influences. *Child Development, 53*, 322–339.

199. Pflaum, S., Pascarella, E., Boswick, M., & Auer, C. (1980). The influence of pupil behaviors and pupil status factors on teacher behaviors during oral reading lessons. *Journal of Educational Research, 74*, 99–105.

200. Purcell, P., & Stewart, I. (1990). Dick and Jane 1989. *Sex Roles, 22* (3/4), 177–185.

201. Putnam, S., & Self, P. A. (1988). *Social Play in Toddlers: Teacher Intrusions.* ERIC ED 319 529.

202. Roberts, E. J. (Ed.). (1980). *Childhood Sexual Learning: The Unwritten Curriculum.* Cambridge, MA: Ballinger.

203. Simpson, A. W., & Erickson, M. T. (1983). Teachers' verbal and nonverbal communication patterns as a function of teacher race, student gender, and student race. *American Educational Research Journal, 20*, 183–198.

204. Stake, J., & Katz, J. (1982). Teacher-pupil relationships in the elementary school classroom: Teacher gender and student gender difference. *American Educational Research Journal, 19,* 465–471.

Ethnic differences in the ways teachers perceive and relate to students are the focus of the following references.

205. Grant, L. (1984). Black females' "place" in desegregated classrooms. *Sociology of Education, 57,* 98–110.

206. Grant, L. (1985). *Uneasy Alliances: Black Males, Teachers, and Peers in Desegregated Classrooms.* Paper presented at the annual meeting of the American Educational Research Association, Chicago.

207. Pollard, D. (1979). Patterns of coping in Black school children. In A. W. Boykin, A. Franklin, & F. Yates (Eds.), *Research Directions of Black Psychologists.* New York: Russell Sage.

208. Washington, V. (1982). Racial differences in teacher perception of first and fourth grade pupils on selected characteristics. *Journal of Negro Education, 51,* 60–72.

The following references deal with the adverse results of gender differences in teacher attention, feedback, and expectations.

209. Brush, L. R. (1980). *Encouraging Girls in Mathematics: The Problems and the Solutions.* Boston: Abt.

210. Fennema, E., & Sherman, J. (1977). Sex-related differences in mathematics achievement, spatial visualization, and affective factors. *American Educational Research Journal, 14,* 51–71.

The references below deal with the fact that teachers encourage different behaviors in male and female students.

211. Caplan, P. J. (1977). Sex, age, behavior, and school subject as determinants of report of learning problems. *Journal of Learning Disabilities, 10,* 60–62.

212. Fagot, B. I. (1977). Consequences of moderate cross-gender behavior in preschool children. *Child Development, 48,* 902–907.

213. Huffine, S., Silvern, S. B., & Brooks, D. M. (1979). Teacher responses to contextually specific sex type behaviors in kindergarten children. *Educational Research Quarterly, 4* (2), 29–35.

214. Schlosser, L., & Algozzine, B. (1980). Sex behavior and teacher expectancies. *Journal of Experimental Education, 48,* 231–236.

The following references detail differences in teachers' tolerance for male and female behavior patterns.

215. Fagot, B. I. (1985). Beyond the reinforcement principle: Another step toward understanding sex roles. *Developmental Psychology, 21,* 1097–1104.

216. Marshall, J. (1983). Developing antisexist initiatives in education. *International Journal of Political Education*, 6, 113–137.

217. Woolridge, P., & Richman, C. L. (1985). Teachers' choice of punishment as a function of a student's gender, age, race, and IQ level. *Journal of School Psychology*, 23, 19–29.

The following references describe how teachers use different classroom management techniques with various ethnic and socioeconomic groups.

218. Glackman, T., Martin, R., Hyman, I., McDowell, E., Berv, V., & Spino, P. (1980). *Corporal Punishment in the Schools As It Relates to Race, Sex, Grade Level and Suspensions*. Philadelphia: Temple University, National Center for the Study of Corporal Punishment in the Schools.

219. Richardson, R. C., & Evans, E. T. (1991). *Empowering Teachers to Eliminate Corporal Punishment in the Schools*. Paper presented at the annual conference of the National Black Child Developmental Institute, Washington, DC.

220. Stevens, L. B. (1983). *Suspension and Corporal Punishment of Students in the Cleveland Public Schools, 1981–1982*. Cleveland, OH: Office of School Monitoring and Community Relations.

221. Woolridge, P., & Richman, C. (1985). Teachers' choice of punishment as a function of a student's gender, age, race and I. Q. level. *Journal of School Psychology*, 23, 19–29.

References that indicate that males exhibit more behavior problems and get into more trouble in school than females are included below.

222. Center, D. B., & Wascom, A. M. (1987). Teacher perceptions of social behavior in behaviorally disordered and socially normal children and youth. *Behavior Disorders*, 12 (3), 200–206.

223. Epstein, M. H., Cullinan, D., & Bursuck, W. D. (1985). Prevalence of behavior problems among learning disabled and nonhandicapped students. *Mental Retardation and Learning Disability Bulletin*, 13, 30–39.

224. Ludwig, G., & Cullinan, D. (1984). Behavior problems of gifted and nongifted elementary school girls and boys. *Gifted Child Quarterly*, 28 (1), 37–39.

225. National Black Child Development Institute. (1990). *The Status of African American Children: Twentieth Anniversary Report*. Washington, DC: Author.

These references provide evidence that female teachers are less tolerant of male behavior patterns than male teachers.

226. McIntyre, L. L. (1988). Teacher gender: A predictor of special education referral. *Journal of Learning Disabilities*, 21, 383.

227. Ritter, D. R. (1989). Teachers' perceptions of problem behavior in general and special education. *Exceptional Children*, 55 (6), 559–564.

Gender segregation and separation are the focus of the following articles.

228. Guttenberg, M., & Gray, H. (1977). Teachers as mediators of sex-role standards. In A. Sargent (Ed.), *Beyond Sex Roles*. St. Paul, MN: West.

229. Lockheed, M. E., & Harris, A. M. (1984). Cross-sex collaborative learning in elementary classrooms. *American Educational Research Journal, 21* (2), 275–294.

The legal definition of nonsexist education is included in the following law.

230. Title IX of the Education Amendments Act, 1972.

The following references discuss various positions on gender differences in school.

231. Bem, S. L. (1983). Traditional sex roles are too restrictive. In G. Leone & M. T. O'Neill (Eds.), *Male-Female Roles: Opposing Viewpoints*. St. Paul, MN: Greenhaven Press.

232. Block, J. H. (1984). *Sex Role Identity and Ego Development*. San Francisco: Jossey-Bass.

233. Brooks-Gunn, J., & Mathews, W. S. (1979). *He & She: How Children Develop Their Sex-Role Identity*. Englewood Cliffs, NJ: Prentice-Hall.

234. Carson, J. C., & Carson, P. (1984). *Any Teacher Can: Practical Suggestions for Effective Classroom Management*. Springfield, IL: Thomas.

235. Giroux, H. A. (1981). Hegemony, resistance, and the paradox of educational reform. In H. A. Giroux, A. N. Penna, & W. F. Pinar (Eds.), *Curriculum & Instruction: Alternatives in Education*. Berkeley, CA: McCutchan.

236. Hyde, J. S. (1984). Gender differences in aggression. In J. S. Hyde & M. C. Linn (Eds.), *The Psychology of Gender: Advances Through Meta-Analysis*. Baltimore: Johns Hopkins Press.

237. Jacklin, C. N. (1989). Female and male: Issues of gender. *American Psychologist, 44* (2), 127–133.

238. Schlafly, P. Personal communication, May 1989.

239. Seward, J. P., & Seward, G. H. (1980). *Sex Differences: Mental and Temperamental*. Lexington, MA: Lexington Books.

240. Wardle, F. (1991). Are we shortchanging boys? *Child Care Information Exchange, 79*, 48–51.

The incident in the self-quiz "An Incident on the Playground" was included in the following reference.

241. Hebert, T. P. (1991). Meeting the affective needs of bright boys through bibliography. *Roeper Review, 13* (4), 207–212.

Opposition to teaching about sexual orientations is documented in the reference below.

242. Columbia Broadcasting System. (1993, April 4). *Sixty Minutes, The Rainbow Curriculum*. Author.

These references describe the plight of gay, lesbian, and bisexual students and possible solutions.

243. Benvenuti, A. (1986). *Assessing and Addressing the Special Challenge of Gay and Lesbian Students for High School Counseling Programs.* ERIC ED 279 958.

244. Cates, J. A. (1987). Adolescent sexuality: Gay and lesbian issues. *Child Welfare, 66,* 353–364.

245. Chang, C. L. (1980). Adolescent homosexual behavior and the health educator. *Journal of School Health, 50* (9), 5117–5121.

246. Coleman, E., & Remafedi, G. (1989). Gay, lesbian, and bisexual adolescents: A critical challenge to counselors. *Journal of Counseling and Development, 68,* 36–40.

247. Dunham, K. L. (1989). *Educated to Be Invisible: The Gay and Lesbian Adolescent.* ERIC ED 336 676.

248. Friends of Project Inc. (1991). *Project 10 Handbook: Addressing Lesbian and Gay Issues in Our Schools. A Resource Directory for Teachers, Guidance Counselors, Parents and School-Based Adolescent Care Providers* (3rd ed.). ERIC ED 337 567.

249. Gonsiorek, J. C. (1988). Mental health issues of gay and lesbian adolescents. *Journal of Adolescent Health Care, 9,* 114–122.

250. Grossman, H. (1972). *Nine Rotten Lousy Kids.* New York: Holt, Rinehart & Winston.

251. Hetrick, E. S., & Martin, A. D. (1987). Developmental issues and their resolution for gay and lesbian adolescents. *Journal of Homosexuality, 14* (1/2), 25–42.

252. Hubbard, B. M. (1989). *Entering Adulthood: Living in Relationships.* Santa Cruz, CA: ETR Associates.

253. Kissen, R. M. (1991). *Listening to Gay and Lesbian Teenagers.* ERIC ED 344 220.

254. Krysiak, G. J. (1987). A very silent and gay minority. *School Counselor, 34* (4), 304–307.

255. Lenton, S. M. (1980). A student development response to the gay issue. In F. B. Newton & K. L. Ender (Eds.), *Student Development Practices.* Springfield, IL: Thomas.

256. Martin, A. D. (1982). Learning to hide: The socialization of the gay adolescent. *Adolescent Psychiatry, 10,* 52–65.

257. Martin, A. D., & Hetrick, E. S. (1988). The stigmatization of the gay and lesbian adolescent. *Journal of Homosexuality, 15* (3), 163–183.

258. Public Broadcasting System. (1993). *Gay By Nature or Nurture.* Author.

259. Powell, R. E. (1987). Homosexual behavior and the school counselor. *School Counselor, 34* (3), 202–208.

260. Remafedi, G. (1987). Adolescent homosexuality: Medical and psychological implications. *Pediatrics, 79* (3), 331–337.

261. Remafedi, G. (1987). Male homosexuality: The adolescent's perspective. *Pediatrics, 79* (3), 326–330.

262. Ross-Reynolds, G. (1982). Issues in counseling the "homosexual" adolescent. In J. Grimes (Ed.), *Psychological Approaches to Problems of Children and Adolescents.* Des Moines: Iowa State Department of Public Instruction, Division of Special Education.

263. Rofes, E. (1989). Opening up the classroom closet: Responding to the educational needs of gay and lesbian youth. *Harvard Educational Review, 59* (4), 444–453.

264. Schneider, M. S., & Tremble, G. (1985). Gay or straight: Working with the confused adolescent. *Journal of Social Work and Human Sexuality, 4,* 631–660.

RESOLVING MOST BEHAVIOR PROBLEMS

Introduction

This part of the book focuses on behavior problems that occur in your classroom even when you're doing a great job of managing your class. You may be following all of the principles already discussed, and one, two, or a few students still call out, talk when they should be listening, refuse to do what you ask of them, scribble and doodle instead of write, get into arguments with other students, "challenge your authority," pay attention for only 30% of the time, and so forth.

When students misbehave despite your best efforts to avoid behavior problems, you can ask four questions to help you decide on a good course of action:

1. *Whose problem is it?* Is it the student's problem or yours?

2. *Should I intervene?* Should you tolerate the behavior or attempt to deal with it?

3. *If so, when?* When would be the most effective time to intervene—as soon as you notice the behavior problem or at some other time?

4. *How should I intervene?* Which of the many strategies would be most likely to work in this particular situation?

Part Two will help you answer these questions so that you can solve most of your classroom behavior problems as quickly and effectively as possible.

PROBLEMS AND WHO OWNS THEM

This chapter will help you become a better observer and evaluator of students' behavior. It explains why teachers sometimes misperceive or misunderstand their students' behavior or interpret behavior differently. Most importantly, the chapter contains exercises that will provide you with insight into your own particular and subjective ways of viewing your students' problems. This will enable you to do a better job of determining if there is a problem, and if so, whose it is.

At first glance, the question of whether a behavior problem exists and whose problem it is may seem superfluous to you. You may believe that educators should be able to tell when a problem exists in their own classroom and who is causing it. These questions, though, are not as straightforward as they may seem (1–12). Sometimes, whether a particular behavior is a "problem" or not is in the eye of the beholder. For example, some teachers think that it's okay for students to converse while doing their seatwork so long as they do not disrupt other students and they stop after a brief exchange. Other teachers would intervene immediately. Certain teachers allow students to call out a question without raising their hands so long as they do not do so habitually and do not take other students' turns. Other teachers do not allow any calling out in their classes. Some teachers intervene just as soon as students begin to be disruptive to make sure things do not get out of hand. Other teachers wait to see if the students will get back on the straight and narrow on their own. Even the strictest teachers do not attend to every infraction of the rules, especially if they think it will be more trouble than it is worth or they are doing something they feel is more important (13–19).

Lawrence, Steed, and Young (15) describe the variables involved in whether certain behaviors will be considered disruptive:

Behavior only becomes disruptive at certain times and in certain places; it is disruptive to wander about in a French lesson but not in Drama, in the corridors at certain hours but not in the craft room; it is disruptive to keep silent in English discussion but not in Mathematics. What is seen as disruption by A may be welcomed as creativity by B and for both the same behavior may change its significance depending on the time of the day or week. . . . There seems to be no easy way of categorizing the precipitating circumstances although in many, the element of teacher stress seems important. Descriptive studies reveal an unending series of circumstances in which the teacher's patience will be exhausted and it is difficult to move from the specific to the general. Time of day, time of the year (especially when examinations make heavy demands on teachers' time), poor health, overwork, domestic upset, previous experience, age, sex, class—all may contribute to explanations of why particular forms of behavior in individuals are sometimes allowed, sometimes stigmatized. (15, p. 17)

While Lawrence, Steed, and Young emphasize that the specific situation as well as the mood of the teacher at the time help determine whether a certain behavior is regarded as disruptive, Gordon (14) stresses a third contributing factor: Some teachers are generally more accepting than others and have shorter lists of what they consider unacceptable behavior.

Two Kinds of Behavior Problems

Student behaviors that educators typically want to change fall into two groups: (1) those that almost all educators agree are problems and (2) those about which they disagree. For example, virtually all educators would agree on the importance of trying to change the following behaviors: rarely staying on-task for more than 5 minutes, cheating during exams, teasing and hitting younger students, coming to school "high" on drugs, constantly calling out answers, and avoiding new or difficult tasks. On the other hand, not all educators would agree that they should necessarily try to change such behaviors as chewing gum in class, boasting to others about one's accomplishments or grades, making extremely frank comments to others about their mistakes or shortcomings, being extremely passive and submissive, or being extremely assertive and competitive.

Behavior that everyone agrees is a problem should definitely be addressed. Not only do educators have the right to try to change such behavior; they have an obligation to do so. But teachers' rights and obligations to try changing behavior are less clear when educators do not agree that a problem exists. Thus, teachers need to consider whether their perceptions of students' behavior are influenced by their own values, priorities, personal likes and dislikes, and life experiences before deciding whether or not to intervene. Learning how to distinguish between the two kinds of behavior problems and what to do about the second kind of behavior are two main themes of this chapter.

Self-Defeating or Harmful Behaviors

Behaviors that harm the students who commit them include provoking rejection by pestering, teasing, or annoying other students; avoiding new or difficult tasks or challenges because of a poor self-concept; being so dependent on the assistance, opinions, or praise of others that this interferes with learning to do things for oneself, to think for oneself, and to decide for oneself; being so cocky, rebellious, defensive, and the like, that the suggestions and criticisms of others are automatically rejected out of hand; and coming to school on drugs. Examples of behaviors that infringe on the rights of others are interrupting what is going on instead of waiting; pushing ahead of others and calling out when it is someone else's turn to answer; taking things that belong to other students, refusing to share, and not returning things that have been borrowed; and hitting others, breaking their things, calling them names, and purposefully doing things to make them feel bad or upset them.

Behaviors That Challenge Values or Expectations

Behaviors that may not conform to educators' expectations and values include being more assertive or passive than some educators feel is okay, working at a pace that makes some educators uncomfortable, and being more competitive than some educators think students should be. Qualities like assertiveness, work speed, and competitiveness are vague and subject to individual judgments.

Even when a behavior is not harmful and does not interfere with the rights of other students, educators do not necessarily have to accept such behavior. Educators are not superhuman, perfect beings. If you try to endure too much, the resentment, anger, and frustration that are bound to build up could impede your ability to teach your class. It could also interfere in your relationship with both the students who prompted these feelings and the other students in the class. But this also does not mean that educators should always try to change behavior that they disapprove of or that bothers them. What it does mean is that educators should examine their reasons for wanting to change behavior before deciding whether or not to intervene.

Differing Perceptions of Behavior

As noted previously, teachers' gender and cultural backgrounds affect the way they perceive and react to their students' behavior. Their values and personalities also radically influence how they "see" certain behavior.

Gender Differences

In previous chapters, we learned that while all teachers want their students to be well behaved, male and female teachers tend to prefer somewhat different student behaviors.

For example, female teachers typically are less tolerant of "male pattern" disruptive behavior. They prefer cooperative rather than competitive behavior and compliant rather than assertive behavior. As a result, whether students' behavior is seen as a problem depends in part on the teacher's gender.

Cultural Differences

Cultural differences can affect whether or not a teacher regards a student's behavior as appropriate, polite, fair, or moral. For example, in some cultures, people are brought up to be *considerate* of others: "Don't play the stereo too loud," "Don't make noise too early, you will wake the people in the next campsite," and "Play outside with your friends so that your brother can study." In other cultures, youngsters are brought up to be *tolerant* of others: "Don't let the radio bother you," "You better go to sleep early—you know that campers make noise in the morning," and "Learn not to be distracted by other people— the world can't stop just because you have to do your homework."

Teachers from cultures that bring up children to be considerate of others are more likely to perceive students as interfering with the rights of others or as unwilling to share, conform, or go along with the group. As a result, they may intervene in situations that other educators would accept as reasonable behavior.

As noted in chapter 5, some of the many areas of behavior influenced by cultural factors include cooperation, competition, sharing, waiting one's turn, apologizing for mistakes or errors, and expressing feelings.

Values Differences

Values are our ideas and feelings about what is good, proper, worthwhile, and desirable and what is bad, improper, worthless, and undesirable. We can state, explain, and justify our values. In that sense, they are rational and intellectual.

All individuals from the same cultural background do not have the same values because they are brought up by different parents in different neighborhoods and schools, belong to different socioeconomic classes, and so on. As a result, educators with similar cultural backgrounds may react very differently to their students' behavior when values are brought into play. For example, educators differ in terms of what they consider appropriate student-teacher relationships. Some expect students to be acquiescent because their teachers are adults: Students are to take in what they are taught, speak when spoken to, and raise questions only about what they do not understand but not about their teachers' beliefs or the way their teachers instruct them. Other educators want their students to play a more active role in what they learn, to question them, and to help determine the way the class is run.

Teachers place different values on the rights of the individual versus the rights of the group. When a conflict arises between the wishes or needs of the individual and those of the group, certain teachers expect the group to be more tolerant of the individual, while others may prefer the individual to be more group oriented. Educators also have differing ideas about how assertively students should seek to obtain what they want and how straightforward and frank students should be about their opinions and feelings when they do not agree with other students. Finally, educators often differ about the best way for students to resolve arguments and disagreements among themselves.

Educators place different values on punctuality and promptness. Some will take credit off for assignments that are turned in late, while others do not consider promptness at all. Educators also disagree about the relative importance of academic subjects, extracurricular activities, sports, the arts, and family activities. As a result, what some educators consider acceptable reasons for not completing an assignment or missing school, others consider a poor excuse or no excuse at all.

Because educators have such differing values, whether a student's behavior is considered a problem will sometimes depend on who his or her teacher is. This means that educators should be aware of when their personal values and expectations influence their perceptions of their students' behavior. They can then take this added information into account when deciding whether or not to treat the behavior as a problem.

Psychological Differences

All people, educators included, are upset by some things that other people can take in stride. Thus, a student's behavior can be seen and treated as a problem in one case and ignored in another, depending on the personality of the educator in charge. For example, imagine that you are an eighth-grade teacher on recess duty. You emerge from the building and spy a large crowd of students in a corner of the school yard. Pushing and elbowing your way through the crowd, you see the school bully beating up the school scapegoat. Now ask yourself who upsets you more—the bully who is constantly taking advantage of weaker students or the scapegoat who is forever allowing himself to be taken advantage of. Stop reading now until you have given yourself time to find an honest answer to the question. *Do not* answer that you are equally upset by both. When you have your answer, read on.

"What's the matter with you? How many times have you been told not to pick on the other children? You ought to be ashamed of yourself! I'm taking you to the principal's office. Let's go," you tell the bully, while trying to control your anger—that is, providing the bully is the one who upsets you most. "What's the matter with you?" you ask the scapegoat—if it is the scapegoat who upsets you—frustration clearly evident in your voice. "How many times are you going to allow yourself to be beaten up before you learn to stand up for yourself? You and I have to have a talk about this," you continue, disregarding the bully for the moment.

Compared to values that we can state, explain, and justify, psychological factors are less intellectual and rational. An individual may experience intense reactions but often without knowing why. When people say things like, "I just can't stand her when she does that" or "That kind of thing drives me up the wall" or when they lose control or explode about some incident that objectively doesn't merit such a strong response, they are often in the dark about why they react the way they do.

There are many reasons why people's psychological makeup affects the way they see things and react to them. To begin with, people are usually comfortable when others act the same way they do and uncomfortable when others behave differently. Educators who are assertive and competitive are likely to accept such behavior from their students, but educators who are more passive and cooperative may react negatively to the same assertive behavior. Likewise, educators who have a very high energy level and are very active may be more accepting of students who have difficulty sitting still in class than educators who are more sedentary.

Educators who strive to be sensitive to the feelings of others may think that students who boast about their talents, grades, achievements, and so on, or are extremely critical of other students should be taught to be more concerned about others' feelings. Other educators who are more straightforward in the way they express their feelings and less concerned about their effects on others may think that these "boastful" and "critical" students are merely proud of their accomplishments and honest about how they see their peers. Instead of wanting to change these students, such educators may believe that the other students should learn to be less sensitive and less insecure about themselves.

Educators who are slow and careful workers may be unable to abide students who work fast because their "frenetic" pace makes them nervous. Other educators may react poorly to students who seem to be working so slowly and meticulously that they may never finish anything on time.

Second, people are comfortable when others behave in ways that complement—or complete—their behavior and uncomfortable when they do not. For example, educators who enjoy helping and supporting others are complemented by students who seek and react positively to their help, approval, and support. But if these same students seek help and approval from educators who prefer to maintain a more aloof, distant, or so-called "professional" relationship with their students, these teachers may see the students as whining, dependent, insecure, and in need of developing more self-confidence and learning to function more independently.

A third explanation for why people see things a certain way is that they often react defensively when confronted with some aspect of their personality they prefer to deny. Educators may create unnecessary conflicts between themselves and their students if they cannot admit the truth about themselves. "Don't ask any more questions," they tell their students, but what they cannot admit to themselves is that they do not know something. "Are you questioning my integrity?" they ask their students when they cannot face the fact that they acted arbitrarily or unfairly.

An associated problem is that educators may avoid seeing their students' problems if the students' behavior requires a response that would be too confronting. Those who have difficulty being disciplinarians may inadvertently permit students to do things they should not be allowed to do in order to avoid having to discipline them. Those who have difficulty accepting their natural inclinations to sometimes place their own desires ahead of those of others may give in to students more than they should to protect themselves from thinking that they are selfish. A few well-chosen words from students, such as "That's not fair, don't you like us? The other teachers don't make us do that," are often all that is necessary to manipulate these educators because they are ready to do almost anything to defend themselves against thinking they are selfish.

Another explanation for some responses is that people who are insecure about some aspect of their personality may be highly sensitive to possible challenges or slights. For example, educators unsure of their ability to maintain order in the class may misperceive students who are unable to adhere to certain rules as being unwilling to do so and purposely challenging the teacher's authority. Those who are unsure of their teaching ability may believe that students who are talking or laughing about something are making fun of them or something they have said or done. Those who are insecure about their self-worth or how

Self-Quiz: Perceptions of Student Behavior

"Yes" answers to the following questions can indicate that your values and personality *may* be causing you to overreact to an existing problem or to perceive a problem where, in fact, none exists.

1. Do you have the same difficulty with many students?
2. Do you feel a lot of anger or resentment toward a particular student?
3. Do you have less control over your actions with certain students?
4. Is the problem something you cannot tolerate in anyone, including yourself?
5. Do you think your students act the way they do to bother or upset you?
6. Do you interpret your students' misconduct as rebellious or disrespectful?
7. Do you resent the freedom and opportunity your students have that were forbidden to you?
8. At times are you moody, tense, edgy, or irritable because things your students do, which shouldn't bother you, do bother you?
9. Are you often concerned about who is really in control—you or your students?
10. Do you vacillate between two extremes, such as permissiveness and strictness?
11. Do you react negatively when students make critical comments about your instructional or management techniques or imply that you are wrong or do not know something?
12. Do you find yourself thinking that some of your students are just like their siblings or others who belong to the same racial, ethnic, or socioeconomic group?

"Yes" answers to the questions below can indicate that you *may* be underestimating the severity of a problem or perhaps denying that a problem exists.

13. Do you find you are particularly solicitous or understanding about a particular student's behavior?
14. Do you believe that your colleagues are too strict?
15. Do you have difficulty admitting that your students have behavior problems because deep down you are afraid you may not be able to help them?
16. Are you so worn out by your own problems that you cannot deal with the possibility that your students may also need your help?
17. Do you tell yourself that your students will soon stop doing what they are doing because you are the kind of person who tries to avoid conflicts with others or who has difficulty admitting that real problems exist?

people perceive them may be quick to interpret their students' behavior as disrespectful. And educators who cannot admit that they have a short fuse may believe that students behave in ways that upset them *in order to upset them.*

An additional factor is that people's perceptions of the present are highly colored by their past experiences in similar situations or with similar people. Thus, educators could be predisposed against certain students because of their experiences with the students' older brothers or sisters or with other students of the same ethnic or racial background.

Finally, some people are more understanding of other people's problems or mistakes if they have gone through similar experiences themselves. In particular, educators who suffered academic or social problems as students or who got into trouble for delinquent behavior yet succeeded despite their problems may be less worried about or threatened by

Self-Quiz: Evaluating Your Perceptions

Your answers to the following questions can provide you with the additional information you need to evaluate your perceptions of and reactions to your students.

1. Do your colleagues have fewer problems than you do with some of your students?

2. Do your colleagues think you overreact to certain problems or students?

3. Do you insist more than your colleagues do that your students' behavior must always conform to your expectations?

4. Do you try to teach your students values that your colleagues do not agree are part of an educator's responsibility?

5. Do your colleagues think you are too lenient with one or more of your students?

6. Do your colleagues disagree with some of your perceptions about your students?

students undergoing similar experiences. As a result, they may be less likely to treat these students' behavior as problems to be corrected or changed, even though the students may actually need their help.

Evaluating Your Perceptions

As the examples indicate, to be human is to be subjective, to make mistakes, to overreact, to deny, to evaluate others in terms of one's own values, and to misperceive and misinterpret others' behavior. Educators are not exempt from this pattern of behavior. When you are an experienced teacher or have completed student teaching, take the self-quiz on perceiving student behavior; it can help you identify when your personal reactions are affecting the way you perceive and experience your students' behavior. Since all teachers are also human beings, it would be surprising if you never experienced any of the problems in the self-quiz.

While "yes" answers to any of the questions can indicate that you may be misperceiving or misinterpreting your students' behavior, it's also possible that your perceptions are correct. One or more of your students may indeed be purposefully trying to annoy you. Some of your students could in fact be disrespectful or rebellious. You may have legitimate reasons for feeling angry or resentful about a particular student. Students can indeed be just like their siblings in some respects. Some parents really do fail in their responsibilities to teach their youngsters the society's value and morals. But there are times when students need understanding and patience, and sometimes we can help a student better by not making an issue of his or her behavior.

A second opinion can often confirm a teacher's perceptions and feelings about students.

Obtaining a Second Opinion

If, after thinking through your answers to the previous self-quiz, you are undecided about whether your values and personality are influencing your perceptions of students' behavior, you might consider seeking a second opinion by asking your colleagues what they think. Sometimes a more objective opinion from someone who knows what is going on in your class or who has had the same students can be extremely helpful.

As you take the self-quiz on evaluating your perceptions, keep in mind that a "yes" answer to one or more of the questions does not necessarily mean that you are misperceiving or misinterpreting your students' behavior. However, that is one possible explanation for the fact that you and your colleagues disagree.

If your answers to the questions indicate that a student of yours does have a problem that you have been avoiding or overlooking, you may feel bad that you haven't provided the needed help. Try to go easy on yourself. The realization that your student has the problem is the first step in doing something about it.

If, in contrast, your answers indicate that you have been overreacting to minor problems or seeing problems where none exists, you may be unhappy about what you have been doing and judge yourself harshly. But your current and more accurate perception of your students' behavior will go a long way toward eliminating the "problem" and, along with it, your need to continue to try to solve it.

Age-Appropriate Objective Instruments

INSTRUMENT	GRADE/AGE RANGE
Behavior Checklist	Kindergarten–second grade
Behavior Evaluation Scale	Kindergarten–twelfth grade
Revised Behavior Problems Checklist	5 years–adolescence
Child Behavior Profile	6–11 years
Child Behavior Rating Scale	Kindergarten–third grade
Devereux Adolescent Behavior Rating Scale	13–18 years
Devereux Elementary School Behavior Rating Scale	Kindergarten–sixth grade
School Behavior Checklist	4–13 years
Walker Problem Behavior Identification Checklist	Preschool–sixth grade

Using Formal Assessments

Most educators rely on their own subjective observations to decide whether their students' behavior is unacceptable and requires their intervention. A few prefer to supplement their personal observations with formal instruments (20–30). Teachers who know their students well may find that formal instruments provide very little additional information, and they may value their own perceptions more than a test that isn't really designed to their particular needs. Formal instruments, however, do have the advantage of objectivity. And when the results they produce agree with a teacher's perceptions, they serve as supportive evidence. When results disagree, they may be an essential check on the teacher's subjective, incorrect perceptions.

Summary

There are two kinds of behavior problems: (1) behavior that is self-defeating or harmful to the student who commits it or that infringes on the rights of others and (2) behavior that does not conform to an educator's personal expectations or values but is not self-defeating or harmful and does not interfere with the rights of others. Educators have the right and obligation to try to change the first kind of behavior. Their right to intervene with the second kind of behavior, however, is less clear. Educators may react personally to their students' behavior because of differing cultural backgrounds, values, and personalities.

Therefore, the first step in dealing with behavior problems is to determine whose problems they are. While most educators rely on their observations to decide whether their students' behavior requires their intervention, some prefer to supplement such observations with formal instruments.

Activities

Review the following report written by a biology teacher about Joan, a 15-year-old student with many problems. State which problems are likely to be hers and which may be the teacher's personal reactions to Joan's behavior.

Initial report: January. At the beginning of the term, Joan was attentive, cooperative, and motivated. She seemed to be genuinely interested in the work. However, by the end of September, she seemed to be exploiting the class and me. It was as if she had been spending the first few weeks developing a good relationship with me that she could exploit at a later date. She began to act as if I were her medical adviser. Three or four times a week she would ask me about minor lacerations on her hands or arms. After a few weeks I began to tell her to see the nurse about them. When I did this, she stopped having accidental injuries to show me.

Joan constantly chews and cracks gum in class in order to get a reaction from me. I told her quite often that although I realized she might need to chew gum, I could not accept the cracking that went along with it. I told her that I had gone halfway by allowing her to chew gum in class and asked her to meet me halfway by not cracking her gum.

I believe that Joan needs structure. This is especially necessary when she refuses to listen to my requests that she start working, open a book, take an examination, and so on. She needs direction and firmness tempered by understanding. Therefore, on these occasions I demand that she work, and I place a pencil in her hand, open her book for her, and tell her that if she does not begin working I will send her to the principal.

Joan has a great many self-doubts. She is constantly asking me questions about heredity, mental illness, amnesia, and various diseases. She appears to be quite worried about this. During one class period, when we were discussing cancer, she began to cry. Suddenly she was screaming and demanding that I stop the discussion. I explained to her why I could not do this and suggested that she stay outside until she had regained control of herself. She left but returned shortly before the end of the period and explained that her mother had died from cancer. Since then, she has never displayed such outbursts when the topic has been discussed.

Biology is probably difficult for Joan because many of the topics upset her. When we begin such a topic, she refuses to attend to the subject matter. This is especially true when we are studying the nervous system. She uses these occasions as excuses for becoming disturbed. Her friend Deborah does the same thing, and then they both use it as an opportunity to ruin the period.

Sometimes the work in class is too difficult for her. This is usually when we are starting a new topic. At these times she becomes agitated, claims that she does not understand the work, and gives up attempting to succeed. When this happens, I point out to her that it is normal for anyone, including her, to be apprehensive about work that is new, and I try to encourage her to overcome her apprehensiveness. To build up her self-confidence, I point out her successes in previous units that were just as difficult for her at first. In fact, I have continually complimented her whenever possible about a nice dress or a new hairdo to help her feel better about herself.

Joan often compares herself to Deborah, whom she thinks is the incarnation of perfection. This, of course, adds to her self-doubts because she is not as good a student as Deborah is. She also joins in whenever Deborah behaves disruptively.

Joan wants sympathy from adults. She believes that no one cares for her. When she feels this way during class, she is extremely melancholy and apathetic. I feel that Joan can certainly be helped. She needs even more acceptance, help, care, and attention than she has been receiving. Unfortunately, Joan has learned that those who make the most noise and cause the greatest disturbance often receive the most attention. This is probably a major reason for her recent outbursts. This is especially bad for her because it does not help her learn self-control.

Report card comment. Joan is doing well. With a little more effort, she should earn an even better grade.

Spring report: April. At the beginning of the second term, Joan attempted to do her work and control her behavior. She attended class and completed most of her assignments. Recently, events outside of school have interfered with her classroom functioning because she brings all her difficulties into the classroom with her. For example, today she was upset when she came to school. She refused to work, tore papers, broke pencils, paced the floor, stared out of the window, and screamed, "Leave me alone!" when I asked her to sit down.

The other day she walked into the classroom and sat in the back of the room instead of in her own seat. I knew that she was disheartened by something. However, I also knew that we must not continue to allow her to withdraw into herself and not function. Hoping to involve her in the work, I asked her if she had a pencil. She said that she was not going to do any work and did not need one. I told her that if she did not want to work in the class she would have to sit in the principal's office. She refused to work, and I placed her name on the misbehavior list. She stated that she was not going to work or leave the room. After I had spent 5 minutes of class time attempting to reason with her, I had to walk up to her and gradually nudge her to the door. She began to scream, curse, and threaten me. Then I told her and the class that the term was drawing to a close, and we no longer could afford to devote class time to her disruptions. I stated very strongly to her and the rest of the class that I would not surrender to her demands just because she was persistent in them. I also let her know that she had better begin helping herself because if she did not make an attempt to improve her habits, she would not pass the course.

Final report: June. Joan made a tremendous amount of progress during the past 3 months. Now she is able to read through the chapter before she asks questions about the work. She had been able to control her behavior even when emotionally upset. Although she is still somewhat disturbed by discussions of disease, she no longer loses control of herself. In the past few weeks, I have heard her compliment her peers, giving them recognition for their accomplishments. This also is a very positive area for her. I have noticed that she no longer looks up to Deborah, who she thought was completely perfect and therefore vastly superior to her. For the past month or so, she has dressed conservatively, using her makeup with extreme reservation.

Biology was a difficult and challenging subject for her. She tried her best to succeed and in doing so has become confident that she can succeed academically. She has also learned to relate to her peers. I believe that she has made a tremendous change for the better.

References

The following references discuss the process of identifying students with behavior problems and the difficulties inherent in this process.

1. Baker, E. H., & Thomas, T. F. (1980). The use of observational procedures in school psychological services. *School Psychology Monographs, 4,* 25–45.

2. Cosper, M. R., & Erickson, M. T. (1984). Relationships among observed classroom behavior and three types of teacher ratings. *Behavior Disorders, 9* (3), 189–194.

3. Epstein, M. H., Cullinan, H. D., & Sabatino, D. A. (1977). State definitions of behavior disorders. *Journal of Special Education, 11,* 417–423.

4. Hartman, D. P. (1982). Using observers to study behavior. *New Directions for Methodology of Social and Behavioral Science, Publication No. 14.* San Francisco: Jossey-Bass.

5. Koppitz, E. M. (1977). Strategies for diagnosis and identification of children with behavior and learning problems. *Behavior Disorders, 2* (3), 136–140.

6. Marcus, S. D., Fox, D., & Brown, D. (1982). Identifying school children with behavior disorders. *Community Mental Health Journal, 18* (4), 249–256.

7. McAuley, R., & McAuley, P. (1977). *Child Behavior Problems.* New York: Free Press.

8. Ollendick, T. H., & Meador, A. E. (1984). Behavioral assessment of children. In G. Goldstein & M. Hersen (Eds.), *Handbook of Psychological Assessment.* New York: Pergamon.

9. Smith, C. R. (1977). *Identification of Youngsters Who Are Chronically Disruptive.* Department of Public Instruction, Special Education Division, Des Moines, IA. Mimeo.

10. Spivack, G., & Swift, M. (1973). The classroom behavior of children: A critical review of teacher administered rating scales. *Journal of Special Education, 7,* 55–89.

11. Walker, H. (1978). Observing and recording child behavior in the classroom: Skills for professionals. *Iowa Perspective, 4,* 1–9.

12. Walls, R. T., Werner, T. J., Bacon, A., & Zane, T. (1977). Behavior checklists. In J. D. Cone & R. P. Hawkins (Eds.), *Behavioral Assessment*. New York: Brunner/Mazel.

The articles below deal with the possibility that the problem may be in the eyes of the beholder.

13. Algozzine, B. (1980). The disturbing child: A matter of opinion. *Behavior Disorders*, 5 (2), 112–115.

14. Gordon, T. (1974). *Teacher Effectiveness Training*. New York: Wyden.

15. Lawrence, J., Steed, D., & Young, P. (1984). *Disruptive Children: Disruptive Schools*. New York: Nichols.

16. Marlin, R., & Lauridsen, D. (1974). *Developing Student Discipline and Motivation: A Series for Teacher In-Service Training*. Champaign, IL: Research Press.

17. Mour, S. (1977). Teaching behaviors and ecological balance. *Behavior Disorders*, 3 (1), 55–58.

18. Swick, K., & Howard, R. (1975, summer). Disruptive behavior: Causes, effects, solutions. *Instructional Psychology*.

19. Thompson, G. (1976). Discipline and the high school teacher. *The Clearing House*, 49, 408–413.

Although an informal approach to evaluating students' behavior problems is recommended in this chapter, many educators prefer to supplement teacher observations with formal instruments. Some of the published instruments currently available are listed below.

20. Cassell, R. (1962). *The Child Behavior Rating Scale*. Los Angeles: Western Psychological Services.

21. Edelbrock, C. S., & Ackenbach, T. M. (1984). The Teacher Version of the Child Behavior Profile. I. Boys 6–11. *Journal of Consulting and Clinical Psychology*, 52, 207–217.

22. McCarney, S. B., Leigh, J. E., & Cornbleet, J. (1983). *Behavior Evaluation Scale*. Columbia, MO: Educational Services.

23. Miller, L. C. (1977). *School Behavior Checklist*. Los Angeles: Western Psychological Services.

24. Quay, H. C. (1977). Measuring dimensions of deviant behavior: The Behavior Problem Checklist. *Journal of Abnormal Child Psychology*, 5, 277–289.

25. Quay, H. C., & Peterson, D. R. (1983). *Revised Behavior Problem Checklist*. Coral Gables, FL: University of Miami.

26. Rubin, E., Simpson, C., & Betwee, M. (1966). *Emotionally Handicapped Children and the Elementary School*. Detroit, MI: Wayne State University Press.

27. Spivack, G., Spotts, J., & Haines, P. E. (1967). *The Devereux Adolescent Behavior Rating Scale.* Devon, PA: Devereux Foundation.

28. Spivack, G., & Swift, M. (1967). *Devereux Elementary School Behavior Rating Scale Manual.* Devon, PA: Devereux Foundation.

29. Von Isser, A., Quay, H. C., & Love, C. T. (1980). Interrelationships among three measures of deviant behavior. *Exceptional Children, 46,* 272–276.

30. Walker, H. (1976). *Walker Problem Behavior Identification Manual.* Los Angeles: Western Psychological Services.

WHETHER, WHEN, AND HOW TO INTERVENE

To Intervene or Not

In the real world, people don't follow the rules 100% of the time. Sometimes adults call out without waiting to be called on during a meeting. Sometimes they cut in and out of traffic lanes on the highway when they are in a hurry. They also "make up" a more socially acceptable reason for not going to work, canceling an appointment, or not accepting an invitation, because for one reason or another, they do not feel comfortable telling the truth.

The same things happen in school. Very few students follow all the rules all the time. At some point in their educational careers—at least once in a while—most students will call out, whisper to their neighbors, run in the hall, lie about why they couldn't do their homework, pass notes, tease someone, pretend they have to go to the bathroom, or do something else that breaks a rule or standard of behavior. Teachers who intervene every time their students do not fulfill the school's behavioral objectives would develop a reputation among students for being overly strict, dominating, inflexible nags. Worse, they would waste considerable precious time dealing with behavior that could and should be overlooked. The following guidelines may help you decide whether or not to intervene when your students do not behave appropriately. These suggestions are based on the experience and opinions of many educators, not on research-derived information.

Unnecessary Intervention

It may come as a surprise, in a book on classroom management, that some situations are better left alone. Consider the following circumstances when it may be either unnecessary or undesirable to intervene:

1. *Minor infractions:* Intervening when behavior is only a minor infraction and isn't disruptive or contagious may be counterproductive. You might be better off overlooking an occasional incident of calling out an answer, whispering to a neighbor, looking out the window, making an innocuous side remark, and so on, than to make an issue of it. The key is that you can do this so long as overlooking the behavior doesn't encourage students to "get into the habit" of doing such things. Experience in the classroom will enable you to make this kind of judgment with a reasonable degree of accuracy.

2. *Accidental, unintentional misbehavior:* When students spill things, bump into others, call out answers, or accidentally take the wrong book or coat, it may not be necessary to intervene unless the students need your help in learning how to avoid accidents. The same principle applies when students say things in the heat of the moment that they quickly regret having said.

3. *Extenuating circumstances:* Misbehavior caused by special conditions should be tolerated. For example, when a normally well behaved student gets argumentative because she has done poorly on an exam for the first time during the school year or she is in a bad mood because of a cold, or when your students cannot settle down because some good news is announced over the public address system or the fire alarm bell goes off accidentally or they will soon be taking standardized tests or a fun trip has been canceled due to inclement weather, it may be more prudent to overlook their atypical behavior than to confront them about it.

4. *Unrealistic expectations:* As we noted in chapter 7, some inappropriate behavior may *only* be inappropriate in the eyes of a particular educator. "Behavior problems" that are problems only because teachers unrealistically expect young students to behave like older students and older students to behave like adults or because educators' personalities and values make them uncomfortable with certain behaviors don't require intervention with students. Instead, the teacher may need to work on changing perceptions or instructional methods. For example, when many of the second-grade class begins to look around the room, talk to each other, and fidget in their seats, it may be time for the teacher to readjust the length of the lesson to their attention span and to give up on trying to get them to concentrate for longer than they are able.

Two Kinds of Flexibility   The preceding discussion of when it might be better to overlook certain behaviors rather than to intervene shows how important flexibility is in applying rules and expectations. But being flexible in situations that require adaptability is one thing; yielding to the temptation to lower your standards to avoid necessary hassles when you are tired, overworked, trying to cover a lot of material in a short time, or being pressured by students trying to intimidate you is another. The first kind of flexibility (adaptability) is helpful to students; the second kind (inconsistency) may encourage your students to misbehave even more. The first kind can help you avoid unnecessary and fruitless confrontations; the second kind will only postpone necessary conflicts until later, when students can become even more difficult to deal with. Learning to distinguish between being inconsistent and being adaptable takes experience and practice.

Necessary Intervention

Some situations clearly call for a response. The following circumstances usually require some form of intervention by teachers:

1. *Harmful behavior:* Students should not be allowed to harm themselves or bully, tease, slander, insult, hit, or provoke other students. Students who are the victims of bullying, insults, and the like, have the right to expect you to intervene quickly and effectively.

2. *Distracting behavior:* Behavior that distracts other students or seriously interferes with their ability to achieve your instructional objectives, such as attention-seeking clowning, note passing, or humming aloud, requires your intervention.

3. *Testing behavior:* Students who are testing you to find out what they can and cannot get away with by challenging your authority, refusing to follow directions, and so on, should be shown by your behavior that you will intervene whenever it's necessary to do so. This is especially important when other students are waiting to see how you will handle the problem.

4. *Contagious behavior:* Disruptive behavior that is likely to be copied by other students in your class should be dealt with before other students become involved.

5. *Consistent misbehavior:* Intervene regularly whenever students' misbehavior represents a consistent regular behavior pattern that requires a consistent response from you.

6. *Anticontractual behavior:* Behavior that represents a student's failure to abide by a commitment when that student has promised not to act in a particular way should not be overlooked (see discussion of contingency contracting in chapter 10).

When to Intervene

Once you decide that your students' behavior does indeed require you to intervene, the next challenge you face is deciding the most effective time to do so. In some situations, you need to intervene immediately; in other situations, a short delay might prove helpful.

Immediate Intervention

Certain guidelines can help you determine when it is important to step in right away to stop what is happening. The following types of behavior require immediate intervention:

1. *Dangerous and harmful behavior:* Intervene instantly when students' behavior is potentially dangerous or harmful to themselves or others. Stop young students if

they start toward the street on their own during a class trip. Prevent older students from hurting themselves or others by misusing science equipment in the laboratories. Even if the situation is not clearly dangerous, in circumstances with much potential for harm, it is better to be safe than sorry. You should also intervene as quickly as possible when students hit, pick on, bully, or victimize others. Finally, despite the saying "sticks and stones will break my bones but names will never hurt me," verbal abuse can often hurt just as much as physical abuse, and it requires your immediate intervention.

2. *Destructive behavior:* Students shouldn't be allowed to damage things that are expensive, that are hard to replace, or that belong to or are used by other students. Your immediate intervention at the first sign of trouble can discourage or prevent students from intentionally or unintentionally acting destructively.

3. *Behavior that can get worse:* Nip behavior problems in the bud if they are likely to intensify if not corrected. Immediately stop an argument between two students if it appears to be leading to a real fight. Students who are backing themselves into corners should be given face-saving ways out of the predicaments they are creating for themselves. Students who are testing you to see just how much you will let them get away with should also be stopped before they get themselves into serious trouble.

4. *Contagious behavior:* Stop misbehavior that is potentially "catching" before it spreads to other students.

5. *Self-perpetuating behavior:* Misbehavior that is intrinsically rewarding—such as cutting ahead in line, taking others' things or money, or teasing—should be stopped before students receive any reinforcement for their actions. Otherwise the reinforcement they receive could strengthen their motivation to continue to misbehave despite any negative consequences you apply.

Delayed Intervention

In some cases, it is better to delay intervention than to respond immediately to students' misbehavior. If students get blamed for things they have not done, the intervention causes more disruption than it avoids. Here are some situations in which immediate intervention can be counterproductive:

1. *When you do not have all the facts:* When you aren't sure of the facts, it might be better to hold off responding to what appears to be a problem until you know enough to intervene appropriately. In our society, we generally follow the principle that it is better to let a guilty person go free than to punish an innocent one. If you are not certain that students who seem to have started down the path of misbehaving will actually misbehave, it may be a good idea to give them the opportunity to control themselves so long as the situation is not likely to be dangerous, destructive, or contagious. For example, if—after handing out test papers to your class—you notice that a student has some notes left on her desk, it might be better to see what she will do instead of intervening right away. Perhaps she was not paying attention

when you told the class to clear their desks, and she will put her notes away before she looks at the test questions. In another example, if you overhear someone say something nasty to another student, you may get angry, but perhaps the other student provoked the response. It may be better not to correct the first student on the basis of an incomplete understanding of the situation; wait until you have found out all the circumstances.

2. *When the timing is wrong:* It may be better to postpone dealing with a problem until a more convenient time if the immediate circumstances will not permit you to deal with it effectively:

- *Insufficient time:* If a student misbehaves at dismissal time, you may have to wait if you want to discuss it with your student without rushing. A simple statement such as "Libby, we'll have to discuss what you just did during your lunch break" is all you need to let her know that you are aware of what she did and plan to handle it.

- *Disruptive effects of intervening:* If you are at a point in a lesson when it would be unwise to stop to handle a behavior problem as you would like to, it may be better to briefly signal your disapproval to the student and deal with it in a more constructive manner at a less disruptive time.

- *When students are too sensitive to expose themselves publicly:* If dealing with students' behavior in public would embarrass them, consider waiting until you can talk to them privately.

- *When students are too upset to deal with their behavior rationally:* When students are extremely angry, jealous, or resentful, it may be more prudent to discuss their behavior with them after they have calmed down.

Weighing the Choices

Unfortunately, in many classroom situations the choices are not as clear as they are in the examples just described. For instance, a student may be doing something that you think will get worse if you do not intervene, but based on your past experience with this student, you also believe that he will respond angrily if you call the class's attention to his behavior. What do you do: allow the situation to get worse or risk the student's ire? What should be your response if a student who reacts defensively to public cricitism has said something insulting to you, and other students are attentively waiting to see how you will handle the situation?

When such situations occur, you should weigh the pros and cons of intervening immediately and make a decision that reflects your best judgment. If it works out well, great! If it does not, change your approach the next time, and try again. Teaching is an art. We all have to learn from experience. When you make a mistake, try to understand where you went wrong. Ask a colleague for feedback if necessary. Whether what you tried worked or not, you are certain to learn something from each experience.

How to Intervene

Once you choose to intervene, your next move is to intervene effectively.

Five Strategies

Redl (3) and others (1, 4) have identified five strategies that educators can use to handle their students' behavior problems: changing, managing, tolerating, preventing, and accommodating.

THEORY FOCUS: REDL ON MANAGING BEHAVIOR PROBLEMS

Fritz Redl founded Pioneer House, a residential program for middle school boys with emotional problems. He also coauthored *The Aggressive Child*, which describes the techniques that the staff at Pioneer House used to rehabilitate these youngsters. Many of the techniques described in chapter 9 for managing students' behavior without consequences were first described by Redl. He is also responsible for the introduction of the life-space interview described in chapter 12. In his other books, *Mental Hygiene in Teaching*, *When We Deal with Children*, and *Understanding Children's Behavior*, Redl has adapted the techniques from Pioneer House

for use in regular classrooms. These techniques include accommodating classroom environments to students' emotional needs, managing their surface behavior without resorting to negative consequences, and preventing dangerous or disruptive behavior in nonpunitive ways. Though his books describe an eclectic approach, he stresses taking students' conscious and unconscious motivation into consideration when handling their disruptive behavior. In doing so, he was one of the first educators to suggest how certain Freudian insights could be applied in the classroom.

Changing   Techniques in the area of changing try to modify the attitudes, values, motives, beliefs, expectations, self-concepts, and so on, of students so that they will not have to behave in the same inappropriate way in given situations. Helping a 10-year-old afraid to stand up to boys who pick on him to overcome his fears is an example of changing. Helping a student who is inappropriately insecure about her abilities and talents to perceive herself more accurately is another.

Managing   Because it takes time to change students, and sometimes educators do not have the power, influence, or time to do this, they usually have to manage their students' behavior problems. Managing refers to techniques that modify a situation enough to make it less likely that a student will exhibit a behavior problem. Managing techniques are not designed to change a student; rather, their effect is to help the students exert more self-control over their behavior until changing techniques can do their job. In the case of the student who is inappropriately insecure about her abilities, an educator would certainly want to change her emotional reaction to the subjects and situations that make her insecure, but until the educator can do this, he might try managing the situation by telling the student that he will give her all the help she needs, that he won't grade her work, or that she can take a makeup exam if she does poorly on a test. These techniques won't change the student's feelings about herself, but they may help her manage her insecurity so it doesn't affect how she functions in school as much.

Educators can also use managing techniques with students who have physiological problems that cannot be changed. For example, a teacher may not be able to change highly active or overactive students, but she can help them manage their behavior by allowing them to release some of their energy when they are restless and fidgety. While this may not make these students any less active overall, it may enable them to avoid problem behaviors for the moment, which can be a blessing for all concerned.

Educators can use management techniques that involve consequences and those that do not. When educators use consequences to manage their students' behavior, they are using power to convince students to control themselves. To do this, they remind students what will happen if they do such and such, or they reward students for behaving the way they want them to behave and punish them for behaving in inappropriate ways. When educators manage students' behavior without consequences, they do not use power. Examples of this approach are diverting students' attention from things that are upsetting them to something unrelated, making a joke out of something they are taking too seriously, and speaking softly and calmly to them when they are nervous or frightened. None of these techniques involves the use of consequences or power.

Students often experience management techniques that involve consequences, especially negative ones, as coercive and manipulative. As a result, these techniques can cause students to resent their teachers and even rebel against them. Therefore, it is preferable to attempt to manage students' behavior with techniques that do not involve consequences. Unfortunately, in school, as in the world beyond the schoolhouse, it is sometimes necessary to use consequences to obtain people's compliance. If this were not true, there would be little need to employ individuals to pass out parking tickets, audit our tax returns, and so on. In keeping with these priorities, management techniques that do not involve consequences are described first, in chapter 9. Then chapter 10 discusses techniques that do make use of consequences.

Teachers can use teacher-managed techniques and student-managed (self-management) techniques. Teacher-managed techniques involve teacher participation in helping students manage their behavior. When teachers remind easily distracted students to remove things that might distract them from their desks before they start to work and ask impulsive students whether they have read all the directions when they are about to start an assignment, they are managing their students' behavior. Students manage their own behavior by using techniques that their teachers have taught them. Examples of self-management include students reminding themselves to remove things that might distract them from their desks and students asking themselves whether they have read all the directions when they are about to start an assignment.

Teaching students to manage their own behavior often involves considerable time and effort. It may not be a feasible approach with students who are too young or too untrustworthy. When feasible, however, it is more desirable to empower students to manage their own behavior than to require them to continue to rely on their teachers. Teacher-managed and student-managed techniques are discussed throughout this text.

Managing and Changing Compared   Managing techniques handle misbehavior for the moment. Changing techniques try to modify students' attitudes, motives, self-concepts, and the like, so they will not misbehave in the future. Convincing students that they have to behave or they will be caught and punished is an example of managing students. But motivating students to want to behave appropriately even when they will not be caught is changing them. Ignoring the attention-seeking behavior of students who play the clown until they stop clowning is managing their behavior because they may play the clown elsewhere and receive attention for doing so. Teaching them how to obtain attention in more acceptable ways is changing them.

Tolerating   Because changing techniques do not change students overnight, and management techniques do not always work, despite educators' best efforts, students will sometimes do just what educators are trying to get them not to do. Adults are the same. When adults resolve not to take their bad moods out on their families, not to complain about some aspect of their spouse's personality, or to make some other behavior change, they often do pretty well for a while, but then they slip. Students generally have less maturity, wisdom, and experience than adults have. If adults cannot be perfect and they slip occasionally, students will probably slip more often. When this happens, educators should tolerate their behavior so long as it is not too self-defeating, unfair, harmful, or dangerous.

To tolerate problem behavior means to accept it temporarily. This is an appropriate strategy when students cannot control *all* their behavior *all* the time, when it will take time for educators and others to eliminate the cause of the problem, or when management techniques won't do the job. When educators tolerate students' behavior problems, they allow students to misbehave, to give up too soon, to withdraw from the group, to pout or cry over nothing, and so on, because the educators know that the students cannot help themselves for the moment. But they tolerate the behavior only temporarily, until they can manage it or until changing techniques affect the students so that they no longer misbehave. It might also be appropriate to tolerate misbehavior due to extenuating circumstances or the heat of the moment if you believe that students are unlikely to repeat this behavior problem.

Preventing   Sometimes it is necessary to prevent students from doing things that will harm them or others or infringe on the rights of others. Specifically, you cannot let depressed or guilt-ridden students harm themselves. Do not let students who behave destructively with temper tantrums disrupt the class for too long or break things that do not belong to them. Preventing students from harming themselves, disrupting the class, or destroying other people's property by removing them from the area, placing yourself between the students and their intended victims, and so on, does not change what is causing their problem. But when an educator's managing techniques do not work, prevention is certainly a necessary strategy while trying to deal with the causes.

Accommodating   The final strategy is accommodating. When educators accept the fact that some of the physiological causes of their students' behaviors are unchangeable, that in some respects students are who they are, educators can help by accommodating demands, expectations, routines, disciplinary techniques, and so on, to the unchangeable aspects of their students. Educators may also want to accommodate their behavioral expectations to their students' culturally influenced behavior patterns so long as their behavior is effective and does not interfere with the rights of others.

Accommodating and Tolerating Compared   Superficially, accommodating and tolerating look similar. In both cases, educators permit their students to behave in ways that differ from how the majority of students behave. The difference between the two is that educators accommodate permanently to the unchangeable aspects of their students' personalities or to their cultural behavior patterns but tolerate only temporarily their changeable yet presently unmanageable unacceptable behavior. For example, one might accommodate the length of in-seat reading assignments to the shorter attention span of a student, but only temporarily tolerate the moodiness of a student who lost a fight during lunch.

Idealistic and Realistic Choices

Ideally, it may be desirable to change students so that they no longer need to behave as they do; realistically, this is a tough goal to achieve. The typical classroom teacher has little time to devote to changing students with behavior propblems, and administrators tend to give more priority to managing students with behavior problems than to changing them (often with justification). In addition, the more students an educator has, the less time he or she will have for the individual attention necessary to eliminate the causes of these behavior problems. Thus, secondary teachers with many classes of different students will have to depend more on managing than on changing techniques. Elementary teachers will be somewhat less dependent on managing techniques. But special educators, resource specialists, and teachers in private schools with small classes will have more opportunity to *change* students who misbehave.

While helping students learn to manage their own behavior is preferable to management by teachers, it is not always a realistic goal. Elementary school teachers usually have fewer students to contend with, but their students may lack the maturity to manage their own behavior successfully. Secondary school teachers work with students who should be mature enough to manage themselves. However, because these teachers usually have to teach large numbers of students, they may lack the time necessary to teach them to manage themselves. Students with emotional problems may become too upset to manage themselves; those with conduct disorders may be unwilling to do so (see chapters 11 and 12). Knowing when to strive for self-management and for which students it is a realistic goal is an important skill that teachers need to develop. Most of the subsequent chapters in this text include material and exercises that will assist you in acquiring this skill.

Class size also affects an educator's ability to accommodate demands and expectations to the unchangeable aspects of a student's personality and to tolerate certain kinds of disruptive behavior. Thus, secondary school teachers may have to resort to preventing some behavior that elementary school teachers might be able to tolerate. Again, special educators, resource specialists, and private school teachers may be able to be more flexible— to tolerate more behavior and accommodate their expectations and routines to their students' individual differences.

Because educators find themselves in different teaching situations, this book includes a variety of techniques for dealing with a given behavior problem. This broad approach to handling problem behaviors will enable you to select the techniques that suit your particular situation. Including techniques that are appropriate for different settings provides other benefits as well. It helps regular education teachers to identify students whose behavior problems may require more individual attention than they can provide, and it enables them to work more cooperatively with resource specialists and others in a team approach to provide the services that mainstreamed students with behavior problems require.

Educators' Response Patterns

Although educators should select techniques and strategies that are appropriate for their particular students and teaching situations, every educator has a personal way of reacting to behavior problems. Clinical experience indicates that most educators follow one or another of five typical patterns in responding to students who are misbehaving.

The first pattern is to use all five strategies. Educators who fall into this group try to understand why their students behave as they do, and then they select strategies that fit the causes of the problems. They generally make the right decisions, but—like everyone else—they sometimes make mistakes.

The second group of educators relies a great deal on changing and managing without consequences. They tend to believe that they can change students by reasoning with them. Thus, they try to find out why students behave as they do, often asking them what the matter is, what's bothering them, why they don't want to do something, and other similar questions. They are usually good at reasoning with, persuading, and cajoling students, but they avoid using negative consequences either because they do not believe it's a good idea to punish students or because they are uncomfortable with being disciplinarians.

A third group uses a lot of preventing and managing without consequences. If these techniques do not work, they tend to tolerate students' behavior problems rather than try to change them. Many of these teachers also have difficulty being authoritative.

The fourth group of educators uses managing with consequences as a primary strategy. They may be behaviorists who believe that this is the best strategy, or they may believe in the philosophy of "spare the rod and spoil the child." Some are perhaps uncomfortable unless they feel themselves to be in control of their students. Finally, they may be so angry and resentful that they have very little patience with their students.

The last group tends to tolerate and accommodate to students' behavior problems. Some of these educators believe that students' behavior problems are just their unique ways of responding to the world and should be accepted as such. Others defensively fool themselves into believing that the students' behavior problems are acceptable. And still others realize that their students have behavior problems, but they do very little to try to change them. This may be because they are so overwhelmed by the behavior that they give up, or else they are so involved in their own problems that they are unable to devote the time and energy needed to deal with their students' problems.

Self-Quiz: How You Handle Behavior Problems

Although it is natural to have your own ways of reacting to students' problems that reflect your own unique personality, at certain times your habitual responses will not be the most effective ones. Insight and awareness about your preferred or usual ways of responding to your students' behavior can enable you to choose consciously instead of reacting automatically. If you are an experienced teacher or have worked with children or teenagers, this activity may give you some insight into how you typically react to behavior problems.

First, list all of the behaviors that you find unacceptable in your students for whatever reason. Second, list the techniques you usually use to handle these behaviors. Third, categorize each of these techniques in terms of the five strategies discussed in this chapter. Then count up the number of techniques in each category. Finally, compare the totals to determine which strategies you use most and least often.

Gordon (2) identifies eight myths about "Good Teachers" that inhibit teachers from using the full range of strategies and techniques available to them when dealing with students' behavior problems. Do you believe in any of these myths? If you do, can you understand how your beliefs might limit your ability to respond appropriately to your students' behavior problems?

1. Good Teachers are calm, unflappable, always even-tempered. They never lose their "cool," never show strong emotions.
2. Good Teachers have no biases or prejudices. Blacks, whites, Chicanos, dumb kids, smart kids, girls and boys all look alike to a Good Teacher. Good Teachers are neither racists nor sexists.
3. Good Teachers can and do hide their real feelings from students.
4. Good Teachers have the same degree of acceptance for all students. They never have "favorites."
5. Good Teachers provide a learning environment that is exciting, stimulating, and free, yet quiet and orderly at all times.
6. Good Teachers, above all, are consistent. They never vary, show partiality, forget, feel high or low, or make mistakes.
7. Good Teachers know the answers. They have greater wisdom than students.
8. Good Teachers support each other, present a "united front" to the students regardless of personal feelings, values, or convictions. (2, p. 22)

Self-Quiz: Unnecessary Limits

Here are some additional questions to ask yourself so you can determine whether your habitual patterns or personal style may limit your range of options:

1. Are you much more concerned than most adults about what others think about you? If you are, do you find that you are reluctant to use certain management techniques that you would like to because you are concerned that they will change how your students feel about you?
2. Are you much less concerned than most adults about the opinion of others? If so, do you disregard your students' complaints about some of the management techniques you use and their suggestions of alternative ways of handling their problems?
3. Are you comfortable with your role as leader of the class, or does your desire to be your students' equal make it difficult for you to use certain techniques?
4. Are you comfortable with your role as an authority figure, or do you have difficulty setting limits and using consequences to help your students control their behavior?
5. Do you enjoy helping others to the point that you would rather have your students dependent on you for your assistance than work independently?

Summary

When students misbehave, educators should determine whether, when, and how to intervene before deciding on a response. Sometimes it's unnecessary or undesirable to intervene; at other times it is essential to do so. In some situations, immediate intervention is imperative; in other situations, it's more prudent to delay.

Educators can use five strategies in responding to their students' behavior problems: changing, managing, tolerating, preventing, and accommodating. Which strategies and techniques are successful depends in part on the educator's teaching situation. Although educators should select strategies and techniques that are appropriate for both their students' problems and their teaching situations, many educators tend to react to their students' behavior partly out of habit.

Activities

I. The exercises that follow should help you apply the concepts just reviewed to practical situations. For each of the incidents below, decide whether you would accept the behavior or intervene. Then, if you feel you would intervene, decide whether you would do so immediately or later.

1. While the class is collecting laboratory equipment, Tina, a 14-year-old, purposely pushes another girl who accidentally bumped her, causing the girl to drop a glass flask.

2. After you have told Steven, an 8-year-old, not to read comic books, you notice him with his head down, apparently reading something in his lap. The last time he disregarded your instructions, you told him he had to let you hold his comic books until dismissal, which caused a long, drawn-out argument.

3. Although the rest of the class has begun to work on an exam you have just handed out, Tony and Jeff, two 10-year-olds, are still talking with their tests unopened and unread.

4. While you are dictating words during a spelling quiz, Alissa, a 12-year-old, returns to class after spending more than 10 minutes in the bathroom despite promising you that she would be back in time to do the spelling.

5. Loretta, a 6-year-old, spills paint all over the table and begins to cry.

6. You see Bob, a 13-year-old, open a switchblade knife on the playground during recess.

7. Jim, a 16-year-old known to have a bad temper and to get into fights, suddenly spins around, tells the person behind him that he better shut his mouth or he will shut it for him, and then goes back to work.

8. Carlos, a 7-year-old who hasn't learned to wait until he is called on to answer, calls out an answer, then puts his hand over his mouth in a way that indicates he realizes his mistake.

9. Alice, a 5-year-old, pushes David off a tricycle when he refuses to let her have a turn.

10. At dismissal time you overhear Ronnie, a 16-year-old, say to Frank, "Now I'm gonna beat the shit out of you."

11. Tim, a 17-year-old who is extremely concerned about not calling attention to himself or his academic problems, is looking at the test of the person next to him.

12. Chris, an 8-year-old, is entertaining the students near him by pretending to put his finger in his nose and then in his mouth.

13. On your way to class late, you notice Jason, a 17-year-old, kissing his girlfriend in the hall just out of sight of anyone in the room.

14. You think that Ralph, a 13-year-old, might be selling drugs when you see him and another student exchange some small objects during recess.

15. Sonia, a 6-year-old, gives one of her usual, seemingly on-purpose, ridiculously incorrect answers to your question, which delights the rest of the class.

II. State whether each of the alternative techniques for dealing with the following behavior problems is an example of changing, managing with consequences, managing without consequences, tolerating, preventing, accommodating, or a combination of these strategies.

1. A preschool student is unwilling to share materials, give someone else a turn on the swing, and the like, without a struggle. The teacher:
   a. explains why children have to share and allow others to have turns.
   b. punishes the student when he refuses to share.
   c. makes sure he doesn't get the toy, swing, or whatever first so that others do not have to wait for him to give it up.
   d. purposely makes him wait extra long so he experiences what others feel when he makes them wait and then discusses his feelings with him.

2. A kindergarten teacher is about to read a story to his class. During story time, he has the group sit around him. One of his students is immature for her age and cannot attend to oral reading for as long as her peers. The teacher:
   a. sits the student up front so he can keep an eye on her and catch her attention if it wanders.
   b. places the student on the periphery of the group so that if her attention wanders, she won't distract the other students as easily.
   c. takes her aside before having the students change their seats and tells her she will get a reward if she listens to the whole story.

3. A second-grader starts teasing a girl working in his group whom he delights in teasing almost any chance he can. The teacher:
   a. tells him to stop.
   b. tells him to stop and punishes him for his behavior.
   c. tells him to stop and describes what will happen if he does it again.
   d. switches him to another group.
   e. takes him aside and explains why he should not tease other children.

4. While a class of second-graders is working in a small group, a student comes up to the desk and complains that another student is teasing her. This student has complained about the same boy and various other students many times before. The teacher:
   a. listens to what she has to say and then suggests that she join a different group.
   b. listens to the student and then asks her if she has any idea why the boy teased her.
   c. tells her that the other children will continue to tease her until she changes the way she reacts to their teasing.

5. While she is taking an arithmetic test, a fourth-grader stretches forward to read what the student in front of her has written. The teacher:
   a. stands near her for a minute or two to indicate that she is being observed.
   b. confiscates her paper and gives her a zero.
   c. calls her up to the desk and explains to her why students should do their own work on tests.

    d. changes her seat so she cannot copy.

    e. calls her up to the desk and tells her to do her own work.

6. A fifth-grader does everything, including her seatwork, so slowly that she is seldom able to complete an assignment within the time allotted. The teacher:

    a. talks to her about the importance of working faster.

    b. offers her a reward if she finishes the work in time.

    c. takes off credit for incomplete items.

    d. allows her to start before the others so she can finish on time.

    e. allows her to finish her class assignments after school.

    f. accepts what she can do within the time allotted without taking off credit.

    g. reminds her periodically to work faster.

7. A seventh-grade student who has been a good student until recently drags himself into class looking like he has no energy, sits down, puts his head on his desk, and appears to be tuning out everything around him. When this happens, the teacher:

    a. calls on him to bring his attention to the work at hand.

    b. allows him to withdraw because he is obviously upset about something.

    c. walks up to him, taps him on the back, and tells him he has to pay attention even if he is upset or go to the office.

8. A ninth-grade student who has only been in this country for 2 years says she wasn't able to do her homework because she had to translate during a meeting her parents had with a community agency. She has made similar statements four or five times in the 2 months she has been in the class. The teacher:

    a. tells her that her excuse isn't acceptable and gives her a zero for the assignment.

    b. gives her extra time to complete the assignment but takes off credit for lateness.

    c. gives her extra time without any penalty.

    d. explains that schoolwork should come before other obligations and suggests she should explain that to her parents.

9. An eleventh-grade student glares at another student and threatens to punch him if he doesn't shut up. The teacher:

    a. sends them to the office.

    b. tells them to cool it and describes the consequences if they don't.

    c. tells them there are better ways of dealing with disagreements and asks them to stay after class for a few minutes to discuss it.

10. A twelfth-grade student resists doing almost anything he is asked to do. The teacher:

    a. asks him if he saw the basketball playoffs on TV the previous night in order to begin to develop a better relationship with him so he can convince him to be less resistive.

    b. tells him he can earn a reward if he agrees to do what he is asked to do.

    c. asks him why he often refuses to do what is asked of him.

    d. allows him to get away with it.

References

1. Fine, M. J., & Walkenshaw, M. R. (1977). *The Teacher's Role in Classroom Management: Humanistic-Behavioral Strategies for Promoting Constructive Classroom Behavior.* Dubuque, IA: Kendall/Hunt.

2. Gordon, T. (1974). *Teacher Effectiveness Training.* New York: Wyden.

3. Redl, F. (1966). *When We Deal with Children.* New York: Free Press.

4. Shirley, R. L. (1979). Strategies in classroom management. *Educational Digest, 45* (4), 7–10.

CHAPTER 9

HELPING STUDENTS BEHAVE APPROPRIATELY

This chapter describes intervention techniques for working with students who are willing to behave appropriately. The techniques discussed here do not require an in-depth knowledge of what causes students' behavior problems, and they do not involve a great deal of time or effort that might better be spent teaching. For the most part, they are designed to deal with the problem at the moment through managing, accommodating, and preventing; they are not concerned with changing students. Part Three describes approaches you can use with students who do not respond to these techniques because the causes of their behavior problems require more individualized, time-consuming, or change-oriented techniques.

The techniques described here are divided into different groups according to the kinds of problems they are designed to handle. They include techniques for:

- Dealing with behavior problems that are partly the result of classroom environmental factors.

- Helping students who cannot conform to classroom rules owing to lack of practice.

- Aiding students who cannot stop themselves from acting out strong feelings inappropriately.

- Providing additional external control to students who want to behave appropriately but cannot because they lack self-control in some situations.

- Helping students realize when and how often they misbehave.

- Issuing desist orders.

- Convincing students open to reason that it would be all right for them to behave appropriately.

Eliminating Environmental Causes of Misbehavior

Chapter 3 described several techniques that good managers can use to eliminate potentially disruptive factors from their classroom environments. This section includes additional suggestions for dealing with behavior problems caused by environmental factors that occur when the techniques listed in chapter 3 do not work. A few examples of how you can make additional modifications in your classroom to handle these problems are described here (1). (Chapters 12 and 13 include suggestions for dealing with environmental factors that require a more in-depth understanding of individual students.)

Restructuring

When students are unable to comply with what you planned for them because they are upset by such unanticipated events as good or bad news announced over the intercom, a fight between two students during recess that brings to the surface racial or ethnic tensions, a conflict between class members, a substitute teacher the previous period, or something equally upsetting, it may be necessary to restructure your plans for the day. Instead of trying to get them to settle down and get to work despite what is bothering them, you may find it more effective to "go with the flow." This might involve adapting your expectations, teaching style, or lesson plan to their mood or taking out one of the emergency lessons you have prepared for just such occasions. In certain cases, it might be even better to depart from the content of your course and deal with whatever is upsetting them in an open and honest way.

Dealing With Competing Diversions

Sometimes events in the classroom can rivet everyone's attention and disrupt the best planned and executed lesson. Rabbits mating in the middle of your lecture, a suggestive description in a novel, a picture from the *National Enquirer*, a joke from a recent comic book, or a drawing by the class cartoonist being passed around can make competing for your students' attention a tough challenge. In such cases, it would be best to remove whatever is diverting their attention. But in cases where the disruptive influence is a fire engine or ambulance across the street, you might allow your students to satisfy their curiosity by looking out the window; then lower the shades and get back to work. Or if the class is excitedly buzzing about something that happened during recess, an event soon to be held in the auditorium, or a program they saw on television, let them get it out of their system by discussing it for a few minutes and then get back to work.

Providing Hurdle Help

Although most students can cope with the normal day-to-day frustrations and delays of school life, some act out because they want help with their work and cannot wait for it. No matter what system you devise to ensure that students who need your help to keep working will get it as soon as possible, chances are that you will sometimes have one or two students who cannot tolerate any significant delay in obtaining your assistance. The frustration they experience may cause them to demand your attention and/or express their feelings in disruptive ways. One effective way to manage this problem is to provide the help such students need to get over the hurdle that is blocking them as quickly as possible. While boosting them over will not help the students learn to cope with normal delays, it does let you manage their disruptive influence while you are using one or more of the changing techniques described in chapters 11 and 12. But if you find yourself having the same problem with a number of students, it may be that the system you have devised or the lesson plan you are following is at fault and not the students' inability to cope with delay. The solution in that case would be to modify your system or lesson plan.

Helping Students Follow Rules

Since, as we noted, there are major differences between how youngsters are allowed and even encouraged to behave outside of school and the way they are required to behave in school, students in the primary grades need time to learn exactly what they are supposed to do and time to practice doing it. Students who have attended schools in other countries where expectations for behavior are different from ours, as well as students who move from one part of the United States to another or are bused from one ethnic neighborhood to another, also require time and practice to learn how to conform to the new expectations (see chapters 4 and 5). The same applies to students faced with new teachers whose standards and expectations differ significantly from those of their previous teachers or to new situations in school that call for new ways of behaving. For example, going from a permissive teacher to a strict disciplinarian or from an unstructured approach that calls for a lot of student interaction, free choice of activities, and free movement between learning centers to an approach that is primarily seatwork and lecture or vice versa can require new ways of behaving that take time to master.

Fine and Walkenshaw (2) have suggested that students who misbehave because they are still in the process of learning how to behave appropriately shold be given "learner's leeway." This involves treating them as students who need to be taught how to follow rules and expectations, not as students who resist doing so, since their "misbehavior" is caused by lack of skill, not lack of motivation.

The following six-step approach is especially appropriate when students—especially young ones who need learner's leeway—misbehave:

1. Make students aware that they are not behaving appropriately. Statements such as "That's not the way to do it," "You're breaking the rule," or "You've forgotten the fourth rule" delivered in a noncritical, supportive tone of voice inform students that they have *inadvertently* behaved inappropriately. But saying the same thing in a complaining, critical, or threatening tone of voice can easily change the message your students receive. Instead of simply hearing that they have made a mistake—which they can correct next time—they may hear that you are dissatisfied with them, that you believe that they could have behaved more appropriately, or that they had better behave more appropriately. Any of these would be an inaccurate and unfair message to give them.

2. Tell students exactly what it was that they did wrong, and if necessary, explain why it was inappropriate—again in a noncritical, nonjudgmental way.

3. Provide students with examples of the right behavior by modeling it yourself or by pointing out when other students are behaving in the appropriate way.

4. Give students additional opportunities to practice the correct behavior.

5. Offer students feedback about how they are doing, but do not praise or reward them for behaving appropriately. (They do not have a motivational problem.) For example, "That's the way to do it," "Now you're on the right track," and "That's much better" are all appropriate statements.

6. If, despite your best effort to be nonjudgmental and noncritical, students act as if they felt criticized or threatened because they had misbehaved, explain that you understand that it was not their fault and that you realize it will take time for them to get used to your particular way of running the classroom.

Helping Students Handle Strong Feelings

When students experience especially strong feelings, they sometimes lose control of themselves. The intensity of their emotions gets the better of them, and they do things they wouldn't normally do. The following are some techniques you can try when students express strong feelings in unacceptable ways (3–9).

Tolerating Inappropriate Behavior

Some things students do in the heat of the moment that they would not ordinarily do are so minor you can overlook them, since this will not increase the chances that students will behave that way when they aren't upset. While educators would certainly disagree about which behaviors are minor or major transgressions, such things as a slammed book, a stomped foot, or an angry look might be included in most of their lists as minor infractions.

Students who occasionally overreact impulsively to strong feelings often realize their mistakes as soon as they have made them or when they calm down. Overlooking their behavior for the moment may give them the opportunity to correct themselves, apologize, or make amends for what they said or did without your intervention.

Managing Strong Feelings

When the expression of strong feelings would be too disruptive to be tolerated, educators can use a number of techniques to help students manage how they express their feelings.

Active Listening   At times, merely listening to students and allowing them to express their feelings can help them regain self-control. Active listening, discussed in chapter 2, can be an effective first step when students are upset.

Acknowledging Feelings   One way to help students manage strong emotions is to acknowledge their feelings and to validate their right to feel the way they do while suggesting alternative ways for them to express themselves (3). Acknowledging their feelings can calm them down somewhat, while providing them with more desirable ways of acting out their feelings still gives them acceptable ways of expressing themselves. For example, if a student has just used a string of four-letter words to express her reaction to what another student has said about her sister, avoid reprimanding or punishing the student. Instead, it may be more effective to tell her that you understand how hurt and angry she must feel about what the other student said but that you hope she can express her anger in language that is more acceptable in school. This approach may get your point across in a way that is less likely to provoke a defensive reaction when the student feels she was in the right and shouldn't be reprimanded or punished for retaliating against the other student.

Discharging Feelings   You can help students who are too upset to control themselves to discharge (get rid of) their feelings in nondisruptive or harmless ways. The idea is to allow them to "let off a little steam" so that the pressure does not make them explode. Running errands, cleaning up work areas, and rearranging storage cabinets are activities that might help angry students work off some tension.

Relaxing Students   Helping students to relax by allowing them to eat something they like, talking to them in a calm manner, allowing them to listen to music with earphones, or even giving them a back rub if you are comfortable doing so can reduce their need to act out their feelings.

Providing Escape   Sometimes merely giving students the chance to postpone or escape a difficult situation by allowing them to use a computer, work at a learning center, or play a game in a free-time area can help them regain control over themselves in a few minutes.

Students who are upset may benefit from some time alone.

Preventing Problem Behavior

You must prevent students with the potential to react to strong feelings in disruptive, dangerous, or destructive ways from doing so even if you cannot help them manage their feelings. Occasionally, you may have to remove students from your classroom until they have calmed down enough to regain their self-control or else protect them from hurting themselves or others, damaging property, or getting into serious trouble.

Minor Problems   Just how flexible educators can be in handling their students' expression of strong feelings depends on how disruptive or dangerous they are. For example, when students say things in the heat of the moment that they wouldn't ordinarily say, you can use any of the techniques previously described. You can, for example, overlook their statements if you think it is possible to do so without repercussions. Otherwise, you can—before intervening—give them the opportunity to correct themselves, apologize, or make amends for what they did once they are calm and have had a chance to reflect. If Harriet says something insulting about your racial, ethnic, or religious background after seeing her failing grade at the top of a test paper, give her a chance to apologize when she has calmed down. And if Sammy walks through the door calling another student four-letter words because of what the other student said about Sammy's mother in the hall, give Sammy a chance to correct himself by saying something like, "What?" "What did you say?" or "I couldn't hear you." As noted in chapter 5, students from some ethnic backgrounds (e.g., Hispanic Americans) may be unaccustomed to making overt and direct apologies for their mistakes or transgressions. Therefore, it is important to be sensitive to their more subtle ways of admitting and saying that they are sorry that they have done something wrong.

You can also acknowledge a student's strong feelings and suggest alternative ways of expressing them. You could, for example, tell Harriet that you understand how bad she feels about failing the test and why she might blame you for failing her. Then, if that defuses the situation a little, you might suggest more acceptable ways of expressing her feelings about her grade, such as saying she thinks you made a mistake, she believes she deserved a better grade, or she feels you were unfair. Applying the same principle to Sammy, you could say that you understand why he is angry and remind him that he could use other language to express himself while in school. If Harriet and Sammy are still unable to control themselves, you could provide them with an escape valve—the opportunity to work at a learning center or in a free-play area until they calm down, telling them that you will deal with their behavior later.

As you read these suggestions, you may have felt that they did not address the real problem. Perhaps you believe it would be more effective to help Harriet accept the responsibility for her failing grade and Sammy to understand that being angry is not an excuse for cursing in class. The problem is that the intensity of their feelings may override their ability to deal with situations rationally, or they may be too angry to be able to appreciate your point of view or too resentful or defensive to admit that they deserve to pay the consequences for their behavior. Later, when they aren't so emotional, they may be more receptive to your intervention techniques. So long as they will not disrupt the class, harm anyone, or destroy something, it may be wise to postpone further action until they have calmed down.

You might also have thought of using consequences to help Harriet and Sammy control themselves or of offering them a reward if they exercised self-control and/or of informing them of the consequences if they continued to behave as they did. Using consequences was purposely omitted here. Although no research evidence supports or refutes this approach, the position taken here is that when students are too upset to control their actions, positive and negative consequences usually have little effect on their behavior. (See chapter 12 for a more detailed discussion of this point of view.)

Serious Problems   Students who react to their strong emotions in dangerous, destructive, or very disruptive ways, or who have the potential to do so, leave educators with little flexibility, since they have to choose techniques that will work immediately. If Harriet were to throw a disruptive temper tantrum or Sammy were to attempt to hit a student he was angry at, your options would be limited because you could not tolerate their behavior. It is also unlikely that they would correct their behavior on their own. In addition, they would probably be too upset to respond to your acknowledgment of their feelings and to your suggestions of alternative ways of expressing themselves. Eventually, they might react favorably to being allowed to escape the situation by spending time in another section of the room until they calmed down, but you would still have to do something immediately to interfere with their disruptive behavior. (See the next section for suggestions on dealing specifically with these kinds of behavior problems.) Considering the intensity of emotion needed to incite students who normally do not throw temper tantrums or hit other students in class, you might have to excuse them from class until they regain enough of their composure to be able to control themselves.

Students do not always "act out" when they are overwhelmed by strong emotions. Sometimes they withdraw psychologically and/or physically from situations that overwhelm them. They are especially likely to withdraw when they are too depressed to relate to external demands or too anxious to confront situations directly. (Chapter 12 describes techniques you can use with students who are too depressed or anxious to conform to the normal demands of school or to relate to the group.)

Providing External Control

This section describes several techniques you can use to provide students who are unable to resist the temptation to misbehave in certain situations with the additional external control they need. These techniques include distracting students, signaling awareness and disapproval of their misbehavior, proximity control, using space and grouping, teaching self-monitoring skills, and issuing mild desist orders and warnings. (10–13)

Distracting Students

Sometimes you can manage students about to lose control by distracting their attention from whatever is overstimulating them. Distracting them does not help them learn self-control, but it does avoid the impending loss of self-control and the immediate problems that could create. For example, you may be able to help a preschooler who comes to class almost in tears because she has had difficulty separating from her mother to forget her troubles by asking her to look at a picture with you or to help decorate a page in the booklet the class is preparing. Or you may be able to distract a student on the verge of escalating a minor disagreement into a major confrontation by asking him to help you do something or run an errand.

Signaling Awareness and Disapproval

Because of your personality, you may prefer to call your students' attention to their misbehavior rather than distract them from it. Signaling that you have noticed that a student is reading a comic book, moving toward off-limits material, or dipping into something in a cooking class before it is time to and making it clear that you disapprove of this behavior by a frown or a movement of your hand or head may be all that is needed to help the student refrain from the behavior.

Proximity Control

When signaling your awareness and disapproval is not enough, positioning yourself close to the students may do the trick (12). For example, you may have signaled your awareness that a student's eyes are roaming in the general direction of her neighbor's papers during an exam, but the student still does not control her behavior; standing closer to her for a few moments may do the job. Your own calm physical presence can help settle students who are upset so that they don't act out their strong emotions. Seating the preschooler on the verge of tears next to you or moving close to the two students arguing about what each said to the other could be a simple, effective intervention technique.

There is virtually no research about which students are likely to be helped by proximity control techniques. However, such techniques may be more effective with younger students and those who are field sensitive because these students are more responsive to and concerned about how their teachers perceive them (see chapter 5).

Using Space and Grouping

You can use the physical space in the classroom to provide students with additional external control (11, 12). The most straightforward example is to separate students who cannot seem to stop talking to each other and seat each of them with nondisruptive students. That decreases the negative effect they have on each other and increases the positive effects the nondisruptive students can have on them. Again, separating two students who are arguing may be more effective than either signaling disapproval or standing near them if they are too upset to control themselves when they are so close together. Finally, placing distractible students where there are few distractions or behind a screen or in a cubicle may help them concentrate better.

Self-Monitoring Skills

Sometimes helping students realize how often, how long, and in what situations they misbehave can give them enough insight to control themselves if they are motivated to behave appropriately (14–17). In certain cases, just learning what they are doing, when they are doing it, and how often is enough to help students modify their behavior. This parallels the cases of those lucky individuals who, once they start counting calories and learn which foods are fattening and how many calories they are consuming, are able to cut down sufficiently to lose weight or people who, having been told that what they are doing bothers others, are able to stop almost immediately.

Because insight alone can sometimes be sufficient, particularly with older students, it might be a good idea to start with seeing if merely helping students discover how often they call out, get up, talk to their neighbors, and so on, will enable them to modify their behavior. To do this, have your students tally the number of times they do a specific, countable behavior such as interrupting, chatting with neighbors, or bringing comic books to class. Or have them keep track of the amount of time they spend in the bathroom, drawing, talking to their neighbors, or carrying on other inappropriate behavior. Hopefully, when they see the total picture, some of them, at least, will change their behavior.

Research indicates that self-monitoring may help students who are mature enough to monitor their behavior accurately and motivated to control themselves. However, research reveals that the positive results of self-monitoring tend not to generalize to other situations and are unlikely to continue when students are not supervised by the teachers who taught them the self-monitoring procedures. In other words, self-monitoring tends to be an effective management technique but typically does little to change students. The following chapter describes additional steps that teachers can take to increase the likelihood that the positive effects of self-monitoring will generalize.

Issuing Desist Orders

At times, a more direct approach may be called for, and you might want to tell students directly to stop doing whatever it is they are doing wrong (10, 13). For example, when it is urgent to get a student to put something fragile down, to not misuse a complex piece of equipment, or to stop provoking a student about to explode, you may have to issue a direct order so that it gets your student's immediate attention and compliance. When you find yourself in such a situation, your desist orders are more likely to be effective if you follow these guidelines (10, 18–22):

1. Clearly identify what it is that you want students to stop. Statements such as "Don't do that" and "John, behave yourself" are too vague and less desirable than "Close the closet door," "Don't call out," and "Don't write on your desk."

2. Suggest appropriate alternatives. When you tell a student to close the closet door, add, "Ask me if you need something inside." When you tell students not to call out, say, "Raise your hand, and I will call on you when it's your turn."

3. When you tell students what to do, your voice and gestures should let them know that you are serious and mean business.

4. Use mild desist orders. While your attitude should be firm and businesslike, it should not be harsh. Do not yell or use sarcasm or ridicule to pressure the student to obey you. And do not express surprise, shock, or disappointment about their behavior. Statements such as "That's a stupid thing to do," "Don't you know better than that?" or "I'm surprised at you" tend to backfire. Even if they work for the moment, they can lower students' self-esteem and increase their resentment.

5. If possible, speak to students privately, not publicly. For example, if a student is drawing something instead of doing her work, walk up to her and whisper your instructions. This would probably be less embarrassing to her and less disruptive to the other students than calling out her name from your desk and ordering her to stop drawing.

6. Focus on your students' behavior, not on them. "Don't tap your foot or your pencil" and "Don't ask again once you have been told no" are better than "Why are you always tapping your foot?" and "Don't be a pest."

7. Avoid challenging or confronting statements that can place you in a win-lose, battle-of-wills situation with your students. "You aren't supposed to go to the restroom

without permission" may be less challenging to a teenager than "You *can't* leave the room." And "Give Mary back her book and see me after class" may be a more acceptable order than "Give Mary back her book and apologize to her right now."

8. If you believe that merely telling students to stop will not be enough, remind them of the consequences if they do not comply with your orders.

9. Make sure that students are aware that you will follow through on what you have said by watching and waiting to make sure the students comply before turning your attention elsewhere and by reminding them of the consequences they incurred the last time they did not comply.

10. Avoid the tendency that many teachers have to speak harshly and publicly to male students and quietly and privately to females (see chapter 6).

Reasoning with Students

Explaining Why Rules Are Necessary

Students who do not understand why certain rules are necessary may be more willing to comply with your expectations if you explain why they should do so. While no research evidence either supports or refutes this commonsense notion (13), it seems to be a sensible approach with students who do not understand the reasons for particular rules. After telling such students that they shouldn't do something, explain why their behavior is unacceptable and why another way of behaving is more appropriate. For example, if the student who opened the door to the storage closet does not understand why you told him to close it, don't leave him thinking he has to close it only because you said so. Instead, explain that some of the equipment inside can break or hurt someone if not handled properly. Or when you tell young students not to talk while someone else is reciting, remind them how hard it is to understand what the speaker is saying when they do not pay attention and how hard it is for the other students to hear when more than one person is speaking.

This does not mean, however, that you should regularly explain the reasons why rules are necessary every time students break them. That would be unnecessary, too time-consuming, disruptive, and counterproductive. But when students truly do not understand why certain rules are needed—perhaps because they attended schools in other countries where the rules were different, or never attended school in the internment camps in which they lived prior to immigrating to the United States, or are inexperienced with school rules—explanations can change students' attitudes about the rules.

Active Listening

If students disagree with a rule they think is unnecessary or they believe that they have not done anything inappropriate—and they aren't the kind of students who habitually challenge your authority whenever they are caught misbehaving—hearing them out and then explaining your perception should increase the likelihood that they will behave appropriately (20). They may be more willing to cooperate because you have listened to their side of the story, which makes them feel more positive toward you. And they may also accept your perception of why the rules really are fair or their behavior really was inappropriate (see chapter 2).

Correcting Misunderstandings

Students who misbehave because they misunderstand situations are likely to correct their behavior once they perceive the situation accurately. With a student who is acting up because she thinks another student unfairly marked one of her answers on a test wrong, explaining that her answer really was incorrect can short-circuit her angry response. Helping a student understand that the reason she was not chosen for a team, part, or group was to give others who are less able a chance and not because she was not good enough or was not wanted, can also avoid a potentially disruptive response.

While misunderstandings can occur for many reasons, they are especially likely to occur between individuals who come from different ethnic and contextual backgrounds, who use different communication styles, or who are different genders. The information in chapters 4 through 6 should help you identify students who are most likely to misunderstand situations, relationships, and communications.

Appealing to Values

When mature students who have been brought up to behave ethically, who usually identify with the group, and who want to behave appropriately misbehave, you can sometimes control them by appealing to the ethical and moral values they already accept. According to Fine and Walkenshaw,

> Some of the values that teachers can appeal to include: (a) an appeal to the mutual respect between teacher and child, as, "You are treating me rudely. Do you think that I have been unfair to you?" (b) an appeal to reality consequences or cause and effect relationships, as, "If you continue to talk, we will not have time to work on our Christmas gifts," (c) an appeal to the child's group code and awareness of peer reactions, as, "If you continue to spoil their fun, you can't expect the other boys and girls to be your friends," and (d) an appeal to the teacher's power of authority, as, "As your teacher, it is my job to see that nobody gets hurt; I cannot allow this behavior to continue and still take good care of you." (25, p. 80)

Role Playing

When students' misbehavior adversely affects others, role playing can be an effective intervention with students old enough to put themselves in other people's shoes (23–26). Having students play the role of the students who lost their turns, were excluded from a

Self-Quiz: Techniques to Help Students

Below are some techniques that do not involve consequences but can help students behave better. Which of these techniques have you used? Which ones would you feel comfortable using? Which ones would you be reluctant to use? Why?

Helping students follow rules:

- Providing learners leeway
- Informing students that their behavior is unacceptable
- Explaining to students why their behavior is unacceptable
- Providing models of appropriate behavior
- Providing students with opportunities to practice acceptable behavior

Helping students cope with strong feelings:

- Overlooking behavior done in the heat of the moment
- Acknowledging students' feelings
- Providing students with opportunities to discharge their feelings
- Relaxing students
- Providing escape

Providing external control:

- Distracting students
- Signaling awareness and disapproval
- Using proximity control
- Using space and grouping
- Teaching students self-monitoring skills
- Using desist orders

Reasoning with students:

- Explaining the "whys" of rules
- Active listening
- Appealing to values
- Role playing

game during recess, or did not get a chance to talk and then asking them how they feel and think can help them appreciate the negative effects of their behavior.

Unfortunately, some students do not profit from learning how their behavior affects others. Some students are too young to be able to place themselves in other people's shoes. Some students with conduct problems do not care about others. Some students with emotional problems enjoy hurting and upsetting others. Chapters 11 and 12 describe techniques that have proved useful for helping these students change their attitudes.

Realistic Thinking Development

Most of the techniques for reasoning with students are more appropriate for older rather than younger students. As Piaget (27) and others have demonstrated, students become more rational as they mature. The thinking of toddlers and preschoolers, for example, is extremely unrealistic; toddlers will hide themselves from others by closing their eyes because they believe that others can't see them since they can't see others. And preschoolers believe in Santa Claus and the Tooth Fairy. By the time children are ready for kindergarten or first grade, their thought processes are more logical. They begin to understand that the world around them and the things that happen to them usually have logical explanations. This helps them overcome their fears of ghosts and monsters, but it also prevents them from continuing to believe in the Tooth Fairy and Santa Claus.

During elementary school, children's logical thinking improves. But they are still prone to blame other people and circumstances for the problems they create for themselves. And they still tend to mistakenly think that their teachers and others treat them unfairly because they cannot yet appreciate other people's preferences and points of view. Youngsters at this age have a better understanding of time, but they still underestimate how long it will take to do certain things like their homework, and they overestimate the time they spend doing unpleasant things like practicing the piano.

Adolescents' thinking processes are much more advanced than students in elementary or intermediate school. To begin with, they are more realistic about time. They are also more able to distinguish among the impossible, the possible, and the probable. They can recognize their own role in the problems they encounter with people, and they are more able to admit when they are the cause of their own difficulties. Though they may not always act like it, adolescents are capable of dealing with issues that arise in the classroom in a much more realistic manner.

To be effective as a classroom manager, you should adjust your techniques to the kind of thinking that characterizes your students. You can do this by spending more time listening to older students' points of view and explaining your perceptions to them and less time bribing, cajoling, insisting, and demanding.

Summary

You can help many students who misbehave without resorting to consequences. You can solve their problems by eliminating the environmental causes of their behavior, teaching them how to follow rules, helping them to cope with strong feelings, providing external controls (such as teaching them how to monitor their behavior, and issuing desist orders), and reasoning with them.

Activities

Each of the following incidents is followed by a number of techniques that could be used to help students modify their behavior. Determine which would be effective solutions to the problems, and describe how you would use them.

1. Van, a 13-year-old student who was exposed to a great deal of trauma during the war in Cambodia before emigrating 2 years ago, becomes very upset whenever wars are discussed in his social studies class. (Eliminating environmental causes of students' behavior, helping students cope with strong emotions, reasoning with students, correcting misunderstandings)

2. Jeff, an 11-year-old who often copies on tests, is allowing his eyes to wander in the direction of another student's paper during an examination. (Teaching students to monitor their behavior, issuing desist orders, reasoning with students)

3. Jane, an immature 5-year-old with a short attention span, starts to talk to the student next to her while you are reading a story to a group of students seated on the floor in front of you. (Eliminating environmental causes of students' behavior, teaching students how to follow rules, issuing desist orders)

4. Warren, a 7-year-old who is a poor sharer, refuses to share some art materials with another student in his group. (Teaching students how to follow rules, providing external control, issuing desist orders, reasoning with students)

5. Francis, a 12-year-old with a bad temper, pushes a student and threatens to hit him in the nose if he does not take back what he said. (Helping students cope with strong feelings, providing external control, issuing desist orders, reasoning with students)

6. When you call on Michael, a 14-year-old who is functioning 3 years below grade level, to recite, he answers angrily that he did not do his homework because it was boring. (Eliminating environmental causes of students' behavior, helping students cope with strong feelings, reasoning with students)

7. Eddie and Carl, two 16-year-olds, hand in virtually identical book reports. When you tell them that, they deny that they worked together or copied. (Using desist orders, reasoning with students)

8. Bertha, a 7-year-old who only attends your class for 3 months because her parents are migrant workers, calls out the answer without waiting to be called on. (Teaching students to follow rules, teaching students how to monitor their behavior, issuing desist orders, reasoning with students)

9. Enrique, a 10-year-old who is limited in his English proficiency because he has only been in the United States for a year and a half, stays in the bathroom for almost 15 minutes while the class is working on oral reading. This is not the first time he has gone to the bathroom to avoid reading aloud. (Eliminating the environmental causes of students' behavior, helping students cope with strong feelings, teaching students to monitor their behavior, issuing desist orders, reasoning with students)

References

The following reference discusses techniques for eliminating environmental causes of misbehavior.

1. Long, N. T., Morse, W. C., & Newman, R. G. (1965). *Conflict in the Classroom: The Education of Emotionally Disturbed Children*. Belmont, CA: Wadsworth.

Helping students follow rules is the focus of the following reference.

2. Fine, M. J., & Walkenshaw, M. R. (1977). *The Teacher's Role in Classroom Management* (2nd ed.). Dubuque, IA: Kendall/Hunt.

Techniques for helping students to handle strong feelings are discussed in the following references.

3. Axline, V. M. (1947). *Play Therapy*. New York: Houghton.

4. Bloom, R. B. (1977). Therapeutic management of children's profanity. *Behavior Disorders, 2* (4), 205–221.

5. Grossman, H. (1965). *Teaching the Emotionally Disturbed: A Casebook*. New York: Holt, Rinehart & Winston.

6. Grossman, H. (1972). *Nine Rotten Lousy Kids*. New York: Holt, Rinehart & Winston.

7. Marshall, H. H. (1972). *Positive Discipline and Classroom Interaction: A Part of the Teaching-Learning Process*. Springfield, IL: Thomas.

8. Morse, W. C. (1985). *The Education and Treatment of Socio-Emotionally Disturbed Children and Youth*. Syracuse, NY: Syracuse University Press.

9. Redl, F., & Wineman, D. (1957). *The Aggressive Child*. New York: Free Press.

Providing external control is discussed in the references below.

10. Kounin, J. S. (1970). *Discipline and Group Management in the Classroom*. New York: Holt, Rinehart & Winston.

11. Stainback, W., Stainback, S., Etscheidt, S., & Doud, J. (1986). A nonintrusive intervention for acting out behavior. *Teaching Exceptional Children, 19* (1), 38–41.

12. Stainback, W., Stainback, S., & Froyen, L. (1987). Structuring the class to prevent disruptive behavior. *Teaching Exceptional Children, 19* (4), 12–16.

13. Weber, W. A., Roff, L. A., Crawford, J., & Robinson, C. (1983). *Classroom Management: Reviews of the Teacher Education and Research Literature*. Princeton, NJ: Educational Testing Service.

Self-monitoring techniques are described in the following references.

14. Lloyd, J. W., Bateman, D. F., Landrum, T. J., & Hallahan, D. P. (1989). Self-recording of attention versus productivity. *Journal of Applied Behavior Analysis, 22* 315–323.

15. McKenzie, T., & Rushall, B. (1974). Effects of self-recording on attendance and performance in a competitive swimming training program. *Journal of Applied Behavior Analysis, 7*, 199–206.

16. Sagotsky, G., Patterson, C. J., & Lepper, M. R. (1978). Training children's self-control: A field experiment in self-monitoring and goal setting in the classroom. *Journal of Experimental Child Psychology, 25*, 242–253.

17. Smith, D. J., Nelson, J. R., Young, K. R., & West, R. P. (1992). The effect of a self-management procedure on the classroom and academic behavior of students with mild handicaps. *School Psychology Review, 21* (1), 59–72.

How to issue desist orders is described in these references.

18. Bordeaux, D. B. (1952). How to get kids to do what's expected of them in the classroom. *Clearing House, 55,* 273–278.

19. Jones, F. H. (1987). *Positive Classroom Discipline.* New York: McGraw-Hill.

20. Lasley, T. J. (1981). Classroom behavior: Some field observations. *High School Journal, 64* (4), 142–149.

21. Masden, C. H., Becker, W. C., Thomas, D. R., Koser, L., & Plager, E. (1968). An analysis of the reinforcing function of "sit down" commands. In R. K. Parker (Ed.), *Readings in Educational Psychology.* Boston: Allyn & Bacon.

22. O'Leary, K. D., & O'Leary, S. G. (Eds.). (1977). *Classroom Management: The Successful Use of Behavior Modification.* New York: Pergamon Press.

The references below can help you learn how to increase students' intrinsic motivation through reasoning.

23. Blackham, G. J., & Silberman, A. (1971). *Modification of Child Behavior.* Belmont, CA: Wadsworth.

24. Brophy, J., & Rohrkemper, M. (1980). *Teachers' Specific Strategies for Dealing with Hostile and Aggressive Students.* Research Series No. 86. East Lansing, MI: Institute on Research in Teaching, Michigan State University.

25. Fine, M. J., & Walkenshaw, M. R. (1977). *The Teacher's Role in Classroom Management* (2nd ed.). Dubuque, IA: Kendall/Hunt.

26. Schmuck, R., & Schmuck, P. A. (1979). *Group Processes in the Classroom.* Dubuque, IA: Brown.

This reference discusses students' realistic thinking development.

27. Piaget, J. (1950). *The Psychology of Intelligence.* New York: Harcourt.

OBTAINING STUDENTS' COMPLIANCE BY USING CONSEQUENCES

As we noted in Part One, teachers who motivate students to want to behave by using effective instructional techniques, satisfying their basic needs, modeling desirable behavior, enhancing their beliefs in the value of school, handling potentially disruptive situations, considering their contextual, ethnic, socioeconomic, and gender characteristics when selecting classroom management approaches, and so on, can avoid many, if not most, behavior problems. Chapter 9 pointed out how many students who misbehave, even when their teachers are doing as much as possible to avoid behavior problems, can be helped to behave appropriately if they are motivated to do so. As you will see in this chapter, some students—younger ones who have not yet learned that it really is necessary to follow rules and conform to standards of acceptable behavior and older ones who are mischievous, interested in seeing what they can get away with, and the like—need to be shown that it is to their advantage to behave appropriately. This chapter describes how you can use consequences to convince these students to behave appropriately. It begins with positive consequences and then moves on to negative consequences, because negative consequences should be used only when positive consequences cannot do the job.

Many of the principles discussed in this chapter are not applicable to all students. As you read this chapter, you should remember that contextual, ethnic, socioeconomic, and gender factors all play a role in determining which principles apply to an individual student.

Positive Consequences— Rewards

All things being equal (which they seldom are), students are more likely to do things they will be rewarded for than punished for. Thus, even though the effects of rewarding as a technique are limited, and one can never know ahead of time whether a particular student will or will not change his or her behavior to obtain a reward, providing and withdrawing positive consequences can be an effective way of handling *some* students' behavior problems.

Two Kinds of Appropriate Behavior

For individual students to learn, they must attend, concentrate, tolerate frustration, stay on task, and participate actively. For entire classes to function smoothly, students must be good group members. They must learn to wait their turn, wait to be called on, share, cooperate, respect the property of others, listen to others, and so on. To date, research about the effects of rewarding desirable behavior has focused primarily on students as learners, not on students as members of a group. Therefore, research can support decisions about when to reward students who are fulfilling their role as learners, but not about when to reward them for fulfilling their roles as members of a group.

Students as Learners   The available evidence indicates that rewarding desirable behavior such as staying on task and completing seatwork when the work is unattractive, boring, repetitive, and involves practicing skills that have already been partially learned does indeed improve student behavior. But when the work is new, interesting, challenging, or not yet learned, rewarding desirable behavior has a detrimental effect on students' behavior (1–7).

The fact that rewarding students increases their motivation to do boring work but not work that is interesting and challenging is common sense. Students probably have little intrinsic motivation to do work that is boring and repetitive, whereas they are much more likely to be self-motivated to master new and challenging information. For example, young children who have already learned how to tie their shoelaces, although poorly, and older students who have partially mastered the basics of multiplication may not be particularly motivated to practice these skills without some extrinsic motivation.

Excessively rewarding students for behaving appropriately even when the work is repetitive, boring, and unattractive may have its shortcomings, too. Even if it does improve students' behavior for the moment, it may not change the students' attitudes. For example, this practice might encourage students to expect extrinsic rewards whenever they cope with the less pleasant aspects of learning instead of learning to accept these as part of any job, in school or out. Perhaps most important, when students are praised and attended to for doing what is expected of them, they can experience this as controlling and manipulative. They may come to feel that they are accepted and cared for only when they fulfill their teachers' expectations and not their own. This can cause them to feel resentful and angry.

What does not at first make sense is why rewarding students who behave appropriately when the work is new, challenging, and as-yet unlearned should encourage poor behavior. A number of reasons have been suggested for why this occurs.

First, superfluous rewards can influence intrinsically motivated students to shift to extrinsic motivation. Then, instead of trying to master the task for its own sake, they become more interested in the reward. Also, when students become so satiated with teacher praise, stickers, smiling faces, and so on, that they lose interest or outgrow them (8–10) and when such rewards just aren't available, students are less motivated to attend, concentrate, or tolerate frustration without the expectation of an extrinsic reward for doing so.

Second, superfluous rewards can make generally independent students lose their ability to function independently by causing them to rely on their teachers' feedback and approval. Teacher rewards can also decrease students' self-confidence if students attribute their success to their teachers' input rather than to their own efforts (11–13).

Finally, research indicates that extrinsic rewards can decrease students' creativity (14–17). Perhaps this happens because extrinsic rewards motivate students to accomplish what they think their teachers want them to accomplish in the way they think their teachers want them to accomplish it rather than to follow their own creative inclinations.

Students as Group Members   Although no direct evidence shows that rewarding students for being good group members can have a detrimental effect on their behavior, the results of the studies cited above regarding the effects of rewards on learning do raise that possibility. The results to date suggest that rewarding students who are already intrinsically motivated to be good group members may train them to do so for extrinsic rewards. Certain well-behaved students may also experience superfluous rewards as controlling and manipulative. Until we know more about these possibilities, educators may be wise to reward students for being good group members sparingly rather than routinely.

How to Reward Appropriate Behavior

Rewarding students is most likely to be effective when you meet certain conditions. *Reward students for behavior you believe deserves to be rewarded, not because students seek it.* Research indicates that some students elicit rewards from their teachers by bringing their completed work up to be praised or by smiling profusely when teachers compliment them to encourage more praise (18, 19). No evidence suggests that students who are so dependent on teacher feedback actually benefit from this praise, as they are already behaving appropriately—perhaps even "too" appropriately.

A second condition is that *the students be aware of the specific behavior that is being rewarded* (20, 21). For example, complimenting a student for working for 40 minutes straight is a much clearer message than praising her for being a "good student," because the feedback focuses the student's attention on the specific behavior that is being rewarded.

Another condition is that *the students agree that the behavior they are being rewarded for deserves to be rewarded.* Some educators praise low-achieving students not only when they succeed, but also when they merely try to succeed, perform well, or give the right answer (22–27). Brophy (18) points out that this may actually worsen, not improve, students' functioning. Students may doubt their own ability or lose confidence in their teachers if they think, "She must really think I'm hopeless if she praises me for that!" or "What's the matter with her? How could she think that was good work?" Similarly, if students are praised, given stickers, stars, or checks every time they sit up straight, wait in line, listen quietly to a story, or engage in any other routine behavior, they may experience the reward as insincere, silly, or simply irrelevant and not credible.

As noted in chapter 6, many teachers tend to reward female students for trying whether or not they succeed, for being neat, and so on. Rewarding students for these kinds of behavior can be very counterproductive. As research summarized in chapter 6 indicates, this can be especially problematic for African American females.

For a reward to work, *your words and actions must be congruent*. Some educators give students verbal rewards for things that they do not truly believe should be rewarded, but they reveal their true feelings by tone of voice, gesture, or body language. Research indicates that students can respond negatively to such confusing double messages (18).

These last two conditions are particularly important in the upper grades. The older students are, the more able they are to see through teachers and to recognize when they are receiving insincere praise or rewards.

Another key condition is that *the students actually experience the reward as rewarding*. Same-age students do not respond equally to the same rewards. For some, teacher praise can exert a powerful influence on their behavior; others may respond better to more materialistic forms of reward, such as stickers, candy, and toys. Students at different developmental levels also experience rewards in different ways. For example, by the time students are in intermediate school, they usually care more about what their peers think of them than about their teachers' opinions. (See the section on motivational development in this chapter for a more detailed discussion of this topic.)

Students and teachers often have different ideas about what is rewarding. What some teachers think are effective rewards students experience as irrelevant, and vice versa. Secondary school teachers, for example, often overrate the rewarding influence of recognizing students for behaving appropriately by mentioning their names in the school newspaper or over the loudspeaker or giving them a chance at special privileges and having contests that they can win. In turn, they tend to underrate the rewarding influence of providing students with the opportunity to achieve their own goals, to be accepted as a person in their own right, and to gain peer approval (28).

As noted in chapters 5 and 6, students' ethnic and socioeconomic backgrounds, as well as their gender, also influence whether or not they will experience a particular consequence as rewarding. Thus, as noted previously, it makes a difference to some students whether "rewards" are materialistic or personal, public or private, group or individual, and so on. The wrong kind of "reward" may not be experienced as rewarding at all if it does not match students' reward preferences and expectations.

Students must understand that the accomplishments for which they are being rewarded were the result of their own intrinsic motivation, efforts, and abilities and not the extrinsic reward. This will increase the likelihood that they will attribute their success to themselves rather than to others (29–33). This is especially important for many female students and for any other students who have an external locus of control or who lack confidence in their own ability (see chapter 6).

For rewards to work they must be timely. The longer teachers wait before rewarding students for behaving appropriately, the less likely it is that the students will connect the reward with the desirable behavior. Thus, rewarding students, especially younger ones, at the end of the day or before lunch for their earlier behavior may be much less effective than rewarding them right at the moment.

A final condition is that the rewards be offered sparingly. This helps ensure that rewards do not lose their effectiveness because students lose interest in them.

Destructive Rewards

We have already noted that rewards used improperly can cause students to become more dependent and less creative or to feel manipulated and change their behavior for the worse. The inappropriate use of rewards can create other problems as well.

Rewarding Undesirable Behavior   Educators sometimes unintentionally reward undesirable behavior. For example, when teachers reward students for completing seatwork assignments, students may conclude that their teachers are more interested in speed and quantity than in the quality of work. But when teachers reward students only *after* evaluating the students' work, the message students receive is quite different. Then they see that quality also counts.

Using Undesirable Rewards   Rewarding students by allowing them to go on errands while others are working at their desks or by excusing them from doing part of their homework may increase appropriate behavior, but it also gives students the message that seatwork and homework are onerous and unnecessary chores that they should avoid if possible.

Creating Competition and Jealousy   If teachers reward students only when they behave appropriately, those who do not receive an equal share of recognition and acceptance may become jealous. Rewarding students for good behavior in hopes that other students will improve the way they behave to get these rewards can also engender resentment and jealousy in the left-out students. Statements intended to motivate students to copy their peers' behavior, such as "Look how well Cecilia is doing her math" may backfire, causing some students to misbehave even more and interfere with group cohesiveness, an important goal in its own right.

Proper Use of Rewards

This discussion on the pitfalls of using rewards improperly is not meant to imply that you should avoid all rewards. Some praise and recognition probably does most of us a lot of good. The point is to encourage you to avoid the superfluous or routine use of rewards.

Motivational Development

What motivates students to behave appropriately in school depends to some extent on their ages (34–37). Preschoolers, kindergartners, and students in the primary grades are usually willing to comply with rules just because teachers say so. They tend to do what they are told to obtain smiles, attention, and praise from their teachers as well and to avoid their teachers' disapproval and lectures. They find such things as candy, stickers, checks, and stars rewarding. At this age, students need immediate reinforcement and gratification.

As they get older, students are less willing to do things just because their teachers say so. This makes their teachers' attention and approval less influential in motivating them,

Self-Quiz: Appropriate Use of Rewards

Your answers to the following questions will help you decide when and how to reward students for behaving appropriately. Rather than asking yourself these questions every time you are inclined to reward a student, which is unnecessary and could destroy your spontaneity, think about them from time to time when the situation warrants.

1. Is the student already motivated? Would a reward be unnecessary and superfluous?
2. Is my goal at the moment to get the student to continue to behave appropriately or to motivate the student to want to behave appropriately?
3. Would rewarding the student further my goal if my objective is to increase his or her intrinsic motivation?
4. Does the student's behavior really merit a reward, or would the reward lack credibility right now?
5. How will the student perceive my attempts to reward her or him—as controlling or manipulative, embarrassing, an indication that I don't expect as much from her or him as I do from other students, or as welcomed signs of my acceptance and recognition of worth, ability, and effort?
6. What kinds of things does the student experience as rewarding—public praise, peer approval, special privileges?

and peer approval becomes more important. Other kinds of material rewards, such as trips, food, and special events, replace stickers, checks, and smiling faces as effective rewards. These students are also better able to accept symbolic rewards that they can turn in for the real thing in the future.

By adolescence, some students may question any rule that seems arbitrary to them. Their teachers' approval can be totally irrelevant compared to the approval of their peers. Rewards that were effective when they were younger may play a much smaller role in motivating them than graduating from school, preparing for a job, or earning the grades necessary to be accepted by the college of their choice.

Hartner (35) provides a theoretical explanation for these observations. According to her, students' motivational systems develop in an orderly way. She suggests that preschool and primary school students are externally oriented; they respond to adult approval of their behavior and use feedback from adults to judge their successes and failures. As a result, they respond positively to being told that they are good students because they raise their hands, wait their turn, and so on. Because of this perspective, they also want to know that their teachers think well of their drawings, paintings, stories, and other efforts.

By the time students are in the upper elementary grades, though, they can reward themselves for behaving appropriately. Now they tell themselves that they are good students because they raise their hands and wait their turn. Thus, while preschool and primary teachers should praise their students for behaving well, upper elementary and secondary teachers should encourage students to reward themselves for "good" behavior. This means focusing comments more on providing students with factual feedback about how they are doing—their strengths and weaknesses, successes and failures.

Hartner claims that by the time students are in secondary school, they have internal-

EFFECTIVE REWARDS	INEFFECTIVE REWARDS
Students rewarded for specific behaviors	Students routinely rewarded
Reward increases students' intrinsic motivation	Reward increases students' extrinsic motivation
All students have adequate opportunity to earn rewards	Some students have little opportunity to earn rewards
Students rewarded for specific behaviors	Students rewarded for being good and well behaved in general
Students aware of specific behavior being rewarded	Students unaware of behavior being rewarded
Students agree that the behavior deserves to be rewarded	Students don't perceive behavior as meriting award
Students aware that they earned reward through own efforts and achievement	Students attribute effort and success to reward
Teachers' words and actions are congruent	Students receive inconsistent message
Students rewarded for significant effort and achievement	Reward based on lowered standards and expectations
Students experience rewards as positive	Students experience rewards as negative
Rewards personalized to students' interests, desires, and developmental level	Students experience reward as irrelevant
Reward is timely	Reward is delayed
Students rewarded only for desirable behavior	Undesirable behavior inadvertently rewarded

ized standards that they can use to evaluate their own accomplishments. As a result, teachers should reduce the amount of feedback they provide their students and instead encourage students to evaluate themselves. In other words, as students mature, teachers can prompt them to function independently to foster their personal growth.

Teachers should also emphasize intrinsic motivation instead of using extrinsic rewards. Hartner has described four kinds of intrinsic motivation that keeps students interested. According to Hartner, students are intrinsically motivated to respond to their environments in new and varied ways; they also have a natural curiosity about the new and different; they look forward to achieving competency; and they prefer challenging, rather than routine, tasks.

An effective classroom manager adjusts motivational techniques to match the stu-

Students tend to be most responsive to approval and disapproval in the primary grades.

Examples of Age-Appropriate Praise

PRIMARY GRADES	UPPER ELEMENTARY GRADES	SECONDARY SCHOOL
That's a beautiful picture.	You should be proud of your picture.	Your picture has great perspective.
You did an outstanding (great) job on the test.	How do you feel about getting almost everything right on the test?	Your reading comprehension score was a little higher than your vocabulary score. Why do you think that is?

dents' developmental levels. Not praising youngsters who need praise or expecting too much of younger students can create disappointment and cause unnecessary behavior problems. Equally ineffective is trying to motivate older students in ways that make them feel like children. A course in developmental psychology, included in almost all teacher preparation programs, will help you understand students' different developmental levels and needs.

Self-Quiz: How You Use Rewards

Your answers to the following questions will help you evaluate the way you intend to reward desirable behavior when you are in the classroom.

1. Is your goal in rewarding students to gain their compliance for the moment or to increase their intrinsic motivation?
2. Do you overemphasize extrinsic rewards rather than techniques that foster intrinsic motivation?
3. How often do you reward students for behaving appropriately—too often, not often enough, about right?
4. Do you reward students routinely out of habit or only when you think the situation calls for it?
5. Do students have other ways of obtaining your acceptance and recognition besides behaving appropriately?
6. Do all of your students get their fair share of acceptance and recognition?
7. Do you individualize feedback by selecting rewards that your students will actually experience as positive, by anticipating how they will react to being rewarded, and by choosing the best way to reward them?
8. Do you reward students merely for completing work and making contributions, or do you reward them for the quality of their efforts, or both?
9. When rewarding students, do you make sure they understand that they have earned the reward through their own efforts?
10. Do you avoid using rewards destructively?
11. Do you reward students for behaving appropriately so that others will follow their example?
12. Do you reward students with positive statements when their work and behavior actually do not merit it in order to balance out the occasions when you criticize them for misbehaving?
13. Do you reward students who seek your praise?

Individual Versus Group Rewards

Teachers tend to reward students individually for their improvement and accomplishments. On the surface this appears to be the rational and logical thing to do, since teachers are often concerned with the behavior and performance of individual students. In many cases, it can be the most motivating approach, especially for European American males and other field-independent students. However, individualistic rewards have a number of potential disadvantages (38–40). As already noted, rewarding students individually can increase rivalry, jealousy, and competition among students. It can also be inappropriate for some students, including many females, Hawaiian Americans, Hispanic Americans, Native Americans, and others who are field sensitive (see chapter 5). Problems can also occur when teachers who want to be fair to all of their students even out the amount or frequency of the individualistic rewards students receive by rewarding some students for accomplishing less or behaving less adequately than their peers. This can cause these students to become less self-confident and less motivated to strive to meet the same standards as their peers.

Rewarding a whole group reduces negative peer comments, jealousy, and resentments among students. It can enhance group cohesiveness and increase desirable group processes and relationships. However, group rewards may be less motivating for field-independent students. And they may be impractical in many situations.

Clearly, both individualistic and group rewards have their place in the classroom. Because teachers tend to overemphasize individualistic rewards, they should consider the possibility of using group rewards, particularly when the rewards appear to be ethnically or gender appropriate.

Rewarding Incompatible Behavior

It's sometimes possible to modify students' unacceptable behavior by rewarding them for behaving appropriately in ways that are incompatible with their undesirable behavior. For example, if students know they can earn rewards for on-task behavior, they may resist the temptation to talk to their neighbors, get up to sharpen their pencils, or write notes to their friends. You can apply this same principle to reduce talking in line by rewarding students for standing quietly; to handle calling out answers by rewarding students for raising their hands; and to discourage lying when being truthful is painful by rewarding telling the truth.

Rewarding students to behave appropriately in ways that are incompatible with their unacceptable behavior often means you can avoid punishing students for misbehaving. Research indicates that positive consequences are more effective than negative consequences and have fewer undesirable side effects.

To use these techniques effectively, you should let students know exactly what they have to do to be rewarded. Also make sure they understand that you will be observing them periodically on an unpredictable, random schedule so that they cannot anticipate when their behavior will be evaluated. Finally, consistently reward students only when they are behaving appropriately.

Although no current research provides evidence about the circumstances under which rewarding incompatible behavior is most likely to be effective, experience indicates that the cause of the students' misbehavior plays an important role. Rewarding students for standing quietly in line would probably be more effective with students who talk out of boredom than with students who want to show their peers that they do not care about school rules. Rewarding students for raising their hands to reduce calling out is more likely to work with students who want to give the right answer and please their teachers than with students who want others to appreciate how smart they are. And rewarding students for on-task behavior to decrease talking may be more effective with students who are talking because they need a short break from their work than with students who are talking because the work is too difficult for them.

Rewarding Improvement

A technique that focuses on the unacceptable behavior is to reward students for improvement (41, 42). You can apply this approach in a number of ways. If a student calls out repeatedly, on the average of eight or nine times a day, you can:

- Reward the student for calling out fewer times a day.

- Give the student increasing numbers of points, tokens, or other recognition for fewer misbehaviors—for example, one point for calling out five times, two points for calling out only four times, three points for calling out only three times.

- Reward the student for spending increasing amounts of time in class without calling out, starting with a half hour, then three quarters of an hour, then an hour, and so on.

- Give the student increasing numbers of points or other rewards, depending on the lapse of time between incidents of calling out—four points if the student does not call out again for an hour, five points if the student does not call out for 2 hours, and so forth.

To use this technique effectively, follow these guidelines:

1. Determine the baseline—the average number of times the student behaves inappropriately during a given period of time or the average interval between incidents of inappropriate behavior.

2. Decide on how much improvement you can realistically expect from the student. Can you expect the student to halve the number of times he or she calls out or gets up from his or her seat or only reduce it by 20% during the first few days of using this technique?

3. Make sure the student knows exactly which behaviors he or she is not supposed to do and what the reward schedule will be for each degree of improvement.

4. Suggest alternative appropriate ways for the student to behave if possible.

5. Reward the student for improvement in behavior according to the schedule.

6. Modify your schedule so that the student has to demonstrate greater and greater degrees of improvement to receive the reward, until you feel that the student's behavior is acceptable.

7. Eliminate the extrinsic rewards and encourage the student to behave appropriately for intrinsic rather than extrinsic reasons.

Using Peers as Models

Students sometimes change their behavior when they observe their prestigious peers behaving in more appropriate ways and they value them and want to be like them. Assigning a student to work with a partner who has a lot of prestige and who stays busy and productive the whole time can encourage the student to put more effort into class assignments. Reminding another student that the other members of the football team come to class on time and do not "horse around" might help him control his behavior. Also, rewarding (praising) peer models for behaving appropriately may motivate another student to modify his or her behavior in order to receive the same reward (44, 45, 47).

Sabatino suggests the following procedure for using peers as models of appropriate behavior:

1. Specify the behaviors to be modeled.
2. Provide situations in which students are likely to observe peers engaged in these specified behaviors.
3. Label target behaviors and draw the students' attention to them, thereby directing behavior toward a desired goal.
4. Identify appropriate behaviors, using peer pressure to recognize and reinforce them.
5. Provide a variety of models and settings so students can practice appropriate behaviors.
6. Identify high-status models (older, same sex) who have a positive influence on student behavior.
7. Remedy situations where students might see other students winning positive consequences by disruptive or inappropriate behavior.
8. Emphasize to students their role as models of appropriate behaviors. (47, p. 11)

Several advantages have been cited for using peers as models. First, students can observe exactly how they are expected to behave. Students can also see that the behavior can be performed and is, in fact, performed by their peers. In addition, students observe other students receiving rewards that they themselves might want. Finally, the prestige of the students serving as models may encourage other students to change their behavior even in the absence of any extrinsic reward.

Although using peers as models can be effective with some students (43, 46), as noted above, it can backfire with others. Instead of motivating certain students to behave appropriately, it can make them resentful and jealous of the student models who are the recipients of their teachers' praise and attention. It can also lead others to label the model students as "teacher's pets" and to abuse and ridicule them. For these reasons, using peers as models may not always be a highly effective way to change students' behavior.

Planned Ignoring

Eliminating rewards when students misbehave can often lead to behavioral improvement. For example, planned ignoring is a technique for managing behavior problems that involves eliminating the attention students receive from their teachers and other students for misbehaving. The assumption underlying this approach is that when the students no longer get the attention that motivates their inappropriate behavior, they will have no reason to continue to misbehave.

The kinds of attention students seek from others varies from student to student. Some just want to know they are being noticed. Others are seeking acceptance and recognition from their peers. Still others hope to gain tokens of love and concern from their teachers. Finally, there are those who are rewarded by signs that they have provoked hostility and rejection from others.

In the past, many authors were overly optimistic about the extent to which planned ignoring could change students' behavior. However, though considerable evidence shows that ignoring behavior can work in certain situations (48, 50, 51, 53, 54), it is also clear that many classroom behavior problems are unaffected or even grow worse when ignored (49, 52). This is because ignoring misbehavior that is not designed to have an effect or to

Students may consider peer models as examples to emulate, but they also may consider them simply teacher's pets.

provoke a reaction may encourage future misbehavior once students learn they can misbehave with impunity.

Although planned ignoring can be an effective technique for temporarily managing certain attention-seeking behavior, it still does not teach students how to gain the attention they want in appropriate ways. It also does not address the causes of their misbehavior. While looking into these causes may not be necessary in every case, students who purposely try to be rejected or laughed at, who curry favor from their peers because they cannot make and keep friends without doing so, or who are overly dependent on teacher praise need help with the emotional problems causing their actions (see chapter 12).

Using Planned Ignoring Effectively   If you keep in mind that planned ignoring is sometimes only a start in working with students who seek inappropriate forms of attention, the following steps will assist you in deciding when and how to use it effectively:

1. *Determine whether students' misbehavior is attention seeking.* Some of the unacceptable ways students may seek attention include whining or crying; acting delinquently by refusing to follow rules, using foul language, and so on; playing the fool (clowning); bragging; pulling practical jokes on others, telling jokes, and making wisecracks; asking teachers to help them when they really do not need help or to

check their work when it is obviously correct; asking to have directions repeated; purposely making careless mistakes; pretending to be sick, hurt, frightened, or upset; making self-derogatory statements; tattling on other students; asking for permission that obviously will not be given.

Students often behave in these ways to have an effect on others. But they may have other reasons as well. When young students whine or cry, they may behave that way because they have not adjusted to the structure and demands of school and the expectations of their teachers. Students may sometimes ask for help they do not need or feedback because they lack confidence in their ability, not just to get attention. Likewise, students who consistently ask to have instructions and explanations repeated may have hearing problems, or they may be so distractible that their attention is elsewhere when the class is being told what to do and how to do it. And some students may actually believe they are sick or hurt and actually feel frightened, even though no "apparent reason" exists for them to feel this way.

When determining whether to ignore attention-seeking students, you should also keep in mind that field-sensitive students, such as Hispanic Americans and many females, tend to seek and need the approval and feedback of adults. Thus, even though they may not appear to require your attention because their work is fine and they "do not need" any help, to ignore their overtures for attention may create a poor match between their preferred learning styles and your teaching style.

Thus, before deciding to manage a behavior problem by ignoring it, be fairly certain that it is actually designed to elicit a reaction from you or your students. Sometimes it is better to give students attention, even though you think they do not need it, than to deny them the attention they require. It may also be more prudent to provide students more help than they seem to need when they ask for assistance, to give them more attention than you think they require when they appear to be feigning illness, and to repeat directions that they should have understood than to erroneously ignore their solicitations when they actually need what they are seeking.

2. *Make sure students know what behavior you want them to change, why the behavior is inappropriate, and why you and/or the other students will be ignoring it.* Students who understand why you and/or their peers are ignoring them are less likely to misinterpret being ignored as a rejection of them rather than of their behavior. When they know what you are doing and why you are doing it, they may be less inclined to resist your efforts.

3. *Obtain the cooperation of the other students in the class if their reactions to the behavior you want to manage is reinforcing it.* Attention-seeking behaviors such as asking for unnecessary help, tattling on others in private, and feigning illness are probably done to obtain a reaction from adults, but acting like a delinquent, playing the fool, making wisecracks, or passing gas as loudly as possible are typically done to get a reaction from other students. When students misbehave to get peer attention, whether or not you ignore the behavior is less important than getting the students to ignore it.

Before soliciting your students' cooperation, determine whether it would be wise to identify the student in question, since some students may feel embarrassed or resentful if their problems are dealt with publicly, and they could then resist your efforts to modify their behavior and even behave worse.

If you think the student can handle it and if the student agrees to be identified, you can explain to the class why they should ignore the student when she or he makes a wisecrack, clowns around, and so on. Then monitor the group's reaction to the student's behavior. Finally, praise and give credit to the group when the student's behavior begins to change.

If you think it would be unwise to identify the student, you still have options. You can select a convenient occasion to meet with your class that is not close in time to any attention-seeking attempts by the student and have a general discussion about why certain kinds of class reactions encourage students to behave inappropriately without mentioning specific students. Make an effort to help your students understand why ignoring attention-seeking behavior is more desirable, and then monitor the group's reaction to the student's behavior. You can also conduct additional discussions as needed.

4. *Eliminate all reinforcement of the attention-seeking behavior.* Make sure you and the other students in the class consistently ignore students' inappropriate behavior. If you only reduce, instead of eliminate, the attention your students receive, they may still get enough attention to maintain their behavior. Their attention-seeking behavior may even increase because they may believe that if they try harder, it will only be a matter of time before they succeed in getting the attention they want.

5. *Expect an initial worsening of the behavior, substitution of other forms of attention-seeking behavior, or spontaneous recovery of the behavior after it has ceased.* When students stop receiving the attention they were used to getting for their misbehavior, they may try harder or switch to some other form of misbehavior to get it before finally giving up. Even after they have given up, they may occasionally try again to see if with the passage of time you or the group have weakened in your resolve.

6. *Evaluate your efforts.* If, after a reasonable period of time, your students' attention-seeking behavior persists even though you and/or the other students in the class have ignored it, determine whether you may be overlooking some other source of reinforcement either in or out of class. If you cannot discover any, it may be that the behavior in question is not attention seeking and requires another type of intervention.

It is not always easy to get students to ignore attention seekers, especially when they behave in obnoxious, disgusting, or provocative ways. In such cases, you may find it necessary to use other techniques to work with the students. It's also difficult to get the cooperation of older students who derive pleasure from the problems of other students, who build themselves up by putting others down, or who are opposed to what school stands for because they are doing poorly or have delinquent attitudes. In such cases, you may have to change their attitudes about school or their motivation so that they will be more willing to cooperate. (See chapter 2.) It's also difficult to use planned ignoring with primary grade students because many of them are too immature to understand why they should ignore their classmates' behavior or to control their natural spontaneous reactions.

Self-Quiz: Choosing Techniques

While you can use the techniques described in this section to handle behavior problems, some are more effective with certain kinds of problems than with others. For example, the attention-seeking antics of the class clown may be improved by planned ignoring; however, if a student takes the things she wants to play with from other students instead of waiting her turn, planned ignoring will probably make the situation worse. Rewarding incompatible behavior would probably be a more effective technique to use.

The following exercise is designed to help you apply the ideas in this section to some typical classroom behavior problems. For each example, decide which technique you would choose: rewarding incompatible behavior, rewarding improvement, using peers as models, or planned ignoring. Justify your choice and describe in detail how you would use the technique.

1. A 10-year-old leaves his lunch bag, orange peels, tray, and other lunch remains at the table when he leaves to play.
2. A 15-year-old, seemingly on purpose, gives obviously ridiculous answers when called on.
3. A 13-year-old complains whenever a less skilled student is chosen for his team during recess and lunch.
4. A 7-year-old pushes and hits other students when she is angry at them.
5. An 8-year-old wanders around the room when she is supposed to be doing her seatwork, especially during math.

Negative Consequences— Punishment

The previous sections described techniques for dealing with behavior problems without using negative consequences to modify students' behavior. Some educators take the position that teachers can handle almost all classroom behavior problems adequately without resorting to negative consequences. Others believe that punishment—or at least the anticipation of punishment—is needed to deal with some students in certain situations. The position taken in this book is that although punishment is an unpleasant and distasteful technique, it is often necessary to use it in combination with other techniques with young students who are still in the first stage of moral development and with older students who think they can get away with things. But when students misbehave because they are immature, distractible, anxious, upset, confused, scapegoated, and so on, you should deal with their misbehavior by means of other, nonpunitive techniques.

Defining Punishment

Educators use the term *punishment* in two different ways. Some educators distinguish between mild consequences such as private statements of disapproval or loss of free time and harsher consequences such as corporal punishment or ridicule. They use the term *negative consequences* for mild consequences and *punishment* for harsh consequences. Others define punishment as the purposeful application of negative consequences of any kind to decrease the frequency of a behavior. According to this definition, mild desist orders and signaling teacher disapproval would not be considered punitive because although they may be distasteful and disagreeable to students, they are intended to provide students with feedback about their behavior and not to add noxious consequences to that behavior. But any extrinsic consequences, whether mild or harsh, intended to be disagreeable do fit the definition. The second definition, treating the terms *negative consequences* and *punishment* synonymously, is the one used in this book. This is because educators and students often perceive the severity/intensity of a particular negative consequence differently. While educators may think they are using mild negative consequences, students may experience them as harsh.

Thus, a teacher may believe that writing students' names on the board when they misbehave is not a harsh punishment. And many students who are used to having their transgressions dealt with publicly may be able to accept having their classmates' attention drawn to their misbehavior. However, students who are not used to such treatment, including many Hispanic Americans, Native Americans, Hawaiian Americans, and members of certain Asian and Pacific groups, may experience their name being placed on the board as a very harsh consequence.

Using Punishment Effectively

The following factors will influence the effectiveness of your efforts when you use negative consequences to modify your students' behavior.

Students' Perceptions of Consequences   Students must experience negative consequences as distasteful, noxious, or disagreeable for them to work. You may, for example, decide to punish a student by sending her to the office or to a time-out area in the classroom, but if the student is uncomfortable in class because she is not prepared and does not want to be called on or because she thinks she cannot do the work, she may experience the time-out as rewarding, not punitive. In the same vein, a student attempting to prove to his delinquent peers that he does not care about school may be encouraged, not discouraged, to misbehave when you reprimand him in front of his classmates. In fact, research has indicated that just about any noxious consequence can be rewarding to certain students (55–57).

Therefore, to use negative consequences effectively, you should select consequences that you believe will be experienced as disagreeable by the particular student you plan to use them with. And once you have applied them, you should check to determine whether they actually have the desired effect on the student.

Providing a Rational Cognitive Structure   Your efforts will be more successful if your students know in advance the specific targeted behavior, why it was inappropriate, why you intend to use punishment rather than another technique to correct the problem, and why you think the particular punishment you have selected is fair (58–60). Identifying the behavior that they need to eliminate helps them comply with your expectations if they decide to do so. Convincing them that their behavior is inappropriate, that punishment is the appropriate way of dealing with the problem, and that this particular punishment is fair may decrease their resistance to your efforts. But if they blame you rather than their behavior for the negative consequences they incur, and if they believe that you are treating them unfairly, they may overtly resist your efforts to modify their behavior. Or they may acquiesce overtly but then covertly act out their resentment by trying to undermine your authority with other students or by trying to get away with other things when your attention is directed elsewhere.

Alternative Behaviors   Students who use unacceptable means of satisfying their desires may be more willing to stop behaving inappropriately if they are offered acceptable ways of obtaining satisfaction (61–63). You may not always be able to suggest alternative ways for students to attain their goals, but when you can, students will be able to both avoid being punished and fulfill their desires. No acceptable alternative behavior may exist for a student who steals other students' possessions, but you can certainly teach the class clown how to get attention in more appropriate ways, and you can teach a young student who grabs things from other students how to ask others to share.

Intensity   Because certain students can experience a public reprimand as positive when they want to impress their peers with their willingness to stand up to their teacher and a period of time-out or a trip to the office can reward students who want to avoid participating in the activity at hand, it is essential to choose consequences that the students in question will actually experience as punishment (55–57). If the students do not perceive a cost, they will not feel a need to change their behavior. Even when students experience consequences as negative, the intensity (severity) of the punishments they receive affects their reactions to them. Punishments that involve very little cost to students compared to the positive reinforcement they receive from misbehaving can have little or no effect on their behavior in comparison to punishments that involve considerable cost (64, 65, 67). This may be one reason some authors conclude that punishments should be as intense (severe) as possible so long as the punishment is not unethical or abusive (64). But research also indicates that harsh punishments can backfire and have serious undesirable side effects.

Most authors who believe that there is a place for punishment in classroom management suggest that the punishment should be only as intense as necessary to motivate students to modify their behavior (66, 68). One of the policies some educators follow to achieve this is to use milder forms of punishment first and then gradually increase the intensity until the desired effect is reached. This is the approach favored here because it helps educators avoid being more punitive than necessary. Some authors, though, feel it is a mistake to gradually escalate the intensity of punishment. According to Morgan and Jenson,

> Erring on the conservative side by using a weak intensity or short duration may be a disservice to the child. Although all educational and clinical procedures should use the least restrictive approach to punishment, we may be doing children great harm by slowly adapting them to greater intensities or duration of a punishing stimulus. For example, to begin by using one minute of time-out and increasing the requirement gradually up to an hour teaches the child to withstand intense punishment, not to change misbehavior. The least restrictive punishing stimulus is one that will not be constantly increased and is effective in reducing an inappropriate behavior. The best strategy is to be familiar with the educational and clinical literature and know what intensities have been successfully used with students in different populations. (68, p. 137)

Reprimanding students privately, in the hall or elsewhere out of sight of the rest of the class, can make a bitter pill a little easier to swallow.

Another policy that educators often follow to avoid being overly punitive is to never decide on students' punishment when they are angry or upset with them. Postponing such decisions until you are calm, relaxed, and rational can help keep you from saying and doing things that both you and your student will soon regret.

Consistency   Many theorists advise educators to be consistent in their use of punishment. They refer to three types of consistency: among teachers, in handling different students, and in response to the same student. Authors who believe that educators should use punishments consistently cite the following reasons for their opinion.

They feel that consistency among teachers is essential because when some teachers permit students to do what other teachers forbid them to do, students can become confused. Students are then unsure whether it's really inappropriate for them to behave in those ways. They may ask themselves why it is not okay to do something in science that is okay to do in social studies. When teachers apply punishments of varying intensities for the same infractions, students may question the fairness of a given punishment. A student may protest that since one of his teachers only holds him back from recess for 5 minutes and only if he calls out more than twice during the period, it's not fair for him to miss the whole recess just because he called out only once in another classroom.

Consistency in handling different students is also essential. Specifically, if some students can get away with doing something, other students may be tempted to try getting away with it as well. Students may also think that they are being punished unfairly if they receive consequences for doing what other students do with impunity—and they may be right.

Consistent responses to the same student are also necessary because if students are punished for doing something one time but not the next time they commit the same infraction, they may not understand, and they may be tempted to take a gamble and misbehave again.

Some educators take the following position:

> Students should know that there will be no allowance for mitigating circumstances (for example, the teacher will not overlook the violation even if Mary forgets her homework for the first time ever or when John acts up after coming back from three days sick in bed). Exceptions to the rules invite manipulative behavior, excuse thinking, and the whining "I didn't mean it" that teachers of young children have grown to dread. (70, p. 133)

While research indicates that consistent punishment is more effective than inconsistent punishment (60, 69–75), and some consistency is essential to avoid arbitrary punishment, the position of this book is that a certain amount of flexibility is also necessary. First, as individuals, educators have their own personalities, cultural backgrounds, values, and philosophies of education, and these variations make it impossible for all educators to feel comfortable handling behavior problems in the same way. Thus, it is both impractical and unfair to expect everyone on a particular teaching staff to agree 100% about what behaviors should be punished, which students should be punished, under what circumstances students should be punished, and which punishments are fair and reasonable.

Second, since different students may break the same rule for different reasons, it is neither fair nor efficient to treat all students alike. It may be appropriate to use punishment to convince students who are not intrinsically motivated to abide by the rules. This lets them know it's necessary for them to do so or else. But students who break rules out of ignorance, in the heat of the moment, in response to a prior provocation, or because of some personal problems at home shouldn't be punished for their transgressions.

Third, you should not punish students who have made a real effort to improve their behavior and have done so if these students give in to temptation after a significant period of good behavior. A reminder or a warning delivered in a nonthreatening way may be more appropriate—and more effective.

Fourth, as noted in chapter 4, the context of students' lives may require flexibility. For example, teachers may have to use a flexible approach with homeless and migrant students, who are not able to function as consistently as most students.

Finally, students' ethnic and contextual backgrounds and their gender influence why they behave as they do and the types of consequences that will be effective with them. Therefore, to treat all students the same invites mistakes.

The reasons just presented support rational, planned, justifiable flexibility, not inconsistency, in the use of negative consequences. Although it is understandable that teachers' moods, burnout, or stress may cause them to react one way to certain behavior on one day and another way the next day, nothing justifies such inconsistency. Nor does anything justify teachers relating differently to different students because of prejudice or personal likes and dislikes. Because justifiable flexibility in the use of punishment can seem like incon-

---

Self-Quiz:
On Flexibility

Review the arguments for and against being flexible about the severity, consistency, and timing of punishment. What are your opinions about these issues? What reasons do you have for your opinion?

---

sistency to students when they see others handled in nonpunitive ways for doing just what they are punished for, it is imperative to explain to students why they are being treated differently. They may not accept the difference at first, but if you explain your reasons each time you punish students, it is likely that they will eventually accept your reasoning.

Timing   Many authors suggest that punishing students as soon as they start to misbehave keeps them from gaining the potential satisfaction of completing the misbehavior—satisfaction that could counteract the negative effects of the punishment. They also argue that the sooner educators intervene, the less likely it is that students' behavior will grow worse because they think they can get away with even more:

> A punishing stimulus should be delivered immediately with as little delay as possible. For optimal effectiveness a punishing stimulus should be presented in the early stages of a misbehavior instead of at its conclusion. Many misbehaviors are linked together like a chain, with less severe responses leading to more intense responses until, at the end of the chain, the child is totally out of control. For example, time-out would be more effective at the beginning of a tantrum than it would be after the child has been screaming and crying for 10 minutes. (68, pp. 136–137)

Although considerable evidence for this position exists, especially in laboratory studies (51, 62, 75–77), others argue against placing too much faith in such evidence:

> Behavioristically based sources of advice for teachers sometimes state that punishment will be more effective when it follows immediately after a transgression rather than when it is delayed, or that it will be more effective if it comes early in a sequence of undesired behavior rather than after completion of the sequence. Principles of this kind do seem to have some application for shaping animal behavior, but they are of doubtful relevance to the classroom, or to human learning generally. Here, punishment is a last resort method for curbing undesired behavior, not a basic method of shaping desired behavior. (43, p. 61)

The position taken in this book is that you should delay punishing students when:

- You are not absolutely sure that students will complete acts of misbehavior that they have just started.

- There may be extenuating circumstances that students might tell you about if given the chance to tell their side of the story.

- Students are too upset emotionally to understand or accept the punishment.

- You are too upset to deal with the situation in a calm, thoughtful manner.

- Punishing the students may be too disruptive to the class.

- It would be better to have the principal or someone else with more authority mete out the punishment.

Natural, Arbitrary, and Logical Consequences

There are three types of negative consequences: natural, arbitrary, and logical (45). Natural consequences occur automatically as the naturally occurring result of a particular behavior. Arbitrary consequences are arranged by an authority figure and are not clearly related to the behavior being punished. Logical consequences are also arranged but are related to the behavior in question.

BEHAVIOR	NATURAL CONSEQUENCE	ARBITRARY CONSEQUENCE	LOGICAL CONSEQUENCE
1. A student constantly complains about his peers.	The student isn't chosen when the class plays during recess.	He loses 3 points or tokens that he has been saving for a prize.	The student is required to sit and play by himself for part of the day.
2. A student lies.	The student's peers don't believe her.	The student loses her snack.	The teacher tells her he doesn't believe her.
3. A student draws graffiti on the bathroom wall.		The student loses free time.	The student has to wash the drawing off the wall.
4. A student calls out answers.		The student misses recess.	The student loses her next turn.
5. A student tries to push ahead in line.	The student is pushed back by another student.	The student is sent to the office.	The student is sent to the end of the line.
6. A student abuses her laboratory equipment.	The equipment breaks, and she can't do the experiment.	She is sent to time-out.	The equipment is confiscated, and the student is not allowed to continue the experiment.

(continued)

(continued)

BEHAVIOR	NATURAL CONSEQUENCE	ARBITRARY CONSEQUENCE	LOGICAL CONSEQUENCE
7. A student hits another student during recess.	The student is hit back.	The student misses a class trip.	The student misses recess for the rest of the week.
8. A student throws a noisy temper tantrum.		The student is sent to the principal to be reprimanded.	The student is removed from class until he calms down.
9. A student teases her peers.	The student has few friends.	She loses her snack.	She is required to sit by herself.
10. The student doesn't return a social studies book to the library.		The student's grade in social studies is lowered.	The student has to pay for the book or work its cost off in the library.
11. A student refuses to participate in the cleanup with her group before recess.	Her share is left undone when the other members of her group go to recess.	The student is reprimanded and loses 10 tokens.	The student remains in the class during recess until she does her share.
12. A student does not show up for three rehearsals in a row.	The other members of the cast treat her poorly.	She is kept in after school.	She loses her part in the play.
13. A student plays the clown when he is called on.	The other students laugh at him.	He is sent to the office.	He isn't called on for an hour.

Sometimes the natural consequences that result from misbehavior are enough to convince students to behave more appropriately. In examples 1, 5, 6, and 7 in the table, it is possible, but not necessarily probable, that the natural consequences of the misbehavior will be distasteful enough to motivate students to change the way they behave. In examples 2, 9, 11, and 12, it is unlikely that the natural consequences alone would motivate students

THEORY FOCUS: DREIKURS RECOMMENDS RESPECT AND OPTIMISM

Rudolf Dreikurs has expressed his views on classroom management in four books: *Psychology in the Classroom: A Manual for Teachers, Discipline Without Tears: What to Do with Children Who Misbehave, Encouraging Children to Learn: The Encouragement Process*, and *Logical Consequences*. According to Dreikurs, teachers can encourage students to behave appropriately by treating them appropriately. Among other things, this includes relating to them respectfully and optimistically and stressing cooperation over competition and improvement over perfection.

He believes that four main reasons explain why students misbehave, and he advises educators to first determine which one is operating and to respond accordingly. For example, when students misbehave to gain attention,

teachers should make sure they do not receive it. When students try to exert power over others, educators should avoid involving themselves in power struggles. If students seek revenge for real or imagined events, they should be treated in ways that reduce their need to be avenged. When they misbehave out of feelings of helplessness and impotency, then teachers should build up their self-confidence.

Dreikurs recognizes that at times these approaches will be ineffective, and then students will have to pay the consequences of their misbehavior in order to learn to behave appropriately. At such times he advises educators to act democratically, not autocratically, and to use logical, not arbitrary, consequences. He equates arbitrary consequences with punishment.

to change. In examples 3, 4, 8, and 10, no natural consequences for the students' misbehavior occur. And in example 13, the natural consequences of playing the clown can actually reinforce the behavior.

When the natural consequences of misbehavior aren't negative enough to bring about a change, educators can use arbitrary or logical consequences to supplement them. Dreikurs and others have suggested that of the two options, logical consequences are preferable (45, 82, 92, 93). They feel that logical consequences are more acceptable to students because they fit the crime and are understandable; they are less likely to create resistance and power struggles because they appear to be the result of the student's behavior, not the teacher's authority; and they tend to be less harsh than many arbitrary punishments.

This line of reasoning appears to have merit, though no research has been carried out to study it (94). In some cases, though, the logical consequences of misbehaving may not be severe enough to counter the intrinsic rewards of students' actions. Examples 2, 3, 5, 9, 11, and 13 in the table may well fit that category. Telling students who lie that one does not believe them, making a student wash graffiti off the wall, sending a student to the end of the line for cutting when he would have been at the end of the line anyway, and requiring a student who teases others to remain isolated may not affect the students as particularly unpleasant. Taking a student's part in a play away from her might actually be rewarding if the student is purposefully attempting to be dropped from the cast. And not moving a student who doesn't do his homework to the next level may merely confirm the student's belief that he is poor at math. In such cases, applying logical consequences could be ineffective, and you would have to resort to other kinds of consequences.

Self-Quiz:
Logical Consequences

Describe a logical consequence that a teacher might apply in each of the following cases.

1. A student calls out answers.
2. A student lies about not getting her snack.
3. A student gets into a fight during recess.
4. A student refuses to clear his place during lunch.
5. A student draws graffiti on the school building.
6. A student pushes ahead in line.
7. A student refuses to do her part of the assignment for the group she has been working in.
8. A student abuses the bathroom pass.
9. A student forges his parent's name to a permission slip for a class trip.

Acceptable Consequences

Considering the fact that negative consequences work because they are distasteful enough to cause students to change their behavior to avoid them, educators should select consequences that are no more unpleasant than is necessary to achieve that goal. To choose punishments more severe than necessary or to use excessively harsh punishments because milder forms prove to be ineffective is an abuse of the educator's authority and an infringement on the rights of the students. Thus, when you use negative consequences with your students, select the least noxious consequences necessary to do the job from among the acceptable alternatives available. If none of the acceptable alternatives work, do not abuse your power. Go on to use the more individualized, in-depth approaches described in Part Three instead.

Disapproval   There is a difference between signaling to students that you are aware of their actions or are issuing desist orders and expressing disapproval and reprimanding them for their behavior. Signaling awareness or giving desist orders provides students with factual information designed to give them the extra external control they require to manage their behavior. In contrast, expressing disapproval and reprimanding students are purposely designed to be noxious enough to motivate students to stop misbehaving. To be effective, the resulting discomfort has to be significant enough to counter the positive reinforcement students can receive from misbehaving.

Research shows that expressing disapproval and reprimanding students in a soft voice and in private so that no one else can hear can be effective so long as it is not done too often (83, 85, 89, 90). But reprimanding students in a loud voice, in front of their peers, or too often can actually lead to a worsening of their behavior. This response may make students angry and resentful, lower their self-esteem, cause them to rebel against the teacher's authority, or cause them to withdraw from class physically and/or psychologically to avoid feeling bad. It can also lead to a worsening in their attitude toward school, a decrease in their time on-task, and lower scores on achievement tests (78, 79, 81, 84, 86). Unfortunately, as noted in chapter 6, research indicates that teachers tend to reprimand males in public and in a harsh, stern voice. Research also indicates that students rank public reprimands among the least acceptable interventions that teachers use (88). Despite these facts, studies of classrooms reveal that teachers tend to criticize and reprimand students to an excessive degree much more often than they praise them (87, 91).

Reprimanding effectively: When you decide that it would benefit your students to express disapproval of their behavior or reprimand them, the following suggestions should help you carry this out more effectively:

1. *Speak to students privately in a calm, soft voice.* Avoid yelling at students from across the room. Speak to them privately at your desk, at their seat, or somewhere where no one else can hear what you say. Speaking to students privately, especially older ones, can protect them from being embarrassed in front of their peers. This also can serve to demonstrate your concern for their feelings, eliminate their need to "stand up to you" to maintain their peer standing, and avoid the negative result possible when students see one of their own being reprimanded publicly. Speaking to students softly in a calm voice instead of yelling makes it less likely that they will react defensively to being reprimanded or become nervous, jumpy, or tense.

2. *Choose your words carefully.* Although little research evidence either supports or refutes the idea, authors of classroom management texts typically suggest that when teachers reprimand students, they should discuss the students' behavior, not the students themselves. In addition, they suggest that teachers describe the behavior, not judge or label it. These authors advise that comments that focus on the students, especially if they are judgmental, can make students feel angry, resentful, and defensive. They can also lower students' self-esteem if they accept their teachers' assertions that they are indeed rude, lazy, dumb, stubborn, and so on. These labels can become self-fulfilling prophecies (80, 82, 89). In addition, judgmental and labeling statements give students little information about what they did wrong compared to statements that describe the inappropriate behavior, which make it clear what needs correcting.

   The advice to describe the students' behavior and to avoid judgmental terms applies to most students, but certain students may require another approach. In particular, when students need to learn to accept responsibility for their behavior, it may be more appropriate to focus in on what *they* did and how *their* behavior affected others. Likewise, when students need to learn to control themselves because it is the right thing to do, it may be desirable to use such terms as *unfair* and *unjust* to describe their behavior. (This rationale, of course, would never justify the use of terms such as *stupid, dumb, lazy, stubborn, bad, jerky,* and the like.)

3. *Do not reprimand students when you are angry or frustrated with them.* The goal of reprimanding is to change students' motivation, not to discharge your feelings. If you are too angry or upset to choose your words wisely or to focus on the students' needs, wait until you have calmed down enough to do so. Otherwise, you may unintentionally reprimand them publicly or use harsh and judgmental terms that you wouldn't normally choose.

Expressing disapproval and reprimanding students tend to work best with younger students and those who value their teachers' opinions of them and seek their teachers' attention and affection (field-sensitive students). Merely signaling to such students awareness

Descriptive: Focus on the Behavior	*Judgmental, Labeling:* Focus on the Student
It was a mistake to start before I finished explaining how to do it.	That was a dumb thing to do.
It's dangerous to put things into the wall socket. You could be electrocuted.	You sure act stupid sometimes. Didn't you know it's dangerous to put things into wall sockets?
Don't interrupt. Wait your turn.	Don't be rude.
You have to finish the rest of the assignment first.	Don't be lazy.
Harold was waiting in line when you pushed ahead of him.	You weren't very nice to Harold. You weren't very fair.
Once the group votes, everyone has to abide by the decision of the majority.	Don't be stubborn.

Self-Quiz: Reprimands

The following are examples of reprimands that can be improved on. In each case, identify the principle or principles that were overlooked, and improve the reprimand accordingly.

1. When the teacher saw Henry taking something from the closet, she called out, "Put that back. How many times do I have to tell you that I'm the only one allowed to remove things from the closet?"
2. When the teacher noticed Katherine looking covertly at her book during a test, she walked up to her and quietly said, "Katherine, I'm surprised at you. I never thought you were a cheat."
3. When Steve refused to let Billy take a turn during recess, his teacher said, "Don't be bad. Let Billy have his turn."
4. The teacher was so angry when he heard Harold make an ethnic comment about Ira that he said, "Harold, you should be ashamed of yourself. You know that we don't say those things in class. Now say you're sorry."
5. When Jim started playing the clown for the class, his teacher reminded the other students that they were supposed to ignore him whenever he did stupid things.

---

of their behavior and/or telling them to stop is often sufficient, so that reprimanding them is unnecessary. But as reprimands may be too inconsequential for students who are very field independent or who require negative consequences to be shown that they can't get away with misbehaving and often unnecessary for students who respond to signals, the position of this book is that their usefulness as a classroom management technique is minimal at best.

Overcorrection   In examples 3, 10, and 11 in the table on natural, arbitrary, and logical consequences, in which students drew graffiti on the wall, failed to return a library book, and refused to participate in cleanup activities, the logical consequences of their misbehavior would be to require them to correct the situation they had caused by removing the graffiti, paying for the library book, and finishing the cleanup during recess. If merely making restitution for misbehavior isn't enough to change their behavior, the teacher could require the students to overcorrect the situation they had created. In the examples cited, overcorrection might consist of having the student clean the complete wall, not just the section with graffiti; spend more time in the library than necessary to pay for the book; and do more than just her fair share of the cleanup. Other situations in which overcorrection might be appropriate include littering, carving school desks, breaking other students' property or projects, purposely excluding children from the group, throwing food in the cafeteria, and refusing to share.

Though overcorrection has been successful (96–99, 102), it has also been criticized for being too punitive and for only being effective in changing behavior so long as the threat of punishment is present (95, 100, 101).

Time-Out   *Time-out* is a term for a number of classroom management procedures that involve removing students from regular classroom activities in ways designed to be unpleasant, distasteful, or boring. This should not be confused with the antiseptic bouncing (117), which is removing students from classroom situations that make them anxious, afraid, or guilty in order to prevent them from experiencing emotional problems.

When students want to take part in the classroom activities they are removed from, removing them can be unpleasant enough to make them modify their behavior. Students who enjoy classroom learning tasks and are motivated to complete their assignments in school instead of at home may want to avoid being sent to a time-out area, and very sociable students may control their talkative behavior if they are denied access to their friends. For such students, making them spend a short period in a time-out area at the back of the room, behind a screen, in the hall, or at their desks with their heads down on their arms may do the trick.

A time-out procedure termed *contingent observation*, which is especially appropriate for preschoolers, has been described by Porterfield, Herbert-Jackson, and Risley (115). In their approach, students who misbehave are first told why their behavior was unacceptable and how they should behave; then they are required to sit on the periphery of the group and watch while teachers call their attention to examples of the desired behavior among their classmates.

When time-out works, a short period of time-out is all that is necessary to create an effective deterrent to misbehavior. White, Nielson, and Johnson (122) report that time-out periods of 1 minute are as effective as lengthy time-out periods. Others have found that from 5 to a maximum of 15 minutes is adequate (105, 106, 111, 113).

But students who are not particularly interested in participating in classroom activities may not mind being removed from a situation they do not find reinforcing to begin with. For these students, some authors have suggested that educators should increase the unpleasant aspects associated with time-out. Suggestions for how to do this include requiring students to sit in a time-out chair facing the corner of the room (a technique some feel is not too different from requiring students to wear a "dunce cap" and sit in the corner or on the dunce's stool), sending students to an area designed to be a boring, unpleasant experience, or having them visit the dean of discipline or the principal's office.

Authors who reject the idea of making time-out worse by having the time-out area be unpleasant advise educators to make time-out unappealing by making "time-in" more appealing. The typical way to do this is to offer students the opportunity to earn points or tokens that can be turned in for a prize, special privileges, or the like, by behaving appropriately and to deny this opportunity to students when they misbehave. In this approach, teachers tell students who have misbehaved that they will be unable to earn points for a specified period of time. Then they place a ribbon on the students or some type of symbol on their desks, signaling that they can't earn points or tokens until it is removed, or else they move students to a time-out area of the room (107).

Considerable evidence shows that various forms of time-out work with some students (103, 106, 109, 110, 114, 115, 118, 119, 122). Weber, Roff, Crawford, and Robinson (121) list 21 texts that recommend time-out procedures to modify students' behavior. Still, the various forms of time-out have received their share of criticism for being overly punitive and unethical (64, 112, 116, 120).

Using time-out effectively: The following general guidelines are designed to help you use time-out techniques effectively:

1. Determine whether the use of negative consequences is the correct procedure. As noted previously, negative consequences are appropriate for some, but some students, such as those who misbehave because they are angry at being teased by others, may require another approach.

2. Decide which type of time-out would be most effective: preventing students from participating in the rewarding aspects of normal classroom activities, denying students the opportunity to earn points or tokens for acceptable behavior, or placing students in an unpleasant time-out area.

3. Establish a baseline of how often the undesirable behavior occurs so that you can measure the effectiveness of your intervention. (Be as accurate as time allows.)

4. Make sure students know which behaviors they have to change and why these are unacceptable.

5. Establish the consequences that students will receive when they misbehave, and be sure students understand both the consequences and what they must do to avoid them.

6. Use the time-out procedure you have chosen, and evaluate its effectiveness in reducing or eliminating the target behavior.

7. If it is not effective, modify your procedure or select a different time-out technique.

8. If it is effective, eliminate the time-out procedure, and see whether students continue to behave appropriately. If the improvement is not maintained, use other procedures to supplement those that you have been using. (See chapters 11 and 12.)

Educators who support time-out procedures offer the following specific suggestions for implementing them:

1. If not permitting students to participate in regular class activities is sufficient punishment to motivate them to modify their behavior, then select the least restrictive

time-out area for the purpose. You can, for example, separate students who are too talkative from their friends by changing their seats. Place attention-seeking students behind a partition or screen, but banish disruptive students to the hall.

2. To use time-out from the opportunity to earn points or tokens, you have to establish a procedure whereby students can both earn points and lose the opportunity to earn them (see the next section on contingency contracting) as well as some signaling device to indicate that students are in time-out for a specified time period. You can use a private signal with students, such as a tap on the shoulder or placing a hand on the desk, to avoid calling attention to the "punishment." Or you can use a more public signal if you believe it is necessary to let other students know that you are "with it" and are handling the problem.

3. If you choose to remove students to an unpleasant time-out area, be sure they experience this as unpleasant. Using such procedures with students who are trying to be kicked out of class or who want to impress other students with their delinquent stance is an ineffective way of handling their misbehavior.

4. When you remove students from class, make sure you are not too angry or frustrated with them to make the right choice of consequences.

5. If necessary, send students to the hall, a detention center that is a regular classroom supervised by an adult, or the dean of discipline or principal's office.

6. Encourage students to do their work during their time-out periods. Make sure they do not have any other reading materials, games, or other objects they can entertain themselves with; advise secretaries and others not to talk to or commiserate with students in time-out.

7. Use the shortest period of time necessary to affect the students' behavior. Most authors consider 5 to 15 minutes reasonable. Do not increase the time students spend in time-out beyond a reasonable period if students resist leaving the classroom or if the procedure is not effective. To do so would be abusive and a misuse of your authority.

Contingency Contracting   Contingency contracts are written out and typically signed by both students and teachers. They specify how students are expected to behave and the positive and negative consequences they will receive when they either comply or fail to comply with their contracts. Ideally, these contracts result from a period of negotiation between teacher and student during which the student participates in determining both the behavioral change expected and the consequences that will occur.

Advantages and disadvantages: Theorists claim several advantages for this approach to setting and enforcing expectations for appropriate behavior (43, 105, 111, 124). First, research indicates that contingency contracting is an effective method of achieving behavioral change in a variety of settings and with a variety of problems (123, 124, 129, 131, 132). A second factor is that students are more willing to abide by contracts they help formulate. They are also more likely to conform to formal agreements than informal ones. Next, writing down behavioral expectations and consequences makes it less likely that students will forget them. Another important point is that students who have agreed that their behavior needs changing are more likely to attribute any negative consequences they may incur to their behavior rather than to the teacher's whims. This is especially helpful with students who resent or resist their teacher's authority. Students participating in the development of contracts are taking a first step toward learning to manage their own behavior. Finally, students themselves prefer contingency contracting over many other classroom management techniques.

But contingency contracting has also been criticized. Some feel that rewarding students for appropriate behavior can create overdependency, loss of creativity, and the like. Also, when used in conjunction with negative consequences, contingency contracting does not produce long-term changes in behavior. This approach can provide the illusion of student participation, when in fact students often only pretend to agree with the contracts they have signed because of their teachers' power over them (43, 73, 127). And as discussed in chapter 5, students from some ethnic backgrounds, such as Southeast Asian Americans, have difficulty disagreeing with their teachers because to do so would be a sign of disrespect or because disagreements create an uncomfortable situation for them. And many female students and students with emotional problems who seek their teachers' approval may agree to a contract verbally without really being committed to it (see chapters 6 and 12). Therefore, teachers should not assume that students who agree to a contingency contract actually think that they should follow through on their commitment. Finally, Tanner asks:

> Can teachers combine contracts with intrinsic motivation? This seems theoretically untenable since contingency management is based on the principle of operant conditioning with the use of extrinsic rewards. . . . Contracts are manipulative. The learner is doing something unappealing for the privilege of doing something less unappealing and so on until the chain is completed. (73, pp. 105–106)

Using contingency contracting effectively: Practitioners of contingency contracting have offered the following suggestions for implementing the technique (111, 125, 126, 128, 130):

1. Develop contracts with students in ways that maximize their participation in order to gain their cooperation and enhance their growth toward self-management. (See the section on self-management later in this chapter.)

2. Specify the desirable and undesirable behaviors and what the consequences of each will be. For example,

   - Each day that I don't call out, I will be allowed to feed the rabbits.

   - I will earn 5 points for each half hour I don't call out. I will lose 5 points each time I speak to other students without permission. When I have 40 points, I will be allowed to feed the rabbits.

   - I will earn 10 points for each day I don't use foul language in class. I will lose 2 points each time I use foul language in class. I will earn 5 points each day I keep my hands to myself. I will lose recess if I hit or push other students.

3. Be realistic about the amount of change you can expect students to make, especially at the start of a contract. Reward small changes of behavior in the right direction so that students can be successful immediately.

4. Emphasize positive rather than negative consequences so that students are likely to profit from their contracts. Emphasize what students will get or earn by behaving appropriately, not what they will lose by misbehaving.

5. Make sure the terms of the agreement are clear.

6. Make sure students agree that the contract is fair.

7. Include a provision that entitles both parties to renegotiate the contract.

8. Include beginning and ending dates.

9. Have both parties to the contract express their agreement by their signature, a handshake, or the like.

10. Evaluate the results periodically. If the contract isn't working, renegotiate the terms; decrease your expectations for behavior change or increase the incentives you are offering students to modify their behavior. If the contract is a success, evaluate your students' behavior after the contract has terminated to determine whether the improvement is maintained without extrinsic consequences. If it isn't, develop new contracts with your students or use some of the techniques designed to motivate students to want to behave appropriately in the absence of consequences.

Unacceptable and Controversial Consequences

The previous section described a number of punitive techniques that many educators feel are acceptable ways of dealing with misbehavior. This section discusses punitive techniques that many authors find unacceptable.

Harsh Reprimands   Numerous authors have reported that harsh reprimands—criticizing students publicly, frequently, angrily, or in a loud voice—can be counterproductive. Instead of reducing disruptive behavior, harsh reprimands often increase undesirable behavior on the part of students who are reprimanded and other class members as well. Research also indicates that harsh reprimands make students more aggressive and anxious and decrease their interest in learning (84, 135, 175).

Serious Consequences for Minor Infractions   Although no research exists as yet on this subject, many educators disapprove of applying serious, time-consuming, or highly distasteful consequences for minor infractions; they feel that "the punishment should fit the crime." Examples of consequences that may not meet this requirement include taking away classroom responsibilities, such as feeding the fish, taking messages to the office, or being the line monitor, for talking in class or in the halls; being kept in school after hours for not completing seatwork; and having to write, "I will not . . . " 100 times for doing something only once or twice.

Negative Practice   Negative practice is a technique in which students are required to repeat an undesirable behavior until it loses its original reinforcing effects. For example, a teacher would require students who spit at other children or on the hallway floors to spit into a toilet or in a grassy area until they feel like they never want to spit again. Another example is making students who throw temper tantrums perform the same antics until they will think twice before doing so the next time they feel angry or frustrated. Though negative practice has its proponents and detractors, there is as yet no evidence of either the effectiveness or the side effects of this technique.

Blame, Shame, Embarrassment, and Ridicule   Purposely calling on inattentive or unprepared students to recite in class in order to embarrass them in front of their peers; using terms such as *stupid, lazy, idiotic, childish, foolish, dumb, egotistical, self-centered,* and the like to describe students or their behavior; and making comments like, "Would you like to sit with the kindergartners?" may suppress students' undesirable behavior for the moment. But using this approach may also seriously damage their self-image and their relationships with their teachers (178).

Peer Pressure   Students' motivation to behave appropriately can be increased by the peer pressure that occurs when the consequences for the entire group depend on the behavior of one or a few individuals (153, 156). This approach can be both advantageous and disadvantageous, as the following statement indicates:

> A well-executed dependent group contingency can have a distinct advantage: Problem students' peers tend to "root for" them and do what they can to encourage improvement because they have something to gain by doing so. A disadvantage is that it can easily be mismanaged, resulting in possible threats, criticism, or harassment from peers when the target student or subgroup does not perform adequately. (149, p. 7)

Telling the class that everyone except Harry and Lenny are ready to leave for recess can get these two to stop talking, but it can also encourage other students to harass them during recess for holding up the class. And this approach is unfair to other students. Due to the inherent possibility that students may exert negative pressure on their peers, peer pressure is not a safe way to motivate nonconforming students. Instead of making the class wait for Harry and Lenny, it would be more prudent to dismiss everyone except the two boys, who must stay behind until they are ready.

A somewhat different form of peer pressure, peer confrontation, has proved to be effective with students whose misbehavior has an adverse effect on their peers (136, 166, 167). This approach involves a three-step process. First, the peers of misbehaving students point out to them the inappropriate behavior and challenge their disruptive classsmates to be aware of their behavior. Then they discuss the harmful effects of the students' inappropriate behavior on their classmates. Finally, they involve the offending students in a process designed to identify alternative ways the students can behave or ways they can solve the problems that led to the undesirable behavior. While this approach has proved useful, its effectiveness may be limited to students in the middle or upper grades.

The potential undesirable side effects of this approach have not been studied in detail. Educators have noted that peers who are supposed to be assisting their classmates to improve their behavior may threaten and abuse them instead if they are too immature to engage in the procedure in constructive ways or are not supervised adequately by their teachers. The technique might cause students to be embarrassed by having their problems discussed publicly. (As noted in chapter 5, this might be the reaction of students from certain ethnic backgrounds.) And the students who are the subject of their peers' confrontation may avoid their peers or retaliate in aggressive ways if they are dissatisfied with or resentful about the way they were treated by them.

Isolation/Seclusion Although many educators consider time-out an acceptable technique, putting students in seclusion or isolation during time-out is highly controversial. Clarizio (45), among others, favors the use of isolation as a technique to control extreme forms of misbehavior:

> To use time-out procedures effectively, a teacher must be sure that removal from the class is a punishment. . . . Ideally, the students should be placed in a dull, unstimulating room containing a chair and a light. The area should be well ventilated, lighted, and consistent with fire code regulations. (45, p. 142)

Gast and Nelson (108) have published guidelines that they believe will enable educators to use seclusion ethically and effectively. These guidelines include the following suggestions:

1. Students should be advised about which behaviors will result in seclusion or time-out beforehand.

2. Teachers should document their attempts to control students' misbehavior by employing milder forms of time-out before using seclusion.

3. Teachers should have a written statement of the procedures to be followed.

4. The time-out room should be at least 6 by 6 feet, properly lighted and ventilated, and free of dangerous objects. It should contain a window for observing the student, and it should be locked only when necessary.

5. Teachers should keep records of all time-out events.

6. Seclusion in excess of 30 minutes should require consultation with supervisory school staff.

7. Teachers should reward students for behaving appropriately after they have completed a period of seclusion.

8. If seclusion appears to be ineffective in suppressing the behavior, an advisory committee should determine whether it should continue to be used.

Locking students in small rooms by themselves and not allowing them to leave until they have stopped crying or screaming should be unacceptable to all educators, and many do consider that kind of treatment as abusive, counterproductive, and wrong. The position of this author is that secluding students in isolation rooms is unjustified regardless of the way they behave in school. Much more humane and effective ways of dealing with behavior problems are readily available.

Corporal Punishment Corporal punishment typically takes the form of a principal or some other school authority administering a paddling on the backside to a student.

While most educators tend to agree that such forms of harsh punishment as ridicule, sarcasm, embarrassment, abusive reprimands, and excessive criticism are undesirable, much less agreement exists about corporal punishment.

Many educators favor using corporal punishment within clearly defined guidelines when, in the judgment of professionals, it is warranted (141, 157, 161, 165). For example, Sabatino, Sabatino, and Mann state:

> This author does not advocate corporal punishment as the best alternative to solving behavioral problems in school. However, in lieu of the ineffectiveness of other tried alternatives, punishment may be necessary as a last resort, and in some cases, may be a better solution than others. (165, p. 12)

The following are two representative statements by superintendents of schools who favor the use of corporal punishment:

> The necessity for the use of corporal punishment as a means of managing behavior in schools arises from two particular sources. First, education is compulsory; children between the ages of 6 and 16 must attend school unless otherwise excused by local or state statute. Secondly, there is often no positive alternative institution to which a child can turn when he/she is suspended from school. If they are suspended from school, where are you going to suggest the parents of the child go for assistance in obtaining a public education for that child? All of us recognize that public education is desirable; it is desirable for children to learn the basic skills that they need to support themselves and to be contributing members of society. The basic knowledge must come from the public school in this country, for there isn't any other source. Therefore, if we suspend a child from school as a possible alternative to corporal punishment, there is no place to send him/her except to the street. (161, p. 11)

> I was not abused by my parents, and they used corporal punishment. I do not consider that I was abused by my teachers who used corporal punishment on me when I was coming up through the public schools. I perceive that I have a positive self-concept and that I have a pretty good attitude toward life. (157, p. 5)

Advantages: Supporters of corporal punishment tend to point out the following facts to bolster their position: Corporal punishment has been approved as a disciplinary technique in schools by the Supreme Court; only a minority of the states have regulations disapproving its use in school (134); national surveys indicate that corporal punishment is widely used and approved of by school personnel and parents (150, 152, 158, 162, 177, 180).

Educators who favor corporal punishment also use a variety of arguments to justify its use (141, 157, 161, 165). They maintain that other techniques do not work with certain students who seem to need to experience pain before they are willing to conform. Even with students who do respond to other management techniques, the process can be so time-consuming that it may be more efficient to use corporal punishment. Also, corporal punishment is the most logical consequence to employ when students behave violently, defiantly, disrespectfully, destructively, or dangerously or when they directly challenge their teachers' authority, lie, refuse to admit their mistakes, and so on. Some suggest that the use of corporal punishment demonstrates that teachers care enough about their students to do what is necessary to help them learn self-control—to do what is best for them and the other members of the class. Others feel that corporal punishment builds character by teaching students to accept the consequences of their actions. It also enables school administrators to handle difficult students without suspending or expelling them. And finally, some believe that corporal punishment is not abusive if used correctly, according to the following guidelines:

- It is administered in a calm, rational atmosphere in private.
- Students are told what they did wrong and why they are being punished.
- Students are not paddled excessively.
- Students are forgiven and consoled immediately afterward to demonstrate to them that they were punished out of love and concern for them, not anger.

Disadvantages: A great many educators oppose corporal punishment in school (66, 80, 120, 140, 142, 143, 145, 147, 148, 151, 162, 173, 174, 176, 179). The following statements exemplify this position:

> If the technology of discipline management could be linked to an animal, then corporal punishment would surely be its ass end. Of all the discipline techniques in existence, corporal punishment distinguishes itself as having the fewest assets and the greatest number of liabilities. In terms of locking adult and child into a series of coercive cycles, it is the all-time champion. (148, p. 344)

> Corporal punishment should never be used to motivate students. It not only is morally questionable, but, of critical importance to the school's mission, it just doesn't work. In fact, it is usually counterproductive. Students obviously do not wish to attend schools where corporal punishment is common, and so any later attempts to motivate them to learn are uphill battles. (120, p. 34)

Educators who are opposed to the use of corporal punishment have offered many reasons for their thinking. First, no evidence shows that corporal punishment decreases off-task behavior (138). They feel that corporal punishment is an unethical, overly punitive, and abusive technique. It is also significant that no legal guidelines have been established to determine when it would be reasonable to use corporal punishment or what type of corporal punishment is reasonable. Specifically, many cases of abusive use of corporal punishment have resulted in physical and psychological damage to students (139, 154). Critics note that corporal punishment tends to be used more with poor, non–European American students and disabled students than with European American, middle-class, nondisabled students (134, 144, 159, 170, 172).

Additional criticism by educators includes the observation that teachers who use corporal punishment tend to be less experienced, less thoughtful, less open-minded, and less educated (164). They posit that using corporal punishment can mask such real causes of students' misbehavior as poor instruction, overcrowded classrooms, cultural and linguistic differences, emotional problems, and learning disabilities. They also feel a danger exists that students may copy the physical aggression their teachers model (66, 133, 137, 165). And corporal punishment can cause students to be truant and drop out of school, to retaliate aggressively against teachers or school property, and to displace their anger onto other convenient victims (66, 137, 142, 147, 152, 160, 165). Corporal punishment can also make students too anxious or too angry to learn effectively (139, 155, 165). And as noted in chapter 5, even when the offense is the same, teachers are more likely to use corporal punishment with African American students and with males than with European American and female students (146, 163, 168, 169). Finally, opponents note that 19 states have banned the use of corporal punishment in schools (171). For all of these reasons, the author is opposed to the use of corporal punishment in school.

Harsh Punishments—Pros and Cons   Many people are against (or at least question) the use of the harsher forms of punishment described in this chapter in both regular and special education (205–211). They believe that it is possible to teach all students, even the ones who demonstrate the most severe forms of behavior problems, without resorting to harsh punishment. They maintain that harsh forms of punishment "only suppress problem behaviors, that they do not produce durable effects, and that their treatment effects do not generalize to other settings" (209, p. 2). They question the moral and ethnical appropriateness of harsh punishments. They note that the most aversive punishments are disproportionately meted out to non-European American and poor students and to students with disabilities. And they argue that the harshness and unfairness of these punishments can lead poor, non-European, and disabled students to demonstrate even more of the kinds of behaviors they are designed to control.

Many individuals favor a total ban on the use of what have been called aversive behavior reduction procedures. Other educators, however, feel that such forms of punishment are necessary with some students who do not respond to the kinds of helping techniques described in the previous chapter or to the rewards or mild forms of punishment discussed in this chapter. They believe that to eliminate or ban the use of harsh aversive behavior reduction procedures would eliminate essential classroom management options for some students (212).

After examining the research on the pros and cons of using harsh punishments, a committee of educators concluded:

> The question of whether totally nonaversive, nonintrusive, or nonrestrictive approaches are superior to strategies incorporating intrusive, aversive, or restrictive procedures for reducing problem behaviors of children with behavior disorders cannot be answered by the current literature. There have simply been too few studies comparing these procedures to provide definitive and conclusive answers. . . .
>
> However, situations will undoubtedly arise in which relatively less aversive, intrusive, and restrictive procedures simply are not effective in reducing behavior. In these cases, practitioners face a moral dilemma of whether to use an ineffective, but personally acceptable procedure, or to use a personally repugnant but aversive procedure to manage severe, intractable, and undesirable behavior. (209, pp. 16–17)

Guidelines   The following guidelines have been offered for using harsh and severe punishments fairly and effectively:

1. Do not use harsh aversive procedures unless all other forms of intervention have failed to achieve the desired behavioral change.

2. Document the other interventions that were attempted.

3. Obtain written permission from students' parents or guardians to implement the particular harsh punishment chosen.

4. Follow the schoolwide or districtwide written policies for administering harsh punishments. Typically, these policies include the legal guidelines that must be followed; the written permission of administrators, student advocates, or human rights commissions that approve and oversee the administration of harsh punishments; the justification for the use of harsh forms of punishments; a procedure for evaluating the effectiveness of the punishment; and procedures for keeping others, including students' parents, apprised of the results of the punishment.

5. Use the least harsh punishment possible.

6. Use a trained staff member to administer the punishment, preferably a person who is not involved with the student on a day-to-day basis.

Mild Punishment—Pros and Cons

The previous section included a discussion of the pros and cons of using various controversial forms of punishment in the classroom. This section summarizes the arguments for and against so-called acceptable forms of mild punishment.

Pros Educators who favor using punishment provide several arguments in support of their position. First, they believe that punishment plays a necessary, inevitable, and pervasive role in socializing children (62) and in the daily lives of both children and adults in the real world. No matter how much educators try not to use punishment, their students are bound to have aversive experiences in the classroom, even if it's just the natural consequences of their own misbehavior. Thus, the question is not whether to punish students but rather how to punish them.

Second, teachers cannot rely on rules alone to manage classroom behavior. Just as sanctions are necessary to make sure adults obey traffic rules, parking and smoking regulations, and other public conventions, it has been demonstrated experimentally that teachers need sanctions to back up school rules (193). Students, especially young ones, need to know that they will be noticed and punished if they misbehave. Once they realize this, most students will behave appropriately without actually having to be punished.

The next argument suggests that punishment also works for students who need the experience of actually being punished to control themselves. Punishment suppresses undesirable behavior quickly and for long periods of time (64, 75, 103, 104, 106, 110, 114, 115, 118, 119, 121, 122–124, 129, 131, 132, 185, 187, 195–197, 201–204). As Walters and Grusec have put it,

> Although punishment does have its undesirable side effects, they are not as detrimental as some people have suggested. Used judiciously, punishment can be quite effective in suppressing unwanted behavior, without adversely affecting desirable behavior. This excludes extremely severe punishment that is administered randomly so that the contingencies are unclear to the recipient, and that which is administered by a hostile and rejecting caretaker. (74, p. 177)

Educators taking this position feel that punishment can have positive side effects on students. For example, behaving more appropriately can improve their relationships with their peers and teachers. As a result, students may experience more affection and acceptance from others, which can improve their self-esteem and self-confidence (181, 192). Also, when students observe their peers being punished, they are less likely to misbehave themselves.

The final argument is that, used appropriately, punishment seldom has the undesirable side effects mentioned in the literature (192).

Cons   Many authors see little, if any, role for punishment in the schools. The following quote is representative of this thinking:

> If punishment works, it does so only under very precise and complicated conditions, much too complicated for us to consistently use in classrooms. The controls that one must utilize to optimize the effectiveness of punishment are not possible in day-to-day operations either within families or schools. I (and, I suspect, you) will continue to respond in punitive ways to frustrating situations. However, I don't expect that the consequence of this punitive action will have the desired effect of helping others function more productively. I therefore will be searching for alternatives. Fortunately, there are other, less complicated, more promising alternatives. (182, pp. 39–40)

These educators feel that punishment does not work because, at best, it suppresses undesirable behavior; it does not teach students how to behave appropriately (43, 111). Also, the effects of punishment last only so long as the risk of it is present. Once the threat of punishment is removed, students tend to revert back to their previous behavior (43, 185, 197). As Clarizio states,

> Punished behavior can come back. . . . How many times have you scolded students, kept them from recess, retained them after school, put them out in the hall, threatened to lower their grades, or sent them to the principal's office only to find that they engage in the very same misbehavior after a short while. (105, p. 130)

Further, they contend that some forms of punishment work best on students who need it least (84). For example, reprimanding students for misbehaving works only for students who are concerned about their teachers' opinions of them. Students who do not care are the ones more likely to misbehave and less likely to be affected by such punishment. Educators opposed to punishment also suggest that punishment doesn't increase students' intrinsic motivation to want to behave appropriately in the absence of consequences. If it did, correctional facilities for adolescents and adults would have much higher success rates than they in fact do. If the goal of education is to prepare students to take their places as law-abiding, moral citizens in a democracy, schools need to increase students' intrinsic motivation (43, 183, 186, 188). Finally, the improved behavior that punishment produces is often illusory, merely reflecting the fact that students are more careful not to get caught, are biding their time until better opportunities present themselves, or are using other equally unacceptable forms of behavior to attain their ends.

Educators who are against using punishment point out that punishment systems can be time-consuming and disruptive. Keeping records of students' points and tokens, arguing with students who resist relinquishing tokens they have already acquired, keeping track of students' on- and off-task behavior, and the like, can use up class time that would better be spent teaching students (43, 46, 182, 189, 200).

Those opposed to punishment argue that punishment can have a negative effect on students. For example, some students copy the punitive approaches that their teachers model (184, 191, 199) and punishing students can cause them to become more aggressive, be less concerned about learning and other school values, be overly concerned about fitting in, have a less rational attitude toward misbehavior, and be less efficient learners (42, 95, 179). Punishment can also increase students' anxiety and decrease their self-esteem (81, 198). In addition, some students avoid their teachers and other school-related activities after they have been punished (194). Punishment can also make students resentful, rebellious, and uncooperative as well as cause them to take pleasure in undermining their teachers' authority (148). And then, punishing students can have a negative ripple effect on their peers, upsetting them, making them anxious, and causing them to be less efficient learners (84, 190).

These educators also point out that punishment can mask the real causes of student problems. Specifically, it can suppress the behavior of students with learning disabilities and/or emotional problems temporarily, thereby concealing the need to use more appropriate techniques for helping such students. It can also coerce students who are teased and victimized because they have disabilities, are members of racial or ethnic minorities, or are too small, passive, or frightened to defend themselves to act as if nothing is bothering them because they fear being punished if they react angrily, physically, or loudly. And it can mask the existence of an irrelevant curriculum, overcrowded classes, and underfinanced school systems.

Finally, punishing students is unpleasurable and distasteful. It is the least desirable form of classroom management and should only be used as a last resort, if at all.

Conclusions   Weighing the arguments for and against punishing students, the author has arrived at three conclusions based on his review of the literature and his personal experiences. First, punishment is a pervasive, inescapable, and necessary part of life. Both in school and out, teachers, parents, and other persons in charge cannot rely on rules alone to ensure that people will behave appropriately. Punishment or the threat of it is necessary for young children who are still in the first stage of moral development. It also plays a minor deterrent role in keeping honest, law-abiding individuals from succumbing to the temptation to copy someone's work, park their car illegally, exaggerate their deductions on their income tax returns, and so on. And it is an important technique to use with those few older youngsters, adolescents, and adults who are likely to break whatever rules they think they can get away with breaking.

In particular, students in the first stage of moral development may need several experiences of mild punishment both in school and elsewhere before learning to behave as expected. For well-behaved students, the mere existence of possible punishment and its occasional use should be enough to help them behave appropriately. Yet, while punishment may be a necessary technique to manage the behavior of students who will misbehave when they think they can get away with it, it does little, if anything, to increase their intrinsic motivation to want to behave in the absence of consequences. These students require the techniques described in chapter 11 that are designed to change their intrinsic motivation.

The second conclusion is that even the so-called acceptable forms of punishment can

Self-Quiz: On Punishment

Decide what your opinion is about the following statement, and list the reasons for your opinion. This may help you clarify your thoughts about the use of punishment to modify students' behavior.

"Punishment is an acceptable classroom management technique if used appropriately."

State whether you think each of the following techniques is appropriate in some situations with some students or inappropriate in all situations and with all students; state the reasons for your opinion.

- Rewarding incompatible behavior
- Rewarding improvement
- Using peers as models
- Planned ignoring
- Expressing disapproval/reprimanding
- Applying logical consequences
- Overcorrection
- Time-out from earning rewards
- Time-out in a time-out area
- Contingency contracting
- Harsh reprimands
- Negative practice
- Blame, shame, embarrassment, and ridicule
- Peer pressure
- Isolation/seclusion
- Corporal punishment

be abused. If used inappropriately or with the wrong students, punishment can have the kinds of undesirable side effects that have been reported in the literature. It can also mask the genuine reason for students' behaviors, which deprives them of the help they require. And it can be used to sustain ineffective teaching, irrelevant curriculum, overcrowded classes, and underfinanced schools.

Finally, punishment should exist more as a possibility than an actuality in the classroom. That is, its primary role should be to deter students from misbehaving because they are aware of the consequences that will result if they do. When teachers have to punish students regularly, this indicates either that they have an unusually large number of students who want to get away with things or—and much more likely—that they are resorting to using punishment to temporarily suppress behavior that could and should be handled more effectively and more pleasantly by other, nonpunitive means.

Self-Management

In recent years, educators have learned that students can manage their own consequences systems to a far greater degree than had originally been thought. This section describes some of the ways students can apply positive and negative consequences to their own behavior and describes what research indicates about the effectiveness of student-managed versus teacher-managed consequences systems.

As the term implies, students are in charge of the consequences when they use self-management techniques. But because students generally know little about the principles of behavior management, they have to be taught how to do it, helped to get started, and supervised periodically to make sure they are doing it correctly. Thus, in a very real sense, self-management requires a collaborative effort between teachers and students.

Using Self-Management Effectively

Practitioners of the self-management approach usually advocate the following steps:

1. Motivate students to want to modify their behavior through active listening, reasoning with them, and other respectful, interactive behaviors so they will cooperate voluntarily.

2. Identify the inappropriate behavior to be modified.

3. Make sure students understand why their behavior is inappropriate.

4. Help students establish a baseline of how often, how long, and in which situations they behave inappropriately.

5. Assist students in identifying appropriate behaviors that they can substitute for inappropriate ones if possible.

6. Help students set *realistic* goals for behavioral change. Discourage students from setting goals that are so unrealistic that they won't be able to earn rewards or avoid punishments.

7. Help students establish consequences that are significant to them and positive if possible, negative if necessary.

8. Teach students how to develop a system for self-observation and record keeping.

   - Teach them how to count the number of times they do behaviors that only last for a short time, such as calling out, bringing comic books to school, pushing other students, or not raising their hands to ask for help.

   - Teach them how to time how long they engage in behavior that is more continuous, such as on- or off-task behavior.

   - Help students develop a schedule for periodic observation that will enable them to spend as much time as possible engaged in productive learning, not self-observation. For example, a timer can be set to go off every 15 or 20 minutes, and the students can record what they were doing at the moment or observe their behavior for the next few minutes.

   - Teach students how to record their observations on charts or graphs so they can monitor their behavior.

9. Supervise students periodically to make sure their observations are accurate.

10. Teach students how to evaluate their behavior so they can determine the kinds and amounts of positive and/or negative consequences they have earned during each

Teachers need to supervise the results of their students' self-management programs.

observation period. Rhode, Morgan, and Young (235) taught students to evaluate the improvement in their behavior accurately by having them compare their evaluations with those of their teacher. If the two were exactly the same, the students received a bonus. If they were close, the students kept the reward they had earned.

11. Make sure students reward themselves as soon as possible after each observation period.

12. Supervise students periodically to make sure they are reinforcing themselves properly and accurately.

13. Teach students to evaluate their progress periodically and to modify their program (goals, consequences, observation schedules, etc.) when necessary.

14. Help students generalize their improved behavior to other situations and to relationships with other people.

15. Eliminate the extrinsic reinforcements, and teach students to reinforce themselves by thinking about how much better they feel, how much better they get along with others, how they stay out of trouble now that they aren't misbehaving, and other internal satisfactions.

16. Help students determine whether their behavioral improvement is maintained in the absence of extrinsic consequences.

Advantages

Educators who favor the application of self-managed rather than teacher-managed consequences offer several reasons to support their position. First, they point out that self-management works as well as, if not better than, teacher-managed consequences (214–216, 218, 220, 227, 229–231, 235–237, 241–243). Specifically, students who are in charge of their own consequences are more motivated to change; rebellious and resistant students are less likely to resent the application of consequences if they are in charge of applying them; students often know better than their teachers what is and isn't rewarding and punishing to them; in some cases, only students know when they are behaving inappropriately (i.e., daydreaming, thinking about going to the bathroom in order to miss class, etc.); and finally, students who have managed their own behavior modification programs are more likely to maintain their improved behavior in the absence of consequences. Second, these educators point out that self-management has positive side effects (219, 224). In particular, it teaches students how to manage their own behavior, which is a necessary skill in the real world; it gives students a sense of being in charge of their own destiny; and students who manage their own consequences are more likely to accept responsibility for their behavior than to blame others.

These educators note that student-managed programs require less teacher time (233, 244). They add that the effects of self-managed consequences are more likely to generalize to other situations and to be maintained when the program of consequences is terminated than are teacher-managed consequences (214, 217, 218, 221, 232, 243). Finally, they comment that self-managed consequences avoid the ethical and legal issues that are sometimes involved in teacher-managed, extrinsic consequences programs (46, 242).

To date, research regarding the effectiveness of self-managed consequences programs indicates that students can modify their behavior to a considerable degree by managing their own reward systems for behaving appropriately and for fulfilling contingency contracts (215, 216, 218, 220, 221, 231, 235, 243). Students can also manage their time-out from the opportunity to earn rewards (225, 226) and the duration they spend in time-out areas to some degree (223, 234). Finally, they can also punish themselves for misbehaving (222).

Disadvantages

Other educators believe that having students manage their own extrinsic consequences systems is not as effective as its proponents claim. They argue that it is no more effective than teacher-managed consequences (228, 230), and it involves a great deal of teacher time. For instance, teachers have to train students to manage their consequences systems and then supervise them periodically or else students will lie, cheat, and make mistakes (233). They suggest that self-management can produce the same negative side effects as systems of external consequences, and it encourages students who aren't really motivated to change their behavior to lie and cheat to gain rewards and avoid punishment (218, 238). In addition, it's more effective at improving academic performance than undesirable behavior (244), and it works best with students who have already been exposed to a teacher-managed consequences system (213, 230). They point out that self-management also works best with students who are motivated to behave appropriately, not students who need to be taught that it is necessary to change (233, 238, 243). Finally, it does not increase students' intrinsic motivation to behave correctly, and it often does not generalize. Even when it is effective in reducing certain target behaviors, it has little or no effect on the undesirable behaviors of students that aren't included in the consequences program. In addition, it does not generalize to other situations, and when the consequences are eliminated, the improvement often disappears (213, 239, 240, 243, 244).

Conclusions   The available evidence suggests that self-management suppresses undesirable behavior as well as teacher management does; however, the effects of both approaches don't generalize very well to other situations. Also, it is unclear how long changes are maintained over time in the absence of consequences. While self-management may require somewhat less teacher time in the long run, it does take considerable teacher time to train and supervise students at the outset. Very little evidence exists regarding the positive and negative side effects claimed for the technique or the types and ages of students it works best with, but the technique does seem to be more effective in keeping students on-task than in reducing their disruptive behavior. Despite these limitations, when it is advisable to use consequences to modify students' behavior, it may be worthwhile to employ a student-managed consequences system before resorting to a teacher-managed one.

Enhancing Generalization and Maintenance

As previously noted, the behavioral improvement that results from using teacher-managed or self-managed consequences to modify students' behavior often does not generalize. That is, students typically do not demonstrate improved behavior in situations in which they are not rewarded for behaving appropriately and do not lose rewards or receive punishments for behaving inappropriately. Moreover, once the extrinsic consequences are eliminated, the improvement is not maintained, and students' original behavioral patterns often return. The reason for this may be that until recently, the most frequent method of achieving generalization and maintenance was "train and hope" (253). That is, teachers trained students to behave appropriately and hoped that in the absence of continued reinforcement the change would be maintained and would generalize to other situations.

A number of procedures that have been shown to increase generalization and maintenance are being used by teachers with increasing frequency. These include sequential modification, variable/intermittent/unpredictable reinforcement schedules, fading, entrapment, and involving students' intrinsic motivation (245–255).

In sequential modification, students are rewarded or punished in multiple settings (in different classrooms, at recess, in the cafeteria, on the bus, etc.), during multiple times (mornings and afternoons), and/or by different individuals (different teachers, bus drivers, tutors, and monitors). Because students experience the consequences of their behavior in a variety of settings, at different times, and with different people, their behavior is more likely to generalize. Sequential modification requires a well-orchestrated, cooperative approach to students. This may be one reason why it is not used as often as it might be.

When teachers use variable/intermittent/unpredictable reinforcement schedules, they apply consequences to students according to an irregular or unpredictable schedule. Because students become accustomed to receiving consequences inconsistently, they are more likely to maintain their behavioral improvement in the absence of extrinsic consequences.

Fading consequences involves the gradual, rather than sudden, elimination of consequences. Slowly eliminating the extrinsic consequences that have led to behavioral improvement provides students the time and opportunity to accustom themselves to behaving appropriately, even in the absence of such consequences.

Entrapment occurs when students' desired behavioral change is maintained through the social behavior of their peers in naturalistic settings (246, 251). For example, the behavioral improvement of students who offer other students a turn because they receive extrinsic arbitrary rewards for doing so can be maintained in the absence of additional arbitrary rewards by the more natural rewards that the other children give them—their smiles, their willingness to reciprocate by offering them a turn, and so on. While these social reinforcers can occur naturally, teachers may also encourage and train students' peers to reinforce the appropriate behavior. This can be done by rewarding students' peers for responding to students' target behaviors in ways that entrap them.

Two behavioral programs that include entrapment and that have proved effective with young elementary school students are RECESS (Reprogramming Environmental Contingencies for Effective Social Skills) and PEERS (Procedures for Establishing Effective Relationship Skills) (248, 255). Research indicates that these programs produce behavioral improvement that generalizes to other environments.

Generalization of behavioral improvement is enhanced when students become intrinsically motivated to behave appropriately. Sometimes it is necessary to use extrinsic consequences to get students to behave in ways that are intrinsically rewarding. For example, until students stop trying to manipulate and intimidate people to get what they want, they may have poor relations with their teachers and peers, and until they stop cheating and try to learn what they are taught, they may not realize that they are capable of doing so. By pointing out to students the positive intrinsic results of their improved behavior in their relationships with others and in their improved self-esteem and self-confidence, teachers may be able to motivate students to continue to behave appropriately even when they are not rewarded for doing so or punished for not doing so.

Teachers who want their students' behavioral improvement to be maintained and to generalize should employ some of the preceding techniques. Training and hoping are insufficient.

Using Consequences Effectively

The techniques for using positive and negative consequences discussed in this chapter are particularly suitable for convincing students that it not only pays to behave appropriately but is also necessary to do so. The following process outlines how to use a number of these techniques in an organized way. In most cases, after following the process for a few weeks, you should see a real improvement in your students' behavior.

1. *Select just a few behaviors to change at first.* To require students to stop doing all the things they should not be doing and start doing all the things they should at once is to invite failure. A much better approach is for you and your students to select a few behaviors (target behaviors) to change *together.* If your students are active participants in the process, if they agree that the behavior should be changed, it is more likely that your efforts will be successful. Then you can manage, tolerate, or prevent the other behaviors until they can be changed. When you select behaviors, pick those that your students are most likely to have success with. Like adults, students find some bad habits easier to break than others, so start with something easy for them. If possible, save the behaviors that annoy you the most for later.

2. *Make sure your students know which specific behaviors they will have to change.* "Play nice with other children" is too vague. "Don't take other children's toys and don't hit other children" is more specific, and it's important to be specific.

3. *Determine how often the targeted behaviors occur to give you a baseline for evaluating the results of your efforts.* Some educators like to chart the frequency of the undesirable behaviors so they can have a visual picture of how this changes as students learn to behave more appropriately.

4. *Make sure, if possible, that your students no longer gain any rewards or positive consequences from their undesirable behaviors.* If you can eliminate the positive consequences of your students' unacceptable behaviors, they may stop the behaviors, because there's no longer any payoff. Unfortunately, this is not always possible. For example, you cannot always prevent students from getting an inherent payoff when they take others' toys or steal things from other students' lockers. In these instances, you may have to resort to extrinsic consequences to control your students' behavior. (See step 6.)

5. *If possible, substitute acceptable behaviors for unacceptable ones.* It is easier for anyone to give up unacceptable ways of achieving satisfaction when they are given other acceptable ways of doing so. Stealing, pushing ahead of others, and lying are unacceptable behaviors that have no acceptable substitutes. So this step does not apply to such behaviors. But students who grab things from others can be taught how to ask in a way that makes it more likely they will hear a "yes," and students who call out answers can learn to raise their hands and be called on.

6. *If necessary, use consequences to get your students to change their behavior.* Reward your students for behaving appropriately. If that does not work, punish students when they behave inappropriately. The specific consequences you choose should depend on which ones will have the desired effect on your students and which ones you are comfortable using. Smiles, pats on the back, praise, and approval can be effective positive rewards. Expressing your disapproval or just ignoring students is sometimes enough to discourage some young students from inappropriate behavior. Often, though, it is necessary to resort to other forms of rewards, such as gold stars,

points, and prizes, and/or the loss of such rewards or a time-out to motivate such students. Whether you use positive or negative consequences, they may work better if your students have a hand in selecting them.

When using consequences to change students' behavior, keep the following principles in mind:

- With older students, self-managed reward systems are generally preferable to those that teachers manage. If possible, teach your students to reward themselves for behaving appropriately. For example, students can reward themselves by reminding themselves that they are in control of their behavior, by focusing on what they are achieving, and by thinking about the positive natural consequences of their changed behavior, such as getting along better with their peers, learning to read better, or getting better grades. If these kinds of intrinsic, mental rewards are not enough, students can give themselves checks or points that can be converted to extrinsic rewards of their choice. But since some students may not be trustworthy enough to reward themselves only when they behave appropriately, you will have to determine whether this technique is feasible with a particular student.

- A successful beginning is essential. Reward students at the start of the program for behavior even if it only approximates the eventual goal in order to give them a feeling of success and to avoid feelings of discouragement and disappointment.

  Remember, some behaviors, especially new ones that students have not practiced, take time to learn correctly. Students may try to do what is expected of them but only accomplish something that resembles the desired behavior. In such cases, you will have to shape your students' behavior by making sure they are rewarded for closer and closer approximations to the desirable behavior. For example, at first young students who have not learned to share their things may only allow others to examine something for a moment. If they have not been willing to do even that before, reward them. Next, reward them for allowing others a short turn and later only when they give other students a fair turn.

- Substitute natural/intrinsic reinforcers for extrinsic reinforcers as soon as possible.

- Positive consequences are preferable to negative consequences.

- When you have to resort to negative consequences, logical, fair, and reasonable ones are more likely to be acceptable to youngsters.

- Apply negative consequences consistently but with flexibility.

- Following through convinces youngsters that you mean business.

- Proper timing enhances the effectiveness of consequences. In general—with some exceptions—reward students immediately for behaving appropriately, and punish them as soon as practical for misbehaving.

7. *Use one or more of the techniques described earlier for enhancing maintenance and generalization.*

8. *Evaluate the results of your efforts.* After a trial period of giving students time to learn the consequences of their behavior, determine whether it has improved. If your students' behavior has changed both in your classroom and outside of it, not only with you but also with others who are not using consequences, your efforts have succeeded.

    But if student behavior has only changed when you are there to administer consequences, then they have not changed their attitude about exercising self-control but only behave appropriately when it is necessary owing to external circumstances—namely, you. In such cases, they still have to change their basic attitude.

    If your students have not changed their behavior even with consequences to pay, your efforts have not worked at all. There are at least three possible explanations:

    - Students may be getting some positive reward from their negative behavior that you have overlooked. If so, eliminate this positive consequence.

    - You may have selected the wrong consequences. They may be too strong or too unfair and so spark rebellion. Or else they may not be significant enough to motivate students to behave differently.

    - It may be more difficult than you realized for students to change the particular behaviors you targeted. If you think this might be the case, continue your efforts a while longer. But if there's still no change, choose some other behavior that will be easier for your students to change.

9. *Eliminate any extrinsic reinforcements that may be maintaining the desired behavior and see if the behavior continues even without these reinforcements.* This is an important step because the ultimate goal is to help students behave appropriately even without external extrinsic consequences.

10. *Work toward attitudinal change.* When your students have changed the few behaviors you have been working on, use these successes to try to get your students to change their basic attitude. Point out how they are better off than before by saying things like: "Now that you are sharing things with other students, you have more friends. How does that make you feel? Don't you think you should wait your turn on the equipment during recess?" "Now that you're doing your own homework instead of copying, you're doing so much better in the course." "Remember all the arguments we used to have because you used to keep asking me for permission when I told you that you couldn't do something? Isn't it much better now that you take 'no' for an answer?"

    This final step is extremely important because the goal of this process is more than getting your students to change a few behaviors; rather, you are trying to change their attitude about the necessity of behaving appropriately.

Self-Quiz: Empowerment
Do you agree that overusing the techniques described in this chapter can lead to the disempowerment of students?

Empowering Students

Students who are empowered by their teachers are helped to believe they can achieve their goals, control their behavior, and meet the challenges that confront them because they themselves have the power to shape their destinies and futures. Those who are disempowered come to believe they lack the ability or potential to do so. Certain behavior management techniques can disempower students.

Deprecating students' backgrounds and treating them prejudicially have a harmful effect on students' self-concept and sense of power. Routinely and unnecessarily rewarding students may teach them to strive to please others rather than to accomplish their own internal motives and may contribute to their "learned helplessness" (256). Praising poor or non-European American students for trying even though they do not succeed or for achieving less than what is expected of others with the same ability can cause them to doubt whether they can succeed or accomplish what others can. And emphasizing teacher-managed techniques over self-managed techniques can lead students to believe that they are unable to manage themselves (256).

Some individuals are concerned that the techniques described in this chapter are being overused at the expense of those described in the previous chapter, believing that the use of extrinsic consequences disempowers students. The following remarks exemplify the view of many African American educators that using extrinsic consequences to modify the behavior of African American students does them more harm than good:

> Perhaps one of the most overriding criticisms of externally oriented management techniques is the tendency of teachers to use these approaches as control tactics rather than teaching students to become self-directing individuals. . . . Many otherwise promising teachers resort to interpreting and utilizing traditional management approaches as control tactics, which then results in making students behaviorally stifled, docile, overcompliant, and further doubt their abilities. Additionally, the use of these approaches in this vein has the tendency to foster impulsive conformity in students and often turns them off to school and learning. . . . Many behaviorally disordered Black children have histories of failure and have developed predispositions to expect failure and, thus, are often unwilling to take chances in learning situations. . . . Given this reality, management approaches which result in these students doubting their abilities further exacerbate an already regressive situation for the life progression of exceptional Black children. (257, pp. 1–14)

Critics of the overuse of extrinsic consequences to modify students' behavior maintain that to empower students, teachers should demonstrate their conviction that students can

Terminology

Many students and even many educators get confused by the terminology used to label techniques that involve using consequences to modify students' behavior. Therefore, it may be helpful to briefly explain the meaning of some of the terms that often appear in the literature but are not used in this text.

Various terms are currently in use to describe procedures for using rewards/positive reinforcement to encourage and increase the rate of students' appropriate behavior. The term *positive reinforcer* is similar to the term *reward* as used in this text. Thus, positively reinforcing students means more or less the same as rewarding students for behaving appropriately.

The terms *extinction* and *nonreinforcement* are similar to the term *planned ignoring* used in this text. They all apply to attempts to reduce undesirable behavior by eliminating any rewards—reinforcements that students may be deriving from their unacceptable behavior.

The term *differential reinforcement* is used to highlight the fact that acceptable/desirable behaviors are rewarded at a different rate than unacceptable/undesirable behaviors are ignored. Thus, differential reinforcement involves two simultaneous procedures: reinforcement/reward of desirable behavior and extinction/ignoring of undesirable behavior.

Response cost refers to procedures in which positive reinforcers (tokens, points, gold stars, credit toward free time, and the like) that are awarded students for behaving appropriately are eliminated when they behave inappropriately.

Educators use different terms for techniques that are designed to decelerate, discourage, or diminish students' inappropriate behavior. Some talk about using *negative reinforcement;* others use terms such as *aversive procedures, behavior reduction procedures,* or *punishment.* In this chapter, the term *punishment* is used for techniques that are designed to make the cost of behaving in undesirable and inappropriate ways high enough that students will choose to modify their behavior rather than pay the cost involved in continuing to misbehave.

and will control their own behavior. And they should assist them to do so without making them dependent on excessive or unnecessary teacher praise, assistance, or supervision:

> Our society thinks that "more discipline" will make a better world and certainly better schools. But doesn't the cry for discipline really translate to "let's try to help people act in a responsible manner"? This society desperately needs people who accept responsibility, not simply accept discipline. (258, p. 188)

Summary

Rewarding desirable behavior encourages students to behave appropriately if the rewards match your students' motivational development levels. Using rewards excessively or inappropriately can stifle students' creativity, cause competition among them, and make them overly dependent on the opinions of others.

In the real world, people conform to rules and regulations not only because they want to but also because they have to. Positive and negative consequences are a necessary and inescapable part of life both in and out of school. Using consequences to obtain students' compliance may be appropriate for young students still in the first stage of moral development. The possibility of incurring negative consequences is sometimes necessary to keep students from yielding to the temptation to misbehave, but with such students, the primary role of consequences should be to deter. Students who are not willing to behave appropriately if they can get away with it have to know that they will have to pay the consequences of their behavior. But punishment alone is not sufficient because it does not deal with the cause of the students' behavior and it does not increase their intrinsic motivation to want to behave appropriately in the absence of consequences. Even when punishment suppresses behavior, it is an abuse of teacher authority to punish students whose misbehavior is caused by other factors besides an unwillingness to conform to rules and regulations or an inability to resist temptations.

Activities

I. Complete the following chart about motivational differences at different developmental levels.

	PRIMARY GRADES	MIDDLE SCHOOL	HIGH SCHOOL
Why students comply with rules			
The forms of positive rewards they respond to			
The roles of extrinsic versus intrinsic rewards			
How much delay students can tolerate before they are rewarded			
The extent to which students can evaluate their behavior and achievements and reward themselves			

II. For each of the following behavior problems, decide whether the use of consequences to modify the behavior might be appropriate or inappropriate. Give the reasons for your opinions.
1. A 13-year-old student becomes angry and defensive whenever he is criticized.
2. A 17-year-old plays the clown.

3. A 7-year-old student has such a short attention span that she begins to talk to her neighbors or look or wander around the room before the seatwork time is half over.

4. A 9-year-old brings electronic games to class, although this is against the rules.

5. An 11-year-old rips up her artwork if she isn't satisfied with it.

6. A 14-year-old refuses to do remedial work at his level, claiming it's too easy.

7. A 6-year-old takes things from other students' cubbies.

8. After failing the last three tests, a 15-year-old has been cutting class two to four times a week.

9. An 8-year-old constantly talks to his neighbor despite being told not to.

10. A 12-year-old regularly comes to class without her homework, claiming she left it at home, lost it, left her books in school, and so forth.

III. List the various classroom/behavior management techniques that your high school and college instructors have tended to use to manage their students. Categorize these techniques as empowering or disempowering approaches.

IV. List the management techniques that you feel most comfortable using, and determine which approach you plan to use with your students.

References

These references discuss the detrimental effects of rewards.

1. Condry, J., & Chambers, J. (1978). Intrinsic motivation and the process of learning. In M. R. Lepper & D. Greene (Eds.), *The Hidden Costs of Reward: New Perspectives on the Psychology of Human Motivation.* New York: Erlbaum.

2. De Charms, R. (1976). *Enhancing Motivation: Change in the Classroom.* New York: Irvington.

3. Deci, E. L. (1976). *Intrinsic Motivation.* New York: Plenum Press.

4. Deci, E. L. (1978). Applications of research on the effects of rewards. In M. R. Lepper & D. Greene (Eds.), *The Hidden Costs of Reward: New Perspectives on the Psychology of Human Motivation.* New York: Erlbaum.

5. McGraw, K. G. (1978). The detrimental effects of reward on performance: A literature review and a prediction model. In M. R. Lepper & D. Greene (Eds.), *The Hidden Costs of Reward: New Perspectives on the Psychology of Human Motivation.* New York: Erlbaum.

6. Pittman, T., Boggiano, A., & Ruble, D. (1982). Intrinsic and extrinsic motivational orientations: Limiting conditions on the undermining and enhancing effects

of reward on intrinsic motivation. In J. Levine & M. Wang (Eds.), *Teacher-Student Perceptions: Implications for Learning.* Morristown, NJ: Erlbaum.

7. Ross, M. (1976). The self-perception of intrinsic motivation. In J. H. Harvey, W. J. Ickes, & R. F. Kidd (Eds.), *New Directions in Attributional Research* (Vol. 1). New York: Erlbaum.

The decreasing effectiveness of repeated rewards is examined in the following reference.

8. Safer, F., & Allen, R. (1976). *Hyperactive Children: Diagnosis and Management.* Baltimore: University Park Press.

The following references focus on developmental differences.

9. Forness, S. R. (1973). The reinforcement hierarchy. *Psychology in the Schools, 10,* 168–177.

10. Stallings, J. (1975). Implementation and child effects of teaching practices in Follow-Through classrooms. *Monograph of the Society for Research in Child Development, 40,* 7–8.

The references that follow describe learned helplessness and dependency.

11. Ginott, H. G. (1972). *Teacher and Child.* New York: Avon.

12. Kruglanski, A. W. (1978). Endogenous attribution and extrinsic motivation. In M. R. Lepper & D. Greene (Eds.), *The Hidden Costs of Reward: New Perspectives on the Psychology of Human Motivation.* New York: Erlbaum.

13. Weiner, B. (1979). A theory of motivation in some classroom experiences. *Journal of Educational Psychology, 71,* 3–25.

The negative effects of excessive unnecessary rewards on students' creativity are discussed in these references.

14. Jenke, S., & Peck, D. (1976). Is immediate reinforcement appropriate? *Arithmetic Teacher, 23,* 32–33.

15. Johnson, D., & Johnson, R. (1975). *Learning Together and Alone: Cooperation, Competition and Individualization.* Englewood Cliffs, NJ: Prentice-Hall.

16. Kruglanski, A. W., Friedman, I., & Zeevi, G. (1971). The effects of extrinsic incentive of some qualitative aspects of task performance. *Journal of Personality, 39,* 606–617.

17. Soar, R., & Soar, R. (1975). Classroom behavior, pupil characteristics, and pupil growth for the school year and summer. *JSAS Catalog of Selected Documents in Psychology, 5,* 873.

The references below discuss students' recruitment of praise.

18. Brophy, J. (1981). Teacher praise: A functional analysis. *Review of Educational Research, 51* (1), 5–32.

19. Stokes, T., Fowler, S., & Baer, D. (1978). Training preschool children to recruit material communities of reinforcement. *Journal of Applied Behavior Analysis, 68,* 488–500.

The importance of identifying the behavior being rewarded is examined in these references.

20. Harris, A., & Kapiche, R. (1978). Problems of quality control in the development and the use of behavior change technology in public school settings. *Education and Treatment of Children, 1,* 43–51.

21. Sharpley, C. F., & Sharpley, A. M. (1978). Contingent vs. noncontingent rewards in the classroom: A review of the literature. *Journal of School Psychology, 19* (3), 250–259.

The following references discuss inappropriate praise.

22. Amato, J. (1975). *Effect of Pupils' Social Class on Teachers' Expectations and Behavior.* Paper presented at the annual meeting of the American Psychological Association, Chicago.

23. Brookover, W., Schweitzer, J., Schneider, J., Beady, C., Flood, P., & Weisenbacker, J. (1978). Elementary school social climate and school achievement. *American Journal of Educational Research, 15,* 301–318.

24. Cooper, H. M. (1979). *Communication of Teacher Expectations to Students.* Paper presented at the conference on Teacher and Student Perceptions of Success and Failure and Applications for Learning and Instruction, University of Pittsburgh, Pittsburgh, PA.

25. Fernandez, C., Espinosa, R., & Dornbusch, S. (1975). *Factors Perpetuating the Low Academic Status of Chicano High School Students* (Memorandum No. 138). Palo Alto, CA: Stanford University, Center for Research and Development in Teaching.

26. Kleinfeld, J. (1975). Effective teachers of Eskimo and Indian students. *School Review, 82,* 301–344.

27. Weinstein, R. (1976). Reading group membership in first grade: Teacher behavior and pupil experience over time. *Journal of Educational Psychology, 68,* 103–116.

How students perceive rewards is discussed in the following reference.

28. Ware, B. (1978). What rewards do students want? *Phi Delta Kappan, 59,* 355–356.

The following references are concerned with students' attributions of the cause of their success.

29. Anderson, L., & Prawat, R. (1983). Responsibility in the classroom: A synthesis of research on self-control. *Educational Leadership, 40* (7), 62–66.

30. Andrews, G., & Debus, R. (1978). Persistence and the causal perception of failure: Modifying cognitive attributions. *Journal of Educational Psychology, 70,* 154–166.

31. Chapin, M., & Dyck, D. (1975). Persistence in children's reading behavior as a function of N length and attribution training. *Journal of Abnormal Psychology, 85,* 511–515.

32. Dweck, C. (1975). The role of expectation and attribution in the alleviation of learned helplessness. *Journal of Personal and Social Psychology, 31,* 674–685.

33. Weier, B. C. (1979). A theory of motivation for some classroom experiences. *Journal of Educational Psychology, 71,* 3–25.

The motivational development of students is discussed in the references below.

34. Brophy, J. E. (1981). Teacher praise: A functional analysis. *Review of Educational Research, 51* (1), 5–32.

35. Hartner, S. (1978). Effectance motivation reconsidered: Toward a developmental model. *Human Development, 21,* 34–64.

36. Meyer, W. U., Bachmann, M., Bierman, U., Hempelmann, M., Plager, F. O., & Spiller, H. (1979). The information value of evaluative behavior: Influences of praise and blame on perceptions of ability. *Journal of Educational Psychology, 79,* 259–268.

37. Walker, H. (1979). *The Acting Out Child: Coping With Classroom Disruption.* Boston: Allyn & Bacon.

The following references relate to the relative effectiveness of individual and group rewards.

38. McLaughlin, T. F. (1981). The effects of individual and group contingencies on reading performance of special education students. *Contemporary Educational Psychology, 6,* 76–79.

39. Salend, S. J., Whittaker, C. R., & Reeder, E. (1992). Group evaluation: Peer-mediated behavior management system. *Exceptional Children, 59* (3), 203–209.

40. Silvernail, D. L. (1986). *Teaching Styles as Related to Student Achievement* (2nd ed.). Washington, DC: National Educational Association.

Rewarding improvement is discussed in the references below.

41. Bolstad, O. D., & Johnson, S. M. (1972). Self-regulation in the modification of disruptive classroom behavior. *Journal of Applied Behavior Analysis, 5,* 443–454.

42. Deitz, S. M., & Repp, R. (1973). Decreasing classroom behavior through DRL schedules of reinforcement. *Journal of Applied Behavior Analysis, 6,* 457–463.

The following references discuss the advantages and disadvantages of using peers as models.

43. Brophy, J. E., & Putnam, J. C. (1978). *Classroom Management in the Elementary Grades.* ERIC ED 167 537.

44. Charles, C. M. (1981). *Building Classroom Discipline: From Models to Practice.* White Plains, NY: Longman.

45. Clarizio, H. F. (1986). *Toward Positive Classroom Discipline* (3rd ed.). New York: Wiley.

46. Long, J. D., & Frye, H. V. (1981). *Making It Till Friday: A Guide to Successful Classroom Management.* Princeton: Princeton Book Company.

47. Sabatino, D. A. (1987). Preventive discipline as a practice in special education. *Teaching Exceptional Children, 19* (4), 8–11.

Planned ignoring is the focus of these references.

48. Hall, R. V., Fox, R., Willard, D., Goldsmith, L., Emerson, M., Owen, M., Davis, F., & Porcia, E. (1971). The teacher as observer and experimenter in the modification of disputing and talking-out behaviors. *Journal of Applied Behavior Analysis, 4,* 141–149.

49. Jones, F., & Miller, W. H. (1971). *The Effective Use of Negative Attention for Reducing Group Disruption in Special Elementary Classrooms.* Department of Psychiatry, University of California at Los Angeles.

50. Kazdin, A. E. (1973). The effect of vicarious reinforcement on attentive behavior in the classroom. *Journal of Applied Behavior Analysis, 6,* 71–78.

51. Masden, C. H., Becker, W. C., Thomas, D. R., Koser, L., & Plager, E. (1968). An analysis of the reinforcing function of "sit down" commands. In R. K. Parker (Ed.), *Readings in Educational Psychology.* Boston: Allyn & Bacon.

52. O'Leary, K. D., Kaufman, K. F., Kass, R. E., & Drabman, R. S. (1970). The effects of loud and soft reprimands on the behavior of disruptive students. *Exceptional Children, 37,* 145–155.

53. Patterson, G. R. (1965). An application of conditioning techniques to the control of a hyperactive child. In L. P. Ullman & L. Krasner (Eds.), *Case Studies in Behavior Modification.* New York: Holt, Rinehart & Winston.

54. Warren, S. A. (1971). Behavior modification—Boon, bane, or both? *Mental Retardation, 9,* 2.

These references deal with students' perceptions of consequences.

55. Burchard, J. D., & Barrera, F. (1972). An analysis of time-out and response cost in a programmed environment. *Journal of Applied Behavior Analysis, 51,* 271–282.

56. Favell, J. E., McGimsey, J. S., & Jones, M. L. (1978). The use of physical restraint in the treatment of self-injury and positive reinforcement. *Journal of Applied Behavior Analysis, 11,* 225–241.

57. Lovaas, I. O., & Bucher, B. D. (1974). *Perspectives in Behavior Modification with Deviant Children.* Englewood Cliffs, NJ: Prentice-Hall.

These references document the importance of providing a rational cognitive structure.

58. MacMillan, D. L., Forness, S., & Trumbull, B. M. (1973). The role of punishment in the classroom. *Exceptional Children, 40,* 85–96.

59. Parke, R. D. (1969). Effectiveness of punishment as an interaction of intensity, timing, and cognitive structuring. *Child Development, 49,* 213–235.

60. Parke, R. D. (1977). Punishment in children: Effects, side effects, and alternative strategies. In H. L. Hom & P. A. Robins (Eds.), *Psychological Processes in Early Education.* New York: Academic Press.

The advantages of providing alternative behaviors are explained in these references.

61. Anderson, L. M., Evertson, C. M., & Emmer, E. T. (1979). *Dimensions in Classroom Management Derived from Recent Research.* ERIC ED 175 860.

62. Aronfreed, J. M. (1968). Aversive control of socialization. In W. J. Arnold (Ed.), *National Symposium on Motivation 1968.* Lincoln, NE: University of Nebraska Press.

63. Knapczyk, D. R. (1992). Effects of developing alternative responses on the aggressive behavior of adolescents. *Behavioral Disorders, 17* (4), 247–263.

The intensity of punishments is a focus of the following references.

64. Arzin, N., & Holz, W. (1966). Punishment. In W. K. Honig (Ed.), *Operant Behavior: Areas of Research and Application.* New York: Appleton-Century-Crofts.

65. Burchard, J. D., & Barrera, F. (1972). An analysis of time-out and response cost in a programmed environment. *Journal of Applied Behavior Analysis, 5,* 271–282.

66. Gnagey, W. J. (1981). *Motivating Classroom Discipline.* New York: Macmillan.

67. Hobbs, S. A., Forehand, R., & Murray, R. G. (1978). Effects of various durations of time-out on the non-compliant behavior of children. *Behavior Therapy, 9,* 652–656.

68. Morgan, D. P., & Jenson, W. R. (1988). *Teaching Behaviorally Disordered Students: Preferred Practice.* Columbus, OH: Merrill.

The pros and cons of consistency are discussed in these references.

69. Deur, J. L., & Parke, R. D. (1970). Effects of inconsistent punishment on aggression in children. *Developmental Psychology, 2* (5).

70. Learning Books (1987). *Classroom Management.* Springhouse, PA: Springhouse.

71. Parke, R. D., & Sawin, D. B. (1975). *The Effects of Inter-agent Inconsistent Discipline and Aggressive Children.* Unpublished manuscript. Fels Research Institute, Wayne State University, Yellow Springs, OH.

72. Stouwie, R. J. (1972). An experimental study of adult dominance and warmth, conflicting verbal instruction and children's moral behavior. *Child Development, 43,* 959–972.

73. Tanner, L. N. (1978). *Classroom Discipline for Effective Teaching and Learning.* New York: Holt, Rinehart & Winston.

74. Walters, G. C., & Grusec, J. E. (1977). *Punishment.* San Francisco: Freeman.

75. Walters, R., Parke, R., & Cane, V. (1965). Timing of punishment and the observation of consequences to others as determinants of response inhibition. *Journal of Experimental Child Psychology, 2,* 10–30.

These references discuss the timing of consequences.

76. Aronfreed, J., & Reber, A. (1965). Internalized behavioral suppression and the timing of social punishment. *Journal of Personality and Social Psychology, 1,* 3–16.

77. Parke, R. D. (1970). The role of punishment in the socialization process. In R. A. Hoppe, G. A. Milton, & E. Simmel (Eds.), *Early Experiences in the Process of Socialization.* New York: Academic Press.

The listings below discuss expressing disapproval of students' actions or behavior.

78. Becker, W., Engelmann, S., & Thomas, D. (1975). *Teaching 1: Classroom Management.* Chicago: Research Press.

79. Berliner, D. (1978). *Changing Academic Learning Time: Clinical Intervention in Four Classrooms.* Paper presented at the annual meeting of the American Education Research Association, Toronto.

80. Cangelosi, J. S. (1988). *Classroom Management Strategies: Gaining and Maintaining Students' Cooperation.* White Plains, NY: Longman.

81. Fisher, C. W., Berliner, D. C., Filby, N. N., Marliave, R., Cahen, L. S., & Dishaw, M. M. (1980). Teaching behaviors, academic learning time, and student achievement: An overview. In C. Denham and A. Lieberman (Eds.), *Time to Learn.* Washington, DC: National Institute of Education.

82. Ginott, H. G. (1972). *Teacher and Child.* New York: Avon.

83. Hall, R. V., Axelrod, S., Foundopoulos, M., Campbell, R. A., & Cranston, S. S. (1971). The effective use of punishment to modify behavior in the classroom. *Educational Technology, 11,* 24–26.

84. Kounin, J. S. (1970). *Discipline and Group Management in Classrooms.* New York: Holt, Rinehart & Winston.

85. O'Leary, K. D., Kaufman, K. F., Kass, R. E., & Drabman, R. S. (1970). The effects of loud and soft reprimands on the behavior of disruptive students. *Exceptional Children, 37,* 145–155.

86. Spear, P. S. (1970). Motivational effects of praise and criticism on children's learning. *Developmental Psychology, 3* (1), 124–132.

87. Thomas, J. D., Presland, I. E., Grant, M. D., & Glynn, T. L. (1978). Natural rates of teacher approval and disapproval in grade 7 classrooms. *Journal of Applied Behavior Analysis, 11* (1), 91–94.

88. Turco, T. L., & Elliott, S. N. (1986). Assessment of students' acceptability ratings of teacher-initiated interventions for classroom misbehavior. *Journal of School Psychology, 24*, 277–283.

89. Van Horn, K. L. (1982). *The Utah Pupil/Teacher Self-Concept Program: Teacher Strategies that Invite Improvement of Pupil and Teacher Self-Concept.* Paper presented at the annual meeting of the American Educational Research Association, New York.

90. Van Houten, R., Mau, P. A., MacKenzie-Keating, S. E., Sameoto, D., & Colavecchia, B. (1980). An analysis of some variables influencing the effectiveness of reprimands. *Journal of Applied Behavior Analysis, 15*, 65–83.

91. White, M. A. (1975). Natural rates of teacher approval and disapproval in the classroom. *Journal of Applied Behavior Analysis, 8* (4), 367–372.

The citations that follow discuss applying logical consequences.

92. Dreikurs, R., Grunwald, B., & Pepper, F. (1982). *Maintaining Sanity in the Classroom* (2nd ed.). New York: Harper & Row.

93. Glasser, W. (1969). *Schools Without Failure.* New York: Harper & Row.

94. Weber, W. A., Roff, L. A., Crawford, J., & Robinson, C. (1983). *Classroom Management: Reviews of the Teacher Education and Research Literature.* Princeton: Educational Testing Service.

Overcorrection is a focus of the references below.

95. Axelrod, S., Branter, J. P., & Meddock, T. D. (1978). Overcorrection: A review and critical analysis. *Journal of Special Education, 12*, 367–391.

96. Arzin, N. H., & Powers, M. A. (1975). Eliminating classroom disturbances of emotionally disturbed children by positive practice procedures. *Behavior Therapy, 6*, 525–534.

97. Barton, E. J., & Osborne, J. G. (1978). The development of classroom sharing by a teacher using positive practice. *Behavior Modification, 2*, 231–250.

98. Doleys, S. M., Wells, K. C., Hobbs, S. A., Roberts, M. W., & Cartelli, L. M. (1976). The effects of social punishment on non-compliance: A comparison of time-out and positive practice. *Journal of Applied Behavior Analysis, 9*, 471–482.

99. Foxx, R. M., & Arzin, N. H. (1972). Restitution: A method of eliminating aggressive-disruptive behavior of mentally retarded and brain damaged patients. *Behavior Research and Therapy, 10*, 15–27.

100. Hobbs, S. A. (1976). Modifying stereotyped behavior by overcorrection: A critical review. *Rehabilitation Psychology, 23*, 1–11.

101. Matson, J. L., Ollendick, T. H., & Martin, J. E. (1979). Overcorrection: A long-term follow-up. *Journal of Behavior Therapy and Experimental Psychiatry, 10*, 11–13.

102. Osborne, J. G. (1976). Overcorrection and behavior therapy: A reply to Hobbs. *Rehabilitation Psychology, 23,* 13–31.

These references discuss time-out.

103. Bean, A. W., & Roberts, M. W. (1981). The effects of time-out release contingencies on changes in child non-compliance. *Journal of Abnormal Child Psychology, 9,* 95–105.

104. Broden, M., Hall, R. V., Dunlap, A., & Clark, R. (1970). Effects of teacher attention and a token reinforcement system in a junior high school special education class. *Exceptional Children, 36,* 341–349.

105. Clarizio, H. F. (1980). *Toward Positive Classroom Discipline* (3rd ed.). New York: Wiley.

106. Clark, H. B., Rowburry, T., Baer, A. M., & Baer, D. M. (1973). Time-out as a punishing stimulus in continuous and intermittent schedules. *Journal of Applied Behavior Analysis, 6,* 443–455.

107. Foxx, R. M., & Shapiro, S. T. (1978). The time-out ribbon: A nonexclusionary time-out procedure. *Journal of Applied Behavior Analysis, 11,* 125–136.

108. Gast, D. L., & Nelson, C. M. (1977). Legal and ethical considerations for the use of time-out in special education settings. *Journal of Special Education, 11* (4), 457–467.

109. Lakey, B. B., McNess, M. P., & McNess, M. C. (1973). Control of an obscene "verbal tic" through time-out in an elementary classroom. *Journal of Applied Behavior Analysis, 6,* 101–104.

110. LeBlanc, J. M., Busby, K. H., & Thomson, C. L. (1974). The function of time-out for changing the aggressive behaviors of a preschool child: A multiple base line analysis. In R. Ulrich, T. Stachnik, & J. Mabry (Eds.), *Control of Human Behavior* (Vol. 3). Glenview, IL: Scott, Foresman.

111. Long, J. D., & Frye, V. H. (1981). *Making It Till Friday: A Guide to Successful Classroom Management* (2nd ed.). Princeton: Princeton Book Company.

112. Mauer, R. E. (1985). *Elementary Discipline Handbook: Solutions for the K–8 Teacher.* West Nyack, NY: Center for Applied Research in Education.

113. Morgan, D. P., & Jenson, D. P. (1988). *Teaching Behaviorally Disordered Students: Preferred Practices.* Columbus, OH: Merrill.

114. Pease, G. A., & Tyler, O. T., Jr. (1979). Self-regulation of time-out duration in the modification of disruptive classroom behavior. *Psychology in the Schools, 16* (27), 101–105.

115. Porterfield, J. K., Herbert-Jackson, E., & Risley, T. R. (1976). Contingent observation: An effective and acceptable procedure for reducing disruptive behavior of young children in a group setting. *Journal of Applied Behavior Analysis, 9,* 55–64.

116. Powell, T. H., & Powell, I. Q. (1982). The use and abuse of using time-out procedures for disruptive pupils. *Pointer, 26,* 18–22.

117. Redl, F., & Wattenberg, W. (1959). *Mental Hygiene in Teaching* (2nd ed.). New York: Harcourt, Brace.

118. Roberts, M. W. (1982). The effects of warned versus unwarned time-out procedures on child noncompliance. *Child and Family Behavior Therapy, 4,* 37–53.

119. Sloane, H. N., Buckholdt, D. R., Jenson, W. R., & Crandal, J. A. (1979). *Structured Teaching: A Design for Classroom Management and Instruction.* Champaign, IL: Research Press.

120. Wallen, C. J., & Wallen, L. L. (1978). *Effective Classroom Management.* Boston: Allyn & Bacon.

121. Weber, W. A., Roff, L. A., Crawford, J., & Robinson, C. (1983). *Classroom Management: Reviews of the Teacher Education and Research Literature.* Princeton: Educational Testing Service.

122. White, G. D., Nielson, G., & Johnson, S. M. (1972). Time-out duration and the suppression of deviant behavior in children. *Journal of Applied Behavior Analysis, 5,* 111–120.

These references discuss contingency contracts.

123. Arwood, B., Williams, R. L., & Long, J. D. (1974). The effects of behavior contracts and behavior proclamations on social conduct and academic achievement in a ninth grade English class. *Adolescence, 9,* 425–436.

124. Clark, L. N. (1978). Let's make a deal: Contingency contracting with adolescents. *American Secondary Education, 8,* 12–23.

125. De Risi, W., & Butz, G. (1975). *Writing Behavioral Contracts.* Champaign, IL: Research Press.

126. Downing, J. A. (1990). Contingency contracts: A step by step format. *Intervention in School and Clinic, 26* (2), 111–113.

127. Good, T. L., Biddle, B. J., & Brophy, J. E. (1975). *Teachers Make a Difference.* New York: Holt, Rinehart & Winston.

128. Hackney, H. (1974). Aplying behavior contracts to chronic problems. *School Counselor, 22,* 23–30.

129. Sapp, G. L. (1971). *The Application of Contingency Management Systems to the Classroom Behavior of Negro Adolescents.* Paper presented at the annual meeting of the American Personnel and Guidance Association, Atlantic City, NJ.

130. Sulzer-Azaroff, B., & Mayer, G. (1977). *Applying Behavior Analysis Procedures with Children.* New York: Holt, Rinehart & Winston.

131. White-Blackburn, G., Semb, S., & Semb, G. (1977). The effects of a good-behavior contract on the classroom behavior of sixth grade students. *Journal of Applied Behavior Analysis, 10,* 312.

132. Williams, R. L., Long, J. D., & Yoakley, R. W. (1972). The utility of behavior contracts and behavior proclamations with advantaged senior high school students. *Journal of School Psychology, 10,* 329–338.

These references discuss techniques that are controversial and thought to be unacceptable by many teachers.

133. Altman, R., & Talkington, L. W. (1971). Modeling: An alternative behavior modification approach for retardates. *Mental Retardation, 9* (3), 20–23.

134. Barba, L. (1979). *A Survey of the Literature on the Attitudes Toward the Administration of Corporal Punishment in Schools.* ERIC ED 186 538.

135. Becker, W. C., Engelmann, S., & Thomas, D. (n.d.) *Teaching I: Classroom Management.* Chicago: Science Research Associates.

136. Bellafiore, L. A., & Salend, S. J. (1983). Modifying inappropriate behavior through a peer confrontation system. *Behavioral Disorders, 8,* 274–279.

137. Bongiovanni, A. F. (1977). A review of research on the effects of punishment: Implications for corporal punishment in the schools. In Wise, J. H. (Ed.), *Proceedings: Conference on Corporal Punishment in the Schools: A National Debate.* ERIC ED 144 185.

138. Bongiovanni, A. F. (1979). An analysis of research on punishment and its relation to the use of corporal punishment in schools. In I. A. Hyman & J. Wise (Eds.), *Corporal Punishment in American Education.* Philadelphia: Temple University Press.

139. Clarke, J., et al. (1984). *Analysis of Recent Corporal Punishment Cases Reported in National Newspapers.* Paper presented at the annual convention of the National Association of School Psychologists, Philadelphia.

140. Cryan, J. R. (1987). The banning of corporal punishment: In child care, school and other educative settings in the U.S. *Childhood Education, 53* (3), 145–153.

141. Dobson, J. (1970). *Dare to Discipline.* Wheaton, IL: Tyndale House Publishers.

142. Dubanoski, R. A., et al. (1983). Corporal punishment in schools: Myths, problems and alternatives. *Child Abuse and Neglect, 7* (3), 271–278.

143. Forness, S. R., & Sinclair, E. (1984). Avoiding corporal punishment in schools: Issues for school counselors. *Elementary School Guidance and Counseling, 18* (4), 268–275.

144. Guess, D., Helmsetter, E., Turnbull, R. H., & Knowlton, S. (1987). *Use of Aversive Procedures with Persons Who Are Disabled: A Historical Review and Critical Analysis.* Seattle: Association for Persons with Severe Handicaps.

145. Henson, K. T. (1985). Corporal punishment: Ten popular myths. *High School Journal, 69* (2), 107–109.

146. Hyman, I. A. (1989). Eliminating corporal punishment in schools: Moving from advocacy to policy implementation. *Discipline, 9* (1), 9–16.

147. Hyman, I. A., & Wise, J. H. (Eds.). (1979). *Corporal Punishment in American Schools*. Philadelphia: Temple University Press.

148. Jones, F. H. (1987). *Positive Classroom Discipline*. New York: McGraw-Hill.

149. Kauffman, J. M., Pullen, P. L., & Akers, E. (1986). Classroom management: Teacher-child-peer relationships. *Focus on Exceptional Children, 19* (1), 1–10.

150. Kelly, P. C., Weir, M. R., & Fearnow, R. G. (1985). A survey of parental opinions of corporal punishment in schools. *Journal of Developmental and Behavioral Pediatrics, 6* (3), 143–145.

151. Kessler, G. (1985). Spanking in schools: Deterrent or barbarism? *Childhood Education, 61* (3), 175–176.

152. Kinnard, K. W., & Rust, J. O. (1981). Corporal punishment in Tennessee schools. *Tennessee Education, 7* (2), 11–17.

153. Litow, L., & Pumroy, D. (1975). A brief review of classroom oriented contingencies. *Journal of Applied Behavior Analysis, 8*, 341–347.

154. Mauer, A. (1977). All in the name of the "last resort." In J. H. Wise (Ed.), *Proceedings: Conference on Corporal Punishment in the Schools: A National Debate*. ERIC ED 144 185.

155. Mauer, A., & Wallerstein, J. S. (1984). *The Influence of Corporal Punishment on Learning: A Statistical Analysis*. Berkeley, CA: Generation Books.

156. Nevin, A., Johnson, D. W., & Johnson, R. (1982). Effects of group and individual contingencies on academic performance and social relation of special needs students. *Journal of Social Psychology, 116* (1), 41–59.

157. Newbold, K. R. (1976). Use of corporal punishment in North Carolina public schools. In R. S. Welsh, et al., *The Supreme Court Spanking Ruling: An Issue in Debate*. ERIC ED 151 644.

158. Patterson, J. (1974). How popular is the paddle? *Phi Delta Kappan, 55*, 707.

159. Ramella, R. (1974). Anatomy of discipline: Should punishment be corporal? *PTA Magazine, 67*, 24–27.

160. Redd, W. H., Morris, E. K., & Martin, J. A. (1975). Effects of positive and negative adult-child interaction on children's social preferences. *Journal of Experimental Child Psychology, 19*, 153–164.

161. Reinholz, L. (1976). A practical defense of corporal punishment. In R. S. Welsh, et al., *The Supreme Court Spanking Ruling: An Issue in Debate*. ERIC ED 151 644.

162. Rose, T. L. (1984). Current uses of corporal punishment in American public schools. *Journal of Educational Psychology, 76* (3), 427–444.

163. Rose, T. L. (1989). Corporal punishment with mildly handicapped students: Five years later. *Remedial and Special Education, 10* (1), 43–52.

164. Rust, J. O., & Kinnard, K. Q. (1983). Personality characteristics of the users of corporal punishment in the schools. *Journal of School Psychology, 21*, 91–105.

165. Sabatino, D. A., Sabatino, A. C., & Mann, L. (1983). *Discipline and Behavioral Management: A Handbook of Tactics, Strategies, and Programs.* Rockville, MD: Aspen.

166. Salend, S. J., Jantzen, N. R., & Giek, K. (1992). Using a peer confrontation system in a group setting. *Behavioral Disorders, 17* (3), 211–218.

167. Sandler, A. G., Arnold, L. B., Gable, R. A., & Strain, P. S. (1987). Effects of peer pressure on disruptive behavior of behaviorally disordered classmates. *Behavioral Disorders, 12*, 104–110.

168. Shaw, S. R., & Braden, J. P. (1990). Race and gender bias in the administration of corporal punishment. *School Psychology Review, 19* (3), 378–383.

169. Simpson, M. (1988). Let the paddler beware. *NEA Today, 6* (1), 27.

170. Smith, J. D., Polloway, E. A., & West, G. K. (1979). Corporal punishment and its implications for exceptional children. *Journal for Exceptional Children, 45* (4), 264–268.

171. Staff. (1990, fall). Nineteen states have banned corporal punishment. *POPS News*, 3.

172. Stevens, L. B. (1983). *Suspension and Corporal Punishment of Students in the Cleveland Public Schools, 1981–1982.* Cleveland, OH: Office of School Monitoring and Community Relations.

173. Strike, K., & Soltis, J. (1986). Who broke the fish tank? And other ethical dilemmas. *Instructor, 95*, 36–37.

174. Sulzer-Azaroff, B., & Mayer, G. R. (1977). *Applying Behavior Analysis Procedures with Children and Youth.* New York: Holt, Rinehart & Winston.

175. Thomas, D. R., Becker, W. C., & Armstrong, M. (1968). Production and elimination of disruptive behavior by systematically varying teachers' behavior. *Journal of Applied Behavior Analysis, 1*, 35–45.

176. Tuhus, M. (1987). It's time we stop paddling kids. *Instructor, 95* (7), 16–19.

177. Van Dyke, H. T. (1984). Corporal punishments in our schools. *Clearing House, 57*, 296–300.

178. Vrederoe, L. E. (1974). Embarrassment and ridicule. In *Discipline in the Classroom* (rev. ed.). Washington, DC: National Education Association.

179. Welsh, R. S. (1985). Spanking: A grand old American tradition. *Children Today, 17*, 25–29.

180. Wright, D., & Moles, O. (1985). *Legal Issues in Educational Order: Principals' Perceptions of School Discipline Policies and Practices.* Paper presented at the annual meeting of the American Educational Research Association, Chicago.

The pros and cons of mild punishments are included in the following references:

181. Drabman, R., & Lakey, B. (1974). Feedback in classroom behavior modification: Effects on the target child and her classmates. *Journal of Applied Behavior Analysis, 7,* 591–598.

182. Englander, M. E. (1986). *Strategies for Classroom Discipline.* New York: Praeger.

183. Garner, H. S. (1976). A truce in the war for the child. *Exceptional Children, 42* (6), 315–320.

184. Gelfand, D. M., Hartmann, D. P., Lamb, A. K., Smith, C. L., Makan, M. A., & Paul, S. C. (1974). The effects of adult models and descriptive alternatives on children's choice of behavior management techniques. *Child Development, 45,* 585–593.

185. Iwata, B. A., & Bailey, J. S. (1974). Reward vs. cost token systems: An analysis of the effects on students and teachers. *Journal of Applied Behavior Analysis, 7,* 567–576.

186. Johnson, L. V., & Bany, M. A. (1976). *Classroom Management: Theory and Skill Training.* New York: Macmillan.

187. Kalish, H. I. (1981). *From Behavioral Science to Behavior Modification.* New York: McGraw-Hill.

188. Lawrence, E. A., & Winschel, J. F. (1975). Locus of control: Implications for special education. *Exceptional Children, 41,* 483–489.

189. McLaughlin, F. T., & Malaby, J. (1972). Reducing and measuring inappropriate verbalizations in a token classroom. *Journal of Applied Behavior Analysis, 5,* 329–333.

190. McManis, D. L. (1967). Marble sorting persistence in mixed verbal incentive and performance level pairings. *American Journal of Mental Deficiency, 71,* 811–817.

191. Mischel, W., & Grusec, J. E. (1966). Determinants of the rehearsal and transmission of neutral and aversive behaviors. *Journal of Personality and Social Psychology, 3,* 197–205.

192. Newsom, C., Favell, J. E., & Rincover, A. (1983). Side effects of punishment. In S. Axelrod & J. Apsche (Eds.), *The Effects of Punishment on Human Behavior.* New York: Academic Press.

193. O'Leary, D., Becker, W., Evans, M., & Saudergas, R. (1969). A token reinforcement program in a public school: A replication and systematic analysis. *Journal of Applied Behavior Analysis, 2,* 3–13.

194. Oliver, S. D., West, R. C., & Sloane, N. H. (1974). Some effects on human behavior of aversive events. *Behavior Therapy, 5,* 481–493.

195. Pace, D. M., & Foreman, S. G. (1982). Variables related to the effectiveness of response cost. *Psychology in the Schools, 19* (3), 365–370.

196. Pazulinec, R., Meyerrose, M., & Sajwaj, T. (1983). Punishment via response cost. In S. Axelrod and J. Apsche (Eds.), *The Effects of Punishment on Human Behavior.* New York: Academic Press.

197. Phillips, E. L., Phillips, E. A., Fixsen, D. L., & Wolf, M. M. (1971). Achievement place: Token reinforcement procedures in a home-styled rehabilitation setting for predelinquent boys. *Journal of Applied Behavior Analysis, 4,* 45–59.

198. Ryan, B. A. (1979). A case against behavior modification in the "ordinary" classroom. *Journal of School Psychology, 17* (2), 131–136.

199. Steuer, F. B., Applefield, J. M., & Smith, R. (1971). Televised aggression and the interpersonal aggression of preschool children. *Journal of Experimental Child Psychology, 11,* 442–447.

200. Sulzer, B., & Mayer, G. B. (1972). *Behavior Modification Procedures for School Personnel.* Hinsdale, IL: Dryden Press.

201. Swanson, L. (1979). Removal of positive reinforcement to alter LD adolescents' preacademic problems. *Psychology in the Schools, 16* (2), 286–292.

202. Walker, H. M. (1983). Application of response costs in school setting: Outcomes, issues and recommendations. *Exceptional Education Quarterly, 3,* 47–55.

203. Warren, S. A. (1971). Behavior modification—Boon, bane, or both? *Mental Retardation, 9,* 2.

204. Witt, J. C., Elliot, S. N. (1982). The response cost lottery: A time efficient and effective classroom intervention. *Journal of School Psychology, 20,* 155–161.

These references discuss the controversy over the use of harsh forms of punishment.

205. Brantinger, E. (1991). Social class distinctions in adolescents' reports of problems and punishments in school. *Behavioral Disorders, 17* (1), 36–46.

206. England, R. E., Meier, K. J., & Fraga, L. R. (1988). Barriers to equal opportunity: Educational practices and minority students. *Urban Affairs Quarterly, 23,* 635–646.

207. Gunter, P. L., Kenton, J., Lack, S. L., Shores, R. E., & Nelson, C. M. (1993). Aversive stimuli in academic interactions between students with serious emotional disturbances and their teachers. *Behavioral Disorders, 18* (4), 265–274.

208. McCarthy, J., & Hoge, D. (1987). The social construction of school punishment: Racial disadvantage out of universalistic process. *Social Forces, 65,* 1101–1220.

209. Polsgrove, L. (Ed.). (1991). *Reducing Undesirable Behavior.* Reston, VA: Council for Exceptional Children.

210. Rose, T. (1988). Current disciplinary practices with handicapped students: Suspensions and expulsions. *Exceptional Children, 55,* 230–239.

211. Rose, T. L. (1989). Corporal punishment with mildly handicapped students: Five years later. *Remedial and Special Education, 10* (1), 43–52.

212. Van Houten, R., Axelrod, S., Bailey, J. S., Favell, J. E., Foxx, R. M., Iwata, B. A., & Lovaas, O. I. (1988). The right to effective behavioral treatment. *Journal of Applied Behavioral Analysis, 21,* 381–384.

Self-management is the focus of these references.

213. Baer, D. M., Fowler, S. A., & Carden-Smith, L. (1984). Using reinforcement and independent grading to promote and maintain task accuracy in a mainstreamed class. *Analysis and Intervention in Developmental Disabilities, 4,* 157–169.

214. Bolstad, O. D., & Johnson, S. M. (1972). Self-regulation in the modification of disruptive classroom behavior. *Journal of Applied Behavior Analysis, 5,* 443–454.

215. Clement, P. W. (1973). Training children to be their own behavior therapists. *Journal of School Health, 43,* 615–620.

216. Drabman, R. S., Spitalnik, R., & O'Leary, K. D. (1973). Teaching self-control to disruptive children. *Journal of Abnormal Psychology, 82,* 10–16.

217. Epstein, R., & Goss, C. M. (1978). A self-control procedure for the maintenance of nondisruptive behavior in an elementary school child. *Behavior Therapy, 9,* 109–117.

218. Felixbrod, J., & O'Leary, K. D. (1973). Effects of reinforcement on children's academic behavior as a function of self-determined and externally imposed contingencies. *Journal of Applied Behavior Analysis, 6,* 241–250.

219. Frith, G. H., & Armstrong, S. W. (1986). Self-monitoring for behavior disordered students. *Teaching Exceptional Children, 18,* 144–148.

220. Glynn, E. L., & Thomas, J. D. (1974). Effects of cueing on self-control of classroom behavior. *Journal of Applied Behavior Analysis, 7,* 299–306.

221. Glynn, E. L., Thomas, J. D., & Shee, S. M. (1973). Behavioral self-control of on-task behavior in an elementary classroom. *Journal of Applied Behavior Analysis, 6,* 105–114.

222. Grusec, J. E., & Kuczynski, L. (1977). Teaching children to punish themselves and effects on subsequent compliance. *Child Development, 48,* 1296–1300.

223. Hall, N. E. (1966). The youth development project: A school based delinquency prevention program. *Journal of School Health, 36,* 97–103.

224. Henker, B., Whalen, C. K., & Henshaw, S. P. (1980). The attributional contexts of cognitive intervention strategies. *Exceptional Education Quarterly, 1,* 17–30.

225. Humphrey, L. L., Karoly, P., & Kirschenbaum, D. S. (1978). Self-management in the classroom: Self-imposed response cost versus self-reward. *Behavior Therapy, 9,* 592–601.

226. Kaufman, K. F., & O'Leary, K. D. (1972). Reward, cost, and self-evaluation procedures for disruptive adolescents in a psychiatric hospital school. *Journal of Applied Behavior Analysis, 5,* 293–309.

227. Kneedler, R. D., & Hallahan, D. P. (1981). Self-monitoring of on-task behavior with learning disabled children: Current studies and directions. *Exceptional Education Quarterly*, 2 (3), 73–82.

228. Ledwidge, B. (1978). Cognitive behavior modification: A step in the wrong direction? *Psychological Bulletin*, 85, 353–375.

229. McKenzie, T., & Rushall, B. (1974). Effects of self-recording on attendance and performance in a competitive swimming training program. *Journal of Applied Behavior Analysis*, 7, 199–206.

230. McLaughlin, T. F. (1976). Self-control in the classroom. *Review of Educational Research*, 46, 631–663.

231. McLaughlin, T. F., & Malaby, J. E. (1974). Increasing and maintaining assignment completion with teacher and pupil controlled individual contingency programs: Three case studies. *Psychology*, 11 (3), 45–51.

232. Molitzky, B. (1974). Behavior recording as treatment: A brief note. *Behavior Therapy*, 5, 107–111.

233. O'Leary, S. G., & Dubey, D. R. (1979). Applications of self-control procedures by children: A review. *Journal of Applied Behavior Analysis*, 12, 449–465.

234. Pease, G. A., & Tyler, O. T., Jr. (1979). Self-regulation of time-out duration in the modification of disruptive behavior. *Psychology in the Schools*, 16, 101–105.

235. Rhode, G., Morgan, D. P., & Young, K. R. (1983). Generalization and maintenance of treatment gains of behaviorally handicapped students from resource rooms to regular classrooms using self-evaluation procedures. *Journal of Applied Behavior Analysis*, 16, 171–188.

236. Rosenbaum, M. S., & Drabman, R. S. (1979). Self-control training in the classroom: A review and critique. *Journal of Applied Behavior Analysis*, 12, 467–485.

237. Sagotsky, G., Patterson, C. J., & Lepper, M. R. (1978). Training children's self-control: A field experiment in self-monitoring and goal setting in the classroom. *Journal of Experimental Child Psychology*, 25, 242–253.

238. Santogrossi, D. A., O'Leary, K. D., Romanczyk, R. G., & Kaufman, K. F. (1973). Self-evaluation by adolescents in a psychiatric hospital school token program. *Journal of Applied Behavior Analysis*, 6, 277–287.

239. Smith, D. J., Nelson, J. R., Young, K. R., & West, R. P. (1992). The effect of a self-management procedure on the classroom and academic behavior of students with mild handicaps. *School Psychology Review*, 21 (1), 59–72.

240. Smith, D. J., Nelson, J. R., Young, K. R., West, R. P., Morgan, D. P., & Rhode, G. (1988). Reducing the disruptive behavior of junior high school students: A classroom self-management procedure. *Behavior Disorders*, 13 (4), 231–239.

241. Sugai, G., & Rowe, P. (1984). The effect of self-recording on out-of-seat behavior of an EMR student. *Education and Training of the Mentally Retarded*, 19, 23–28.

242. Thomas, J. W. (1980). Agency and achievement: Self-management and self-regard. *Review of Educational Research, 50,* 213–240.

243. Turkewitz, H., O'Leary, K. D., & Ironsmith, M. (1975). Generalization and maintenance of appropriate behavior through self-control. *Journal of Consulting and Clinical Psychology, 43,* 577–583.

244. Workman, E. A., & Hector, M. A. (1978). Behavioral self-control in classroom settings: A review of the literature. *Journal of School Psychology, 16,* 227–236.

The following references describe methods for increasing maintenance and generalization.

245. Baer, M., Fowler, S. A., & Carden-Smith, L. (1984). Using reinforcement and independent grading to promote and maintain task accuracy in a mainstreamed class. *Analysis and Intervention in Developmental Disabilities, 4,* 157–169.

246. Chandler, L. K., Fowler, S. A., & Lubeck, R. C. (1992). An analysis of the effects of multiple setting events on the social behavior of preschool children with special needs. *Journal of Applied Behavior Analysis, 25* (2), 249–263.

247. Fox, J., Shores, R., Lindeman, D., & Strain, P. (1986). Maintaining social initiations of withdrawn handicapped and nonhandicapped preschoolers through a response-dependent fading tactic. *Journal of Abnormal Child Psychology, 14* (3), 387–396.

248. Hops, J., Guild, J. J., Fleischman, D. H., Paine, S. C., Street, A., Walker, H. M., & Greenwood, C. R. (1978). *PEERS (Procedures for Establishing Effective Relationship Skills).* Manual for Consultants. Eugene, OR: Unpublished manuscript. University of Oregon, Center at Oregon for Behavioral Education of the Handicapped.

249. Kohler, F. W., & Fowler, S. A. (1985). Training prosocial behaviors to young children: An analysis of reciprocity with untrained peers. *Journal of Applied Behavior Analysis, 18,* 187–200.

250. Kohler, F. W., & Greenwood, C. R. (1986). Toward a technology of generalization: The identification of natural contingencies of reinforcement. *Behavior Analyst, 9,* 9–26.

251. McConnell, S. R. (1987). Entrapment effects and the generalization and maintenance of social skills training for elementary school students with behavioral disorders. *Behavior Disorders, 12,* 252–263.

252. Rhode, G., Morgan, D. P., & Young, K. R. (1983). Generalization and maintenance of treatment gains of behaviorally handicapped students from resource rooms to regular classrooms using self-evaluation procedures. *Journal of Applied Behavior Analysis, 16* (2), 171–188.

253. Stokes, T. F., & Baer, D. M. (1977). An implicit technology of generalization. *Journal of Applied Behavior Analysis, 10* (2), 349–367.

254. Strain, P. S., Odom, S. L., & McDonnell, S. (1984). Promoting social reciprocity of exceptional children: Identification, target behavior selection, and intervention. *Remedial and Special Education, 5* (1), 21–28.

255. Walker, H. M., Street, A., Garrett, B., Crossen, J., Hops, H., & Greenwood, C. R. (1978). *RECESS (Reprogramming Environmental Contingencies for Effective Social Skills)*. Manual for Consultants. Eugene, OR: Unpublished manuscript. University of Oregon, Center at Oregon for Behavioral Education of the Handicapped.

The importance of empowering students is discussed in these references.

256. Grossman, H. (1990). *Trouble Free Teaching: Solutions to Behavior Problems in the Classroom*. Mountain View, CA: Mayfield.

257. Patton, J. M. (1981). *A Critique of Externally Oriented Behavior Management Approaches as Applied to Exceptional Black Children*. ERIC ED 204 902.

258. Sleeter, C. E., & Grant, C. A. (1988). *Making Choices for Multicultural Education: Five Approaches to Race, Class, and Gender*. Columbus, OH: Merrill.

SOLUTIONS TO INDIVIDUAL BEHAVIOR PROBLEMS

Introduction

Part Three is designed to help you deal with the behavior problems of the few students in your class who do not respond to the techniques described in the previous chapters because they need a more individualized, in-depth approach. The chapters in this part will help you determine what specifically causes these students' problems so that you can then provide them with the appropriate individualized approach they require. Chapter 11 discusses students with conduct problems, who appear to be unwilling to conform to the necessary demands of school, such as waiting their turn and respecting other people's property, because they are not concerned about the rights of others. Chapter 12 describes techniques you can use with students whose emotional problems—fear, anxiety, anger, depression, and so on—cause them to behave inappropriately. Chapter 13 explains how you can use managing and accommodating techniques to help students who lack the physiological characteristics to conform to and fulfill the demands of most teachers and school systems. These students may be developmentally immature for their age or temperamentally different. They may have problems sustaining attention or controlling their impulses. They may be suffering from the unfortunate results of prenatal exposure to harmful drugs or alcohol or the like.

In the past, many of these students would have been truants or dropouts. Some would have been suspended from school or placed on home instruction. Others would have been advised, pressured, or assigned to follow an educational track in which they would have been out of the sight and mind of most educators. Still others would have been assigned or relegated to self-contained special education classes and programs in which they were segregated from their more successful and better behaved peers. Today research suggests that many of these students can succeed in regular education and in nontracked programs if they are given the individualized approaches they require. To assist you to do that is the goal of this part of the book.

Although many educators believe that it is important to individualize classroom management techniques with some students (1–6), others do not agree. They advocate a set response for each of the behavior problems they confront. For example, when they catch students cheating during an exam, they invariably punish them. Or when students answer without waiting to be called on, they reprimand them. If students turn in their assignments late, they routinely lower their grades.

But different students can behave the same way for entirely different reasons. Students cheat during exams for a whole range of reasons. For some, cheating, lying, getting away with things, and taking the easy way out are how they do things. Others cheat because their parents put tremendous pressure on them to earn high grades, or they set unrealistically high goals for themselves, or they don't have the background or skills necessary to learn what is being taught in class without additional help.

While students should not be allowed to cheat on exams, punishing them for doing so may not deal with the cause of the problem. Punishment may be a reasonable first step with students who lie, cheat, and steal as a way of life, helping them learn that "crime doesn't pay." But with the other students, appropriate solutions might involve convincing their parents to put less pressure on them, helping them develop realistic standards, or making sure they get the extra help they need so they can do well on exams without cheating.

Some Typical Concerns

While you are reading this part of the book, one or more of the following questions about the feasibility of handling students' behavior problems on an individual basis will probably cross your mind:

1. *Is it really necessary to know the cause of students' inappropriate behavior to deal effectively with it?* Research clearly supports the approach that it is possible for educators to choose the correct solution to students' behavior problems without knowing what causes them. But it is much more likely that educators will choose the appropriate techniques and avoid those that are ineffective or that make the problems worse if they consider the causes of their students' problems when choosing how to respond. For example, using consequences to teach students not to steal, cheat, lie, or take advantage of younger children may work if their misconduct is caused by a lack of exposure to appropriate consequences. But it will not change the attitudes of students who act this way because they have not received enough love, attention, and caring to want to behave ethically. Likewise, providing added assistance may help anxious students with poor self-concepts who believe they cannot succeed on their own get started or continue to work and so teach them that they can succeed. But giving such assistance will only aggravate the problems of students who are not used to working on frustrating, difficult, or tedious things on their own because they have been able to manipulate adults into doing such things for them. Finally, requiring students to behave themselves "or else" may work with students who know what appropriate behavior is. But nonassimilated immigrant students may need to be taught how to behave in new ways and told why behavior that is acceptable in their homes and neighborhoods is not acceptable in school.

2. *Is it really possible to know why students behave as they do?* Teachers with access to information about their students' developmental histories, home lives, previous school records, and the ways they behave outside of school are in a good position to understand why their students behave as they do. Teachers with some of this information can make educated guesses about what causes their students' behavior problems. Even teachers who know very little about their students except what they learn from their own observations have at least that much information on which to base their judgments.

   Special education teachers who work with 8 to 20 students and elementary school teachers who may have 25 to 30 students in their classes are in excellent positions to get the information they need to draw reasonably accurate conclusions about the causes of their students' behavior problems. In contrast, secondary school teachers, who deal with six or seven different classes of 25 or more students each, may have more difficulty finding the time to gather adequate information about their students, especially if they have large numbers of students with behavior problems. If they only have a few students with behavior problems in each of their classes, though, the individualized approach described in this part of the text is quite feasible.

While it's best if educators have all the necessary information at their disposal, they are still better off making an educated guess based on the information they have and adapting their strategies and techniques to what they think causes the problems than using the same techniques with all students. Even educated guesses increase the odds that the strategies and techniques they choose will be effective.

3. *Can one person relate to students in so many different ways?* It is absolutely true that educators are all individuals with their own unique personalities that in turn determine which techniques they will and will not be comfortable using with their students. But it is also true that what usually limits the range of techniques that educators use is not teachers' personalities but rather a lack of understanding about the causes of their students' behavior problems, too little information about alternative strategies and techniques, and an absence of self-awareness about how they habitually respond to their students' behavior. As educators grow more knowledgeable about what causes different behavior problems, which techniques work best with each of them, and what approaches they typically use from force of habit, they will be better able to select techniques that suit both their personalities and the causes of their students' behavior problems.

4. *Can students accept different rules, expectations, and consequences for other students without becoming jealous, resentful, or rebellious?* If different rules and expectations and different consequences for various students are used in an arbitrary manner, without rhyme or reason, then they probably will make students jealous, resentful, angry, or rebellious. But if teachers tailor their expectations to the needs of each of their students, and students can see that they are all being treated fairly, then they will be more accepting of this approach because they will all be getting what they need.

References

1. Brophy, J., & Evertson, S. M. (1976). *Learning from Teaching: A Developmental Perspective.* Boston: Allyn & Bacon.

2. Morse, W. C., & Smith, J. M. (1980). *Understanding Child Variance.* Reston, VA: Council for Exceptional Children.

3. Rhodes, W. C., & Tracy, M. (1975). *A Study of Child Variance.* Ann Arbor, MI: University of Michigan Press.

4. Rich, H. L. (1978). A matching model for educating the emotionally disturbed and behavior disordered. *Focus on Exceptional Children, 10* (3), 1–11.

5. Shea, T. M., & Bauer, A. M. (1987). *Teaching Children and Youth with Behavior Disorders* (2nd ed.). Englewood Cliffs, NJ: Prentice-Hall.

6. Quay, H. C. (1969). Dimensions of problem behavior in educational programming. In P. S. Graubard (Ed.), *Children Against Schools*. Chicago: Follet.

CONDUCT PROBLEMS

This chapter begins by defining conduct problems from a developmental point of view. It then goes on to explain why some students have conduct problems and offers guidelines for identifying such students. The remainder of the chapter describes techniques you can use to deal with conduct problems in your classroom.

Humans are social beings, born completely dependent on others to care for them. Even when fully grown, they almost always continue to live with or near other people. While different groups (societies and cultures) expect different things from their members, they all require that, at certain times, their members submit to authority, adhere to norms of acceptable behavior, and sacrifice personal desires for the benefit of the entire group. Individuals in any society who have not accepted these three obligations and who do not exercise the necessary control over their behavior to meet these obligations have conduct problems. Put another way, individuals with conduct problems are unwilling to control their behavior when it interferes with the rights of others.

People generally fulfill these three obligations for several reasons. First, they anticipate positive consequences if they do so and negative consequences if they do not. Second, they are emulating others whose behavior is acceptable to society. Also, most understand that groups cannot function properly if each individual does as she or he pleases. Finally, they internalize the values and morals that the society instills in them, which in turn make them want to behave in ways approved by society even when it is clear that no negative consequences will occur if they do not.

Defining Conduct Problems

Individuals with conduct problems are unwilling to control their behavior for three reasons. First, they haven't learned that they will suffer undesirable consequences if they don't. Second, they do not understand or care that society cannot function unless people exercise self-control. And third, they have not internalized the morals and values necessary to help them control their behavior in the absence of consequences.

Modern society cannot rely on consequences in most situations because most people are not under constant surveillance. No one watches to see whether people give money to charity or add a tip for the waiter when they pay restaurant bills with credit cards. No one makes people return the extra change the clerk in the department store hands them by mistake. And no one forces parents to give their children the best care possible even to the point of making considerable financial sacrifices to put them through college. People do these things not because they have to by law but because they see the necessity of doing so and accept the morals and values that make them believe it's right and good to do these things.

No society can rely on rewards and punishments alone to control its members' behavior for very long. It would take more enforcement agents to do the job well than would be practical. But society cannot rely on values and morals alone either. Societies must use a combination of both forms of influence to make sure that its members fulfill their obligations to each other.

Students with conduct disorders are described in this section as "appearing" to be unwilling to respect the rights of others and conform to the norms of their society because their unwillingness to do so is a matter of controversy. Some people believe that they choose to misbehave (1). Others maintain that a combination of physiological characteristics and life experiences *cause* students with conduct disorders to be unwilling to behave as expected. They claim that if teachers and others knew what caused these students to seem to voluntarily choose to take advantage of others, they would understand that their "choice" is actually shaped by factors and events beyond their control (2, 3). This argument has not been resolved. In fact, no one has been able to prove whether people in general, including those who have conduct disorders, are free to choose to behave as they do or only appear to exercise free will.

Research indicates that some children may be biologically predisposed to have difficulty learning to control themselves because they are born with a temperament that makes them more stubborn or active, an attention deficit disorder, unusually high levels of male hormones, cognitive deficiencies that make it difficult for them to understand social cues and communication, or other unusual physical characteristics (2, 8) (also see chapter 13). Such physiological characteristics can also make it difficult for well-meaning and competent parents to bring up such children and youth to conform to the wishes of others (see chapter 13).

There is also evidence that environmental factors can play a significant role in causing conduct problems (4–7). Thus, students with conduct disorders are more likely to have parents and grandparents who also have conduct disorders. These students' parents do not teach them to control themselves and to respect the rights of others because they themselves do not. Instead, they model disrespect for the rights of others and aggressive behavior as a means of exerting power over others.

Some students with conduct disorders are brought up by parents who because of their own psychological problems have abused, rejected, or neglected them or failed to provide the emotional involvement and affection that they needed. Some students develop conduct disorders because their parents used ineffective disciplinary techniques and neglected to supervise them adequately. And finally, as already noted, there is evidence that difficult children with the kinds of physiological characteristics listed previously make it difficult for parents to do their job or cause parents to respond in unhelpful ways.

It is not clear from the evidence summarized in this section whether the various factors mentioned necessarily cause students to behave in unacceptable ways. The data can be interpreted in two ways. One possible interpretation is that these factors do indeed cause students to demonstrate conduct disorders. But an alternative hypothesis is that they merely predispose, not require, students to misbehave.

The author of this text assumes that students with conduct disorders only appear to choose to behave in undesirable ways. He believes that if society and its representatives—in this case, the educators—want students with conduct disorders to behave differently, they must expose them to experiences that will correct or reshape the motivation that causes them to behave as they do.

The School's Role

Whether or not schools should teach moral values is controversial. Many educators believe that it is the school's role to improve the values of students, especially those who have conduct disorders: "Because the major point of contact between such children and society is the school, it seems reasonable to argue that public schools are the societal institutions in the best position to provide corrective programming" (10, p. 78).

Some individuals and organizations who believe that the schools are not the place to correct students' attitudes about their obligations to society and others oppose the inclusion of moral education in the curriculum. The following two rights from the *Student's Bill of Rights*, published by the Eagle Forum, illustrate this position:

> 1. *The right to privacy.* School persons may not force me to discuss, or play magic circle, or answer questions, write assignments, or keep journals about my religion, moral values, family, attitudes and feelings, sex behavior and private parts of the body, political attitudes, or what I and my family do at home.

> 5. *The right to have and hold my moral values and standards, my political opinions, and my cultural attitudes.* School persons may not impose on me the value system that ethics are situational or that moral dilemmas have no right or wrong answers; may not ask me to make personal decisions whether to lie, to cheat, to steal, to take drugs, to drink alcohol, to engage in premarital sex with either gender or to kill (as promoted in the "lifeboat game" or in discussions of abortion, euthanasia, and suicide); may not require me to role play open-ended psychological problems. (9, pp. 1–2)

Those who favor inclusion of moral education do not necessarily agree with the perception of moral education put forth in the *Student's Bill of Rights*:

> Teaching values does not mean using the classroom to push a particular point of view on any political issue—say, abortion or the death penalty—that has worked its way to the core of the values debate. We're not even talking about school prayer or requiring

the Pledge of Allegiance. It's much simpler than that: teaching values means quietly helping kids to learn honesty, responsibility, respect for others, the importance of serving one's community and nation—ideals that have sufficiently universal appeal to serve as the founding and guiding principles of this country. In the schools, values education means lessons about friendship and anger, stealing and integrity, simply being polite, helping those who may be less fortunate—all lessons sadly absent from today's curriculum. (11, p. 2)

As previously noted, some educators would argue that moral development is the sole responsibility of parents and religious leaders and not the schools. But American schools have always been active in the moral development of their students merely by establishing rules, procedures, and expectations for students to live up to. Today's educators, like their predecessors, have an important—though not primary—role to play in ensuring that students develop morality. This is especially true of students with conduct problems. As you will see, although it is unlikely that you will be able to eliminate your students' conduct problems on your own, you can make an important contribution if their problems are not serious enough to require the services of other professionals.

Developmental Approach

The approach to helping students with conduct problems recommended in this book is developmental. It assumes that students with conduct problems misbehave because they have not attained the stage of moral development that is appropriate for their age (see chapter 3), so the solution to their problem is to help them in reaching their age-appropriate stage of moral development. You can assist students to achieve this goal by using classroom management techniques that will enhance their moral growth and by using managing, tolerating, and preventing techniques while assisting your students to reach their appropriate stage of moral development.

Although moral development theorists such as Loevinger and Wessler, Kohlberg, and Piaget identify a number of stages in the moral development of children and adolescents, for purposes of discussion, three stages of moral development are particularly relevant here (12–14). The descriptions that follow represent an educationally relevant synthesis of the different theories of moral development.

First Stage—
Extrinsic Consequences

When children are very young, the adults caring for them are more concerned about satisfying their physical and emotional needs than teaching them to control themselves and do things independently. As children get older, though, caretaking adults become less willing to permit them to behave in an uncontrolled way or to do everything for them. To teach young children self-control, adults use several approaches: They model the behavior they expect youngsters to emulate, communicate their expectations that youngsters will control themselves, reward them when they do, and punish them when they do not. As a result, little by little, youngsters adjust to the fact that they have to control their behavior and become more independent. Primary-grade students who have not learned this, and who therefore resist conforming to adult expectations, have conduct problems.

Identification

Few real children are angels—they all misbehave occasionally. Students who have not yet reached the first stage of moral development and have not learned that it's necessary to behave appropriately are less likely than older students to do what they are told to do without first ignoring the teacher in charge, resorting to some delaying tactic, or resisting in some way. For example, they may balk at putting their things away, stopping an activity they enjoy, or starting an activity they dislike. They may play with things they have been told not to touch or else break things they are told to be careful with unless you keep them from doing so. They would rather be "done for" than to "do" for themselves. For instance, they may insist that their teachers help them dress, tie their shoes, or straighten up after them. The idea that whoever messes up should straighten up is totally unacceptable to them. They also tend to take things from others and resist sharing or cooperating with others and taking turns. In fact, they often act as if they expect to have their desires satisfied immediately and become upset if they do not get what they want, *when* they want it. They call out answers or push ahead of others instead of waiting to be called on or attended to. For them, waiting is a deprivation they are unwilling to accept unless absolutely necessary.

They have not yet been taught that they have to "control their behavior or else." So when they are told to do something they do not want to do, they often do not believe they really have to comply. Instead, they pretend that they have not heard their teachers, in the hope that the adults will do it for them, or they play up to their teachers or else try to intimidate them to get them to change their minds. They will sometimes also disregard what they are told until it becomes obvious to them that they had better listen.

Students who have learned that they have to control their behavior usually acquiesce to authority without experiencing a lot of anger or resentment. In contrast, children who have not yet learned that it is necessary to do so may whine, cry, and throw temper tantrums as an expression of their anger at being controlled. Adolescents who have not adjusted to these obligations may sulk, start arguments, or throw temper tantrums as well for the same reason.

Research indicates that teachers can, with a high degree of accuracy, informally iden-

Students who have not reached the first stage of moral development become upset if they don't get what they want when they want it.

tify students in regular classes who have conduct problems (15). Educators can also supplement their own observations with the results of formal assessment instruments, such as the Behavior Problems Checklist (16) and the Devereaux Child Behavior Rating Scale (17).

Behaviors that may indicate that students have conduct problems include the following:

- Ignoring the teacher's directions
- Using delaying tactics
- Resisting following directions
- Trying to get others to do their chores for them
- Taking things from others
- Refusing to share or cooperate with others
- Demanding immediate gratification
- Calling out answers
- Pushing ahead in line
- Trying to manipulate teachers
- Whining, crying, or throwing temper tantrums when required to acquiesce

There is considerable ethnic and gender bias in the identification of students with conduct disorders. At both elementary and secondary levels, four times as many male students as females are labeled conduct disordered. And the disproportionality is even greater for African American males (8, 18). To avoid ethnic and gender bias, it is important to look beyond behavior to its cause. Students may behave in ways that teachers disapprove of for many reasons. As noted in chapters 5 and 6, teachers and school officials tend to be intolerant of male behavior patterns, especially the culturally influenced more assertive and aggressive behavior of African American males. Youngsters who have accepted the fact that they need to conform to the behavioral expectations of their parents and the other adults in their neighborhoods do not have conduct disorders, even though their behavior in school meets with their teachers' disapproval. They have attained the first stage of moral development. Their problem is that some of their behavior is acceptable at home, but not in school. You may want such students to modify their behavior in school. If you do, the techniques described in chapter 5 for dealing with cultural incompatibilities are more appropriate than the techniques discussed in this chapter for dealing with conduct disorders.

Chris: A Case Example   Chris was a 6-year-old who had conduct problems because he had not reached the first stage of moral development. He was not readmitted by the two preschools he attended because of his behavior problems and was enrolled in a public school kindergarten because he wasn't accepted by any of the private schools in the area. In kindergarten he was described as "unruly," "stubborn," and "lacking in social skills." His first-grade teacher reported that he had difficulty sharing and taking turns. He hit other children when they did not give him his way and often rebelled or had temper tantrums when his teacher reprimanded him or enforced the consequences that resulted from his misbehavior.

Interviews with Chris's parents indicated that they were both career-oriented individuals with little time to devote to Chris, their only child, who was basically being brought up by four child-care workers. During the time they did spend with Chris, they indulged him without setting limits rather than disciplining him because they believed that whatever time they spent with him should be quality time, which they interpreted as always being fun or feeling good.

Fostering Moral Development

Educators can help students like Chris attain the moral development appropriate for their chronological age. They can do this by relating to them in ways that counteract the effects of the experiences that delayed their moral development in the first place.

Causes of Delayed Moral Development   The following are some of the typical reasons why certain students' moral development is delayed. Consider how these relate to Chris's situation.

Models: Youngsters often learn as much or more from what adults do as from what they say. For example, if adults tell young children not to lie, not to interrupt, and not to be selfish with their things, but then they themselves lie to children, interrupt them, and avoid sharing with them, children will probably learn from what they see and experience, not from what they are told is right.

Expectations: Children and teenagers learn to control themselves when adults require them to do so. But some parents do not require that their youngsters control themselves. And youngsters who do not learn to control their behavior for the benefit of others at home are not prepared to do so in school.

Also, some adults are inconsistent in their expectations and rules. This means that they allow youngsters to get away with things either when they are in a good mood or a bad mood. As a result, their children do not learn that it is actually necessary to follow rules or obey adults. In addition, parents may disagree about what youngsters should and shouldn't be allowed to do and countermand each other's orders. When this happens, youngsters learn who to ask for what, or they play one adult against the other instead of complying when they are told to do something.

Consequences: Some parents do not use consequences effectively. Specifically, once parents have told youngsters to do or not to do something, they have to follow through. And the consequences of the children's noncompliance have to be strong enough to make a difference. A mild reprimand or another slight consequence may have very little effect on youngsters who have just gotten great satisfaction from some forbidden pleasure.

Negative consequences may also be ineffective if they do not have the intended effect. Parents who really "lay the law down" to youngsters by shouting and screaming threats about what will happen to them if they ever dare to do the same thing again may believe that their youngsters will certainly think twice about repeating the behavior. In reality, though, their children could be so accustomed to such angry outbursts and empty threats that they hardly listen to them. Youngsters who have not been exposed to effective consequences at home may have conduct problems at school and elsewhere because they do not expect to have to pay any serious consequences for misbehaving.

Individual differences: As noted earlier, physiological factors can also impede a child's moral development. Youngsters born with stubborn or persistent temperaments may find it especially difficult to do what others tell them to do. Immature children may be unable to exercise the kind of self-control typical of their more mature peers. In addition, extenuating circumstances, such as illness, poverty, or pressure on the job, can prevent parents from bringing up youngsters as they would like to. Thus, although parents are responsible for the moral development of their children, they are not necessarily to blame when their youngsters have conduct problems.

Enhancing Moral Growth

As already noted, children can develop conduct problems if the adults who care for them do not model the behavior that society expects of its members, if they do not expect youngsters to behave appropriately, or if they do not use consequences properly. Teachers can help students with conduct problems change their attitudes and behavior by relating to them in ways that make up for what they have missed.

Appropriate models and expectations: Your students may change their attitudes and behavior if you truly expect them to wait their turn, share, speak respectfully, take "no" for an answer, and so on, and if you yourself behave that way. For this reason, when working with a student who has conduct problems, begin by exposing the student to expectations for correct behavior. Point out that both you and the other students in the class behave the way you expect this student to behave.

The following are some general principles to consider when exposing students to appropriate expectations in order to change their attitudes toward good behavior:

1. Base your expectations on how much and what kinds of self-control are appropriate for children or adolescents of their age.

2. Make your expectations clear—avoid any vagueness.

3. Maintain consistent expectations. While it may be necessary to occasionally be flexible, for the most part your expectations should be consistent.

4. Maintain a good balance between justifying your expectations and insisting that your students do what they are told because you are the teacher in charge.

5. Do not weaken if they cry, throw a temper tantrum, say nasty things, or promise to do better next time.

6. Do not expect your students to always comply the first time they are told to do something or to comply without occasionally testing you to see how serious you are. And do not expect your students to be able to change overnight, to control all of their inappropriate behaviors at once, or to show continual progress without occasionally slipping back into old patterns.

7. It is unrealistic to expect your students to change their behaviors without feeling resentful or angry and occasionally showing these strong feelings by pouting, having a temper tantrum, claiming you are mean or unfair, and the like. Anger is a natural reaction to being forced to do what one does not want to do. All children go through this phase until they finally accept the fact that they have to submit, conform, and sacrifice some of their personal desires. In certain cases, students are just passing through this phase at an older age.

Effective consequences: Providing good role models and appropriate expectations is sometimes all you need to change a student's behavior. But if your students were not exposed to appropriate consequences at home, it will be necessary to teach them the positive consequences of desirable behavior as well as the negative consequences of any misbehavior. The techniques for using positive and negative consequences discussed in chapter 10 are particularly suitable for convincing students that it not only pays to behave appropriately but also is necessary to do so.

Second Stage— Natural Consequences

By the time students leave the primary grades to enter upper elementary, they can understand why rules are necessary. Now instead of behaving appropriately primarily because of what will happen as a result, they also follow rules and procedures because they can appreciate their reasonableness. For example, primary-grade students raise their hands and wait to be called on, keep silent while others are reciting, keep working at boring tasks, share with others, and put things away where they belong when they do not really want to in order to gain their teachers' approval and avoid disapproval. Upper elementary students do these things because they understand that only one student can recite at a time, that students can't hear the speaker when others are talking, that it is necessary to stay on-task even when assignments are boring in order to learn or complete the work during the allotted time, that if they want others to share with them then they have to share with others, and that they have to put things where they belong so that they and others can find them again. Unlike students in the first stage of moral development, who exercise self-control because of the extrinsic consequences of their actions, students in the second stage exercise self-control not only because of extrinsic consequences but also because they appreciate the natural consequences of their behavior.

Identification

Students who are in upper elementary but have not reached the second stage of moral development still need consequences to motivate them to behave appropriately. They seem to base their decisions about how to behave on a "what's-in-it-for-me" standard. Sometimes they may actually ask their teachers what will happen if they do not comply. They often complain about having to conform to rules and question their necessity. When they are caught misbehaving, they resist paying the consequences, claiming they are unfair. They may feign regret or guilt, but they rarely experience these emotions to the same degree as their classmates. They also commonly maintain a double standard in their relationships. They expect others to listen to them, share with them, and treat them nicely even though they don't behave in these ways themselves. They do this because they do not yet understand that others will treat them the way they treat others.

Audrey: A Case Example   Audrey, a 10-year-old, has been a problem since she entered school. She came late, attended irregularly, was disobedient toward her teachers, and complained that they were too strict and unfair when they insisted that she abide by the same rules and do the same assignments as her classmates.

Audrey's parents were described as suspicious of school authorities and uncooperative. During the few parent-teacher conferences they attended, they said they did not believe in the rigidity of school because it stunted children's creativity and development. One of the teachers described them as artists who did not believe in rules either at home or at school. They claimed to be bringing up Audrey to question authority and to think for herself so that she could discover who she was and become self-directing and self-actualizing. Knowing Audrey's background, it is understandable that she resisted her teachers' authority, truly believed that they treated her unfairly, and exhibited conduct problems in school.

Fostering Moral Development

Causes of Delayed Moral Development   Unfortunately, no studies presently explain why some youngsters do not progress to the second stage of moral development. The following criteria have been mentioned as possible causes by educators and psychologists.

Poor modeling: As noted, children may learn more from what adults do than from what they say. Children who see adults cheating at games, breaking traffic rules, and lying to others may learn to mock rules and procedures in the same way.

Lack of explanations: Youngsters need to be taught why rules and procedures are necessary so they can learn to appreciate why everyone cannot do as he or she pleases. If adults merely tell youngsters, "Do it because I say so," or "Do it or else," these children may learn to obey but not to reason. It is important to teach youngsters the practical reasons to behave appropriately.

Lack of group identification: If youngsters do not identify with the group—their friends and classmates—they may not care how their actions impede or infringe on the rights and goals of others. This means that they may understand quite well that others cannot hear the speaker when they themselves are talking and that others may not get their share or turn if they take too much or too long, but they may simply not care enough about "others" to control their own desires.

Immaturity: Youngsters who develop at slower rates than their peers may be too immature socially and emotionally to understand or appreciate the practical reasons why they should abide by rules and procedures in the absence of extrinsic consequences.

Enhancing Moral Growth   Educators can help students with conduct problems to acquire the kind of moral self-control characteristic of second-stage development by modeling appropriate behavior, explaining the practical necessity for rules and procedures, helping students understand the effects of their behavior on others through role playing, providing students with cooperative learning experiences, and fostering group identification.

As the following quotation aptly explains, students may learn to behave morally by following their teachers' examples:

> Students do not learn moral values solely through reasoned debate. They may learn by example and from behavioral reinforcement. For example, if teachers praise students for helping one another understand their assignments, the children may come to value cooperative learning. Or students who consistently see the teacher listening respectfully to everybody's point of view adopt this practice too. Teachers need to show young children how to be fair in concrete ways, for children seem to learn situation-specific rules of behavior before they are able to grasp universal principles of justice. (21, pp. 45–46)

To encourage the second stage of moral development, deemphasize your role as the authority and your use of extrinsic consequences as management techniques. Instead of telling students about the extrinsic consequences of various behaviors, explain the practical reasons why it's necessary to share, take turns, raise one's hand, and so forth. When students ask what will happen to them if they do or do not follow rules, explain that the issue isn't what will happen to them but rather how their actions will affect others. Make sure students know and understand why the rules and procedures established for the class are necessary, not arbitrary, and why acceptable alternative ways of behavior are more appropriate than undesirable ones.

You can help your students develop to the second stage by asking them to think about the implications of their actions for the group. Direct them to imagine what would happen if:

Everyone called out whenever they wanted to.

No one cleaned up or put things back where others could find them.

No one listened to the umpires when they were told they were out.

Help students understand the principle of reciprocity in human relationships. You can do this by explaining the kinds of reactions their behavior evokes in others. Another approach is to ask students to imagine how they would feel, what they would think, and how they might react if someone did to them what they do to others. For example:

You had been waiting 10 minutes and someone cut in line ahead of you.

The school library had no books for you to do your report because someone had taken more than they needed.

Someone called out the correct answer to a difficult question when it was your turn, and you knew the answer.

Someone took your book because he had lost his.

No one chose you for the team during recess.

Deemphasize competition and individual assignments. Instead, involve students in cooperative learning experiences so that they learn how they can benefit from helping each other and working together. Remind students often that others are more likely to help them if they help others.

Research indicates that using role playing and having students who behave inappropriately assume the role of the victim or injured party can improve the way some of them relate to their peers (19, 20, 22, 23). But these studies are not clear about which students are most likely to benefit from role playing and exactly why they benefit from the technique. It may be that role playing works best with students who are unaware of or try not to think about how their actions affect others because they get a firsthand experience of what it feels like to be treated as they usually treat others.

You can also help students identify with their classmates so that they care about the effects their misbehavior has on the group. Use the techniques described in chapter 2 to foster group cohesiveness and group identity.

Third Stage—
Intrinsic Consequences

Adolescents who have reached the third stage of moral development behave appropriately because it is the right thing to do. They do this even when they would have no extrinsic consequences to pay. They do it for the intrinsic consequences they feel. In particular, when they do the right thing, they feel good about themselves; when they misbehave, they feel bad, guilty, or ashamed of themselves. Because many adolescents and adults exhibit this type of morality only some of the time, even honest, law-abiding citizens require the watchful eye of parking meter attendants, IRS agents, and the highway patrol from time to time.

Identification

Older students who have internalized or accepted the values and moral behavior they need to control themselves in the absence of consequences feel good about doing so and bad when they do not. Students who haven't yet internalized these values and morals do not experience these feelings as intrinsic consequences of their behavior. They often cheat on exams, in sports, and in competitive games and are apparently not bothered by this. It also does not upset them to allow others to do their share of the work. They do not seem to care about other people's feelings and feel little remorse or guilt about taking advantage of others who are younger or weaker. If caught lying, cheating, or stealing, they only regret being caught, not what they did. They may feign remorse and guilt, but unless they are good actors, it is usually obvious that they really do not experience these feelings.

Ernie: A Case Example   When Ernie, a 15-year-old, was caught breaking into his school, he and two others had removed audiovisual, musical, and office equipment worth several thousand dollars. Ernie had a history of stealing from other students when he was in elementary school, but that appeared to have stopped once he entered junior high, though one of his teachers suspected, but could not prove, that he continued to steal. In junior and senior high, he was suspected of copying homework, and he was observed cheating on tests a number of times, but he denied doing so when confronted by his teachers. His teachers considered him devious, dishonest, and manipulative but also bright enough to avoid being caught with the "smoking gun." When asked why he had broken into the school, Ernie claimed that he stole the equipment to get money to buy the clothes and other things he needed for school and a guitar to take guitar lessons because there were no jobs for someone his age, and his mother wouldn't help him out.

Ernie lived with his mother and two sisters in a rundown neighborhood. His father was serving a second sentence for robbery. His mother advised the authorities to lock up Ernie with his father, since he had turned out to be "just like him."

Fostering Moral Development

Adolescents are motivated to behave appropriately for moral reasons. This happens as a result of adults teaching them the moral principles that guide behavior, modeling the kind of behavior they want them to copy, and giving them the love and attention they need in order to learn to care about others. Clearly, this did not happen in Ernie's case.

Causes of Delayed Moral Development   Adults who reward or punish youngsters like Ernie for respecting or not respecting others' rights without explaining the ethical reasons behind their actions may succeed in convincing young people that they should behave appropriately when there are consequences to pay. This approach does not, however, help youngsters learn to control themselves in the absence of consequences. In addition, adults who model immoral behavior because they themselves have conduct problems tend to raise adolescents with conduct problems. And finally, youngsters who are not treated lovingly with caring attention often have less love to give. It's as if we need to have our own batteries charged before we are able to give to or care about others.

Enhancing Moral Growth   Hersh, Miller, and Fielding (21) believe that the type of self-control characterizing the third level of moral development has three aspects: judging, caring, and behaving. According to their theory, to function at the stage of moral development where one acts appropriately for intrinsic reasons, individuals must have certain abilities. Specifically, they have to be able to reason or judge moral issues by weighing conflicting interests and principles and choosing in favor of the higher morality. They must care enough about others on a basic, emotional level to want to help, support, and protect them regardless of whether a payoff is in it for them. They must also be able to act on their moral feelings and judgments in situations where internal and external pressures push them not to act.

Take, for example, a student offered a great deal of money by a drug dealer to help him sell drugs to his classmates. The student might refuse if he is afraid of being caught (a nonmoral decision), but he might also refuse if he *judged* that it was wrong to sell illegal drugs or if he *cared* enough about his fellow students not to want to profit from their misery. If he was poor and needed the money or if the drug dealer threatened to harm him if he did not cooperate, he would then also have to face internal and external pressures on him not to *act* on his feelings or moral judgments.

Another example is a teenager who, having lost the textbook for an upcoming exam, sees someone else's on an empty table in the lunchroom. She would either have to *judge* that it was wrong to take someone else's book or *care* enough about the unknown individual to decide not to take it for moral reasons. If the exam was really important to her or she desperately needed a good grade, she would also have to cope with internal pressures on her not to *act* on her judgment and feeling that it is wrong to steal.

You can help teenagers who have not yet reached the third stage of moral development by working with them to improve their moral judgment or reasoning, which means working at the cognitive level. You can encourage their caring for others, the affective level of experience. Finally, you can help them act on their judgments and feelings, to fulfill themselves as moral people on the behavioral level.

Cognitive level—judging: Explain to students why they should behave morally. For example, give them reasons why they should treat others as they would like to be treated, why they should not take things that belong to others, and why they shouldn't copy on tests. Point out to them when other students or newsworthy adults behave morally. Model the behavior you want them to copy, and tell them how and why you live by the principles you do. Tell them you would like the same principles to guide their behavior. Or if you are uncomfortable discussing your personal beliefs and lifestyle with your students, use other people they can identify with as examples for them to emulate.

When students argue that other people behave immorally, explain that life is not perfect and that each person has to live his or her life in the best way possible. Help students think about how they could handle situations in which moral behavior does not seem to "pay" because others are not acting ethically. Examples might include students copying from each other during an exam while the teacher is out of the room or students grabbing what they need when there aren't enough materials to go around.

Numerous moral education programs for use in the schools have been published in recent years (12, 24–32). Most of these programs are based on two assumptions: (1) If students do not know moral principles, then they cannot apply them to moral issues, such as competing unfairly, lying, or respecting the rights of the majority; and (2) students who do know such principles will apply them to moral issues. Although these programs are designed to be used with groups of students, you can use many of these materials with individual students.

These programs typically present students with situations involving moral dilemmas that they are then asked to solve. To use this technique, you can make up your own situations as well. For example, you can ask your students what they think would be the best thing to do if:

Paul's friend makes a wisecrack to a third student in front of Paul about the student's excessive weight and expects Paul to laugh at his remark.

Teresa's best friend asks to copy her homework because even though she wanted to do her report, she had to go somewhere with her parents, and she can't afford to get a zero. Teresa believes that allowing someone to copy one's homework is wrong.

Someone hits Armando first, and he knows the boy will continue to hit him if he doesn't defend himself, but Armando has been taught that fighting isn't a good way to solve problems between people.

Harvey wants to help his parents, who are abusing drugs to the point that they are hurting themselves, his brother, and him. To do this he wants to turn them in for their own benefit, but they have ordered him not to do this.

Lupe, a little girl that Helen takes care of after school, gets into the medicine cabinet and swallows something a few minutes before her parents return. Helen thinks she ought to tell them in case Lupe swallowed something dangerous, but she is afraid she will lose her job if she does. Besides, she tells herself, she doesn't really know if it was dangerous.

Some of these programs also teach values that are necessary in a democratic society. You can adopt this approach with students by giving them reasons why all students should have the right to state their opinions and be *listened* to, why it is necessary for individuals to generally accept the decisions of the majority even when they don't agree with them, and why all students should do their fair share of the work the group is assigned. Using role playing as well can give students the experiences necessary to understand the explanations you have given them.

Research (40) indicates that these cognitive approaches (moral education) increase students' scores on such tests of moral reasoning as Kohlberg's Standard Moral Judgment Interview (33) and the Defining Issues Test (34). Yet no clear relationship shows up between students' scores on tests of moral reasoning and their behavior either in or out of the classroom (35, 37, 39, 42, 50, 54). The finding relating directly to behavior is that only some delinquents and students with conduct problems score low on tests of moral reasoning. But many students who score low on such tests do not exhibit conduct problems in school or delinquent behavior outside of school (38, 41, 43, 44, 46, 48, 49). As Junell explains, while moral education produces increased moral awareness and the ability to reason morally, "The fact remains that the link between moral reasoning and behaving morally is very weak if not virtually nonexistent" (47, p. 79). The current state of affairs is summarized succinctly by Rest: "To date, no studies have demonstrated directly that changes wrought by these moral education programs have brought about changes in behavior" (34, p. 87).

And Coleman, Pfeiffer, and Oakland add that "advanced moral reasoning may be a necessary but not sufficient condition for moral behavior" (42, p. 56).

Perhaps the cognitive approach is only appropriate for teenagers who misbehave because they have not been taught that they should behave morally. It may be that most students with conduct problems need to be able to care about others and withstand the internal and external pressures that inhibit them from acting morally. It is now clear that cognitive development alone will not bring about behavioral change (36–38, 45, 51, 53, 55, 59). Adults must also motivate students to want to behave morally (52, 56–58).

Affective level—caring: The moral development literature includes a variety of techniques, mostly not yet researched, that educators can use to help students learn to care enough about others so that they want to treat them morally (60–67). One involves students in activities where they learn firsthand about the feelings and experiences of others. For example, students with conduct problems can visit programs that serve abused children or impoverished families. Or they can talk to students who have been beaten up, had their money stolen, been exposed to racial abuse, and so on, so that they can learn what it feels like to be the victim of someone else's misbehavior. Or the students they have victimized can confront them directly. These techniques seem to have the potential of affecting students more powerfully than role-playing the victim, but their actual effectiveness has not been researched. One possible shortcoming of providing students with direct experiences or involving them in role playing is that if they don't care enough about their victims to feel for them, learning about their suffering isn't going to change their behavior.

Another technique for helping students to care more about others is to give them the chance to help others so they can learn from experience how helping people can make them feel good about themselves. Newman and others (11, 64, 65) have described techniques for involving students in worthwhile projects designed to achieve this goal. However, no current research shows that students with conduct problems would behave differently after having been involved in such a program.

A third approach is to involve students in cooperative learning projects. In theory, working together in small groups will give students enough satisfaction so that they will want to relate better to their peers. Again, the effectiveness of such an approach with students who have conduct problems is as yet unresearched.

Many educators believe that teachers can increase the caring behavior of students by acting in a caring manner toward them. During class, teachers can demonstrate their interest and concern for certain students by providing them with a little extra attention, writing extra or more detailed comments on their work, and actively listening when the students voice their personal concerns. Teachers can also spend time with students doing things that the students choose, whether it's shooting baskets, having a soda, or lending a sympathetic ear to what the students have to say.

The idea that caring for students can indeed "charge up their batteries" is very appealing. It certainly appears that youngsters who are well cared for and who receive love and affection are more likely to love and care for others than youngsters who have been abused, neglected, or rejected. But there are real limits involved. Secondary school teachers with 30 or more students per period for six periods can model caring behavior, but they can only provide so much actual care, love, and attention to individual students. Since anecdotal reports of successful programs for students with serious conduct problems indicate that they need lots of individual attention, it does not appear feasible for regular education teachers to provide such individual attention to adolescents who have serious conduct problems. Often these students require abundant extra care if they have experienced serious neglect or deprivation. On the other hand, teenagers with mild conduct problems may decide to behave better if they are exposed to caring and concerned educators. Thus, you can sometimes help teenagers with mild conduct problems. Adolescents with serious problems, though, will probably require additional services from other professionals.

Behavioral level—acting: As already noted, people do not always act on their moral convictions. Certain situations bring out the best in people; others the worst. Some adolescents who have sound moral reasoning and care for others may nevertheless misbehave because they cannot resist the pressures to behave inappropriately. They may be unable to resist a request from a good friend to copy their answers during a test, even though they believe it's wrong to do this. Or they may be unable to do anything but defend their honor physically when someone makes a derogatory remark about their mother, even though they agree that students shouldn't fight in school. Students who have difficulty acting on their beliefs need to have their resolve strengthened. They also need to practice how to resolve situations in more acceptable ways so that they don't keep giving in to pressures to behave inappropriately.

A number of educators have suggested that teachers can help students decide to behave morally in conflict situations by helping them clarify their values (69, 70, 72, 73). The assumption underlying this "values clarification" approach is that students will be able to use their values to make decisions about how to behave better when they are clear about them. One way to use this approach with students who do not yet act on their values is to teach them to apply the following process to conflict situations:

- *List the alternative ways of behaving.* In the example about copying on a test, a student could either allow a friend to copy her test answers or not.

- *Consider the consequences of each alternative way of behaving both to oneself and to others.* If the student cooperates with her friend, she might feel bad about cheating and anxious that she would be caught. She might also be caught and get into trouble, but her friend would be appreciative. Possible consequences for her friend might be that she would get a better grade on the exam, but she might also be tempted to continue to rely on her instead of doing her own work, which would be bad for her friend in the long run.

- *Identify one's personal values that are involved.* The personal values that the student identifies might include not cheating, helping a friend, being liked by a friend, and doing what one thinks is right.

- *Identify the values that are most important or significant, and select the alternative that fits these values.* If the student identifies not cheating as her highest value, she would probably agree that not cooperating with her friend would be the best alternative. If she identifies being liked by a friend as first, she would probably believe that cooperating would be the alternative to choose. If she identifies helping a friend as paramount, she might choose either alternative, depending on which she thinks is more helpful—assisting her friend to get a higher grade or encouraging her to do her own work.

You can also use this process with students after they have misbehaved to help them evaluate what they did and to help them understand why they should or could have behaved differently. For example, you could guide Alex, who hit another student who had said something about Alex's mother, to examine and evaluate alternative ways he could have reacted to the situation:

- *In what alternative ways could Alex have reacted to the situation?* He could have fought in school, fought after school, or not fought.

- *What would have been the consequences of each alternative to Alex and the other student?* By fighting in school, Alex defended his honor, but he also got into trouble. The other student received a bloody nose, got into trouble for fighting, and may have learned not to provoke Alex and others. If they had fought after school, the consequences may have been roughly the same except that they wouldn't have gotten into trouble. If Alex hadn't fought the other student, he would have felt shame for not defending his honor physically, and the other student might have lost respect for him and might continue to provoke him.

- *What personal values were involved in the situation?* To defend one's honor and to do well in school.

- *Which values were most important to Alex, and which alternative would have fit these values?* Fighting after school would have satisfied both values and led to the greatest number of desirable consequences.

Helping students clarify their values is no guarantee, however, that they will either choose values that parallel the school's or act on their values when pressure exists not to do so. In fact, current research does not indicate that helping students in groups to clarify their values results in improved behavior (71). As Beach points out, "The values a student prizes may not be the ones he or she ought to prize" (68, p. 31).

The process just described is a modification of the group process. While there is as yet no research evidence regarding the effectiveness of this individualized approach with students who have conduct problems, many teachers believe that it has been useful with such students.

The Role of Consequences

Some teachers believe that rewarding students with conduct problems for behaving appropriately and denying them rewards or punishing them when they misbehave can change them. In reality, while extrinsic consequences may be necessary to manage students' behavior, they are unlikely to affect students' basic attitudes about life or the extent to which they care about others.

Harsh punishments are particularly counterproductive with students with conduct problems. In recent years, it has become increasingly clear that harsh punishments often

Self-Quiz:
Techniques
for Handling
Conduct Problems

How would you feel about employing each of the following techniques with teenage students who have conduct problems?

Discussing moral dilemmas in class

Teaching the values that are assumed to be necessary in a democratic society

Involving students in activities in which they learn firsthand about the feelings and experiences of individuals who are the victims of injustice

Providing students opportunities to help others

Involving students in cooperative learning projects

Providing students with extra attention after school

Utilizing values clarification techniques

do not produce behavioral improvement. When they do, the improvement tends not to generalize to other situations and often backfires (2, 8). As Lytton puts it, "Different reactions to punishment have been demonstrated in CD [conduct disordered] and non-CD children. Antisocial behavior of CD children has been found to increase after punishment, whereas for normal children it decreases" (2, p. 688).

It may be that harsh treatment confirms students' perceptions that aggression is the way to obtain what one wants, that the world is not a nice place, and that other people do not really care about them. In fact, doing the opposite of punishing students with conduct disorders seems to be the most effective approach, as Erickson and Egeland point out:

> Children's behavior showed improvement when teachers specifically and persistently contradicted the student's expectations about how adults would respond to him/her. For example, teachers made a special effort to stay close to, and become involved with, children who had a family history of avoidant, detached behavior. And they remained calm and consistently supportive of children even in the face of aggressive, acting-out behavior. (74, p. 165)

Thus, "blaming these students for their behavior and threatening them with punishment and exclusion from education should not take the place of planning an appropriate education for them" (8, p. 22).

Managing, Tolerating, and Preventing

While you are attempting to change them, you can work with students who have conduct problems using three approaches. You may use more than one at a time, depending on the circumstances.

Managing

While fostering your students' moral development—and waiting for the results—you may have to manage their inappropriate behavior. The following examples of managing techniques might work for you during this transition time:

1. When you see students on the verge of doing something wrong, distract their attention to something else. Ask them to do something for you or engage them in a conversation about something that will hold their interest.

2. Remind the students about the acceptable alternative ways they could accomplish the same goal.

3. Stay near at hand when students appear to be about to get into trouble. The knowledge that you are watching may be all that is needed to help them control their impulse.

4. If that does not deter the students, signal your disapproval by a look or a gesture that conveys your attitude. Remind students that what they are about to do is wrong.

5. If the students are about to commit a target behavior you are trying to modify through consequences, remind them of the consequences.

6. Help students manage their own behavior. Explain the importance of avoiding situations that are so tempting or where so much pressure is on them to misbehave. Help them draw up a list of situations that they should try to avoid.

Tolerating

You will not be able to manage all of your students' inappropriate behaviors, so you will have to tolerate or prevent some. Certainly you will want to prevent behaviors that are dangerous or that seriously interfere with the rights of others. Whether you should tolerate or try to prevent behaviors that are not so serious is a matter for you to decide based on your own preferences.

The following are some general principles to keep in mind when you tolerate your students' behaviors:

1. *Try not to feel resentful or disappointed that you have to tolerate their behavior.* It may help you to remember the reason you are doing this—because the students cannot control all of their behavior immediately. If you get angry or disappointed, you will give your students conflicting messages. You may try to communicate temporary acceptance of their behavior, but this will not work if you really feel resentful and they sense this.

2. *Tolerate behavior only temporarily.* Sometimes it is easier to tolerate students' behavior problems than to continue to try to change them. However, since conduct problems can be changed, do not tolerate behavior as a substitute for trying to change it.

3. *Make sure your students know which behavior you are tolerating and which you are not.* Both you and your students should be clear about this distinction.

Preventing

Behaviors that are unfair to other youngsters or that seriously interfere with their rights should be prevented if possible. "If possible" is included because educators cannot be in more than one place at a time; they do not—regardless of what their students sometimes think—have eyes in the back of their heads, and they cannot anticipate each and every thing that students will do. All they can do is their best.

The following are some techniques you can use to prevent students from behaving inappropriately while you are fostering their moral development:

1. Schedule activities that usually generate misbehavior for times when you or some-one else can provide the needed supervision.

2. Supervise students closely in situations likely to cause problems. Keep a ready eye out for trouble and intervene before anything happens. For example, if a student is a poor loser and will cheat or lie to win, try to be watchful when she or he is play-ing competitive games.

3. Protect students from situations they cannot handle without supervision when you are not in a position to provide close supervision. For example, do not allow stu-dents to borrow things from other students or books from the class library if they do not yet take care of other things well or return them. Do not place students who take advantage of others in charge of groups. Do not allow students to use valuable or irreplaceable equipment when you know they will not be careful. Do not allow students who will not share or give up things to others to have the first turn.

4. When your intervention is not effective and the problem is threatening to get out of hand, remove students from the situation before they seriously interfere with the rights of others.

5. Use physical control if necessary to make sure students do not harm anyone. Do not hesitate to call on the authorities for help when students are on the verge of doing something dangerous. Many educators are wary of using physical force with their students because of possible litigation. But when all else fails or it is obvious that nothing else will work and you need an immediate response, consider physi-cally preventing your students from doing harm. Use the minimum amount of force necessary, but make sure you use enough. Then get help from others as soon as possible. Since many school districts have written policies and guidelines for how to use physical restraint with students, you should become familiar with them as soon as possible.

Whether these or other techniques will work depends on such factors as your students' ages, the kinds of behaviors you want to prevent, and your personality. Thus, you may be able to physically prevent a young student from taking something that belongs to another student; but if your student is a teenager, this technique may be totally inappropriate. If a student is about to do something that is not so serious, you might be okay trying a technique that has only a reasonable chance of succeeding. But if your student might hurt someone or get into serious trouble, choose a technique that is guaranteed to be effective even if it is a drastic solution to the problem. Finally, your particular personality will influence your choice of the preventive techniques you use. When a student is on the verge of getting into trouble, you may feel comfortable allowing the student to remain in the situation while you maintain a watchful eye and prepare to intervene if necessary. Or you may prefer to remove the student from the situation.

Case Studies

The following case studies illustrate how you can use the techniques described in this chapter to help students with conduct problems.

Randi

Randi, an 8-year-old, was considered "disruptive and unmanageable" by Ms. Finney, her third-grade teacher. At the start of the second month of the school year, Ms. Finney asked for consultation with a district behavior therapist. The specific behaviors she listed on the referral forms included "calling out, not waiting her turn, difficulty sharing, taking things from other students' cubbies, aggressive behavior toward peers, resisting cleaning up and putting things away." After meeting with Ms. Finney, Randi's first-grade teacher, and her parents, as well as observing Randi in class and reviewing her cumulative folder, the behavior specialist, Mr. Singfield, thought that they should deal with Randi's behavior problems as conduct problems, and he devised the following program.

Before saying anything to Randi, Ms. Finney determined how often each of the behaviors occurred during two mornings and two afternoons over a 4-day period. Following this she met with Randi, listed five of her undesirable behaviors, and clearly explained why they were unacceptable. Together they selected two behaviors from the list that Randi agreed to modify—calling out and refusing to put her things away. They also identified two alternative acceptable behaviors—raising her hand and waiting to be called on and putting her things away. In addition, they selected the rewards that Randi would receive for behaving in an acceptable way and the negative consequences that would result when she behaved inappropriately. For raising her hand instead of calling out and for putting her things away, she was awarded points that she could later use for playing jacks with Ms. Finney. She received 1 point each time she raised her hand and 5 points each time she put her things away. But she lost 1 point each time she called out and 5 points each time she refused to put her things away. She could purchase a minute of jacks-playing time with 5 points. In addition, Ms. Finney told Randi that she would ignore her whenever she called out. (Mr. Singfield had observed that Ms. Finney often acknowledged Randi's contributions when she called out, thereby reinforcing her behavior.) Randi was also told that the other three unacceptable behaviors on the list were not a part of the deal for the time being. She would not receive any positive or negative consequences regarding them except that if she hit or pushed other students, she would be sent to the principal's office (a technique that Ms. Finney had been using without any observable success).

During the first 3 days of the program, Randi called out only four times and put her things away each time she was required to. During the morning of the fourth day, she was sent to the office for hitting, and when she returned, she reverted to her previous level of calling out. Her behavior improved again during the fifth day. By the end of the second week, Randi raised her hand and put her things away consistently. But the program had little effect on her other undesirable classroom behaviors.

After the third week, during which Randi had five almost perfect days, Ms. Finney and Mr. Singfield decided to eliminate the extrinsic consequences. This resulted in a rapid deterioration of Randi's behavior, and they reinstated the point system. The two target behaviors improved immediately, and waiting her turn and participating in group cleanup improved somewhat. But Randi continued to take things from other students' cubbies and to resist sharing materials and equipment.

At this point, Mr. Singfield decided it would be necessary to include Randi's parents in the program. During his initial interview with them, he had noted that Randi's parents presented a "divided front" in that her father permitted her to get away with a great deal, and he often "undercut" her mother's efforts to discipline her. As a result of their second meeting with Mr. Singfield, Randi's parents adopted a consistent approach with her. In addition, Ms. Finney began to place more emphasis on consistently praising Randi for behaving appropriately and pointing out how much better it would be for her if she also modified the three other undesirable behaviors on her list. After two additional weeks, all of Randi's undesirable behaviors in school improved considerably. Her parents also reported that her behavior at home had improved a little.

Six weeks later, the program was discontinued in school but maintained at home with very little deterioration in Randi's behavior in class. She seldom called out, consistently put her things away, and participated in group cleanup. No instances of taking things from other students' cubbies were observed. She still resisted sharing with others on occasion, however, and infrequently hit or pushed other students when they wouldn't acquiesce to her wishes.

Barry

Barry, a 16-year-old, was a bright student who was just barely passing in school. He was 2 years behind in math and 3 in reading. Although he had been a disruptive student until the eighth grade, his behavior changed drastically when he entered high school. He stopped "defying" his teachers and fighting with other students. His teachers felt that he had gone "underground." They suspected him of copying his homework, stealing equipment from science labs, forging his mother's signature on absence reports, and selling drugs, but they were unable to prove anything.

When some inexpensive equipment from the science laboratory was discovered in his locker, two letters requesting a meeting were sent to his home without an answer. In response to a telephone call, his mother told the school authorities that they could do as they

Terminology

The problems of the students discussed in this chapter have been given different labels. The term *conduct disorders* is used by psychiatrists, psychologists, and others who employ the American Psychiatric Association's *Diagnostic and Statistical Manual of Mental Disorders*. The manual defines conduct disorder as "a persistent pattern of conduct in which the basic rights of others and major age-appropriate societal norms or rules are violated" (75, p. 53).

Some individuals use the term *socially maladjusted* for these students because they do not follow society's rules. The term *behav-* *ior disorders* is used by many educators for students who might be identified as having conduct disorders. However, *behavior disorders* is also used by some educators as a generic term for any misbehavior, regardless of its cause. Although *juvenile delinquency* is a quasi-legal label for the behavior of students who have problems with the legal system, some individuals mistakenly use the term *juvenile delinquents* for all students with conduct disorders or behavior disorders. Research indicates that while the majority of youth in the juvenile correctional system have been identified as having conduct disorders, many have emotional disorders, developmental disabilities, or other problems (76).

pleased with Barry. She could not afford to take a day off from work, and her husband was in prison for the third time.

Mr. Johnson, Barry's science teacher who had grown up in the same neighborhood as Barry, volunteered to be his mentor if he was not suspended or referred to the police. Given the option of working with Mr. Johnson or having his case referred to the police, Barry chose Mr. Johnson.

During the first few meetings, Barry said nothing about the science equipment. They talked mostly about Barry's poor grades and irregular attendance. Mr. Johnson offered to obtain a tutor for Barry, but he declined, saying he did not need one because he just wanted to finish high school and get a job. But it turned out that the jobs Barry was interested in required more than a high school diploma. In response to Mr. Johnson's question about what he liked to do, Barry answered sports and art, both of which he was good at.

Mr. Johnson located a commercial artist who hired Barry part-time after school, and Mr. Johnson took Barry to two basketball games before Barry brought up the subject of the stolen science equipment. When Barry justified his behavior on the grounds that kids like him had to survive in any way they could, since they could not make it in the system, Mr. Johnson let him know that he had also grown up in Barry's neighborhood—without, however, communicating an attitude of "Look at me, I made it, why can't you?"

Two months later Barry asked Mr. Johnson if he could still find him a tutor, since he had decided that he wanted to study commercial art in college.

Summary

Youngsters must learn to accept the fact that there are times when they must submit to authority, conform to norms of acceptable behavior, and sacrifice their personal desires for the benefit of others. To teach them to accept these obligations when they are young, adults provide good models for youngsters to follow, motivate them to copy appropriate adult behaviors, and teach them that desirable consequences follow when they submit, conform, or sacrifice, and negative consequences follow when they do not. When children are older, adults motivate them to accept these three obligations even when they do not have to suffer the consequences of their actions by explaining the reasons why they should do so, teaching them ethical principles, and providing them with the affection and concerned caring needed to motivate them to want to behave morally. Young children who do not fulfill these three obligations, and older children and adolescents who do so only when there are consequences to pay, have conduct problems.

To help students who have conduct problems, you should use techniques that will assist them in attaining the stage of moral development that is appropriate for their age. While you are doing this, you can also use managing, tolerating, and preventing techniques.

Activities

Read each of the following descriptions and decide whether the behavior described was more likely caused by conduct problems or some other kinds of problems.

1. John was a 9-year-old who had been behaving poorly since kindergarten. He was slow to do what he was told and did so only under pressure. He argued and fought with the other students in his classes and seldom shared, waited his turn, or allowed others to speak if he wanted to say something. His parents reported that he refused to listen to them, demanded their complete and immediate attention, and did not get along with his younger brother and sister. Some of the specific behaviors they described were nagging them and making a general nuisance of himself until he either got what he wanted or was punished, interrupting them whenever he felt like it, and taking his siblings' toys without permission.

2. Ophelia was a 5-year-old preschool student who was well behaved at school. However, her teachers were concerned about the fact that she seldom interacted with other children and almost never spoke to anyone about anything. On a few occasions, she even wet herself rather than ask to go to the bathroom. What struck them was the difference between her behavior when she was with her mother at the beginning of the school day and then after her mother left. In her mother's presence, she was lively, energetic, full of smiles, spontaneous, and talkative. As soon as her mother left, she became quiet and never smiled. Ophelia's parents were also worried about her behavior. Their three main concerns were that she was still unable to fall asleep unless one of them kept her company, she cried and threw temper tantrums when they left her with her baby-sitter, and she showed little interest in playing with other children her age. On the other hand, she got along well with her younger sister and older brother and was well behaved except when she was put to bed or left with baby-sitters.

3. Tyrone, a 13-year-old, got along well with his teachers but not with the other students. He was often in trouble for getting into fights that he invariably started because of some slight insult he imagined he had suffered at the hands of his peers. His parents reported that he always listened to them except when it came to his two younger sisters. Although his parents had warned and punished him repeatedly, he still made life miserable for his sisters. He hit them, teased them, took things away from them, called them names, and did anything he could to upset them. The more they cried and complained to their parents, the more he annoyed them. When he was younger, the neighbors complained that he shot their pets with his pellet gun, tied things to their pets' tails, and set fires in the street. However, except for one neighbor who suspected that Tyrone had broken some windows of his cottage, it had been over 2 years since any of the neighbors had complained about him.

References

These references discuss whether students with conduct disorders choose to misbehave.

1. Kelly, E. J. (1988). *The Differential Problem Sorter Manual: Rationales and Procedures Distinguishing Between Conduct Problem and Emotionally Disturbed Students and Populations*. Las Vegas: University of Nevada, Department of Special Education.

2. Lytton, H. (1990). Child and parent effects in boys' conduct disorder: A reinterpretation. *Developmental Psychology, 26* (5), 683–697.

3. Weinberg, L. A. (1992). The relevancy of choice is distinguishing seriously emotionally disturbed from socially maladjusted students. *Behavioral Disorders, 17* (2), 99–106.

The following references provide evidence that biological and environmental factors contribute to the development of students' conduct disorders.

4. Beardslee, W. R., Schultz, L. H., & Selman, R. L. (1987). Levels of social-cognitive development, adaptive functioning, and DSM-III diagnoses in adolescent offspring of parents with affective disorders: Implications of the development of the capacity for mutuality. *Developmental Psychology, 23,* 807–815.

5. Emery, R. E. (1982). Interparental conflict and the children of discord and divorce. *Psychological Bulletin, 92,* 310–330.

6. Loeber, R., & Stouthamer-Loeber, M. (1986). Family factors as correlates and predictors of juvenile conduct problems and delinquency. In M. Tronry & N. Morris (Eds.), *Crime and Justice: An Annual Review of Research* (Vol. 7). Chicago: University of Chicago Press.

7. Rutter, M., & Garmezy, N. (1983). Developmental psychopathology. In E. M. Hetherington (Ed.), *Handbook of Child Psychology* (Vol. 4). New York: Wiley.

8. Wood, F. H., Cheney, C. O., Cline, D. H., Sampson, K., Smith, C. R., & Guetzloe, E. C. (1991). *Conduct Disorders and Social Maladjustments: Policies, Politics, and Programming.* Reston, VA: Council for Exceptional Children.

The schools' role in working with students who have conduct disorders is discussed in these references.

9. Eagle Forum. (n.d.) *The Student's Bill of Rights.* Box 618, Alton, IL.

10. Nelson, C. M., Center, D. B., Rutherford, R. B., & Walker, H. M. (1991). Serving troubled youth in a troubled society: A reply to Maag and Howell. *Exceptional Children, 58* (1), 77–79.

11. Townsend, K. K. (1993, January 31). Teaching right from wrong. *San Francisco Examiner.*

These references describe theories of moral development.

12. Kohlberg, L. (1984). Moral stages and moralization. In A. Garrod, R. Bartell, W. Rampaul, & K. Siefert (Eds.), *Perspective on Teaching, Learning and Development.* Dubuque, IA: Kendall/Hunt.

13. Loevinger, J., & Wessler, R. (1979). *Measuring Ego Development* (Vol. 1). San Francisco: Jossey-Bass.

14. Piaget, J. (1965). *The Moral Judgment of Children.* New York: Free Press.

These references describe techniques for identifying students with conduct disorders.

15. Nelson, C. M. (1971). Techniques for screening conduct disturbed children. *Exceptional Children, 37,* 501–507.

16. Quay, H. C., & Peterson, D. R. (1979). *Manual for the Behavior Problems Checklist.* Miami: Quay & Peterson.

17. Spivack, G., & Spotts, J. (1966). *Devereux Child Behavior Rating Scale.* Devon, PA: Devereux Foundation.

This reference documents bias in the identification of students with conduct disorders.

18. Ludwig, G., & Cullinan, D. (1984). Behavior problems of gifted and nongifted elementary school girls and boys. *Gifted Child Quarterly, 28* (1), 37–39.

Fostering moral development in the second stage is discussed in these references.

19. Chandler, M. (1973). Egocentrism and antisocial behavior: The assessment and training of social perspective-taking skills. *Developmental Psychology, 9,* 326–332.

20. Feshbach, N. (1978). Studies in developing empathy. In B. Maker (Ed.), *Progress in Experimental Personality Research.* New York: Academic Press.

21. Hersh, R. H., Miller, J. P., & Fielding, G. D. (1980). *Models of Moral Education*. White Plains, NY: Longman.

22. Schmuck, R., & Schmuck, P. (1984). *Group Process in the Classroom* (4th ed.). Dubuque, IA: Brown.

23. Selman, R. L. (1976). Social cognitive understanding: A guide to educational and clinical practice. In T. Lickona (Ed.), *Moral Development: Theory Research and Social Issues*. New York: Holt, Rinehart & Winston.

Moral education programs and techniques are described in the following references.

24. Fraenkel, J. R. (1977). *How to Teach About Values: An Analytic Approach*. Englewood Cliffs, NJ: Prentice-Hall.

25. Gardner, E. M. (1983). *Moral Education for Emotionally Disturbed Adolescents: An Application of Kohlbergian Techniques and Spiritual Principles*. Lexington, MA: Lexington Books.

26. Hersh, R. H., Miller, J. P., & Fielding, G. D. (1980). *Models of Moral Education: An Appraisal*. White Plains, NY: Longman.

27. McPhail, P., Ungoed-Thomas, J. R., & Chapman, H. (1975). *Lifeline*. Niles, IL: Argus Communications.

28. Presno, V., & Presno, C. (1980). *The Values Realm: Activities for Helping Students Develop Values*. New York: Teachers College Press.

29. Reimer, J., Paolitto, D. P., & Hersch, R. H. (1983). *Promoting Moral Growth: From Piaget to Kohlberg* (2nd ed.). White Plains, NY: Longman.

30. Shaver, J., & Strong, W. (1976). *Facing Value Decisions: Rationale Building for Teachers*. Belmont, CA: Wadsworth.

31. Silver, M. (1976). *Values Education*. Washington, DC: National Education Association.

32. Sullivan, E. V. (1975). *Moral Learning: Finding Issues and Questions*. New York: Paulist Press.

These references describe tests of moral reasoning.

33. Kohlberg, L., Colby, A., Gibbs, J., & Speicher-Dubin, B. (1978). *Standard Form Scoring Manual*. Cambridge, MA: Harvard University, Center for Moral Education.

34. Rest, J. R. (1986). *Moral Development: Advances in Research and Theory*. New York: Praeger.

Research on the effectiveness of moral education is the focus of these references.

35. Arbuthnot, J., & Gordon, D. A. (1986). Behavioral and cognitive effects of a moral reasoning development intervention for high risk behaviorally disordered adolescents. *Journal of Consulting and Clinical Psychology, 54,* 208–216.

36. Arndt, A. W., Jr. (1976). Maturity of moral reasoning about hypothetical dilemmas and behavior in an actual setting. *Dissertation Abstracts International, 37*, 435B. (University Microfilms No. 75-15, 009).

37. Bear, G. G. (1980). The relationship of moral reasoning to conduct problems and intelligence. *Dissertation Abstracts International, 40*, 4961A. (University Microfilms No. 80-04, 677).

38. Bear, G. G., & Richards, H. C. (1981). Moral reasoning and conduct problems in the classroom. *Journal of Educational Psychology, 73* (5), 644–670.

39. Blakeney, C. D., Jr., & Blakeney, R. A. (1991). Understanding and reforming misbehavior among behaviorally disordered adolescents. *Behavioral Disorders, 16* (2), 120–126.

40. Blatt, M., & Kohlberg, L. (1975). The effects of classroom moral discussion upon children's level of moral judgment. In L. Kohlberg & E. Toriel (Eds.), *Recent Research in Moral Development*. New York: Holt, Rinehart & Winston.

41. Campagna, A. F., & Hartner, S. (1975). Moral judgment in socio-pathic and normal children. *Journal of Personality and Social Psychology, 31*, 199–205.

42. Coleman, M., Pfeiffer, S., & Oakland, T. (1992). Aggression replacement training with behaviorally disordered adolescents. *Behavioral Disorders, 18* (1), 54–66.

43. Fodor, E. M. (1972). Delinquency and susceptibility to social influence among adolescents as a function of level of moral development. *Journal of Social Psychology, 86*, 257–260.

44. Hickey, J. E. (1972). The effects of guided moral discussion upon youthful offender's level of moral judgment. *Dissertation Abstracts International, 33*, 1551A. (University Microfilms No. 72-25, 438).

45. Hogan, R. (1975). The structure of moral character and the explanation of moral action. *Journal of Youth and Adolescence, 4*, 1–15.

46. Hudgins, W., & Prentice, N. M. (1973). Moral judgment in delinquent and non-delinquent adolescents and their mothers. *Journal of Abnormal Psychology, 82*, 145–152.

47. Junell, J. S. (1979). *Matters of Feeling: Values Education Reconsidered*. Bloomington, IN: Phi Delta Kappa Educational Foundation.

48. Jurkovic, G., & Prentice, N. M. (1974). Dimensions of moral interaction and moral judgment in delinquent and nondelinquent families. *Journal of Consulting and Clinical Psychology, 42*, 256–262.

49. Kohlberg, L. (1958). *The Development of Modes of Moral Thinking and Choice in the Years 10 to 16*. Unpublished doctoral dissertation, University of Chicago.

50. Kohlberg, L., & Candee, D. (1984). The relationship of moral judgment to moral action. In L. Kohlberg (Ed.), *The Psychology of Moral Development*. San Francisco: Harper & Row.

51. Kohlberg, L., & Hersch, R. H. (1977). Moral development: A review of the theory. *Theory into Practice, 16,* 53–58.

52. Kohlberg, L., Kauffman, K., Scharf, P., & Hickey, J. (1974). *The Just Community Approach to Corrections: A Manual* (Part I). Unpublished manuscript, Harvard University, Cambridge, MA.

53. Leming, J. S. (1978). Intrapersonal variations in stage of moral reasoning among adolescents as a function of situational context. *Journal of Youth and Adolescence, 4,* 405–416.

54. Maag, J. W. (1989). Moral discussion group interventions: Promising technique or wishful thinking? *Behavioral Disorders, 14,* 97–105.

55. Muson, H. (1979, February). Moral thinking: Can it be taught? *Psychology Today,* 48–68.

56. Power, C., & Reimer, J. (1978). Moral atmosphere: An educational bridge between moral judgment and action. In W. Damon (Ed.), *New Directions in Child Development: Moral Development.* San Francisco: Jossey-Bass.

57. Scharf, P. (1978). *Moral Education.* Davis, CA: Responsible Action.

58. Scharf, P., Hickey, J. E., & Moriarty, T. (1973). Moral conflict and change in correctional settings. *Personnel and Guidance Journal, 51,* 660–663.

59. Stein, J. L. (1973). *Adolescent Reasoning About Moral and Sex Dilemmas: A Longitudinal Study.* Unpublished doctoral dissertation, Harvard University, Cambridge, MA.

The following references discuss enhancing moral growth on the affective level through increasing caring and empathy.

60. Gibbs, J. C. (1987). Social processes in delinquency: The need to facilitate empathy as well as sociomoral reasoning. In W. M. Kurtines & J. L. Gewirtz (Eds.), *Moral Development Through Social Interaction.* New York: Wiley.

61. Kurtines, W. M., & Gewirtz, J. L. (Eds.). (1987). *Moral Development Through Social Interaction.* New York: Wiley.

62. Lickona, T. (1977). Creating the just community with children. *Theory into Practice, 16* (2), 103.

63. McPhail, P. (1975). *Learning to Care.* Niles, IL: Argus Communications.

64. Newman, F. (1975). *Education for Citizen Action: Challenge for Secondary Curriculum.* Berkeley, CA: McCutchan.

65. Newman, F., Bertocci, T. A., & Landsness, R. M. (1977). *Skills in Citizen Action.* Skokie, IL: National Textbook.

66. Panella, D., & Henggeler, S. W. (1986). Peer interaction of conduct-disordered, anxious-withdrawn, and well-adjusted black adolescents. *Journal of Abnormal Child Psychology, 14,* 1–11.

67. Schonert-Reichl, K. A. (1993). Empathy and social relationships in adolescents with behavioral disorders. *Behavioral Disorders, 18* (3), 189–204.

Values clarification is discussed in the following references.

68. Beach, W. (1992). *Ethical Education in American Public School.* Washington, DC: National Education Association.

69. Kirschenbaum, H. (1977). *Advanced Value Clarification.* La Jolla, CA: University Associates.

70. Kirschenbaum, H., & Simon, S. (1973). *Readings in Values Clarification.* Minneapolis, MN: Winston Press.

71. Lockwood, A. L. (1978). The effects of values clarification and moral development curricula on school age subjects. *Review of Educational Research, 48,* 325–364.

72. Raths, L., Harmin, M., & Simon, S. (1966). *Values and Teaching: Working with Values in the Classroom.* Columbus, OH: Merrill.

73. Simon, S., Howe, L., & Kirschenbaum, H. (1972). *Values Clarification: A Handbook of Practical Strategies for Teachers and Students.* New York: Hart.

The following reference discusses why the application of consequences does not change students with conduct disorders.

74. Erickson, M. F., & Egeland, B. (1987). A developmental view of the psychological consequences of maltreatment. *School Psychology Review, 16,* 156–168.

These references are cited in the discussion of terminology.

75. American Psychiatric Association. (1987). *Diagnostic and Statistical Manual of Mental Disorders* (3rd ed., rev.). Washington, DC: Author.

76. Leone, P. E., Rutherford, R. B., Jr., & Nelson, C. M. (1991). *Special Education in Juvenile Corrections.* Reston, VA: Council for Exceptional Children.

EMOTIONAL PROBLEMS

This chapter is concerned with students who misbehave in the classroom because they come to school with emotional problems that originate elsewhere. It discusses what emotional problems are, how they cause students to misbehave, and what educators can do to help such students in school.

Role of Emotions

Emotions both stimulate us to react to events and help us select appropriate responses to these events. Consider the following example of how the process works.

The bell signaling the end of the period will ring in 2 minutes, and the teacher in charge hasn't quite finished returning the class test papers. Mary, Jaime, and Latanya are about to receive their papers. Mary looks apprehensively at the top of the page—C. She is relieved. "I finally passed," she announces to her friend sitting alongside her. Jaime looks at his paper, sees a C, and moans. Latanya examines her paper—C. "Oh no!" she thinks. "I can't show this to my dad. He'll kill me."

The bell rings. Mary walks out of the room happy. Jaime stops at the door, anxiously waiting for his friend, Carlos. Carlos sees the worried look on his face. "Hey, man," Jaime says to him, "you gotta help me with this sucker." Latanya is still sitting in her seat, stunned. She is in no hurry to go home where she will have to fulfill the family ritual of showing her parents her test papers, because she is petrified of the consequences.

With each of these three students and their test grades, the process is the same. First, something happens that is given meaning by the student's intellect. In this example, they see their grades. For Mary, the C is good; for Jaime and Latanya, the C is a disaster.

Next, each student has an emotional experience, including a bodily response that prepares them to react to the situation. Mary feels happy, Jaime becomes anxious, and Latanya is afraid.

Then their intellect determines how they will react, based on their previous experiences, training, expectations, and the like. Mary bounds out of the room humming; Jaime seeks assistance; and Latanya sits motionless, trying to summon up the courage to face her parents.

Emotional Problems

This process of an event, a feeling, and a behavior is the way things should happen and the way they usually do happen. But some students' emotional responses do not guide their behavior appropriately. As a result, we say that they have emotional problems.

Overly Intense Emotions

Certain students have emotional responses that are too strong. For example, you may know students with whom you really have to be careful about what you say because they are devastated by the slightest criticism. Or you may have students who feel intensely anxious when they have to talk in front of a group. Some students build up the little positive things in their lives all out of proportion, so that other students can't understand what they are so excited about. Students who experience their emotions too intensely and so behave inappropriately usually have emotional problems.

Most of the time, you will have to make on-the-spot decisions about your students' emotional responses. You can make fairly accurate informal assessments by using their behaviors to indicate whether their responses are appropriate or not.

Emotional responses that are too intense are characterized by extreme reactions to small or relatively inconsequential events or events that, at the student's current age or developmental level, should no longer evoke such strong responses. Here are examples of behaviors from students whose emotional responses are too intense:

They are petrified by a little blood from a scrape on the knee or a small cut on the finger.

They become extremely anxious when they have to answer questions, take tests, make a report, or the like.

They are easily upset by even a minor criticism or correction of their work or behavior.

They become very angry about small things and seem to have a chip on their shoulder.

They are frustrated over very minor delays, small obstacles, and other irritants.

They get depressed over the little disappointments that other students seem to take in stride.

If, for example, Jaime's emotional response had been too intense, he might have felt so anxious that he would have avoided talking about the exam or asking Carlos for help so he would do better the next time he took a test because it would have made him much more anxious. If Latanya's emotional response had been too strong, she might have stayed out all night or thrown away her test and told her parents she received an A but lost the paper. In both cases, Jaime and Latanya would have overreacted to their grades and behaved inappropriately.

Weak Emotions

Certain students have just the opposite problem. Instead of being too strong, their emotional responses are too weak. For example, most students mistreated or abused by their peers will eventually rise up and protest such treatment. But students with weak emotional responses just feel a little resentful but not resentful enough to do something about it. Then again, most students have their ups and downs; but some seem incapable of feeling really happy. Though nice things happen to them, these things don't excite or energize them as they would other people. Educators with a student that fits this description sometimes feel like shaking the student and saying, "Wake up, you're alive, you've got feelings, stand up for yourself, enjoy yourself, live a little."

The following are examples of students' emotional responses that are too weak:

They do not experience enough anger to defend or protect themselves when others take advantage of them.

They are not upset enough by their mistakes and failures to try to correct them or do better.

They are not particularly pleased by the pleasant things they experience.

If Mary's emotional response had been weak, she would not have felt good, despite the fact that she had passed her first test in the course thanks to tutoring sessions. If Jaime's response had been too weak, he would not have cared enough that he was earning a C average in the course instead of the B he needed to earn a college scholarship. As a result of their weak responses, neither Mary nor Jaime would have been motivated or energized to respond positively to their grades.

Incorrect Emotions

Many students experience unwarranted emotional responses. Some are insecure about their abilities to do well even though no objective reason exists for them to think this way. Other students seem to love to be unhappy and virtually wallow in their misery. They never seem "happier" than when relating some misfortune or complaint. Some students enjoy hurting others. Instead of empathizing with their peers' pain, they take pleasure in it. They seem to delight in putting others down, ridiculing them for their mistakes, and teasing and abusing weaker students.

The following are examples of students' unwarranted emotional responses:

They worry about things they know are extremely unlikely to happen. For instance, they may worry about failing a test they have studied for in a course that they are doing well in.

They torment other children, pets, or animals and laugh at the pain they inflict on them.

They do dangerous things and appear exhilarated by the possibility of being hurt.

They seem uncomfortable and anxious when others show that they like or respect them.

Latanya could have experienced an unwarranted emotion. Instead of being afraid of her parents' reaction to her C grade, she could have convinced herself that she had been marked unfairly and complained angrily about her teacher to her parents. It is obvious that such a mistaken view of reality can cause problems for the student as well as for the teacher who has to deal with such a student on a day-to-day basis.

Conflicting Emotions

Students sometimes experience conflicting emotions. They get angry at someone, but then they feel too guilty to act on their anger. Or they think they know the answer and want to participate, but then they are too afraid of being wrong to raise their hands. They may be afraid to do something dangerous, but they are also too ashamed to tell their friends that they do not want to do it. To experience conflicting emotions is natural. It only becomes a problem for students when they can't sort out their emotions enough to act one way or the other.

Students with conflicting emotions often appear to be immobilized by their problems:

Instead of showing resentment or anger when taken advantage of, they may act as if nothing bothers them because they are too guilty to admit to themselves that they are resentful.

Instead of trying to learn to play an instrument, build a project, or make a team, they act as if they didn't care one way or the other because down deep they are afraid of failure.

Rather than ask for help when they need it, they persist even though they know that what they are doing is inadequate or wrong.

If Jaime, for example, had experienced conflicting emotions, he might have felt both anxious about his average and also too ashamed to ask anyone for help.

At times, intense, weak, and conflicting emotions can be appropriate. Intense emotional responses fit intense situations. When students are having serious problems in school, when something wonderful and unexpected happens to them, or when they have done something terrible that they regret, it is appropriate that they experience strong emotional responses. Weak emotional responses are also natural in the rhythm of life. If every event produced the same level of response, little delays, obstacles, or disappointments would upset students as much as major frustrations, and they would be overwhelmed by the little problems that confront everyone from time to time. Conflicting emotions are a part of life, too. Students should feel too guilty or too ashamed to act on some of their feelings if these actions would hurt or be unfair to others. Emotional responses only cause students problems when they are *too* strong, *too* weak, or *incorrect* for the situations at hand or when, instead of dealing with their conflicting emotions, students can't act on them.

Inappropriate Emotions and Inappropriate Behavior

When students experience emotional responses that are too strong, too weak, incorrect, or in conflict, their behavior is appropriate for their emotional response but inappropriate for the situation. Because of this mismatch between emotion and situation, these students usually use ineffective solutions or they adopt one of three strategies instead of applying appropriate solutions to the problems and opportunities of daily living. They either avoid facing up to the situations, defend against the situations, or merely suffer through the situations without being able to even try dealing with them.

Using Ineffective Solutions   When students are under the sway of emotional problems, they may use less effective techniques than they would otherwise employ to deal with a challenge, problem, or opportunity. For example, a student who is anxious before a test may start to work before reading all of the directions in order to relieve her tension by getting started. Another student may be so angry at what another student said to him about his religion, ethnic background, parents, and such, that instead of responding in a way that is commensurate with what the other student did and keeping out of trouble, he overreacts and stabs him.

Avoiding   Students may avoid situations if they cannot cope with the emotions these situations arouse. For example, they may feign illness to avoid a test, a teacher, or a bully on the bus who is too threatening to handle. Avoiding these situations may temporarily alleviate their fears and anxieties, but it doesn't solve the problem they are too anxious or too afraid to handle.

The following examples of avoidance behavior characterize many students with emotional problems:

They cut classes or are truant.

They do not try to accomplish things that they anticipate will be difficult, or they stop attempting things as soon as they reach a difficult stage or obstacle in the process.

Instead of discussing the things that bother them, they retreat into themselves and give others the silent treatment.

They tend to break up relationships rather than try to work on them when they run into difficulties with other people.

When their peers do annoying things or interfere with what they are doing, they let them have their way to avoid confrontations.

They may hide their true feelings and attitudes because they are too afraid of the consequences that may occur if they reveal them.

Defending   While the word *defend* has many meanings, here it means to fool oneself, to pretend to oneself that one does not feel or think the way one in fact does. By being defensive, people keep themselves from experiencing feelings and thoughts that are too threatening or unacceptable. Students act defensively when they convince themselves that their teachers cannot teach when in fact they actually have not made an effort to learn. Another example is when students persuade themselves that a test they failed owing to lack of preparation was unfair and picayune.

Students are especially likely to act defensively when they experience conflicting emotions. For example, if a student is afraid of failing an audition for the school play, she can skip the audition. If she also feels ashamed about being insecure, she may overcome her fear enough to show up. But if the student cannot admit to herself that she is insecure because she can't deal with the shame such an admission would produce, she may "forget" to show up for the audition. Then the student can blame a poor memory for the fact that she did not show up, thereby missing the audition and avoiding the shame she might feel if she had missed it intentionally.

Defending oneself to oneself and lying to others are different behaviors. When students act defensively, they delude themselves. At least on one level, they really believe their self-deceptions. But when students lie to others, they know the truth yet prefer not to admit it to others.

Like all of us, students have a variety of ways they can act defensively:

They blame their teachers and peers for their own mistakes and shortcomings, fail to see how they play a role in their own rejection and failure, or believe the constructive criticism and necessary punishment they receive is unjustified and uncalled for.

They justify inappropriate behavior to themselves with a variety of excuses that are obviously false to others.

When things do not turn out as they expect them to or when they do not succeed in doing what they attempted to do, they adopt a sour grapes attitude, saying things like "It didn't really matter" and "Who needed it anyway?"

They feel too sick or too tired to try doing something so as not to have to face up to the fact that they really don't want to do it or are afraid to do it.

Suffering   Suffering an emotion means experiencing it so intensely that one cannot do anything about it except suffer. Students who suffer with emotions or emotional problems may experience emotional blocks when they are extremely anxious about taking a test, speaking in front of a group, or reading answers aloud. Other students may be immobilized by depression or guilt.

The unproductive, unhelpful suffering some students experience can take many forms:

They bite their nails, twitch, develop a variety of facial grimaces, or simply cry when they are anxious or afraid.

More extreme suffering can cause them to have blocks when they have to talk, read, or perform before a group.

They fall apart on examinations and are unable to do what would be easy for them to do if they weren't so anxious.

When their work is difficult, they rip up their papers, throw their books across the room, or take their frustration and tension out on inanimate objects in other ways.

They sit silently, stare out the window, draw at their desk, and so on, when they are too depressed to mobilize themselves to do anything.

Only excessive use of ineffective solutions, avoiding, defending, or suffering causes problems. The examples given in this section illustrate some of the nonconstructive ways students react to the daily problems and challenges in their lives. That does not mean, however, that avoiding, defending, and suffering are always inappropriate. For example, students often have to experiment with ineffective solutions to learn from their mistakes. Avoidance may sometimes be necessary. Students cannot always face up to every challenge as soon as it presents itself—they do not operate that way. Students need to take breaks from the difficulties they encounter in school so that they can return to them refreshed and ready to do battle again. In these cases, avoidance is natural and necessary.

Defensive behavior can also be appropriate at times. For instance, when students are learning a new skill or sport, it sometimes helps them to believe they are doing better than they are. If beginners knew how poorly they wrote, how clumsy they looked on the basketball court, or how their violin playing really sounded, they might be too discouraged to continue to strive to achieve their goals.

Suffering is a normal part of life, too. Students may have to suffer for a time before they can act. Sometimes they have to fail badly at or feel bad about something before they are moved enough to change their behavior. A little suffering may not stir them to action. Instead they need to suffer a lot first.

Students' emotional problems are caused by emotional responses that lead them to consistently use ineffective solutions, avoid, defend, and suffer with their problems instead of trying to solve them. Everyone experiences inappropriate emotional responses from time to time. And at times, everyone avoids, defends, and suffers instead of trying to solve their problems. But when students do these things to excess, too often, and in situations that are nonconstructive, so that they have few successes and fail to develop competency or confidence, they have emotional problems.

Students use ineffective solutions, avoid, defend, and suffer inappropriately when doing so impedes rather than fosters their progress. Experienced teachers usually know when a student who is avoiding a challenge should be allowed to take a break from it and when the student should be encouraged or required to tackle it head-on. They can also tell when to go along with a student's behavior because the student is not prepared to accept the truth and when that student needs a dose of reality. And most teachers know when allowing a student to suffer the results of his or her mistakes and inappropriate behavior would be good for the student and when it would be better to provide the student with support, understanding, and forgiveness.

Self-Quiz: Behavior Adjustment Mechanisms

Categorize each of the following behaviors in terms of the four adjustment mechanisms (avoiding, suffering, defending, solving appropriately or inappropriately).

1. She leaves the room to go to the bathroom when the work is difficult.
2. He convinces himself that what one does not know is not important.
3. He asks the teacher for help when he does not understand the problem.
4. He believes that his teacher is too strict when it is obvious to others that he is not.
5. She scribbles on the page instead of working.
6. She studies before the examination.
7. He has a stomach pain or a headache when he has to go to school.
8. She pretends to her parents that she is sick when she has to go to school.
9. He believes that school is not important because he is going to be a professional football player, so it does not matter that he is flunking three subjects.
10. She becomes so nervous when she has to give a report in front of the class that she can't speak.

Identification

If a student's behavior problem is caused by an inappropriate emotional response, you need to be able to identify the emotion and decide whether it is too strong, too weak, incorrect, or in conflict with another feeling. For example, you might realize that a student is hitting someone else because she is extremely jealous (too intense). Or you may discover that a student is being teased by other youngsters because he doesn't become angry enough to defend himself (too weak). You might conclude that a third student won't answer in class because he is afraid for no good reason that you and the other students are going to make fun of him (incorrect). And you may learn that a fourth student has not been doing any homework for the last month because she is worried that she might be pregnant, but at the same time she is afraid to confide in anyone or take a pregnancy test because she feels ashamed (conflicting emotions). In each example, it is possible to both identify the emotion that is causing the behavior and to know whether it is too strong, too weak, incorrect, or in conflict.

Informal Assessment

If a student's behavior is caused by an emotional problem, you should also be able to determine whether she or he is using ineffective solutions, avoiding, defending, or suffering. It may be clear to you, for example, that a teenager spends less time with her girlfriends because she is *avoiding* situations where she has to relate to boys. Or you may discover that a student's anger and vindictiveness when you point out what he has done wrong is his way of *defending* himself because he can't admit that he has made a mistake. Or you may realize that even though a student has written a good composition, if you try to make her read it to the class, she may *suffer* a panic attack and do a terrible job of reading it aloud.

Self-Quiz: Causes of Problem Behaviors

Below are five descriptions of problem behaviors. Imagine at least one emotional cause and one nonemotional cause for each behavior.

1. When the teacher asks her a question, she continues to look out the window.

2. He never plays soccer with the other students during recess.
3. When the teacher does not do what he wants, he makes angry noises, shouts, and on occasion threatens the teacher.
4. When it is her turn to be called on, she lowers her head and looks down at her desk.
5. When she has seatwork, she often asks her neighbors to do it for her.

Formal Assessment

You can also use formal assessment instruments to identify students with emotional problems. Such instruments as the Behavior Checklist (3), the Behavior Problems Checklist (1, 2, 6), the Devereaux Elementary School and Adolescent Behavior Rating Scales (4, 5), and the Walker Problem Identification Checklist (7, 8) can help you determine when the causes of students' behavior problems are emotional.

Biased Assessment

When evaluating students' emotional problems, it is important to avoid the kinds of gender and ethnic biases described in chapters 5 and 6. Studies reported in the 1960s, 1980s, and 1990s indicate that females account for only between 12% and 16% of the students in programs for students with emotional problems (9–11). Yet there is evidence that females have as many if not more emotional problems than males. As noted in chapter 5, school-age girls are more fearful and anxious than boys and are also more likely to experience themselves as sad or depressed than boys.

It appears that teachers either are less likely to notice female students' emotional problems or choose not to attend to them. The studies cited above found that the type of behavior most likely to call teachers' and school officials' attention to students' emotional problems are acting out, disruptive, externalizing behaviors that are typically characteristic of angry, resentful, jealous, and rebellious students and male students. Withdrawal and other internalizing behaviors, which are more typical of anxious, fearful, and especially depressed students and female students, are much less likely to provoke responses from teachers. In general, females are attended to when their emotional problems are expressed in typical male ways. These results are similar to the findings reported in chapter 6 that indicate that teachers, especially female teachers, tend to be less tolerant of "male-typical" behaviors.

Ethnic bias in the identification of students with emotional problems should also be avoided. For example, Asian Pacific American students tend to be underidentified as having emotional problems, whereas African American students are overidentified. As noted in chapter 5, many teachers are unable to determine when Asian Pacific American students are fulfilling culturally appropriate behavior styles and when they are truly shy, anxious, timid, or fearful. And as noted in chapter 5, African American males are especially likely to suffer the consequences of teachers' intolerance of male behavior patterns.

Emotional Versus Conduct Problems

Students have emotional problems because their emotional responses to situations are too intense, too weak, incorrect, or in conflict, and they commonly use ineffective solutions, avoid, defend, and suffer rather than trying to solve the problems and challenges of their daily lives. In contrast, students with conduct problems appear to be unwilling to control their behavior. They know how adults expect them to behave, but they do not believe they need to or should behave that way. Conduct problems and emotional problems differ in two important respects.

First, students with conduct problems may be able to behave differently, but they neither want to do so nor think it is necessary to do so. Students with emotional problems, however, cannot behave differently. Thus, if students have conduct problems, they need a change in their attitudes to change their conduct. If students have emotional problems, however, they need to have chances to experience more appropriate emotional responses and to be able to avoid, defend, and suffer less and resolve their problems more.

The second way in which conduct and emotional problems differ is that students with conduct problems do things to benefit themselves even at the expense of others. But students with emotional problems may do things even though they benefit no one, not even themselves. Thus, for change to take place, students with conduct problems have to learn that they can't and shouldn't always place their own benefit before the welfare of others. Students with emotional problems, however, need help so that they don't continue to do things that aren't beneficial to themselves.

Now let's look at some examples of these differences. Two students may both act as if they do not hear their teacher ask them to move a cage with a harmless garden snake inside, but each may have a different reason. A student with conduct problems may not want to do his share of the classroom chores. But a student with emotional problems may want to do his share yet be too afraid of snakes to be able to follow through. In another example, a student with conduct problems may copy test answers because she thinks it's okay to do so. A student with emotional problems may be so anxious about doing poorly on the test that she copies someone else's answers even though she knows it's wrong to do so. In a third example, a student with conduct problems pushes in front of another student to avoid waiting his turn. A student with emotional problems may do the same because he enjoys dominating weaker students.

Two Kinds of Emotional Problems

Some students' emotional problems are part of their personalities, and they bring their problems with them wherever they go. They are anxious and insecure in situations that most students can take in stride. They are angry, sullen, and resentful in situations that do not upset most other children and teenagers. Or they fear all authority figures, not just those that are punitive. Other students without such personality problems and who are doing well in general may have problems dealing with particular situations. The necessity of adjusting to a divorce, a new stepparent and perhaps stepbrothers and sisters, a death in the family, a serious illness, a move to a new neighborhood, and other life crises cause them to react in ways that can create additional difficulties for themselves and others. They may suddenly become anxious, angry, rebellious, or depressed, but they are not basically anxious, angry, rebellious, or depressed young people. Because difficult situations rather than their personalities cause their emotional problems, mental health professionals often label their difficulties adjustment problems or reactive problems.

Students with adjustment, or reactive, problems that affect their functioning in school need individualized attention from their teachers. Students with personality problems require a somewhat different approach than students who have situational problems because the cause of their problems is different. Thus, educators need to distinguish between these two types of emotional problems because this distinction is critical to coming up with a sensitive and effective response.

Comparing Personality and Situational Problems

Your answers to the following questions will help you determine whether a student's emotional problems are situational or part of the student's personality:

1. *Did the student's emotional problems appear suddenly or are they long-standing?* Did the student suddenly change from well adjusted to anxious or from easy to get along with to angry and disobedient? One indication that a student's emotional problems are situational is that they tend to be recent. Often what happens is that the student does quite well until a particular situation or event causes a sudden emotional change.

2. *Can you identify a particular event or circumstance that triggered the change in the student's emotions?* When a student has problems that arise outside of school, a

teacher can often get the student to talk about the problem if the teacher approaches the student in the right way. Sometimes when a student is obviously troubled but is reluctant to discuss the problem, a call home often confirms a teacher's suspicion that something outside of school is interfering with a student's classroom functioning.

3. *Does the problem affect all aspects of the student's life or is it restricted to a single or a few situations?* Sometimes a student's situational emotional problem affects the student's life in general. For example, a student who becomes depressed because of the death of a parent will probably be depressed in most situations. However, in many cases a student's situational problem affects only those areas that are directly related to the cause of the problem. A student who has not made an athletic team may avoid only former friends who did make the team. A student who was raped may avoid only persons who remind her of the rapist who victimized her. And a student who failed a final exam in one subject may have an adverse reaction to that subject, not school, academic classes, or examinations in general.

Situational Problems

Since not all students are alike, some can handle situations that cause others to have problems. Certain situations, though, are so challenging, threatening, or emotionally charged that they are likely to cause most students to have some situational problems. For example, the death of a parent usually has a profound effect on people, regardless of their age. Students of any age may suffer extreme forms of anxiety, panic, sadness, depression, or a combination of all these feelings if one of their parents dies. Adolescents—being less dependent on and attached to their parents—may have these reactions to a lesser degree, but they may suffer from bouts of guilt and remorse for the way they had behaved toward the parent.

Divorce has a similar effect on students, especially young ones, though it is usually less severe than an actual death. Concerns about who will take care of them, who will support them, whether they will lose the parent they are not living with, is it their fault that their parents separated, and so on, cause most youngsters to feel frightened, anxious, guilty, resentful, angry, sad, or depressed. If their parents put them in the middle of their own conflicts and require them to take sides, they may experience even more problems. Students experiencing the emotional side effects of a death or divorce in the family typically have difficulty functioning well in school.

Many other home-based problems can influence school behavior, too. A new sibling can be a problem for young "only children" who are suddenly no longer the center of attention. Especially vulnerable youngsters may become jealous of their peers in school or try to make up for what they are missing at home by seeking extra attention from their teachers. Or deteriorations in students' relationships with their parents can affect the way they function in school. In particular, students who become the victims of physical or

Self-Quiz: Is It a Situational or Personality Problem?

The following examples illustrate the difference between situational and personality problems. Read each one and decide whether the emotional problem causing the behavior is more likely to be a situational or personality problem.

1. Rocco, a 7-year-old who is afraid of his older brother and sister, the children in his neighborhood, and the other children his age or older in school, only plays with younger children during recess.
2. After having heard for the last 5 years that she cannot and should not try to do what normal children do because of her heart condition, Cindy, a 9-year-old, is afraid to run, play ball, walk up hilly streets, or do anything that requires a lot of physical exertion. But she is not at all hesitant about engaging in challenging activities that do not involve physical exertion.
3. Michael, an 11-year-old student, lies both at home and at school whenever he is confronted with his inappropriate behavior.
4. Harry, a 12-year-old, lies to a teacher who punishes the students in her class rather severely for the infractions they commit, but he is as honest as most students his age with his other teachers.
5. Vincente, a 13-year-old student in the honors program of his intermediate school, has been inattentive in class for the last few days. He does not volunteer answers, and when called on, says he does not know the answer, gives his teachers a blank look, or glares at them. In one of his classes, he either reads comic books surreptitiously or lays his head down on his desk and tunes out the world.

sexual abuse at home or whose parents start to abuse alcohol or drugs may demonstrate the psychological effects of such situations in school.

In addition, experiences unrelated to the home can create situational emotional problems that can interfere with students' classroom functioning. For example, a serious illness or prolonged hospitalization, preoccupation with an unwanted pregnancy, or racial or ethnic conflicts on the school bus or in the streets can take their toll on student performance in school.

If a well-behaved student suddenly comes to class looking tired, depressed, or sullen, withdraws from his or her peers, stops participating in class and turning in homework, and cuts class or acts rebellious for no apparent reason, and if you suspect that this behavior may be due to situational problems outside of school, a good first step is to try finding out what the student is reacting to. A very young child may respond to a question such as, "What's the matter, Betty? You seem so sad." An older child might be approached with a question like, "Everything seems to upset you lately, Billy. Is something wrong?" An inquiry to a teenager might be phrased, "You have really had a short fuse the last couple of weeks. Is something bothering you that you want to talk about?" or "You really seem down. Has something happened to upset you?"

If a student seems hesitant to discuss the cause of the problem with you, let your student know that your goal is to be helpful, not critical. Assure the student that you want to help the student decide how she or he wants to handle the problem, not tell the student what to do. If your intuition tells you that the problem may be serious or confidential, inform the student that if she or he wants to talk with you, you will not interfere by going

Some students welcome the opportunity to discuss their problems with an understanding teacher.

to talk to anyone else involved without the student's consent unless it is absolutely necessary. You might have to explain what these circumstances are.

If the student still will not confide in you, the problem may be the kind that students typically prefer to talk over with someone besides their teachers. Sexual problems, discord at home, drug-related problems, unwanted pregnancies, and abuse at home are topics that many students feel uncomfortable discussing with teachers, even when they and their teachers have had excellent relationships. If you think your student is unable to confide in you, you might suggest someone else she or he could talk to or an agency or organization that might be able to help.

If your student does confide in you, you may learn that the student is reacting to a situation that cannot be changed, such as a death or divorce. If that is the case, you may be able to help the student deal with his or her feelings and also adapt your expectations to the student's current emotional state. Also treat your student with understanding, patience, and compassion. You can readily adjust your expectations and demands until the passage of time heals the wounds.

If, in contrast, your student is confronted by a situation that can be remedied, you will have to decide whether you can help or whether the student should be referred to another individual, agency, or organization. In dealing with a minor problem, you may be able to provide your student with the needed advice. But if your student is confronting a serious problem that requires the attention of other professionals and is not yet receiving such assistance, the most helpful thing you could probably do would be to help that student contact the appropriate agency or professional. In particular, if your student's difficulty in school is caused by conflicts at home, you would need to determine whether you have the

Self-Quiz: Choosing Responses to Situational Problems

Which of the following techniques would you feel comfortable using if you thought one of your students was experiencing situational problems?

Asking students if something is bothering them and what it might be.

Temporarily adjusting your expectations to the student's emotional state.

Counseling the student about how to deal with the problem.

Suggesting specific agencies that provide help to an older student.

Contacting a younger student's parents for additional information.

Contacting an older student's parents for additional information.

Counseling the student's parents.

Referring the student's parents to specific agencies that provide the assistance they require.

Informing the appropriate school personnel about the student's problem.

Informing the appropriate authorities if you suspect child abuse.

---

training and time to counsel the student's parents about the problem or whether you should refer the family to an agency that provides such services. Also, if your student's problems in school stem from some kind of abuse, you may be required by law to inform the proper authorities of what you have learned.

Sometimes the situational emotional problems that interfere with students' ability to function effectively in school arise in the schools themselves. Students whose ethnic, religious, or socioeconomic backgrounds differ from those of their peers and/or teachers may experience anxiety and discomfort because they do not know how to behave in certain situations and do not understand what others think or why they behave as they do.

Attending school can create situational problems for students who are different from their peers. Being different at school can be a problem. To stand out from the crowd is not always pleasant. Children and teenagers can be very cruel to those who do not look, act, or think like them. They may discriminate against, tease, reject, and even abuse students with disabilities, gifted students, those from different ethnic, religious, or socioeconomic backgrounds, gay and lesbian students, overweight students, or any students who do not fit the mold.

A supportive multicultural school environment that helps students appreciate diversity can go a long way to counter these forces. A nonsupportive school environment may do nothing to ameliorate them. In such cases, different students often feel anxious, fearful, angry, or alienated. They may fight back, play the clown, ingratiate themselves with their peers, or withdraw. Students with disabilities may resist being mainstreamed and integrated into programs with students who do not have disabilities. Gifted and talented students may pretend that they do not know as much as they do or think as they do to fit in with their peers. Students from different ethnic, religious, or socioeconomic backgrounds may stand up to their peers' pressure and even fight back both psychologically and physically. Or they may strive to become like their peers, rejecting what is different about themselves and their families and thus suffering guilt and shame and placing themselves in conflict with those family members who would rather maintain their identities.

Personality Problems

Students whose emotional problems are part of their personalities present teachers with two related, but different, challenges. The first is to overcome the learning and behavior problems caused by their students' emotional problems. The second is to contribute toward eliminating—or at least reducing—the emotional problems themselves. Many educators doubt that classroom teachers can handle the learning and behavior problems of students with even mild emotional problems, let alone make a contribution toward eliminating the problems. However, the view in this book is well expressed by Brophy and Putnam: "Teachers with the willingness and skills to do so can play important roles in helping their disturbed students to improve their general personal adjustments, in addition to helping them cope with the demands of the student role" (12, p. 13).

Helping Students Change

Like all emotional responses, an emotional response that is problematic typically consists of an idea, a feeling and the accompanying physiological changes that are evoked by the idea, and then a behavior. An example follows.

Bo, a student who mistakenly thinks he is a terrible math student, scans the items on a math test he is about to take and decides that the test is much too difficult for him to pass. He becomes fearful, and his physiological state changes to reflect his fear. He rips up his exam and runs out of the room.

To help students with emotional problems, teachers can help change the ideas that are the basis of their emotional reactions. If a teacher can help Bo understand that he is a capable math student, Bo will not become inappropriately fearful. Teacher can also help students by modifying their physiological state. If Bo is too upset to think rationally about his math ability, the teacher may succeed in calming him down sufficiently by using relaxation techniques, enabling Bo to take the test despite his imagined inability. Finally, teachers can work on the behavioral level. The teacher could offer Bo enough of a reward or incentive for taking the test that he does so despite his imagined inability and inappropriate fears.

Teachers can also use a combination of techniques to help students. In this case, a teacher might try to calm Bo down and offer him a reward. Whichever technique or combination of techniques succeeds in enabling Bo to take the test, passing the test will provide Bo with evidence that his fears were unfounded. And that will make it less likely that he will have the same reaction with the next math test.

This section describes various techniques for changing students' ideas and modifying their physiological states. It includes a number of behavioral interventions and approaches that employ a combination of techniques. Subsequent sections describe techniques you can use to improve students' behavior despite their problems (managing, tolerating, and preventing).

Because you will see and interact with your students daily, you are a key figure in their lives. You have an opportunity to influence not only how they behave but also how they feel about themselves.

Enhancing Self-Concepts   People's self-concepts, the characteristics they attribute to themselves, have a highly significant effect on the way they behave. Virtually no limits restrict the types of characteristics individual students can attribute to themselves—how tall they are, who they take after, whether or not they are good eaters, how intelligent they are, and so on. Despite this, four groups of attributes appear particularly relevant for understanding students' behavior (13–15):

- Ability or competency: the extent to which students believe they can attain, achieve, and succeed.

- Power or locus of control: the extent to which they believe they, not others, are in control of their lives.

- Virtuousness: the extent to which they think they have lived up to the moral and ethical standards they have acquired.

- Acceptance: The degree to which they experience others as liking, respecting, and wanting them.

Self-esteem, which is related to self-defining characteristics but is actually a different concept, refers to students' appraisal of the qualities they attribute to themselves. Specifically, if their self-concept matches what they think they should be like (ideal self), then they are likely to esteem themselves highly. If, however, a great discrepancy occurs between their self-concept and their ideal self, they may disparage themselves (16).

Research indicates that students with poor self-concepts or low self-esteem often develop emotional problems that in turn create learning and behavior problems (17–27). For example, students who believe they are unable to do things or are incompetent—who think they cannot learn or solve problems because they are stupid, or think they cannot play sports because they are clumsy and uncoordinated—can become anxious or fearful when confronted with the very things they mistakenly believe they will not be able to succeed at. Their anxiety or fear may be so strong that they avoid the task or challenges altogether. Or they may try to rise to the challenge but experience an emotional block. They might also give up at the first sign of difficulty because they are convinced they will fail if they persist. If they do this, they may give up quietly and feel sad or depressed, fly into a rage and rip up or destroy whatever they were working on, or take their anger and frustration out on others who only want to help them succeed.

Feeling incapable and inept, some students develop "learned helplessness" and come to believe that the locus of control over their lives is external. That is, they assume that they are not the masters of their own destiny. Instead of taking charge, they give up setting goals for themselves and become passive.

In the same circumstances, other students become defensive. They fool around in class, forget to do their homework, cut school, and are generally negligent so they can blame their failure on lack of effort rather than lack of ability. They tend to have difficulty accepting criticism no matter how constructive, well meaning, or well put it may be. Instead of accepting the truth, they defend themselves against the hurt they experience by blaming others and feeling angry. These reactions of avoiding, blocking, giving up easily, and acting defensively all cause students to fail. And this only fulfills or confirms their original fear that they are unable to succeed and makes it likely that they will experience even more anxiety and fear the next time.

Students who believe they are not virtuous have their own type of emotional problems. They may think that they are spoiled, selfish, mean, uncooperative, stubborn, or willful when in reality they are not. But thinking that they are bad and prone to blame themselves when things go wrong, they often feel guilty, ashamed, and depressed. Students with these burdensome feelings have difficulty keeping their minds on their work or mobilizing the energy they need to function adequately. Some try extra hard to be good to combat their notion that they are bad. This can prevent them from defending themselves when their peers take advantage of them because they think that it is bad to do so.

Students who believe they are not worthy of attention, respect, love, or acceptance tend to either avoid relationships with their peers and teachers or try currying favor with them. They feel they have to work hard or do something special to be accepted. Such students often feel sorry for themselves and can become sad and even depressed. Whatever specific form students' poor self-concepts take, so long as they think poorly of themselves, they experience emotional problems that can affect how well they function in school.

The good news is that research indicates that dedicated teachers can improve their students' self-concepts and self-esteem when they make the effort to do so (28–34). As Knoblock states, "Students can be assisted to feel better about themselves as a specific aspect of the school day. Self-awareness and understanding can be put into the context of skill development and can be taught systematically over time." (31, p. 158). The process of change, however, takes time. Canfield and Wells offer this caution: "It is possible to change self-concepts, and it is possible for teachers to effect the changes. . . . It isn't easy. Changes take place slowly over a long period of time" (28, p. 4).

Although in theory it is possible for students to attribute only negative characteristics to themselves, more typically they attribute both positive and negative qualities to themselves. Thus, one student may think of himself as competent and powerful but not as accepted or virtuous, while another believes just the opposite of herself. So to target your efforts at improving students' self-concepts accurately, it is essential to first know what they think of themselves in various areas.

You can gather this kind of information informally by observing students at work, at play, and during their interactions with others. You can also talk with them about what they think of themselves.

It is important to avoid ethnic bias when you evaluate your students' self-concepts. For example, you should not conclude that Asian Pacific Americans who do not volunteer answers or field-sensitive Hispanic Americans who seek what may seem unnecessary teacher feedback and approval lack self-confidence. They may function that way for cultural reasons (see chapter 5). Moreover, you should not assume that African American and Hispanic American students have low self-esteem because they are treated in a discriminatory manner and exposed to the prejudicial opinions that others have of them. And you should not jump to the conclusion that African American and Hispanic American students who are not doing well in school have low opinions of themselves and their abilities. Most studies of African American, Hispanic American, and poor students indicate that their self-concepts are at least as high, if not higher, than those of middle-class European Americans (35–49).

There are three common explanations for why African American and Hispanic American students, including those from poor backgrounds, do not necessarily have low self-concepts, even if they live in poor neighborhoods, experience discrimination, or do not do well in school:

1. The prevailing view that African Americans and other non-European Americans suffer from poor self-concepts is a product of a European American perspective. European American teachers and others do not realize that most non-European American children and their parents do not accept the dominant society's view that they are inferior and incapable. European Americans are not aware that African American, Native American, Hispanic American, and other non-European American families have always attempted to counteract the messages that students receive about their "inferiority" and have done so with increasing success since the black, brown, and red power movements of the late 1960s and 1970s (44, 46):

   > To act as if the only influence upon the formation of self-concepts is that of the dominant culture negates the idea of the child having any other culture or a socialization process that might counteract such a negative view. Such conclusions assume that all a Black or Indian child will get from his family socialization is a carbon copy of the negative stereotyping and evaluation of the white racist culture. . . . Either from ethnocentric distortion or from the negation of the culture of the minority group, researchers leave only psychopathological explanations for observed behavior (i.e., academic failure due to "poor self-concept." (44, p. 17)

   > Blacks have not really believed that white equals goodness and purity. Their self-concept has never entirely been controlled by whites . . . . Blacks have struggled to show their children that the white view of blacks as inferior is incorrect as well as immoral. (46, p. 139)

2. Non-European American and poor students believe that the environment they encounter both in and out of school is so hostile and prejudiced that despite their best efforts, skills, and abilities, they will not be able to accomplish their goals. That is, they do not see lack of effort or ability as the cause of many of their problems. As a result, they do not accept blame for not doing well and do not lose self-respect and self-confidence (50, 51).

   In a society that is fair, as it tends to be for most middle-class European Americans, students with an internal locus of control (who believe that they are in control of their lives) do better in school, because they try harder to succeed and to improve when they do poorly. However, in the case of poor students, African Americans, Hispanic Americans, and Native Americans, who exist in a racist and prejudiced environment, an internal locus of control may be self-destructive because it may lead students to blame themselves or hold themselves responsible for failure caused by unfairness, prejudice, and economic injustice. Students with an internal locus of control who are not doing well because of discrimination may blame themselves and give up; but students who correctly understand that external factors are to blame may strive to change them, especially if they are supported by others who hold similar beliefs and have similar characteristics.

3. Many poor non-European American students do not have poor self-concepts because they experience less academic stress than middle-class European American students. Unlike middle-class students, they are not trying to live up to high expectations, since their family's, their teachers', and their own expectations are not as high.

Several formal assessment instruments can be used to evaluate students' self concepts (13, 52–55). The Piers-Harris Children's Self-Concept Scale (55) and the Self-Observation Scales (53) provide information about students' overall perceptions of themselves. Other instruments have a more narrow focus: the Perceived Competency Scale for Children (52), the Nowicki Strickland Locus of Control Scale for Children (54), and the Coopersmith Self-Esteem Inventory (13). These instruments have been shown to be valid with European American students. However, for the reasons already discussed, their validity with non-European Americans is questionable.

Your daily interactions with your students give you lots of opportunities to make a significant contribution toward helping them improve their self-concept. This is actually important for all students, but it is crucial for students with poor self-concepts and low self-esteem. The recommended way to best help such students is to provide them with information and experiences that contradict the negative ways they currently perceive themselves. If they think they are inadequate or stupid, help them learn that they are capable and smart. If they believe they are powerless, help them see that they have some control over their own destinies. If they believe they are bad, help them realize that they are not. And if they feel they are not accepted by others, treat them with acceptance and respect.

Negative self-concepts that have built up over many years will not be changed overnight by a few well-chosen words. It takes consistent and determined effort for a considerable period of time to help students think better of themselves. The following suggestions are designed to assist you in achieving this goal.

Lack of ability: You can employ the following techniques with students who believe they do not have the capacity to attain their goals:

1. If your students think they are incapable or stupid, good instructional techniques individualized to their strengths and weaknesses are probably the most effective way to work with these students. Selecting work at their ability levels, organizing their assignments to ensure success, and providing support and information when they need it can help many students with poor self-concepts succeed despite their beliefs that they cannot.

2. You may be able to counteract students' pessimistic self-perceptions by helping them see the strengths and skills they bring to each task, by expressing your personal belief that they can succeed, and by explaining how their past experiences can be poor predictors of the present if they practice, study, and concentrate more and learn from their mistakes.

3. Students with emotional problems can be helped by reading books and seeing films and videos about others who have had experiences and problems like theirs (18, 26,

56–66). Using fictional or nonfictional material to enable students to learn vicariously about the experiences of others is called bibliotherapy.

Hebert describes bibliotherapy in the following way:

> Bibliotherapy is a counseling technique for helping people deal with their problems through reading novels or stories about characters who have similar problems. . . . Since reading appeals to the imagination, bibliotherapy provides an interaction between the reader and the story which can be less threatening than a direct confrontation. The real value of bibliotherapy is that it is a vicarious experience. Through the imagination, a young person has the opportunity to try various approaches to a problem without real life consequences should a wrong decision be made. (61, p. 209)

Exposing students who do not believe that they can overcome their past experiences or present problems to stories of real people who have actually done so can be inspirational. Providing students with the opportunity to identify with characters in fiction who have overcome problems similar to theirs can also be very beneficial.

Materials that are especially suited for use in a bibliotherapy approach with students at different age and grade levels are included in the references at the end of the chapter.

4. If students see their accomplishments as inadequate because they judge themselves by perfectionistic standards, help them be more realistic about what to expect of themselves. Explain that no one can do well in everything.

5. According to research, providing students with opportunities to succeed in areas where they feel adequate improves their general perceptions of their ability in other areas (67). An example of how you might put this to use with students who are anxious about reading or social studies is to encourage them to decorate their reports with artwork or maps or prepare dioramas if that is an area in which they have talent or skill.

6. Merely encouraging students to make positive rather than negative statements about themselves and reinforcing them when they do so can improve their self-concepts (30, 32). While this approach alone may not be enough to solve the problem, it does help.

Lack of power: You can help students who think that the control over their lives is external to believe they can influence their own destinies in a variety of ways:

1. Demonstrate your trust and faith that they can be self-managing and self-motivating enough to attain the goals they determine themselves with a minimum of external guidance.

2. In keeping with their maturity level, allow students to choose among alternative learning activities, centers, manipulatives, and instructional materials and permit them to generate or develop some of the alternatives themselves within limits you set. This will enhance their perceptions that they, and not others, are responsible for what they do in class. This also gives them another opportunity to experience your faith in them.

3. Allow students to work at their own pace within limits set by the needs of the group as a whole.

4. Provide dependent students with assistance only when they request it, and gradually wean them from needing your assistance.

5. Ask students what they think about their own work rather than expressing your opinion. This demonstrates your faith that they can evaluate themselves.

6. Teach students who seek extrinsic rewards to reward themselves.

Lack of virtue: The first thing you can do to help students who feel guilty and depressed because they think that they are bad is to avoid saying or doing things that will feed their guilt. Accentuate the positive in your relationships with them. If you have to say something negative, try to mention something positive first by saying such things as, "You were doing really well putting your art work away until you began to . . . " or "Sometimes you do wait patiently until you're called on and other times, like now, you don't." When talking about unacceptable behavior, instead of saying that a young student is naughty or a teenager is irresponsible, say that the student's *behavior* or the way the student acted was wrong or unacceptable. This condemns the action, not the person (see the section on reprimands in chapter 10).

Lack of acceptance: Students who believe that they are not respected, cared for, or loved by others will grow to feel better about themselves as they experience acceptance from others. Coopersmith and Feldman describe acceptance in the following terms:

> Acceptance implies liking and showing concern for the child as he is, with his capacities, limitations, strengths, and weaknesses. This acceptance is expressed by interest in the child, concern for his welfare, involvement in his activities and development, support for him in his times of stress and appreciation of what he is, and can do. Acceptance is also expressed by recognition of the child's frailties and difficulties and by the awareness that the child can only do so much and be his particular kind of person at this time of his life. . . . It is the quality of expression rather than the sheer quantity that is critical. Children can sense concern, interest, and appreciation and are not easily fooled by mere words of praise and affection or by insincere demonstrations of physical affection. (20, p. 206)

Your daily interaction gives you many chances to demonstrate your interest, concern, and acceptance of students. While you should do this with all students, students who feel they are not accepted and loved by others especially need such caring, compassionate treatment.

Self-concept enhancement programs: There are numerous structured programs that are designed to enhance students' self-concepts (28, 29, 34, 68–70). Typically, they involve self-concept-enhancing activities as a regular part of the curriculum. One of the better known ones, rational-emotive therapy, includes group activities that foster attitudes of self-acceptance, willingness to take risks, acceptance of uncertainty, tolerance of imperfections in one's personality, behavior, and achievement, and so on (69, 72, 73). Another approach includes group activities such as having students say something nice about themselves and making collages about their positive attributes, making positive statements about others in the class, and overcoming obstacles in an obstacle course. In another program, called Social Contact Exercise/Positive Bombardment, the class prepares a "Happiness Booklet" for each student, in which each class member and teacher writes something positive about the student; the class produces a video showing the students "doing their best thing"; and the students engage in various cooperative learning activities. Many programs incorporate their own particular selection of self-concept-enhancing activities suggested by authors who have published books and articles about how to improve students' self-concepts.

The results of these programs suggest that they may have a modest effect on the self-concepts of some students who do not have serious self-concept problems (71–74). It appears that long-term intervention—10 or more weeks using programs that are integrated into the ongoing curriculum and reinforced by it—are more effective than short-term efforts using programs that are added on to the curriculum (75). There is suggestive evidence that these programs may be more effective with males than with females.

Unfortunately, the results of these programs with students who have emotional problems have been mixed at best (76, 77). They seem to help some students, but they do not produce consistent positive results. As Morse explains, "There are programs to improve self-concept, but self-concept is so much a part of a person's totality that it is hard to imagine a specific curricular method that could accomplish this" (14, p. 255).

Correcting Overgeneralizations   Some students have emotional problems in school because they overgeneralize their emotional reactions. For example, students abused at home may fear and avoid adults in general, including their teachers. Or students who have learned to say as little as possible at home to avoid being criticized or ridiculed may be too anxious to volunteer opinions or answers in school if they anticipate a similar response. It's not that they think they are bad or ridiculous, but rather that they expect to be treated badly or ridiculed. They transfer their experience at home to similar situations and assume that the outcome will be the same.

It is not necessary to delve into the histories of students who flinch at a sudden move in their vicinity, act startled at a sudden noise, seem devastated by the slightest criticism, or tremble when called on to recite. Their reactions in class are enough to make you realize that their past experiences—whatever they were—caused them to respond inappropriately. Nor is it necessary to know the details in order to develop a plan to help them change their emotional responses, though such knowledge could certainly assist the process. Two approaches in particular can make a contribution toward changing the emotional reactions of such students: a helping relationship and gradual desensitization.

Helping relationships: Just telling students they have nothing to worry about, be angry about, or feel jealous about and explaining why is rarely enough to change their expectations. The saying "Actions speak louder than words" is operative here. You can show these students that all adults or all authority figures are not alike by relating to them in ways that disprove their expectations. The suggestions in chapter 2 for relating to students in non-authoritarian ways, being fair, listening actively, being friendly, communicating acceptance and empathy, and avoiding negative and destructive consequences are particularly relevant for students with emotional problems.

Gradual desensitization: You can begin to help students who will not volunteer in class because they are afraid others will laugh at them by convincing them that they have nothing to be afraid of. You could also help them feel relaxed enough so that despite their idea that they may be laughed at, they still volunteer to answer. If they do well on one try, and no one laughs or ridicules them, the experience will change their original apprehension. Then the next time they know the answer, they will be more likely to raise their hands.

The difficulty with this approach is helping to relax students who are highly upset because they anticipate dire consequences. Gradual desensitization, which is one way to accomplish this, is based on the fact that people are less likely to feel upset about something that usually bothers them if they take tranquilizers or sedatives, eat a very satisfying meal, or have a good massage. The physical effects these activities have on them counteract the effects of the anxiety and anger-producing ideas and experiences that are upsetting them. They may still remember what it was that made them anxious or angry—they may still be aware that they are not ready for a test or that someone treated them unfairly—but they just are not bothered as much.

Gradual desensitization is a technique in which students are first relaxed and then gradually desensitized to the experience they cannot deal with. Proceeding gradually is extremely important because although at times some people can jump right into upsetting situations, more often they have to first test out the waters, then accustom themselves to the temperature, and finally jump into the challenging experience.

To use gradual desensitization effectively with your students, follow these six steps:

1. Identify the situation that arouses the wrong emotional response, such as taking a test, reading aloud, trying out for a play, and so on.

2. Determine how you can best help your students to feel calm, relaxed, and comfortable. Techniques that help students relax include:
   Deep rhythmic breathing, stretching, or vigorous exercise
   Thinking about something pleasant that happened or that the student would like to happen (emotive imagery)
   A favorite snack
   Calm, soothing music
   A favorite toy, stuffed animal, and the like (for younger children)
   The physical presence of a friend, parent, or teacher

3. Identify a series of small, gradual steps that your students can take on the way toward confronting the actual stimulus they can't cope with. You have several options here. You can graduate steps in terms of how close students are to actually doing the threatening challenge, how close they are in time to the threat, or whether they are going through the steps in the threatening situation in their imagination or in reality. (You may choose to have them do the steps in their imagination first as a safe way to start.)

4. Help your students attain each step while they are feeling relaxed and calm. Be sure not to pressure them to proceed more rapidly than they are ready to.

5. Call your students' attention to the fact that they accomplished the goal without experiencing any negative results.

6. Encourage them to try to do the same thing again.

Two examples of this approach follow. Clara, an anxious third-grade student, is unwilling to participate in the class play because she is afraid she will forget her poem and everyone will laugh at her. The last time she participated, she was so anxious that she forgot her lines. How can her teacher use gradual desensitization to help Clara overcome her problem? First, he could help relax Clara by having her think about something pleasant, giving her a favorite snack, or waiting until she was feeling very good about something and then asking her to recite her poem for him when none of the other students were present. If she did this and it was a positive experience for her, the teacher might wait to catch her in a good mood next time or do something to put her in a good mood and then ask her to recite the poem in front of one or two students. Finally, he would work up to having Clara do it in front of the whole class. Then if that worked out well, he could ask her to think about participating when the class performs for the whole school in the auditorium. He would have to do everything possible to make her feel calm and relaxed before she goes on stage, however.

The second example involves a sixth-grade student named Steve, who after repeatedly suffering "test anxiety" and blocking on examinations, announces he will not take any more tests because he always fails. How can a teacher gradually desensitize Steve to taking tests? First, the teacher can identify a series of steps leading up to taking tests that Steve can proceed through gradually and use an appropriate way of helping Steve during each step. For example, after making sure Steve is relaxed, the teacher can ask him to imagine the following situations one by one: You have just been told that there will be a test in 3 days. You are studying for the test at home 2 days before the test. You are studying for the test the night before you are to take it. It's the morning of the test. You have completed your studies, and you feel confident that you will do well. You are in class waiting for the tests to be distributed. You receive your copy and begin. You complete the test and pass it in. Now, it is the day after the test, and you are waiting for the test papers to be returned. You look at your grade—it is an A.

After completing these imaginary steps, which may take a few days, the teacher can help Steve get used to real tests in stages. The teacher can ask Steve to read the test over without taking it. Then the next few times Steve takes a test, he can first take it without handing it in, take the test with the understanding that he can have a makeup if he isn't satisfied with how he did, and finally take the test under the same conditions as the other students.

Some educators feel that gradual desensitization is outside the scope and role of classroom teachers, but research indicates that teachers can use it effectively with students who have emotional problems (78–83). Moreover, once students learn how to relax themselves and how to develop their own series of graduated steps, they can use these techniques independently for any subsequent challenges they encounter.

Resolving Conflicting Emotions   Students can have emotional problems because their values and standards of behavior prevent them from acting out their emotions in appropriate ways. For example, students may learn at home that nice boys and girls discuss their differences instead of fighting, and when someone teases, pesters, annoys, or pushes them, they should try to find out why, ignore the provocation, or walk away, but never tease or push back. The idea that it's wrong to act out their anger or even feel angry can put them in a bind because feeling angry also makes them feel guilty. Then if the guilt is strong enough to keep them from asserting or defending themselves when they feel angry or resentful, other students may take advantage of, pick on, or scapegoat them. Similarly, students who have been taught that they should always want to share their things with others, always be considerate of others, and always allow others to go first may feel too guilty to stick up for their own rights or speak out for their own interests when it's appropriate to do so.

You can help such inhibited students by giving them more realistic expectations and standards of behavior that allow for flexibility when the situation calls for it. Consider telling students who believe that good boys *never* fight that they try not to fight or do not fight unless they have to. Help students who think that good children *always* share their things with others by telling them that good children share *most* things *most* of the time with others who also share their things with them. Explain to your students that it is natural to feel angry when they are treated unfairly or punished unjustly, and help them express these feelings appropriately. One way to do this is to model the appropriate behavior yourself. When the opportunity presents itself, you can also point out when other students behave in ways that you and most people find acceptable even if your student does not. This helps them see and accept a broader range of behavior.

Correcting Defensive Behavior   As we noted earlier, students can defend themselves against experiencing uncomfortable emotions by distorting the way they see and experience the world. Specifically, students can defend themselves against taking responsibility for their low grades in school by believing that their teachers are inadequate, their exams are unfair, or their assignments are tricky. They can also defend themselves against thinking that they are bad when they lash out at others in anger or pick on other students for the fun of it by believing "the other student started the problem," "they had it coming to them," "it was an accident," "everyone else does it anyway," or similar rationalizations.

Defensive students can be highly exasperating. Teachers often want to confront them with the truth to clear away their excuses and self-deceptions. But such direct attacks on students' defenses often backfire. Instead of helping students face reality, such attacks often cause students who are highly motivated to defend themselves to become even more defensive. To escape such painful confrontations with teachers, students may cause incidents that result in being excluded from class, or they may cut class or drop out of school.

Life-space interview: Students who misbehave because of their emotional problems sometimes feel too guilty or anxious to assume responsibility for their actions or face the implications of their behavior and its effects on others. They would rather think that what they have done "was an accident," that it "isn't a big deal," that it "wasn't their fault," that the other person "had it coming because he started it," and so on. Because they are too threatened by the guilt and anxiety that the real implications of their behavior would provoke, they resist their teachers' direct attempts to discuss their behavior with them. The life-space interview, a nonconfrontational technique to assist students to examine their behavior, can be effective with such students.

Life-space interviewing was developed to assist teachers to deal with their students' defenses (85–89, 95). Somewhat like Gordon's (84) concept of active listening (chapter 2), the life-space interview is designed to engage defensive students in a communication process with their teachers that will lead them to correct their misperceptions and modify their behavior. The technique is designed to help students gradually face the truth they have been hiding from without forcing them to give up their defenses before they are ready to do so. This approach is based on the assumption that students will be more open to modifying their inappropriate behavior once they have admitted to themselves what they really have been doing and the real reasons they have been doing it. By helping students perceive

THEORY FOCUS: MORSE ON UNDERSTANDING CHILD VARIANCE

William Morse began training educators to work with students who had emotional problems in the 1950s. The training program he directed was especially noted for preparing educators to use the "life-space interview" and many other techniques first described by Redl to help students deal with emotional crises in the classroom. *Public School Classes for the Emotionally Handicapped: A Research Analysis*, which Morse coauthored, was the first detailed study of how students with emotional problems were handled and mishandled in the public schools. His book *Understanding Child Variance* suggests that behavior problems can be the result of a variety of causes, with each cause more amenable to some solutions than to others. Two of the many other books he has written that contain a wealth of suggestions for how to help students with emotional and conduct problems are *The Education and Treatment of Socio-Emotionally Impaired Children and Youth* and *Affective Education for Special Children and Youth*.

themselves and their experiences more accurately and by aiding them in developing alternative ways of coping with their feelings, the life-space interview enhances feelings of being in control of one's life (89).

What follows is a description of the major aspects of life-space interviewing and an example of how it is used with defensive students. Although the concepts are presented in a logical order, they are not thought of as fixed steps but rather as aspects to be considered and included at some point in the process.

Harold is a 15-year-old who breaks other students' things "by accident," says nasty things to them "without realizing it," interrupts them when they are talking, and constantly gets himself rejected. But he never admits either that he starts things or that he brings about his own rejection. As far as he is concerned, he is always the victim, never the instigator.

Harold's parents always found him to be much more difficult to deal with than his older brother. By the time Harold was 3, his parents were already engaged in fruitless battles with him. By now, they and his older brother rely almost exclusively on threats and punishments to manage his behavior. When he was younger, Harold showed his anger toward them because of how he was treated. But as he got older, he began to defend himself against experiencing his anger by doing the things he did to bother his family and others "accidentally."

Establish a relationship of confidence and acceptance with your students. Students are much more likely to admit the truth to you if they believe that you won't laugh, feel disgusted, or react punitively but instead will say that what they tell you is not nearly as bad, wrong, disgusting, or difficult as the students think. If you establish a trusting, accepting relationship before you broach a subject that may make a student defensive, it is less likely that the student will feel it necessary to maintain his or her defenses during the discussion.

In Harold's case, you might establish a relationship of confidence and acceptance by telling him the good things about himself and, most importantly, by trying not to respond negatively and punitively when he "accidentally" does obnoxious and provocative things in class.

Choose problems or incidents that your students can deal with realistically and cooperatively. After you have established a relationship of trust, select a situation that is not too threatening for your student to deal with. Helping a student face the truth about something that is less threatening is usually more effective than tackling something that would make a student feel really terrible to admit. With Harold, you might pick an incident when he caused a student to yell at him by "accidentally" sticking his feet out just as the student walked by.

Interview students under circumstances that encourage their participation. Students are more likely to discuss their thoughts and feelings in private. Long and Frye (85) advise allowing 10 to 20 minutes to provide enough time for such a conversation.

Find out your students' perceptions. After you have selected an incident or situation to discuss with your student, find out how the student sees it. Listen as long as necessary and ask whatever questions you need to in order to be sure you understand the students' point of view. Do this in a nonjudgmental way, without any sign of disagreement or disapproval. Remember that your students will distort the situation not because they want to but because they have to defend against the truth for the moment. This step is critical because you have to understand the student's point of view if you want to correct it. It's also important because you communicate your interest and respect by listening to what your student has to say. As Morse points out,

> We want to know how the youngster sees and thinks about an event. . . . Once we are clear how the child perceives the problem (even if the pupil's view cannot be accepted as satisfactory), we are in a position to work out, hopefully with concurrence, a possible resolution. (86, p. 214)

Tanner (89) also recommends that the teacher try to determine the meaning of the incident to the student. Is it really a central issue? Is it related to a particular vulnerability or concern, such as jealousy, pride, ethnic or racial sensitivity, or issues over power? If a student explodes in anger when a group of students laughs at him, is it because he was laughed at by his peers or because his teacher failed to protect him from their ridicule?

In Harold's case, you would listen while Harold complained that the student yelled at him, that no one likes him, and that he feels left out. Then you would ask what he thought caused the student to yell at him. When Harold answered that the student just liked to yell at him, you wouldn't try to correct him.

Communicate your understanding and acceptance of both the students' perception of the incident and their feelings about it (without expressing agreement). Few things are more satisfying in our relationships with others than knowing that we are understood and accepted—except perhaps when others also agree with us. Communicating your understanding and acceptance of your students' perceptions can motivate them to want to discuss their feelings with you. Keep in mind that acceptance is not agreement, however. Acceptance means you can appreciate that they think and feel the way they do because of the way they experienced the incident. Acceptance also means listening in a noncritical and nonjudgmental manner. It does not necessarily mean that you see things the same way the student does.

In working with Harold, you could express your acceptance of his feelings by saying that you understand that he was angry about being yelled at for no reason. You could add that he would be justified to feel that way *if* the incident happened as he described it. You are not saying here that you agree with his perception, only that you can understand and appreciate the way he feels given how he sees the situation.

Explore other possible perceptions of the incident or situation. After you have indicated that you understand your student's point of view and accept how he or she feels or thinks about what happened, ask if your student can think of any other way to look at or understand the event. Do this without suggesting that the student's point of view is incorrect. If the student does not come up with an alternative, you can suggest one or two. For example, you might say, "I can understand why you think that you had a right to hit Molly for laughing at what you said when I called on you, but how do you know she was laughing at what you said? Is it possible that someone else had just said something funny to her or had told her a joke?" If the student is adamant that there is no other possible explanation, do not make an issue of it. This indicates that the student is not ready to face the truth. But if your student can admit that other possibilities might make sense, then together you can look at which alternative is the most likely or plausible one. Again, do this in a nonjudgmental way.

After communicating your understanding and acceptance of Harold's feelings, you would ask him whether it was possible that the student had some other reason for yelling at him. If he says "no," you would ask him if he remembers the student saying, "You almost tripped me with your stupid, fat feet." If Harold does not want to discuss it, let it drop. But if he seems receptive, you would ask Harold to think about why he decided to stretch his feet out in the aisle at the very moment the student walked by. If he is willing to admit that he might have been at fault after all, you would proceed to the next step.

Maximize your students' motivation to perceive things realistically rather than defensively. Students are more likely to admit that they made a mistake, that they were wrong, or that they were responsible for what happened if they will benefit by facing the truth or at least if nothing too terrible will result if they do look at what really happened. Therefore, to encourage students to give up their defenses, help them see the benefit in doing so. For example, you can explain that by not admitting their mistakes, students are forced to repeat them over and over again. You can also say that by not giving their peers the benefit of the doubt, they are making it difficult for themselves to make and keep friends. Being clear that you are willing and eager to help them avoid making the same mistakes over again might also help them be less defensive.

At this step in the process, you could help Harold understand that if he actually started the problem by almost tripping the other student—and he can admit it and stop doing this kind of thing—he will be taking the first step toward having the student as a friend. On the other hand, if he cannot admit it, keeps on doing it, and complains that the student is picking on him, he will continue to have the student as an enemy. Be positive as you explain this. Mention all the positive benefits Harold might derive from seeing things more clearly. Avoid pressuring him by suggesting any type of negative repercussions if he doesn't change his ways.

Provide the help, support, and rewards your students need to face the truth they have been denying. If students admit that they are worried and anxious about not being able to succeed at things, give them extra help, sign them up for an after-school program, or arrange for peer tutoring. If students feel guilty or ashamed about the "bad" things they have been doing to you, forgive them and give them extra attention in class. Regardless of what they admit to, do not scold them for what they did. Instead, reward them for confronting things that they couldn't face before.

In Harold's case, you could praise him for being willing to admit his role in his problems. Remind him that this takes real courage, and help him see how his relationship with other students improves over time as his behavior toward them changes.

Assist students in identifying more appropriate ways of behaving that are in tune with their nondefensive perceptions of themselves and their experiences. Tanner advises:

> Elicit from the pupil how the pupil thinks he or she might be helped and what the teacher might be able to do to help the pupil control the behavior impulse in question. Develop a follow-through plan with the pupil. What will we have to do if this happens again? . . . any plan must be concerned within the limitations of school resources. (89, p. 168)

Student-identified and -managed solutions are preferable to those that teachers select and enforce because the students are more motivated to follow through on plans they determine or help determine. But as Morse (14) suggests, the teacher should also approve any plan.

With Harold, you could ask him what he thinks he should do if he believes it was his responsibility that his feet tripped the student. If he decides that he should apologize to the student for tripping him, congratulate him for deciding on such a mature response and praise him when he actually does apologize.

Evaluate the effectiveness of your efforts. You should evaluate your attempts to change your students' behavior using the same types of criteria you would use to evaluate any technique: Does the unacceptable behavior occur less often? Is it less severe or less serious? Has it been replaced by more appropriate behavior? Include any other questions that help you objectively assess possible improvement.

You can evaluate Harold's progress by observing any change in how often he inflicts accidental mishaps on others and by comparing the number of times he is willing to admit that he was at fault with the number of times he blames others for things he does to them.

To summarize, the steps in the life-space interview process are:

1. Establish a relationship of confidence and acceptance with your students.

2. Choose situations or incidents that your students can deal with realistically and cooperatively.

3. Interview students under circumstances that encourage their participation.

4. Find out your students' perceptions.

5. Communicate your understanding and acceptance of both the students' perception of the incident and their feelings about it (without expressing agreement).

6. Explore other possible perceptions of the incident or situation.

7. Maximize your students' motivation to perceive things realistically rather than defensively.

8. Provide the help, support, and rewards your students need to face the truth they have been denying.

9. Assist students in identifying more appropriate ways of behaving that are in tune with their nondefensive perceptions of themselves and their experiences.

10. Evaluate the effectiveness of your efforts.

Numerous educators have recommended the life-space interview to teachers (85–89, 90, 92–95). They claim that the life-space interview

1. enables students to express their feelings in a nonjudgmental environment;
2. helps students learn to problem solve;
3. provides a technique that is readily available for use in most crisis situations;
4. helps students identify those feelings that "cause" the acting out;
5. teaches students that they can change their behavior; and
6. enables the professional that is in the proximity to the problem to aid the client in a close temporal relationship to the problem. (91, p. 111)

Some educators question the feasibility of using the life-space interview in classroom situations (91). They are concerned that attending to students' misbehavior by means of the life-space interview can reinforce attention-seeking students. This possibility can be avoided by not using it with the small percentage of students who act out to obtain their teachers' attention.

Critics are also concerned that life-space interviews can use up time that may be more profitably spent on academic studies, that it requires more individual attention than teachers can provide, and that the cost of training teachers to use it is significant. Proponents of the life-space interview claim that since research indicates that it can be a helpful tool when working with students with emotional problems, its use is justified despite the time involved both in training teachers and in using it with individual students (90–95).

There have been no studies about possible ethnic or gender differences in the effectiveness of the life-space interview. However, as noted in chapters 5 and 6, students from some ethnic backgrounds (e.g., Asian Pacific Americans and Native Americans) and male students in general tend to be less comfortable discussing their feelings than European American and female students. And since the life-space interview technique is designed to elicit students' feelings, these students may be more resistant to the technique.

Confronting students' defenses: When educators need to get results faster than they can with the indirect life-space interview, they can be more direct. For example, they can present students with a true picture of reality without pressuring them to accept it. This approach is more confronting than life-space interviewing because the student is presented with the educator's perception without any real preparation. It's not, however, as confronting as it could be because the teacher does not pressure the student to accept the teacher's perception.

One way to use this technique is to behave in ways that contradict what your student believes or actually say that you disagree with the student without getting into an argument about it. For example, if you think that a student might be worried that she cannot do something but cannot admit it and so cannot ask for help, you can just say to her, "Don't forget, I'm here to help you" or "It's all right to ask for help if you get stuck." If necessary, you can be even more direct and say, "I really don't think you can do that by yourself." If a student causes his own problems with other students and then runs to you to complain, hoping to receive sympathy, you can say, "I can't give you sympathy because it's your own fault. You are making them act mean by the way you are treating them." Another option is to say, "You don't have to agree with me, but I think they act mean to you because you try to boss them around. If you stop acting the way you do, maybe they will stop acting the way they do." The important thing in this approach is to give the student a clearer picture of reality *without* insisting or even trying to convince the student to accept your point of view unless the student continues the conversation voluntarily.

Some educators are even more confrontational. They not only tell students how they perceive situations, but they also present their evidence and arguments until the students either see the truth or escape from the situation by refusing to continue the discussion, starting an argument, pretending to agree, calling them liars, or some other diversion. While this head-on approach can work, it also has the potential for making the situation worse. Even when teachers succeed in making students see things more objectively, the students may be so overwhelmed by the guilt, shame, fear, or anxiety they were defending against that they do something drastic. For this reason, it is best to avoid pressured, direct confrontation.

Social Skills Training   Researchers have found that social skills training—teaching students the social skills they need to know to behave more appropriately—helps students who do not relate well to others to improve their behavior (96–101). Moreover, there is some evidence that once they change their behavior, their peers relate better to them, thus reinforcing and maintaining the behavioral improvement to some degree.

The list of social skills that students may lack is very long. They may need to learn to share, to wait their turn, to ask permission, to function cooperatively, to do their share of the work, to acknowledge their mistakes, to smile, to express their anger and resentment in acceptable ways, and so on.

Social skills training is based on three assumptions:

> (a) Individuals who have difficulty establishing or sustaining mutually rewarding relationships have not learned to behave in the ways that their peers judge to be appropriate and rewarding, (b) these individuals can be taught how to behave differently, and (c) unaccepted individuals will elicit more positive reactions and evaluations from peers as they acquire and perform more socially approved behavior. (96, pp. 229–330)

It is unclear whether students with emotional problems fit the description of students who may profit from social skills training. Many of them know how to behave appropriately. Their difficulty lies in the fact that their emotional problems interfere with their ability to do so. As Elliot and Gresham remind teachers, "It is important to distinguish between interfering problem behaviors that prevent *skill acquisition* from those that interfere with the *skill performance*" (98, p. 295).

Social skills training may be helpful for students whose emotional problems have prevented them from acquiring the skills they need to relate positively to others. It may be especially timely for such students once the emotional problems that have interfered with their acquisition of the skills have been eliminated. However, teaching social skills to students who know them but cannot act on them appears unnecessary. If you feel that some of your students may be helped by social skills training, consult the references at the end of this chapter for sources of additional information.

Bieman and Montminy have pointed out the importance of adapting social skills training procedures, target behaviors, and goals to students' developmental levels: "Developmental changes (changes in children's normative peer interactions, in their social reasoning, and in peer group structure and influence) must be considered together in planning developmentally sensitive interventions" (96, p. 249). They have also described specific modifications that teachers should consider implementing for students at different developmental levels.

Managing Emotional Problems

This section describes techniques you can use to make it less likely that students will act out their emotions in class in nonconstructive ways. Unlike the techniques described so far, they are designed to manage students' misbehavior, not solve it.

As noted in Part Two, educators can use four kinds of techniques to manage students' behavior: teacher-managed techniques with and without consequences, and self-managed techniques with and without consequences. The application of these techniques to students with emotional problems is discussed here.

Managing Without Consequences   Although it is often possible to manage students' behavior by the use of consequences, there are a number of reasons why it's preferable for educators to manage their students' *emotional* problems without using positive or negative consequences whenever possible.

First, trying to pressure or coerce students with emotional problems to change their behavior when they are too upset to do so is like pushing them into the deep end of a pool without letting them get used to the cold water in the shallow end first. Educators can certainly make the consequences of not participating in the school play, not reading a composition to the rest of the class, or not answering when called on so distasteful that students who would otherwise be too embarrassed, ashamed, or anxious to participate feel compelled to do so. Sometimes this works, and students participate and learn that they were concerned about nothing. But many times this approach fails because working only on the behavioral level without changing the students' physical responses does not counteract the effects of their incorrect emotions. As a result, their intense embarrassment, shame, or anxiety causes them to block, stammer, clutch up, and so fail.

A second reason to avoid using consequences with these students is that students who experience incorrect emotions often misperceive things. This means that they may not be able to understand why their teachers are trying to pressure or coerce them to do things that these youngsters mistakenly—but firmly—believe they cannot do or will harm them in some way.

Students whose emotions are too strong may also be too afraid to face something, too anxious to try something, too angry to make peace with someone, or too upset to sit down and talk calmly about something, regardless of the rewards they are offered or the negative consequences educators may impose on them. Promising such students positive consequences if they change behavior that is often beyond their control or negative consequences if they do not may create unbearable conflicts in these students, drive them to tears, cause them to develop such "nervous" symptoms as twitches and sniffles, and push them to become truant or drop out of school.

Even if using techniques with consequences does get students to change their behavior for the moment, the price may not be worth it. When educators can get students to control their behavior without correcting their misperceptions or calming their emotional overreactions, they may actually be putting even more pressure on the students to act out their feelings until they explode.

The use of consequences is also likely to prove ineffective or even counterproductive with students who are angry and resentful about being under the control of others or who are suspicious about others' motives. Even attempts to change these students' behavior by using only positive consequences can make them angrier, more resentful and suspicious, and cause them to rebel against one more dose of the very type of external control they can't accept.

Finally, the use of consequences can increase learned helplessness and foster an external locus of control. Many students with emotional problems already experience these and they do not need any reinforcement.

The following lists contain examples of managing techniques without consequences (102–106). They are divided into three groups. The first group involves ways in which *you* can adapt to the students. The second group focuses on suggestions for calming *students* down, or draining off part of their emotions so they are less likely to cause an inappropriate reaction. The third group provides ways of adapting the *situation* to accomplish this end. The choice of which techniques would be the most appropriate for you to use depends both on the kinds of problems your students exhibit and the kinds of techniques you are comfortable using.

Adapting to students: These are some of the things you can do to manage your students with emotional problems.

1. *Impersonalize your commands.* Older, rebellious, angry, or resentful students often react better when orders and directions are given in an impersonal way. You may get a more positive response from students if you say, "You are supposed to raise your hand" or "You are supposed to put away the equipment you use" instead of "I want you to raise your hand" or "Didn't I tell you to straighten up?" Likewise, they may react better to statements such as "That's nothing to be proud of" than to statements like "I'm not very proud of you."

2. *Avoid challenging statements.* Students, especially teenagers, with emotional problems may rebel when they are told what they can and cannot do. When they hear the word *can't*, it's as if they experience a challenge to their independence. Sometimes it helps to phrase statements differently. "You aren't supposed to" can sound more acceptable than either "You can't" or "I won't allow you to."

3. *Suggest rather than order.* Students may also react better if you make suggestions rather than give orders.

These first three techniques are only temporary measures to manage behavior problems. In the long run, your students should be able to accept statements that reflect *your* authority or that state clearly what they are or are not allowed to do. But while you are helping these students grow and change so that they don't become resentful, angry, or rebellious when you "tell it like it is," you can make life easier for everyone concerned by rephrasing statements that could cause problems.

4. *Avoid moralizing.* Students who have problems with excessive guilt and shame may have difficulty coping with criticism that is expressed in moral terms. When they are told they are bad, unfair, and so on, they may feel so devastated that they

become too defensive to accept the truth. It may be much easier for them to hear that their actions are not helpful, appropriate, or acceptable. These words are less moralistic and focus on and describe the behavior rather than the person.

5. *Ignore provocative or argumentative behavior.* Some students create incidents so they have a chance to express their angry feelings. It's as if they are looking for an excuse to be angry and are trying to pick a fight. When students do this, you may be able to avoid these predictable outbursts by ignoring their behavior. Certain students purposely provoke teachers into punishing or rejecting them so they can then feel sorry for themselves. Others who cannot cope with schoolwork may use provocative and argumentative behavior to get sent to the office or study hall. You may be able to manage these behaviors easily simply by ignoring them. This may not deal with the cause of the problem, but ignoring attempts to provoke a reaction from you may enable you to manage the situation until you can use some of the techniques described in the previous section to help these students change.

6. *Relieve tension using humor.* Sometimes, when they are very upset, students with emotional problems say things they do not mean and do not believe. They can also unwittingly take positions they know are wrong or blow things out of proportion. Then, later, they cannot admit their mistakes gracefully. When educators take these situations seriously and respond by trying to maintain their own positions and points of view, this aggravates things. The results would be ludicrous if they were not so unfortunate—two individuals unable to extricate themselves from a situation that both realize is ridiculous. At such times, making light of the situation, pointing out the humor in it, and laughing *at* oneself but *with* one's student can turn a potential confrontation into a moment of shared humor.

Calming students: The following approaches are aimed at calming students. You can use these three techniques to help diminish the strength of your students' emotional overreactions so they are less likely to cause inappropriate behavior.

1. *Use relaxation techniques to counteract strong emotions.* You can try the relaxation methods described in the section on gradual desensitization when students are so afraid, angry, anxious, or upset that they are on the verge of misbehaving. You can also use relaxation techniques before students engage in activities that are potentially upsetting.

2. *Assure students that they will receive the support they need.* If students are anxious about not being able to do something alone, offer to help them whenever it becomes necessary.

3. *Prepare students for upsetting events ahead of time.* If you give students advance notice about something that may upset them and help them work through their anxieties and fears, they may be able to handle the event by the time it actually occurs.

Adapting the situation: Adapting the situation is a third way to work with students who have emotional problems. These techniques include ways you can modify the situations confronting your students to make their emotional reactions more manageable.

1. *Use the space to your students' advantage.* If certain students tease others or get into arguments with them over small things, separate them from their peers as much as possible. If they are anxious about being in school without the support of their parents, seat them close to you.

2. *Arrange the timing of activities to your students' advantage.* Schedule confrontations with students so they don't occur at difficult times, such as the end of the day or right before tests. If students are so anxious that they can only do certain activities when they can count on your help, then schedule such activities for times you can give them the attention they need.

3. *Distract students before their emotions get too strong to control.* When students are about to have a frustration fit over something they are trying to do or are starting to have an argument with another student, distract them from the problem situation to another activity. This technique is especially effective with younger students.

Managing with Consequences   Unfortunately, like many things in life, techniques for managing without consequences only work some of the time. If you believe that your students will be able to accept and profit from consequences, you may decide to try using management techniques with consequences. If so, look at some of the management techniques described in chapter 10, which you can also use with students who have emotional problems. However, be mindful of the potential problems discussed earlier and also avoid the use of negative or harsh consequences (102, 106). The rationale for avoiding such consequences with students in general and especially students who have emotional problems is expressed very well by Hewett:

> Teaching children to behave in certain ways and to acquire complex skills such as reading because they are afraid not to represents an educational "dead end" since our major goal is to make appropriate behavior and acquisition of reading eventually rewarding in and of itself. (102, p. 71)

Self-Management   Research indicates that educators can teach some students who have emotional problems to self-correct and self-moderate their emotional reactions by using techniques that are labeled self-control, self-mediation, self-instruction, self-management, cognitive behavior therapy, and cognitive behavior modification by various practitioners of this approach. The literature on self-control approaches for students with emotional problems includes a wide variety of techniques (108, 110, 112, 115, 116, 119, 121, 122, 124–126, 128, 130). Typically these involve teaching students to do some, but not necessarily all, of the following:

- To delay acting out their feelings and impulses
- To relax
- To examine the reasons for their feelings and correct their misperceptions
- To identify alternative ways of reacting to their feelings
- To consider the consequences that are likely to result from each alternative
- To select the most appropriate alternative

- To instruct themselves about appropriate ways of reacting to their feelings

- To evaluate their behavior and reinforce themselves for appropriate behavior

This section describes some of the ways students can implement procedures to manage their emotional reactions. It also discusses approaches that educators have used to teach students how to follow these procedures. Finally, it reviews the research on the effectiveness of self-management techniques.

Delay: Students can try to delay acting out their emotions until they can think about their behavior by counting to 10, reminding themselves not to say or do anything while they are upset, instructing themselves to walk away when they are tempted to "lay hands on" someone else, and telling themselves that rule number 1 is always to "cool off" before you say or do anything. Any other helpful self-reminders that create a time gap between the emotional response and follow-up behavior can help the student cope.

Relaxation: Once students have inhibited their initial impulsive reactions, they can relax themselves in any of the ways already described, such as deep breathing or muscle-relaxing exercises, allowing the body to go limp, emotive imagery, or vigorous physical exercise.

Reasoning: Once they are relaxed rather than upset, students will be able to think reasonably about their reactions. One way to do this is for them to label their feelings and/ or question their appropriateness. This is particularly important for students who are not "in touch with" their feelings, such as students who act out their anger or frustration without even realizing that they are angry or frustrated. A student who gets easily frustrated whenever he runs into trouble in his schoolwork and rips up his papers without realizing why he does so can be taught to monitor himself. You can teach him to tell himself, "Oh, oh! I am getting frustrated. I fell like throwing my paper away again. Why should I feel frustrated? There's always a hard part to learning something new." Another student, disappointed that she was not called on when she knew the answer to a tough question and about to complain, can remind herself that students cannot expect to be called on whenever they raise their hands. A student who gets angry whenever he receives a poor grade on a test and blames the teacher or the test in a loud, disruptive manner can remind himself that he should check the answers marked wrong with another student before deciding that his answers are absolutely right. A student who gets jealous when students she tends to play with are playing with someone else can remind herself that students, including herself, do not play with the same friend all the time. And a student who tends to believe that others pick on him unfairly can ask himself if he did anything to cause another student to reject him.

A second approach is for students to develop a set of alternative behaviors, explore the possible results of each, and select the most beneficial or effective one. For example, a student who gets so angry when she drops the ball playing poison ball that she wants to throw the ball over the fence can ask herself how the other students will react if she does this. Or a student who experiences the urge to hit another student for something he said can remind himself that if he does, he will get into trouble; but if he only says something nasty back to the student, there won't be any repercussions.

Self-instruction: Just as in creating a delay, students can instruct themselves to react more appropriately. Self-instructions can remind students how to react to their emotions in more constructive ways. Examples of self-instructions give an idea of how many situations they cover: "Tell people how you feel; don't act your feelings out," "Tell people you're angry with them; don't hit others," "Don't rip up your paper; ask the teacher for help," and "Take a short break when you feel tense."

Self-evaluation and reinforcement: Each time students follow self-management procedures, they should evaluate the results in terms of how they feel about their behavior and their increased self-control. They also need to look at the favorable consequences that resulted from their behavior as well as the unfavorable consequences they avoided by controlling themselves. Noting the positive results of following self-management procedures should be intrinsically rewarding. But students can also reward themselves for modifying their behavior with a positive reinforcement of their choice. (See chapter 10 for examples of positive rewards.)

There is evidence that when students are taught to manage their own behavior, rewarding them for doing so is unnecessary (114, 142, 143). It may be that the intrinsic satisfaction they experience from the behavioral improvement is sufficiently rewarding to make extrinsic rewards unnecessary.

Anger Control Program Model: The Anger Control Program Model is an example of a structured approach to self-management to help students reduce inappropriate expressions of anger (114). There are five steps in the approach: ·

> Step 1. MOTOR CUE/IMPULSE DELAY; *stop* and *think* before you act, *cue* yourself.
> Step 2. PROBLEM DEFINITION; say how you *feel* and exactly what the problem is.
> Step 3. GENERATION OF ALTERNATIVES; think of as many *solutions* as you can.
> Step 4. CONSIDERATION OF CONSEQUENCES; *think* ahead to what might happen next.
> Step 5. IMPLEMENTATION; when you have a good solution, *try it!*
> (114, p. 111)

Turtle Technique: The Turtle Technique, another structured program for helping students manage their emotions, has been successful with some elementary school students (128). In this technique, the teacher tells the students a story about a little turtle who gets into trouble in school for becoming angry and fighting with other students until a tortoise tells him to withdraw into his shell whenever he gets angry and just rest until he feels better. The teacher then shows the students how to pull their arms and legs in close to their bodies, lay their heads on their desks, put their arms over their heads, and relax. They also learn to use problem-solving approaches for selecting appropriate ways to react to their feelings before coming out of their "shells."

Teaching self-management: It is possible to teach students to correct and moderate their behavior when they experience strong emotions that they would otherwise act out nonconstructively. Meichenbaum and Goodman (124–126) suggest using the following approach to train students to control their own behavior:

1. The teacher models the behavior that students should copy while saying aloud the things that students should eventually think.

2. Students perform the same behavior under the teacher's supervision.

THEORY FOCUS: MEICHENBAUM ON SELF-MANAGEMENT

Donald Meichenbaum is one of the founders of cognitive behavior modification, a self-management strategy that emphasizes helping students think before acting. His published works have helped educators appreciate the fact that students are more capable of managing their own behavior than was originally thought. In a number of articles and books, including *Cognitive Behavior Modification: An Integrative Approach*, Meichenbaum describes self-management techniques that students can use to gain control over their actions as well as effective procedures for teaching students to employ these techniques correctly and consistently in school.

Meichenbaum has stated:

Consider the child in the classroom who "knows what to do and does it," who has a series of adaptive routines and procedural scripts to perform both academic and social tasks. If teachers had their wish they would "clone" such children. My present research efforts are designed to understand such children and the learning conditions under which self-directed behavior can be nurtured.

In contrast, children who evidence attentional problems, such as hyperactive children, tend to have difficulty in following rules, especially when those rules are designed to sustain their behavior over a period of time and when there is not continual feedback. Similarly, conduct disorder children have difficulty complying with teacher requests. Our work on teaching children self-control strategies, under the headings of cognitive behavior modification and metacognitive training (cognitive strategy instruction), is designed to help make both teaching and learning trouble free. (Donald Meichenbaum, personal communication)

3. Students perform the behavior while instructing themselves aloud.

4. Students perform the behavior while whispering the instructions to themselves.

5. Students perform the behavior and instruct themselves.

Educators have used bibliotherapy—stories of how others have managed similar emotions and overcome similar problems—to provide models for students to learn from. Educators have also had students observe how others in class handle similar problems or watch videotapes with helpful models. Having students role-play the parts of others affected by their inappropriate emotional reactions also helps enhance students' understanding of the consequences that their inappropriate behavior has had.

Effectiveness: Self-managing techniques have been effective for some, but not all, of the students they have been used with. Specifically, they have helped some students control behavior that is angry and aggressive (110, 118, 123, 128), anxious (124, 129), and fearful (120, 127). Research reviews of the efficacy of self-management techniques with students who have emotional problems indicate that their effectiveness is limited (107, 109, 111, 117, 131). It also is not clear which techniques will work with which students and why. As Bornstein has said,

Self-instructional training will probably be of great benefit to some, moderate benefit to others, and minimal or no benefit to yet a final grouping of individuals. Our job is to identify those variables that substantially affect the success of our treatment. (109, p. 71)

Epanchin and Paul arrived at virtually the same conclusion about self-managing techniques: "Given the paucity of information, it is not yet possible to say how and for whom this approach works best, although it appears to be promising" (113, p. 187).

Although many conceivable reasons might explain why self-management techniques are not equally effective with all students, four explanations appear particularly plausible. First, older students appear to profit more than younger ones from self-management techniques (139, 140). This may be because children's abilities to control themselves mature as they do. Older children are also better able to remember and follow a number of instructions, develop their own plans of action, and generate their own visual images.

While a number of studies indicate that preschoolers can be taught to control their motor behavior, resist temptations, and influence their emotional states (132, 135–138, 141), they require more training than older children on identifying the cues that indicate they should begin to self-instruct themselves. They require a specific, uncomplicated, short set of instructions from adults that they can tell themselves to follow (they are relatively unable to formulate instructional commands on their own). They also respond better to self-instruction if they receive extrinsic rewards for doing it (134, 140).

Also, some students may not be mature enough to follow the procedures that self-management requires. In particular, since many students with emotional problems are immature, they may not be able to use self-management techniques that are appropriate for their ages but not their developmental levels. As Pressley has stated, "Cognitive rationales can increase children's self-control, but only if the content of the rationale is consistent with what the child can comprehend (as a function of developmental level)" (140, p. 347).

A second possible explanation for why self-management is effective with some students but not others is that these techniques appear to work better with students whose locus of control is internal (133). Students with an internal locus believe that they are in control of their own lives, but students with emotional problems who have poor self-concepts may not believe in their self-power and efficacy enough to put self-management techniques to use effectively.

A third explanation is that some students become too upset to delay their reactions long enough to think before acting. Others may be unable to control themselves in the intensity of feeling even though they know full well the possible negative consequences that could follow. The same happens with adults who are so angry that they lose control and say things they are sorry for or do things that they know will cause them grief. The satisfaction they get from expressing their anger at the moment simply outweighs the more distant, undesirable results they anticipate later.

Finally, defensive students who misperceive both themselves and their experiences may not be able to objectively perceive and evaluate alternative ways of behaving even though they delay acting out their feelings. This can happen if they are too defensive to correct their perceptions on their own.

Developmental level. It is best to decide on the types of self-management techniques you teach students to use, how you teach them to use these techniques, and the extent to which you rely on self-management rather than teacher-initiated techniques partly based on your students' developmental levels.

Self-control. Preschool and primary-grade students may be able to exercise some self-control, but it is generally more effective to emphasize teacher-initiated managing techniques at this level. Secondary school students may be able to manage much more of their emotional reactions providing they are not immature or defensive and they believe they can control their own lives.

Number of instructions. Younger students may only be able to give themselves simple directives that involve a single idea, such as: work slow, ask for help, think of fun things. Older students should be able to remember increasingly longer series of instructions. For example: Count to ten before saying or doing anything, then breathe deeply and let your body go limp; next, ask yourself if the other person could somehow be right and you wrong; then think of all the different ways you might react, and choose the best one.

Specificity of instructions. Young students require teachers to formulate the directives they will use to self-instruct themselves. Teachers need to say, "When you want to hit somebody, say 'Count to ten.'" Or "When you want to stop working because the work is too hard, say to yourself, 'Ask the teacher for help.'" A final example: "When you're afraid about going to recess, say to yourself, 'Think of fun things you like to do during recess.'" In contrast, teachers can give older students general directives to follow. Instead of telling older students exactly what to say to delay their reactions, they might tell students that they can choose from a number of things to do, such as counting to 10, thinking about something else, turning and walking away from the person, and so on. Then the teacher can encourage students to find out which approach works best for them.

Cues. Preschool and primary-grade students usually cannot generalize self-instructional techniques they have learned to use in one situation (to one cue) to other situations (with other cues). Thus, they need practice using the technique in each different situation where it applies. You also have to teach older students to generalize the self-management techniques they have learned with one set of cues to other possible situations, but their training may not have to be so concrete and repetitious.

Monitoring and evaluating. Young students may not be able to evaluate how well their self-managing efforts are working and can require close supervision. But you can teach older students how to monitor and evaluate the results of their efforts to manage their own behavior.

Reinforcement. As noted, preschool and primary-grade students may implement their self-management systems more consistently if teachers give them extrinsic rewards. Older students, however, may be able to reward themselves by observing the improvement in their behavior and thinking about how much better off they are as a result.

Maintenance and generalization: The positive results of self-management approaches with students who have emotional problems are not routinely maintained or generalized to other situations and individuals (100, 101, 143–146). Positive results are more likely to be maintained and generalized when teachers use specific techniques designed to foster maintenance and generalization, such as those described in chapter 10.

Tolerating Emotional Problems

Students who cannot yet manage their own behavior and who don't respond to their teachers' management techniques all the time will occasionally act out inappropriately. At such times, teachers can either tolerate this behavior or try to prevent it from occurring. Sometimes it is especially appropriate to tolerate students' misbehavior.

To begin with, it is unrealistic to expect that you and your students will be able to manage all of their inappropriate behaviors. You and your students may be able to manage many such potential instances, but you may have to tolerate others.

Tolerating may also be appropriate if the behavior will not harm your students, hurt others, or seriously interfere with their rights. For example, you might decide to tolerate a student's occasional show of temper or complaint that you are unfair. But you would certainly try to prevent a student from hitting another student in anger or destroying something in a fit of jealousy that another student has made.

Even when your students' behavior improves owing to your efforts, you may have to occasionally tolerate their misbehavior when they slip back into old patterns temporarily because the going gets too rough or a situation is particularly upsetting. Likewise, as students attempt to cope with more and more of what would once have been too threatening to face or as they move closer to a goal that is very frightening, they may find it necessary to take a step back.

Another time tolerance is called for is when students who have been inhibited from doing things due to excessive fear, guilt, or shame begin to do things that others their age have been doing for a long time. Often these students don't know how to behave appropriately. Under such circumstances, it is a good idea to tolerate their incorrect behavior until they learn to behave more appropriately. For example, when students who have been timid about standing up to their peers finally begin to do so, they often overreact or use highly aggressive ways of defending themselves due to their lack of experience. Tolerate this behavior (if it is not dangerous) while you teach your students more acceptable ways of standing up to others.

Finally, if you use consequences to manage your students' behavior, you may have more success with this approach if you tolerate their expression of anger or resentment. They are likely to be upset with you for requiring them to behave more appropriately, even though you are doing it for their benefit. Let them express these negative feelings as a by-product of the goal you are striving toward.

When you choose to tolerate behavior, the principles for tolerating conduct problems discussed in chapter 11 apply to tolerating emotional problems as well. They are:

1. Try not to feel resentful or discouraged that you have to tolerate behavior, since you have no other option for the moment.

2. Tolerate behavior only temporarily.

3. Make sure the student understands which behaviors you are tolerating and which you are not.

4. Never tolerate behavior that you can manage.

Preventing Emotional Problems

Preventing emotional problems from occurring is the best strategy for behavior that would be harmful or significantly interfere with the rights of others. You have a great many ways to prevent students from acting out their emotional problems. The number is limited only by the creativeness and ingenuity you apply to the task. This section includes examples of certain techniques you can use with your students, but your personality and the situation will suggest others that can be just as effective with your particular students.

1. *Remove upsetting stimuli from your students' environment.* Remove things that are too upsetting or threatening for students to cope with. These might include pictures of war, disease, famine, and death.

2. *Protect students from situations they cannot handle.* Extricate students from situations that are disintegrating before the students become too anxious, too angry, or too afraid to maintain their self-control. Don't allow students to try things when you know they can't succeed.

3. *Provide the assistance your students need in order that they not experience frustration or anxiety.* Helping your students succeed when they are on the verge of misbehaving due to frustration or anxiety about something they are trying to accomplish is a good prevention technique. If you know that your students will need your help, provide it even before they begin to feel frustrated or anxious. This may mean giving students a calculator to do math problems or providing a peer tutor in algebra, even though students need them for emotional rather than academic reasons.

4. *Adapt your demands and expectations to fit your students' emotional states.* When students are anxious, angry, or resentful, accept what they are capable of doing at the moment, not what they can do when they aren't upset.

5. *Excuse students from situations that they will be unable to handle.* Allow students to decline from participating in class plays, reading their work aloud, and similar situations. Provide alternative activities for students who cannot handle discussions or films about disease, war, crime, or kidnapping. Use cubicles and earphones to protect students from activities they cannot deal with. If necessary, permit students to leave the room, run an errand, or otherwise get some distance to avoid a stressful situation.

6. *Depersonalize your teaching techniques when students cannot handle attention from others.* Use such impersonal teaching materials as computers and programmed instruction texts for students who are uncomfortable with personal help.

7. *Use physical control if necessary to make sure students do not harm anyone.* Do not hesitate to call authorities for help when students appear on the verge of doing something dangerous. Many educators are wary of using physical force with their students due to the possibility of litigation. But if all else fails and the situation calls for an immediate response, you might consider physically preventing your students from doing harm. In doing so, always use the least amount of force necessary, but make sure you use enough. Then get help from others as soon as possible.

Prevention should not be punitive. Students with emotional problems misbehave because their emotions are inappropriate. They do not mean to be willful, disobedient, mean, or nasty. When they have to be sent out of the room, physically restrained, and so on, it is because they *cannot* control themselves, not because they *do not want to.* They do not deserve to be punished, nor will punishing them help them solve their emotional problems. Thus, if you have to prevent students from misbehaving, treat them with kindness and understanding as you do so. And if at all possible, have your words, tone of voice, and actions all convey this attitude while you do what you have to. This may be an unrealistic goal at times, but it is a goal worth striving for.

Matching Techniques and Problems

Educators can help improve the behavior of students with emotional problems by correcting the ideas that cause their inappropriate emotions, by calming and relaxing them so their upsetting emotions do not affect them as much, by using consequences to convince them to behave in acceptable ways despite their emotional problems, or by using a combination of these approaches. When educators give students more information, try to talk sense with them, or tell them to try being less defensive, they are working on the students' incorrect ideas. When they allow students to listen to calm music or eat a snack when they are anxious or have them do relaxation exercises to reduce the tension they have built up during the day, they are working on modifying the students' physical state. These physical interventions do not do anything about the ideas and situations that made the students tense or caused their worrisome thoughts, but they counteract the effects that the students' ideas have on their bodies. This enables the students to relax and to function temporarily as if these troubling thoughts or situations didn't exist. Finally, when educators pressure students to attempt to do something even though the students believe they have almost no chance of succeeding, or when they force students to move onward despite their fears, they are working on the students' behavior itself.

Educators who tend to habitually emphasize one or another of these alternatives sometimes make the mistake of using their usual approach even when it is not effective. For example, educators who rely almost exclusively on words to explain to students why they should not be so upset, afraid, anxious, or angry may have a difficult time helping students when they are just too upset to respond to ideas and logic. This is clearly the case when students are too angry to discuss something no matter how much their teachers try to get them to think about the problem rationally. The students first need to relax before they can relate to ideas, no matter how clearly the teacher presents them.

Educators who overuse relaxing their students when they are upset or afraid may do a good job of calming them down. But if they do not also deal with the ideas that cause their students' inappropriate behaviors, they will not be able to do anything to help these students avoid repeating the same behaviors again and again.

Finally, educators who push anxious, fearful students to do things can sometimes help them overcome their hesitancy. It is just as likely, though, that this may upset students even more, causing them to fail at things they are not ready for or to mistrust their teachers, whom they see as insensitive to their feelings.

To be genuinely effective with students who have emotional problems, you need to be knowledgeable about a variety of techniques. From these, you should choose the ones that you believe are most likely to work well with an individual student.

Self-Quiz: Handling Emotional Problems

To determine the range of techniques you would use with students who have emotional problems, answer the following questions about the techniques listed below.

1. How comfortable would you feel about using each of the techniques?
2. How often have you used each of the techniques?
3. Which techniques do you overemphasize?
4. Which techniques would you like to use more often?

Improving students' self-concepts by:

Ensuring their success through selecting work at their levels, providing extra help, and so on

Expressing your belief that they can succeed

Having students read stories about others who have overcome similar obstacles and problems

Correcting students' perfectionistic standards

Providing opportunities for students to succeed in alternative activities

Encouraging students to make positive rather than negative statements about themselves

Helping students believe they have power over their own lives by:

Allowing them to select the activities they engage in, the materials they use, the pace at which they work, and other self-determining decisions

Providing as little assistance as possible to dependent students

Encouraging students to evaluate their own work and efforts

Correcting students' overgeneralizations by:

Gradually desensitizing them to threatening stimuli

Encouraging inhibited students to act out their emotions without feeling guilty or embarrassed

(continued)

Summary

When students' emotions function properly, they help guide their actions so that they can adequately handle the many different situations they face daily. When their emotions do not perform this function or perform it inadequately, then students have emotional problems. A student's behavioral problems have an emotional basis if the student's emotional responses are often inappropriate for the situation and the student often avoids, defends, suffers, or uses ineffective solutions instead of solving the problems of daily living.

If a student's behavior problems are caused by emotional factors, you should be able to identify the inappropriate emotions; state whether they are too strong, too weak, incorrect, or in conflict; and determine if the student uses ineffective solutions, avoids, defends, or suffers *too much* and *too often*. Though some educators doubt that classroom teachers can handle the behavior problems of students with emotional problems, much less make

Correcting students' defensive behavior by:

Life-space interview techniques

Confronting students' defenses directly

Managing students' behavior by:

Impersonalizing your directives

Suggesting rather than ordering

Avoiding moralizing

Ignoring provocative and argumentative behavior

Releasing tensions through humor

Using relaxation techniques

Preparing students for impending upsetting events

Using space advantageously

Distracting students before they become upset

Using consequences to encourage students to control themselves despite their emotional reactions

Teaching students to manage their own behavior by:

Delaying their responses

Relaxing themselves

Reasoning through problems

Reinforcing themselves for behaving appropriately

Tolerating behavior problems that can't be managed

Preventing students from harming themselves or others or from infringing on others' rights by:

Removing upsetting stimuli from the environment

Protecting students from situations they can't handle

Adapting demands and expectations to students' emotional states

Allowing students to escape from upsetting situations

Depersonalizing teaching techniques

Using physical restraint when necessary

Employing nonpunitive preventive techniques

a contribution toward eliminating these emotional problems, research and classroom experience indicate otherwise.

Activities

I. Reread the three case studies in the activities section in chapter 11 and decide which, if any, of the students described had emotional problems.

II. Decide whether each of the following behavior patterns is more likely to be a conduct problem or an emotional problem, and state the reasons for your opinion.

1. Harry pushes ahead of smaller children in line when the teacher is not supervising the group.

2. Carlotta seldom participates in group cleanup activities unless her teacher uses consequences to motivate her.

3. Matilda teases weaker children and laughs when they act upset.

4. Although he has never been caught at it, Rudy has been selling drugs in school, according to reports from three students.

5. Although Placido is a bright student and can do the work on his own without any difficulty, he often copies other students' homework.

6. Antonia thinks so little of her math abilities that she often gives up whenever she encounters a difficult problem.

III. Decide whether each of the six problems described below is more likely to be a personality problem or a situational problem. Give reasons for your choices.

1. Because of the neglect and abuse she received since her early childhood, Barbara is very suspicious of children and adults and doesn't trust anyone.

2. Because he was not selected for the varsity football team, Peter feels very bad and no longer associates with any of his friends who made the team.

3. Mark is afraid of his brothers and sisters and the other children in the school. He always sits in the back row and does not play with anyone his own age or older.

4. Since she was hit by a car a few months ago, Maria shakes whenever she has to cross the street.

5. The other children in the class laughed at Jason because he did so poorly on an exam. Now he doesn't want to go to school.

6. Because Susan is so anxious and dependent, she always tries to get attention from adults.

IV. Imagine a behavior problem that can result when students experience each of the following emotions in class: anger, fear, anxiety, jealousy, depression, guilt, shame. Suggest two management techniques that educators can use to make it less likely that these potential behavior problems will occur.

References

Formal assessment instruments are described in the following references.

1. Quay, H. C. (1977). Measuring dimensions of deviant behavior: The Behavior Problem Checklist. *Journal of Abnormal Child Psychology, 5,* 277–289.

2. Quay, H. C. & Peterson, D. R. (1983). *Revised Behavior Problem Checklist*. Coral Gables, FL: University of Miami.

3. Rubin, E., Simpson, C., & Betwee, M. (1966). *Emotionally Handicapped Children and the Elementary School*. Detroit: Wayne State University Press.

4. Spivack, G., Spotts, J., & Haines, P. E. (1967). *The Devereux Adolescent Behavior Rating Scale*. Devon, PA: Devereux Foundation.

5. Spivack, G., & Swift, M. (1967). *Devereux Elementary School Behavior Rating Scale Manual*. Devon, PA: Devereux Foundation.

6. Von Isser, A., Quay, H. C., & Love, C. T. (1980). Interrelationships among three measures of deviant behavior. *Exceptional Children, 46*, 272–276.

7. Walker, H. (1969). Empirical assessment of deviant behavior in children. *Psychology in the Schools, 6*, 93–97.

8. Walker, H. (1976). *Walker Problem Behavior Identification Manual*. Los Angeles: Western Psychological Services.

These references document the underrepresentation of females in programs for students with emotional problems.

9. Jennings, K. D., Mendelson, S. R., May, K., & Brown, G. M. (1988). Elementary students in classes for the emotionally disturbed: Characteristics and classroom behavior. *American Journal of Orthopsychiatry, 58*, 65–76.

10. Mattison, R. E., & Morales, J. (1991). Elementary and secondary socially and/or emotionally disturbed girls: Characteristics and identification. *Journal of School Psychology, 29*, 121–134.

11. Morse, W. C., Cutler, R. L., & Fink, A. H. (1964). *Public School Classes for the Emotionally Handicapped: A Research Analysis*. Reston, VA: Council for Exceptional Children.

The ability of teachers to help students with personality problems is discussed in the following reference.

12. Brophy, J. E., & Putnam, J. G. (1978). *Classroom Management in the Elementary Grades*. ERIC ED 167 537.

Attributes that comprise students' self-concepts are discussed in the following references.

13. Coopersmith, S. (1981). *The Antecedents of Self-Esteem* (2nd ed.). Palo Alto, CA: Consulting Psychologists.

14. Morse, W. C. (1985). *The Education and Treatment of Socioemotionally Impaired Children and Youth*. Syracuse, NY: Syracuse University Press.

15. Wells, L., & Maxwell, G. (1976). *Self-Esteem: Its Conceptualization and Measurement*. Beverly Hills, CA: Sage.

This reference discusses the relationship between self-concept and self-esteem.

16. Rosenberg, M. (1979). *Conceiving the Self.* New York: Basic Books.

The relationship between low self-concept or low self-esteem and the development of emotional problems is documented in the following references.

17. Bandina, A. (1982). Self-efficacy mechanism in human agency. *American Psychologist, 37*, 122–148.

18. Baskin, B. H., & Harris, K. S. (1977). *Notes from a Different Drummer: A Guide to Juvenile Fiction Portraying the Handicapped.* New York: Bowker.

19. Burdett, K., & Jensen, L. C. (1983). The self-concept and aggressive behavior among elementary school children from two socioeconomic areas and two grade levels. *Psychology in the Schools, 20*, 370–375.

20. Coopersmith, S., & Feldman, R. (1974). Fostering a positive self-concept and high self-esteem in the classroom. In R. H. Coop & K. White (Eds.), *Psychological Concepts in the Classroom.* New York: Harper & Row.

21. Gose, A., Wooden, A., & Muller, D. (1980). The relative potential of self-concept and intelligence as predictors of achievement. *Journal of Psychology, 104*, 279–287.

22. Hansford, B. C., & Hattie, J. E. (1982). The relationship between self and achievement/performance measures. *Review of Educational Research, 52*, 123–142.

23. Kinard, E. M. (1980). Emotional development in physically abused children. *American Journal of Orthopsychiatry, 50*, 686–696.

24. Reynolds, W. M. (1980). Self-esteem and classroom behavior in elementary school children. *Psychology in the Schools, 17*, 273–277.

25. Rosenberg, F. R., & Rosenberg, M. (1978). Self-esteem and delinquency. *Journal of Youth and Adolescence, 7*, 279–291.

26. Russell, A., & Russell, W. A. (1979). Using bibliotherapy with emotionally disturbed children. *Teaching Exceptional Children, 11*, 168–171.

27. Yauman, B. E. (1980). Special education placements and the self-concepts of elementary school-age children. *Learning Disabilities Quarterly, 3*, 30–35.

The fact that teachers can improve students' self-concepts and self-esteem is supported in the references below.

28. Canfield, J., & Wells, H. C. (1994). *100 Ways to Enhance Self-Concept in the Classroom.* Englewood Cliffs, NJ: Prentice Hall.

29. De Charms, R. (1976). *Enhancing Motivation.* New York: Irvington.

30. Hauserman, N., Mitler, J. S., & Bond, F. T. (1976). A behavioral approach to changing self-concept in elementary school children. *Psychological Record, 26*, 111–116.

31. Knoblock, P. (1983). *Teaching Emotionally Disturbed Children*. Boston: Houghton Mifflin.

32. Lane, J., & Muller, D. (1977). The effect of altering self-descriptive behavior on self-concept and classroom behavior. *Journal of Psychology, 97,* 115–125.

33. Scheier, M. A., & Kraut, R. E. (1979). Increasing educational achievement via self-concept change. *Review of Educational Research, 49,* 131–149.

34. Schulman, J. L., Ford, R. C., & Busk, P. (1973). A classroom program to improve self-concept. *Psychology in the Schools, 10,* 481–487.

The relationship between ethnic and socioeconomic background and self-concept is the focus of the references below.

35. Arnez, N. (1972). Enhancing the black self-concept through literature. In J. Banks (Ed.), *Black Self-Concept: Implications for Education and Social Science.* New York: McGraw-Hill.

36. Banks, J. A., & Grambs, D. (Eds.). (1972). *Black Self-Concept: Implications for Education and Social Sciences.* New York: McGraw-Hill.

37. Braroe, N. W. (1975). *Indian and White: Self Image and Interaction in a Canadian Plains Community.* Stanford, CA: Stanford University Press.

38. Evans, F. B., & Anderson, J. G. (1973). The psychocultural origins of achievement and achievement motivation: The Mexican-American family. *Sociology of Education, 46,* 396–416.

39. Healy, G. W., & DeBlassie, R. R. (1974). A comparison of Negro, Anglo, and Spanish American adolescents' self concepts. *Adolescence, 33,* 15–24.

40. Heaps, R. A., & Morrill, S. G. (1979). Comparing the self-concepts of Navajo and white high school students. *Journal of American Indian Education, 18* (3), 12–14.

41. Larned, D. T., & Muller, D. (1979). Development of self-concept in Mexican American and Anglo students. *Hispanic Journal of Behavioral Sciences, 1* (2), 179–185.

42. Luftig, R. L. (1982), *The Effects of Schooling on the Self-Concept of Native American Students.* ERIC ED 220 227.

43. Muller, D., & Leonetti, R. (1974). Self-concepts of primary level Chicano and Anglo students. *California Journal of Educational Research, 25,* 57–60.

44. Parry, R. (1982). Poor self-concept and differential academic achievement: An inadequate explanation of school performance of black and Native American children. *Canadian Journal of Native Education, 10* (1), 11–24.

45. Patton, S. M., Walberg, H. J., & Yeh, E. G. (1973). Ethnicity, environmental control, and academic self-concept in Chicago. *American Educational Research Journal, 10,* 85–91.

46. Poussaint, A. R. (1974, August). Building a strong self-image in the black child. *Ebony*, 136–143.

47. Trowbridge, N. T. (1973). Self-concept and socioeconomic status in elementary-school children. *American Educational Research Journal, 9*, 525–537.

48. Wells, E. E. (1978). *The Mythical Negative Black Self Concept*. San Francisco: R & E Research Associates.

49. Zirkel, P. A. (1973). Self-concept and the "disadvantage" of ethnic group membership and mixture. *Review of Educational Research, 41*, 211–225.

Students' locus of control is the focus of the references below.

50. Cummings, S. (1977). Family socialization and fatalism among black adolescents. *Journal of Negro Education, 46* (1), 62–75.

51. Gurin, P., Gurin, G., Lao, R. C., & Beattie, M. (1969). Internal-external control in the motivational dynamics of negro youth. *Journal of Social Issues, 25* (3), 29–53.

The following references describe formal assessment instruments for evaluating students' self-concepts.

52. Harter, S. (1982). The perceived competency scale for children. *Child Development, 53*, 87–97.

53. Katzenmer, W. G., & Stenner, A. J. (1970). *Self-Observation Scales*. Durham, NC: NTS Research Corporation.

54. Nowicki, S., & Strickland, B. (1973). A locus of control scale for children. *Journal of Consulting and Clinical Psychology, 40*, 148–154.

55. Piers, E. V., & Harris, D. B. (1969). *Children's Self-Concept Scale (The Way I Feel About Myself)*. Nashville, TN: Counselor Recordings and Tests.

The following references describe the effective use of bibliotherapy and provide lists of useful reading materials.

56. Bohning, G. (1981). Bibliotherapy: Fitting the resources together. *Elementary School Journal, 82* (2), 166–170.

57. D'Alessandro, M. (1990). Accommodating emotionally handicapped children through a literature-based reading program. *Reading Teacher, 44* (4), 288–293.

58. Dreyer, S. S. (1977). *The Bookfinder: A Guide to Children's Literature About the Needs and Problems of Youth Aged Two Through Fifteen*. Circle Pines, MN: American Guidance Service.

59. Fassler, J. (1978). *Helping Children Cope*. New York: Free Press.

60. Frasier, M., & McCannon, C. (1981). Using bibliotherapy with gifted children. *Gifted Child Quarterly, 25*, 81–84.

61. Hebert, T. P. (1991). Meeting the affective needs of bright boys through bibliotherapy, *Roeper Review, 13* (4), 207–212.

62. Lenkowsky, R. (1987). Bibliotherapy: A review and analysis of the literature. *Journal of Special Education, 21* (2), 123–132.

63. Pardeck, J. T. (1991). Using books to prevent and treat adolescent chemical dependency. *Adolescence, 26* (101), 201–208.

64. Pardeck, J. A., & Pardeck, J. T. (1986). *Young People with Problems: A Guide to Bibliotherapy.* Westport, CT: Greenwood Press.

65. Riordan, R. J., & Wilson, J. S. (1989). Bibliotherapy: Does it work? *Journal of Counseling and Development, 67,* 506–508.

66. Schrank, F. A., & Engles, D. W. (1981). Bibliotherapy as a counseling adjunct: Research findings. Personnel and Guidance Journal, 60,143–147.

Techniques for helping students think more positively about their abilities are included in the reference below.

67. White, K., & Allen, R. (1971). Art counseling in an educational setting: Self-concept change among preadolescent boys. *Journal of School Psychology, 9* (2), 218–225.

The following references describe self-concept enhancement programs.

68. Felker, D. W. (1974). *Building Positive Self-Concepts.* Minneapolis: Burgess.

69. Vernon, A. (1989). *Thinking, Feeling, Behaving: An Emotional Education Curriculum for Adolescents.* Champaign, IL: Research Press.

70. Weinstein, G., & Fantini, M. (1970). *Toward Humanistic Education.* New York: Praeger.

The effectiveness of self-concept enhancement programs with students with emotional problems is discussed in these references.

71. Baskin, E. J., & Hess, R. D. (1980). Does affective education work? A review of seven programs. *Journal of School Psychology, 18* (1), 40–50.

72. DiGiuseppe, R., & Bernard, M. E. (1990). The application of rational-emotive theory and therapy to school-aged children. *School Psychology Review, 19,* 268–286.

73. Laconte, M. A., Shaw, D., & D. I. (1993). The effects of a rational-emotive affective education program for high-risk middle school students. *Psychology in the Schools, 30,* 274–281.

74. Strein, W. (1988). Classroom-based elementary school affective education programs: A critical review. *Psychology in the Schools, 25,* 288–296.

These references provide evidence that some self-concept enhancement approaches are more effective with males than with females.

75. Calsyn, R. J., Pennell, C., & Harter, M. (1984). Are affective education programs more effective with girls than boys? *Elementary School Guidance and Counseling, 19* (2), 133–140.

76. Calsyn, R., & Prost, B. (1983). Evaluation of an affective education curriculum: Sex and treatment effects. *Journal of Humanistic Education and Development, 22*, 58–69.

77. Stilwell, W., & Barclay, J. (1979). Effects of affective education intervention in the elementary school. *Psychology in the Schools, 16*, 80–87.

The use of gradual desensitization is described in these references.

78. Deffenbacher, J., & Kemper, C. (1974). Systematic desensitization of test anxiety in junior high school students. *The School Counselor, 21*, 216–222.

79. Hosford, C. (1979). Overcoming of fear of speaking in a group. In J. Krumboltz & C. Thoresen (Eds.), *Behavioral Counseling*. New York: Holt, Rinehart & Winston.

80. Johnson, S. (1979). Children's fears in the classroom setting. *School Psychologist Digest, 8*, 382–396.

81. Lazarus, A. A., Davidson, G. C., & Polefka, D. A. (1965). Classical and operant factors in the treatment of a school phobia. *Journal of Abnormal Psychology, 70*, 225–229.

82. Mann, J. (1972). Vicarious desensitization of test anxiety through observation of videotaped treatment. *Journal of Counseling Psychology, 19*, 1–7.

83. Montenegro, H. (1968). Severe separation anxiety in two preschool children: Successfully treated by reciprocal inhibition. *Journal of Child Psychology and Psychiatry, 9*, 93–103.

Active listening is discussed in this reference.

84. Gordon, R. (1974). *Teacher Effectiveness Training*. New York: Wyden.

These authors describe and recommend the life-space interview to teachers.

85. Long, J. D., & Frye, V. H. (1981). *Making It Till Friday: A Guide to Successful Classroom Management* (2nd ed.). Princeton: Princeton Book Company.

86. Long, N. J., Morse, W. C., & Newman, R. G. (Eds.). (1980). *Conflict in the Classroom: The Education of Emotionally Disturbed Children* (4th ed.). Belmont, CA: Wadsworth.

87. Morse, W. C. (1963). Working paper: Training teachers in life-space interviewing. *American Journal of Orthopsychiatry, 33*, 727–730.

88. Redl, F. (1959). The concept of the life-space interview. *American Journal of Orthopsychiatry, 29*, 1–18.

89. Tanner, L. N. (1978). *Classroom Discipline for Effective Teaching and Learning*. New York: Holt, Rinehart & Winston.

Evidence of the effectiveness of the life-space interview is included in the following references.

90. De Magistris, R. J., & Imber, S. C. (1980). The effects of life-space interviewing on academic and social performance of behaviorally disordered children. *Behavior Disorders, 6,* 12–25.

91. Gardner, R., III. (1990). Life space interviewing: It can be effective, but don't . . . *Behavioral Disorders, 15,* 111–118.

92. Long, N. J. (1990). Comments on Ralph Gardner's article "Life space interviewing: It can be effective, but don't. . . ." *Behavioral Disorders, 15,* 119–125.

93. Naslund, S. R. (1987). Life space interviewing: A psychoeducational interviewing model for teaching pupils insights and measuring program effectiveness. *Pointer, 31* (2), 12–15.

94. Reilly, M. J., Imber, S. C., & Cremins, J. (1978). *The Effects of Life-Space Interviews on Social Behaviors of Junior High School Special Needs Students.* Paper presented at the 56th International Conference of the Council for Exceptional Children, Kansas City.

95. Wood, M. M., & Long, N. J. (1990). *Life Space Intervention: Talking with Children and Youth in Crisis.* Austin, TX: Pro-Ed.

These references describe social skills training techniques and discuss their effectiveness.

96. Bierman, K. L., & Montminy, H. P. (1993). Developmental issues in social-skills assessment and intervention with children and adolescents. *Behavior Modification, 17* (3), 229–254.

97. Christopher, J. S., Nangle, D. W., & Hansen, D. J. (1993). Social-skills intervention with adolescents. *Behavior Modification, 17* (3), 314–338.

98. Elliot, S. N., & Gresham, F. M. (1993). Social skills intervention for children. *Behavior Modification, 17* (3), 287–313.

99. Fox, J. J., & McEvoy, M. A. (1993). Assessing and enhancing generalization and social validity of social-skills interventions with children and adolescents. *Behavior Modification, 17* (3), 339–366.

100. Sasso, G. M., Melloy, K. J., & Kavale, K. A. (1990). Generalization, maintenance, and behavioral covariation associated with social skills training through structured learning. *Behavioral Disorders, 16* (1), 9–22.

101. Zaragoza, N., Vaughn, S., & McIntosh, R. (1991). Social skills interventions and children with behavior problems: A review. *Behavioral Disorders, 16* (4), 260–275.

Techniques for managing the behavior of students with emotional problems without using consequences are described in the references below.

102. Hewett, F. M. (1968). *The Emotionally Disturbed Child in the Classroom.* Boston: Allyn & Bacon.

103. Jacobson, S., & Falgre, C. (1953). Neutralization: A tool for the teacher of disturbed children. *American Journal of Orthopsychiatry, 23,* 684–690.

104. Long, N. J., & Newman, R. G. (1965). Managing surface behavior of children in school. In N. J. Long, W. C. Morse, & R. G. Newman (Eds.), *Conflict in the Classroom.* Belmont, CA: Wadsworth.

105. Redl, F., & Wineman, D. (1957). *The Aggressive Child.* New York: Free Press.

106. Wood, F. H. (1978). Punishment and special education: Some concluding remarks. In F. H. Wood & K. C. Lakin (Eds.), *Punishment and Aversive Stimulation in Special Education: Legal, Theoretical, and Practical Issues in Their Use with Emotionally Disturbed Children and Youth.* Minneapolis, MN: Advanced Training Institute for Trainers of Teachers for Seriously Emotionally Disturbed Children and Youth.

Self-management techniques are the focus of these references.

107. Albion, F. M. (1983). A methodological analysis of self-control in applied settings. *Behavior Disorders, 8,* 87–102.

108. Beck, A. T. (1976). *Cognitive Therapy and Emotional Disorders.* New York: International University Press.

109. Bornstein, P. H. (1985). Self-instructional training: A commentary and state of the art. *Journal of Applied Behavior Analysis, 18,* 69–72.

110. Camp, B., Blom, G., Herbert, F., & Van Doornenck, W. (1977). "Think Aloud": A program for developing self-control in young aggressive boys. *Journal of Abnormal Child Psychology, 5,* 192–199.

111. Carpenter, R. L., & Apter, S. J. (1987). Research in integration of cognitive-emotional interventions for behaviorally disordered children and youth. In M. C. Wang, H. J. Walberg, & M. C. Reynolds (Eds.), *Handbook of Special Education: Research and Practice.* Oxford, England: Pergamon Press.

112. Emery, G., Hollon, D. S., & Bedrosian, R. D. (1981). *New Directions in Cognitive Therapy.* New York: Guilford Press.

113. Epanchin, B. C., & Paul, J. L. (1987). *Emotional Problems of Childhood and Adolescence: A Multidisciplinary Prospective.* Columbus, OH: Merrill.

114. Etscheidt, S. (1991). Reducing aggressive behavior and improving self-control: A cognitive-behavioral training program for behaviorally disordered adolescents. *Behavior Disorders, 16* (2), 107–115.

115. Fagan, S. (1979). Psychoeducational management and self-control. In D. Cullinan & M. Epstein (Eds.), *Special Education for Adolescents: Issues and Perspectives.* Columbus, OH: Merrill.

116. Fagan, S. A., Long, N. J., & Stevens, D. J. (1975). *Teaching Children Self-Control in the Classroom: A Psychoeducational Curriculum.* Columbus, OH: Merrill.

117. Fick, L. (1979, May). Self-control strategies for emotionally disabled students. *Iowa Perspective.*

118. Goodwin, S., & Mahoney, M. (1975). Modification of aggression through modeling: An experimental probe. *Journal of Behavior Therapy and Experimental Psychiatry, 6,* 200–202.

119. Hallahan, D. P. (Ed.). (1980). Teaching exceptional children to use cognitive strategies. *Exceptional Education Quarterly, 1.*

120. Kanfer, F. H., Karoly, P., & Newman, A. (1975). Reduction of children's fear of the dark by competence-related and situation threat-related verbal cues. *Journal of Consulting and Clinical Psychology, 43,* 251–258.

121. Knaus, W. (1974). *Rational-Emotive Education: A Manual for Elementary School Teachers.* New York: Institute for Rational Living.

122. Kurtz, P. D., & Neisworth, J. T. (1976). Self-control possibilities for exceptional children. *Exceptional Children, 42,* 213–217.

123. McCullough, J. P., Huntsinger, G. N., & Nay, W. R. (1977). Self-controlled treatment of aggression in a 16-year-old male: Case study. *Journal of Consulting and Clinical Psychology, 45,* 322–331.

124. Meichenbaum, D. (1973). Cognitive factors in behavior modification: Modifying what clients say about themselves. In R. Rubin, J. Brady, & J. Henderson (Eds.), *Advances in Behavior Therapy* (Vol. 4). New York: Academic Press.

125. Meichenbaum, D. (1977). *Cognitive-Behavior Modification: An Integrative Approach.* New York: Plenum.

126. Meichenbaum, D., & Goodman, J. (1971). Training impulsive children to talk to themselves: A means of developing self-control. *Journal of Abnormal Psychology, 77,* 115–126.

127. Prout, H. T., & Harvey, J. R. (1976). Applications of desensitization procedures for school related problems. A review. *Psychology in the Schools, 13,* 533–540.

128. Robin, A., Schneider, M., & Dolnick, M. (1976). The Turtle Technique: An extended case study of self-control in the classroom. *Psychology in the Schools, 13,* 449–453.

129. Warren, R., Deffenbacher, J., & Brading, P. (1976). Rational emotive therapy and the reduction of test anxiety in elementary school children. *Rational Living, 11,* 26–29.

130. Workman, E. (1982). *Teaching Behavior Self-Control to Students.* Austin, TX: Pro-Ed.

131. Workman, E. A., & Hector, M. A. (1982). Behavior self-control in classroom settings: A review of the literature. *Journal of School Psychology, 16,* 227–236.

The following references deal with developmental issues in self-management.

132. Bornstein, P. H., & Quevillon, R. P. (1976). The effects of a self-instructional package on overactive preschool boys. *Journal of Applied Behavior Analysis, 9,* 179–188.

133. Bugenthal, D. B., Whalen, C. K., & Hencker, B. (1977). Casual attributions of hyperactive children and motivational assumptions of two behavior-change assumptions: Evidence for an interactionist position. *Child Development, 48,* 874–884.

134. Hartig, M., & Kanfer, F. (1973). The role of verbal self-instructions on children's resistance to temptation. *Journal of Personality and Social Psychology, 25,* 259–267.

135. Meacham, J. A. (1978). A verbal guidance through remembering the goals of actions. *Child Development, 49,* 188–193.

136. Mischel, W., Ebbensen, E. B., & Zeiss, A. (1972). Cognitive and attentional mechanisms in delay of gratification. *Journal of Personality and Social Psychology, 21,* 204–218.

137. Mischel, W., & Patterson, C. J. (1976). Substantive and structural elements of effective plans for self-control. *Journal of Personality and Social Psychology, 34,* 942–950.

138. Mischel, W., & Patterson, C. J. (1978). Effect plans for self-control in children. In W. A. Collins (Ed.), *Minnesota Symposium on Child Psychology* (Vol. 2). Hillsdale, NJ: Erlbaum.

139. O'Leary, S. G., & Dubey, D. R. (1979). Application of self-control procedures by children: A review. *Journal of Applied Behavior Analysis, 12* (3), 449–465.

140. Pressley, M. (1979). Increasing children's self-control through cognitive interventions. *Review of Educational Research, 49* (2), 319–370.

141. Yates, B. T., & Mischel, W. C. (1979). Young children's preferred attentional strategies for delaying gratification. *Journal of Personality and Social Psychology, 37,* 286–300.

These references present evidence that the intrinsic satisfaction that students experience from behavioral improvement is sufficiently rewarding to make extrinsic rewards unnecessary when students manage their own behavior.

142. DiGangi, S. A., & Maag, J. W. (1992). A component analysis of self-management training with behaviorally disordered youth. *Behavioral Disorders, 17* (4), 281–290.

143. Nelson, J. R., Smith, D. J., Young, K. R., & Young, J. M. (1991). A review of self-management outcome research conducted with students who exhibit behavioral disorders. *Behavioral Disorders, 16* (3), 169–179.

These references discuss the maintenance and generalization of the positive effects of self-management.

144. Ager, C. L., & Cole, C. L. (1991). A review of cognitive-behavioral interventions for children and adolescents with behavioral disorders. *Behavioral Disorders, 16* (4), 276–287.

145. Billings, D. C., & Wasik, B. H. (1985). Self-instructional training with preschoolers: An attempt to replicate. *Journal of Applied Behavior Analysis, 18,* 61–67.

146. Smith, D. J., Young, K. R., West, R. P., Morgan, D. P., & Rhode, G. (1988). Reducing the disruptive behavior of junior high school students: A classroom management procedure. *Behavioral Disorders, 13,* 231–239.

PHYSIOLOGICAL FACTORS

Some students don't comply with the rules and procedures that are appropriate for most students because they are physiologically unable to do so. This chapter discusses four of the major physiological factors that make it difficult for certain students to fulfill their teachers' expectations—developmental lag, temperamental differences, attention deficit hyperactivity disorder, and prenatal exposure to dangerous substances. The chapter explains how these factors can affect students' behavior, describes how you can help identify students whose behavior problems are caused by these factors, and offers suggestions for dealing with such problems in your classroom.

Developmental Lag

Infants, children, and teenagers all develop at their own unique biologically determined rates. Children not only learn to crawl, walk, talk, and control their bowel and bladder movements at different ages, they also develop the skills necessary for success in kindergarten and elementary school at different ages. Unfortunately—with few exceptions—students all begin kindergarten in September when they are approximately 5 and first grade the following fall when they are close to 6 despite their different levels of maturity. As a result, significant numbers of children with developmental delays start school almost predestined to experience difficulty, frustration, and failure in the lower grades. Thus, by the time they catch up to their peers developmentally, they may lag far behind academically and be in trouble behaviorally.

Identification

Because the consequences of developmental lag can influence a student's entire education, it is both valuable and important to discover these students as early as possible.

471

Informal Assessment You can identify developmentally delayed, immature students informally by whether or not their behavior is age inappropriate. The examples in the following paragraphs describe the immature behavior of students with developmental lag.

Preschoolers: Behaviors that characterize preschool children with developmental lag include speaking very little compared with their peers or speaking in "baby talk"; playing alone or engaging in parallel play rather than playing with children, and showing a preference to play outdoors or with toys and games rather than to engage in activities that require more concentration and self-control; difficulty in waiting their turn and controlling their impulses to hit others or take what others have; tending not to follow directions; trouble settling into an activity; and once they settle in, not sitting still or paying attention for as long as other children their age. In addition, they may also cry more often and more easily than their peers and be unwilling to attend school without bringing along their "security blanket" or favorite stuffed animal.

Steve is an example of an immature preschool student. Although he had turned 4 in May, he was kept back with the 3-year-olds in September due to immaturity. Specifically, he was unable to sit still during circle time and demonstrated no interest in table work that involved art projects, puzzles, or any structured activities. He would play instead in the playhouse or on the rug with blocks. He had "great difficulty with delay of gratification" when it came to waiting for other students to have their turns at things.

Elementary school students: Some of the behaviors that characterize immature elementary school students include having a short attention span and not being able to sit still for very long; becoming easily frustrated; and preferring playing, drawing, talking, and so on, to academic activities. They also lack the social skills necessary to get along with their peers, such as sharing with others, waiting their turn, and keeping their hands to themselves, and they demand a great deal of teacher attention.

Melany is an example of a youngster whose development was delayed. She did not sit up until she was 6 months old, did not start to crawl until she was 13 months, did not walk until her 19th month, and did not talk until she was almost 3. At 6 years of age, her physical development still lagged behind her peers except for her fine-motor coordination.

Her attention span was extremely short both at home and at school. At home she would shift from one toy or game to another or one activity to another. In school she was observed looking at eight different books within a five-minute period.

Her social behavior was more like a 4-year-old's than a 6-year-old's. She never expressed any interest in inviting children to her house. When her schoolmates invited her to play, she only accepted after being coaxed and cajoled by her parents. In school she was often in difficulty with other students because she took things they were playing with, pushed them out of the way to get where she wanted to go, and interrupted them during sharing time to talk about herself.

Secondary school students: Secondary school students can also be developmentally immature, although their immaturity is sometimes less obvious to their teachers and parents. Teenagers with developmental lags may prefer to spend time with younger children and have few friends among their classmates. They are often less motivated to do well in school because they are not mature enough to be concerned that what they learn and the grades they receive can affect their future. They tend to avoid activities that involve the opposite sex, and aren't as independent as many teenagers. Thus, while many adolescents are already acting as if they know it all and can go it alone, suggesting that parental guidance is

Parallel play is characteristic of young and immature students.

an unnecessary interference, immature adolescents are unable to venture forth without a great deal of parental support.

Sonia is an example of an immature teenager. At almost 16, she still decorated her bedroom like a child's room and wore clothing styled for preteens. She lived very much in the present, never thinking of her future either at home or in school. She never demonstrated any interest in boys, whom she shunned like a contagious disease. She had been adamant about not having any kind of sweet 16 celebration until her parents suggested that she could invite a few close girlfriends for a weekend outing. In school she usually kept to herself, almost never attending school functions such as dances, athletic events, and after-school trips.

If your student's actions fit one of these descriptions, her or his behavior problem may be caused by a development lag. But you should ask yourself three additional questions before arriving at this conclusion:

1. *Does your student behave immaturely in all situations?* The truly immature child or teenager will seem immature in any situation that calls for mature behavior. Other teachers and the student's parents can either confirm the fact that your student behaves immaturely or let you know that the student behaves one way with your and another way with them.

2. *Has your student always behaved immaturely, or did the student behave more maturely for a while and then regress to an earlier, more immature form of behavior?*

A child or teenager who is developmentally immature doesn't waver, first behaving maturely, then reverting back to immature behavior. A student who regresses certainly requires the teacher's attention, but the cause is unlikely to be developmental delay.

3. *Is your student's immaturity caused by environmental rather than physiological factors?* Immature behavior can also be caused by environmental factors. For example, students who have unpleasant or traumatic experiences with other children may lose interest in playing with them. Or students who have never been urged to keep trying when things get difficult or to accept the disappointments and frustrations of life without excessive complaining may have little or no tolerance for frustration. Also, traumatic experiences with the opposite sex can cause teenagers to avoid any male-female relationships, and insecurity can cause an adolescent to prefer the company of younger students, who are not so threatening because they are not seen as competitors with more academic or social skills, strength, knowledge, beauty, and the like.

Formal Assessment   A number of valid developmental tests are available to help you identify preschool and primary-grade students who are developmentally delayed. No instruments are currently available, however, for testing upper elementary and secondary school students. Here are several developmental tests for younger students:

Batelle Developmental Inventory, birth–8 years. DLM Teaching Resources, Allen, Texas.

Denver Developmental Screening Test, 2 weeks–6 years. LADOCO Publishing Foundation, Denver, Colorado.

Developmental Profile II, birth–9 years. Psychological Development Publications, Aspen, Colorado.

Minnesota Child Development Inventory, birth–6 years. Behavior Science Systems, Inc., Minneapolis, Minnesota.

VISCO Child Development Screening Test, 3–7 years. Educational Activities, Inc., Freeport, New York.

It is important to note that these instruments can provide misleading information about poor students, immigrant students, and others who grow up in a different environment than the European American children on whom they were normed. For example, a young child who has not yet learned to ride a tricycle may not be developmentally delayed. She may come from a family that is too poor to afford one. Likewise, a boy who cannot throw a ball may have learned how to kick a soccer ball instead. And a youngster who does not go to the store to buy things may not be too immature to be relied on. Rather, she may not be allowed to go to the store because her parents think that the neighborhood is too dangerous to allow her out on the street alone.

Helping Developmentally Delayed Students

Research indicates that educators can help developmentally delayed students succeed in school despite their immaturity by adapting instructional and classroom management techniques to their students' developmental levels (1, 2). The discussion that follows describes some techniques you can use to accomplish this with students at different school levels.

Preschool and Elementary School Students The speech problems and poor motor coordination that interfere with young developmentally delayed students' abilities to communicate with others and run, climb, ride tricycles, cut, paste, draw, print, and so on, aren't behavior problems in themselves. But given the low frustration tolerance of children in general and especially those with developmental lags, these obstacles can certainly lead young students to behave inappropriately. By providing such students with the assistance they need to achieve what the other students do, educators can help keep them from becoming frustrated and venting their feelings in school.

You can provide poorly coordinated youngsters with equipment that is especially suitable for their motor problems and the help they need to succeed in such activities as climbing, cutting, pasting, and printing. This may improve their behavior. If they cannot succeed even with your help, directing them to alternative activities is another option. Teaching other students not to make negative comments about the way developmentally delayed students do things can help protect such students from having their self-concept damaged by their peers.

Educators can also help developmentally delayed students avoid behavior problems by accommodating the length of seatwork assignments to their shorter attention spans, assigning them to a quiet nonstimulating area where they can be free of distractions, and providing them with alternative activities when they can't sit still. Placing these students on the periphery of the group during circle time or when telling or reading stories may make it easier for their attention to wander, but this also allows them to leave the group mentally or physically when they can no longer concentrate without distracting others.

You can manage students who have not developed the social skills necessary to get along with others by keeping them under close supervision. Remind such students in advance not to hit, take things, or push ahead of others. It is unlikely, though, that these kinds of techniques will completely eliminate their behavior problems. Thus, be prepared to accept some immature, infantile, and even antisocial behavior so long as it doesn't seriously interfere with the rights of others. Certainly, praise students when they conform to rules and procedures and make them aware when they don't, but don't use consequences to try to speed up the maturational process or scold students for behaving immaturely.

Secondary School Students Secondary school students who are too immature to care about their future and lack the maturity to function independently in school shouldn't be allowed to fall by the wayside. Teachers should do whatever is possible to ensure that such students make enough progress in school so they will be able to move ahead when they mature. To do this, provide students with the extra support, structure, and guidance they need to participate and succeed despite their immaturity. But it is important to do this without pressuring them to "act their age." Immature teenagers cannot be more responsible in school than they really are. Requiring them to function independently may cause them to fall flat on their faces. Nor can they be motivated to want to participate in social activities that are only attractive to their more mature peers. Manipulating them into positions where they must participate in such activities can result in unnecessary embarrassment and shame for them.

Self-Quiz:
Developmental Delays

What kinds of developmental delays are you most and least able to accept? Review the problems that tend to characterize students with developmental delays, and state whether you react positively or negatively to each one.

Temperamental Differences

Ask a group of mothers and fathers what kinds of differences they observed among their sons and daughters when they were infants. One mother might tell you that her firstborn was so full of energy that the infant hardly slept, couldn't be kept in her crib and playpen, was totally unpredictable, and got into everything in the house, but then the second child slept through the night when he was 2 months old, was almost never cranky, and spent hours playing by himself in his crib. A father might focus on the fact that one child was finicky about foods, frightened of strangers, and just downright difficult to please, while the other was just the opposite. Ask the parents if these differences continued as their children grew, and they will tell you how little they were able to change them over the years.

Such informal observations of basic ways of being have been supported by formal research. Studies have demonstrated that infants have consistent, individual patterns of sleeping, eating, body movements, and physiological functioning. They differ in terms of whether they typically approach or withdraw from new things in their environment, such as foods and strangers, in how active they are, and in how often they smile or cry. Studies that have followed groups of infants through childhood and adolescence have also found that some, but not all, individuals maintain these earliest behavior patterns. Studies of identical twins reared apart from birth also show evidence of inborn behavioral styles. These persistent, apparently inborn differences among infants have been called *temperamental traits* by theorists who believe that they help account for many of the personality differences among people.

Temperamental Traits

Although authors have tended to agree on the definition of temperament, they vary considerably in the lists of temperamental traits and temperamental types they provide (3–7). Presently, research evidence does not clearly support any particular list of temperamental traits.

One of the most ambitious attempts to document temperamental differences among infants and to examine their effects on the development of personality is the New York Longitudinal Study, initiated by Thomas, Chess, and Birch (18). These researchers followed a group of infants through to young adulthood. They used nine temperamental traits to characterize the differences among the individuals they followed.

As they studied the life spans of these individuals, they discovered that youngsters with temperamental characteristics that didn't match the behavior styles commonly expected of students in school were more likely than others to have problems adjusting to school rules and procedures. The following are descriptions of the nine temperamental characteristics they included in their studies and the kinds of classroom behavior problems some are associated with (8–21):

Activity—the amount and tempo of motor activity. Highly active infants were described by their parents as so active that they couldn't be left alone on the bed. They crawled or ran around so much that they exhausted their parents. Nonactive babies lay quietly in bed, in the bath, and when they were being dressed, and they remained in the same position all night.

In school, highly active students wriggle around in their seats, start conversations with students sitting alongside them, and move around the classroom. They listen to only the first part of directions before starting an assignment. They do not hear what their teachers say when they are actively involved in doing something they should not be doing because they are too energetic to sit still and listen.

Students with low activity levels usually work at a slow pace. They may not finish classroom assignments, timed tests, or lengthy homework assignments during the time allotted. When other students are ready for the next class or activity, they may still be putting their materials away. Sometimes they are misperceived as sluggish, apathetic, or even retarded because of their inability to accomplish the expected amount of work in the standard time.

Rhythmicity—the regularity of functions such as sleeping, eating, and bowel and bladder movement. Regular children fell asleep and woke up at approximately the same time each day or moved their bowels on a regularly predictable schedule. Irregular infants were unpredictable. Rhythmicity has not been found to cause behavior problems in school.

Approach or withdrawal—the initial response to newness. Children who approached new aspects in the environment were described as smiling at strangers or loving new toys. Those who withdrew were slow to accept new toys, people, places, or foods.

Withdrawers tend to react negatively to new teachers, new subjects, and new activities. If they are also slow to adapt, it may take them an inordinately long time to get involved in new tasks and activities, which could negatively impact their performance in school.

Adaptability—the extent to which an individual changes her or his initial responses in the ways desired by parents and other adults. Highly adaptable babies changed their initial avoidance responses to bathing, new foods, toys, and the like, after a short time. Low-adaptable babies continued to reject new things even after they were no longer strange or new.

Low adaptability has been found to be related to behavior problems only when students also have certain other temperamental traits (see the discussions of difficult children and those slow to warm up).

Intensity of reaction—the energy of response. Highly intense children screamed and spit out food they did not like. Low-intensity children whimpered and let the food drool out.

Students who react intensely seem as if they love some teachers or some subjects and hate others. These students' intense ways of reacting do not actually reflect their true feelings, nor do they predict how they will actually deal with a teacher, subject, or task because it is just their style of responding. Nevertheless, educators and sometimes the students themselves are fooled into believing that these reactions express how they really feel about things.

Students who characteristically react with low intensity do not show others how they really feel because their words, facial expressions, and gestures are misleading. This means that educators may not realize when these students are upset, frustrated, or frightened. They also may not recognize the subtle clues that indicate that these seemingly disinterested students are actually quite motivated to learn.

Threshold of responsiveness—the amount of stimulation required to cause a reaction. Babies with a high threshold of responsiveness were difficult to startle and inattentive to new foods mixed in with their meals. Babies with low thresholds seemed to notice anything new, any change, or any noise.

Students with high thresholds of responsiveness are slow to pick up both the subtle and not-so-subtle clues in their environments. Relatively insensitive to body language and other social clues, they often misread the feelings of peers and teachers. They may also have difficulty distinguishing the important from the unimportant and the central from the trivial in their teachers' lectures. In a general sense, they may not know what their teachers want or are driving at unless it's spelled out for them.

Mood—positive, pleasant, joyful, friendly, in contrast to negative, unpleasant, crying, unfriendly. Infants who had positive moods cooed, laughed, and smiled much more than average. Children with negative moods whined, cried, and fussed a lot.

Students with negative moods can allow their moods to affect how they function in school. If their moodiness puts their teachers off, they may be called on less often, praised less often, and given less attention by teachers who are unlikely to extend themselves for "ill-humored," "unfriendly" students.

Distractibility—the ease with which irrelevant events change ongoing actions. Distractible children stopped crying when they were picked up, even though they were still hungry, and they stopped playing with one toy when they spied another one. Non-distractible children continued to cry in their mothers' arms or continued to play with the same toy despite possible distractions.

Highly distractible students have difficulty attending to lectures and completing seatwork. The end result is often poor grades and arguments with teachers about paying attention and staying on-task.

Attention span and persistence—attention span: the length of time an individual continues in self-initiated activities; persistence: the extent to which a child continues an activity despite obstacles. Children with long attention spans maintained interest in their activities much longer than children with short attention spans, who quickly switched from one activity to another.

Persistent toddlers continued to try to walk, though they repeatedly fell, and they continued to do something even though their parents said "no." Nonpersistent children gave up easily and stopped when their parents told them to.

Students with short attention spans have problems staying on-task. Persistent students are usually well received by their teachers when they persist in trying to

THEORY FOCUS: CHESS AND THOMAS ON TEMPERAMENTAL CHARACTERISTICS

Stella Chess and Alexander Thomas have collaborated on a wide variety of research projects, including the New York Longitudinal Study, which investigates the role of temperament during the life span. This ongoing study of individuals from their early years through young adulthood has contributed immensely to our understanding of what types of behavior can be influenced by temperament. The study has also helped us learn more about the stability of temperamental characteristics over time and the relationship between extreme temperamental characteristics and the development of behavior problems. Through such books as *Temperament in Clinical Practice, Temperament and Development, Temperamental and Behavior Disorders,* and *Your Child Is a Person,* as well as a large number of articles, these researchers have helped both professionals and parents realize the role that physiological factors can play in determining people's personalities.

Chess describes the role of temperament and the purpose of her research as follows:

The many individual styles children bring to their everyday responses to the people and actions of their environment are to be seen in the classroom, too. Temperamental features will characterize their varied approaches both to social demands and expectations and also to the educational tasks of the educational institutions. This is a complicated set of ongoing interactions with mutual influences: the youngster's temperamental style, together with intellectual abilities and other features of personality, will influence the educators and the decisions they make—in ever continuing cycles. And, along with this, one must be aware that both expectations and abilities will depend also on the child, adolescent, or adult's developmental status. Only by following the same individuals through life can we distinguish their changing adaptations, see "winners" who coped well from infancy on as well as those with poor beginnings who discovered strengths and became "winners" as adults! Unfortunately the opposite also occurred.

Temperament, we found, plays a powerful part in filtering meaning and hopes, and even lighting educational fires well after none were expected any longer. (Stella Chess, personal communication)

solve problems and complete assignments despite difficulties and frustrations. But when they persist in doing what the teacher tells them to stop doing or when they nag their teachers after they have been told "no" repeatedly, the same temperamental characteristic can cause problems.

The results of the New York Longitudinal Study also indicated that youngsters who had certain combinations of temperamental characteristics were especially likely to have problems adapting to school. Thomas, Chess, and Birch (18) labeled two of these groups of youngsters "difficult children" and "slow-to-warm-up children."

Difficult children: Students who are characteristically irregular in their biological functioning, put off by new aspects of their environment, slow to adapt to changing expectations, negative in mood, and intense in their reactions were the most likely to develop problems during childhood and adolescence. Seventy percent of the infants in this group had adjustment problems by age 10.

Since they had irregular functioning, they did not develop patterns of eating, sleeping, and so on, that their parents could plan their day around. Instead of adjusting to the schedules their parents attempted to set for them, they required their parents to adjust to their irregularity. Likely to withdraw from new situations and slow to adapt, they required many gently familiarizing exposures to new experiences before they could adjust to each new situation. Without this gentle lead-in, they tended to react with screams, temper tantrums, and threats. Since they often overreacted to even minor frustrations, parents were unable to judge how they really felt about things.

In school they reacted negatively to the beginning of the new school year, a new teacher, or a new social or academic demand. Teachers tended to misperceive their temperamentally determined, intensely negative responses as willful defiance or else emotional overreaction.

Slow-to-warm-up children: Children who were characterized by low activity levels, initial withdrawal responses, slow adaptability, low-intensity reactions, and negative moods initially responded to newness and strangers with mild fussing or turning away. When they started nursery school, they often wanted to have one of their parents remain for a while. Even with their parents present, they tended to remain on the sidelines, watching the other children until they felt comfortable enough to join in.

In grade school they often met new situations and new tasks with an "I don't like it" announcement or, more typically, a silent refusal to participate. Because these students are quietly passive in their negativism, their reluctance often goes unnoticed. When it is noticed and teachers push them to participate by cajoling or coaxing them or by engaging in a battle of wills with them, the students tend to either retreat further into themselves or become less quiet and more intensely negative. On the other hand, when adults are able to wait while these youngsters adapt at their own slower pace, these students often overcome their initial negativism to participate.

Identification

Temperamentally different children need to be identified so that you can work with them in the classroom appropriately. Without such identification, you may respond to them with techniques that will not help the students or you.

Informal Assessment   Once you realize that your students' behavior is influenced by temperamental factors, you can help them succeed in situations even when their temperament is a disadvantage, and you can help eliminate adjustment problems they may already have. But first you need to find out if a temperamental factor is involved. To informally determine whether a student's problems are caused by temperamental differences, you should ask yourself four questions:

1. *Does the problem fit descriptions that research suggests can be the result of temperamental differences?* Below is a list of 15 traits substantiated by research as being possible aspects of temperament (3–7, 18). If your student's behavior does not appear on the list, it is unlikely that it is caused by temperamental factors. But if your student's behavior does appear on the list, it may be a reflection of his or her temperament. For example, it is unlikely that students who are jealous of their peers or poor sharers behave that way for temperamental reasons, since no evidence shows that such behaviors have a temperamental base.

Daringness—fearful versus courageous responses to challenging or risky situations

Sociability—an individual's desire to be with or avoid contact with others

Reflectiveness—the tendency to respond impulsively (spontaneously) or thoughtfully

Flexibility—stubbornness or pliability in relationships with others

Diurnal-nocturnal—whether an individual functions better early or late in the day

Activity level—the amount and tempo of motor activity

Rhythmicity—the regularity of functions

Approach-withdrawal—an individual's initial response to newness

Adaptability—ability to modify an initial response in light of additional information

Intensity of reaction—the energy of an individual's response

Threshold of responsiveness—the amount of stimulation required to evoke a reaction

Mood—usual or customary emotional state

Distractibility—the ease with which irrelevant events change ongoing activities

Persistence—the tendency to continue an activity despite obstacles or difficulties

Attention span—the length of time an individual engages in self-directed activities

2. *Is the behavior present in all aspects of the student's life?* Consult with your student's other teachers to determine whether the student consistently behaves the way he or she does in your class. Ask your student's parents how the student behaves at home, or request the school social worker to obtain that information from them for you. Parents can be asked to informally describe their youngster's behavior or to complete a formal questionnaire designed to elicit the information from them (23).

3. *Has the student behaved that way since he or she was young?* Although research indicates that parents' recollections of their youngsters' behavior as infants and toddlers are sometimes distorted, in most instances your students' parents should be able to provide you with the information you require to determine whether their behavior has been consistent over time. The Dimensions of Temperament Survey (23) may also prove helpful. Again, consider working with the school social worker to obtain this information. Keep in mind that some parents have difficulty remembering how their youngsters behaved when they were infants and toddlers, while others may not remember their youngsters' behavior accurately. Most parents, however, recall their youngsters' behavior fairly accurately (27–31).

4. *Using appropriate techniques, have adults and teachers been unable to change the student's behavior?* To determine this, you would want to know what techniques were tried, when, where, under what conditions, and with what degree of success. Your student's parents and other teachers can give you the information you need to answer this question.

The following case examples illustrate an informal procedure to determine whether a student's behavior problems have a temperamental basis. You can use similar procedures with your own students.

Larry was a 7-year-old whose first- and second-grade teachers used words such as "shy," "withdrawn," "timid," "insecure," and "frightened" to describe him. They reported that he avoided new tasks and had trouble making friends. Three months into the school year, his second-grade teacher was trying unsuccessfully to get him to overcome his "insecurity." His first-grade teacher said, however, that if left alone, Larry got over his initial fears and learned that he was able to succeed. Then he did as well, if not better, both academically and socially than many of his peers.

Larry's parents also saw him as "shy" and "timid." They reported that he had difficulty making friends and often stayed in his room with the door closed when guests were in the house unless he knew them very well. He balked at accompanying the family on visits to other people's houses and exasperated his parents on vacation trips abroad, during which he seemed especially ill at ease. He often refused to try new foods when they went out to restaurants or to other people's homes. When he visited amusement parks, he would adamantly refuse to go on most rides designed for children his age. On the other hand, he had excellent relationships with his younger brother and two school friends and behaved perfectly normally with people he knew well and in situations where he was comfortable.

Larry's parents recalled that he had always been uncomfortable with strangers. Even as an infant, he would cry when handed over to or picked up by anyone except his parents. Each change of housekeeper or baby-sitter and the two times they had relocated had been traumatic for him. He had great difficulty adjusting to nursery school and preschool, and his mother had to remain with him in both programs for quite some time before he felt comfortable being left by himself. Until then, her attempts to coax him or pressure him to allow her to just drop him off were unsuccessful. Yet he eventually adjusted to the new program, housekeeper, or baby-sitter and could be left without any problem. Larry's parents also recalled that he was a finicky eater who tended to reject any new food out of hand. He also didn't seem to be interested in new toys, pets, or anything else at first sight. An evaluation of the techniques his parents had been using to try to get him to accept new neighborhoods, children, housekeepers, baby-sitters, schools, food, and so on, indicated that they were totally appropriate and would probably have worked quite well with an average child.

Larry's behavior fits the description of a youngster whose temperamental makeup included initial negative reactions to new things and a slowness to adapt. Background information about him revealed that the way he behaved at school was similar to the way he behaved at home and consistent with how he had been behaving his whole life. This information also indicated that neither Larry's parents nor his teachers had been able to change his behavior. These facts make it clear that the behavior problems his teachers and parents noted were indeed the result of his temperament.

Mary was a 9-year-old who was having difficulty in fourth grade. Her teacher stated that she refused to do as she was told. Instead, she would continue working on activities she liked long after the other students had moved on, and she wouldn't do things she didn't want to do until she was pressured or threatened. She interrupted when others were speaking and called out answers without raising her hand. Her teacher's major complaint was that she would do almost anything in her power to get her way. Interviews with her other teachers indicated that she had been particularly willful and stubborn with her second-grade teacher, who was rather inexperienced, easygoing, and not a strict disciplinarian. But she had not been a problem with her first- and third-grade teachers, who "knew how to control" their students.

Her parents reported that at home she interrupted them no matter what they were doing whenever she wished and pestered them until she either got her way or was punished. If she wanted to watch television when they thought she should be doing something else, or if she wanted a new dress or toy that they thought she did not need, she would whine, throw temper tantrums, slam doors, and generally make their lives miserable until they either hit her or gave in to her in order to have some peace in the house. Her parents described themselves as alternating between feeling extreme rage at their inability to control her and feeling extremely bad about how punitive they had become toward her. At times they blamed her for not being able to "take 'no' for an answer." At other times they blamed themselves for not making sure that she did so.

Mary's parents remembered having had the same difficulty with her since she was able to get into things. She always tried to have things her own way. They didn't think, though, that she was particularly motivated to overcome obstacles, nor did she have an unusual amount of persistence about difficult tasks. Like other children, when things got difficult she became bored or frustrated and gave up.

During an extended conversation. Mary's parents admitted that when she was little, they had both been so busy with their careers that they often gave in to her or did things for her that she should have done for herself because it was easier and less trouble. Her mother agreed that she still handled Mary the same way at times because, although she was no longer working, she was suffering from "battle fatigue" and preferred to avoid confrontations if possible.

The information available from Mary's parents and teachers indicates that her behavior was not consistent in all situations. In addition, the techniques her parents used to change her behavior were inappropriate. Thus, it is likely that the cause of Mary's persistent behavior wasn't temperamental. Judging from how Mary's parents tried to discipline her, her behavior would probably improve if her parents and teachers used techniques such as the ones suggested in chapter 11 to teach her to take "no" for an answer.

Formal Assessment   A number of instruments have been specifically designed to help educators assess their students' temperaments (22–26). Research indicates that educators can use these assessments to arrive at valid conclusions about their students' temperaments (22–27).

INSTRUMENT	RATER	AGE RANGE
Behavior Style Questionnaire	Parents	3–7 years
Dimensions of Temperamental Survey	Parents	3–adult
Preschool Temperament Inventory	Teachers	3–6 years
Teacher Temperament Questionnaire	Teachers	3–7 years

Helping Temperamentally Different Students

When teachers adjust their expectations to the unmodifiable aspects of youngsters' personalities, the youngsters do well. But many teachers don't recognize when youngsters' behavior problems are in fact caused by their temperaments. It is often much easier for teachers to accept the fact that youngsters have been born with certain physiological aptitudes (or "gifts") that will help them do well in sports, music, art, or academics than it is for them to accept the fact that youngsters' responses to new situations, as well as their persistence, activity levels, and the pace at which they do things, can also be influenced by physiological factors.

Two Problems   The belief that youngsters can change their behavior if they try when in fact they really cannot and the perception that they are willful, disobedient, rebellious, lazy, spoiled, selfish, and so on, when they aren't can easily lead teachers to engage in fruitless battles with their students. This can, in turn, create additional problems for youngsters who are already experiencing difficulty in adjusting to the demands of family, school, and society. This was clearly seen in the studies of Chess, Thomas, Birch, and their associates (8, 11, 18) and has been confirmed by others (36–47). As they followed the development of the youngsters in their study, Thomas, Chess, and Birch found that those who had extremes of certain temperamental traits were more likely than others to have adjustment problems at home and school. The authors concluded that these extreme temperamental characteristics tended to interfere with the youngsters' normal development because these children were temperamentally unable to behave the way adults expected them to.

When adults tried to require these youngsters to behave according to their expectations, the youngsters were likely to respond by becoming negative, aggressive, or withdrawn. But when adults adapted their methods and expectations to the youngsters' temperaments, then they did not develop these additional problems. Instead they adjusted well but still behaved somewhat differently than most youngsters because of their temperamental makeup (15, 18, 32–35).

This research shows that extreme temperamental differences can add two types of behavior problems. First, students may have difficulty "adjusting" to school unless their teachers individualize both instructional and classroom management techniques to the unique temperaments of these students. Second, students may develop additional problems if their teachers misperceive the cause of their behavior and so use inappropriate techniques to try to change it. Educators who mistakenly believe that such students are willful, disobedient, stubborn, lazy, or rebellious may resort to punitive approaches to force them to change what in reality are relatively fixed aspects of their personalities. Such futile attempts to get students to change can lead to unnecessary conflicts and can also cause students to believe that they actually *are* bad, selfish, stubborn, uncooperative, lazy, and the like.

But avoiding unnecessary conflicts with temperamentally different students does not mean that teachers should merely accept their students' temperamentally determined behavior styles. If left totally to their own devices, students whose temperaments are characterized by withdrawal tendencies, slow adaptability, negative moods, or extreme distractibility may experience problems at school. Thus, it is especially important that their teachers help them succeed in school despite their temperamental differences. Such help may prevent them from developing additional problems stemming from mismatches between the demands of school and their temperaments.

Self-Management Techniques   Virtually no research has been done on the ability of temperamentally different students to use self-management techniques to modify their behavior. Thus, the discussion that follows on helping students manage their behavior is based on several reasonable, but unproved, assumptions. The most basic assumption is that students who are aware of their temperamental makeups are better able to manage their behavior. A corollary is that educators should help increase students' awareness about their temperamental traits. To do this most effectively, educators should use techniques for enhancing students' self-awareness that are suitable for the students' developmental levels. For example, preschool and primary-grade students cannot yet understand that individuals have different behavioral styles. Students in the upper elementary grades can begin to understand that people are all different, and secondary school students can comprehend the concept of temperamental traits in more or less the form it's presented in this chapter. Given these concepts, it seems reasonable that temperamentally different students can use the techniques for self-reinforcement described in chapter 10 and the techniques for self-instruction described in chapter 12 to gain some degree of self-control over their temperamentally determined behavior styles. In addition, secondary school students can select school activities, courses, hobbies, and ultimately occupations that suit their temperaments.

To assist temperamentally different students to manage their behavior, you should help them become aware of their temperamental makeups and teach them self-management skills. The following techniques for accomplishing these goals have proved successful with some students who have other kinds of problems. They may also be effective with temperamentally different students.

Self-awareness: Help students become aware of their temperamental characteristics. Adapt your techniques for enhancing students' awareness of their temperamental traits to the cognitive levels of elementary-grade students by talking to them on a concrete rather than abstract level. High-activity students might be told, "Wow, you have a lot of energy," or "You don't like to sit still for a long time like the other students, do you?" or "Where do you get all your energy from? Are you always like that?" If students are slow to warm up, you might say, "At first you didn't want to try the new game, but after a while you changed your mind, and you liked it, didn't you?" or, "You did the same thing the first few times the music specialist came to the class. Now you're practically the first one to choose an instrument from the box. I guess it takes you a little longer than other students to get to like something new." Students with negative moods can be told, "Seems like you woke up in a bad mood today. I guess some days are better than others for you."

Have students read stories with characters who have temperaments similar to theirs. Then ask, "Did Mitzy remind you of anyone?" or, "Do you think Danny is like you?" Teach students to monitor their behavior, and discuss what they have learned about themselves with them. High-activity students can record how many times they get out of their seats. Low-activity students can record how many times they fail to complete seatwork during the time allotted. Moody students can assign themselves frowning and happy faces each day. Persistent students can monitor the number of times they were told to stop doing something or change activities more than once before they complied.

You can talk to secondary school students more directly about individual differences among people and engage them in discussions of their behavior styles in class. Such discussions, however, will probably be more acceptable and successful if you give the strengths and advantages of their temperamental characteristics at least as much if not more emphasis than the behavior problems their temperaments create. It is also important to explain to students as soon as possible how they can manage their temperaments and turn their own behavior styles to their advantage.

Self-managing specific temperamental traits: You can use the self-management techniques described in chapters 10 and 12 with students who have the kinds of temperaments that research indicates are likely to cause difficulties for students in school.

High activity level. Teach students to identify when they are becoming restless or tense. Show them how to relax, take a quiet break at their seats, stretch, or ask permission to leave the room if necessary.

Low activity level. Guide students to understand the advantage of using part of their recess or lunchtime to catch up and to set aside more time than others need to complete their homework assignments.

Initial withdrawal and/or slow adapting. Teach students to remind themselves that they react negatively at first to new experiences, to question the validity of their initial responses, and to instruct themselves to join in new experiences despite initial negative reactions to them.

High-intensity of reactions. Help students learn to instruct themselves to:

- Identify when they are about to respond intensely

- Delay their responses

- Question whether their intense feelings actually reflect their true reactions

- Express their feelings in less intense words, such as "I feel anger," "This doesn't hold my interest," and "I don't want to be with you right now" instead of "I hate you," "This is the most boring class I have ever had," and "I can't stand you"

Low-intensity reactions. Help students practice expressing their opinions and feelings more directly and clearly. Teach students to monitor the reactions of others when they express their feelings and opinions in order to determine whether they have gotten their messages across. Have students practice asking themselves, "Does the person act like he or she really understands how I feel or think, or do I have to make myself clearer?"

Negative mood. Teach students to question their negative feelings and opinions about people, events, tasks, and so on, when they are in a negative mood. Prepare them to use guided imagery to think about happy, optimistic, or pleasant experiences when they feel moody or pessimistic. Teach them to instruct themselves to avoid making negative comments and to tell others that they are in a bad mood when they think that it will help others to know when their moods are affecting how they relate to others.

High persistence. Help students instruct themselves to think that others are not necessarily bossy or unfair when they issue desist orders or deny students' requests. Explain that requiring others to give them the same directives repeatedly is disruptive and that others may have good reasons for saying "no."

Teacher-Initiated Techniques   Because we have no reason to believe that students can completely modify their behavior styles by using self-management techniques, teachers can help temperamentally different students by using teacher-initiated techniques to manage some of their behavior problems. They can also help by accommodating their expectations and routines to aspects of their students' behavior styles that can't be managed. Finally, they can prevent students' extreme temperamental differences from causing serious problems in school. In the absence of research on the effectiveness of specific classroom management techniques with such students, the following techniques are reasonable suggestions rather than proven solutions.

High activity level:

1. If possible, schedule sedentary activities, such as reading and math, after activities like physical education, lunch, and recess so that students can discharge some of their energy before having to sit for long periods of time. If you use this technique, be sure to provide a relaxing, cooling-off transition period between the two activities to prepare students to be less active.

2. Provide students with plenty of desk room so they can stretch out and fidget without bothering other students.

3. Permit students to discharge some of their energy by taking breaks from sedentary activities. Allow them to stand, stretch, sharpen pencils, run errands—whatever does not cause a problem or disrupt other students. Encourage responsible students to take breaks as needed. With less responsible students, though, you might have to schedule breaks at regular intervals. While most students should be able to take breaks without having to be supervised, some may abuse the privilege. If they do, you may have to convince them to control any inclinations to take advantage of their temperament by reasoning with them or by taking away the privilege (logical consequence).

4. Locating students in the back of the room may make it less likely that their high activity level will distract other students, but seating them close to you may decrease their overactive behavior.

5. If possible, use teaching techniques that require students to learn by doing, manipulating, moving around, or using other hands-on approaches.

6. Do not require students to sit still for long stretches of time during class trips. If students must eat together on trips or in school, allow your active students to leave the table as soon as they become restless.

7. Do not assume that students hear and understand you when you say something while they are busily engaged in high-energy activities. Ask them to respond to a

Students with highly active temperaments need to let off a little steam occasionally.

question or to follow directions to determine whether they understand. Better yet, have them stop what they are doing and attend before you say anything important.

8. Guide students into high-energy extracurricular activities, hobbies, sports, and so on.

9. If the students' parents or other teachers are not aware of their temperament, advise them that the students are not willful or disobedient but rather highly energetic.

Low activity level:

1. Give students extra time to complete things that other students can finish in less time when you aren't on a strict schedule. If you do have a schedule to keep, have

these students start earlier than the others. If students are required to keep up with a group, remind them to try to stay with the group, but do so without nagging or complaining.

2. Do not schedule activities that have to be finished in school for the final period of the day when there is no chance of extra time for the activity.

3. Except under extenuating circumstances, do not pitch in and help students complete things because they take too long—even when you or the class are late or in a rush. If you are too helpful too often, students may learn to expect you to do things for them.

4. Do not take it personally when students make you or the class wait—even when you give them a head start and remind them about the time. It's perfectly natural to feel angry and frustrated at such times, but don't treat the students as if they are unfair, inconsiderate, or selfish.

5. Use untimed power tests, not timed tests. If students do poorly on standarized tests, find out whether they didn't know the work or didn't have enough time to demonstrate what they knew.

6. Advise other adults who may not be aware of the students' temperaments that they are slow moving, not slow learners, slow thinkers, or perfectionists.

Initial withdrawal:

1. Keep in mind that these students' initial reaction is to withdraw, but they will eventually get involved if they are allowed to do so at their own pace, especially if the activity is intrinsically interesting or rewarding.

2. Allow students to withdraw from you and/or their peers if that is what they need to do. Keep your distance until they signal their readiness to be engaged, but be sure they understand that you are available if and when they need you.

3. If these students are just starting school and having difficulty adjusting to new situations, don't view their behavior as an indication that they are too dependent on their parents, suffering from separation anxiety, or afraid of school. If necessary, tell the appropriate school officials that their difficulty is only a temperamentally determined inability to jump right into a new situation and that these students need patience, understanding, and encouragement, not therapy.

4. Give students advance notice about impending changes. If possible, familiarize them with new activities before they are introduced by showing them pictures, telling them anecdotes, and so forth. Put new or novel situations in their best light by highlighting the positive, attractive, and advantageous. But do not hide any negatives because unpleasant surprises can be devastating.

5. If possible, introduce students to new things in a pleasant, familiar setting or in the company of a trusted friend.

6. If possible, allow students—especially young ones—to watch an activity a few times before getting involved in it. Although the students may seem only to be watching disinterestedly, more than likely they are actually learning and preparing to join in.

7. Praise students when they react positively to new situations, even if it takes a while for them to do so, but don't scold or pressure them when they don't.

8. If students are also slow to adapt and take even longer to get over their initial negative reactions, keep at it. Muster up even more patience and understanding.

9. Guide students toward activities, hobbies, subjects, and careers that do not involve constant change and novelty.

10. Give students insight into their temperaments. Remind them of the many times they didn't like something at first but then changed their opinions.

Slow-adapting students: Most of the techniques for helping students with initial-withdrawal temperaments also apply to these students.

High-intensity reactions:

1. Warm students in advance that something will occur that may displease them, and remind them that they tend to overreact to such situations. You might say something like "I know you don't like achievement tests because you think they are difficult for you. However, everyone will have to take the test on Thursday. And you will see it will be just as easy for you as the one you took last time."

2. Give students practice in thinking before acting, counting to 10 before saying anything, saying how they feel rather than acting out their feelings, and toning down the emotional content of the words they choose.

3. If you believe that techniques such as these won't work, you can wait until the other students have left the room or else ask intense reactors to step out into the hall before you give them upsetting news so their reactions do not disrupt the class. If you cannot do these things, try to postpone the communication until you can.

4. When, despite your best efforts, students overreact, do not let the intensity of their responses fool you into thinking they really are disgusted, petrified, furious, or in some other extreme state. Remind yourself that their intense reactions are only temporary and don't reflect their true feelings. This realization should help you avoid taking comments such as "I hate your class" or "You're the most boring teacher I have ever had" personally.

5. After the students have calmed down, find a convenient time and place to discuss their overreaction so that they, too, do not take their overreaction seriously. (See the section on self-management.)

Low-intensity reactions:

1. Tune in to the subtle ways students with low-intensity reactions express their feelings and attitudes. Especially watch for signals that they need your support and encouragement, that they are having difficulty with a task, or that they are especially interested in some topic or subject.

2. Explain to them how their low-intensity reactions affect others. For example, teach them that weak hellos and unenthusiastic responses to peers lead others to think they are unfriendly. You can also point out that their low-intensity reactions to things that bother them may encourage students to take advantage of them because they do not really seem to be angry or annoyed at the way they are being treated. (See the section on self-management.)

3. Encourage students to consciously attempt to express their feelings and attitudes more directly.

4. Provide them with opportunities to role-play and practice how to express themselves more directly and forcefully.

High threshold of response:

1. Make sure you have your students' attention before saying important things, and accentuate what you say strongly enough so they get the message.

2. Give them practice attending to and interpreting body language, gestures, and the subtle, polite, and indirect ways people often express themselves by having them read stories that contain such material, observing and interpreting the interactions of others, and role-playing.

3. Encourage students to ask questions when they are uncertain or confused about what others are communicating.

4. Give them the extra instruction and practice they need to be able to distinguish important information from less essential peripheral material, especially before important lessons and examinations.

Negative mood:

1. One of the most important things you can do when you have temperamentally moody students in your class is to analyze your own reaction to them. Do their negative moods affect your own moods? Do you find being with students when they are moody exasperating? Do you avoid them, exhort them to behave better, or take their complaints personally? To react in these ways some of the time is unavoidable; every educator has limits. But if you react in these ways often, you may be causing unnecessary problems for your students and yourself.

2. Try not to take your students' moodiness personally. You are not the cause of it, and you probably can't change it.

3. Avoid moralizing or penalizing students for being moody.

4. If possible, adjust your students' schedules so that their moodiness does not interfere, postponing what can be delayed until they are in a better mood.

5. Try to kid them into feeling better. Your sense of humor could snap them out of a bad mood. Even if it does not, it may help you cope with the problem. See if some

personal attention, words of praise, or a favorite activity changes your students' moods.

6. If that does not work, remind them that they are in a bad mood, and ask them to do the best they can under the circumstances.

7. Do what you can to ensure that their moodiness does not interfere with other students, but be especially tuned to involving them in group activities with others when they are in a good mood.

8. Although there probably are not any activities, hobbies, or careers for which a negative mood is an advantage, moody students would probably profit from being guided toward activities where they can work alone. Careers that involve meeting the public or putting on a happy, smiling face probably are not a good fit.

9. Help them understand how their moodiness affects others. Say things both nicely and in a complaining, whining voice and call attention to the difference. Discuss how it feels to be around someone who is nasty, crabby, or unhappy.

10. Help your students recognize when they are in a bad mood. Teach them to wait, if possible, until the bad mood passes before making important or irrevocable decisions. Teach them to say as little as possible when they are in a bad mood and to tell the people they are involved with not to pay attention to their bad mood. And teach them not to blame others for their moodiness. (See the section on self-management.)

High persistence:

1. Strike a balance between firmness and flexibility when dealing with persistent students. Stand firm when persistent students pressure you to allow them to do things they shouldn't do or if they don't want to stop when it's necessary in order to keep the group together or keep on schedule. Giving in because you are too busy to deal with the students' persistence only makes it more likely that they will pester you even more next time. But be flexible when temperamentally persistent students do not want to stop what they are doing if it won't inconvenience the group and if it makes good educational sense. The goal should be to avoid unnecessary arguments while helping persistent students realize that rules and schedules exist, others have rights, and people will not always wait for them. You may have to frustrate these students from time to time, but that is preferable to their developing conduct problems.

2. Suggest that students postpone starting on a project that they will not be able to complete during the time available if you think they will have difficulty stopping.

3. When students are already working on something, give them advance warning that they will soon have to stop even though they won't be finished.

4. Direct students toward activities, hobbies, and careers that allow them to work as long as they wish on tasks that require persistence for success. Activities involving rigid schedules, group effort, or constantly shifting activities may be especially difficult for them.

5. Provide students with the insight they need to understand that people are not unfair or impatient just because they insist that the students stick to an established schedule or will not take "no" for an answer. (See the section on self-management.)

Low persistence:

1. Encourage students to keep trying when things become difficult.

2. Provide the assistance they need to continue as soon as they start becoming frustrated or anxious.

3. Praise and reward students whenever they persevere.

4. If they quit too soon, let them take a break; then encourage them to start again.

5. If students fail because of lack of perseverance, help them understand that the cause was lack of persistence, not lack of ability. This is especially important when students fail tests because they quit before finishing. (See the section on self-management.)

Self-Quiz: Temperamental Makeup

What is your temperamental makeup? Review the list of 15 temperamental characteristics and the four criteria for determining an individual's temperamental characteristics and determine your temperamental makeup.

What kinds of temperamental traits in your students are you most and least able to accept? Review the list of temperamental traits and decide which ones evoke positive or negative reactions in you. *What can you do to avoid causing temperamentally different students additional problems?* List the self-management techniques you could use to improve and control your own reactions to your students' temperamental characteristics.

Attention Deficit Hyperactivity Disorders

Students with attention deficit hyperactivity disorders have some, but not necessarily all, of the following characteristics: short attention span, poor power of concentration, distractibility, constant motion and restlessness (hyperactivity), and impulsivity (48–50). Estimates of the percentage of students who have attention deficit hyperactivity disorders range from 3% to 5% (51, 52).

To understand the physiological nature of attention deficit hyperactivity disorders, it will be helpful to review briefly and in a simplified form how the body's neuroendocrine system works. The neuroendocrine system is composed of two interrelated units—the nervous system and the endocrine system. The nervous system is like an extremely complex information-transmitting circuitry system. The brain receives and processes information it has received from nerve cells throughout the body; "decides" what various specialized cell groups, such as the heart and muscles, should do; then sends commands to them through the spinal cord and the nerves in contact with them. The brain also influences the way the body functions by affecting the rate at which the endocrine glands secrete hormones into the blood. The following vignette illustrates how the neuroendocrine system works.

Leticia, a teenager, is walking home from school reading a flyer about a rally for the basketball team. As she reads, nerve cells are transmitting various kinds of information to her brain. Her eyes are sending sensations that the brain translates into letters, words, and meanings. The brain is also receiving information about the smells of the nearby pizza parlor, the movement of the people around her, and the sounds of the traffic. The brain keeps most of this information out of her awareness, though, so that she can read without distraction as she strolls along. She is relaxed, so her endocrine glands are secreting their various hormones at levels appropriate for her calm state.

When she comes to the end of the sidewalk, she steps into the street. Suddenly a horn blasts. Her brain directs her legs to stop and her auditory and visual systems to attend to the traffic. Because of the fear she experiences, it also directs her endocrine system to adjust the rates of secretion of its various hormones to the potential danger.

Leticia jumps back onto the sidewalk out of the path of an oncoming car that just misses her, waits for the light to change, crosses the street, and continues walking with her newspaper tucked under her arm. After a while, her circulating hormones readjust to a level more typical of a leisurely stroll home in the city during the day, and once again she feels relaxed.

A few minutes later Leticia walks into the house, where she sees her mother preparing supper. She greets her mother and is about to ask if she can attend the rally when her brain remembers something. The last time she went to a rally, she had promised to come straight home afterward and finish her homework, but she had not done either. "Wait!" her brain tells her, "If you want to go, you better do your homework first, then ask." So she goes up to her room and begins to study. After a few minutes, one of Leticia's friends calls to tell her the latest news. It is already a quarter past four, and she still has to finish a good hour of geometry homework, change clothes, and eat supper before six if she is going to get to the rally on time. So she tells her friend that she will call her back after she finishes her homework. A short while later, her older brother comes home and blasts his stereo in the room next to her. Her attention drifts from her assignment to the music, but her brain gets her back on track. She continues working until nothing is sinking in. She takes a short break, goes back to studying, and finishes her work in plenty of time to call her friend. Afterward she explains to her mother that she has already finished all of her homework, not like last time, and is allowed to attend the rally.

Leticia seems to have the ability to control herself, but when the neuroendocrine system does not function correctly, people may lose the ability to control their impulses, attend to their environments, talk, understand spoken or written language, and so on. Until a few years ago, children and adolescents with neuroendocrine dysfunctions that cause attention problems (lack of concentration, distractibility, and short attention span), constant motion and restlessness, and impulsivity were labeled hyperactive. Now they are said to have an attention deficit hyperactivity disorder.

Attention Problems

Attention problems can result when the brain doesn't do an adequate job of censoring out irrelevant information sent to it. This is one of the reasons why some students are easily distracted while doing seatwork. A problem like this would have interfered with Leticia's ability to concentrate on the flyer in the busy street or on her homework in the noisy house.

Students experience another kind of attention problem when they try to read but their mind wanders or when they are unable to concentrate on desk work, homework, or even their favorite television programs for as long as they should. If Leticia had this problem, she would not have been able to concentrate long enough to complete her homework, even without distractions at home.

Constant Motion and Restlessness

One way children and adolescents show hyperactivity—or constant motion and restlessness—is by being unable to remain still in situations that require prolonged periods of sitting, such as working on seat assignments, watching audiovisual materials, or attending to lectures in class or to long programs in the auditorium. If Leticia had been hyperactive, she might not have been able to sit still long enough to complete her homework.

Impulsivity

Youngsters act impulsively when they do not stop to think about the possible consequences of their actions before they act. Another expression of this quality is that they begin things without planning or organizing ahead of time. If Leticia had been impulsive, she may not have been able to wait before asking her mother for permission to go to the rally or to hear the latest news from her friend until after she had completed her homework.

Identification

To manage students with attention deficit hyperactivity disorders in the classroom, you need to know if they do indeed have such a disorder or if some other cause explains their behavior. Identifying such students is the first step in helping them manage their behavior.

Informal Assessment   The following discussion describes behaviors characteristic of children and adolescents with attention deficit hyperactivity disorders. A student could have an attention deficit hyperactivity disorder if she or he behaves in a number of these ways *more often* and *more consistently* than other youngsters and does so in *most* situations both in and out of school.

Attention span: Youngsters with attention deficit hyperactivity disorders are often unable to stick to one thing very long. At school they often fail to complete tasks that require sustained attention. At home they get bored with their games and toys easily and even stop watching television programs they like before they end. In addition, although they seem to enjoy great amounts of physical activity, mental work tires them easily, and the results of their mental efforts deteriorate rapidly after a short period of time.

Distractibility: These students commonly stop doing what they are involved in to do something else that catches their eye. Thus, they shift from one activity to another within a short period of time. They also have difficulty distinguishing the relevant from the irrelevant.

Constant motion and restlessness: Youngsters with this disorder are often on the go—running, jumping, climbing, or moving about in some way. They have difficulty sitting quietly for prolonged periods of time in school and elsewhere. Even when they do sit, they are very fidgety. They also break things, often without meaning to, because of their high energy level.

Impulsivity: Such students do things on the spur of the moment, act before thinking, seldom plan ahead, and rarely stop to organize their work. Characteristically, they do not wait their turn. In school they call out answers or raise their hand to answer, but when called on, they often do not know the answer. At home they grab and push ahead.

Formal Assessment   Conners and his associates (55–57) have developed two rating scales that teachers and parents can use to evaluate the hyperactive behavior of students. Although these scales do not give a definitive conclusion about what causes students' attention and activity problems, they do provide valuable information that can be used in conjunction with information from professionals to decide how to deal with students' behavior problems.

If you believe that a student may have an attention deficit hyperactivity disorder, you should refer this student to the appropriate school personnel who can initiate a process to determine what actually causes the student's behavior problems. There are three reasons why you shouldn't attempt to arrive at this decision on your own. First, educators generally tend to overestimate the number of students who have attention and activity problems (53, 58, 59). Second, many of the behaviors that students with attention deficit hyperactivity disorders exhibit can also have non-physiological causes. For example, the distractible, fidgety, tense behavior of anxious students sometimes closely parallels the behavior of students with attention problems. Next, three of the temperamental factors identified by Thomas, Chess, and Birch (18)—high activity level, short attention span, and distractibility—are highly similar to some of the symptoms of attention deficit hyperactivity disorder (54, 60). Finally, only a physician is qualified to determine whether a student's behavior problems are caused by physiological factors.

Students' ethnic and gender characteristics appear to influence the rate at which they are labeled as having attention deficit hyperactivity disorder. Teachers are especially likely to overidentify African American males and other males who are brought up by adults who encourage a higher level of active behavior than many teachers find acceptable in school. In fact, prevalence studies indicate that males who have been identified as having attention

---

Self-Quiz: Response to Attention Deficits

What problems of students with attention deficits are you most and least able to accept? Describe how you typically react to the attention problems, constant motion and restlessness, and impulsivity of students with attention deficit hyperactivity disorders. *What could you do to improve the way you react to these problems?* Describe the specific techniques you could use to manage your reactions to these problems.

---

deficit hyperactivity disorder outnumber females by between 4 to 1 and 10 to 1, depending on the study (63).

While boys and girls who have attention deficit hyperactivity disorder experience the same degree of difficulty sustaining attention and demonstrate similar degrees of academic difficulties, they differ in other respects (61–64). Girls are more impulsive than boys. However, boys are more hyperactive and exhibit more behavior problems than girls. Girls with attention deficit hyperactivity disorder exhibit fewer behaviors that disrupt the class or call attention to themselves and are rated by their peers as less deviant than boys. Perhaps this is one reason why fewer girls are identified as having attention deficit hyperactivity disorder and are identified later than boys. As deHaas suggests, "Because of the disruptive problems they present, hyperactive boys may then get remedial help, whereas hyperactive girls, in spite of their attentional deficits, may not be referred for help" (62, p. 465).

Managing Attention Deficit Hyperactivity Disorders

Physicians themselves are often unable to determine whether students' attention problems (short attention span and distractibility) and activity problems (restlessness and fidgetiness) are due to temperamental factors or attention deficit hyperactivity disorder (54). Research studies regarding the effectiveness of techniques for dealing with these problems do not differentiate between temperamentally different students and those with attention deficit hyperactivity disorders. Thus, the techniques for dealing with the problems of temperamentally different students should apply equally to students with either condition.

Self-Management Techniques   You can teach students with attention deficit hyperactivity disorders to use the self-management techniques described in chapters 10 and 12 and earlier in this chapter. Following are examples of how you can teach these students to manage their impulsivity, attention problems, and activity problems.

Impulsivity: Impulsive students can learn to slow themselves down a little and look before they leap. While there is no sure-fire, certain way of doing this every time, the following process can help.

1. *Help students see the problem.* You can do this by explaining how their impulsive behavior causes them to make mistakes, gets them into trouble, or makes them do things they are sorry for later. Teaching students to monitor their own behavior can

help them appreciate how often they act impulsively by saying things they later wished they hadn't said, calling out without being called on, volunteering to answer a question without being sure they know the answer, and answering a question on a test or starting a seat assignment before either reading the directions or allowing teachers to complete their instructions.

2. *Teach students to recognize when they are in situations that call for well-thought-out responses and the times they are on the verge of acting impulsively and how to control themselves from acting impulsively in such situations.* Tell younger students the instructions they should give themselves to control themselves. For example, you can tell students to first instruct themselves to wait and ask themselves if they have thought through what they are about to do before responding.

3. *Help students to develop a plan of action and follow it.* Teach them to rehearse their answers to determine whether they really know the answer before they volunteer. Teach them how to formulate alternative ways of reacting to situations and to weigh the pros and cons of each one. Encourage them to slow themselves down by reminding themselves that they will do a better job if they work slowly and carefully. Train them to ask themselves questions such as: "Do I really know the answer?" "Do I know exactly what I'm supposed to do?" "Have I read all of the directions?" "Do I have a plan?" "Am I following my plan?" "Have I thought things through?" "What will happen if I do it?" "How else can I do it?" "What do I do next?"

4. *Teach students to reward themselves when they have controlled their impulsivity.* They can do this by congratulating themselves for their achievements, by feeling good about their newfound self-control, by keeping a record of how well they have done, and other forms of self-acknowledgment. If intrinsic rewards aren't effective, allow them to earn some extrinsic reward that they have chosen themselves.

A number of published systems exist for helping students manage their own impulsive behavior. Palkes, Stewart, and Kahana (91) describe how students can use cards that say "stop," "listen," and "think" placed on their desks to remind themselves to *stop* before doing or deciding, to *listen* to everything first, and to *think* before acting. Camp and Bash (69) describe a Think Aloud Program that trains students to ask themselves a series of self-managing questions while they work. Sample questions include: "What am I supposed to be doing?" "How do I do it?" "What is my plan?" "Am I sticking to my plan?" "How well did I do?" Fagan (74) and Fagan, Long, and Stevens (75) have published a game- and skill-oriented curriculum designed to teach the self-control skills described above.

Attention problems: Argulewicz, Elliot, and Spencer (65) have described a practical three-step procedure—tell, show, and do—for teaching young students to manage their attention problems. In the "tell" step, students are told what is involved in paying attention while the teacher models the appropriate behavior. In this case, appropriate behavior includes such things as facing the person or material, maintaining eye contact, and repeating a series of attention-maintaining self-instructions. In the "show" step, students are shown pictures and asked to identify the ones in which people are paying attention. In the "do" step, students rehearse attending behavior under the teachers' supervision until they have learned the technique.

Students can learn to maintain their attention in class by using a timer that emits a soft sound which doesn't distract other students. When the sound tones, they are to monitor whether they are paying attention. Using this device, students can earn rewards by increasing their on-task time (86). Varni and Henker (95) had students monitor their time on-task by using a wrist counter.

Students can also manage their distractibility by instructing themselves to clear their desks of any materials that might divert their attention before they begin. They can also choose to work in a cubicle or in a screened-off area if they feel they cannot continue to concentrate on their work without such aids.

Activity problems: The suggestions covered earlier in this chapter for helping students manage high activity levels are also appropriate for restless and fidgety students. You can also find more detailed discussions of these and other self-management techniques in the literature (76, 80–83, 87, 88, 92).

Effectiveness: Ample evidence shows that certain students can use self-management techniques to modify their behavior to some degree. Students have demonstrated improvement in attention, activity, and impulse problems after being taught to use various self-management techniques (65–73, 78, 79, 82, 85, 86, 90, 91, 95). While the results are not conclusive, it appears that these techniques are more effective in improving students' academic skills than their social skills (78). They are also more effective with younger students when they are given extrinsic rewards for using the procedure they have been taught (68, 77, 103).

Although these techniques are effective with many students (68, 82, 85, 86), this effectiveness doesn't generalize to tasks and situations in which students have not been specifically trained to apply them (70, 78, 84, 89). As Pressley concludes,

> These studies showed that cognitive strategies could be used by children to affect their self-control, but the studies did not show that children would (could) apply the strategies in new situations. In fact, the available data suggest that subjects do not generalize the strategies to new situations. (93, pp. 361–362)

Another limitation of self-management techniques is that their effectiveness often diminishes or disappears over time, especially when teachers permit students to supervise themselves (72, 93, 95). A final drawback is that educators are unable to predict in advance which students will and which won't profit from training in self-management techniques. As Rosenbaum and Drabman suggest, "Methods for identifying children for whom self-control is not an appropriate goal need to be developed" (94, p. 481).

Teacher-Initiated Techniques   In addition to helping these students learn self-management techniques, you can also take action to help modify their behavior.

Managing without consequences: You can help manage students' impulsive behaviors in the following ways:

1. Require students to leave their pencils and pens on the desk until you have finished giving directions.

2. Require them to delay answering questions or beginning problems for a few seconds so they can think through their answers and approaches.

3. Remind them to be careful and to take their time before they begin assignments and while working on them.

To help distractible students:

1. Require students, especially young ones, to keep such things as toys, lunch boxes, and other items in another section of the room until recess or lunchtime.

2. Have students keep their desks free of all materials except those they need for the work at hand.

3. Instruct students to fold their paper or cover up part of it so they only see part of it at a time. Give them place markers to use while reading. Put arithmetic problems in boxes or in folded columns to help them focus attention on just one problem at a time. Don't put too much on one page.

4. Supervise your students closely to keep them on-task.

5. When you tell students to do something, make sure they haven't been too distracted to hear you. Make eye contact if possible. Also, have them acknowledge that they heard you so you don't assume they did when they were actually distracted by something else.

Managing with consequences: A significant amount of research has been conducted on the effectiveness of using positive and negative consequences to modify the behavior problems of students with attention deficit hyperactivity disorders (96–109). Researchers have rewarded students for behavioral improvement, ignored students exhibiting undesirable behavior and praised and attended them for desirable behavior, rewarded other students who were modeling appropriate behavior, used peer pressure by applying group consequences for individual students' behavior, and had parents reward students for behavioral improvement in school based on daily reports sent home.

The results of these studies suggest that students appear to be able to exert some degree of control over their inattentive and hyperactive behavior when they are motivated to do so by extrinsic consequences. Students seem to be able to attend better when they are rewarded for doing so. However, praise may have less effect on the behavior of students with attention deficit hyperactivity disorder than reprimands and other mild negative consequences. It is unclear whether this difference would apply to public reprimands, because like most other students, students with attention deficit hyperactivity disorders respond better to negative feedback when they receive it privately rather than in front of their peers.

It is important to note that while all of these studies reported some success with certain students, the overall effectiveness of these programs was difficult to maintain when the extrinsic reinforcements were ended (97, 100, 101, 108). This problem has led many reviewers of the research to conclude that student self-management procedures are preferable to teacher-initiated management procedures that involve extrinsic consequences (65, 104).

Peer tutoring: There is evidence that tutoring helps students with attention deficit hyperactivity disorders to attend better to their work and also reduces their time off-task and eliminates some of their fidgety behavior. However, it appears that the behavioral improvement is not maintained when the tutor is not present (110). The benefits of peer tutoring may result from any and all of the following conditions: Students are given instructions, directions, and assistance in a one-to-one situation; they are able to work at their own pace; and they receive more immediate and private feedback about their work.

Accommodating to Attention Deficit Hyperactivity Disorders

Because neither self-management nor teacher-initiated management techniques are effective with all students who have attention deficit hyperactivity disorders, you will sometimes need to accommodate your classroom management techniques to certain students.

Short Attention Spans   Here are some of the many ways you can accommodate your expectations, classroom routines, instruction, and the like, to those aspects of students' attention problems that can't be managed:

1. Shorten the length of students' work sessions to fit their attention spans and allow them extra time to complete their work whenever possible.

2. Select activities that suit students with short attention spans. For example, short stories may work better than books, and short chapters may be better than long ones. Or you can have a folder of different, but relevant, activities that students can do in a short period of time. Allow students to use this folder quietly when they need a change.

3. Allow students to get up quietly when they feel it is necessary. A short break in the classroom or out in the hall may help these students get ready for another work session.

4. If students do poorly on activities that require sustained attention, determine whether the cause is lack of ability, motivation, or effort or another cause or a short attention span. This is especially important if students do poorly on standardized tests.

You can also find more detailed descriptions of these and other techniques in the literature on the education of students with attention deficit disorders (111–125).

Distractibility   In addition to techniques listed earlier for distractible students, you can accommodate to their needs by using the following techniques:

1. Provide students with an environment as free from distracting stimuli as possible.

2. Seat students in the front of the room so they are less likely to be distracted by the actions of other students.

3. Place display materials as far away from students as possible.

4. Assign students to work in cubicles when they cannot concentrate.

5. Use filmstrip viewers, computers, recordings, and earphones to cut down on auditory and visual distractions.

6. If necessary, allow more time for students to complete things that are likely to involve distractions. If you can plan more time for such activities, you won't have to remind them to get back on-task so often.

7. Do not attribute students' inattention to boredom, lack of motivation, or inability if it is caused by distractibility.

Substance Abuse

Substance abuse can cause both severe and subtle birth defects and a variety of learning and behavioral problems (126–128, 131, 135–137, 139, 141–144, 147, 148, 150, 152–155, 161, 162). Even supposedly less severe forms of substance abuse, such as smoking cigarettes during pregnancy, can cause children to develop learning, social adjustment, and behavior problems (133, 139).

Fortunately, only some substance-exposed children actually develop the difficulties that these dangerous substances may cause (158, 162). The reasons for this are largely unknown. However, it has been determined that good prenatal care reduces the likelihood that substance-exposed children will actually suffer the potential problems for which they are at risk (141, 150).

Substance-exposed children do not suffer all the possible problems that their exposure can cause (136, 141, 150, 158). The problems that children of substance-abusing parents can experience vary. Approximately 2% to 17% will suffer from severe congenital defects, including developmental disabilities, cerebral palsy, and seizure disorders (132, 158). Many others will develop normally at first, then demonstrate learning and behavior problems as they approach school age.

Substance-exposed students often function adequately under adult guidance and in structured learning and play situations. They have great difficulty, however, adjusting to situations that require them to provide their own structure, initiative, or organization. They do much better in one-to-one situations or when they have to cope with only one individual, task, or toy. When they have to deal with group situations or multiple activities, materials, tasks, or people, they quickly become overstimulated, overwhelmed, and disorganized.

Many, but not all, substance-exposed children suffer additional insults and injuries (130, 132, 138, 140, 141, 143, 151, 152). Their parents tend to have a host of additional medical and social problems. Mothers who are unable to stop abusing drugs for their children's sake during their pregnancy are often unable to care for them after they have been born. The fact that mothers abuse drugs during pregnancy is often an indication that their children will receive insufficient care. Those who are poor tend to abandon their children in the hospital, which often leads to eventual foster care placement. Mothers who do decide to care for their children often provide inadequate care for them because of their drug problems:

Potential Problems of Substance-Exposed Children

Congenital Defects
   Central nervous system damage
   Retarded physical growth
   Abnormal facial and cranial features
   Severe and mild developmental disabilities
   Seizure disorders

Language Disabilities
   Expressive language difficulties
   Communicative difficulties and language delays
   Perceptual difficulties and auditory processing and word retrieval difficulties

Impaired conceptualizing abilities
Difficulty organizing information

Emotional and Behavioral Problems
   Irritability, hypersensitivity
   Avoidance of eye contact
   Difficulty in forming attachments with adults and establishing and maintaining relationships with peers
   Behavioral extremes and emotional instability
   Constant testing of limits set by adults
   Difficulty understanding social cues
   Perseveration and low tolerance for change
   Difficulty adjusting to simultaneous stimulations
   Distractibility, hyperactivity, poor impulse control, low frustration tolerance
   Short attention span and decreased ability to focus attention and concentrate

Growing numbers of crack babies simply are being abandoned in hospitals by their crack-smoking mothers. As for those babies who are discharged, the vast majority go from the hospital nursery to chaotic home environments characterized by deep poverty and little physical or emotional nurturing. With one strike already against them, these babies are at high risk for the second strike—neglect and abuse by crack-using adults. (152, p. 19)

Excluding those children who are born with obvious and serious disabilities, presently we are unable to determine when and to what extent substance-exposed children's learning, behavior, and emotional problems are caused by physiological factors or the environmental disadvantages often associated with being born into a family of substance-abusing parents. For now, the prudent position is that these students' learning and behavior problems can best be understood as resulting from the interaction of both biological and environmental factors.

The future for drug-exposed children may not be quite as bleak as originally thought. As already noted, we now know that only a portion of substance-exposed children will be born with or develop problems. In addition, because some of these problems are the result of environmental, rather than physiological, factors, they may be more reversible than originally thought. As Vincent and colleagues put it:

The media have painted a dire picture of infants who were exposed to alcohol and other drugs in utero. . . . Children who were prenatally exposed to substances are unique, but as a whole they are more like than different from other children. . . . There is a danger in this label in that it can engender a self-fulfilling prophecy: Children will become what their parents and teachers expect them to become. Given the current view of drug exposure this would be an unfair prophecy. (158, pp. 1, 24)

The actual number of mothers who abuse drugs while pregnant and the number of drug-exposed infants are unknown. Surveys of parents who expose their fetuses to harmful substances have yielded results that range from 0.4% to 27% of the parents tested or questioned, depending on the hospital and the neighborhood surveyed (130, 134, 146, 157, 160). What is known is that their number is growing at an alarming rate (145). Estimates of the number of infants that may be affected yearly by crack alone range from 48,000 to 375,000 (129, 130, 152, 156, 160).

Some individuals believe that parental substance abuse contributes to the fact that African American, Native American, and poor students get into more difficulty in school. They claim that African American, Native American, and poor parents abuse alcohol, marijuana, cocaine, and other dangerous drugs during pregnancy more frequently than middle-class European American parents. And as a result, their children have more birth defects, perform less adequately in school, are more likely to suffer from attention deficit hyperactivity disorders, and are more likely to become discipline problems.

Statistics do indicate that poor, African American, Native American, and inner-city mothers in general abuse these substances while pregnant more frequently than other mothers (149, 152, 158, 159). However, some researchers believe that the difference between their rates of drug abuse and those of European American middle-class mothers is overstated, if not incorrect, because European American middle-class mothers are better able to hide their substance-abusing behavior from the authorities (133, 152):

> A minority woman who uses drugs or alcohol during pregnancy is almost ten times more likely to be reported to child-abuse authorities than is a white woman. White middle-class mothers—along with other white middle-class cocaine users—find it easier to hide their substance abuse than do poor, minority women. (152, p. 21)

There is evidence that substance-abusing poor parents in general, and non-European American parents in particular, are less able to obtain the good prenatal care that reduces the likelihood that substance-exposed children will actually suffer the potential problems for which they are at risk. Thus, it may be that their children are at even greater risk than European American middle-class children.

It is unclear whether substance-exposed students who have difficulty adjusting to the rules and routines of school should be treated differently from other students with similar problems. Our experience with these students is too limited, and our ability to determine which of their difficulties is caused by environmental or physiological factors is too rudimentary. Thus, for the present, teachers of substance-exposed students are advised to handle their emotional and behavior problems the same way they would handle these problems with any other students.

More detailed discussions of techniques for working with the learning and behavior problems of substance-exposed students and descriptions of educational programs that appear to be effective with these students are included in the references at the end of the chapter (136, 150, 158).

Summary

Educators or other professionals are limited in what they can do to modify a student's physiological makeup. They cannot, for example, hurry the maturational process of a student who is developmentally delayed, change the temperament of a low-active student, completely control the short attention span, distractibility, and fidgety behavior of students with attention deficit hyperactivity disorders, or undo the damage to students caused by prenatal exposure to harmful substances. Thus, with most students whose behavior problems are caused by physiological factors, changing is not a feasible strategy. Teachers can, however, teach students to manage their biological makeup to some degree, manage some of the behavior their students cannot manage themselves, and finally, accommodate their expectations and demands to aspects of their students' personalities that neither they nor their students can manage. Doing this will enable students to make the most of their physiological makeup, help teachers avoid unnecessary and fruitless conflicts with students, and reduce the chances that their students will develop additional problems.

Activities

For each of the following behavior problems, state the kind of physiological factors that might be causing the behavior (developmental delay, temperament, or attention deficit hyperactivity disorder), and describe the additional information you would need before deciding that the cause of the problem is indeed physiological.

1. Carlos, a 6-year-old, seldom spends more than 4 or 5 minutes at any task before his attention begins to wander. This is especially true when the class is seated on the floor in front of the teacher while she is reading aloud to them.

2. Beth, an 8-year-old who is a slow worker compared to other students, typically refuses to stop working on seat assignments that she has not completed when it is time to change activities. She also tends to reject her teacher's suggestions that she try another approach when her way of doing something isn't working.

3. Sheila, a fourth-grader, usually avoids or reacts negatively to new situations and tasks. When coaxed or pressured to become involved, she will dig her heels in and stubbornly refuse.

4. Jimmy, a 12-year-old, doesn't spend more than 6 or 7 minutes doing seatwork before looking around the room or playing with something in his desk. Whenever someone says something to someone else or there is some movement in the room, he is the first to lift his head from his work to see what is going on.

5. Consuela, a 16-year-old who has been in the United States for a year and a half, spends very little time with her peers, especially boys. She seems unconcerned

about her future, at least so far as school is concerned, and is not at all interested in her schoolwork.

References

Developmental lag is discussed in these references.

1. Ames, L., & Ilg, F. (1965). *School Readiness*. New York: Harper & Row.

2. Spollen, J. C., & Ballif, B. L. (1971). Effectiveness of individualized instruction for kindergarten children with a developmental lag. *Exceptional Children*, 28 (3), 205–209.

The references below discuss various theories of temperament.

3. Brown, G. W. (1973). Temperament and child development. *Journal of Learning Disabilities*, 6 (9), 557–561.

4. Buss, A. H. (1984). *Temperament: Early Developing Personality Traits*. Hillsdale, NJ: Erlbaum.

5. Buss, A. H., & Plomin, R. (1975). A *Temperament Theory of Personality Development*. New York: John Wiley & Sons.

6. Diamond, S. (1957). *Personality and Temperament*. New York: Harper & Brothers.

7. Plomin, R., & Dunn, J. (Eds.). (1986). *The Study of Temperament: Changes, Continuities and Challenges*. Hillsdale, NJ: Erlbaum.

These citations describe the New York Longitudinal Study.

8. Chess, S. (1968). Temperament and learning ability in school children. *American Journal of Public Health*, 58 (12), 231–239.

9. Chess, S. (1971). *Preschool Behavior Style and Later Academic Achievement—Final Report*. ERIC ED 054 511.

10. Chess, S., & Thomas, A. (1986). *Temperament in Clinical Practice*. New York: Guilford Press.

11. Chess, S., Thomas, A., & Cameron, M. (1976, spring). Temperament: Its significance for early schooling. *New York University Educational Quarterly*, 24–29.

12. Kagan, J. (1982). The construct of difficult temperament: A reply to Thomas, Chess, and Korn. *Merrill-Palmer Quarterly*, 28, 21–24.

13. Lerner, J. V., Chess, S., & Lenerz, K. (1986). Early temperament and later educational outcome. In National Institute of Education, *Temperament and School Learning*. ERIC ED 267 078.

14. Lerner, J. V., & Vicary, J. R. (1984). Difficult temperament and drug use: Analysis from the New York Longitudinal Study. *Journal of Drug Education, 14* (1), 1–8.

15. Thomas, A., & Chess, S. (1976). Evolution of behavior disorders into adolescents. *American Journal of Psychiatry, 133* (5), 339–542.

16. Thomas, A., & Chess, S. (1977). *Temperament and Development.* New York: Brunner/Mazel.

17. Thomas, A., & Chess, S. (1984). Genesis and evolution of behavior disorders: From infancy to early adult life. *American Journal of Psychiatry, III,* 1–9.

18. Thomas, A., Chess, S., & Birch, H. G. (1968). *Temperament and Behavior Disorders.* New York: New York University Press.

19. Thomas, A., Chess, S., & Birch, H. G. (1972). *Your Child Is A Person.* New York: Viking Press.

20. Thomas, A., Chess, S., & Korn, S. J. (1982). The reality of difficult temperament. *Merrill-Palmer Quarterly, 28,* 1–20.

21. Thomas, A., Chess. S., Sillen, J., & Mendez, O. (1974). Cross-cultural study of behavior in children with special vulnerabilities to stress. In D. F. Ricks, A. Thomas, & M. Roff (Eds.), *Life History Research in Psychopathology (Vol. 3).* Minneapolis: Minnesota Press.

The listings below discuss specific assessment instruments.

22. Behavior Style Questionnaire: McDevitt, S. C., & Carey, W. B. (1978). The measurement of temperament in 3–7 year old children. *Journal of Child Psychology and Psychiatry and Allied Professions, 19,* 245–253.

23. The Dimensions of Temperament Survey: Lerner, R. M., Palermo, M., Spiro, A., III, & Nesselrode, J. R. (1982). Assessing the dimensions of temperamental individuality across the life span: The Dimensions of Temperament Survey. *Child Development, 53* (1), 149–159.

24. The Preschool Temperament Inventory: Billman, J. (1981). *The Preschool Temperament Inventory: Construction and Standardization of a Teacher-Rated Instrument for Assessing Temperament of Three- to Six-Year-Old Children.* ERIC ED 224, 592.

25. Teacher Temperament Questionnaire. Sobesky, W. E., List, K. R., Holden, D. L., & Braucht, W. G. (1981). *Dimensions of Child Temperament in School Settings.* ERIC ED 200 315.

26. Thomas, A., & Chess, S. (1977). *Temperament and Development.* New York: Brunner/Mazel.

The references that follow discuss the validity of temperament assessment instruments.

27. Billman, J., & McDevitt, S. C. (1980). Convergence of parent and observer ratings of temperament with observations of peer interactions in nursery school. *Child Development, 51* (2), 395–400.

28. Corsini, D. A., & Doyle, K. (1979). *Temperamental Traits of Preschool Children: Across Setting Consistency.* ERIC ED 183 265.

29. Hubert, N. C., Wachs, T. D., Peters-Martin, P., & Gandour, M. J. (1982). The study of early temperament measurement and conceptual issues. *Child Development*, 53 (3), 571–600.

30. Lyon, M. E., & Plomiss, R. (1981). The measurement of temperament using parent ratings. *Journal of Child Psychology and Psychiatry and Allied Disciplines*, 22 (1), 47–53.

31. Pfeffer, J., & Martin, R. P. (1983). Comparison of mothers' and fathers' temperament ratings of referred and non-referred preschool children. *Journal of Clinical Psychology*, 39 (6), 1013–1020.

The references below discuss additional problems that can result when temperamentally different youngsters aren't handled properly.

32. Barron, A. P., & Earls, F. (1984). The relation of temperament and social factors to behavior problems in three-year-old children. *Journal of Child Psychology and Psychiatry and Related Disciplines*, 25 (1), 23–33.

33. Cameron, J. R. (1977). Parental treatment, children's temperament and the risk of childhood behavior problems: Relationship between parental characteristics and changes in children's temperament over time. *American Journal of Orthopsychiatry*, 47 (4), 568–576.

34. Nelson, J. A. N. (1985). *Toward Quality of Match: Relationship between Children's Temperament and Specific Aspects of Parent Behavior.* ERIC ED 260 817.

35. Nelson, J. A. N., & Simmer, N. J. (1984). Correlational study of children's temperament and parent behavior. *Early Childhood Development and Care*, 16 (3), 230–250.

The following references deal with the problems that temperamentally different students experience in school.

36. Barclay, L. K. (1985). *Skill Development and Temperament in Kindergarten Children: A Cross-Cultural Study.* ERIC ED 262 878.

37. Barclay, J. R. (1978). *Temperamental Clusters and Individual Differences in the Elementary Classroom: A Summary.* ERIC ED 160 202, ED 157 600.

38. Carey, W. B., Fox, M., & McDevitt, S. C. (1977). Temperament as a factor in early school adjustment. *Pediatrics*, 60, 621–624.

39. Garside, R., Birch, H., Scott, D., Chamber, S., Kolvin, I., Tweddle, N., & Barber, L. (1975). Dimensions of temperament in infant school children. *Journal of Child Psychology and Allied Disciplines*, 13, 219–231.

40. Keogh, B. K. (1986). Temperament and schooling: Meaning of "goodness of fit." *New Directions for Child Development*, 31, 89–108.

41. Keogh, B. K., & Pullis, M. (1980). Temperament influences on the development of exceptional children. In B. K. Keogh (Ed.), *Advances in Special Education*. Greenwich, CT: JAI Press.

42. Klein, H. A. (1983). The relationship between children's temperament and adjustment to kindergarten and headstart settings. *Journal of Psychology, 112* (2), 259–268.

43. National Institute of Education. (1985). *Temperament and School Learning*. ERIC ED 267 078.

44. Nelson, J. A. N., & Simmerer, N. J. (1983). *Individuality and the Development of Social Competence among Preschool Children*. ERIC ED 246 994.

45. Palsin, H. (1986). Preschool temperament and performance on achievement tests. *Developmental Psychology, 22* (6), 766–770.

46. Pullis, M., & Caldwell, J. (1982). The influence of children's temperament characteristics on teachers' decision strategies. *American Educational Research Journal, 19*, 165–181.

47. Soderman, H. K. (1985). Dealing with difficult young children: Strategies for teachers and parents. *Young Children, 4* (5), 15–20.

References below provide a definition of attention deficit hyperactivity disorders.

48. American Psychiatric Association. (1987). *Diagnostic and Statistical Manual of Mental Disorders* (3rd ed.). Washington, DC: American Psychiatric Association.

49. Barkley, R. A. (1982). Guidelines for defining hyperactivity in children: Attention deficit disorders with hyperactivity. In B. Lahey & A. E. Kazdin (Eds.), *Advances in Clinical Child Psychology* (Vol. 5). New York: Plenum.

50. Whalen, C. K. (1983). Hyperactivity, learning problems and the attention deficit disorders. In T. H. Ollendick & M. Herson (Eds.), *Handbook of Child Psychopathology*. New York: Plenum.

These references describe the prevalence of attention deficit hyperactivity disorder.

51. Barkley, R. A. (1990). *Attention Deficit Hyperactivity Disorder: A Handbook for Diagnosis and Treatment*. New York: Guilford Press.

52. Hakola, S. R. (1992). Legal rights of students with attention deficit disorder. *School Psychology Quarterly, 7* (4), 285–297.

The following citations describe the identification process with these students.

53. Bax, J. (1978). The active and overactive school child. *Developmental Medicine and Neurology, 14*, 83–86.

54. Carey, W. B., McDevitt, S. C., & Baker, D. (1979). Differentiating minimal brain dysfunction and temperament. *Developmental Medicine and Child Neurology, 21* (6), 765–772.

55. Conners, C. K. (1969). A teacher's rating scale for use in drug studies with children. *American Journal of Psychiatry, 126,* 152–156.

56. Conners, C. K. (1973). Rating scales for use in drug studies with children [Special issue, Pharmacology of Children]. *Psychopharmacology Bulletin,* 24–84.

57. Goyette, C. H., Conners, C. K., & Ulrich, R. F. (1978). Normative data on Revised Conners Parent and Teaching Rating Scales. *Journal of Abnormal Child Psychology, 6,* 221–236.

58. Rich, H. L. (1978). Teachers' perception of motor activity and related behaviors. *Exceptional Children, 45,* 210–211.

59. Rich, H. L. (1979). The syndrome of hyperactivity among elementary resource students. *Education and Treatment of Children, 2,* 91–100.

60. Victor, J. B., & Halverson, C. F. (1976). Distractibility and hypersensitivity: Two behavior factors in elementary school children. *Journal of Abnormal Child Psychology, 3,* 83–94.

These references discuss gender differences among students with attention deficit hyperactivity disorders.

61. Ackerman, P. T., Dykman, R. A., & Oglesby, D. M. (1983). Sex and group differences in reading and attention disordered children with and without hyperkenesis. *Journal of Learning Disabilities, 16,* 407–415.

62. deHaas, P. A. (1986). Attention styles and peer relationships of hyperactive and normal boys and girls. *Journal of Abnormal Child Psychology, 14* (3), 457–467.

63. Milch, R., & Landau, S. (1982). Socialization and peer relations in hyperactive children. In K. D. Gandnow & I. Bialer (Ed.), *Advances in Learning and Behavioral Disabilities* (Vol. 1). Greenwich, CT: JAI Press.

64. Pelham, W. E., & Bender, M. E., (1982). Peer relationships in hyperactive children: Description and treatment. In K. D. Gadow & I. Bialer (Eds.), *Advances in Learning and Behavioral Disabilities: A Research Annual* (Vol. 1). Greenwich, CT: JAI Press.

Self-managing techniques are discussed in these references.

65. Argulewicz, E. N., Elliot, S. N., & Spencer, D. (1982). Application of a cognitive-behavioral intervention for improving classroom attention. *School Psychology Review, 11* (1), 90–95.

66. Bender, N. N. (1976). Self-verbalization versus tutor verbalization in modifying impulsivity. *Journal of Educational Psychology, 68,* 347–354.

67. Bolstad, O., & Johnson, S. (1972). Self-regulation in the modification of disruptive classroom behavior. *Journal of Applied Behavior Analysis, 5,* 443–454.

68. Bornstein, P. H., & Quevillon, R. P. (1976). The effects of a self-instructional package on overactive preschool boys. *Journal of Applied Behavior Analysis, 9,* 179–188.

69. Camp, B. W., & Bash, M. A. (1981). *Think Aloud: Increasing Social and Cognitive Skill, A Problem-Solving Program for Children*. Champaign, IL: Research Press.

70. Camp, B. W., Blom, G. E., Hebert, F., & van Doorninck, W. F. (1977). Think aloud: A program for developing self-control in young aggressive boys. *Journal of Abnormal Child Psychology, 5*, 157–169.

71. Cole, P. M., & Hartley, D. G. (1978). The effects of reinforcement and strategy training on impulsive responding. *Child Development, 49*, 381–384.

72. Cullinan, D., Epstein, M. H., & Silver, L. (1977). Modification of impulsive tempo in learning-disabled pupils. *Journal of Abnormal Child Psychology, 5*, 437–444.

73. Douglas, V. I., Parry, P., Maiton, P., & Garson, C. (1976). Assessment of cognitive training program for hyperactive children. *Journal of Abnormal Child Psychology, 4* (4), 389–410.

74. Fagan, S. (1979). Psychoeducational management and self-control. In D. Cullinan & M. Epstein (Eds.), *Special Education for Adolescents: Issues and Perspectives*. Columbus, OH: Merrill.

75. Fagan, S., Long, N., & Stevens, D. (1975). *Teaching Children Self-Control*. Columbus, OH: Merrill.

76. Finch, A. J., & Spirito, A. (1980). Use of cognitive training to train cognitive processes. *Exceptional Education Quarterly, 1* (1), 31–39.

77. Friedling, C., & O'Leary, S. G. (1979). Effects of self-instructional training on second and third grade hyperactive students: A failure to replicate. *Journal of Applied Behavior Analysis, 12*, 211–219.

78. Glenwick, U. S., & Barocas, R. (1979). Training impulsive children in verbal self-control by use of natural change agents. *Journal of Special Education, 13* (4), 387–397.

79. Glynn, E. L., Thomas, J. E., & Shee, S. M. (1973). Behavioral self-control of on-task behavior in an elementary classroom. *Journal of Applied Behavior Analysis, 6*, 105–113.

80. Hallahan, D. P. (Ed.). (1980). Teaching exceptional children to use cognitive strategies. *Exceptional Education Quarterly, 1*, 1–94.

81. Hallahan, D. P., Lloyd, J. W., Kauffman, J. M., & Lopez, A. B. (1983). Academic problems. In R. J. Morris & T. R. Kratochwill (Eds.), *The Practice of Child Therapy*. New York: Pergamon.

82. Hallahan, D. P., Lloyd, J., Kosiewicz, M. M., Kauffman, J. M., & Graves, A. W. (1979). Self-monitoring of attention as a treatment for a learning disabled boy's off-task behavior. *Learning Disabilities Quarterly, 2*, 24–32.

83. Hallahan, D. P., Lloyd, J. W., & Stoller, L. (1982). *Improving Attention with Self-Monitoring: A Manual for Teachers*. Charlottesville, VA: Learning Disabilities Institute, University of Virginia.

84. Kagen, R. M. (1976). Generalization of verbal self-instructional training in cognitive impulsive children. *Dissertation Abstracts International, 37,* 4148B (University Microfilms No. 77-3926).

85. Kendall, P. C., Zupan, B. A., & Braswell, L. (1981). Self-control in children: Further analysis of the self-control rating scale. *Behavior Therapy, 12,* 667–681.

86. Kneedler, R. D., & Hallahan, D. P. (1984). Self-monitoring as an attentional strategy for academic tasks with learning disabled children. In B. Gholson and T. Rosenthal (Eds.), *Applications of Cognitive Development Theory.* New York: Academic Press.

87. Meichenbaum, D. H. (1979). Teaching children self-control. In B. B. Lahey & A. E. Kazdin (Eds.), *Advances in Clinical Child Psychology* (Vol. 2). New York: Plenum.

88. Meichenbaum, D. H. (1980). Cognitive behavior modification: A promise yet unfulfilled. *Exceptional Education Quarterly, 1* (1), 83–88.

89. Meichenbaum, D. H., & Goodman, J. (1971). Training impulsive children to talk to themselves. *Journal of Abnormal Psychology, 77,* 115–126.

90. Palkes, H., Stewart, M., & Freedman, J. (1971). Improvement in maze performance of hyperactive boys as a function of verbal training procedures. *Journal of Special Education, 5,* 337–342.

91. Palkes, H., Stewart, M., & Kahana, B. (1968). Porteus maze performance of hyperactive boys after training in self-directed verbal commands. *Child Development, 39,* 817–826.

92. Polsgrove, L. (1979). Self-control: Methods for child training. *Behavior Disorders, 4,* 116–130.

93. Pressley, M. (1979). Increasing children's self-control through cognitive interventions. *Review of Educational Research, 49* (2), 319–370.

94. Rosenbaum, M. S., & Drabman, R. S. (1979). Self-control training in the classroom: A review and critique.

95. Varni, J. W., & Henker, B. (1979). A self-regulation approach to the treatment of three hyperactive boys. *Child Behavior Therapy, 1,* 171–191.

The following references describe teacher-managed techniques with consequences.

96. Abramowitz, A. J., & O'Leary, S. G. (1991). Behavioral interventions for the classroom: Implications for students with ADHD. *School Psychology Review, 20* (2), 220–234.

97. Anderson, A., Foder, I., & Alpert, M. A. (1976). A comparison of methods for training self-control. *Behavior Therapy, 7,* 649–658.

98. Broden, M., Bruce, C., Mitchell, M. A., Carter, V., & Hall, R. V. (1970). Effects of teacher attention on attending behavior of two boys at adjacent desks. *Journal of Applied Behavior Analysis, 3,* 199–204.

99. Coleman, R. A. (1970). A conditioning technique applicable to elementary school classrooms. *Journal of Applied Behavior Analysis, 3,* 293–297.

100. Drabman, R. S., Spitalnik, R. S., & O'Leary, K. D. (1973). Teaching self-control to disruptive children. *Journal of Abnormal Psychology, 82,* 10–16.

101. Gordon, M., Thomason, F., Cooper, S., & Ivers, C. L. (1991). Nonmedical treatment of ADHD? Hyperactivity: The attention training system. *Journal of School Psychology, 29,* 151–159.

102. Hallahan, D. P., & Kauffman, J. M. (1975). Research on the education of distractible and hyperactive children. In W. M. Cruickshank & D. P. Hallahan (Eds.), *Perceptual and Learning Disabilities in Children, Vol. 2: Research and Theory.* Syracuse, NY: Syracuse University Press.

103. O'Leary, K. D., Pelham, W. E., Rosenbaum, A., & Price, G. H. (1976). Behavioral treatment of hyperkinetic children: An experimental evaluation of its usefulness. *Clinical Pediatrics, 15,* 510–575.

104. O'Leary, S. G., & Dubey, D. R. (1979). Application of self-control procedures by children: A review. *Journal of Applied Behavior Analysis, 12,* 449–465.

105. Pfiffner, L. J., & Barkley, R. A. (1990). Educational placement and classroom management. In R. A. Barkley (Ed.), *Attention Deficit Hyperactivity Disorder: A Handbook for Diagnosis and Treatment.* New York: Guilford Press.

106. Rosen, L. A., O'Leary, S. G., Joyce, S. A., Conway, G., & Pfiffner, L. J. (1984). The importance of prudent negative consequences for maintaining the appropriate behavior of hyperactive children. *Journal of Abnormal Child Psychology, 12,* 581–604.

107. Rosenbaum, A., O'Leary, K. D., & Jacob, R. G. (1975). Behavioral intervention with hyperactive children: Group consequences as a supplement to individual contingencies. *Behavior Therapy, 6,* 315–322.

108. Turkewitz, H., O'Leary, K. D., & Ironsmith, M. (1975). Generalization and maintenance of appropriate behavior through self-control. *Journal of Consulting and Clinical Psychiatry, 43,* 577–583.

109. Walker, H. M., & Buckley, N. K. (1968). The use of positive reinforcement in conditioning attending behavior. *Journal of Applied Behavior Analysis, 1,* 245–250.

Peer tutoring with these students is discussed in the following reference.

110. DuPaul, G. J., & Henningson, P. N. (1993). Peer tutoring effects on the classroom performance of children with attention deficit hyperactivity disorder. *School Psychology Review, 22* (1), 134–143.

Techniques for accommodating to students are the focus of the citations below.

111. Conners, C. K., & Wells, K. C. (1986). *Hyperkinetic Children: A Neuropsychosocial Approach.* Beverly Hills, CA: Sage.

112. Connors, J. P. (1974). *Classroom Activities for Helping Hyperactive Children*. New York: Center for Applied Research in Education.

113. Cruickshank, W. M. (1975). The learning environment. In W. M. Cruickshank & D. P. Hallahan (Eds.), *Perceptual and Learning Disabilities in Children, Vol. 1: Psychoeducational Practices*. Syracuse, NY: Syracuse University Press.

114. Cruickshank, W. M., Bentzen, F., Retzeburg, F., & Tannhauser, M. A. (1961). A *Teaching Method for Brain-Injured and Hyperactive Children*. Syracuse, NY: Syracuse University Press.

115. Cruickshank, W. M., & Hallahan, D. P. (Eds.). (1975). *Perceptual and Learning Disabilities in Children, Vol. 2: Research and Theory*. Syracuse, NY: Syracuse University Press.

116. Digate, G., Epstein, M. H., Cullinan, D., & Switzky, H. N. (1978). Modification of impulsivity: Implications for improved efficiency in learning for exceptional children. *Journal of Special Education, 12*, 459–468.

117. Fairchild, T. N. (1975). *Managing the Hyperactive Child in the Classroom*. Austin, TX: Learning Concepts.

118. Fine, M. J. (Ed.). (1977). *Principles and Techniques of Intervention with Hyperactive Children*. Springfield, IL: Thomas.

119. Fontenelle, D. (1983). *A Guide for Parents and Teachers*. Englewood Cliffs, NJ: Prentice-Hall.

120. Jacob, R. G., O'Leary, K. D., & Rosenblad, C. (1978). Formal and informal classroom settings: Effects on hyperactivity. *Journal of Abnormal Child Psychology, 6*, 47–59.

121. Kauffman, J. M., & Hallahan, D. P. (1979). Learning disabilities and hyperactivity (with comments on minimal brain dysfunction). In B. B. Lahey & A. E. Kazdin (Eds.), *Advances in Clinical Child Psychology*. New York: Plenum.

122. Lahey, B. B. (Ed.). (1979). *Behavior Therapy with Hyperactive and Learning Disabled Children*. New York: Oxford University Press.

123. Margolis, H., Brannigan, G. G., & Poston, M. A. (1977). Modification of impulsivity: Implications for teaching. *Elementary School Journal, 77*, 231–237.

124. Pick, A. D., Cristy, M. D., & Frankel, G. W. (1972). A developmental study of visual selective attention. *Journal of Experimental Child Psychology, 14*, 165–175.

125. Vallet, R. E. (1974). *The Psychoeducational Treatment of Hyperactive Children*. Belmont, CA: Fearon.

The following references discuss the prevalence of parental substance abuse and its effects on children.

126. Adler, T. (1989). Cocaine babies face behavior deficits. *American Psychological Association Monitor, 20* (7), 14.

127. Archer, L. D. (1987). *Program Strategies for Preventing Fetal Alcohol Syndrome and Alcohol Related Birth Defects.* DHHS Publication No. (ADM) 87-1482.

128. Aronson, M., Kyllerman, M., Sobel, J. G., Sandin, B., & Olegard, R. (1985). Children of alcoholic mothers: Developmental, perceptual, and behavioral characteristics as compared to matched controls. *Acta Paediatricia Scandinavica, 74,* 27–35.

129. Besharov, D. J. (1989). The children of crack, will we protect them. *Public Welfare, 47* (4), 6–11.

130. Besharov, D. J. (1990). Crack children in foster care. *Children Today, 19,* 21–35.

131. Brooks-Gunn, J., & McCarton, C. (1991). *Effects of Drugs In-Utero on Infant Development.* Washington, DC: National Institute of Child Health and Human Development, Report to Congress.

132. Burkett, B., Yasin, S., & Palow, D. (1990). Perinatal implications of cocaine exposure. *Journal of Reproductive Medicine, 35* (1), 35–42.

133. Chasnoff, I., Landress, H., & Barrett, M. (1990). The prevalence of illicit drug and/or alcohol use during pregnancy and discrepancies in mandatory reporting in Pinellas County, Florida. *New England Journal of Medicine, 322,* 1202–1206.

134. Chavin, W., & Kandall, S. R. (1990). Between a rock and a hard place: Perinatal drug abuse. *Pediatrics, 85,* 223–225.

135. Cohen, S. (1985). *The Substance Abuse Problems, Vol. II. New Issues for the 1980's.* Redding, CA: Hawthorn Press.

136. Cole, C., Ferara, V., Johnson, D., Jones, M., Schoenbaum, M., Tyler, R., Wallace, V., & Poulsen, M. (1989). *Today's Challenge: Teaching Strategies for Working with Young Children Pre-natally Exposed to Drugs/Alcohol.* Los Angeles: Los Angeles Unified School District.

137. Dow-Edwards, D. L. (1988). Developmental effects of cocaine. *National Institute of Drug Abuse Research Monographs, 88,* 290–303.

138. Finnegan, L. (1989). *Drug Dependency in Pregnancy: Clinical Management of Mother and Child.* Washington, DC: National Institute of Drug Abuse Service Research Monograph Service, U.S. Government Printing Office.

139. Fried, P. A., & O'Connell, C. M. (1987). A comparison of the effects of prenatal exposure to tobacco, alcohol, cannabis, and caffeine on birthsize and subsequent growth. *Neurotoxicology and Teratology, 9,* 79–85.

140. Gittler, J., & McPherson, M. (1990). Prenatal substance abuse. *Children Today, 19,* 3–7.

141. Griffith, D. (1991, May). *Intervention Needs of Children Prenatally Exposed to Drugs,* Congressional testimony before the House Select Committee on Special Education.

142. Haflon, N. (1989). *Hearing: Born Hooked, Confronting the Impact of Perinatal Substance Abuse.* Select Committee on Children, Youth and Families, U.S. House of Representatives. April 27, 1989.

143. Howard J., Beckwith, L., Rodning, C., & Kropenske, V. (1989). Development of young children of substance-abusing parents: Insights from seven years of intervention and research. *Zero to Three, 9,* 8–12.

144. Kronstadt, D. (1989). *Pregnancy and Cocaine Addiction: An Overview of Impact and Treatment.* San Francisco: Far West Laboratory for Educational Research and Development.

145. Miller, G. (1989). *Hearing: Born Hooked, Confronting the Impact of Perinatal Substance Abuse.* Select Committee on Children, Youth and Families, U.S. House of Representatives. April 27, 1989.

146. New York City HRA Office of Management Analysis (1990). *Report issued on January 31, 1990.* New York.

147. New York Times (1989, September 17), *Crack's Toll Among Babies: A Joyless View of Even Toys.* New York.

148. Petitti, D. B., & Coleman, C. (1990). Cocaine and the risk of low birth weight. *American Journal of Public Health, 80* (1), 25–28.

149. Phillipson, R. (1988). The fetal alcohol syndrome: Recent international statistics. *Australia and New Zealand Journal of Developmental Psychology, 14* (34), 211–221.

150. Poulsen, M. (1991). *Schools Meet the Challenge: Educational Needs of Children at Risk Due to Substance Exposure.* Sacramento: Resources in Special Education.

151. Reed, B. (1987). Developing women-sensitive drug dependent treatment services: Why so difficult? *Journal of Psychoactive Drugs, 19* (2), 151–164.

152. Rist, M. C. (1990). The shadow children. *American School Board Journal, 177* (1), 19–24.

153. Straus, A. (1981). Neonatal manifestations of maternal phencyclidine (PCP) abuse. *Pediatrics, 66,* 4.

154. Streisstguth, A. P. (1989). *Prenatal Alcohol Exposure and Child IQ Achievement and Classroom Behavior at Age 7.* Paper presented at the annual conference of the Society for Research in Child Development, Kansas City, MO.

155. Streisstguth, A. P., Clarren, S. K., & Jones, K. L. (1985). Natural history of the fetal alcohol syndrome: A 10-year follow-up of eleven patients. *Lancet, 2* (8446), 85–91.

156. U.S. Department of Health and Human Services, Office of Inspector General. (1990). *Crack Babies.* Washington, DC: Author.

157. U.S. National Center for Health Statistics. (1989). *Advance Report of Final Natality Statistics, 1987.* Vol. 38, No. 3, Supplement, June 29, 1989. Washington, DC: U.S. Department of Health and Human Services.

158. Vincent, L. J., Poulsen, M. K., Cole, C. K., Woodruff, G., & Griffith, D. R. (1991). *Born Substance Exposed, Educationally Vulnerable*. Reston, VA: Council for Exceptional Children.

159. Wescott, S. M. (1990). Time to address a preventable tragedy. *Winds of Change, 5* (3), 30–34.

160. Weston, R. R., Ivins, B., Zuckerman, B., Jones, C., & Lopez, R. (1989). Drug-exposed babies: Research and clinical issues. *Zero to Three, 9*, 1–7.

161. Wilson, G. S. (1989). Clinical studies of infants and children exposed prenatally to heroin. *Annals of the New York Academy of Sciences, 562*, 183–194.

162. Zuckerman, B. (1991). Drug-exposed infants: Understanding the medical risk. *The Future of Children, 1* (1), 26–35.

INDEX